Praise for *The Torture Machine*

"If it was not for Flint Taylor I would still be languishing in prison. He brought hope to a hopeless place. . . . All the struggles that we lived through are captured in perfect detail here. Thank you, Flint for writing this book."
—Darrell Cannon, Chicago police torture survivor

"It is impossible to fully understand the continuing challenges created by unjustifiable police violence against Black and Brown people without appreciating the historical backdrop that sustains this national crisis. Flint Taylor's powerful new book, informed by his decades as one of the most effective advocates addressing these issues, is a must read."
—Bryan Stevenson, bestselling author of *Just Mercy*

"If you want to understand what actually happened to those Jon Burge tortured, read this book. *Torture Machine* is the truth for all to read. Flint Taylor and this book are a godsend."
—Anthony Holmes, Chicago police torture survivor

"This book is a powerful testament to [the survivors'] courage and determination and is essential reading for anyone wanting to understand what can happen when those in power condone violations of civil and constitutional rights for political expediency."
—Mary E. Howell, preeminent New Orleans civil rights attorney

"A stunning, sweeping history of police violence in Chicago and Flint Taylor's lifelong pursuit of racial justice. Quite literally the work of a lifetime."
—Alison Flowers, author of *Exoneree Diaries: The Fight for Innocence, Independence, and Identity*

"An indispensable and searing account of the barbarous regime of policing under Jon Burge and the ongoing fight for justice."
—Martha Biondi, author of *To Stand and Fight: The Struggle for Civil Rights in Postwar New York City*, and James Thindwa, labor activist and board member, *In These Times*

"An unsparing dissection of foundational racism in the criminal justice system. . . . It could not be more timely."
—Jamie Kalven, investigative reporter and executive director of the Invisible Institute

"Powerfully and excitingly presented, Flint Taylor narrates the legal battle that he pioneered and pursued for more than thirty years to expose and ultimately incarcerate Chicago police commander and torturer Jon Burge.

Flint's work with others at the People's Law Office has led to the freeing of many wrongly convicted torture survivors, the paying of more than $40 million in damages to these survivors, and reparations that include the teaching of the torture scandal in the Chicago public schools.

"Flint's dogged legal advocacy exposed the racist pathology of the Chicago Police Department as well as the collaboration and support by those at the highest level of city and county government. It is an honor and inspiration to have worked with Flint through the first twenty years of these legal battles."

—Jeff Haas, author of *The Assassination of Fred Hampton: How the FBI and the Chicago Police Murdered a Black Panther*

"Flint Taylor's searing memoir is a chilling reminder of American law enforcement's enduring commitment to silencing Black voices and torturing Black bodies in the name of 'order.' It is also a most powerful and moving account of the courageous community members, activists, and movement lawyers who have given their lives to make sure that those same voices are heard, and that some measure of justice can be had. From the moment, fifty years ago, when law enforcement murdered twenty-one-year-old Fred Hampton as he slept in bed, to the more recent fight to hold Jon Burge and the Chicago PD accountable for brutalizing hundreds of people in their custody over the last thirty years, *The Torture Machine* is essential reading for all who care about this country—past and future."

—Heather Ann Thompson, Pulitzer Prize–winning author of *Blood in the Water: The Attica Prison Uprising of 1971 and Its Legacy*

THE TORTURE MACHINE

Racism and Police Violence in Chicago

Flint Taylor

Haymarket Books
Chicago, Illinois

Published in 2019 by
Haymarket Books
P.O. Box 180165
Chicago, IL 60618
773-583-7884
www.haymarketbooks.org
info@haymarketbooks.org

ISBN: 978-1-60846-895-9

Distributed to the trade in the US through Consortium Book Sales and Distri-
bution (www.cbsd.com) and internationally through Ingram Publisher Services
International (www.ingramcontent.com).

This book was published with the generous support of Lannan Foundation and
Wallace Action Fund.

Special discounts are available for bulk purchases by organizations and institutions. Please call 773-583-7884 or email info@haymarketbooks.org for more
information.

Cover design by Rachel Cohen

Printed in Canada by union labor.

Library of Congress Cataloging-in-Publication data is available.

10 9 8 7 6 5 4 3 2 1

To Pat, Kate, Laurie, and Wally;
to my sisters and brothers of the People's Law Office;
to the survivors of Chicago police torture and their families

To the memory of my parents, Elly and Flint Sr.

And to the spirit of Fred Hampton and his family

CONTENTS

1. Murder by Darkness:
   The Assassination of Fred Hampton and Mark Clark   1

2. The *Wilson* Case:
   And He Just Kept on Cranking and Cranking . . .   35

3. Street Files and Important Trials   52

4. The First *Wilson* Civil Rights Trial   65

5. The Cover-Up Begins to Unravel   87

6. Déjà Vu   103

7. The Fight for Justice Broadens   135

8. Out of the Court and into the Streets   148

9. Fire Burge!   159

10. Burge on Trial Again   175

11. A Parade and an Appeal   194

12. The *Vigilante*, Aaron Patterson, and a Judgment against Burge   203

13. The Marcus Wiggins Case:
    "They're Supposed to Serve and Protect, Right?"   212

14. Decisions, Decisions   221

15. And It Seemed Like They Blew My Brains Out   234

16. Those Idiots from the People's Law Office   245

17. A Landmark Victory, a Plea, and a Tragedy   268

18. Special Prosecutors, Clemencies, and Pardons   280

19. Free at Last   293

20. Freedom Denied — 302

21. An Open Secret — 313

22. The Daley Show — 322

23. Broadening the Struggle against Police Torture — 326

24. The Tale of Two Reports — 333

25. Beyond All Reasonable Doubt — 344

26. The Art of the No Deal — 360

27. Hearings, Hearings, and More Hearings — 370

28. The Feds Come Marching In — 382

29. The Worm Turns — 393

30. Exonerations — 402

31. Burge in the Dock — 410

32. A Modicum of Justice — 426

33. Daley the Defendant — 438

34. On What Planet . . . — 453

35. Reparations Now! — 460

36. Never Before in America — 473

37. Coming Full Circle — 482

38. Wilson Walks — 496

Epilogue — 508

Acknowledgments — 511

Index — 516

If you dare to struggle, then you dare to win, if you dare not to struggle, then, goddamnit, you don't deserve to win!

—Fred Hampton, Illinois Black Panther Party chairman, November 1969

CHAPTER 1

Murder by Darkness

The Assassination of Fred Hampton and Mark Clark

The call came in the early morning hours of December 4, 1969. "Come to the crib" was the command. "The police have murdered Chairman Fred." I was a second-year law student at Northwestern Law School, working with a group of young lawyers, law students, and legal workers in a highly unusual law firm, founded just months before. Our firm, located in a converted sausage shop on Chicago's north side, was grounded in principles of collectivity, and, inspired by our Black Panther Party clients, we named it the People's Law Office. As young radicals, we devoted ourselves to aggressively fighting, in the courtrooms of Cook County, Illinois, against racial injustice and the war in Vietnam. Our clients also included a revolutionary Puerto Rican organization, the Young Lords; a radical organization of white youth called Rising Up Angry; the Weatherman faction of the Students for a Democratic Society; and, most notably, the charismatic young chairman of the Chicago chapter of the Black Panther Party, Fred Hampton.

After I stopped at the law school to pull fellow student Jack Welsh out of class, we drove to the small west side Panther apartment known to us as "the chairman's crib." The car radio was blaring that the Panthers and the police had engaged in a shootout that would have done Al Capone proud. Fred and Peoria chapter chairman Mark Clark were dead, several of the seven survivors were wounded and hospitalized, and the others were in jail. All the surviving Panthers had been charged with attempted murder.

Jack and I entered the bloody, bullet-riddled apartment. The raiding officers had left it unsealed, inexplicably, after the pre-dawn attack.

The plasterboard walls looked like Swiss cheese, ripped by scores of bullets from police weapons that, as we soon learned, included a machine gun, a semiautomatic rifle, and several shotguns. A large pool of blood stained the floor at the doorway where Fred's body had been dragged after he was shot in the head, and there were fresh bloodstains on all the beds in the apartment. Shock and grief soon met with the dawning realization that the police claims of a shootout were bold-faced lies. We were looking at a murder scene.

I had met Chairman Fred a few months before, when I escorted him to Northwestern Law School to speak to the student body. As we traveled from the Panther offices on Chicago's west side to the school, Fred was obsessing on the "pigs" who were out to get him, and in my relative naiveté I thought perhaps he was being a little paranoid. But he was, in fact, prophetic. At Northwestern's Lincoln Hall, in my first attempt at public speaking, I stumbled as I introduced him to the eager student crowd. Only twenty-one years old, Fred captivated the audience with his dynamic and analytical oratory, a mesmerizing intersection of Malcolm X, Martin Luther King, and a present-day hip-hop poet.

Although Fred and I were contemporaries, our backgrounds were a study in contrasts. I grew up in a small, all-white town in central Massachusetts, while Fred grew up in Maywood, a racially divided suburb of Chicago. My ancestors came voluntarily to this country, some on the *Mayflower* and others later, from Italy; Fred's came in chains and were enslaved in Louisiana. My father was a teacher, my mother a part-time librarian; Fred's mother and father were factory workers. While I was a jock and honor student in high school, Fred was an NAACP youth leader and organizer, spearheading demonstrations against segregated facilities in his high school and hometown. As I was trying to find myself in an alienating Ivy League college, Fred and former Student Nonviolent Coordinating Committee (SNCC) leader Bobby Rush were organizing the Chicago chapter of the Black Panther Party. The previous summer, while Fred served a prison sentence in a maximum-security prison in downstate Illinois for allegedly stealing seventy-one dollars' worth of ice cream and distributing it to neighborhood kids, I was meeting Fred's family and other Panther family members as a fledging intern with the brand-new People's Law Office. And on December 4, 1969, I stood in his blood.

Starting that day, my comrades at the People's Law Office (PLO) and I embarked on a thirteen-year legal battle—a crusade, no doubt—to uncover and expose the truth about that murderous raid. In the process we established a narrative that documented the violent lengths that the US government, working with local police, would go to with the aim of crushing radical and revolutionary Black organizations and their leaders in the United States. This journey would galvanize our commitment to fighting for radical change and against racism and violence by law enforcement.

We spent almost two weeks taking evidence in the apartment, carefully cataloging and photographing each item, and then transporting much of it, cloak-and-dagger style, to the attic of a north side church for safekeeping. As we tracked nearly one hundred bullet holes made by police weapons, Panther members narrated guided tours of the tiny apartment for thousands of stunned Chicagoans. Each morning, the bloody mattress on which the sleeping Fred Hampton was slain was taken from its secure hiding place and displayed to those who had come to view the crime scene. Bobby Rush publicly laid the blame on the FBI and its director J. Edgar Hoover, whom Rush mocked as "J. Who Edgar." At a press conference shortly after the raid, Renault Robinson and Howard Saffold, co-leaders of the Afro American Patrolmen's League, condemned the raid as "murder." In a moment that I will never forget, an older Black woman, touring the apartment, shook her head and said, "Ain't nothin' but a northern lynching."

The apartment stood as a physical testament to the truth about what had happened in the early morning of December 4, 1969, but from the outset the local establishment media, with the exception of one *Sun Times* reporter, wholeheartedly bought state's attorney Edward Hanrahan's version of events. Without challenge, the front pages of all four daily papers trumpeted the law enforcement narrative that the police raiders had been met with a barrage of gunfire from the Panthers, provoking a shootout that lasted twenty minutes.

The skeptical *Sun Times* reporter, Brian Boyer, had visited the apartment and wrote a story that questioned Hanrahan's version. His editors buried the story in the back pages, prompting Boyer to quit. In response, *Sun Times* editor in chief Jim Hoge was motivated to visit the crime scene, coming straight from the opera to the apartment, dressed to the nines, his wife clad in an expensive fur. We showed them, by floodlight, the evidence that had convinced Boyer. From that point forward the *Sun Times* and its evening sibling, the *Chicago Daily News*, adopted a more questioning stance, while the *Chicago Tribune* continued to back Hanrahan—who had ordered the raid—and his men. Hanrahan reacted to the conflicting media coverage by giving an exclusive to the *Tribune*, in which the police raiders reiterated their lies that the raid had been a gun battle initiated by the Panthers. The *Trib*'s exclusive was accompanied by photos of the apartment's back door, with encircled marks, which Hanrahan claimed were bullet holes made by Panther weapons. We went to the back door, found those marks, and discovered that they were nail heads.

We also secured another crucial piece of evidence: the door panel from the front entry door to the apartment. Hanrahan and the police had claimed that only one shot had penetrated the door, and that it had come from within, from a Panther gun. We saw that there were in fact two holes, one of which went into the apartment rather than out. PLO lawyer Francis "Skip" Andrew—who, with the invaluable assistance of PLO intern and law student Ray McClain, was coordinating our evidence gathering—and ballistics expert Herb McDonnell directed that the intact door be photographed, then carefully removed the panel. McDonnell plotted the trajectories of the two shots and then took the panel to his lab in Corning, New York, where he ran tests and concluded that the first bullet was fired into the door by the police. A few weeks later, over Christmas break, Seva Dubuar, who, like me, was a Northwestern law student working at the PLO, picked up the panel from McDonnell in Corning, and she and I drove the panel—wrapped to look like a Christmas present—back to Chicago.

The Panther defense team included Jeff Haas, Skip Andrew, our PLO mentor Dennis Cunningham, and an all-star lineup of Chicago defense lawyers. With the evidence of the door panel, we were able to establish that a key component of the State's ballistics evidence was fabricated, and, as a result, Hanrahan dropped the attempted murder charges against the seven surviving Panthers in April 1970. Our vehicle then became a civil rights damages suit, brought on behalf of the Hampton and Clark families and the surviving Panthers. We sued the fourteen raiding officers, State's Attorney Hanrahan, and his first assistant, Richard Jalovec, for a racially and politically motivated conspiracy to plan and execute the murderous raid, and added another set of police officers and prosecutors in an interrelated conspiracy to cover up the murders and to maliciously prosecute the survivors. Under the tutelage of several leading National Lawyers Guild attorneys—Arthur Kinoy, Bill Goodman, and Bill Bender—I drafted the original civil rights complaint for damages in longhand, and we filed the finished version in federal district court in June 1970.

Around this time, a federal grand jury, specially empaneled by the US Justice Department to investigate the bloody raid, returned its findings. The grand jury was controlled by the head of president Richard Nixon's Civil Rights Division, a Wisconsin lawyer named Jerris Leonard, who had said, the previous summer, that the Panthers were "nothing but hoodlums, and we've got to get them." Despite acknowledging that the police had fired more than ninety bullets to a single bullet fired by the Panthers, the grand jury—which included only one Black member out of twenty-three—issued a lengthy report constructed by Leonard, his associates, and the FBI that found there was not sufficient probable cause to charge anyone for the crimes. The surviving Panthers had decided not to testify before the grand jury, and the report claimed that the jury's decision not to indict was therefore the Panthers' fault.

These life-changing events motivated me to withdraw from law school. US troops had just invaded Cambodia, and, amid all the governmental inhumanity, as I later told a *New York Times* reporter, I needed to find out whether I could "be a lawyer and a human being at the same time."

I was now working full-time at the PLO. Michael Deutsch, a brilliant and committed young lawyer, had recently joined the office. In November 1970, Michael, Jeff Haas, and I were called down to Carbondale, Illinois, some 350 miles south of Chicago, to represent six Panthers who had been arrested for engaging in a shootout with the local police. There I met student activist Patricia Handlin, who would go on to start a branch of the PLO south in Carbondale and would also later become my wife.

Jeff and Michael tried the Carbondale case in the summer of 1971, with my assistance (wearing an ill-fitting red wig to hide my shoulder-length hair). As Carbondale was a university town, we were treated to a very sympathetic, multiracial jury that embraced the Panthers' claims of self-defense, and, after a month-long trial, quickly acquitted the Panthers on trial of all charges. We celebrated with the jury at a post-verdict party and learned that a young, white Vietnam veteran had demonstrated to his fellow jurors how the Panthers had defended themselves against the police attack.

That September we became involved in an epic law enforcement murder case arising from the bloody assault at Attica Correctional Facility that killed thirty-four prisoners and nine guards. The prisoners had risen up and taken over the facility on September 9, 1971, in their demands for more humane treatment, and in the days that followed were attempting to negotiate with New York governor Nelson Rockefeller and prison officials. On September 13, Rockefeller ordered the National Guard and New York State Police to attack. In the aftermath, the surviving prisoners were forced to crawl in the mud through a gauntlet of guards, who physically and verbally abused them. Some of the leaders of the uprising, including Frank "Big Black" Smith, were singled out for individual torture and abuse. Sixty of the rebelling prisoners were charged with felonies, including murder of the nine guards—who were, in fact, killed by law enforcement bullets.

Almost all of us from the PLO, at one time or another, traveled to Attica to meet with many of the surviving Attica brothers, who were being held in solitary confinement. Now back for my final year of law school and resolved to become a "people's lawyer," I met with Big Black, Mariano "Dalu" Gonzalez, Roger "Champ" Champen, and several other leaders who had been tortured and charged with crimes. The strength and humanity of these men inspired us and fueled our dedication and resolve. Mara Siegel, a Buffalo college student who later moved to Chicago and became part of our office, joined the efforts. As the Attica cases progressed, Dennis and Michael moved to Buffalo to work on their defense, a commitment that would last for more than thirty years.

The Feds' refusal to obtain indictments for civil rights violations in the *Hampton* case rekindled widespread community outrage and led to the appointment of a Cook County special prosecutor, Barnabas Sears. In the face of great political pressure, Sears returned indictments against State's Attorney Hanrahan, Assistant State's Attorney Jalovec, and the police raiders, not for murder or attempted murder—on which the grand jury deadlocked, 10–10—but for conspiracy to obstruct justice. The case was assigned to a loyal Democratic machine judge, Philip Romiti, and the defendants, represented by a contingent of politically connected and high-powered criminal defense lawyers, wisely chose to waive a jury and take a bench trial before Romiti.

The trial began in the summer of 1972, in advance of the November elections. Hanrahan, who before the raid had been the heir apparent to mayor Richard J. Daley, was running against a reform-minded Republican, Bernard Carey, and desperately needed to be acquitted before Election Day. Daley, at least publicly, continued to strongly back Hanrahan. Special Prosecutor Sears presented a very strong case, but it was clear from the start that the political fix, Chicago-style, was in.

While studying for the bar exam and continuing my work at the People's Law Office, I was asked, on a late July day, to open the Hampton files, at that time housed at the Northwestern Law School legal clinic, for the special prosecutor to inspect. Several statements by Panther survivors were among the files, and some of the statements contained inconsistencies with the Panthers' testimony before the special grand jury: most consequentially, one of the survivors, in a moment of false braggadocio, claimed to have fired two shots. Although these statements, one of which was sworn, should have been protected from disclosure by the attorney-client privilege, Special Prosecutor Sears demanded that we turn them over so that he could provide them to the defense. We reluctantly did so, and the defense lawyers gleefully put us on trial. "Charge Perjury in Indictment of Hanrahan," the *Sun Times* blared in a headline. There was absolutely no physical evidence that these shots were fired, but it made no difference; on the eve of the bar exam, I was grilled consecutively by three of the defense lawyers, one of whom, John Coghlan, would soon be one of our chief adversaries in the Hampton civil rights trial.

On Wednesday, November 1, 1972, after thirteen weeks of evidence, Judge Romiti acquitted all the defendants of conspiracy to obstruct justice. The ruling required the judge to conclude that there was essentially no evidence to support the charges. Like the federal grand jury's finding of no probable cause, it was indefensible from a factual and legal point of view, but totally explicable politically. Mayor Daley exclaimed, "The verdict speaks for itself. The great lesson here is not to be too willing to believe charges before the evidence is in. I think the black people of Chicago feel the same way."

Six days later, the Black people of Chicago showed how they actually felt, as they crossed party lines en masse and voted Hanrahan out of office. This marked the start of a movement that, a decade later, would result in the election of Harold Washington as Chicago's first Black mayor.

For the civil case, we had drawn federal judge J. Sam Perry. Perry, originally from Alabama, was seventy-four years old, short-tempered, hard of hearing, and about to go on senior status. He had served in the Illinois State Legislature with Richard J. Daley before ascending to the federal bench. In February 1972, Judge Perry, in his first important decision, dismissed Hanrahan, Jalovec, and the other prosecutors from the case on the grounds of absolute immunity from suit; Mayor Daley and police superintendent James Conlisk for lack of personal involvement; and numerous other Chicago police officials involved in the cover-up, on other legal grounds. He did not dismiss the case against the fourteen raiders, but he stayed all proceedings while we appealed his dismissals. The highly publicized drama about our clients' statements and Judge Romiti's acquittals capped a depressing year. That I passed the bar in November and became a real lawyer (while still striving to be a human being) was only small solace.

Then the tide turned. In February 1973, a front-page *Tribune* headline announced, "Panther Tip on 'Hit Squad.'" The story named Panther William O'Neal as someone "who for four years has worked as an FBI informant in the ranks of the Black Panther Party," and had led the FBI to "members of a police murder squad." The 1970 federal grand jury report had referenced an unnamed FBI informant who had supplied information that led to the raid, and the *Tribune*'s article raised our suspicions to near certainty that O'Neal was that informant.

In June, the front page of the *Chicago Daily News* featured a story headlined "New Story of Panther Raid Told." I eagerly put a dime in the newspaper box slot, grabbed a copy, and read that the alleged ringleader of the murder squad, former Chicago police sergeant Stanley Robinson, had alleged that O'Neal had told him "he [O'Neal] killed Fred Hampton" by "engineering the Panther raid with FBI agent Roy Mitchell."

Two months later, the Seventh Circuit Court of Appeals overturned Judge Perry's dismissal of Hanrahan, Jalovec, and the officers involved in the cover-up, and we were free to pursue O'Neal, Roy Mitchell, and the FBI connection in Perry's court. Our first move was to seek O'Neal's FBI file and other FBI documents pertaining to the raid and the Panthers, and to take his deposition. The government, which had given O'Neal a new identity and relocated him after he testified against Stanley Robinson, claimed at first that they could not find O'Neal, then claimed that giving a deposition would jeopardize his new identity. After public pressure, led by the Reverend Jesse Jackson, was brought to bear on US attorney James Thompson, the government backtracked and said they would produce O'Neal at a secret location in Detroit.

Jeff Haas, Bill Bender, Dennis Cunningham, and I were met in Detroit by government officials and taken to the secret location to question O'Neal. We had not yet received any FBI documents, so O'Neal was able to minimize his role in planning the raid. An independent toxicological report had found a large amount of secobarbital in Fred's bloodstream, and we suspected O'Neal of drugging him, but O'Neal denied it. He did admit to being in the apartment the night before the raid and to being the informant who supplied information to the FBI about the Panthers.

The government was at first represented by an assistant US attorney from the Chicago office named Sheldon Waxman. Waxman was troubled by what he was learning about the FBI's role in the raid and wanted no part of a cover-up, so, a short time after the O'Neal deposition, he announced in open court that the government was reviewing a "truckload, possibly a semi-trailer" of documents. Five weeks later, Waxman, apparently countermanded by the federal powers that be, produced thirty-four FBI documents that he said were responsive to our document request. Jeff told the *Chicago Sun Times,* "I don't think we got all the documents. . . . We were promised a truckload of documents and all we got was a tricycle full."

Among the documents Waxman turned over was one that O'Neal had assiduously avoided mentioning: a detailed, hand-drawn floor plan of Fred's apartment that specifically designated the back bedroom as the "room of Hampton and [Deborah] Johnson when they stay here." The FBI cover sheet revealed that Roy Mitchell had drafted the floor plan with O'Neal's assistance, and Mitchell had distributed it to Hanrahan and Jalovec before the raid. This document was a crucial building block in establishing the breadth of this intergovernmental conspiracy.

Two years earlier, in 1971, a break-in at an FBI office in Media, Pennsylvania, by peace activists, followed by a Freedom of Information Act request by NBC reporter Carl Stern, had revealed the existence of a secret, illegal, domestic FBI counterintelligence program, COINTELPRO, the brainchild of longtime FBI director J. Edgar Hoover. During the 1960s, COINTELPRO had been directed at progressive and revolutionary Black leaders and organizations: two of Hoover's directives, issued in August 1967 and March 1968, named as specific targets, past and present, Malcolm X, Martin Luther King, Stokely Carmichael, Elijah Muhammad, and H. Rap Brown, and the organizations they led. Hoover commanded his field offices, including Chicago, to "expose, disrupt, misdirect, discredit, and otherwise neutralize" these leaders and organizations and to "prevent the rise of a 'messiah' who could unify and electrify the militant black-nationalist movement."

We set out to establish that the Black Panther Party had become COINTELPRO's main target; that Fred Hampton, as a "messianic" young leader, had also become a target; and that COINTELPRO was responsible for the December 4 raid. We climbed the FBI's chain of command in

Chicago, first deposing Roy Mitchell, the crew-cut mainstay of Chicago's Racial Matters Squad. We established that O'Neal had supplied the floor plan information to Mitchell, immediately after the Panthers and police had engaged in a deadly shootout on November 19 that left one Panther and two police officers dead, and that Mitchell, had, in late November, attempted to sell the raid on the Hampton apartment to the Chicago Police Departments's Gang Intelligence Unit. When this failed, he found a willing partner in Hanrahan, Jalovec, and their handpicked unit of specially assigned Chicago police officers, known as the "state's attorney's police."

When I attempted to question Mitchell at his deposition about COINTELPRO, I met with government objections, but Mitchell volunteered that "Cointel had no part" of the raid. "It was not in any way, shape or form even remotely connected to it," he added.

During Mitchell's three-day deposition, Sheldon Waxman was abruptly replaced by another assistant US attorney, Arnold Kanter, who was more willing to implement the FBI's and Justice Department's strategy of stonewalling and cover-up. When we deposed Roy Mitchell's supervisor at the Racial Matters Squad, Robert Piper, and the special agent in charge of the Chicago FBI office, Marlin Johnson, Kanter instructed them not to answer any questions about COINTELPRO. Nonetheless, we added Piper and Johnson, along with O'Neal and Mitchell, as defendants in our suit, alleging that these FBI operatives had

> directed and implemented a counterintelligence program in Chicago which included the use of illegal wiretaps, burglary, agent-provocateurs [sic], false arrest and prosecution, and illegal raids against the Black Panther Party in Chicago and specifically against the Plaintiffs, that the aims and goals of this program were to disrupt and neutralize the Party, and to prevent the rise of leadership within its ranks; and that an important tactic of this program was to provoke and solicit law enforcement agencies to raids and violence against the Party and thereby cause its destruction.

In the spring of 1975 we sought to depose O'Neal a second time, so we could grill him about the floor plan. When the government claimed they could not locate O'Neal, I told *Chicago Daily Defender* reporter Robert McClory that, if the judge would not order O'Neal's production, "We'll have to go looking ourselves, and that could be dangerous." After former US attorney Waxman was publicly quoted as saying that the government knew how to find O'Neal, and Judge Perry ordered Arnold Kanter to do so, the government produced him for a second secret deposition, this time in Chicago in the lockup of the Dirksen Federal Building. A decidedly more hostile O'Neal grudgingly admitted to supplying Mitchell with the floor plan information.

We also formally requested the complete Chicago COINTELPRO file. The government resisted, arguing that the documents were not relevant. Then, without first informing us, Kanter took the file to the judge for a secret in camera inspection at Judge Perry's house. Perry denied us access, ruling that the documents were "irrelevant and immaterial." He also severely limited our questioning of Hoover's high-level assistants, including William C. Sullivan, who was in charge of FBI Domestic Intelligence and Counterintelligence, and barred us from asking about COINTELPRO's focus on Black leaders and groups, including the Black Panthers. These decisions cemented our conviction that Judge Perry was a willing partner to the FBI defendants and their lawyers.

Fortunately, our efforts were aided by a US Senate Committee investigation, chaired by Idaho senator Frank Church, that, in the wake of the Watergate scandal, was investigating the domestic intelligence and counterintelligence activities of the FBI and the CIA. A young Black Senate committee lawyer named Arthur Jefferson was aggressively pursuing the FBI's counterintelligence activities against the Panthers and had obtained the Chicago COINTELPRO files that the judge had kept from us. I established a confidential relationship with Jefferson—he shared with me the contents of the COINTELPRO files, while I supplied him with documentation about the FBI's role in the raid and gave him access to a Panther witness, who testified (under the pseudonym of JX King) about O'Neal's attempts to provoke illegal activity by the Panthers.

In a face-to-face meeting in Washington, DC, Jefferson described a number of particularly explosive documents. Two were what later became known as the "hit letter" documents—an anonymous letter, written in faux-Black bureau speak, that had been sent to the powerful Blackstone Ranger street gang leader Jeff Fort, claiming the Panthers had a "hit" out on Fort, and a cover memo explaining that the letter's stated intent was to provoke Fort to take "retaliatory action" against the Panthers and its leaders. Another series of documents from Hoover called on Chicago and other FBI field offices to devise measures to "cripple" the BPP, while other documents established that O'Neal was acting as part of COINTELPRO when he assumed the role of agent provocateur within the BPP. The most damning document of those that Jefferson discussed with me was dated December 3, 1969, the day before Fred Hampton and Mark Clark were murdered, and claimed the impending raid as a counterintelligence action.

Soon after, the joint efforts of Judge Perry and the government to suppress the Chicago COINTELPRO documents were publicly exposed. In the fall of 1975, Arthur Jefferson convinced the committee chair, senator Frank Church, to formally request access to our evidence from attorney general Edward Levi, while I was able to convince Jefferson to include the hit letter and cover memo in the passel of damning COINTELPRO documents that the committee publicly released in late November. Armed with the cover memo, in a fiery motion crafted by Dennis, we again moved for the documents that the judge had secreted in his chambers. We alleged that after the murders of Malcolm X and Dr. King, "Fred Hampton became, to the agents responsible for suppression of the movement, Number One on the Hit Parade, and thus he met his end." We specifically accused Judge Perry of suppressing the hit letter and memo, as well as, in general terms, the December 3, 1969, memo, which the Senate committee had not yet publicly released. Standing on the eve of trial, we concluded, "It remains an arbitrary and oppressive abuse of judicial discretion to thus fetter plaintiffs' discovery, and eviscerate their case."

Judge Perry was not pleased with our accusations. A few weeks before, he had flown into a rage when we had filed a motion to remove him from the case. (That motion was later denied by a close judicial associate of Mayor Daley.) Two weeks after filing the motion for production of the withheld COINTELPRO documents, we appeared before Judge Perry and presented three hours of heated argument. Afterward, an agitated Perry hurried off the bench, promising to rule the next week. In his written order he once again found the documents to be "irrelevant." For good measure, he also refused our request to continue the trial date. (We would later learn that the judge had confided to former US attorney Sheldon Waxman, in a chance meeting, that we would "never prove that the FBI killed those fellas.")

While the judge and the government were doing everything in their power to keep the emerging evidence secret, our opposite strategy of exposure was having some real success, as the local press was showing rising interest in our battles and our increasingly credible claims that the Hampton raid was part of a nationwide plan to destroy the Panthers and wipe out its leadership. Veteran *Tribune* police reporter Bob Wiedrich, who, six years earlier, had penned the now discredited *Tribune* exclusive from

Hanrahan and his raiders, filed a column entitled "FBI Placed Itself Above the Law." Wiedrich wrote that the FBI had "only one purpose in mind" when it concocted the "hit" letter: to "provoke the Rangers to kill the Panthers before they were killed themselves."

On January 5, 1976, we sat in the cavernous courtroom on the twenty-fifth floor of the Dirksen Federal Building, about to embark on the longest jury trial in federal court history. James Montgomery, described in the *Chicago Reader* as "black, in his mid-thirties and one of Chicago's hottest young trial lawyers," had joined the trial team. Jim, who had previously defended raid survivor (and Fred's partner) Deborah Johnson, was of the mind that his cachet with the judge would win us points, the trial's length and scope could be minimized, and we could either win a jury verdict or convince the City, County, and Feds to settle. We were also joined by NAACP lawyer Herbert Reid, "one of the nation's foremost black lawyers and dean of the Howard Law School," who had several years earlier co-chaired, with former US attorney general Ramsey Clark and NAACP leader Roy Wilkins, an independent investigation of the raid, which resulted in a report aptly tited *Search and Destroy.* The NAACP, in particular staff attorney Jimmy Myerson, had supported us throughout the pretrial phase of the case.

In less flattering terms, Jeff Haas and I were described as, respectively, "a long haired academic radical" and "looking like everyone's kid brother." We were aided by PLO lawyers even younger—Peter Schmiedel, Hollis Hill, Charles "Chick" Hoffman, and Ralph Hurvitz—who performed invaluable support work on the case and kept the office running, so we could all continue to collect our $75-per-week salaries as equal law partners. Also working closely with us was our political, public relations, and fundraising arm, a group of dedicated volunteers, led by Prexy Nesbitt, Diane Rappaport, and Linda Webber, known as the December 4th Committee.

Before jury selection began, I stepped to the lectern and argued that we be permitted to file an amended complaint, based on the recent revelations of the Church Senate Committee, that would join the Estate of J. Edgar Hoover; his top COINTELPRO assistants William Sullivan and Charles Brennan; former Nixon administration attorney general (and Watergate principal) John Mitchell; and former assistant US attorney general Jerris Leonard as conspiring co-defendants in our case. Not surprisingly, Judge Perry denied the motion and called into the courtroom the venire (panel) of 150 prospective jurors, only fifteen of whom were Black. In his opening remarks to the courtroom full of prospective jurors, Perry referred to the events of December 4, 1969, as a "gun battle," and, in a most inappropriate assertion, noted "a certain amount of prejudice against police officers."

Judge Perry was prone to calling Black potential jurors "colored" and "Negro" as he conducted the voir dire questioning, and he did his best to rehabilitate those jurors who articulated an obvious bias against the Panthers or a connection to the police. After three weeks of questioning, a jury of six jurors and four alternates was chosen. Nine of the ten were white, and the sole African American member selected was Sallie Jones, an older, conservative woman whose son was a Los Angeles police officer. After she was reluctantly approved by defense counsel, Perry called her in and lectured her on prejudice, telling her, "Color is an illusion."

As jury selection drew to a close, Judge Perry, declaring that he was "not Solomon," did an about-face and ordered the government to produce the COINTELPRO documents. Among them was the December 3, 1969, memo that claimed the raid as a COINTELPRO activity.

First, we called Marlin Johnson, the special agent in charge of the Chicago FBI office, to the stand. The newly produced documents revealed that Johnson, as Chicago's top dog, had to approve all local COINTEL-PRO activities. Johnson was, in lawyer-speak, a "fog machine," claiming to remember precious little. In addition, to the utter amazement of everyone save the judge, Johnson defined a "hit" as a "nonviolent act" and claimed that the direction to O'Neal to "compel" criminal activities by the Panthers meant to "restrain" those activities. *Sun Times* columnist Bob Greene scorned Johnson's testimony using baseball terms: "No Guns, No Hits, No Terror," he wrote.

Next up was FBI agent Roy Martin Mitchell of the Racial Matters Squad. Mitchell, a complex man who played his cards close to the vest, had previously denied that the raid had any connection to COINTEL-PRO. It was mid-March when the otherwise very careful FBI agent made a blunder. Mitchell, in his haste to slander Fred Hampton and the Panthers, volunteered that informant O'Neal had told him about an alleged Panther plan to ambush a state trooper. We had no documentation of such a serious alleged plot, and we knew that if O'Neal had reported anything close to it—true or not—Mitchell would have written a memo to the file. Judge Perry directed Mitchell to look for the document, and, over the next week, as Jeff and I requested it repeatedly, Mitchell professed time and again that he had not found it yet. Then, on the last day of his testimony, Mitchell informed us in open court that he had found the document and would produce it later in the day, after he left the stand. Judge Perry, under the scrutiny of the newly awakened media, ordered the government to bring up all of the Hampton, O'Neal, and Black Panther files, and ordered Mitchell to retake the stand to explain his search.

Assistant US Attorney Kanter had been joined by a high-ranking Justice Department lawyer named Edward Christenbury. Apparently unwilling to continue the government's cover-up, Christenbury told the court that their team would produce all of the files we had been fighting for over the past two years. The next morning, our jaws dropped as the government lawyers paraded into court, wheeling carts loaded with nearly two hundred volumes of FBI documents. In total there were close to 35,000 pages of previously withheld documents, including 14 volumes on Fred Hampton, 16 on O'Neal, and 135 on the Black Panther Party. The judge, nonplused by what he had wrought, granted the government's request to retain the documents for the purpose of making deletions before producing the sanitized versions to us on a rolling basis.

Now, we thought, there was no way the trial could proceed. We would need weeks, if not months, to review and digest the contents of these materials, re-question the FBI principals who had generated them, and make the fundamental adjustments to our trial presentation that this newly discovered evidence would require. But Judge Perry refused to stop the train, which was already careening out of control; he was more determined than ever to protect the defendants and aid them in their quest to defeat our conspiracy case. So, for the next three weeks, the government produced sanitized files, a few each day, while we spent the mornings conducting hearings on those documents and the afternoons trying our radically evolving case before the jury. We sought sanctions against the government and the FBI defendants for the massive cover-up, but the judge refused to hold a sanctions hearing and barred us from asking the FBI defendants before the jury about their role in the cover-up. He told the jurors that it was his mistake alone that caused the suppression of evidence.

The documents were under a protective order and the judge had gagged us as well, so the courtroom was the only place where this explosive new evidence could be publicly exposed. To operate within these strictures, we devised a strategy of introducing a wide range of these documents into evidence while confronting the FBI witnesses on the stand with the contents. In this way we got startling new evidence to the public, such as documents that called for the crippling of the Panthers' Breakfast for Children Program, their political education classes, and their liberation school.

On April 8, 1976, the government lawyers produced the last two volumes of O'Neal's files. Roy Mitchell's supervisor on the Racial Matters Squad, Robert Piper, was on the stand. Our colleague Jim Montgomery had excused himself from much of the day-to-day conflict to tend to his law practice, so Jeff Haas stepped into his shoes as the lead witness interrogator, while I attempted to comprehend, organize, and manage the steady stream of evidence that was multiplying by the day; recorded the testimony coming from the witness stand; and handled the examination of a few witnesses.

As I thumbed through the O'Neal files at counsel table, I realized why the government had saved these for last. In the sixteenth file was a set of documents that definitively established O'Neal as a COINTELPRO agent. It also revealed that FBI headquarters had approved Robert Piper's request for a $300 bonus for O'Neal's work in obtaining the floor plan of the Hampton apartment and setting up the raid. In justification for O'Neal's thirty pieces of silver, Piper had lauded O'Neal's information as being of "tremendous value." When Jeff confronted Piper on the witness stand with his own language, Piper, perhaps not understanding the gravity of his words, admitted that, thanks to O'Neal, the raid was "successful."

Tension had continued to escalate inside the courtroom. Judge Perry rescinded his order on the government to give us the voluminous Chicago Black Panther files, the government "discovered" forty-five more files, Perry accused us of stalling, and then he held me in contempt for protesting the accusation. The $100 fine, which he later rescinded, would have cost a third of my monthly draw.

In the real world, on April 23, 1976, the Church Senate Committee released its *Final Report With Respect to Intelligence Activities*. The 989-page volume dealt with the illegal and unconstitutional transgressions of the FBI, CIA, NSA, IRS, and the US military. More than half the report covered FBI "black bag" jobs, wiretaps, use of informants/agents provocateur, and COINTELPRO. One chapter studied the FBI's plan to "neutralize" Martin Luther King Jr. In the very next chapter came "The FBI's Covert Action Program to Destroy the Black Panther Party." As promised by Arthur Jefferson, the chapter relied on a combination of the evidence we had shared with the committee and they with us, and, quoting from Robert Piper's bonus document, placed the responsibility for the murders of Fred Hampton and

Mark Clark squarely on the shoulders of the FBI and its COINTELPRO.

We received another public boost when we convinced US congressman Harold Washington and Illinois state senator Richard Newhouse to sign a letter, addressed to US attorney general Edward Levi, calling for an independent investigation of the "massive" and "illegal" governmental cover-up and for the firings of Kanter and Christenbury. The front page of the *Chicago Daily News* featured an article by Rob Warden with the headline "2 Charge FBI Hid Panther Death Role," and quoted from the letter, which we had supplied Warden.

Two weeks later, US attorney Sam Skinner announced that he had opened an internal investigation into the cover-up. To our befuddlement, he appointed assistant US attorney Charles Korcoras, the prosecutor who had worked hand in glove with Mitchell and O'Neal in the trial, a few years before, of disgraced "murder squad" sergeant Stanley Robinson. In the *Daily News* Rob Warden quoted me as saying appointing Korcoras was like "naming John Mitchell to investigate Watergate." We learned later that, regarding our letter calling for a special investigation, Judge Perry had sent secret letters to Korcoras and US attorney general Edward Levi, stating that the government attorneys' withholding of documents "could not have been intentional," that they all "acted in good faith," that only one of the multitude of withheld documents was relevant, and that all of the government lawyers and FBI defendants "should be complimented for their high standard of conduct in the case." For good measure, he pointed out that he had sentenced Harold Washington to probation in a tax evasion case a few years back.

Perry's boldness also extended to off-the-cuff remarks in public. He told Reverend Streitor, a suburban minister, at a local Memorial Day parade that the conspiracy involving Hanrahan and the FBI was "impossible," could not be true, and there was "no earthly way to establish it."

Two weeks after Memorial Day, we received the last volumes of FBI documents—files on the Panthers' Breakfast for Children Program and BPP wiretap files—and finished with our case against the FBI defendants. Rob Warden, who, along with Bob McClory, had been covering the trial on a daily basis, ran a front-page *Daily News* story detailing a statement circulated to courtroom reporters by another Mitchell informant, Maria Fisher. Fisher claimed that she had been solicited by Marlin Johnson, head of the Chicago FBI office, to drug Fred the night before the raid. Her credibility was suspect, but the issue of "who drugged Fred" had been a vexing issue ever since the independent toxicology report, performed in connection with a second autopsy, had revealed a large quantity of seco-barbital in his bloodstream. We had always felt that O'Neal had done the drugging, given the fact that he had fed Fred hot dogs and Kool-Aid the night before. Like all the Panthers who were asked, O'Neal strongly denied that Fred had used drugs, but, not surprisingly, he also denied that he had done the drugging.

The next four months of trial were devoted to the testimony of the seven raid survivors, starting with Ronald "Doc" Satchel. Doc was instrumental in setting up and running the Panthers' free medical clinic. He was inspired to join the Panthers when, as a nineteen-year-old pre-med student at the University of Illinois, he heard Fred speak. Doc had been asleep in the middle bedroom of the apartment, along with seventeen-year-old Verlina Brewer and former Blackstone Ranger Blair Anderson, when the raiders burst in firing. He later described what transpired when gunfire coming from the front and back of the tiny apartment roused him from sleep:

> I was on the bed nearest the door. Bullets started coming through the wall. Plaster was falling to the floor. When I got fully awake, the first thing I thought of was to get on the floor. Blair and Verlina were in my room. We all got down there, in between the two beds. I was hit with a Thompson submachine gun, forty-five caliber. I got hit once in the leg and three times in the pelvic area. I got wounded in my finger and thumb. My thumb was split wide open. So I had blood all over both hands.

He then described what happened after raider Joe Gorman stopped spraying the room:

> I saw two people in the doorway with guns pointed at me. I remember hear-ing a voice say, "If Panthers kill police, police will kill Panthers." They told me to turn the light on. I said I was hit and hurting and couldn't get up. They said, "If you don't get up, we're going to kill you." I tried to make my way around the foot of the bed, using the wall to support myself, and limped to the doorway. They started calling me "Nigger!" "Black bastard!" "Mother-fucker!" I hopped once or twice more toward the back of the house—then I was kicked in the rear. I fell flat on the floor in the dining room area, on my chest and stomach.

He described suffering intense pain:

I was told to put both of my hands behind my neck, and handcuffs were placed on my wrists, real tight. I was in a very awkward position. My stomach was in pain. I had pain in my leg. Raising my arms over my neck caused more intense pain. The cuffs cut off circulation in my arms. Blair was put on the floor next to me. I seemed to be passing out. I thought I was going to die. I heard Blair say, "Be strong. You'll be all right." I was kicked on one of my feet and told, "Get up, nigger." I tried. But I was dizzy and blacking out periodically. The same voice said, "Get up or I'll kick your ass." I don't know how I managed to get up—maybe it was a rush of adrenalin—but I did. I had to walk to the front door and down the stairs and all the way to the paddy wagon. It was freezing cold. I was in excruciating pain, and I kept passing out.

Doc spent two weeks in Cook County Hospital, chained to a bed, and part of his colon was removed. He "kept wondering what happened to Fred. When I found out Fred had died, I cried. I felt real bad, and I wished that I had died, too."

The other Panther raid survivors followed: Vietnam vet Harold Bell, who described experiencing a domestic search-and-destroy mission; Blair Anderson and Verlina Brewer, both wounded by machine gun and shotgun fire; and Louis Truelock, a forty-six-year-old ex-prisoner Fred had met while incarcerated and was widely suspected of being a police informant. Truelock disappeared during his days of testimony and Jeff had to hunt for him in the west side drug houses. Brenda Harris and Deborah Johnson completed the procession of survivors who took the stand. Brenda, like Verlina a diminutive teenager, was shot upon the raiders' violent entrance after they had fatally shot Mark Clark, the Peoria Panther sitting as security at the front door, through the heart. As Brenda lay wounded on the bed in the front room, Joe Gorman stitched the wall above her with machine gun fire.

Fred's partner, Deborah Johnson, eight and a half months pregnant, was asleep in the rear bedroom when the raiders came through in the back, firing. She described how Fred had fallen asleep:

We got in bed. He said, "You better call my mom and tell her we're not going to come." So I called her, and we talked for a while. Fred fell asleep while he was talking to his mother. It was unusual, but I didn't think it was anything really strange.

At 4:30 a.m. Deborah was awakened:

The first thing I remember was Louis Truelock on the side of the bed, shaking Fred: "Chairman, Chairman, wake up! The pigs are vamping!" I looked up and saw bullets coming from what looked like the front of the apartment and the kitchen area. The only movement that Fred made was to lift his head up slowly. He looked up, then laid his head back down. That was all the movement that he did. He never said a word. For him to move his head up that slowly and just lay it back down was real unusual. Especially if somebody was saying, "The pigs are vamping." If he had heard that, he would have flown up. Although Fred was big, he was very swift on his feet.

She continued:

All this time, the bed was vibrating. Bullets were going into the mattress. I looked up at the doorway, and I could see sparks of light, because it was dark back in that area. I thought I was dead then and I was just seeing this as a spirit or something. I didn't feel any pain. I wasn't shot, but I just knew, with all this going on, it was all over. Then Louis Truelock yelled out: "Stop shooting! Stop shooting! We have a pregnant sister in here." At some point, they stopped shooting. Fred didn't move anymore. That was it, the one time he raised his head and laid it back down, like a slow-motion movie.

After the shooting stopped, Deborah came out of the bedroom:

There were two lines of police that I had to walk through. One of them grabbed my robe and pulled it open and said, "Well, what do you know—we have a pregnant broad." Another policeman grabbed me by the hair and slung me into the kitchen area.

She then described the assassination of Fred Hampton:

I stood facing the wall by the refrigerator, next to the open door. Then the shooting started up again. I heard a woman scream. Then it stopped. I looked around and saw Ronald Satchel on the dining room floor. He had blood all over him. They brought Verlina Brewer in from the front bedroom area and threw her against the refrigerator. She was bleeding. She started to fall. They grabbed her and threw her against the refrigerator again. Ron Satchel wasn't moving. I thought he was dead. I mean, I couldn't even see his body breathe. There was more shooting. I heard a voice that wasn't familiar to me say, "He's barely alive. He'll barely make it." I assumed they were talking about Fred. The shooting started again, just for a brief period. It stopped. Then another unfamiliar voice said, "He's good and dead now."

Tensions continued to rise as the trial headed into its eleventh month. FBI firearms expert Robert Zimmers painstakingly established that only one of the nearly one hundred shots fired came from a Panther weapon. A subplot concerned the wildly disparate resources of the two sides. The County and City were paying the lawyers for Hanrahan and the police an hourly rate that would, when all was said and done, exceed a total of two million dollars, while we were scuffling to survive. The entire force of the US attorneys' office, Department of Justice, and FBI was arrayed against us. The defense lawyers received copies of the transcript within hours of the testimony, while we were relegated to reading the court's copy in the courtroom—when Perry deigned to let us do so. We also learned that these lawyers had struck a secret, unethical deal with the court reporter, paying more per page, in order to keep us from getting a cheaper copy.

Against this backdrop arose the "raid" controversy. John Coghlan, Hanrahan's lead lawyer, and Camillo Volini, who represented the police raiders, had convinced Judge Perry to bar us from using the word "raid." Instead, the event could only, and exclusively, be called "the service of a search warrant." Yet, in an agreed stipulation, Coghlan and Volini consented to the use of the word "raid," and the forbidden word was read to the jury. They then accused us of willfully violating the court's order; the judge agreed, over our protests, and told the jury we had done so.

Outraged, I went through the transcript and found exactly where Coghlan and Volini had agreed to the use of the word "raid," and attempted to present an emergency motion to have Judge Perry correct his prejudicial statement to the jury. Over the course of the trial, Perry had repeatedly told me to "shut up," accused me of "not knowing anything," accused Jeff and me of "disrupting" the trial, and otherwise heaped abuse upon us.

When I attempted to present the motion, Judge Perry refused to hear it and called for the jury. Exasperated, we returned to our counsel table, located in front of the jury box. I tossed my files and papers onto the table in a sweeping motion that propelled a glass-lined water pitcher off the table and into the side of the empty jury box. The glass splintered, water splashed onto the floor, and the judge said, "Let the record show the conduct of both counsel in throwing papers around and one of them—what is it that is broken over there?" Attorney Coghlan, "ever the snitch," as Dennis later wrote, pointed out that it was a broken glass pitcher, and the judge shouted, "Mr. Taylor, you did that, and you are now held in contempt and the court now orders you committed to the attorney general of the United

States for a period of twenty-four hours and orders the marshal to take you into custody forthwith."

As the marshal dragged me out of the courtroom, I vainly demanded that I be permitted to speak in my defense. The judge recessed so that photos could be taken of the crime scene. The story, accompanied by the judge's photos, was splashed all over television and the newspapers. Four jurors admitted to seeing the water pitcher story on the ten o'clock news; one newspaper reported that I had "flung" the pitcher across the courtroom.

As I sat in a jail cell at the Metropolitan Correctional Center (MCC) a block away from the courthouse, with only a pen, I took brown paper towels from the wall dispenser and wrote out a motion exposing the defense lawyers' secret court transcript deal and demanding that they be sanctioned for it. Then I composed an angry song, the "J. Sam Piggy Blues."

> I'm a racist through and through,
> And a goddamned fascist too,
> My name is J. Sam Piggy Blue.

Judge Perry, in a written order, refused to admit that he was wrong about the "raid" stipulation. In a polemic drafted by Dennis, we—unsuccessfully—beseeched the Seventh Circuit Court of Appeals to remove Perry from the case. We cited an "unholy alliance" between Perry and the defense and blasted him for "gross unfairness," "wrongheaded prejudicial actions," "exasperated temper and bias," and an "infinite tolerance of brazenly obvious and obfuscating defense tactics." The *Daily Defender* opined:

> If the 11 month old Black Panther trial is to be anything more than another long, agonizing whitewash, U.S. District Judge Joseph Sam Perry must step out of the case or be politely removed, courtroom observers and a growing number of legal experts agree. At 80, Perry is too old, too ill tempered, too emotionally involved in defending his dignity and too antagonistic toward some of the attorneys to handle the subtleties of the complicated affair, they believe.

Two weeks later, informant O'Neal took the stand. Jeff took him on with relish. We had successfully demanded additional O'Neal documents from the government—this time, the file that showed he had received tens of thousands of dollars from the government since his role in setting up the raid was publicly exposed. The government called it "relocation" and "witness protection expenses"; we branded it hush money.

On the stand, O'Neal downplayed his relationship with Roy Mitchell and mixed "I don't recalls" with denials that he was a provocateur. We had lined up two of O'Neal's former Panther buddies to give firsthand accounts of his violent schemes, and Jeff confronted O'Neal with his attempts to "discourage" them from testifying. Jeff also brought out that O'Neal was paid six times more than an average FBI informant and that he had received his "Judas" bonus payment directly after serving as a pall-bearer at Fred's funeral. During his testimony, which stretched into the New Year, O'Neal vanished for several days. The government and O'Neal offered up inconsistent explanations, but the judge refused to let us probe. We surmised that O'Neal was threatening to tell the actual truth if he did not get some additional compensation.

Later that January, more than a year into the trial, we called raid leader Daniel Groth to the stand. Sergeant Groth, rumored to have connections to the CIA, had led the charge through the front door of Fred's apartment together with a notoriously brutal Black cop named James "Gloves" Davis. Crucial to the raid's legal cover was the search warrant that Groth and Jalovec had drafted. In the warrant, issued by a judge who had previously been Hanrahan's first assistant, Sergeant Groth swore that there were two sources of information: the FBI, and an informant of his own. We were convinced that Groth did not have an informant, that the warrant was based entirely on O'Neal's triple-hearsay information. If that were true, the warrant was illegal, Groth was a perjurer, and the FBI–police conspiracy would be more powerfully established.

We had begun to establish this theory two and a half years earlier, when I had attempted, in a smoke-filled deposition room, to question Groth about this informant. He refused to answer, repeating that to reveal the informant's name, or anything about him or her, would "endanger the lives of other people." He did, however, reveal that he had a floor plan of Fred Hampton's apartment, sketched on a yellow piece of paper, which had disappeared. In a pretrial ruling Judge Perry had refused to order Groth to answer questions about his alleged informant, but he had left the door open for us to revisit the question at trial.

Given my familiarity with Groth and the informant issue, I drew the assignment of cross-examining him. Somehow, I had to challenge Groth's assertion that he had an informant while making a record for an almost certain appeal. This was compounded by Attorney Coghlan interspersing objections and directions to Groth not to answer, and the judge upbraiding me for crossing the ever-shifting line of what would supposedly endanger the life of some unknown person. This cat-and-mouse game went on, as I built to the ultimate question:

> Mr. Taylor: Now, you have discussed with your purported informant when he intends to come in here and verify the testimony you have given?
> Groth: At the direction of Special State's Attorney Coghlan and Corporation Counsel Volini, because of my promise to my informant, I respectfully decline to answer that question because my answer may endanger the lives of other persons.

After a heated exchange with the judge, I continued:

> Mr. Taylor: How does it endanger the lives of other people?

Judge Perry barked, "Objection sustained" before Coghlan and Volini could open their mouths to object. I asked for a sidebar outside the jury's presence, but Perry refused, so I headed to the precipice:

> Mr. Taylor: You didn't have an informant, did you, Mr. Groth?
> Groth: That is a total untruth.
> Mr. Taylor: Well, who is he?

All hell broke loose. Perry loudly chastised me for asking the question and summarily cut me off: "You are through, you are through. I am terminating your examination." As the jury filed out, I put my head down on the podium.

The next day, in Perry's chambers, I was taken to the woodshed. Coghlan called me stupid and incompetent, accused me of "boo-hooing" before the jury and of using "Hitler tactics." I made a statement defending my actions and my integrity that felt like I was speaking at my own sentencing. The judge demanded a blanket apology in exchange for my right to continue with questioning, and I reluctantly agreed to apologize, but only for asking the final question.

Next was state's attorney Edward Vincent Hanrahan. Having fallen from grace after the raid, "Hammyhands," as acerbic *Daily News* columnist Mike Royko had dubbed him, was attempting to rekindle his political career by running to replace his former mentor, recently deceased mayor Richard J. Daley, in the Democratic primary against Michael Bilandic—the machine's candidate—and Harold Washington. The December 4th Committee had sprung into action, and Hanrahan was greeted by a courthouse demonstration with leaflets and picket signs proclaiming "Wanted for Murder Not for Mayor" and "Hanrahan=Ku Klux Klan." After the defense lawyers complained, Perry issued an order that barred the demonstrators from the sidewalk surrounding the Federal Building and sent US marshals up and down the aisles of the courtroom, looking for spectators with leaflets.

The confrontation between Jeff and Hanrahan started slowly, almost politely. Hanrahan admitted that he had a close working relationship with Roy Mitchell and Marlin Johnson while he was the US attorney for the Northern District of Illinois but attempted to restrict his pre-raid involvement to a December 3 meeting with Jalovec, where he had tacitly approved the raid by telling Jalovec to caution the raiders to "be careful." He took no responsibility for the raid's pre-dawn timing or the decision not to use tear gas, floodlights, or bullhorns. The courtroom tension escalated as Jeff confronted Hanrahan with his racist "war on gangs"; his deceitful and hateful post-raid pronouncements about the "vicious" Black Panthers, the "gun battle," and his "courageous" raiders; his refusal to admit or deny whether he had consulted Mayor Daley before or after the raid; and the carefully orchestrated exclusive he had given to the *Tribune,* where nailheads and police bullet holes were falsely identified as evidence of Panther firing.

The showdown reached its apex when Jeff attempted to question Hanrahan about a deal struck in the spring of 1970 between Civil Rights Division chief Jerris Leonard and Hanrahan, which spared Hanrahan, Jalovec, and their raiders from federal indictment in exchange for Hanrahan's agreement to dismiss the charges against the Panther survivors. (Leonard had consulted with his boss, attorney general John Mitchell.) The contours of this deal were outlined in an FBI document that, days before, Judge Perry had barred me from introducing into evidence when I had questioned its author. The unwritten third tenet of this deal was that Hanrahan and the raiders would remain silent about the FBI's role in the raid. When Jeff probed Hanrahan's denial of knowledge of the deal, using evidence I had managed to elicit from the document's author, Judge Perry cut him off and forbade him from further questioning about the deal. Jeff replied, "Judge, we can't cover up the cover-up."

Perry held Jeff in contempt and sentenced him to twenty-four hours in the MCC. On his way to jail, Jeff said, "I think all the people who have spoken the truth have always ended up in contempt, and the cover-up goes on and on." When Jeff was freed the next morning, he told the press that while the food was bland at the MCC, he found "the company there more congenial than that of some persons in the courtroom."

As we moved into March, the pressure to finish our case mounted, and Perry continually threatened to cut us off. We called as witnesses the BPP minister of defense Bobby Rush, national Panther leader Elaine Brown, the head of the Afro American Patrolmen's League, and the former mayor of Maywood to talk about Fred's history as a young NAACP organizer and his unique leadership qualities as a Panther. Panther veterans Rush and Brown also attempted to dispel the false, media-driven image of the Panthers as a "racist" and violent street gang, to give a true depiction of the Black Panther Party, with its "serve the people" ten-point program, its philosophy of self-defense in the face of rampant police brutality in the Black community, and its building, through Fred, of the original Rainbow Coalition—Black, white, Puerto Rican, and poor people—in Chicago. Unlike Hanrahan's appearance, unfortunately, this evidence drew little press attention, with more attention paid to the expensive Gucci boots Elaine Brown wore to the stand.

In early April, Judge Perry terminated our evidence, and the twenty-eight defendants filed nine voluminous motions for directed verdicts in their favor. Perry gave us less than a week to respond, and our frantically compiled fact-laden responses were submitted, in part, in handwriting. After a few hours of argument from Jeff and me, the judge took a long lunch break, and, upon return read from several written orders. As Judge Romiti had done before him, Perry usurped the function of the jury and dismissed Hanrahan on the eve of an election, along with all our conspiracy claims, those against the FBI defendants, and the cover-up claims, leaving only the claims against the seven raiding officers who had admitted to firing their weapons at the apartment. Although we were not shocked, we were outraged, and ignored Perry's gag order to publicly say so. Hanrahan, for his part, crowed about his judge-conferred blamelessness, but he still overwhelmingly lost his bid for mayor to Bilandic a week later.

As the case against the seven triggermen continued, Perry granted us the right to call the mothers of Fred Hampton and Mark Clark to the stand. Both mothers were strong and loving women who exuded a quiet strength. They had both sat, stoically, through the painful reliving of their sons' brutal murders and the constant slander and abuse that the defense lawyers heaped upon their sons. Their appearances on the stand were brief but powerful. Iberia Hampton talked about Fred and the late-night call, just past midnight on December 4, when Fred told her he would not be coming home that night as promised. She broke down in tears as she recounted Fred's telling her that Deborah was pregnant and that she should look after the baby if anything happened to him.

Judge Perry's decision had angered many in the community who had been following the trial, and a large demonstration took place across the street from the courthouse while "Machine Gun" Joe Gorman was testifying for the defense. Attorneys Coghlan and Volini informed the judge and accused us of organizing the event. They also recited to the judge some of the picket signs: "Reverse Perry's Racist Outrage" and "Co-conspirators: FBI, Hanrahan, Local Police and Now Perry."

We were resigned to the fact that there was no way the judge would let us win what was left of the case; nevertheless we pressed on to make of record all the evidence that he was barring us from presenting to the jury, and to contest at every opportunity his blatant unfairness. The abuse—not only from the judge but also from the defendants—was unremitting. Several of the raiders attended court each day, on the City's dime. Early on, Gloves Davis, who shot Mark Clark and Brenda Harris, pulled a gun on Doc Satchel in the courtroom cafeteria. Each day, the raiders stared us down and, as we walked by them in the hall, whispered, "Jeff sucks" and "Flint sucks." This was part of a conscious plan on the defense's part to bait us that Coghlan executed with reckless glee. He accused Jeff of being "limp-wristed," a "sissy," and "sashaying around the courtroom" and called me a "fairy." According to Coghlan, Jeff and I were everything from "insolent" and "gutless" "fakers," arguing "drivel" and "foolishness," to "revolutionary" lawyers bent on destroying the entire judicial system.

During the last few months of the trial, Jeff took on most of the raiding cops, while I dealt with the expert witnesses called by the raiders in an effort to undermine our toxicological evidence that Fred had been drugged. We presented a strong circumstantial case, conforming with Deborah Johnson's testimony, that Fred had been executed by Edward Carmody, the raider who had led the charge through the back door. Carmody had admitted to firing several shots from his handgun into the back bedroom where Fred was sleeping. We unsuccessfully fought to introduce evidence that showed Gloves Davis had amassed sixty-six complaints for brutality and misconduct, and that he had thrown our associate, attorney Marc Kadish, up against the wall in the Criminal Courts Building on the morning of December 4, 1969, when Marc referred to the "murder" of Fred Hampton. The judge also refused to admit a police radio tape on which unknown officers cheered when it was announced that Fred was taken to the morgue, and on which one said, in unwitting affirmation of our evidence, "That is the time to catch them—when they are in bed." We also offered as evidence the chilling picture of smiling cops, carrying Fred's body out of the apartment.

After the evidence was closed in early June, Coghlan and Volini made what is normally a perfunctory motion, asking Perry to decide that there was insufficient evidence for the remaining skeleton of our case to be decided by the jury. Brief arguments were heard, and the judge deferred his ruling until after the jury made its decision. This would give him a final opportunity to erase the verdict, in the unlikely event that the jury ruled in our favor. But the undeniable evidence was so strong—ninety bullets to one—that it would take a monumental abuse of the law and facts for Perry to do so.

Jim Montgomery returned to the courtroom to make the first of our closing arguments. With the mothers of Fred and Mark, most of the Panther survivors, and the six-and-a-half-year-old son of Fred and Deborah sitting on one side of the courtroom and the raiders on the other, we listened uncomfortably as Jim separated his view of the case from ours. Calling it a simple case, he told the jury to ignore what the Panthers and Fred stood for. In a significant rejection of the large amount of unfinished business created by Judge Perry's dismissals, Montgomery called upon the jury to "put to rest finally and forever what happened on December 4th."

I followed, focusing on humanizing Fred, Mark, and the survivors, emphasizing their youthful idealism, and detailing the racially motivated torture that they suffered. I highlighted the many positive aspects of the Black Panther Party and its programs. I explained how the toxicological evidence definitively established that Fred was drugged, and I noted that the raiders were armed not only with a battery of high-powered weapons but also with a floor plan of the apartment. In conclusion, I argued:

> We come to you and ask you to enforce the law because if it is not enforced here when will it be enforced? Are police officers going to be allowed to shoot from 90 to 100 bullets into an apartment of citizens of this country, whether they be black or white, poor, rich, Panthers or not Panthers, to use the color of our laws to do that, to tear the place asunder, to beat people, to shoot them, to maim them for life, to kill them? Are they going to be able to? That is the question that you have to ask yourselves. These defendants, as police officers,

are they going to be allowed to violate those rights in the face of the law, in the face of our Constitution, in the face of the Bill of Rights? I say you won't let them, and you will come back with a just and fair verdict which history will be proud of. That is what we ask and that is what the evidence demands.

Jeff argued powerfully that the targeting of Fred by the raiders, the angles of the bullets in Fred's head, the admissions that Carmody had made in reports and earlier testimony, and Deborah Johnson's testimony all established that Fred was murdered, indeed assassinated, as he lay drugged on his bed at 4:30 in the morning of December 4, 1969. After all the arguments were concluded, the judge granted Coghlan an additional argument so he could tell the jury that he was formerly a Chicago police officer and had left the force to become a lawyer after his Black partner had taken five bullets in the stomach.

On Friday, June 16, 1977, at 7:15 p.m., the jury was sequestered at a nearby hotel and began its deliberations. When we returned to court on Monday morning, Perry informed us that he had received several notes from the jury over the weekend, starting on Saturday. Each note asserted that the jurors were "hopelessly deadlocked." Without consulting us, he had instructed the marshal to tell them to continue to deliberate. The notes became more and more definitive, stating that further deliberations would be futile. Surprised that the jury was divided despite all that had transpired, Jeff, Dennis, and I agreed with the defendants that a mistrial should be declared. Jim Montgomery, seeking finality, disagreed and wanted the judge to instruct the jury to continue to deliberate. All of our positions were presented to the judge. We made it clear that we believed that the proper approach was to declare the jury hung, and a new trial ordered. As weary as we were, we thought that we might be able to escape Perry on retrial and be able to fairly present our case. Coghlan, for the defense, told Judge Perry that before he declared the jury hung he should grant the defense motions for directed verdicts.

It was as if a light bulb went off in Perry's head. He quickly called in the jury and followed Coghlan's instructions, dismissing the case for "insufficient evidence." So ended the longest trial in federal court history.

The *Daily Defender*'s banner headline the next day read: "Verdict in Panther Case Called 'Racist.'" Iberia Hampton was quoted by Bob McClory as angrily saying, "My son's name is cleared no matter what that judge said. Anybody in his right mind knows the truth by now, but nothing that man does would surprise me." I said that Perry's verdict "was an incredible insult to the black community. It was an outrageous ruling." Jeff summed up the trial: "The law has been turned upside down and stretched every which way to defeat us. We can't underestimate the vengeful side of Judge Perry."

We later learned that the jury was split 4–2 for the defendants. Sallie Jones, the jury's only Black member, and Collette Barbosa, a white woman whose husband had died during jury selection, were firmly in our corner. Now it was on to the appeal.

Not so fast, decreed Perry. He required that we post a $100,000 bond as a prerequisite to appealing. The Court of Appeals lifted the bond, and we began the mammoth task of reading and outlining the 37,000-page trial transcript, and researching, writing, typing, and producing a brief 246 pages in length. The signature page listed fifteen lawyers and several law students, ten of whom were from the PLO, and acknowledged the work of fourteen additional people who had also contributed to the final product. Among those named were Jon Moore and Jani Hoft, who would go on to be important members of our office, and Linda Turner, who typed and retyped, at all times of the day and night, the mammoth brief. Jeff and I boldly put photos of Fred and Mark on the inside front cover. The brief concluded with a series of demands that reflected Dennis's rhetorical skill:

> The case made out by Plaintiffs was easily sufficient in all respects to go to the jury on each Defendant with every count. Equally clear is the vengeful disposition of the judge who so assiduously sought to hold back the tide of that reality. . . . He must be reversed in every wrongful action below which is not moot, and rebuked for those acts which are; and Appellants must be made whole upon the record for a new trial under the detailed supervision of this Court. Their rights to all the evidence on discovery must be spelled out and enforced; all the proper Defendants in the conspiracy must be joined; the admissibility of critical items suppressed by Judge Perry must be pronounced; the propriety of challenge on cross-examination, and of admissions and prior statements as evidence, must be upheld; and the Defendants properly punished for their brazen misconduct and obstruction which is underscored by their massive cover-up of documents and their repeated lying to the Court about them.
>
> Indeed the judgment of this Court of Appeals must be upon Judge Perry for his partisan defense of those caught murdering FRED HAMPTON and MARK CLARK, and violating the basic human rights of young, black people,

and covering up the truth about it to this day—all by conspiracy, plotting and racism of the most frightening sort.

This Court must see to it that the conspiracy proceeds no further, as well as that those shown to be responsible are made accountable. Plaintiffs have sought to prosecute this case for eight years in the public interest as well as their own. The case they managed to make out in this trial more than vindicates the worthiness of their claims. It is a conclusive judgment on the failure of the entire apparatus of law enforcement, government, and justice, to rise to the occasion created by the facts in this case, and in the case of the campaign against the Panther Party nationwide. F.B.I. racial "counterintelligence" was a star-spangled blueprint for genocide, and still is if allowed to exist, and if those who operate it are still allowed to do so. They still have the mission of "neutralization" against their perceived political opponents, and they still demand immunity for their operations. They still purport to be protecting our country; and they still do not accept the Bill of Rights.

For all this, the undersigned demand detailed and determined redress, to be ordered and guaranteed by this Honorable Court through the full and timely exercise of its judicial responsibility, upon the authority of the truth and the People of the United States, until full justice is finally done. **All power to the People**.

On August 14, 1978, the Seventh Circuit Court of Appeals convened a highly unusual special session to hear a full day of oral arguments on our appeal. A week before, the *Chicago Reader* had published a front-page article by Bob McClory, with a photo of Jeff and me looking as tough as we could, entitled "Why Don't Jeff Haas and Flint Taylor Just Give Up?" McClory wrote: "Both are young, talented, and aggressive. By rights, they should be comfortable attorneys in prestigious LaSalle Street offices. Instead, 9 years after the infamous Black Panther raid, they're making $125 a week and still fighting to bring the killers of Fred Hampton and Mark Clark to justice."

We were thrilled when the three Seventh Circuit judges assigned to the case took the bench. Two of the three had liberal reputations, and one, judge Luther Swygert, had been a friend of the radical National Lawyers Guild as a young attorney. The third was the conservative judge Wilbur Pell, who, we would later learn, was a former FBI agent. Jim Montgomery, Jeff, and I all argued, as did a battery of defense lawyers, and Dennis argued the contempt cases. Tension was at its highest when Judge Pell confronted Dennis with our implied conclusion that if the Court of Appeals ruled against us it, too, would be part of the conspiracy. In response, Dennis did his best lawyer's imitation of Muhammad Ali's "rope-a-dope," giving an equivocal response that Dennis rues to this day. In Dennis's considered view, the only principled answer was "yes."

We awaited the court's decision with guarded optimism. On April 23, 1979, the court issued its seventy-one-page opinion. As soon as we saw that Judge Swygert had written the opinion, our spirits soared. In a 2–1 decision, with Judge Pell filing a vitriolic dissent, the court found that we had presented "considerable evidence"—the "most damning from the files of the FBI itself"—that the FBI had a national counterintelligence program seemingly aimed at "neutralizing the Black Panther Party as a political entity. . . . Among the tactics used by the FBI was to discredit the BPP among liberal whites, the promotion of violent conflicts between the BPP and other groups, the encouragement of dissension within the BPP, and the disruption of the Breakfast for Children Program."

The court also found that "one of the key figures in the Chicago program to disrupt the Panthers was William O'Neal," through whom the other FBI defendants "effectuated many of their programs" and who encouraged the Panthers to initiate and "participate in various criminal activities, obtain more weapons, and to increase their use of violent tactics." It also recognized that "the FBI in Washington urged its offices implementing COINTELPRO to develop . . . working relationships with local law enforcement officials . . . to help effectuate the FBI's counterintelligence goals." The Court noted that on December 3, 1969, the FBI defendants notified bureau headquarters in a counterintelligence memorandum that "a positive course of action" was planned on Hampton's apartment and later claimed credit for the raid in a post-raid memo that sought a $300 bonus for O'Neal for his work in setting up the raid. The court further recounted a complex federal and state effort to cover up and falsify the evidence, a conspiracy that continued through the trial.

The Seventh Circuit found that we had presented evidence of two conspiracies between and among the FBI, the police, and the prosecutor defendants. The first encompassed the planning of the raid and the raid itself, and was designed "to subvert and eliminate the Black Panther Party and its members, thereby suppressing . . . a vital, radical black political organization." The second conspiracy, which included the post-raid cover-up and legal harassment of the plaintiffs, "was intended to frustrate any redress the Plaintiffs might seek and, more importantly, to conceal the true character of the pre-raid and raid activities of the defendants involved in the first conspiracy." The court further found that there was no doubt that "the evidence demonstrated a commingling of racial and political motives on the part of the defendants." As to the federal defendants, the court found that COINTELPRO, as indicated by the FBI's own documents, "directed against the BPP transcended mere 'law enforcement' and [was] designed to 'neutralize' the BPP as a political voice on racial issues."

The court also sided with us on the issue of Groth's informant:

> There is a serious factual controversy focusing on the existence or identity of Groth's informant, and a resolution of this controversy is essential to a just adjudication of Plaintiffs' claims. Thus, we conclude that the public's interest in encouraging the flow of information to law enforcement officials cannot prevail in this case, and that Groth must disclose the identity of his informant.

We also won a hearing on whether the federal defendants and their lawyers should be punished for their suppression of the FBI files:

> [Marlin] Johnson, [Robert] Piper and [Roy] Mitchell, and their counsel, rather than promptly furnishing relevant documents as requested, deliberately impeded discovery and actively obstructed the judicial process, thus denying the Plaintiffs the fair trial to which they were entitled. Regrettably, the trial judge permitted these tactics . . . [and] repeatedly exonerated the federal defendants for these derelictions.

The court of appeals also absolved Jeff and me of our contempt citations. While not "condoning" my "gesture of anger," the court found that Judge Perry's course of prior conduct had caused me to "reach the breaking point" of my "patience and forbearance." In absolving Jeff, the court stated that attorneys had the right to be "persistent, vociferous, contentious, and imposing, even to the point of appearing obnoxious, when acting on their client's behalf."

We were elated and felt a deep sense of vindication. Chick Hoffman had T-shirts made, with "Right On Luther" emblazoned on the front. It was a complete victory, but it wasn't final yet. The defendants moved for a rehearing before all of the judges of the Seventh Circuit; we escaped with a tie vote. The Burger Supreme Court refused to hear the case, voting 5–3 against granting certiorari on the federal defendants' petition and 7–1 against Hanrahan and the raiders. The Supreme Court did see fit to take away the $100,000 in attorneys' fees that the court of appeals had awarded us.

In an act of justified mercy, the court of appeals had directed in its decision that the case be assigned to a different trial court judge for a prompt retrial. Initially, it was assigned at random to Milton Shadur, one of the most liberal and brilliant judges on the bench. However, Judge Shadur recused himself because, while a lawyer, his office had signed an amicus brief supporting our side of the case.

The case was then assigned to John Grady, a moderate Republican judge with no ax to grind. We moved to implement the court of appeals decision by holding a hearing on the federal cover-up and to compel Groth and Coghlan to name their phantom informant. Coghlan at first resisted, then, after Judge Grady ordered Groth to comply, I found myself, in the summer of 1981, once again facing Groth in a tension-filled deposition, asking him once again about his informant. This time, Groth named a former Panther who had been killed in a failed bombing attempt soon after the raid. This designation was demonstrably false, and both Groth and Coghlan were caught in a web of lies and intimidation that included the brow-beating of the mother and brother of the deceased former Panther. Judge Grady expressed "surprise" that the named informant was long since dead, and we asked him, in a sixty-page motion that carefully detailed Groth's and Coghlan's pattern of misconduct, to formally declare that Groth did not have an informant. Coincidence or not, the County fired Coghlan soon after Groth's deposition.

With all of the defendants now between a rock and a hard place, we entered into settlement negotiations with US attorney Dan Webb and lawyers from Cook County and the City of Chicago. In November 1982, the *New York Times* announced that we had reached a record $1.85 million settlement with the City, County, and federal government. Bill Hampton, Fred's brother, told the *Times,* "At times when we had to go to court almost daily and when all the decisions were coming down against us, [it seemed] we should just give up, but we in the family knew that we were right and the police were wrong, so we just kept praying and kept fighting." I added that the historic settlement was "an admission of a conspiracy between the FBI and the police" and that the case would "live on as a reminder of how far the government can and will go to suppress those whose philosophies it does not like." After thirteen years of intense struggle, we had changed the historical narrative and added a harrowing chapter to the people's history of racist police violence in Chicago.

CHAPTER 2

The *Wilson* Case

And He Just Kept on Cranking and Cranking . . .

Just months before we finally settled the *Hampton* case, Chicago was rocked by a series of fatal shootings of police officers in broad daylight. On February 9, 1982, two uniformed CPD officers, Richard O'Brien and William Fahey, were shot and killed during a routine traffic stop on Chicago's south side. They had just attended the funeral of a Chicago police officer who had been shot only days before. Two Black men fled the scene in a brown Chevy, and mayor Jane Byrne and her police superintendent, Richard Brzeczek, mandated what would become the most massive manhunt in the City's history. Brzeczek designated lieutenant Jon Burge, who headed up the Violent Crimes Unit at Area 2, to direct the search for the killers. The geographical area policed by Area 2, which covered most of Chicago's predominantly African American far south side, became the main focus of the manhunt.

Under Burge's command, incensed CPD officers kicked in doors, ransacked homes, beat up numerous residents, and, once suspects were in custody, tortured those Black men they suspected of either being involved in or having knowledge of the crime. Several had bags placed over their heads in what is known in the international torture lexicon as "dry submarino," at least one man was beaten on the bottoms of his feet and testicles, and another was taken to a police station roof, where one of his hands was placed in a bolt cutter. Upward of two hundred complaints were filed with the CPD by abused persons, ranging from mothers and a fireman and a taxi cab driver to alleged street gang members. Local civil rights leader the Reverend Jesse Jackson publicly likened the manhunt to Kristallnacht,

35

the bloody nighttime raids on Jewish homes and synagogues that were perpetrated by the Nazis in November 1938. Many of the complaints were collected by the president of the well-respected Black Bar Association, Ronald Samuels, who made several phone calls and sent urgent letters and a telegram to Superintendent Brzeczek in an unsuccessful attempt to speak directly with him about the "explosive situation" in the Black community. A Fraternal Order of Police (FOP) leader offered a $10,000 reward, while admitting that there was "a lot of anger among the men," and lamenting, "There is no respect out there for the man in blue. When policemen in full uniform are getting shot in broad daylight, the uniform means nothing."

By February 12, the investigation had zeroed in on a group of young men who lived close to the murder scene. A contingent of Area 2 detectives, including Frank Laverty—a stand-up cop who believed in telling the truth—went to the men's house and took six of them into custody. Laverty was about to transport them to Area 2 when Burge approached him and directed him to relinquish custody because Burge intended to take them to police headquarters at 11th and State for interrogation. All too aware of Burge's reputation, Laverty pointedly told his boss, "He's cuffed, he ain't hurt, he ain't been touched." Laverty later told me that he "cared more about the case being done right than about some punch in the head."

Burge scowled at Laverty and went off with a few trusted detectives and the captured suspects to 11th and State, which housed both the CPD's detective headquarters and Superintendent Brzeczek's office. Burge was met by the chief of detectives, Bill Hanhardt (who would later spend ten years in federal prison on corruption charges). Primary among the suspects was Donald White, who Burge and his men had concluded was one of the killers. Donald, his brothers Lamont and Walter, Anthony Williams, and two other associates were put in separate rooms. Donald, a slight and nervous man who went by the incongruous nickname of "Kojak," repeatedly told the room full of menacing detectives that he "didn't shoot no police." Detective Fred Hill, who Laverty claimed had a reputation as a violent racist, told Donald that he was "tired of this fucking shit," and pulled out a plastic bag. Hill placed the bag over Donald's head, and while he was gasping for air, the detectives beat him all over his head, "just beating me, beating me." When he persisted in denying that he shot Fahey and O'Brien, Hill·and his cohorts again subjected Donald to dry submarino. With his head pounding, Donald, who had asthma, started to scream and plead for the detectives to stop. At this point, Hill shifted his interrogation tactics, declaring that Donald "knew who killed the police." Further denials led to Hill pulling out his revolver, declaring that he should make Donald run and "shoot the shit out of you and say you tried to escape."

Donald's brothers were spared the submarino treatment, suffering instead only brutal beatings. Donald was taken to the polygraph office in the headquarters building for a lie detector test. The civilian examiner was outraged by Donald's bloodied physical appearance and engaged in a heated argument with the Area 2 detectives who had brought him there. This argument later led to the examiner's being fired.

Meanwhile, screams were also emanating from the other interrogation locations as Burge and his detectives moved from room to room. Anthony Williams, nicknamed "Mertz," later identified Burge as one of his interrogators. Burge cuffed Anthony to a chair, beat him with a phone book, and placed a plastic bag over his head. He then said, "Let's take the cuffs off him, take him to the staircase, shoot him, and say he was trying to escape." After consulting with a detective for a moment, Burge returned to the room, pulled out a long silver-barreled gun, said that he was "going to shoot this nigger," and put the gun to Anthony's head. Anthony was saved from further abuse when a Black cop entered the room. After Burge left, the officer told Anthony to pretend that he was being beaten, in case Burge was listening.

A high-ranking Cook County assistant prosecutor from Richard M. Daley's state's attorney's office, Mike Angarola, was also present at 11th and State during the interrogations and was reporting to Daley's first assistant, Richard Devine. According to Walter White, Angarola was present when detective Fred Hill beat him. In contrast, a Black Area 2 detective named Sammy Lacey and the Black commander of Area 2, Milton Deas, who had reported to headquarters after hearing that the cop killers had supposedly been captured, were relegated to an office distant from the interrogations.

As a result of the brutal torture, Anthony Williams, Donald White, and Donald's brothers gave the detectives information that linked two of their associates, Andrew Wilson and his brother Jackie, to the killing of officers Fahey and O'Brien. Attorneys Devine and Angarola then arranged for the White brothers to be placed in protective custody, with a financial reward that was accompanied by the implicit understanding that their torture would not be revealed.

By now, both Mayor Byrne and Superintendent Brzeczek were actively involved. Both had visited Area 2, and Byrne had given Burge and his detectives a pep talk that urged them to solve the crimes by any means necessary. Byrne had offered a $50,000 reward for information leading to the apprehension of the killers; she met with an informant who gave her relevant information that was passed on to Brzeczek and, in turn, to Burge. In response to the groundswell of complaints from the Black community, Brzeczek chose to call in his Black command staff and urged them to help cool out the community, but he made no effort to tell his white command staff—or Burge—to stop the brutality.

Accompanied by a deputy superintendent and a battery of Area 2 detectives, Burge led a 5:00 a.m. raid on a basement apartment on Chicago's west side. Shirtless and asleep on a couch, Andrew Wilson was awakened as the raiders kicked the door down. Burge and his men threw Andrew to the floor and Burge "walked over" his neck. As they dragged him to a police car, Burge told the arresting detectives not to "mess with him" now; they would "get him at the station."

Andrew was transported by a car full of detectives back to an old police edifice at the corner of 91st Street and Cottage Grove. He was dragged up to the second floor, where Area 2 was located, to a room full of screaming and hollering officers. As Andrew later described it:

> They beat me up. They was kicking me around and slapping me on the floor. They grabbed a bag out of the garbage can, a gray garbage bag, and put it over my head. I was scuffling with them. I bit through it. They took it off of my head and one of them burned me on my arm. They slapped me back down on the floor but the big one, he kicked me, that's how I got my eye messed up.

Burge then entered the room and voiced his displeasure, saying that he had told the detectives not to "mess his face up." He admonished them that there would not have been any marks on Andrew if he had administered the abuse.

In the room next to Andrew was Doris Miller, a postal carrier who had lived in the same neighborhood as the Wilson brothers on Chicago's far south side and had watched them grow up. The investigating detectives had information that Doris, who had never before been arrested, might have transported Jackie Wilson to an apartment hideout sometime after the killings, so they had raided her house at about 1:25 a.m. and took her into custody for being an "accessory to murder." She was taken up the back stairs, to avoid the TV camera crews that were already encamped at the front of the building, and was handcuffed to a ring on the wall, where she remained until, around dawn, she was moved. The door to the adjoining room was open, and she saw Andrew, bare-chested and covered with sweat, sitting on a stool. Soon after, she heard the sounds of a body hitting the floor, and a voice that she recognized as Andrew's "moaning, pleading, and begging for mercy," and repeatedly denying that he did anything.

Doris heard a detective tell Andrew, "Look, motherfucker, we are going to take you out of here now, and if you try anything, we will blow your head off." Andrew was then taken to a small interrogation room with a window that faced south onto 91st Street. Under the window stood an old-fashioned ribbed steam radiator, which Andrew, who had only a first-grade education, referred to as a "heaterator." On each side of the window above the radiator was a handcuff ring. Across the street was a Chicago Fire Department station.

Andrew asked for a lawyer. Burge ignored his request, telling Andrew that he was going to confess, because Burge's reputation was at stake. Detective John Yucaitis, a longtime Burge associate, then entered the room with a brown shopping bag. As Andrew described it, the bag contained Burge's "little gizmos"—a black box that had a crank and wires, and another device that was round and black, looked something like a hair dryer, and "had a plug on it." The wires that came out of the box had small clamps at the ends, which Yucaitis attached to Andrew's nose and ears. Then the torture by electric shock began.

Andrew reacted to the shocking by kicking Yucaitis, who was squatting in front of him, cranking the black shock box. Yucaitis responded by punching Andrew in the mouth and then administered another round of shocks by turning the crank on the box, causing Andrew to start shouting. Sammy Lacey, who had come into Area 2 to submit his overtime sheets, heard the shouting, as, no doubt, did many of the high-level CPD brass and assistant prosecutors who had flocked to Area 2 after the arrest was announced. Apparently in response to the cries, someone came to the interrogation room door, the shocking stopped, and the interrogators left the room.

The detectives then took Andrew to another room where assistant state's attorney (ASA) Larry Hyman was sitting. Hyman was a supervisor in the Cook County state's attorneys' Felony Review Unit—a unit of lawyers whose assignment it was to take confessions obtained by police interrogators. Hyman and the detectives fully expected that Andrew was ready to give a full confession. Instead, Andrew said, in the presence of several of his torturers, "You expect me to make a statement after all of them tortured me?" Hyman asked, "What?" But Andrew, intimidated by all the detectives in the room, said no more. Hyman then angrily told the detectives to "get the jagoff out of here."

Back in the interrogation room, Andrew sat in the chair, handcuffed to a ring on the wall. After about half an hour, Burge returned and declared that it was "fun time." Burge, with the aid of another officer, put a second set of cuffs on Andrew, attaching one set to each wrist, had him kick off his boots, and cuffed his ankles together. Burge then took out the black box, attached a wire to each of Andrew's ears, and cranked. Andrew knocked the wires off his ears, and after they were reattached, he knocked them off again and fell out of the chair. Frustrated, Burge and the other officer cuffed him to the rings on the wall, one arm on each ring, stretching him across the radiator, and reattached the wires, this time to his pinky fingers. Burge, now sitting in the chair with the box in his lap, started "cranking and cranking and cranking."

Although the shocking forced Andrew's body against the hot radiator, he did not feel the burning heat because the shocking was "in his head," flickering like a light, causing him pain and to constantly grind his teeth. As Andrew described it:

> I wasn't paying no attention, but it burned me still. But I didn't even feel it. All you could feel was that machine he was running, that box with the wires on it. That took over. The radiator didn't even exist then. The box existed.

Andrew was screaming and shouting as Burge continued to shock him, while the other officer kicked Andrew in the back. They then stood him up and rearranged his cuffs. Burge, brandishing the hair-dryer-like device, ran it gently between Andrew's legs. A tingling sensation gave way to a sharp jolt when Burge jabbed this shocking device into Andrew's back. Andrew's face smashed into the grill that covered the window, and he started to spit up blood. Only then did the torture session stop.

That same morning, Jackie Wilson was arrested at a south side apartment. Transported to another room on the second floor at Area 2, he heard Andrew hollering and moaning for what seemed like "forever." Surrounded by a dozen white Area 2 detectives, he asked to speak with his lawyer and refused to talk, which resulted in his being repeatedly hit on the head with a telephone book, kicked and poked in the chest and ribs, slapped, and kicked in the testicles. The detectives tried in vain to coerce Jackie into helping them get his brother to confess, and when he refused, they twisted his fingers, stepped on his hand, and stuck a revolver in his mouth, cocking it back and forth. At one point Burge entered the room, and at his direction, Jackie was electric-shocked on his hand. Finally, Jackie agreed to confess. He was brought to ASA Hyman, but, after he gave a court-reported statement, he refused to sign it until he spoke with his lawyer. A threat to break his fingers brought Jackie back in line, and he signed at about two o'clock in the afternoon.

Andrew, however, continued to resist giving a formal confession. That afternoon, he and Jackie were taken to another police station to stand in line-ups. While Andrew sat in a room, Burge entered, started talking to Andrew about his criminal background, and began to play with his gun. He then stuck the four-inch barrel into Andrew's mouth and repeatedly clicked it.

After the lineups, Andrew was returned to an interrogation room at Area 2. Burge entered the room and delivered an ultimatum—either give a court-reported confession or suffer another round of torture. Andrew succumbed and gave a transcribed confession to ASA Hyman at about 6:30 p.m. Burge entered the room while Andrew was giving the confession. Hyman asked him to leave, but Burge remained, and after the statement was complete, triumphantly told Andrew, "We are going to fry your Black ass now."

At about nine o'clock, Burge and his men finally released Doris Miller from custody. She had been handcuffed to the ring on the wall the entire day, her requests to go to the bathroom had been rejected, and she had to resort to peeing in an ashtray in the room in the presence of an unknown male arrestee. At about the same time, two uniformed police "wagon men," Mario Ferro and John Mulvaney, responded to a radio call to report to Area 2 for the purpose of transporting Andrew to the lock-up at police headquarters. They entered the room where Andrew was being held, surrounded by Burge and several detectives, and Burge told them, "That's the man." Ferro and Mulvaney started to hit Andrew, and Mulvaney grabbed his penis and squeezed it. One of the detectives told the wagon men to "put him in a cell with some other prisoners so it would look like they did it to him."

After re-handcuffing Andrew's hands behind his back, the wagon men led him to the stairway, where Mulvaney attempted to trip him from behind so that he would fall down the stairs. Failing in that effort, they slammed him against the wall at the bottom of the stairs. This reopened the cut over his right eye that he had suffered earlier in the day.

At police headquarters Andrew was led to the elevator at gunpoint. On the way up in the elevator, Mulvaney threw him to the floor, twisted his arm, and cracked him on the back of his head with his .45. At the eleventh floor, only a few floors from Superintendent Brzeczek's office, Mulvaney pulled Andrew up to his feet, the elevator door opened, and a bleeding and badly beaten Andrew Wilson was presented to the lockup keepers. Afraid that they would be blamed for the torture, they refused to accept him into custody. An argument ensued between the lockup keepers, who threatened to "call the brass," and the wagon men, who, apparently scared by the threat, reluctantly changed course and said that they would take Andrew to the hospital. Andrew was placed in leg irons. On the way down in the elevator Mulvaney told Andrew that he would refuse treatment at the hospital if "he knew what was good for him."

Ferro and Mulvaney then placed Andrew back into the police wagon and headed for Mercy Hospital, about two miles away. They brought Andrew into the emergency room, and Ferro told a nurse named Patricia Reynolds they had a dangerous criminal with them. She noticed that Wilson was bleeding from his forehead and brought him into the treatment room. Ferro then told her, "If this guy knows what is good for him, he will refuse treatment." Nurse Reynolds and a clerk began the admission process, but when asked if he wanted to be treated, Wilson shook his head "no." However, when Ferro and Mulvaney looked away for a moment, the clerk, who was Black, asked again, while nodding his head "yes," Wilson responded with an affirmative nod and signed the consent form that the clerk presented to him.

After the nurses cleaned his head wounds and gave him a tetanus shot, the ER doctor, Geoffrey Korn, surrounded by the wagon men, and several hospital security guards, examined Wilson amid the charged atmosphere. He observed approximately fifteen fresh injuries, including a black and bleeding eye; lacerations to the face, forehead, and back of the head; redness of the wrists; a six-inch second-degree burn on the thigh; and linear injuries to the face and chest that would subsequently be diagnosed as burns.

Dr. Korn then began to treat Andrew's wounds. Mulvaney, looking nervous, was at the doctor's back when Korn noticed that Mulvaney had pulled his gun out and was pointing it to the floor. Concerned that Andrew might jump or flinch during treatment, and thereby draw fire, he asked Mulvaney to put the gun away. Mulvaney refused; an angry Dr. Korn told Mulvaney that he could not treat a patient in such circumstances and left the room. Ferro tried to mediate, but Mulvaney again told Andrew to refuse treatment, which he did when Dr. Korn came back and attempted to convince him otherwise. Ferro told Korn that they would take Andrew to Cook County Hospital, but their actual destination was back to the lockup at 11th and State, where Andrew was accepted into custody without complaint, presumably because he had been taken to the hospital and had a bandage on his forehead.

The next morning, Andrew was transported to holiday bond court, where he was herded into the "bullpen," where dozens of men, including his brother Jackie, awaited their appearances before judge Thaddeus Kowalski for bond hearings. Public defender Barbara Steinberg, on duty that day, spoke briefly to Andrew before his appearance. Andrew pulled up his shirt, showing her his burned chest, and told her that he had been electric-shocked on his genitals by the police.

Shortly, Andrew and Jackie were called before the judge, who appointed Steinberg to represent Andrew at the hearing. Jackie's bond hearing proceeded while Steinberg held a whispered conversation with Andrew. After Jackie was denied bond, the prosecutor recited Andrew's substantial criminal background. Asked if she wanted to address this recitation, Steinberg instead asked Andrew to pull up his shirt for the judge. She then requested that he

> receive proper medical care. The same medical care any defendant who is injured would receive without the attendant notoriety that accompanies this case. He says that he simply has not received medical care, and he is in fair discomfort, so I would like an order for that.

The judge granted her request. Andrew and Jackie were taken to Cermak Hospital, part of the Cook County Jail, an old and overcrowded compound of buildings that stood just south of the criminal courts on Chicago's southwest side. Instead of the pro forma screening to which most prisoners were subjected, intake personnel took a series of photos of Andrew's obvious injuries before Dr. Goodman, the only physician on duty over the Lincoln's Birthday holiday, examined Andrew in the hospital's makeshift emergency room. After recording the most obvious of Andrew's injuries, Goodman called Dr. Jack Raba, director of medical services at the jail, at home, because he was treating a man with "unusual injuries that may have included burns." That evening, Raba went to the jail to see Andrew, who was being held in an 8' x 10' cell. Raba, accompanied by a paramedic and two correctional officers, sat on Andrew's bunk and examined him. By the light of the bulb that hung from the ceiling of the cell, he observed that the wounds on Andrew's face and chest had blistered and, unlike the previous doctors, recorded them as burns rather than as lacerations. Andrew told him that the burns had come from being pushed onto a radiator, and said that he had been electric-shocked.

On the morning of February 16, Andrew was taken from the jail to the adjoining Criminal Courts Building and the courtroom known as Branch 66. The judge assigned to Branch 66 on that day, Joseph Urso, conducted preliminary hearings in murder cases. Also assigned to Branch 66 that day was public defender Dale Coventry. Coventry, a high school American literature teacher before he became a lawyer, was a member of an elite team of trial lawyers known as the Murder Task Force. The task force had been following the manhunt and had received numerous complaints of police violence from their clients during that supercharged five days. Information had come from Barbara Steinberg to the supervisor of the task force, who raised the possibility that Andrew be neurologically examined because of his allegations of electric shock.

Judge Urso appointed Dale Coventry to represent Andrew, who still had a large bandage over his eye. When Coventry whispered, "How did you get the injuries?" Andrew said, "The police." Coventry then obtained a court order to allow him to take photographs of the injuries.

As soon as Andrew was returned to the jail, Coventry and his investigator, armed with the court order and a Polaroid camera, appeared for a legal visit. They were escorted to a concrete block room in the jail's musty basement. The contrast was stark—the five-foot-eight, 140-pound Black prisoner with an obvious learning disability being interviewed by a balding, middle-aged, white former teacher, accompanied by a six-foot-five investigator and his camera.

Andrew detailed his torture as the investigator took a series of photos that would form a cornerstone of the proof of Andrew's torture for decades to come. When Andrew described the alligator clips being attached from Burge's black box to his ears and nose, Coventry examined his ears and nose carefully and directed that a series of photos be taken from different angles. His examination revealed several small semicircular marks that appeared to be either burn marks or tiny scabs on the inside of Andrew's earlobes as well as corresponding marks on the outside of his ears. He also found a similar semicircular mark at the bottom of Andrew's left nostril.

That evening, Dr. Raba conducted a follow-up examination of Andrew at his cell. He confirmed that the burns were still blistered but not infected, and observed the status of the other injuries. Troubled by the seriousness of what he had seen and heard, Raba wrote a letter to CPD superintendent Richard Brzeczek the following day, demanding an investigation. In his letter, copies of which he also sent to the sheriff of Cook County and the executive director of the Cook County Department of Corrections, Raba wrote:

> I examined Mr. Andrew Wilson on February 15 and 16, 1982. He had multiple bruises, swellings and abrasions on his face and head. His right eye was battered and had a superficial laceration. Andrew Wilson had several linear blisters on his right thigh, right cheek and anterior chest which were consistent with radiator burns. He stated that he had been cuffed to a radiator and pushed into it. He also stated that electrical shocks had been administered to his gums, lips and genitals.
>
> All these injuries occurred prior to his arrival at the jail. There must [be] a thorough investigation of this matter.

Brzeczek now was between a rock and a hard place. Trained as a lawyer, and as a patron of Mayor Byrne—who had been a primary cheerleader for the manhunt—Brzeczek knew that a legitimate investigation would most likely jeopardize the prosecution of the Wilson brothers, a result that would make him public enemy number one with Byrne, to say nothing of with his entire department. Having been close to the manhunt, he in all likelihood knew about the torture, as well as about the hundreds of complaints against his officers. In fact, he would later claim that after he had received Dr. Raba's letter, he had privately "read the riot act" to his brass for being present at Area 2 while the torture was proceeding and doing nothing to stop it. Brzeczek further revealed that the brass defended themselves by saying that the wagon men were the culprits, but he wasn't buying it. He told them not to give him "any of that bullshit," because the Raba letter convinced him that the blame lay at the doorstep of Area 2.

After mulling Raba's letter for a week and sharing it with Mayor Byrne, Brzeczek came to the obvious, if less than admirable, conclusion that he needed to cover his ass and pass the decision about whether to open this can of worms to someone else. He had the perfect candidate—Mr. "law and order" himself, state's attorney Richie Daley. Daley was Brzeczek's and Byrne's political archenemy, so Brzeczek took the unusual step of sending Raba's complaint directly to Daley, with a cover letter informing Daley that he had opened an administrative investigation based on Raba's allegations, but, because Andrew was "one of the defendants in a matter presently pending before the Criminal Division of Cook County, I am seeking your direction as to how the Department should proceed in the investigation of these allegations." Brzeczek concluded:

> I have publicly stated that we will scrupulously investigate every allegation of police misconduct brought to our attention. However, in pursuing this posture, I also do not want to jeopardize the prosecution's case in any way. I will forbear from taking any steps other than the one previously mentioned in connection with these allegations until I hear from you or one of your assistants.

Brzeczek's letter became an instant topic of conversation among Daley, his first assistant, Richard Devine, and his chief deputy, Bill Kunkle. Devine was a machine Democrat who had been an administrative assistant to Richie's father, Mayor Richard the First, whereas Kunkle was a Republican holdover from the prior administration of state's attorney Bernard Carey. Daley and Devine had already entrusted the prosecution of the Wilson brothers to Kunkle and Angarola. Brzeczek's letter posed a number of pressing problems to these prosecutors who were hell-bent on sending Andrew Wilson to the death chamber. They instantly sensed that Brzeczek was setting them up. They also knew that they had a huge conflict-of-interest problem: How could they defend the interrogation of the Wilson brothers against a motion that their confessions were tortured from them, while at the same time investigating their interrogators for the torture? Even more important, from their point of view, was the reality that a legitimate investigation of the crimes committed by Burge and his men would jeopardize the Wilson prosecutions and the careers of Jon Burge and any number of his confederates.

Their solution was not unlike the one that Brzeczek and his command staff adopted—they passed the case along to a trusted supervisor in the Special Prosecutions Unit, intentionally and specifically bypassing the chief of that unit, a former US attorney known as a straight shooter. In so doing, they were assured that their "investigation" would die aborning, as it did a short time later, with the explanation that Andrew Wilson would not cooperate with Special Prosecutions because he faced a capital murder charge.

Daley, Devine, and Kunkle also did not respond to Brzeczek, who, true to his word, made sure that the department's internal investigation was put on an indefinite hold. He subsequently issued an official superintendent's commendation to Burge and all his men at Area 2 for their work in solving the police murders, citing among their main accomplishments the confessions that they obtained. The internal investigation was finally and quietly closed, three years later, with a finding of "not sustained."

In the fall of 1982, judge John J. Crowley conducted a two-week hearing in his courtroom, on the fifth floor of the Criminal Courts Building at 26th and California, on the Wilson brothers' motion to suppress their allegedly coerced confessions. Andrew and Jackie testified in detail about their torture. When Andrew started to describe being strapped across the "heaterator," he broke down on the stand, and a recess was taken. Andrew's testimony was supported by doctors Raba and Korn, Nurse Reynolds, and Doris Miller, as well as by the graphic photos taken by Coventry's investigator. Raba testified, despite having received a phone call from his ultimate boss and Chicago's second most powerful Democratic leader—Cook County board chairman George Dunne —asking him to stand down from his charges. The call had come at about the same time that Daley received Raba's letter, back in February, and was the only instance in Raba's career that Dunne had spoken to him. Raba politely told him at the time that he would do nothing of the sort.

A parade of Area 2 officers, led by Burge, as well as ASA Larry Hyman and the state's attorneys' court reporter who had transcribed the statements, took the stand. They all uniformly denied that any physical abuse had occurred. Remarkably, Burge denied even being in the same room with Andrew from the time Andrew arrived at Area 2 in the early morning until after he gave his court-reported statement that evening. Polaroid pictures taken by the court reporter of Andrew and Jackie, which showed only their faces, were also offered as evidence by the prosecution that there had been little or no abuse.

Kunkle suggested that the injuries happened before and during Andrew's arrest, and, later, at the hands of the wagon men, arguing:

> It would be a sad thing indeed if there were a police officer on the Chicago police department insensitive enough and stupid enough to do one-tenth of the things that the defense in this motion suggest that these officers did, but to have one that would do these things in front of civilian witnesses or where others could hear is beyond the pale. I cannot imagine the Court accepting such testimony as fact.

Judge Crowley, a law-and-order machine judge who had previously worked as a city lawyer, wasted little time denying the motion to suppress.

In an oral ruling from the bench, he first found that there was "no credible evidence" that Jackie's statement was taken by "force or compulsion," or that he had been denied his right to a lawyer. With regard to Andrew, he adopted Kunkle's arguments, finding that one of Andrew's injuries happened during his arrest, while the remainder occurred after his court-reported statement was taken in the evening—and, by implication, were inflicted by the wagon men. Without expressly addressing the testimonial and photographic evidence of electric shock, the judge found Andrew's testimony to "be an exaggeration—I do not think those matters took place."

Thus the court found no violation of Andrew's or Jackie's Fifth, Sixth, or Fourteenth Amendment rights had occurred, and that their confessions could therefore be admitted at trial.

Two months later, in January 1983, Andrew and Jackie were put on trial together. Andrew's conviction seemed preordained, but Jackie had a puncher's chance, as the State's evidence, based exclusively on Jackie's coerced confession, showed that he had done little more than tell Andrew one of the officers was still alive and drive the getaway car. Remarkably, the State's only eyewitness testified that Jackie "stood by in shock" while Andrew shot the two officers. Neither Andrew nor Jackie testified, but both of their confessions were read to the jury. After prosecutor Mike Angarola detailed all the evidence against the defendants, defense attorney Dale Coventry took a highly unusual tack. He argued, "It's apparent that the hope here is that these two Black defendants will be convicted by this all-white jury."

Coventry continued:

> I think the jury should consider why you were picked. Blacks were excluded. It was clear from the start. What does your common sense tell you why the prosecution would want an all-white jury to deliberate on the shooting deaths of two police officers when two black men are on trial. I think it's cheap and it's an insult. It's an insult to your intelligence.

Relying on ASA Hyman's delay in obtaining Andrew's statement and Doris Miller's testimony, Coventry pushed the envelope, first arguing that Andrew was "beaten, beaten, and beaten." After he survived an objection, he pushed further:

> Coventry: Wilson was beaten and when he was in that room—
> Mr. Kunkle: Objection, your Honor. No evidence of that.
> The Court: No evidence whatsoever. Sustained.

Coventry circled around again, detailing Doris Miller's abuse at Area 2, and asserted, over Kunkle's objection, "Andrew Wilson signed a statement to keep from being beaten, tortured." Later on, Coventry attempted to argue that the marks on Andrew's face, as shown in a lineup photo, were burn marks, but the court squelched that argument as well.

Coventry then emphasized that the Area 2 detectives, during this intensive investigation in which numerous witnesses were interviewed, supposedly destroyed all their notes and retained only official reports that they had selectively reconstructed from their notes. (These notes, as well as other unofficial reports and memos, were, in all likelihood, placed in a secret "street file" and destroyed sometime prior to trial. This was the long time, illegal practice of Chicago police detectives since time immemorial.)

On Jackie's behalf, defense attorney Richard Kling laid the blame for the murders entirely on Andrew, an understandable tactic that underscored the egregious injustice of the judge's decision to deny Andrew and Jackie separate trials.

In rebuttal, Kunkle argued, with the court's blessing, "These men are evil, yes, these men are dangerous, yes, these men are killers, but they are also vile and contemptible cowards." Wrapping himself in the Constitution and the police department's motto to "serve and protect," he praised Burge and his men: "The police in this investigation did a tremendous job, they did a thankless job, they did a remarkable job." The jury was sent to deliberate at 9:00 p.m.

The sequestered jury did not linger long—at 11:00 a.m. the next morning they returned with unanimous verdicts, finding both Andrew and Jackie guilty on all counts of murder and armed robbery. The judge then set the death penalty hearing for 1:30 the same afternoon and accused the defense of stalling when they sought more time to prepare their case. The court then denied the defense the right to call several experts on the death penalty, as well as the right to call doctors Korn and Raba and Nurse Reynolds. The same jury then found both Andrew and Jackie eligible for the death penalty.

Court was reconvened the next Monday to hear aggravation and mitigation evidence. But before the hearing started, Judge Crowley accused Jackie's attorney of making "spurious, irresponsible, unprofessional, unfounded" and "evil" comments. The judge began to read quotes from the *Southtown Economist*:

Jackie Wilson's attorney, Richard Kling, also leveled a charge that there was pressure for a conviction due to the February 22nd mayoral primary. State's Attorney Richard Daley is considered Mayor Jane Byrne's primary opponent.

An agitated Judge Crowley continued reading from the article:

I think this is one more indication that the State and the judge, parentheses John J. Crowley, close parentheses, are interested in having a conviction just before election time since there obviously was no concern as to whether the conviction will be reversed, Kling said. He said that the jury was also prejudiced by "the attitude toward conviction" on the part of Crowley.

In response to Kling's denials, Crowley blustered: "Well, those are outrageous comments on the part of a lawyer. They are outrageous and unfounded."

The hearing proceeded. Kunkle, who had sent notorious serial murderer John Wayne Gacy to death row, and was a rabid advocate of the death penalty, was completely in his element:

What sort of justice respects equally the life of Abraham Lincoln and John Wilkes Booth, or Martin Luther King and James Earl Ray, or Robert Kennedy and Sirhan Sirhan? To say that these men, some great, and some unspeakably vile, equally possess human dignity is to demonstrate an inability to make any moral judgment derived from human dignity.

Coventry's co-counsel, assistant public defender Jamie Kunz, attempted to combat the emotional storm that Kunkle had rekindled, but his moral imperative was blunted by the station of the victims, the racial undercurrents that churned, and the truncating of Andrew's torture evidence:

If the executive branch, including the state's attorney, and the police, are going to come to me and say here is a man who committed a certain crime and for this reason we want you to say yes, kill him, that if they are going to ask that of me, the juror, I want them to come with their hands clean, I don't want them to come with a case where they have lost or destroyed police reports. I don't want them to come to me with a case where they have beaten and bloodied the defendant. For that reason alone, I will not impose the death penalty in this case.

Jackie Wilson was, relatively speaking, in a much stronger position on the question of the death penalty because his conviction, as Kling argued, was based only on accountability for Andrew's actions as the triggerman. Kling urged the jury to show compassion for his client, and painted a stark picture of an execution:

What Mr. Kunkle is asking you to do is to kill Jackie Wilson. It's as simple as that. He is asking you to cause the State of Illinois to pull a switch which will put five thousand volts of electricity through the body of Jackie Wilson. Not the way Jackie looks as he sits there today, but only after his head is first shaved so that they can put on the oil which will allow the electricity to flow more surely through the electric chair. Not the way he looks today, but after they put him in a diaper, because when you are electrocuted, you lose control of your body functions and they want to make sure that the death room is clean. Not the way he looks today, but after they put a mask over his head, not so he can't see what is going to happen, but so that the witnesses who by law view the electrocution can't see what's going to happen, because it is so horrible a happening.

Angarola made the state's final argument. Rebutting Kling's argument that life without parole was a viable alternative to voting for death, he invoked the Attica prison uprising and argued that the Wilsons were likely to kill correctional guards if they were spared execution. Quoting a death penalty advocate, Angarola concluded that if the United States may "rightly honor its heroes, it may rightly execute the worst of its criminals. By doing so, it will remind its citizens that it is a country worthy of heroes."

After deliberating, the jury, almost exactly one year after the murders, mandated death for Andrew, and a double life sentence for Jackie.

CHAPTER 3

Street Files
and Important Trials

On April 8, 1982, Area 2 detective Frank Laverty, at great cost to his professional career, made a decision that would establish him as a true hero to many but as a villain to the Chicago Police Department and the state's attorney's office. On his way to O'Hare airport to fly to Denver for a vacation, Frank picked up the *Chicago Tribune* and read about the George Jones murder case, which was being defended by PLO attorneys Jeff Haas and Peter Schmiedel. The article recounted that Jones, the eighteen-year-old son of a Black Chicago police officer, was on trial for raping and murdering an eleven-year-old girl. Laverty had done some of the investigation in the case. Months before, he had informed his Area 2 supervisors and commander, in person and by interoffice memo, that the detectives had charged the wrong man and that the real culprit was a gang member who had subsequently committed another rape and murder. The commander assured Laverty that the situation would be taken care of, and Laverty gave the case no further thought until he saw the *Tribune* article.

Laverty called the commander, an old-school Black officer named Milton Deas, who had ceded responsibility to Burge when Burge had returned to Area 2 to head up the Violent Crimes Unit in November 1981. Deas was not helpful, telling Laverty, "Do what you have to do," so Laverty called the courtroom where George Jones was being tried. It was lunchtime; Peter and Jeff were eating lunch in the vacant courtroom, and Jeff happened to answer the phone. Amazed that Laverty had evidence that could free their client, Jeff and Peter asked him to come directly to court.

Scrapping his vacation plans, Laverty rushed to the courthouse, where Peter served him with a subpoena to testify. On the stand in a special hearing outside the presence of the jury, Laverty told the judge and a stunned courtroom that, months before, he had found the true killer, identified him to his superiors and to ASA Larry Hyman, and had written reports detailing the evidence that supported his findings. Peter and Jeff had not received Laverty's reports during discovery, and his courageous revelations led to the granting of a mistrial in the case.

Despite the newly revealed evidence, the prosecutors were determined to retry Jones, who had been arrested on the eve of his high school graduation and spent five months in Cook County Jail before making bond. Mike Angarola called Laverty, told him he was in deep trouble with the department, and attempted to coerce him into falsely stating that he had colluded with Jeff and Peter. Laverty refused, and the case was dismissed.

True enough, Laverty, who had been an honest homicide detective for nearly a decade, was in hot water with the department. He had exposed a frame-up of an innocent young Black man, the first of a string of such exonerations that would make Illinois the capital of wrongful convictions. But that was the lesser of his perceived transgressions—his revelations also established that CPD detectives had a department-wide practice of keeping secret files, called "street files," in which they kept memos such as the ones that Laverty wrote in the Jones case, their notes, and other unofficial reports. These files and their contents were not made available to defense lawyers in criminal cases as required by the US Constitution.

Burge was outraged by Laverty's flagrant violation of the police code of silence. He made his feelings known to his detectives when Laverty walked through the common area where the detectives typed their reports. As Laverty left the room, Burge pulled out his gun, pointed it at Laverty's back, and said, "Bang." For its part, the department launched an investigation—not of the detectives who framed an innocent young man, but of Laverty, and Brzeczek transferred Laverty to the Personnel Division, where his assignment was to watch recruits give urine samples.

Directly after the George Jones case was dismissed, we filed suit in federal court seeking an injunction against the street files practice. From the outset, the department was ordered to preserve all of the files, and in the fall of 1982, we conducted an extensive evidentiary hearing before one of the most astute judges in the Northern District of Illinois, Milton Shadur. Laverty was a key witness for us, and the commanders of each of the six detective areas were forced to admit that, in one form or another, the street files practice had existed under their commands for many years. Superintendent Brzeczek testified that he was unaware of the practice, and had mandated, after the initial court order was entered, that officers preserve everything, even if written on a matchbook cover. Bill Kunkle, on behalf of the state's attorney's office, admitted he was aware that police officers kept their own files but gave classic "hear no evil, see no evil, speak no evil" testimony that we—and many defense attorneys—found patently unbelievable. In response to Laverty's revelations and our lawsuit, the CPD changed its written policies to require that all notes must be recorded and preserved, and that all notes, reports, and files, whether official or not, be maintained for the purpose of production to criminal defense lawyers. In May 1983, Judge Shadur made the CPD's changes mandatory by entering an injunction.

As the street files hearing was proceeding, a political movement born in response to the murder of Fred Hampton and fueled, in part, by the brutality of the Wilson manhunt, was focusing on mayor Jane Byrne and her police superintendent. A coalition of forces had convinced US congressman Harold Washington, a progressive African American, to run against Byrne and Richie Daley in the upcoming Democratic mayoral primary, in a three-way race. Electoral politics was not our ideological cup of tea, but Washington—who had supported us during the *Hampton* civil trial—and his campaign caught our attention and won our guarded support.

Only weeks before the primary in February 1983, Washington's campaign caught fire, and he addressed a massive rally at the Chicago campus of the University of Illinois. Brzeczek had already fanned the anti-police sentiments in the Black community by claiming that the streets would not be safe if Washington were elected and that the police department would be a "circus." The twelve thousand supporters in attendance roared their approval as Harold joined the voices, chanting, "Fire Brzeczek! Fire Brzeczek!"

Washington, at the urging of his press secretary, sought to capitalize on the police brutality issue by staging a press conference at which victims of police violence would tell their stories. We arranged to bring several of our clients to the gathering. Harold first met privately with the victims, about forty in number, then I questioned several of them before a packed house of reporters. Harold followed with a promise to establish an independent citizens' review board to investigate police misconduct. Although the event occasioned a big news story and helped to further galvanize the Black community, Washington was apparently concerned that he had alienated the powerful Fraternal Order of Police.

In Chicago, it has almost always been the case that the candidate who wins the Democratic primary is assured of winning the office for which she is running, since Republican opposition is either token or nonexistent.

This was not the case in 1983, despite the fact that the Republicans had slated a nondescript politician named Bernie Epton whose only "qualification" was that he was white. After Washington won the primary, the six weeks leading up to the general election became a racial battleground. Most of the white politicians, including Richie Daley and Democratic Party chairman Ed Vrdolyak, either openly supported Bernard Epton or quietly directed their captains to work for him in their wards. The predominately white northwest and southwest sides were awash in a sea of Epton signs, but Washington prevailed, with 51.5 percent of the vote.

Unfortunately, Harold's election and the appointments of James Montgomery as the first Black corporation counsel and Fred Rice as the first Black police superintendent would have no effect on the systemic racist torture that continued under Jon Burge's command, with the knowing complicity of Richie Daley.

Throughout the 1980s we gained more significant trial experience in cases involving high-profile police violence, prisoner rights, and wrongful prosecution. In 1981, Michael Deutsch, Peter Schmiedel, and I tried the Humboldt Park case. The legendary federal judge Prentice Marshall, with whom we had forged a mutually respectful relationship, presided over the jury trial. We represented the families of two young Puerto Rican men, Julio Osorio and Raphael Cruz, who were gunned down by a Chicago police sergeant during the June 1977 Puerto Rican Day uprising in Humboldt Park. Both were unarmed; Cruz was walking with a cane and was shot in the back. Police sergeant Thomas Walton, who fired the fatal shots, claimed that Osorio had a gun, but none was found. According to an eyewitness, Walton had admitted at the scene that the "gun" was in reality a hairbrush.

We were not optimistic, despite our compelling evidence, as one of the jurors, an older, white veteran of World War II, consistently scowled and would not make eye contact with us. More than three weeks into the trial, Judge Marshall suffered a serious heart attack. From his hospital bed, he offered us two options: finish the trial before another federal judge, or have him declare a mistrial, with a promised retrial before Judge Marshall after he recovered. The three of us voted 2 to 1, with Michael dissenting, to retry the case before Judge Marshall. After the jury was discharged, we spoke to several of them, and learned that five of the six were on our side. The World War II veteran told us Walton "shot them down like ducks in a pond" and would have voted to award the full $10 million we were seeking on behalf of the families. The likely error of our ways was made clearer when, after Judge Marshall returned to the bench, he informed us that he was transferring the case because his doctor had forbidden him from any lengthy trials. The case was cast into legal limbo; several years later, we settled with the City for a fraction of the suggested $10 million.

Judge Marshall was healthy enough, though, to try two shorter cases after he returned. In 1982, Jon Moore, a young PLO lawyer who had worked on the *Hampton* appeal, and I obtained a $44,000 jury verdict for a Chilean refugee family abused by the Chicago police after they'd fled the repressive regime of Augusto Pinochet. In 1983, Jan Susler, who had joined the office the year before, and I tried two important civil rights cases. First, we obtained a $60,000 jury verdict for our colleague Chick Hoffman's sister Hinda, a court reporter who had been humiliated in a voyeuristic stationhouse strip search by the police after she was arrested for a traffic offense.

A few months later, we tried Maxine Smith's damages case in Peoria, Illinois. An older African American woman, Maxine was doing time for killing an abusive boyfriend. While housed at the women's prison in Dwight, Illinois, she distinguished herself as the first woman jailhouse lawyer, working in the prison library on behalf of other prisoners. When Maxine was banished to solitary confinement because of her work, we brought suit. She remained in segregation for two years before the court ordered her immediate release in 1978. I had argued the case before the Seventh Circuit that summer. Now, five years later, her damages case "played in Peoria," and we obtained a $100,000 jury verdict for Maxine, who was finally out on parole.

The Greensboro Massacre

In the summer of 1984, I headed south to Greensboro, North Carolina, to work on a massive civil rights case that alleged a conspiracy to murder and cover-up against Ku Klux Klan and American Nazi Party members, local Greensboro police officers, FBI and BATF (Bureau of Alcohol, Tobacco, and Firearms) agents, and the City of Greensboro. On November 3, 1979, five anti-Klan demonstrators and leaders in the Communist Workers Party (CWP) were murdered in broad daylight while gathering for a "Death to the Klan" march and conference. Thirty-five heavily armed members of the Klan and American Nazi Party drove a vehicle caravan through the streets of Greensboro and opened fire on the demonstrators, killing five and wounding seven. The attacks had been captured on videotape by local news stations, but the Klan and Nazi perpetrators had subsequently been acquitted, first for murder, then for civil rights violations, by all-white juries. The City of Greensboro's official position was that the demonstrators had sought a confrontation with the Klan and thus brought the murderous attacks on themselves.

During nine months of pretrial discovery, we wrested evidence from the law enforcement defendants that exposed the depth and contours of official involvement. Greensboro police informant Eddie Dawson had also been a longtime FBI agent provocateur in the Klan and had encouraged other acts of violence by his longtime associate, Grand Dragon Virgil Griffin, with whom he planned the November 3 attack. Dawson not only acted with the knowledge of the Greensboro police in planning the attack, but he had also informed his FBI contact that violence was likely on November 3, and Greensboro police had been informed that the Klan was coming to the town with a machine gun "to shoot up the place." BATF provocateur Bernard Butkovich had informed his superiors about the Nazis' plan for violence, that they possessed several high-powered weapons, and that Klansman Jerry Paul Smith had bragged at the Nazi planning meeting of having manufactured a pipe bomb that "could work good thrown into a crowd of niggers." Evidence also showed that Butkovich's encouragement of violence was pursuant to BATF policy and conducted with his superior's advice and consent.

Jury selection began in March 1985 in Winston-Salem, North Carolina. Judge Robert Merhige, a liberal Johnson appointee from Virginia, had been specially assigned to ensure a modicum of justice in this nationally high-profile case. In voir dire Judge Merhige examined more than three hundred prospective jurors, asking wide-ranging questions designed to reveal their attitudes toward race, communism, Klansmen, Nazis, labor organizers, "outside agitators," guns, and agents provocateur. Most of the prospective white jurors exhibited a great degree of racism, anticommunism, anti-unionism, and tolerance for the Klan. After disqualifying more than 250 jurors for cause, he employed a system of exercising preemptory challenges that prevented the defendants from removing every Black person qualified by the court, as would be their strategy. As a result, the six-person jury included a Black man who had participated in civil rights demonstrations in the early 1960s and had boldly said in voir dire that he "can't respect any man who has to hide his face to express his beliefs."

Our in-court presentation was handled by Lewis Pitts, a fearless movement attorney who would become a lifelong friend; Carolyn McAllister, a terrific lawyer from Durham; and me. The team also included attorneys Gayle Korotkin (the glue that held the mammoth case together), Pam DiStefano, Danny Sheehan, and Victoria Osk; Curtis Pierce, a young paralegal from the People's Law Office; and three of the murdered demonstrators' widows, Dale Sampson, Marty Nathan, and Signe Waller.

In our opening statements, Lewis focused on the right to equal protection of the laws and emphasized that law enforcement should have prevented the bloody attack. I pointed out that law enforcement had formed the "head and tail" of the murderous caravan, and described how, when told of the imminent violence, Greensboro police officers continued to stand in line for biscuits at a local restaurant. Carolyn described our clients as young people committed to helping minorities and those without a voice. Several of the Klan and Nazi defendants were also granted the right to speak. Nazi leader Gorrell Pierce asserted, "What we have here is two different ideologies, one extreme right, one extreme left. . . . When those two forces get together, there's potential for sparks to fly."

We called two television reporters who shot footage of the attack. They described what they had captured on videotape, including scenes of the defendants calmly going to the trunks of their cars, pulling out their weapons, and firing at the demonstrators. The tapes would be shown repeatedly, often in slow motion, throughout the trial. The tapes also showed Jerry Paul Smith running up to a car and firing the fatal bullets point blank into the off-camera body of CWP leader Cesar Cauce.

Early on we had decided that, as possible, we would call a victim of the attack to the stand, followed by a Klan or Nazi defendant, so the jury could compare their beliefs, attitudes, demeanors, and actions.

One of the first in-court confrontations occurred when we called Mark Sherer to the stand to establish that he had fired the first shots. Sherer first invoked the Fifth Amendment when I asked him whether he had constructed a pipe bomb and committed acts of violence in order to be admitted to the underground arm of the Klan, but the judge forbade him from further doing so. I read him his most damaging prior admissions, which established a preplanned conspiratorial intent to commit violence, and he claimed that he was coerced into making the statements. He admitted that he fired the first shot, but backed off his prior admission that he had fired three shots, admitting to only two. He did admit that, as he touched off the attack, he shouted, "Show me a nigger with some guts and I'll show you a Klansman with a gun."

We elicited prior admissions from the Klansmen and Nazis about their membership in a violent underground Klan, their anti-Black and anticommunist attitudes and activities, and their desire to retaliate for their public embarrassment at the hands of the CWP months before, when they had tried to screen the racist film "A Birth of a Nation." Defendant Jerry Paul Smith claimed amnesia when I showed him the portion of the videotape that captured his firing the fatal shots into Cesar Cauce's body. Klan security guard David Wayne Matthews could not remember bragging in the presence of the police that he had shot three demonstrators. Lewis Pitts and Carolyn McAllister confronted Grand Dragon Griffin and his co-conspirators with their prior admissions that they buried the murder weapons and hid in the swamps of South Carolina for a week after the massacre.

I examined caravan leader Eddie Dawson. He detailed his long and complex history as a police and FBI provocateur while acting as an influential Klan leader. He testified that as a police informant he recruited local Klansmen to go to Greensboro on November 3, and that he gave an inflammatory speech at a statewide planning meeting during which he urged Klansmen to bring weapons. He recounted that he and Greensboro police detective Jerry "Rooster" Cooper, his control agent, had obtained the demonstrators' march plans from the police department and he and his Klan associates used those plans to map out the attack. He explained how he kept Cooper informed of the Klan's plans, including the number of weapons on board, and how he charted the plans with his Klan and Nazi co-conspirators. He admitted that he shouted the first provocations at the demonstrators, yelling at Paul Bermanzohn, who would later be shot in the head and partially paralyzed, "You commie son of a bitch, you asked for the Klan, here we are!" Finally, he told how the Greensboro police kept him from testifying at the state criminal trial after he threatened to expose their role in the attacks and cover-up.

Thanks in large part to the Greensboro Civil Rights Fund, local papers provided daily coverage, and the *New York Times*, *Boston Globe*, *Washington Post*, *LA Times*, and *Chicago Tribune* also wrote about the case. On the Saturday that Eddie Dawson testified, Reverend Jesse Jackson, who, decades before, had been a student activist and athlete at North Carolina A&T in Greensboro, addressed the media at the street corner where the slayings had occurred. Jackson branded the Klan and Nazi onslaught a "massacre" in which "five people were shot down in cold blood."

We also called numerous police defendants, including Greensboro's chief of police. Their testimony revealed extensive foreknowledge about the plans for serious violence by the Klan and Nazis, as well as about Dawson's involvement in these plans. Nonetheless, no police defendant stopped the caravan, searched or arrested the defendants, or was at the scene when the Klan arrived. While the caravan was en route, the lieutenant in charge of monitoring the march was incommunicado, several officers were finishing their breakfasts, a sergeant drove in the opposite direction when he saw the caravan, and several officers were ordered out of the area only minutes before the attack.

As our case in chief neared conclusion, we called Paul Bermanzohn to the stand. He entered the courtroom in a wheelchair, described his background as the son of Holocaust survivors, and told how he was shot down in Greensboro. We then called defendant Roland Wayne Wood, a huge man with a menacing presence, who appeared in a three-piece suit and white tennis shoes. He had been one of the main shooters on November 3. I confronted him with some of his prior anticommunist and anti-Semitic statements and a prior court appearance at which he wore an "Eat lead you lousy Red" T-shirt. When I had him recite a Nazi song that included the chilling refrain "Kill a Commie for Christ," the jury laughed. I asked for a recess, and Dr. Bermanzohn told me that Wood was close to coming down off the stand and attacking me. It was late on a Friday afternoon, and I wanted to confront Wood before the weekend about the five white skulls he was wearing pinned to his lapel. After court reconvened, I suggested that the skulls represented the five slain demonstrators. Wood's denial seemed both implausible and irrelevant.

The thrust of the defendants' presentation was to discredit the victims, highlight their communist beliefs, tie them to weapons and to a few of the many shots fired, and emphasize that the plaintiffs had publicly dared the Klan to come to their "Death to the Klan" march.

In our closing arguments, Lewis urged the jury to reject the notion that Black people, civil rights advocates, and communists "are so undeserving of constitutional rights that it's okay to kill them" and argued that "our forefathers and foremothers would be as mad as a hornet in a jar that these plaintiffs were killed, not because they were communists, but because it erodes all our rights." I emphasized the role of the agents provocateur and asserted that we had presented "some of the most powerful and damning evidence that you are ever going to see in a court of law." I urged the jury to "stand up and say to the Klan and the Nazis, 'You can't do this in America.'" Carolyn concluded: "Regardless of whether you agree with [the plaintiffs], their motivation was to work for a better world."

On June 6, 1985, the jury began deliberations. We were confident in the power of our case, and, fully cognizant of the violent propensities of the Klan, imported a shotgun to our collective house in Winston-Salem in case they attacked us. Police snipers were perched on the rooftop of the building facing the courthouse. The next morning, the Black juror, who had been elected foreperson, reported that the jury was deadlocked on the civil rights conspiracy claim and asked, "What do we do now?" A woman who had moved to the South from New England was in tears. The judge directed the jury to continue its deliberations. Late that afternoon, the jury returned with a very disappointing verdict: they found for all the defendants on all of the federal civil rights claims. They did find, under North Carolina law, wrongful death liability for conspiracy to assault and batter in favor of Michael Nathan's estate, and against Lieutenant Spoon, in charge of police protection on November 3; Edward Dawson; Jerry Cooper; Klansmen Mark Sherer, David Wayne Matthews, and Jerry Paul Smith; and Nazis Roland Wayne Wood and Jack Fowler; and found state assault and battery in favor of two surviving plaintiffs and Nathan's estate, and against four Klansmen and Nazis. The jury found against the other four estates and nine of the survivors on all claims. The next day, the jury awarded $355,100 to Nathan's estate and $40,450 to the two survivors.

Despite our extreme disappointment, we decided that we should rightfully claim the verdict as a major victory. After nearly six years and three trials, a Southern jury had finally convicted a good number of the main actors in the November 3 massacre and had found a conspiracy between police officials, their provocateur, and the Klan and Nazi killers. Community reaction was positive because an intense six-year struggle—waged by the widows, the families, the survivors, and numerous political, religious, and community organizations, and prosecuted by people's lawyers, law students, and paralegals—had resulted in a rare victory against the Klan and the police. The Klan could no longer claim, as they had previously, that November 3 in Greensboro upheld the principle that they could kill Blacks and communists with complete impunity.

The verdict was national news. The *New York Times* editorialized, "The recompense for the victims may be limited as well as late, but this is no time to complain about inadequate justice. The criminal acquittals set back American principles of law and civil rights; the civil verdict goes a long way to reassert them." The Greensboro Civil Rights Fund put out the statement, "It's a tremendous victory that a North Carolina jury found against North Carolina policemen. However, the fact that only certain plaintiffs were found for can only be attributed to racial or political prejudice." CWP leader Nelson Johnson, whose claims, like those of all six Black plaintiffs, had been rejected by the jury, put the verdicts in perspective: "No dollar amount can measure the significance of this historic victory."

Lewis Pitts and I interviewed the Black jury foreman. He told us he and the white woman from New England strongly supported a verdict on the civil rights conspiracy charges in favor of most of the victims, against the BATF provocateurs and several of the police and federal defendants, and substantially higher damage awards. The Southern white faction was unable to put their anticommunism and racism aside, however, and wanted a narrow verdict or none at all. They feared the community reaction to a verdict for the CWP plaintiffs. In the case of Sandy Smith, an unarmed Black woman who was shot between the eyes and killed, they refused to support liability because they disliked her husband, a Black doctor, and did not want him to recover. They also severely limited Dr. Paul Bermanzohn's recovery, despite his permanent paralysis, because they feared that any additional money would go to the CWP.

As in all the major cases I would be involved in throughout my career, exposing the whole truth, and in the process establishing a people's narrative, was of paramount importance. The verdict placed the Greensboro massacre in the historical context of racist Klan violence, all too often fomented by FBI and police provocateurs and countenanced by law enforcement. More personally, through the Greensboro trial experience, our legal team formed a lifelong bond and comradeship that was forged in the legal and political battle that we fought together.

The Supremes and More Street Files

In October 1985, Chick Hoffman and I journeyed to Washington, DC, to argue the *Saxner* case before the US Supreme Court. David Saxner and Albert Cain were federal prisoners in Terre Haute, Indiana, banished to disciplinary segregation for protesting the deaths of several fellow prisoners, who had died as a direct result of inadequate medical care. Back in

1981, my wife, Pat, now a lawyer, and I had convinced an Indiana jury that the prison disciplinary committee had violated Saxner's and Cain's due process rights, and the jury had awarded them the paltry sum of $9,000. Rather than pay the judgment, Ronald Reagan's justice department took the case all the way to the high court. The bench was transitioning from the liberal court of Earl Warren to the more conservative Warren Burger court, but elderly liberal icons Thurgood Marshall and William Brennan were still on the bench. When the government lawyer argued that prison guards who sat on the disciplinary committees should be afforded the same absolute immunity as judges, Justice Marshall, in his gravelly voice, asked with indignation: "Are you saying that prison guards are like us?" Two months later, we were able to share with David Saxner, who had embarked on a post-prison career of fighting for prisoner rights, that the Supreme Court had affirmed our verdict in a 6 to 3 decision.

In April 1986, Peter and I tried a police killing case in which the shooter, a "repeater" cop with a background of brutality, fatally shot our African American client, Gary Lee, in a south side alley. Before judge Prentice Marshall we presented a strong circumstantial case that the officer was lying when he said that Lee was wielding a razor, and had planted a razorblade near Lee's body after he shot him. Unbeknownst to us, however, the jury's foreman was closely connected to the Chicago police and had lied about that fact during voir dire. He swung the jury against us, but we discovered the truth about this juror the next week and moved for a new trial, which Judge Marshall granted. We later settled the case for a modest amount.

Also that April, death row prisoner Andrew Wilson, with the assistance of Dale Coventry, filed a handwritten civil rights complaint in Chicago Federal District Court. The complaint alleged that Wilson's torture violated his constitutional rights and requested monetary damages, the reversal of his conviction, and release from prison. Among the defendants named were Jon Burge, Chicago police superintendent Richard Brzeczek, and the City of Chicago. The case was assigned to judge Brian Barnett Duff, whose erratic behavior on the bench was well known. Coventry, a criminal defense lawyer, requested that Duff appoint a civil lawyer for Wilson, who was indigent, and Duff obliged. A succession of three appointed lawyers, each disinterested and unwilling, appeared over the next year while the case languished.

In January 1987, Jeff and I began a seven-week damages trial for George Jones, who, thanks to Frank Laverty, had been exonerated five years earlier. This was the third in a trilogy of street files trials. Jeff and I were joined on the trial team by John Stainthorp, a young PLO lawyer who had grown up in central England and connected with us by volunteering to work in Buffalo on the Attica cases. George Jones was desperate to avoid reliving his nightmare in court, so we had offered to settle the case for $90,000, but Mayor Washington's lawyers had refused. The case was tried before a fair, albeit conservative, judge, who was convinced, as was the jury, that George had been falsely arrested and maliciously prosecuted by a crew of Area 2 detectives and supervisors who had hidden the evidence that proved his innocence. Instead of graduating from high school, George had spent five hellish weeks in Cook County Jail, and his life was changed forever.

This was the first case in which we developed and presented psychological and psychiatric evidence of posttraumatic stress disorder (PTSD), evidence that would later be instrumental in the police torture cases. The jury returned an $800,000 verdict, and after court-ordered attorneys' fees were added, the total amount recovered was $1.5 million. This unprecedented verdict paved the way for the numerous exoneration cases that have followed.

CHAPTER 4

The First *Wilson*
Civil Rights Trial

In April 1987 the Illinois Supreme Court issued its decision on Andrew Wilson's criminal appeal. Clearly swayed by the uncontroverted evidence of Wilson's injuries, as attested to by the doctors and nurses who had treated him, the court held that the state had *not* shown by "clear and convincing" evidence that Andrew's confession was *not* a product of his physical abuse. The court reversed his conviction and death sentence—something the law did not permit Judge Duff to do even if he were so inclined—and ordered a new criminal trial, at which his confession would be barred.

A few days later I received a call from Pontiac Correctional Center's death row. It was Andrew Wilson. He wanted to know if we would take over his civil case. Knowing the case would be a massive undertaking with little chance of success, our office collectively agreed, nevertheless, that torture was a human rights violation, period. End of story, no matter how unpopular the victim. I appeared before Judge Duff at the next court date only to discover that Andrew and Dale Coventry had hedged their bets— Andrew had also contacted a former associate of Dale's on the public defender's Murder Task Force, and he was in court as well. Duff told us to work it out with Andrew, and the former public defender initially won the day. But Andrew soon became disenchanted with him, and we became his lawyers in August 1987. Our thirty-one-year-and-counting commitment to fighting against Chicago police torture began.

Our relationship with Judge Duff was doomed from the beginning. Early on, he called the case "a bad penny"; profusely praised Bill Kunkle, who was reprosecuting Andrew in criminal court as a specially appointed private lawyer; belittled our most important allegation against the City— that the police department had a practice of abusing suspects in police injury cases; accused Andrew of not cooperating with the court; alleged that the mild-mannered John Stainthorp had misrepresented the status of the case; and threatened to remove us as counsel if John continued "to be a problem." Stunned, John apologized, even though he was right.

In June, Andrew was retried for the double murder, with Kunkle as prosecutor. In a strange twist, Dale Coventry called Jon Burge as a defense witness to establish that he had destroyed all the police memos and notes—the street file—generated during the manhunt, only months before his Area 2 nemesis Frank Laverty exposed this illegal practice. Even with his confession barred from evidence, Andrew was once again convicted, but one juror held out against reimposing the death penalty. Andrew's brutal torture had, ironically, served to save him from execution.

Kunkle, who had followed Richard Devine from the top echelon of Daley's state's attorney's office to the staunchly Democratic law firm of Phelan, Pope and John, billed Cook County the relatively modest amount of $36,000 for his reprosecution of Andrew Wilson. But he and Burge were angling for a bigger financial plum: the appointment of Kunkle and his law firm as the lawyers for Burge and his cohorts in our civil rights case. Kunkle first wrote a letter of commendation to superintendent of police LeRoy Martin, citing Burge and his men for swiftly arresting Andrew and Jackie Wilson "without incident," and for performing "at all times with the highest degree of professionalism and work ethic imaginable." Burge followed up by meeting with Martin and a high-ranking deputy from the city's law department, who blessed his effort to seek Kunkle's appointment as their lawyer. Burge then wrote to the powerful chair of the city council's finance committee, Burt Natarus, asserting that "due to the magnitude of the case," the "potential of a significant judgment against the defendants," and "possible adverse publicity," the committee should retain Kunkle because he was "by far, the most knowledgeable and qualified person due to his intricate knowledge of the evidence and idiosyncrasies of the case."

The deal was struck, and Kunkle and his junior associate Jeff Rubin entered the case just in time to represent Burge and his Area 2 co-defendants at a week of intense depositions at our downtown office, in September. In an attempt to intimidate John and me, all of the defendants attended each of the depositions, a right to which defendants in civil cases are entitled but very rarely exercise. The white, chain-smoking, and physically imposing "torturers' row" of four, arrayed across the table with the equally burly Kunkle, reminded me of the Daniel Groth deposition in the *Hampton* case, nearly fifteen years before.

I challenged Kunkle's entry into the case, asserting that, as the highest-ranking trial prosecutor in Andrew's and Jackie's criminal cases, he was a potential witness on the question of the destroyed street file and therefore had a conflict of interest. Kunkle responded with his trademark smirk, and the depositions continued. After we questioned officers John Yucairis, Patrick O'Hara, and Thomas McKenna at length, it was my turn to question Burge. Dressed in a sports coat and tie, chain-smoking Pall Malls, the six-foot, 250-pound, red-haired Burge was imposing, to say the least. An experienced witness, he loved to intimidate lawyers, lecturing the "counselors," as he dismissively called them, while demonstrating his superior knowledge of all things police oriented.

With the deposition we learned a great deal about Burge's background that would inform our understanding of his racist motivations and dehumanizing interrogation techniques. Burge grew up in a racially changing neighborhood on Chicago's south side, was an ROTC cadet at Bowen High School, and, when he flunked out of college, joined the US Army. He became a military police (MP) sergeant and was assigned to a prisoner of war camp in South Vietnam's Mekong Delta during the height of the Vietnam War. He interrogated soldiers and stood security for the military intelligence officers when they interrogated enemy soldiers and Vietnamese civilians—interrogations that the Winter Soldier investigation revealed to have included murder and torture with electric shock. Burge claimed to have killed an unknown number of the "enemy" and left Vietnam with a leg wound. Like so many Vietnam veterans, he received no treatment for PTSD, which he belittled as "gobbledygook" in his testimony.

He joined the Chicago police department and, in 1972, became a detective on the midnight shift at Area 2. He proudly admitted that he was a skilled and experienced interrogator and utilized the techniques he had employed as an MP in Vietnam. After a stint with the intelligence division, he shot up the ranks from detective to commander in what would later be described as record time, but, he boasted, he remained a "hands-on" supervisor, who often observed interrogations conducted by his detectives. Area 2 became a model detective division as Burge and his men gave meaning to the "war on crime" politics that was gripping Chicago and the nation, churning out an impressive record of arrests, confessions, and convictions that fueled the mass incarceration of young African American men. Unmarried, except to the department, Burge's main investment was a $100,000 boat that he kept moored at a downtown harbor on Lake Michigan.

Burge contended that he told his detectives to handle Andrew "with kid gloves" and never entered the interview room (which was next door to his office) the entire time Andrew was being interrogated and tortured. He flatly denied having been accused of any other acts of torture, except for a claim by a man named Michael Johnson, made a year and a half or two after Andrew's, and scoffed at the notion of having possessed or used any torture devices. He attempted to stretch the meaning of "next door" to refer to an interview room two doors down from his office, in order to make his testimony consistent with that of his fellow defendants, who claimed that the radiator in the room in which Andrew was interrogated did not work. Burge also claimed that back in 1982 he had measured the distance between the two handcuff rings in that room, and that they were wider apart than the span of his outstretched arms. The rings were no longer there, but Burge's defense did not account for the length of the handcuff chains that extended from the handcuffs on Andrew's wrists to the rings on the wall.

Judge Duff had set a firm trial date for early November 1988, but Kunkle used his considerable influence over Duff to obtain a three-month continuance. Just before Christmas, John and I traveled to Pontiac Correctional Center, a maximum-security prison some one hundred miles south of Chicago, for the deposition of Andrew Wilson. More than a decade before, Pontiac had been the location of a prison uprising that had led to the deaths of two guards. Jeff, Michael, and Peter had played primary roles on a stellar defense team that ultimately won exonerations of seventeen prisoners, and I joined them to successfully challenge the oppressive lockdown conditions imposed at Pontiac in the aftermath of the killings.

As the deposition started, Kunkle was at his bloodthirsty best. A devout death penalty advocate, he was smarting from the loss of the death sentence in Andrew's case and relished the opportunity to again rake Andrew over the coals. Andrew stood up well, recounting in detail his harrowing ordeal. He described Burge's torturing him with the hair-dryer device:

Kunkle: What happened next?
Andrew: He shocked me. He stuck it on me. He put it between my legs, under my groin area and he was rubbing it real gentle, and you could feel it tingling and stuff. I think I was standing there, and he stood up and he was just rubbing it on me, and you could feel the damn thing. Excuse me, you could feel it.
Kunkle: And then what happened?
Andrew: Oh—

Andrew then broke down crying, a classic symptom of torture-induced PTSD, and Dale, who was present as Andrew's criminal defense lawyer, called for a recess. Kunkle could not suppress his glee. When the deposition went back on the record, John described Kunkle's reaction:

> John: The record should reflect that immediately before the recess, Mr. Wilson became very upset while talking about being electrocuted and left the room, and when he did so, Mr. Kunkle was smiling broadly, and when I noted that, hoping to get it on the record, Mr. Kunkle said, "Yeah, I love to see him cry. It is too late to get it on the record, you are too late."
>
> Kunkle: You can put it on the record now, and I will affirm it. There is no question about it.

In December, the pretrial deposition schedule intensified, and I first questioned Deputy Superintendent McCarthy, who'd had the two fallen officers, Fahey and O'Brien, under his direct command. We learned that McCarthy had insisted that he and several other supervisors from the Gang Crimes Unit be present at Andrew's predawn arrest and, along with Burge, had led the charge. The show of force echoed the Hampton raid, both in the heavy armaments used, including the department's "war wagon," and the personal relationships some of the raiders had with the slain officers. Given the build-up, Andrew's arrest was "anticlimactic," as Burge termed it, no doubt because Andrew did not offer them the opportunity to kill him.

Next was former superintendent Brzeczek. Despite Judge Duff's initial disparaging remarks concerning our claim that the department had a pattern, practice, or custom of brutalizing persons suspected of killing police officers, the judge had subsequently denied a motion by the City and Brzeczek to dismiss that claim. In the time since the torture of Andrew Wilson in February 1982, much had happened in Brzeczek's professional and personal life. After Harold Washington was elected, Brzeczek had resigned as superintendent and the next year unsuccessfully ran as a Republican against Richie Daley for Cook County state's attorney. His personal life had spiraled downward as he became embroiled in a secret affair, drank heavily, and was under psychiatric care. Daley, perhaps as political retribution, indicted him for fraud—using police funds to help finance his affair—but in 1987 Brzeczek was acquitted by a Cook County judge. When I questioned him just before Christmas, he was on the rebound but not yet ready to tell the whole truth concerning our claims of pattern and practice, and cover-up. ("Policy, pattern, or practice" claims, sometimes referred to as "policy, practice, or custom" claims, are also known as *Monell* claims, based on the 1978 US Supreme Court decision of that name. Establishing a *Monell* claim [section 1983] is a requirement for suing a municipality under the federal Civil Rights Act.)

Prior to the deposition we had obtained the file of the department's Office of Professional Standards (OPS) "investigation" of Andrew's torture. The file revealed that the OPS had opened its investigation of Burge and Yucaitis at Brzeczek's behest eight days after he had received the letter from Dr. Raba documenting Andrew's torture, the same day that Brzeczek had informed Daley he had opened an OPS investigation but would "forbear from taking any steps other than the one previously mentioned" until he heard back from Daley. The OPS investigator was Keith Griffiths, who obtained Andrew's medical records and the transcript of all the testimony at the November 1982 motion to suppress hearing, then did nothing more for three years. At that time the OPS director had quietly approved a finding of "not sustained," an administrative limbo that dismissed the charges because there was not enough evidence to either prove or disprove the allegations. This "tie goes to the police officer" ruling was a convenient method to dispose of troublesome complaints of brutality, used by the OPS in a vast majority of its cases, earning OPS the characterization of a "washing machine" that perpetuated the police "code of silence."

At this early stage we focused on Brzeczek and the department's role rather than that of Daley, in large part because Daley was not a defendant in our suit. Not surprisingly, in his testimony Brzeczek made a concerted effort to protect himself and the department. He claimed that he had not heard the complaints about brutality during the manhunt or Jesse Jackson's cry that the police department had turned the Black community into a "war zone," but only remembered claims of searches and questioning on the street. He said that when he heard about these complaints, he called in his Black command personnel to enlist them in an effort to calm the community, but "did not recall" if he had talked to his white command staff. I attempted to establish through questioning Brzeczek that when he informed Daley he would take no further steps, he meant that he would direct the OPS to desist from further investigating Burge and his men, beyond opening the OPS file, unless Daley told him to do otherwise. After conceding that Daley never responded, Brzeczek would not admit to this interpretation of his letter, but maintained, rather, that what he meant was that the department would not pursue a criminal investigation of Burge and his men without Daley's approval. In so doing, he admitted that Dr. Raba's letter set forth allegations that, if proven, were criminal offenses; and, in what we rightly felt was a significant first, admitted, as the superintendent of police, that electric shock and burning on a radiator were a "form of torture."

As 1988 began, with an impending trial date a little more than a month away, we gathered in Judge Duff's courtroom for a pretrial conference. Like me, Duff had grown up in a Massachusetts factory town and come to the Midwest as a young man, but the similarities ended there. Duff, a classic Boston Irishman, was a Republican politician who had served as minority whip in the Illinois House of Representatives and developed a close relationship with liberal US senator Chuck Percy. Duff had next become a Cook County judge, where his mercurial behavior was on display: in one instance, angered by how his clerk had handed him up a file, he held her in contempt, fined her, and detained her in custody for an hour. In 1985, Senator Percy pulled some strings with then president Ronald Reagan, and Duff was appointed to the federal bench, where he started his lifetime term by referring to a litigant as a "wetback."

Duff's attitude at the early January conference gave us a hint of what lay ahead. He denied us the right to call Afro American Patrolmen's League president Renault Robinson to testify about the complaints of brutality during the manhunt; he also denied my request to argue the point, told me to "be quiet," and accused me of talking to Jeff, walking away "with a body language of disdain for the court," and "walking on the edge of contempt."

The weeks before trial were filled with a flurry of more than twenty depositions. Back in 1982, Dale Coventry had subpoenaed OPS files related to the violent manhunt. He had received the cover sheets to about twenty-five files but not the files themselves. We had recently obtained these sheets from Dale. When we asked the City for the corresponding files, officials claimed there were none, and that they had nothing as to the approximately 175 other cases of alleged brutality. From the cover sheets and newspaper reports we gleaned the names of several victims who alleged that they were brutalized, and we listed them as witnesses. Most prominent was Roy Brown, a former Gangster Disciples gang member. Roy testified at his February deposition that he was taken by a red-haired officer from his home near the scene of the police murders to Area 1 detective headquarters, accused of knowing "who killed those cops," and tortured. He further described his ordeal:

He smacked me in the head, and then he took his two thumbs and stuck them back here and kept punching them back there. It felt like my brain was going to explode. Then he put a plastic bag over my head, and they took these big lock cutters out of this big gray cabinet and they said, "We are going to cut your fucking finger." They put my finger in there. I kept telling them "I don't know nothing."

His fingers spared, Roy's torture continued:

Then they took this stick and they started whacking me. The next thing I know I was in a hallway and I was going up these steps with this bag over my head fighting for air. Every now and then, they would take it up and give me some air. I said, in the name of Jesus God, I don't know nothing.

Then, at the top of the stairs,

I was on the roof of the police station, and he would whack me with the sticks on the backs of my legs. I was, you know, dying for air.

Desperate and on his knees, Roy was broken. He stopped the torture by saying, "I tell you something." He gave them the name and address of a rival gang member named Paul, who knew no more about the murders than Roy did. As they locked up Roy that night, the officers told him, "Nigger, you better not tell anybody about this or we'll throw you in the river."

About a week before the trial was to begin, a letter in an official police department envelope appeared in my office mailbox. It read as follows [all *sic*]:

Mr Flint Taylor:
I understand that you are representing Andrew Wilson in his civil action against several police officers for brutality.
Check the following:
Several witnesses, including the White's were severely beaten at 1121 S. State Street in front of the Chief of Detectives, the Superintendent of Police and the State's Attorneys.
Mayor Byrne and State's Attorney Daley were aware of the actions of the detectives. ASA Angarola told both of them and condoned the actions.
Several of the detectives named in the suit have been previously accused of using torture machines at complaints given to OPS and in motions filed in Criminal trials.
The device was destroyed by throwing it off of Lt. Burge's boat.
Mayor Byrne and State's Attorney Daley ordered that the numerous complaints filed against the police as a result of this crime not be investigated.

This order was carried out by an OPS investigator named Buckley who is close to Alderman Burke.

You should interview everyone assigned to Area 2 Violent Crimes at that time because some of them were disgusted and will tell all. The torture was not necessary.

Russ Ewing of Channel 7 was investigating this matter and you should talk to him.

DO NOT SHOW THIS TO ANYONE. IF YOU WANT MORE INFORMATION PUT AN AD IN THE SOUTHTOWN ECONOMIST. YOU DO NOT HAVE PERMISSION TO SHOW THIS TO ANYONE IT IS PRIVLEDGED

Ty

Struck both by the information and its cloak-and-dagger presentation, John and I, as instructed, placed an ad in the *Southtown Economist*, a community newspaper that was a favorite of the many Chicago cops who lived on the southwest side of Chicago. Buried in the personals, the ad read, "Further information sought on Wilson case. Call: 663-5046."

A week later—seven years to the day after Andrew Wilson was tortured—Judge Duff swore in six jurors and four alternates to hear what he told them would be, at most, a three-week trial. Jurors from the Northern District of Illinois were drawn not only from racially diverse Cook County but also from numerous predominantly white-collar counties. Normally, a jury venire (the pool of potential jurors) would thereby include only 10 to 20 percent Black and Latinx people. At Duff's direction, the clerk had summoned sixty potential jurors, and, remarkably, about thirty-five of them were people of color. Duff told us that we should "thank our lucky stars" we had such a diverse group, and Kunkle acknowledged this unusual circumstance. The defendants were confronted with a playing field to which they were unaccustomed, and after they exercised all five of their peremptory challenges on Black people, the six-person jury that was empaneled still included two Black men and two Black women.

Brzeczek was our first main witness, and I cross-examined him. He again admitted, this time in open court, that Andrew's allegations amounted to torture, and that he had deferred to Daley concerning whether to conduct a criminal investigation into these uniquely serious allegations. I read his letter to Daley to the jury and grilled him about its evident meaning. When I repeatedly attempted to establish through the OPS file, which the City had previously agreed could be admitted into evidence, that the investigation had been closed after three and a half years, Duff shut me down, holding me in contempt and fining me a hundred dollars. I finished by establishing that rather than disciplining Burge or criminally investigating him, Brzeczek issued a unit commendation with Burge as the lead name.

Andrew was our next witness. Earlier that day, Kunkle convened the deposition of Duane Jensen. Duane, a Vietnam veteran, was a carpenter by trade and had a working knowledge of electrical wiring. He had done some work on our house, and I had described Burge's shock box to him. Having grown up in rural Wisconsin, Duane was familiar with a hand-crank generator used during his youth to make phone calls. It sounded exactly like what Andrew was describing, so I enlisted Duane to construct a facsimile from Andrew's description of the box. Duane found a crank phone generator at an antique shop, constructed the box, placed the generator inside it, and attached two wires with alligator clips at the ends to the generator. During Duane's deposition, Kunkle, armed with voltage and amperage meters, established what we already knew—that the shock box would deliver a shock. Duff barred us from presenting the box as demonstrative evidence, a common method of using facsimiles constructed to scale. But over the following decades, Duane's box would serve as an important demonstrative aid that we often used at press conferences, public testimony, and speaking engagements.

John carefully led Andrew, flanked by his current public defender, Alan Sincox, through his now familiar testimony. When Andrew started to recount that Burge reentered the interrogation room with the torture box, he began to break down and pleaded, "I want to leave, can I get a recess, I want to leave for a while." Duff reluctantly granted the request and then chastised John: "Speak to your client . . . I don't want this to be a repetitive thing." He later accused Andrew of being on drugs. Kunkle tore into Andrew on cross-examination, spending hour after hour questioning him about the murders of Fahey and O'Brien and the contents of his tortured confession. At Alan's direction, Andrew invoked his Fifth Amendment right not to incriminate himself in response to most of these questions.

After Roy Brown and several other victims of the manhunt had testified, much of our remaining case was devoted to testimony from the doctors and lawyers who corroborated Andrew's injuries. We also called the commander of Area 2, Milton Deas. An older Black man who had been a central figure in the George Jones street files cover-up, Deas was Burge's boss in title only, as it was common knowledge that Burge ran the show. I was able to get Deas to contradict a key component of Burge's defense by establishing through him that all the radiators at Area 2 were working. Deas reinforced the police code of silence when he said he had not been concerned when he saw Andrew with blood on his face, and that his entire investigation of his officers consisted of asking Burge if he did it. When I confronted him with the evidence of Andrew's torture, he retorted, "I am still proud of my men, let there be no doubt about it."

As Duff put pressure on us to finish our case, a second letter arrived in my mailbox from "Ty." After chiding us for being a little "to obvious [*sic*]" in our ad, the anonymous source asked us to place a second ad, this time answering whether we would keep the letters secret and never use them in court. Ty then continued:

> I believe I have learned something that will blow the lid off your case. You should check for other cases which Lt. Burge was accussed [*sic*] of using this device. I believe he started right after becoming a detective many years ago. I will not give any specifics until I am assured that these letters are not going to be used ever.
>
> I have checked who was in Area 2 when this was going on, and have some comments on the people assigned. You must remember that they all knew, as did all of the State's Attorneys, and many judges and attorneys in private practice.

He (or she?) then listed seven Area 2 detectives, including Yucaitis, as "Burge's asskickers," and thirteen others, including Laverty, as "weak links," who might be open to talking.

We planned on closing our case with Dr. Robert Kirschner, deputy chief Cook County medical examiner, who was also an internationally known expert on torture and human rights. The defendants objected to the portion of his testimony that drew on his torture-related expertise, and Duff convened a three-hour nighttime examination of Kirschner outside the presence of the jury to determine whether to bar that portion of his testimony.

Kirschner testified that Andrew's account of how he felt when he was shocked, his description of the pain going through his brain with his teeth clenching and chattering, was "very consistent with what other people who have been tortured report when they have received similar electric shocks," and was unlikely to be manufactured testimony. He also testified that Andrew's crying when he testified about being shocked was characteristic of a torture victim, especially as Andrew was a streetwise "cop killer" who was otherwise unlikely to break down.

Duff barred Dr. Kirschner from giving this testimony, but the portion that Duff allowed was nonetheless very powerful. Kirschner had examined Andrew, his medical records, and photos of his injuries, and testified that Andrew had suffered burns consistent with being caused by a hot radiator, and with being inflicted two days before February 16. He had also recently visited the Area 2 facility, and although it had not been in use as a police station since 1983, the radiators remained. He measured them, and we took pictures of him kneeling with his body against the radiator as Andrew had described. He told the jury that his demonstration established that Andrew could have suffered burns to his face, chest, and thigh from one of the Area 2 radiators. He also testified that the photos of Andrew's ears showed patterned abrasions consistent with being caused by alligator clips. In dramatic testimony that was a surprise even to us, he had discovered, using a magnifying glass, an electrical spark burn when he examined a blow-up of the photo of Andrew's right ear.

The night before Kirschner's voir dire, Judge Duff had conducted another nighttime hearing for the purpose of determining whether we could present certain documents and pretrial depositions to the jury. Duff had sent Lois Lacorte, the court reporter, home early so there was no transcribed record of the proceedings. We were joined that night by Mariel Nanasi, a former law student intern at our office. When Mariel commented that the case was interesting, Duff responded, in our presence, "Yes, this is a constitutional case where it will be determined whether the Constitution will protect the 'scum of the earth' against government misconduct."

The morning after the voir dire, the *Chicago Lawyer*, a well-respected investigative monthly, published its March issue, with two front-page articles. The first, "Torture in Chicago," featured pictures of Andrew's wounds, recounted Andrew's and Roy Brown's testimony in great detail, and previewed Kirschner's. The second article, headlined "Judges under a Microscope" and featuring a picture of Duff, detailed the results of the publication's survey of 348 federal court lawyers concerning the performance of Chicago's twenty federal judges. Of the eight questions in the survey, Duff was rated worst on five and second-worst on one. Seventy-six percent of lawyers surveyed thought his understanding of complex issues was either "poor" or "very poor," 74 percent thought he was not courteous to lawyers and litigants, and 71 percent disagreed or strongly disagreed with the statement that Duff's legal opinions were "clear and well-reasoned."

Duff was incensed. He blamed us for supplying the photos that appeared in the article—they were in the public record—and bemoaned the fact that the *Chicago Lawyer* made him appear to be "dumber than a box of rocks." Then Jeff, arguing in open court that Kirschner should be allowed to offer his expert opinions, made reference to Duff's "scum of the earth" comment. "That's a lie!" Duff shouted. He then defended his comment, explaining that what he said was "Each of you feels that the other is the scum of the earth. I'm going to let the jury decide." When Jeff tried to assert that the judge was discussing the issue of Andrew's credibility, he summoned us into his chambers, where he accused Jeff of making the reference deliberately, for the benefit of the press. He sent Lois to search for the transcript, which, of course, she could not find, because he'd made the comment when there was no court reporter present. Duff told us that it was "terribly important to his reputation," and predicted that the ten o'clock news would broadcast that the "judge called the plaintiff 'scum of the earth.'" He asked each lawyer if they had heard the remarks. John and I both said we had, and I told him he had said it on two separate occasions, one of which was off the record. All the defense lawyers, following Kunkle's lead, either said they did not recall his making the comment or that they were not present.

Duff then paraded us back into the courtroom, where he stated, "We have checked the record and have found no instance that would suggest that the Court has called anyone any names." He then publicly sanitized his prior words, declaring that "in talking to lawyers, one of the important concepts here—and I'll repeat it again, what I said before, what I did say—this is an exquisite case because it puts at issue whether or not if the jury believes a reprehensible citizen or a citizen believed to be reprehensible was tortured by the government, will the constitution protect him?"

We rested our case the next day. The trial was about to extend well beyond the three weeks the judge had told the jury it would take, and when Duff informed the jury, a Black woman juror told him that she had plans to travel to Detroit the following weekend. Duff questioned the juror, who said she would cut her visit short if necessary. Duff refused to accept her offer, or to work out scheduling that would make it easier for her to continue to serve, and excused her without hearing argument on the subject. After he had made his decision, he reluctantly let Jeff argue why she need not have been excused. Jeff pointed out that the juror was a Black woman, while the alternate who would take her place was a white man.

Duff professed ignorance of this fact, cited his "sensitivity" to the juror's needs, and claimed that he thought that the first alternate was a young Black woman. He proposed that the excused juror, as a "middle-aged Black woman" in all likelihood would be "very seriously opposed to crime," and therefore not necessarily sympathetic to our case.

Kunkle had previously moved for a mistrial, and Duff asked us if we wanted to join in the request on the basis of our claims that he was hopelessly biased and prejudiced against us. Jeff responded that we felt like the accused at the Salem witch trials: "If you're not guilty, you get drowned, and if you're guilty, you survive and you get hung." He continued, "We have put six weeks of our time and a tremendous amount of our resources into this case. Our client is indigent. We are not funded by anybody as the defendants are. They can go to trial after trial after trial and we are not in a position to do that." Duff, who no doubt believed that our rejection of his offer exonerated him from our accusations of bias, could barely hide his pleasure.

Kunkle began his defense by calling commander Jon Burge to the stand. On direct, Burge flatly denied any involvement in Andrew's torture. He went on, with the judge's blessing, to recount, in graphic detail, all the evidence they had gathered or heard about that implicated Andrew, not only in the police murders but in other crimes as well. Duff overruled all of our objections, and, after Kunkle finished by eliciting another round of denials, I began my cross-examination. After establishing that Burge dealt with electricity as an auto mechanic and became familiar with hand-crank phone generators while he was in Vietnam, I asked him to affirm his prior deposition testimony that he was a "hands-on" supervisor. The judge sustained Kunkle's objection and rebuffed several additional attempts on my part to introduce what should have been permitted under the federal rules of evidence.

In continuing to sustain nearly all of Kunkle's objections, Duff often ignored black-letter rules of evidence and humiliated me before the jury for pointing that out. After one particularly maddening exchange, I lingered before following the other counsel out of the courtroom in order to cool off a bit. When I came into the chambers, Duff accused me of staring at the jurors and of "lying for the record" when I offered an explanation. Back before the jury, Burge said that he had never heard of the police code of silence except in the movies. He said his only knowledge of the use of electric shock was during stationhouse discussions of the "old times," and that he "took lightly" that Andrew had been rejected from police lockup and had been depicted in the media with large bandages on his face and head.

After Burge left the witness stand on March 16, we returned to the office, where a phone message and a letter from Ty awaited us. The message said, "Melvin Jones is at Cook County Jail, you should check the dates." The letter, in a CPD envelope like the previous ones, read [all *sic*]:

> Mr. Taylor,
>
> As I have said previously, I do not want to be involved in this affair. This is why I asked for the reassurance that these letters would be kept private. I do not wish to be shunned like officer Laverty has been since he cooperated with you.
>
> The following points should be made.
>
> Burge hates black people and is an ego-maniac. He would do anything to further himself.
>
> Almost all of the detectives and police officers know the Wilson's did the murders but they do not approve of the beatings and the torture.
>
> No one wants to see the Wilson's get any money but they would like to see the families of the police officers get any funds that the Wilson's get.

The letter continued:

> I advise you to immediately interview a Melvin Jones who is in Cook County Jail on a murder charge. He is being re-tried in Markham. When you speak with him compare the dates from 1982 and you will see why it is important. You will also find that the State's Attorney knew that he was complaining and that is why his charges were dropped then. That decision was made in the top levels at 26th and California.
>
> There is something else but I am not quite sure of the facts if you need it contact me by the same means.
>
> TY

We had dubbed the faceless police officer "Deep Badge" (in a nod to "Deep Throat," the anonymous source of Watergate fame). I contacted Dale Coventry, and he enlisted Alan Sincox, Andrew's current public defender, in our endeavor to find Melvin Jones. Sure enough, Melvin was in Cook County Jail. Dale and Alan also obtained the transcript from Melvin's 1982 motion to suppress hearing from his current lawyer. Dale visited Melvin in jail and confirmed that he was the Melvin Jones mentioned by Deep Badge. In the meantime, Jeff spoke with Cassandra Watson, who had been Melvin's lawyer back in 1982. Watson was a former

Black Panther who had gone on to be an assistant state's attorney and then a defense lawyer.

In the transcript of his August 1982 hearing, Melvin, who had been picked up as a suspect in a high-profile murder case, described being electric-shocked by Burge at Area 2 on February 5, 1982—only nine days before Andrew Wilson had been tortured. Melvin testified that Burge had entered the interrogation room where he was being held, asked him if he knew who Burge was, and said that before it was over he would "wish that he had never set eyes on him." Burge handcuffed Melvin to a ring on the wall and produced a device similar to the hair-dryer instrument that Andrew had described. After Burge plugged it in, he told Jones that he hoped he'd had sex the night before. He produced a spark by touching the device to the interrogation room radiator, then pulled down Melvin's pants. In response to questioning by Cassandra Watson, Melvin described his torture:

> Watson: And where did he touch you with the electrical device?
> Melvin Jones: First he touched the electrical device on my left foot.
> Watson: Did he have an occasion to put the electrical device on you again?
> Jones: Yes he did.
> Watson: Where did he put it on you the second time?
> Jones: Right on my right thigh, right here.
> Watson: Indicating the left side of the right thigh.
> Watson: And did he have occasion to put the electrical device on you again?
> Jones: Yes he did.
> Watson: Where did he place it to your body at that time?
> Jones: At that time he placed it on my penis.

Melvin added that he began to scream when Burge shocked him on his foot, exclaiming, "You ain't supposed to be doing this to me," to which Burge replied that Melvin "had no proof." To demonstrate his point, Burge turned to a detective in the room and asked, "Do you see anything?" The detective looked up at the ceiling and replied, "I didn't see nothing." Burge then declared, "No court and no state are going to take your word over a lieutenant's word." In his 1982 testimony, Melvin had also added another crucial detail: before he tortured Melvin, Burge predicted that he would have him "crawling on the floor" like Burge had "Satan and Cochise."

We were in a quandary about how to proceed with this game-changing evidence. Deep Badge had insisted that we not reveal the letters, and we had implicitly promised not to when we published the ads in the *Southtown Economist*. But we considered our greater responsibility to be to Andrew Wilson and the public record.

The trial was in its last week when we concluded our week-long investigation into the explosive Jones evidence. We decided that we would not reveal Deep Badge's letters but would refer only to the anonymous phone call, and would attach Melvin Jones's 1982 testimony to a motion we hastily prepared the night after Dale gave me the transcript. In the motion we asked for the right to call Melvin Jones as a witness before the conclusion of the trial, to take Burge's deposition that weekend, and for Burge to be punished for perjuring himself at his earlier deposition when he denied knowing about any other allegations of electric shock made against him, with the exception of those made by Michael Johnson.

We had decided to file and argue the motion in Duff's chambers in order to avoid publicity that might prejudice the jury. Both the judge and Kunkle were shocked by Melvin Jones's testimony. Duff recognized that Melvin's torture was "extraordinarily similar" to and had occurred in timing close to Andrew's, two crucial factors in making the testimony admissible as evidence. Kunkle, after huddling with Burge and his co-defendants, told the judge that if he permitted Melvin to testify, it would create a conflict of interest between Burge and his co-defendants so serious that Kunkle might have to withdraw as the lawyer for those defendants whom Melvin did not implicate. He said that he needed to consult with his law partners. He also questioned why this information had not surfaced until so late in the trial and accused us of "sandbagging" him and the court, a charge that I deflected, pointing out that it was Burge who was sitting on this information after having falsely denied knowledge at his deposition.

Judge Duff seemed preoccupied with logistics and timing, saying that we had put him in an "extraordinary position" in an "extraordinary trial" that "boggled his mind." He agreed with Kunkle that it was "manifestly true" that the evidence created a conflict of interest, and asked if the evidence also went to the claim against the City. We said we would not be contending that it did, while noting that if we had obtained this evidence in a more timely way, we would have broadened our claim of a pattern and practice of torture to one not limited to persons suspected of attacking police.

Duff admitted that the evidence was compellingly powerful, called it a "hand grenade on the doorstep," and promised that he would "cogitate hard" on the question over the Easter holiday that weekend. Monday morning, after declaring that the question was "extremely complicated" and that his decision was made while "surrounded by alligators," Judge Duff informed us that Melvin Jones, like Michael Johnson, would not be permitted to testify, and that he was deferring resolution of our claim that Burge had committed perjury until after the trial.

Kunkle concluded his defense by calling ASA Lawrence Hyman, who denied that Andrew told him he was being tortured; detective George Karl, whose function was to introduce into evidence "roach clips" that Kunkle claimed could easily have been accessed by Andrew in Cook County Jail to self-inflict the injuries to his ears and nose; and Dr. Raymond Warpeha, a burn expert from the Loyola Hospital Burn Center. For $500 per hour, an almost unheard-of hourly rate for a doctor in 1989, Warpeha, after looking at the pictures of Andrew's injuries, contradicted the opinions of four treating doctors, a treating nurse, and Dr. Kirschner by claiming that the injuries on Andrew's face, chest, and leg were "friction abrasions" rather than burns. The defendants ended their case by reading a string of Andrew Wilson's convictions for violent felonies.

At 1:00 p.m. on Wednesday, March 29, 1989, after the jury had waited all morning in the jury room, closing arguments began. To our surprise, we had convinced Duff that we should be permitted to use Duane Jensen's black shock box as demonstrative evidence during our argument because Kunkle intended to use the roach clips in a similar way. The victory was short-lived, however. The jury had already seen the clips, and Kunkle told the judge he would not use them in closing, so Duff reversed his decision, banishing the box, which had never been displayed to the jury, from sight.

John began by invoking the jury's "promise to justice," asking, in this "important case," "if a jury in Chicago, Illinois, in 1989 can apply the Constitution to Andrew Wilson?" In a statement none of us fully comprehended at the time, John declared that there were "a lot of things hidden that we don't know about." He then addressed all the theories Kunkle had presented during the trial, in order: the "injuries happened during the police killings" theory; the "cold radiator" theory; the "wagon men did it" theory; the "roach clips" theory; the "self-infliction" theory; and the "friction abrasions not burns" theory. He recited to the jury an instruction we had convinced the judge to give—that the fact that Andrew was convicted of killing two police officers was not a defense available to Burge and his confederates. He then took the jury through all the evidence that corroborated Andrew's chilling story, concluding by pointing out that Burge and his men had done this together, they had covered it up, and "the conspiracy continues."

Jeff addressed the City's liability for the police department's pattern and practice of abusing suspects accused of harming police officers. Constrained by a fifteen-minute time limit, Jeff emphasized that Superintendent Brzeczek's fingerprints were all over the case, as were those of his top assistants, and that our evidence showed a CPD run amok: crashing down doors; beating and torturing people such as Roy Brown; refusing to investigate and promoting Burge. He asserted that the officers at Area 2 had used "Gestapo tactics" against Andrew Wilson and Chicago's Black community in the aftermath of the police murders.

Jeff, whose grandfather had represented Leo Frank, a Jewish man lynched in Georgia in the early 1900s, returned to the theme as he concluded. His voice rising, he intoned "You know, when people use Gestapo tactics, they always have a reason. 'Well, there was a policeman killed.' I think in Germany they said a Jew had assassinated somebody who—" Defense counsel James McCarthy jumped to his feet and successfully objected, bringing Jeff's argument to an abrupt end.

After his colleagues gave a short and unremarkable argument in defense of the City and Brzeczek as its superintendent, Kunkle took the stage. He first invoked his role in sending serial child murderer John Wayne Gacy to the death chamber. He then turned the Constitution on its head, imploring the jury to respect the constitutional rights of Burge and the slain officers. In his two hours of argument, during which he repeatedly waved the officers' guns before the jury, he wove Andrew's criminal background, his alleged plan to break a cop-killer friend out of custody, and the details of the officers' murders into nearly every point. He pounded away on the fact that Andrew took the Fifth Amendment on all the questions concerning the police killings. He highlighted the contradictions among the testimony of the various doctors. He seized upon Andrew's concession that he had seen electric shock in a movie and suggested that Andrew had constructed his story from that movie. He also suggested that the idea for the crank box came from a movie Dale Coventry had seen. He dismissed our evidence of conspiracy, saying, "This conspiracy is going to get to the whole city of Chicago pretty soon." Kunkle concluded:

> It is said that the evil men do lives after them. Well it sure does with Andrew
> Wilson. And Andrew Wilson's lack of concern for human life and human

property and human rights and the laws and the Constitution of this country has been demonstrated by him throughout his entire life.

I was tasked with delivering our rebuttal argument. John and Jeff gave me a pep talk while the jury ate supper during a thirty-minute recess. I took the podium in a bit of a daze, but then the adrenaline began to flow:

> This case is about what happened to Andrew Wilson, not what's supposition, what's fantasy by a creative lawyer, what movie. It is evidence versus suppostion. It is evidence versus cover-up, it is evidence versus the failure to investigate. . . . This case is about whether they can torture a man, they can beat a man, they can injure a man and feel no bar because of who he is. Just because you think that Andrew Wilson should get the death penalty doesn't mean that you can electroshock him and start the process.

I expressed disbelief in Burge's claim that he could not remember ever entering the room where Andrew was being tortured, and I condemned the terror visited by the CPD on Andrew and the entire Black community:

> What does it say about the rule of law? What does it say about the Constitution of the United States? This isn't South Africa. This isn't the South before the civil rights movement. This isn't Chile. This isn't El Salvador. This is the United States of America, in Chicago, in 1989. And this case is about whether that kind of conduct can be condoned.

I emphasized Brzeczek's admission that Dr. Raba had described torture that should have been criminally investigated, but that he and his entire command structure did nothing other than cover up the crime and exonerate the perpetrators. I pointed out that it was inconceivable that Andrew, with his first-grade education, could have pulled off the deception of which Kunkle had accused him.

As I drew to the finish, I talked about how saddened and angry the evidence made me, but also how heartened I was by the courage of Dr. Raba and our other witnesses who had "bucked the code of silence" and defied "the big lie" in an attempt to "get justice for the least of the persons who live on this planet, and by that, get justice for all of us."

At 8:45 p.m. the jury retired to pick a foreperson and then went home for the night. We would later learn that they elected Mr. Reed, a white, college-educated social worker, who worked for the juvenile correctional system of the state of Illinois. During voir dire he had revealed that on the evening of the police murders, he had been stopped for going a few miles over the speed limit, was treated rudely, and attributed it to the manhunt.

The jury returned the next morning and asked the marshal for paper and pencils, a ruler, and a magnifying glass, which, in a slip from protocol, he brought them without first asking the judge or informing the lawyers. The speculation was that they wanted to look at the photos of the ears and perform some sort of measurements with regard to the radiator and the injuries to Andrew's chest. At 3:54 p.m., the jury sent out its first of a series of notes, which read: "We have apparently reached an impasse in this important case and feel that we will not be coming to any unanimous verdict."

Jeff, John, and I huddled to discuss our position. One one hand, we had given it our best shot, would never get another jury composed of 50 percent Black jurors, and we just could not envision having the resources or the emotional energy to retry the case. On the other hand, if the judge declared the jury hung, we could start over, perhaps with another less biased judge, and a very real possibility of introducing the Melvin Jones evidence. We were divided on the question, so we passed when the judge asked us how we suggested that he proceed.

Jeff Rubin, who was standing in for Kunkle, urged the judge to declare a mistrial on the spot. McCarthy concurred on behalf of the City, after which we resolved our internal differences and John urged Duff to tell them to "try and reach a verdict." Duff asked the jury whether they had reached a verdict on any of the four counts in the complaint. The answer came back at 5:00 p.m.: "No, we are at a total impasse." Forty minutes later, the jury sent out another note: "We have come to [a] unanimous decision on one of the counts regarding the defendant(s)." The judge told them to continue their deliberations.

Two hours later, they sent out another note: "Judge, we continue to remain at an impasse. It does not appear that any other movement will be taking place. May we fill out the proper form?" Ten minutes later they sent an even more definitive note: ". . . We can not come to a decision regarding this matter."

The writing was on the wall. Twenty-four hours after the jury had chosen a foreperson, Duff called the jury into open court. Ms. Smither, a Black electrical engineer from the suburbs, looked visibly upset. Foreperson Reed announced that they had reached a verdict absolving Yucaitis and O'Hara from the torture count but were hung as to Burge on that claim.

They were also hung as to the City on the pattern and practice count, and as to Burge, Yucaitis, and O'Hara on the conspiracy count.

Duff praised the jury for its work, and they departed without speaking to us. He ominously said, on the record, "I do not intend to wait very long to start this trial again." Exhausted, we had lived to fight another day, but not as soon as Duff had in store. He invited us into his chambers and announced that he intended to start the retrial the next week. We went ballistic.

CHAPTER 5

The Cover-Up Begins to Unravel

The next Monday, the *Chicago Sun Times* headline read: "Jurors Think a Retrial Useless for Cop Killer." Douglas Coffey, a Black juror, was quoted as saying that a retrial "would be a waste of taxpayers' money because the results would be the same." According to the article, the jury, although conceding that Andrew "might have been subjected to police mishandling . . . refused to consider awarding him any money and suggested another jury panel would reach the same conclusion." One of the two female jurors was quoted as saying, anonymously, "It would be hard to override a natural feeling that the police may have suffered justifiable rage over their colleagues' murders." In conclusion, the article asserted, "Two of the jurors believed that Wilson was tortured but concluded that the ends justified the means. He deserved it. In the end they caught the killer."

The judge summoned us to court the following day. I was absent owing to a family matter, but John and Jeff continued to battle the judge around the retrial date. We needed time to further develop not only the Melvin Jones evidence but also what we were recognizing as a pattern and practice of torture by Burge and his associates. After a flurry of personal attacks, rejoinders, and a threat from the judge to dismiss the case if we did not proceed on his schedule, Duff granted a short reprieve, setting the trial to start eight days later, with arguments on the Melvin Jones question to proceed the day before.

In spite of the financial and workload strain the case had placed upon our law partners and office, as well as on our families, we were not about to give up in midstream. Several of us were convinced we were sitting on an iceberg of torture evidence. Our commitment to continuing was bolstered by an interview we conducted with one of the Black jurors, who told us that at least one juror had wanted to award punitive damages against Burge; most of them agreed that Andrew was tortured; and that all of them would have agreed upon liability against the City if they believed they could have done so without finding Burge liable.

Spurred by the Melvin Jones revelation, we had begun to gather evidence of other torture victims that supported a pattern and practice by Burge and his associates. Melvin told us that "Satan" was Anthony Holmes, and "Cochise" was Roger Collins. "Satan" was in Stateville Penitentiary, a maximum-security prison in nearby Joliet, while "Cochise" was in Menard, a maximum-security prison three hundred miles south of Chicago. Through a phone call and a letter, "Cochise" gave us more information. He told us about his brother, Howard Collins, who, he said, was victimized by Burge. In a letter to Jeff, he wrote [all *sic*]:

> Check out George Powell. Burgers beat him real bad and did him wrong. Everybody who know about the case know that guy and they beat him and made him sign a confession. This has been going on for years, going back almost 20 years to '72 or '73, and no one act like it's happening. I would have thought they would have been caught and/or busted them a long time ago, but it seem as if they fellow officers cover up and keep they mouths close for them.

George Powell was a prisoner in Danville Penitentiary, located in southeast Illinois, near Terre Haute, Indiana. He called me collect and named Lawrence Poree, Edward James, Leroy Sanford, and James Lewis as additional Burge victims. Poree and Lewis were in Pontiac, the same prison as Andrew Wilson; Edward James was also in Stateville.

On April 6, less than a week from the trial start date, George Powell, an Army veteran, described his torture to me over the phone. In November 1979, Burge and detectives named Hoke and McGuire had repeatedly beaten him, placed a bag over his head, and electric-shocked him on the chest, genitals, and stomach with a cattle prod–like shocking device. It was a Sears and Roebuck bag, and when he could no longer breathe, he tried to bite a hole in the bag, prompting his torturers to slap him. They tried to get him to implicate his co-defendants, and finally got him to admit knowledge and minimal involvement in the crime. He was then taken to another south side station, where he gave a false confession to a female assistant state's attorney that led to his conviction for murder on an accountability theory and a forty-year sentence. He had told his mother about his torture; she had attempted to file a complaint with the OPS but told him she had been turned away on the pretext that George was in jail.

That same day, Jeff spoke with Lawrence Poree, collect, from Pontiac. Poree told him about two separate occasions, one in 1972 or 1973, and a second, in 1979, when he was tortured by Burge and several other Area 2 detectives. Poree said that on both occasions he was shocked on his body and genitals with a shocking device housed in a black box. He also claimed that during one of the sessions, he was told that it was "fun time again," that he should "ask Satan about the box," and that "this is what we got for niggers like you." Water was poured over his head, and he was hit in the face with a pistol and over the head with a telephone book. Poree said that he had bitten his tongue bloody and that he had scars on his stomach from being burned on the interrogation room radiator.

In another April 6 phone call, Edward James told Jeff that, in 1979, Burge had gone to Memphis, Tennessee, to arrest him on an armed robbery warrant, and told him that once they got him back to the "horror chamber" in Chicago, he would "talk before midnight." "We know how to squeeze your nuts and make you talk," Burge said. "I have made guys tougher than you talk—I've made Satan talk." When they got Edward back to Area 2, Burge first introduced him to "'Machine Gun' Joe Gorman, the one who killed Fred Hampton and Mark Clark." Gorman, who had become an Area 2 detective after the 1969 raid, looked on as Edward was choked and punched in the jaw and neck. As Burge had predicted, Edward confessed before midnight.

Racing against the clock, we burned the midnight oil to finish and file a written continuance motion the next day. We listed Anthony "Satan" Holmes, whom we hoped to interview by phone that day; Lawrence Poree; George Powell and his mother; and Edward James as newly discovered torture witnesses. We also listed several other witnesses brutalized and tortured during the Wilson manhunt whom we had located in the past few weeks. We had found the "Mike" to whom Roy Brown had referred. His full name was Paul Mike, and he told us of being taken to the same detective station as Brown, having his legs spread wide, and being beaten with a stick on his testicles, then on the bottoms of his feet, all the while being told that he knew who killed the officers. After Paul was held for several days, he was released without charge. He said that he had filed an OPS complaint but heard nothing.

We also listed as a newly discovered witness Walter Johnson, another victim of the manhunt. Like Paul Mike, he had filed an OPS complaint, and his one-page cover sheet had been among those obtained by Dale

Coventry back in 1982. Johnson told us that he was first taken to 51st Street, where detectives put a bag over his head, kicked him in the testicles, and punched him in the jaw. He was later taken to Area 2, where he was further abused and then released after it was clear that he knew nothing about the police murders.

Jeff spoke with Anthony "Satan" Holmes on the phone from Stateville. Anthony said that in May 1973, at about 3:30 in the morning, Burge and several other Area 2 detectives awakened him and took him to the second floor of Area 2. He then described being tortured by Burge and his fellow detectives for the next three to four hours. He was handcuffed hand and foot, and pushed into a chair. Burge produced a black box with what looked like a generator in it. A bag was placed over Anthony's head and he was choked. He bit through the bag, and a second bag was placed over his head. Burge started cranking the box, touched the clips attached to the wires that ran from the box to Anthony's handcuffs, and began to shock him.

Anthony told Jeff that he was jolted out of the chair and passed out. He also described "rolling around on the ground." His torturers put him back in the chair and the shocking continued for two more rounds. He passed out again, and described a throbbing pain and a numbness as his jaws tightened and he gritted his teeth. He thought he was about to die. According to Anthony, he told people about his torture, including his public defenders, one of whom was a young attorney named Larry Suffredin.

We spent the weekend drafting a formal motion asking Judge Duff to recuse himself from the case, while preparing for Monday's deposition of Burge. Once again Burge and Kunkle came to our offices, this time to be questioned about the newly discovered evidence. At the outset, Kunkle made it clear that Burge would only answer questions about the Melvin Jones case. Kunkle considered anything involving Satan, Cochise, Michael Johnson, or our other newly discovered witnesses to be "irrelevant," and therefore the defense was mandating, contrary to the federal rules of discovery, that these subjects were out of bounds.

With the black box sitting on the conference table in front of me, I grilled Burge at length about how he could have neglected to mention the Melvin Jones case when I asked at his pretrial deposition about other allegations of electric shock. My questioning demonstrated that it was absurd to think that he would not remember an allegation of electric shock that had occurred only days before Andrew's torture, particularly since he was compelled to testify about it at Melvin's motion to suppress hearing only months later. Burge admitted that he was "very surprised" when Melvin made the allegations against him, and that he had not forgotten Michael Johnson's allegations of electric shock, but at Kunkle's direction he refused to answer whether he remembered the allegations made by George Powell, "Satan," "Cochise," and Lawrence Poree, or whether those allegations were true. He further admitted that he had testified in Melvin's case at about the same time that Andrew Wilson had formalized his allegations of electric shock by filing his motion to suppress. Not only did this further discredit Burge's "forgetfulness," but it also gave credence to Deep Badge's assertion that the Melvin Jones case must have been known at the highest levels of the state's attorney's office, as it would have presented a major problem for Andrew's prosecution if the case became known to Andrew's defense lawyers.

Burge conceded that he knew who "Cochise" and "Satan" were, but refused to answer whether he had them "crawling all over the floor," as Melvin had quoted him. He linked Melvin Jones to Michael Johnson, saying that Melvin was being questioned for the murder of a witness against Johnson, another detail that made his professed lapse of memory about Melvin's torture even more unbelievable. As with Andrew, he denied being involved in Melvin's interrogation, but he did admit to entering the interrogation room and telling Melvin that he "did not take kindly to people who killed state's witnesses." He revealed that Brzeczek and his first deputy had come to Area 2 on an unrelated case while Melvin was being held there, but denied that he told Brzeczek about Melvin.

Burge admitted that he became familiar with how hand-crank telephones worked while he was in Vietnam but denied that he had ever possessed or used any electric-shock device, including one similar to the black box sitting on the conference room table. He also denied that he had thrown a similar such device off his boat into Lake Michigan. Burge also denied Melvin Jones's allegation that he had threatened to "blow" Melvin's "black head off."

We appeared the next day in Duff's courtroom, twenty-four hours before he had scheduled the start of jury selection, to argue our continuance motion. First, though, we filed our motion to remove Duff for "systematic bias." We relied on two federal statutes, one of which required that Duff transfer the motion to another judge to determine whether he should be removed. Despite not having a copy of the complete trial transcript, we were able to list more than forty specific examples of Duff's bias. We attached an affidavit from Mariel Nanasi, attesting to the "scum of the earth" statement; we also pointed out that Duff had suggested that Andrew Wilson was on drugs when he broke down on the stand, and that Duff had also surmised, unprompted by Kunkle, that Andrew might have been fabricating his testimony based on purported gang member experiences. We decried how Duff had repeatedly humiliated us both in front of the jury and outside its presence, cut off our examinations of witnesses, did not allow us to finish our case, unfairly dismissed a Black woman juror during the trial, and, on several occasions, accepted Kunkle's obvious misrepresentations in order to punish us for being in the right. And, of course, we also highlighted his treatment of the Melvin Jones evidence.

On our way to court, we saw a copy of that morning's *Chicago Tribune*, which featured the headline "Cop Killer's Attorneys, Judge at Odds Over Start of New Trial." The article began by discussing that day's court date, reporting that we had requested a six-month delay because we had "discovered only recently about a dozen other people who say that they were beaten and subjected to electric shock torture at Area 2 during the 1970s and 1980s." Relying on our continuance motion, the article also publicized our recusal request: "Wilson's lawyers have also asked Judge Brian Barnett Duff to step aside, charging that he was attempting to shove new evidence under the rug by rushing into the second trial less than two weeks after the first trial resulted in a partial verdict." The *Tribune* quoted Jeff as saying that the time was needed "to develop this evidence of systematic abuse under Burge's command. This has become a case not about Andrew Wilson but about Jon Burge and police misconduct—about police getting away with this type of stuff."

After Kunkle made sure that the judge saw the article, Duff heard arguments on our recusal motion. Within minutes, Duff was shaking his pencil and yelling at me:

> Duff: You know, and I know, that there have been many trials in this building which have had to go up to the appellate court involving your appeals and your behavior.
> Taylor: That is false, Judge. Name one.
> Duff: Judge Perry.
> Taylor: Didn't they reverse Judge Perry because of the way he treated me? And you are treating me the same way Judge Perry did.

Duff refused to name any other cases. I continued to call out Duff for his false statements, he threatened me with contempt, and I backed off (after Jeff whispered to me that I was playing into the judge's hands). John then attempted to lay out the evidence of the court's bias and prejudice, but at every turn, the judge interjected his defense to the charge, often with a long and revisionist soliloquy, designed to make his record both for the press and the Court of Appeals. When the argument turned to his "scum of the earth" comment, Duff gave yet another explanation:

> What I said, and I'll say it again, if I believed you, then the police officers in this case are bestial torturers, sadists, and people of low order of humanity, and if we would believe what everybody else says about your client, then your client is, if it's believed—and that's the thing that you are leaving out—a killer, a person who would shoot a dying man on the street, a person who made his living as an armed robber, a person who would plot invasions of jails, a person who would do many things, and if a jury would believe that of him, they would believe that he was the scum of the earth.

When the argument turned to Melvin Jones and the newly discovered torture evidence, Duff's again revealed his skeptical view of the credibility of this testimony:

> They're all in jail, and they all say that Commander Burge did all these same things, and you believe them all, and you want me to believe them all.

When John returned to Duff's handling of the Melvin Jones evidence at the first trial, Duff interjected:

> I consider the allegations that were made about Mr. Burge to be very, very important and not necessarily to be dealt with within the context of this trial. I'm very concerned about that in other contexts as well, but not necessarily in the context of what problems we have here. If they are true they are devastatingly important. They're criminal. And criminal sanctions don't have anything to do with this trial. They may also be criminal as respects more than one person. They are potentially conspiratorial outside of this courtroom in a fashion that would make them subject, I think, to possible criminal sanctions, including RICO.

At 5:20 p.m., Duff announced: "I'm denying your motion for recusal." Jeff then gave a brief opening argument on our continuance motion, the only thing standing between us and jury selection the next morning. He quoted a member of the press, who had told him that "he could not understand it, the judge says that the evidence is significant," then gives as his reason for proceeding "his schedule and the fact that he has planned vacations for his staff." Jeff urged that a substantial adjournment to the fall was "absolutely required" for there to be "any semblance of a fair trial."

Kunkle and the City, aware that the immediate trial date put us at an extreme disadvantage, opposed our motion. Kunkle used the occasion to lay the groundwork for his attack on Melvin Jones and the other newly discovered torture victims—that they were violent gang members with long criminal records, who fabricated and shared their torture stories while in jail and therefore could not be believed.

Jeff answered Kunkle's argument by throwing down the gauntlet, saying that if we were forced to go to trial the next day without the newly discovered electric-shock evidence, the trial would be reduced to a "farce," a "sham," a "show of a trial," where Burge would be able to "laugh off" his crimes once again. "We choose not to participate in that, your Honor, because it doesn't mean anything!"

At 7:00 p.m. that night, Duff granted what seemed like a stay of execution, continuing the trial to June 5—about seven weeks away. The next day, he dismissed the sixty prospective jurors he had summoned, charged us $2,400 for the cost of paying them for the day, and set aside three days in the middle of May to address the related questions of Melvin Jones, the other recently discovered victims, and our intention to amend our complaint against the City.

The next weekend, Jeff traveled to Stateville to meet with Anthony "Satan" Holmes, then to Pontiac to see Andrew Wilson and several of the newly discovered electric-shock survivors. Jeff also appeared on journalist Lu Palmer's radio show, and during the discussion of the case, a man named Willie Porch called in and revealed that he, too, was a Burge torture victim. When Jeff later interviewed him off the air, Willie told him that he and three other associates had been arrested for the attempted murder of two off-duty police officers and were taken to Area 2, where Burge smashed him on the head with a long silver gun. Porch also described how one of his co-defendants, Raymond Golden, was hit in the eye with a shotgun. According to Porch, another detective identified himself as "Joe Gorman, a famous man." Burge then added, "He [Gorman] killed Fred Hampton and Mark Clark and he wishes he could kill you." Burge and Gorman then hung Porch by the handcuffs on a hook on the interrogation room door.

Porch also told Jeff that his two co-defendants, brothers Tony and Timothy Thompson, were also beaten—Tony so badly about the face that the detectives referred to him as "Tony Puff-Face."

The word had spread, both in Illinois prisons and among defense lawyers, that we were seeking Area 2 torture victims. We quickly learned about several additional men who had been subjected to brutal interrogations at Area 2. Darrell Cannon talked to John from Menard Penitentiary. He told of being taken to a remote area on the far southeast side of Chicago in November 1983, where he was electric-shocked on his genitals and subjected to a mock execution and repeated racial epithets by Area 2 sergeant John Byrne and detectives Peter Dignan and Charles Grunhard. He also told John that he had testified to this at his trial in 1984.

We finally located the correct Michael Johnson from about seventeen men of that same name imprisoned in Illinois. Michael told Jeff how he had been beaten bloody and subjected to electric shock by Burge, only months after Andrew Wilson and Melvin Jones were tortured. He also said that his mother, longtime community activist Mary L. Johnson, was at Area 2 attempting to see him while Burge was brutalizing him. We also obtained the OPS complaint filed by Michael, as well as an FBI file revealing that the FBI had been specifically informed, in 1982, of Burge's alleged actions in the Michael Johnson case. Both the FBI and the OPS had exonerated Burge without so much as questioning him or seeking to determine Burge's history.

Tom Geraghty, a cofounder of the Northwestern Legal Clinic with former PLO lawyer Susan Jordan, told us about the testimony of his death-row client, Leroy Orange, and Leroy's co-defendant, Leonard Kidd. Both men claimed that Burge had electric-shocked them in January 1984. We also were told of several other victims of Byrne and Dignan, including Gregory Banks and Lee Holmes, who had been subjected to baggings, beatings, and racial epithets while being questioned at Area 2 in the early 1980s. Detective Michael Hoke, now a commander, was named by several of Burge's earlier victims, including Cochise's brother Howard Collins. Howard told us that Burge and Hoke pointed their guns at his head and pulled the triggers (the chambers were, unbeknownst to Howard, empty) while transporting him to Area 2, where they placed a noose around his neck and beat him.

These cases confirmed what Deep Badge had been telling us: the torture was systemic rather than isolated; Burge was a racist; and his crew of "asskickers" and fellow travelers were repeat perpetrators. Armed with this information, we moved to amend our complaint against the City, broadening our definition of its "longstanding policy, practice, and custom" of torture, "coordinated, and executed by, Jon Burge and detectives of Area 2," to include "torturing certain black suspects in serious felony cases, inter alia, by shocking them with electrical devices." We further alleged that these policies, practices, and customs were "known, approved, and ratified by defendant Brzeczek," who "specifically ratified the torture of Andrew Wilson." We added that an "additional aspect" of these practices was that "no disciplinary action would be taken against police officers who inflicted the beatings and torture," that none was imposed in Andrew's case, and that Burge was commended and promoted rather than disciplined for these "brutal practices."

Two days before the arguments were set to begin, Melvin Jones was deposed in the basement of Cook County Jail. His incarceration there was a result of a long and winding legal path that began when he was found not guilty of possessing a weapon in September 1982. When tortured by Burge the previous February, Melvin did not confess to the crime for which he was being questioned—the murder of Geoffrey Mayfield, the state's witness against Michael Johnson in another murder case. Nevertheless, there was a gun at the scene of the arrest (or so Burge and his detectives said), so Melvin was prosecuted, and later acquitted, on a gun possession charge. Shortly after his release, detectives Flood and McGuire, who had been involved with Melvin's February interrogation, picked him up—supposedly for questioning on a triple murder. With no reports or written statements to back them up, Flood and McGuire claimed that Melvin—who had steadfastly refused in February to crack under torture—now willingly and voluntarily confessed to the murder of Geoffrey Mayfield. On the detectives' testimony, Melvin was convicted and sentenced to natural life.

On appeal, Melvin was fortunate to draw African American judge Eugene Pincham as one of the three judges on his appellate panel. Gene, as we called him, was an iconic defense lawyer before taking the bench and had been co-counsel with us in the criminal defense of the Black Panther raid survivors in 1970. Judge Pincham sensed a "frame-up," as he termed it in his written decision, and decried what he strongly suspected was perjury by Flood and McGuire. One of the other two judges on the panel was similarly convinced, and consequently the Illinois Appellate Court overturned Melvin's conviction and returned the case for a new trial, which Melvin was awaiting in Cook County Jail.

When we reconvened in Judge Duff's courtroom on the afternoon of May 17, we were feeling quietly confident. The week before, we had filed a proffer that detailed the evidence we had uncovered and gathered in the wake of Deep Badge's revelation two months before. The proffer set forth the allegations of twenty-seven African American victims of Area 2 torture, spanning a twelve-year period, accusing Burge and twelve of Burge's associates of a chilling list of draconian torture tactics. Kunkle was in Washington, so he sent his senior law partner and former Daley first assistant Richard Devine to file an appearance and sit at counsel table.

Duff announced at the outset that he was denying our motion to sanction Burge for what we had argued was Burge's perjury or willful deception when he did not disclose Melvin Jones and numerous other allegations of torture at his pretrial deposition. Jeff argued that Melvin's testimony was admissible against Burge under the federal rules of evidence because the incident was close in time to Andrew's torture, was similar to the torture perpetrated against Andrew, showed opportunity and preparation, demonstrated a modus operandi, and reflected an intent to torture. I followed by arguing that the evidence was also admissible against the City because it supported a pattern and practice of torture, and further established that the City did not discipline Burge for his pattern of torture but rather ratified his conduct.

Devine left the courtroom and Rubin began his argument. Relying on Melvin's partially completed deposition, he argued that the electric-shock device as described by Melvin, "if it does exist, is without doubt, a different device than either of the two devices that Andrew Wilson has described." He reinforced Duff's legally erroneous view that he first had to decide whether Melvin's testimony was believable, a premise that allowed him to hammer home, in excruciating detail, Melvin's criminal background, his alleged connection to Michael Johnson, and his implication in several murders, including Geoffrey Mayfield's. At one point, Duff demonstrated that Rubin's character assassination was having its desired effect, saying, "So, however reprehensible Mr. Jones may be, should I let it reflect on his credibility in my determination?"

Rubin then played on a theme first suggested by Duff—that Andrew Wilson and Melvin Jones had somehow conspired to concoct similar stories while they were both housed in Cook County Jail in 1982. At that point Jeff rose and pointed out that the men were housed in different parts of the jail, could not have had contact with each other, and in fact did not know each other then or now. Jousting with Rubin, Duff showed a clear understanding of the issue of intent:

> All right, you have got a lieutenant in the station house, the same station house, and you got a man who has used electrical torturing devices on persons who are in for murder, they're black, they're from the same neighborhood, they're under the aegis or responsibility of Burge, who is in charge of all the investigations, that the actions themselves might suggest an animus built in, racial, experiential, motivated by a desire for success, ambition, general hatred, neurotic attitude.

Rubin emphasized that the evidence would enormously prejudice Burge and would operate to show Burge's propensity to torture, something that the law prohibited concerning other, similar bad acts. He closed his argument by saying that the Melvin Jones evidence was a "bomb" that we wanted to "blow up in the case."

On rebuttal, Jeff countered the credibility argument by saying that Burge "didn't get his victims from LaSalle Street in three-piece suits. By and large they were people who were charged with serious crimes. That's one of the reasons he thought he could get away with it." He pointed out that we had not yet had the opportunity to question Melvin about the similarities between the torture devices, and, in any event, under the applicable case law they did not have to be the same device: "[Burge] might have had five devices at Area 2, and maybe he used modifications." In fact, it was becoming clear to us that Burge and his men had, over the years, used at least three or four different electric-shock devices, with the black box being the most notorious. Electric shock against Black persons accused of murder in order to get confessions was Burge's unique imprint and signature, Jeff argued in conclusion.

Next, it was my turn to rebut the City's arguments. I was met with a barrage of questions from Duff, who refused to consider the fact that there were now a multitude of other allegations of torture, saying we would take up that evidence later. When I argued that the pattern and practice of torture must have been an "open secret" within the department, known to its policymakers, Duff reacted skeptically, saying, "If it were going on for fifteen or twenty years, why does it all come to the front now?" I replied, "Code of silence, Judge. They all knew about it, but they weren't about to let it get outside of the department."

The next day, Duff asked us to address a "due diligence" argument raised by Rubin and the City: whether we had done as much as we could, as soon as we could, to discover and bring to light the newly discovered torture evidence. It seemed absurd that we could be accused of not being diligent, given how many requests we had made for torture evidence and how uniformly we had been stonewalled by Burge, his associates, and the City.

Burge's team had gotten ahold of an internal letter that Alan Sincox had written to his fellow public defenders, seeking information on other torture cases, and had been made aware of our ads in the *Southtown Economist* as well as Jeff's appearance on WVON. Duff asked us about the ads. I told him about Deep Badge's letter requesting that we place the ad, the second letter telling us to run a different ad, and the third letter and phone call informing us of Melvin Jones. "Obviously this fellow didn't want to be known," I said, "so he put us through those kinds of challenges in order to get ultimately the name of Melvin Jones, which has certainly changed the entire face of this case."

Rubin called my recitation "very suspicious" and asked why the letters were not in court. Duff said that the divulgence "filled him with curiosity" and wondered why our anonymous source did not call us in the "middle of the night" and say, "'Check Melvin Jones.'" I responded, "I wish he did." When Duff asked why I thought it was a police officer, I pointed out the CPD return address. Duff suggested, as an alternative, that "he wanted you to think he was," opining, "It's all pretty speculative, isn't it?"

The argument then turned to our motion to amend our complaint against the City to conform our pattern and practice allegations to the newly discovered torture evidence. I pointed out, "It's not very often that you're going to have proof that a lieutenant in charge of the Violent Crimes Unit in a big police area in the City of Chicago had a pattern and practice over twelve years of allegedly electroshocking and torturing people in serious cases and you can prove that." Referring to prior statements by the court, I added, "I think it's serious enough that the court indicated that it referred it to the US attorney for possible inquiry, and I think it's . . . highly relevant to the plaintiff's claim."

Duff then corrected me, offering an addendum to his prior statements that only served to make it clearer than ever that we needed to watch our backs:

> Mr. Taylor, let's at all times, if you will, when you're referring to what this court is doing, as you love to do so often, and interpret my actions in terms of what you believe, make it clear that I referred it to the US attorney because

I said if it's true, it's very, very serious, and if it's not true, there may be a conspiracy to obstruct justice on the other side.

After a short recess, Duff returned to announce his rulings:

I am going to deny the admissibility of Jones' evidence against Burge under Rule 404 (b). I find that a reasonable jury could conclude from this evidence that the Jones incident occurred and that it is close enough in time to the Wilson evidence. However, the evidence doesn't go to intent, the intent in the Wilson incident is self-evident. It doesn't go to motive, as the Jones incident has no causal connection to the Wilson incident. It doesn't go to opportunity or preparation, as Jones has apparently testified that the device used against him was dissimilar to the two devices used against Wilson. The evidence can't be used as a modus operandi. Modus operandi is a means of indicating identity, and up to this point no one is contesting Burge's identity.

He threw us a bone, saying that the Jones incident was "possibly relevant to punitive damages," and thus he was separating the issue of punitive damages from the rest of the trial. He also ruled that the Jones evidence was not relevant to our pattern and practice claim as it stood against the City. Duff also denied our motion to amend our pattern and practice claim, saying that our arguments, while "eloquent and intelligent" were not "persuasive."

As Duff prepared to leave the bench, I asked, "What about the other instances where the black box was used?" "I don't want to discuss it any further," Duff responded. "I have ruled." In fact, he had not ruled on the admissibility of this evidence, although his ruling on Melvin Jones certainly foreshadowed his intent. We told him we wished him to stay the trial and certify his rulings so that we could immediately appeal them.

Duff: Well, it's now five minutes to six and you have never mentioned that until this very minute.
Taylor: You didn't rule on it until one minute ago, so it's kind of hard. We had felt that you were going to rule the other way.
Duff: That's ridiculous. You are so ungracious when you lose an argument, Mr. Taylor.

When I attempted to explain our position, Duff stormed off the bench.

Our next stop was the basement of Cook County Jail to finish Melvin Jones's deposition. Melvin was not an eloquent speaker, but his description of his forty-eight-hour ordeal was remarkable. Under Rubin's questioning,

Melvin filled in more details about his initial interrogation. When he asked for a lawyer, he was told that he had only two rights—"to get his ass kicked or confess"—and that Burge said, of Melvin's attorney, Cassandra Watson, "That bitch will never get upstairs" to see him. Melvin testified that after he had been shocked on the thigh, foot, and penis, Burge continued to threaten him; then, after about an hour, told him that he was getting a reprieve. Burge warned that when he returned, it would be "just [you] and [me]."

Burge came back to Area 2 in the early morning hours, and, after talking to Superintendent Brzeczek, returned to interrogating Melvin Jones. Stripped down to a sleeveless T-shirt, Burge sat at a table in the interrogation room and told Melvin that he was about to shock him again. Burge then left the room, and returned with a large gray staple gun. When Melvin continued to deny any knowledge of the Mayfield murder, Burge came around the table and cracked Jones on the top of his head with the stapler, leaving a knot that remained seven years later. When Melvin covered his head, Burge hit him a second time, this time on his hand.

Burge then left Jones alone until morning, but Melvin could not sleep and kept his eyes open at all times. After an unidentified officer who accompanied detective Daniel McWeeny into the interrogation room slapped and kicked Melvin, he was again left alone in the room until after nightfall. The door was open, detectives looked in and laughed at him, and Melvin thought he was on display. That night, detectives Flood and McGuire took him to a nearby station for fingerprinting, and he told the uniformed lockup keeper, "I don't want to go back to that station because they are misusing and threatening me and torturing me and everything."

Flood and McGuire returned Melvin to an Area 2 interrogation room for a final attempt to crack him. He was handcuffed to the wall, and Burge and his detectives then took the "good cop/bad cop" approach to the interrogation. McWeeny told Melvin that Burge could be "a real asshole" and also suggested that he might be able to pull some political strings to help with Melvin's parole violation, if he cooperated. When Melvin refused to talk, Burge came into the room, closed the door, and asked, "Has he talked yet?" McWeeny shook his head "no," and Burge pulled out a gun. He pointed it at Melvin's head from about three or four inches away. Melvin heard three clicks, ducked, and looked away. Burge called him a "Black motherfucker" and said, "I should kill your Black ass." McWeeny then moved between them and told Burge to "get out of here."

Burge left, and McWeeny told Melvin that Flood and McGuire were going to put the gun on him if he didn't talk. For the next few hours, a smiling Burge peeked into the room on several occasions but did not reenter. At about three in the morning, Melvin, in desperation, took a few pages from a miniature phone diary he had in his pocket and wrote on them, with a broken pencil he kept in another pocket, "Help, my name is Melvin Jones. I'm being tortured." The window in the second-floor room was partially open, and Melvin tossed the pages out the window. The notes were found—unfortunately, by a detective, who came into the interrogation room later that morning, said, "The motherfucker is throwing help signals out the window," and shut the window. Shortly, forty-eight hours after Melvin's ordeal had begun, Burge and his detectives gave up on the interrogation, charged Melvin with possession of a gun, and sent him off to jail.

Melvin described the effects of the torture—the electric shock buzzed through his body, he said, and he felt a "heavy sting," which caused him to grit his teeth. He told a paramedic at the jail that he had been shocked on his penis and bashed on the head, but the paramedic showed no concern. The criminal court judge also rejected his testimony that he was tortured. The torture caused him to have nightmares about Burge, waking him in a cold sweat. He sought psychiatric help, both in prison and at the jail, but never received any.

Keeping in mind Duff's ruling based on the dissimilarity between the Wilson and Jones electric-shock devices, Jeff asked three questions when it was his turn. Melvin agreed that the device used on him by Burge was similar to a curling iron. Drawing a connection to the "hair dryer" device described by Andrew, we now had a basis to ask Duff to reconsider his exclusion of the Melvin Jones evidence.

CHAPTER 6

Déjà Vu

We returned to the tiny federal courtroom on the eighteenth floor of the Dirksen Building on Monday, June 5, 1989, to pick a jury for the retrial. In his chambers, Duff informed us that he intended to change his opening remarks about the case to the jurors—in contrast to his relatively neutral description at the first trial—to include that Andrew had been convicted of the murders of two Chicago police officers, and that the defendants "suggest . . . that the plaintiff was an experienced criminal who would know that he was facing the death penalty and was the sort of person who would have self-inflicted his wounds."

We strenuously objected, then returned to the courtroom, where the judge introduced everyone. Unlike in the first trial, the vast majority of the sixty prospective jurors sitting in the cramped courtroom were white, with three of the African Americans sitting in the first row. When we returned to chambers to further discuss what Duff would tell the venire about the case, he sprung on us a change in how the jury would be selected. Unlike in the first trial, when we got four challenges and the City and the individual defendants, combined, also got four, this time the defendants would get a total of six challenges and we would get three. Duff's intent seemed obvious—he wanted to make sure that the jury would not include any Black people.

John reacted first:

Judge, that's an outrageous decision . . . there is a very few number of Black people in the jury pool. Clearly the defendants are going to wipe them out. . . . Certainly you know it was very hard for us to get a jury that could even come close to fair consideration of this matter and for you to make this decision at the start of this trial, just further illustrates Judge, that this is not going to be a fair trial, especially in light of you having barred the highly relevant evidence of Melvin Jones.

In an astounding statement, Duff responded, "That subject is still open, isn't it?"

"Excuse me?" John exclaimed in disbelief. Citing to the three-day hearing of the previous month, John said, "I understood you made a ruling in which you were going to bar it."

In either a telling demonstration of his lack of recall or a classic bait-and-switch, Duff said, "Wait a minute. I don't know what you are talking about." After we continued to protest, Duff tossed us a crumb: we would get four challenges to the defendants' total of six.

Jury selection is one of the most intriguing and challenging aspects of being a trial lawyer. During voir dire, depending on the judge, you learn a little or a lot about a potential juror's background and attitudes. From that information, you seek to select those persons who are most apt to side with your client. When it is a racially charged case with an unpopular client, it is crucially important to expose biases and demonstrate that a biased juror cannot set those biases aside to approach the case with an open mind. After the judge excuses those who are shown to be so biased, a fast-paced chess game follows, with the lawyers for each side using their precious peremptory challenges to remove those prospective jurors who appear to be the most likely to vote against their client, especially if they also appear to be strong-willed.

As the first trial made clear, we were representing one of the most unpopular clients imaginable, and the prejudice against him was strongly reinforced by racial and pro-law-enforcement biases. Now we had fewer challenges, a venire that was 80 percent white, and Duff had topped it off by refusing to ask the questions we had proposed that were designed to most directly expose these biases. Nonetheless, more than ten were disqualified for cause during Duff's group questioning, all but one because they admitted that they could not be fair to a convicted cop killer. The exception was a man who had worked with the FBI and said that he could believe from his own experience that law enforcement officers might sometimes act outside the law when interrogating suspects. Having a realistically open mind disqualified him in Duff's eyes.

One of the three Black prospective jurors in the first row failed to show up the next morning, and Duff quickly struck her from the venire and issued a contempt order against her in absentia—an order he later rescinded when she called in to say that she could not find a babysitter. The other two Black women were the first persons to be individually questioned by the judge. The first was a middle-aged woman who worked at AT&T, was a union steward, and was married to a minister who was also a prison guard. The other was an older widow whose family were farmers who had moved from Arkansas. They were followed by a Japanese American man who was born in 1936 and left Hiroshima in 1960, an older white man who had vacation plans, and an educated suburban white woman who was a teacher and married to a lawyer.

On the third day of jury selection, we started the process of exercising our challenges. The City struck one of the Black women and Kunkle struck the other. By noon we had picked the six persons who would sit as our jury. There were no Black members; the jury would be the white woman teacher, the Japanese American man, a Filipino American man who had fled martial law and the "communist" insurgency in the early 1970s, a white woman clerk who had moved from the city to the suburbs, and a young white man who lived in the suburbs and worked for a printing company.

Given our experience in the first trial, the first and second alternates might prove to be important, as, in another long trial (this time in the summer), we might lose at least one juror along the way. The first three alternates chosen were white but seemed to have some liberal tendencies. One was a college graduate who was reading *Presumed Innocent*, by the wrongful conviction lawyer Scott Turow; the second had studied in Brazil and spoke Portuguese; and the third was a retired waitress with an eighth-grade education, who worked with people with mental disabilities and also regularly visited nursing homes. Finally, a young Black woman, with nearly no possibility of ascending to a decision-making role, was seated as the fourth alternate. The defendants had struck two more Black people, a white woman who was an animal rights activist, and a white man who grew up in the racially torn neighborhood of Marquette Park.

Judge Duff then recessed the trial for two weeks. But before he did, he took a parting shot by issuing a gag order that forbade us from speaking to the press about the case for the duration of the trial. The two-week hiatus was filled with more depositions. Jeff made the long trip to Menard Penitentiary to attend the deposition of Michael Johnson. During the deposition, Jeff received more documents from Johnson's OPS and FBI files, including a statement given to OPS investigators by his mother, Mary, the same day that Michael was brutalized. The statement revealed that she had been permitted to visit with Michael at Area 2 earlier that day, that he looked okay, and that he told her that he had been threatened with torture if he did not talk.

She said that Burge, who smelled of alcohol, came into the room and told her to get out of his police station. She left, and when Michael was released a few hours later, his face "was all swollen, and he was shaking all over." Michael told her that Burge had "blazed" him. She called Cassandra Watson, Michael's attorney, then took Michael to the hospital, and after that to OPS, where photos were taken of his injuries. Later that night the Johnsons lodged a battery report with the CPD, naming Burge as the offender. The originals of the photos had been destroyed years before, and only a light, washed-out black-and-white Xerox copy remained in the file.

Rubin questioned Michael Johnson in the same way he had questioned Melvin Jones, zeroing in on the murder of Geoffrey Mayfield and Michael's alleged ties to Melvin Jones and the Gangster Disciples street gang. As with Melvin, he elicited numerous assertions of the Fifth Amendment. Michael managed to recount in detail how he had been brutally beaten by Burge, how Burge cursed out the detectives who had let his mother see him, and then hurled a chair at him, saying, "You thought that your black-ass, fat mother was going to save you, but you were wrong." As Burge pummeled him, Michael said that Burge bragged about having worked over "Satan" and "Cochise." At the very end of the questioning, Rubin showed Michael his 1982 statement to the OPS, in which he stated that a drunken Burge also called him a "nigger dog"; threatened to kill him; said that although Geoffrey Mayfield was "just another nigger" they cared about him because he was a state's witness; and said, "If I see that pretty little nigger bitch Cassandra today, I'll kill you."

Back in Chicago, the next day Rubin took on Cassandra Watson. His goal was to link the diminutive African American lawyer with Melvin Jones, Michael Johnson, and Larry Hoover, the reputed leader of the Black Gangster Disciples, in an effort to discredit Melvin's and Michael's accounts of having been tortured by Burge. While Rubin was able to confirm the obvious—that Cassandra had been Melvin's and Michael's lawyer in 1982, and that she had also represented Hoover at one time—Cassandra was able to utilize the attorney-client privilege to block Rubin's attempts to discover what she had discussed with her clients.

Cassandra first revealed that Detective Flood—the same detective Flood present when Burge tortured Melvin Jones—had recently visited her mother's house on two occasions, in a highly irregular attempt to serve the defendants' subpoena for deposition on her. She rightly interpreted this abuse of police power as an attempt by Burge and his lawyers to intimidate her, and complained to the commander of Area 2, who, she said, was "shocked" by what she told him about one of his men's attempts to serve a subpoena on her. She also emphasized that she did not want to be a witness in our case and had told Jeff this six weeks earlier, when he contacted her after Melvin Jones's name was revealed to us by Deep Badge. She also explained why she had not come forward voluntarily to reveal what she knew—she had been very ill and had recently undergone two major surgeries.

Cassandra testified that when Melvin Jones told her about his torture, he described one of the aftereffects as involuntary convulsion-like movements in his shoulders. She also said that she had heard about a half-dozen other instances of Burge and his associates torturing suspects with his black box. When Rubin asked whether she had made complaints in any of the cases, she answered that she had, on one occasion: Burge had then called her, told her he was investigating the allegations, and they "both began laughing hysterically" at the absurdity of Burge—who was "part of a conspiracy of brutality"—investigating his henhouse. She confirmed that Michael Johnson's face was badly swollen and both of his lips were busted when she saw him after he was released from Area 2; that he identified Burge as the perpetrator; and that she decided he should go to OPS, and later to the FBI, because she wanted to make a record of Burge's threat to kill Michael if he saw him on the street. She also said that she firmly believed Burge and his men had framed Michael for the murder on which he was serving life as retribution for "telling on Burge," and she detailed how Burge and his detectives had used drugs, money, and physical violence to procure false testimony against Michael. She also said that she told the chief judge of Cook County about this conspiracy, that the judge threatened contempts, and that the intimidation then stopped.

Cassandra said it was "common knowledge" that Burge was shocking people and that the entire Area had a reputation for beating and shocking people. She told of an occasion when she brought a sleeping bag to Area 2 and slept there overnight in a successful attempt to keep one of her clients from being shocked by Burge. She said that she would get calls from clients being held at Area 2, asking her to "hurry up and get here before I get shocked with this box." She also told how she had visited clients parched and drenched with perspiration, who had been "sweated" in temperatures of 90 to 100 degrees in one of the radiator-heated interrogation rooms. She told of passing conversations she would have with Burge, with her saying "You got the box?" and his smiling and saying, "No boxes today."

She also recounted that she saw Burge with Richie Daley before Daley ran for mayor in 1988, and Burge said to her "Don't start any shit, Watson." She said that James "Bulljive" Taylor, a longtime Black machine Democrat who had served as mayor Jane Byrne's chief of staff, was present for the conversation, and she commented to Taylor, "That is the one that shocks people with the box." Bulljive, without emotion, simply responded, "Oh yeah?" She also said that she'd had a conversation with Flood about police perjury and the box, and she was positive from his responses that he knew what she was talking about.

When Rubin asked her if, in any of their conversations, Burge had admitted to shocking people, she said no, but that he would laugh instead, and never denied it. She then snapped her fingers, in a moment of self-described "sudden recollection," and told of one exchange with Burge in which he told her, while standing at the door that "this box [didn't] leave any marks." She continued:

> Nobody makes up that anybody shocks them on their genitals. These men haven't ever been in any wars. They don't know anything about torture. Burge is the one that has all the experience with the war in Vietnam. He is the one that knows about those kinds of things.

Cassandra concluded her testimony by saying that Burge was "a phenomenon unto himself with this box." Her clients were in a "state of amazement that he was doing this and nobody did anything about it."

Deep Badge must have been following the trial closely. His (or her) fourth and final letter appeared, again in an official police department envelope, on June 19, the day opening statements were to begin. The letter began, "There is much consternation at Area 2 since your latest briefs have arrived." He said that Hoke, who was named by several of the victims, was particularly perturbed because, according to Deep Badge, he "was not the beating type and had stood up to Burge." Deep Badge cautioned us that not all the complaints lodged by those who had confessed were true, but then went on to say:

> The common cord is Burge. The machines and the plastic bags were his, and he is the person who encouraged their use. You will find that the people with him were either weak and easily led or sadists. He probably did this because it was easier than spending the time and the effort talking the people into confessing.

Deep Badge concluded with the familiar admonition: "This is not to be shown to anyone."

Just before the jury was ushered in for opening statements, Duff issued his latest ruling concerning Melvin Jones and the other torture victims we had listed in our May proffer of evidence: the evidence was too prejudicial to be admitted as to the liability of the defendants; it might be relevant as to the issue of punitive damages, so he was severing that portion of the case until after liability and compensatory damages were decided by the jury. Perhaps unwittingly, he cracked open the door for us to attempt to get the evidence in, despite his ruling, by adding, "I am not going to preclude the plaintiff developing the issue or the evidence in the liability area although I can't see it totally now."

John delivered our opening once again and got into hot water when he made an indirect reference to the "verboten" Illinois Supreme Court decision that had reversed Andrew's conviction, and when he stated that the families of the slain officers had filed suit against Andrew. (The latter was out of bounds because it could lead the jurors to conclude that damages awarded to Andrew might end up going to the officers' families.) Duff referred to John's references as "errors" but refused to grant Kunkle's motion for a mistrial. Kunkle then offered the police defendants' opening. It became clear from Kunkle's argument that they were abandoning the "friction abrasions, not burns" theory for an elaborate self-infliction defense.

We then began to present our pattern and practice evidence against the City. The judge was much less deferential to the City and its case than he was to Kunkle and Burge, and, as a result, we were able to broaden and deepen our proof against the City this time around. When we called Ronald Samuels, who had collected nearly two hundred misconduct complaints for the Cook County Bar Association during the manhunt, we were able to get before the jury that he had called the OPS and spoken to someone who admitted that the office had "lost" 120 complaints.

Just before former superintendent Brzeczek took the stand, Judge Duff informed us that the morning's proceedings had been delayed because he had received a call from one of the jurors, who said his car had been stolen the night before. The car was uninsured for theft, and the juror said, "This situation may hinder me from paying close attention to testimony and may in fact bias my train of thought. You might consider excusing me from this particular jury." After a brief huddle, I told the judge we thought the juror should be excused. This would elevate the first alternate, who seemed more open-minded, to take his place. The defense lawyers all supported his continuing as a juror, so Duff decided to question him. He was called into the courtroom and told us his car was a 1980 Cutlass Supreme in "mint condition," the "most valuable thing" that he owned. He was "so aggravated" that "I just want to choke someone." "I'm not sure I can sit here and listen to people who have been convicted of crimes and think that they might have stolen my car."

Duff asked, "Are you telling me that you don't think you can be fair as a juror?" Nodding his head (as if "yes"), he answered "no," which Duff and we took to mean that he was saying he could not be fair. Duff then excused him for cause and sent him out of the courtroom. Kunkle objected, maintaining that he was in fact saying he could be fair, so Duff called him back in and asked again if he was saying that he would be biased. Amid reiterating how upset he was, and how he blamed being on jury duty for the theft, he said, "I can be fair, I consider myself always fair. I am a good judge of character." Duff, saying that he "wished he could be a mind reader," permitted the juror to remain, and he ended up as the foreperson of the jury.

Early on, we called three torture survivors whom we had discovered since the first trial. Paul Mike told about being in bed with his girlfriend, asleep, when unidentified white detectives broke through his door and burglar bars at 3:00 a.m. the morning after Fahey and O'Brien were murdered. They smacked him around while he tried to dress, hit his girlfriend on the leg, and took money from their pants pockets. They took Paul to his car and searched it, then took him to the station at 51st and Wentworth, where they handcuffed him to the wall in an interrogation room next to the room where they were holding Roy Brown. The detectives hit him in the face, on the bottoms of his feet, and on his scrotum with a billy club. He heard Brown screaming, and after Brown said, "It was him" [meaning Paul Mike], Paul's beating was resumed.

After Paul Mike told his interrogators whom he was with the day of the murders, they took him to a large holding cell in the basement, where a large number of young Black men were also being held. Paul testified that "everybody was in there moaning, a few guys was crying"; they had been questioned about the murders and accused of "having something to do" with them. Some of them "had been whipped real bad, they were laying on the floor hunching." Later, he was moved to a smaller cell, where he remained for two days, lying on a cold bench without food for the first day. When the police finally released him without charge, he was brought to a desk, where the desk officer tore up his arrest slip and threw it into a big garbage can. Paul Mike subsequently gave a statement to the OPS but never heard back from them, and his money was never returned.

Next was Walter Johnson, who at the time of the officers' murders was a fifteen-year-old student at Calumet High School on the south side of Chicago. He was playing hooky from school down the street from the murders when they occurred, and, like Paul Mike, was paid an unwelcome visit by police officers in the early morning hours of February 10, 1982. Later that morning he was taken to 51st and Wentworth by a battery of detectives and questioned. When he denied any knowledge of the crimes, an unidentified white detective punched him in the mouth and accused him of lying. He fell to the floor, where the detectives handcuffed him and kicked him in the testicles and stomach while calling him a "Black motherfucker" and "stinking son of a bitch." Then they dragged him into a hallway, put a plastic bag over his head, and kicked him again in the stomach and groin. They pulled the bag halfway off, letting him gasp for air, called him a liar when he continued to deny involvement, then pulled the bag over his face again. He was terrified and "crying out for fear." When they could not get him to confess, they took him to Area 2, where he was threatened with further abuse and held overnight; ultimately, after standing in two lineups, he was released without charge. Like Paul Mike, he made an OPS complaint but no action was taken.

Willie Porch was the third new pattern and practice witness. He posed an interesting problem for Judge Duff because he, unlike the others, had specifically identified Burge as the sergeant who, in 1979, interrogated and tortured him. Duff ruled that Porch's testimony was admissible against the City because he had been arrested for the armed robbery and attempted murder of two police officers, a distinction that placed him in the category of victims we had originally included in our pattern and practice claim. However, according to Duff's prior rulings concerning Melvin Jones and the other newly discovered torture victims, Willie Porch's testimony was not admissible against Burge. Duff's eventual solution was to require that Willie refer to Burge generically as "the sergeant," and to Machine Gun Joe Gorman, who was also involved in the interrogation, as "the detective." This decision hurt us on two fronts—not only did it keep us from introducing the evidence against Burge individually, but it also prevented us from linking Burge to the City's pattern and practice.

Willie had been transported from Menard Penitentiary at 3:00 a.m. a few days before, and was subjected to a full day of deposition questioning once he arrived. Like many of our witnesses, Willie was soft-spoken, and could barely be heard when he told of being a postal employee for the seven years before he was convicted and sent away on a thirty-year sentence. Jeff had previously told Willie he could call Burge "Sergeant X" and that he could name Joe Gorman. When he did so, Duff interrupted to say that no names should be used. Jeff then asked Willie, "You know their names, but you're not giving their names, is that right?" Kunkle jumped to his feet to object, and Duff said, "I think that's entirely improper. The jury is instructed to disregard that. It's an attempt at evasion of the court's ruling."

Willie then described the actions of "the sergeant" and "the detective." He and his co-arrestee, Raymond Golden, were ordered to sit on the floor in an Area 2 interrogation room. The sergeant stepped on Willie's groin with his full weight, and Willie shouted and screamed in response. The sergeant then took him into the case management office, where the detective told him that he was "a machine gun detective" and that he "killed Fred Hampton." When Willie denied any involvement in the robbery and attempted murder, the sergeant grabbed him on one side, the detective on the other; they opened the closet door and attempted to lift Willie up to put him on the door's coat hook. Willie felt pain so great in his arms, shoulders, and wrist that he started screaming and shouting. His body was a foot or two off the ground before they relented and put him in a chair.

The sergeant took a long, silver or chrome, brown-handled revolver out of his holster and hit Willie three or four times on the top and side of his head. The detective hit him with his hands at the same time. They led him into another room, where Raymond Golden was being held, and brought them face to face. Raymond remained silent, so the sergeant hit him in the left side of his head with a shotgun. Now bleeding from his head, Raymond fingered Willie as having been with him during the crime. When they took Willie out of that room he saw Tony Thompson, whose face and head were swollen and his eyes closed, like a pummeled prizefighter. When Willie continued to refuse to cooperate, he was threatened with looking like "Tony Puff Face."

Finally, at about one in the morning, an assistant Cook County state's attorney named Thomas Davy came into the room. Davy, who would later go on to become a Cook County criminal court judge, said that he had heard that Willie had something to tell him. Willie testified that he told Davy he didn't have anything to say, that in Davy's presence the sergeant and detective started hitting and kneeing him again, and that the sergeant hit him several times on the head with his gun.

Mr. Haas: What if anything did you say or do while this was going on?
Porch: I asked the Assistant State's Attorney Davy did he see that.
Haas: What happened after that?
Porch: He kept his head down and told me all he wanted was a statement.
Haas: What happened after that?
Porch: I asked him if he could make them stop.
Haas: What did he say?
Porch: He said all he wanted was a statement.

Later that morning Willie was taken to the police station, where the officers he was accused of attempting to murder were assigned, and was paraded in front of a shift roll call. Five days later he made bail and went straight to the hospital for treatment. He also made a statement to OPS, but nothing ever came of it. That file, like so many others, no longer existed.

While Willie was being cross-examined, assistant corporation counsel Maureen Murphy and I excused ourselves and headed to the offices of the OPS, to depose chief OPS administrator David Fogel. Appointed by mayor Harold Washington in 1984, Fogel's directive was to reform the OPS. In a confidential memo Fogel sent the mayor in 1987—which we did not have access to until several years later—Fogel condemned his own agency, saying that it had a "politically corrupt heritage" and "a good number of irremediably incompetent investigators." Moreover, Fogel wrote, the OPS "immunized police from internal discipline," and "institutionalized lying, subterfuge, and injustice."

Although Fogel had not been in charge when Dr. Raba's letter was forwarded to the OPS in 1982, and had no hand in the failure to investigate the hundreds of complaints that arose from the manhunt, he was the boss in September 1985, when the OPS quietly, after three and a half years, closed its investigation into Andrew Wilson's allegations of torture by Burge, with a finding of "not sustained." We had what was represented to us to be the complete OPS file in Andrew's case, and it reflected that the commander of Area 2, the chief and deputy chiefs of detectives, and a deputy superintendent had all approved the finding. Fogel's name did not appear anywhere in the file, and he therefore was able to deny involvement in the finding. He said he was not in any way aware of the investigation of "Andrew . . . what's his name?"'s case while it remained open in 1984 and 1985. (Much later we would obtain a letter, not included in the file given to us by the City, written on police department stationery, signed by Fogel and addressed to Dr. Raba, which informed Dr. Raba of the "not sustained" finding.)

When I asked Fogel whether he was aware of other electric-shock cases, he said, "None in the last three years, but in the time I have been here, there have been half a dozen such allegations throughout the city. And so I keep track of that whenever those allegations come up." He claimed he had not heard of any torture cases arising from Area 2, acknowledged that identifying patterns of brutality was important, and denied that his information revealed a pattern of torture by electric shock or compelled him to "do any back-investigation" to see if there were torture cases that preceded his time at OPS.

I asked if he had records of the electric-shock cases he had mentioned, and Fogel said he did, and that they were accessible in the very office where we were sparring. "Would you obtain them now?" I asked. Maureen Murphy said no. I then looked Fogel directly in the eye and said "Are you willing to do that?" Not about to countermand the City's lawyer, Fogel said, "You can just subpoena them."

I went on to confront Fogel with the two aces up my sleeve—our proffer listing twenty-five cases of Area 2–related torture and the Illinois Supreme Court's decision in Andrew's case. I gave Fogel, a very intelligent man, time to read and absorb the information in both documents. Back on the record, I specifically called Fogel's attention to the Supreme Court's finding that Andrew's multitude of injuries happened while in police custody and asked him if that would be sufficient to reopen the Wilson investigation. He said that with "something this sensitive" he would "have to think more" about it. He conceded that the proffer, if the allegations were true, would show a pattern, but that he "didn't think that he could do anything" with that information, supposedly because the documentation would no longer exist. I concluded by asking Fogel to make a determination about reopening the investigation and inform me of it.

When we returned to court the next morning, Kunkle was fuming. He was incensed by Jeff's instruction to Willie Porch to refer to Burge as "Sergeant X," and by his informing the jury that Willie knew the sergeant's name but had been instructed not to name him. Arguing that this scenario had pointed the finger at Burge and his co-defendant detectives, Kunkle moved for a mistrial. Alternatively, he presented an instruction to be given to the jury that was false on its face: "There is no evidence that any of the defendant police officers—commander Jon Burge, detective John Yucaitis, and detective Patrick O'Hara—were personally involved in any of the incidents Willie Porch testified about." Now it was Jeff's turn to become irate:

It's a complete and total lie. . . . to give the jury an instruction that the man who tortured Porch had nothing to do with it is so far from the truth, it takes us so far out of reality, that it reduces the case almost to an absurdity. . . . To tell the jury an outright lie, Judge, I can't participate in that.

Duff, appearing reasonable, said that he was not inclined to give the instruction to the jury, resorting to an old saw about the lady who told her children not to put beans up their noses, which, naturally, they did as soon as she left the house.

Kunkle then presented the judge with a second motion, this one focused on a nearly two-week-old article in the *Daily Defender*. We had backed Duff off from his blanket gag order by citing a 1975 Seventh Circuit Court of Appeals decision, written by judge Luther Swygert, that recognized that attorneys, particularly in civil cases brought in the public interest, had a First Amendment right to speak about the trial unless their statements presented a "clear and present danger of a serious and imminent threat to the administration of justice."

Duff, in a gruff voice, read from the article:

Mr. Taylor is concerned that the court will, again, deny the submission of evidence that he says will prove that Wilson was tortured in the horror chambers by officers seeking a confession. Quote, "if the judge does not allow this evidence [of physical torture] into court, it will be a completely unfair trial" Taylor said. "What they [the police] did to Wilson was just as bad as what Wilson was convicted of doing."

After acknowledging that Judge Swygert's decision was still controlling law, Duff went on:

The right to talk to the press does not include the right to denigrate justice. It does not include the right to talk in a way which would reflect on the court in an adverse fashion directly. It also does not include the right to attempt to intimidate the court if, indeed, it was even possible by references to the court's fairness in a public forum prior to his making a decision.

After Willie completed his testimony, Duff revisited the *Daily Defender* article and gave me a direct order to "make no comments denigrating the fairness of the trial or trying to put this court into disrepute," adding, "If I see any further allegations in the public media that you have tried to suggest that this court is not fair in this trial, I will consider it contemptuous."

In my baseball-playing days, we had a phrase for an umpire who acted like Duff—that he had "rabbit ears."

After court, we rushed to our offices to depose Burge once again—Duff had, inexplicably, allowed us to question him about the other torture victims listed in our proffer, rekindling our hope that we might get this evidence before the jury. Burge showed a sharp memory of almost all of the men listed in the proffer, but uniformly denied witnessing or participating in any torture or abuse. In Burge's world, all of these men confessed willy-nilly, and, when there were physical injuries, they had happened at another time and place, at the hands of unknown officers who were trying to subdue a violent suspect. He offered that he considered almost all of his alleged victims during the 1970s to be leaders or members of the "Royal Family," which he described as an organization that engaged in robberies and "patterned itself after the Mafia." In our view, this suggested a motive for Burge, who was in the department's robbery section at that time, to torture these men. He also admitted that he had called Michael Johnson a "piece of human garbage" because he was angry that Michael was on the street after the witness against him had been killed.

When asked if, at the time of his 1988 deposition, he had been aware of any other allegations of torture and abuse made against him, Burge suddenly lost his sharp memory, in order to avoid our charge that he had covered up those allegations under oath. Remarkably, Burge admitted that Gorman was "the butt end of a lot of blue-humor jokes over the years" about the Panther raid, which Burge pointedly called a "shootout," and that Gorman was specifically teased about the fact that the officers had left the crime scene unsealed after the raid, but he "could not honestly recall" if Gorman was referred to as "Machine Gun Joe."

Things were tense throughout, and at one point Kunkle told me to "stop fucking around." I concluded my questioning with one of those "When did you stop beating your wife?" type of questions that went to the heart of the truth:

> Taylor: Do you think that someone who has been repeatedly accused with electric-shocking people should be entitled to much credibility?
> Burge: I don't know anybody who falls into that category, so I could not render an answer to that question.
> Taylor: Making that assumption—if someone was, would he be entitled to much credibility?
> Burge: I can't answer that question.

Taylor: Why is that?

Burge: Because I don't feel I could give you a forthright and honest answer.

Taylor: Why?

Burge: Because it doesn't make any sense.

With the July 4 holiday approaching, Judge Duff recessed the trial until the next Wednesday. On Monday, July 3, I drove about 250 miles to the medium-security prison in downstate Centralia, Illinois, to visit Donald White. Because we suspected that Donald had been treated similarly to Andrew Wilson, we had been on his trail since before the first trial. We had intensified our search after Deep Badge had informed us in early February that "several witnesses, including the Whites, were severely beaten at 1121 S. State Street in front of the Chief of Detectives, the Superintendent of Police and the State's Attorneys."

It was a little after noon when Donald entered the interview room. I was surprised at how small and scared he looked. When he showed some reluctance to tell me what happened to him at police headquarters, I earnestly told him that Burge had "done this to a lot of people" and that "somebody sooner or later" had to come forward and "tell the truth." He then told me in detail about how he had been arrested along with his brothers and three other friends, taken to police headquarters, accused of killing Fahey and O'Brien, and subjected to brutal beatings and torture by Burge, Hill, O'Hara, and several other Area 2 detectives. He was only spared, he said, after he was not identified by an eyewitness in a lineup and passed a lie detector test.

I urged Donald to testify for us. He paused, then made a proposal. He was about to be released on parole and feared for himself and his family if he testified. Detective Hill had recently visited the prison, he said, and suggested in no uncertain terms that he remain quiet. He would testify, Donald promised, if we would defray his moving costs and one month's rent so that he could move his family out of Illinois, an amount of approximately $1,000. He reminded me that the state's attorney's office had invested much more than that to keep him appeased after he became a potential witness against Andrew Wilson in 1982—more than $10,000, we would later learn. I swallowed hard, thought about how John—whom I had affectionately nicknamed "Dr. No," for his cautious and considered approach to almost all issues—would react, and nervously agreed to Donald's proposal.

When we returned to court on July 5, Kunkle greeted us with a leaflet that he said had been handed out by Willie Porch's brother at a suburban courthouse and by unknown people downtown near the federal court-house. The bright yellow leaflet, which he tendered to Judge Duff, was signed by Citizens Alert—an organization headed by Mary Powers, a sub-urban warrior for police accountability who had been religiously attending the trials. The leaflet called out Richie Daley, the police superintendent, OPS, and the US attorney's office. It detailed the torture of Andrew Wilson, Anthony Holmes, Melvin Jones, and several other victims under the bold headline, "Burge's Known History of Torture." It called on the community to demand a police investigation of Burge and his immediate suspension, and urged a letter-writing campaign to Judge Duff to "express your outrage at the blatant disregard for the law and human rights of people accused of committing crimes."

Duff sent a chill down our spines when he threatened a mistrial and the moving of a subsequent trial out of the city:

> It is an unfortunate attempt by some persons to influence the case in their way which is non-legal and non-judicious, and I suppose in a sense to politicize the trial. . . . It would be most unfortunate if we had to cause a mistrial because if community interference can do that, I will tell you that I would seriously consider taking the venue to another city, and I don't think any of us would particularly enjoy that.

A quick questioning of the jurors confirmed that no one had seen the leaflet, and we called Dr. Jack Raba to the stand. Raba reiterated much of what he said at the first trial: that the linear and parallel marks on Andrew's body were burns in a unique pattern consistent with the radiator; that Andrew had showed him his injuries and told him of the electric shock; that he had written Brzeczek and requested an investigation; and that three and a half years later he had received a letter from Fogel telling him his complaint had been rejected as "not sustained." In addition, I also asked him to draw on his extensive experience, as a jail doctor and administrator who had seen more than a hundred self-inflicted wounds during his career, to offer his opinion that Andrew's wounds were not self-inflicted. The defendants objected, saying that they had not been given notice and that Raba had not been identified as an expert; and Duff, after hearing arguments and telling me that "every single time you say I've been prejudicial if I rule against you," sustained the objection.

Next, we sought to call Phillip Adkins as a witness. Phillip was arrested on June 7, 1984, at 5:00 a.m., by three members of Area 2's midnight crew, identified by Deep Badge as "Burge's asskickers," for armed robbery and attempted murder of an off-duty Chicago cop. He was placed in the detectives' car, driven by Burge henchman Peter Dignan, and questioned about the crime. When he refused to cooperate, one of the detectives called him a "smart-ass nigger," and after repeating that slur several times, they announced they were going to "take him to their spot and beat the hell out of him."

They drove to a parking lot of a Chicago Housing Authority low-income high-rise building, and parked by a viaduct facing some railroad tracks. Without warning, the detective sitting next to Phillip slugged him "with great force" in the stomach, causing him to double over. The detective in the front passenger seat said to straighten "the smart-ass nigger" up so they could "get some balls." He then proceeded to poke Phillip repeatedly in his groin area with a long metal flashlight. Handcuffed behind his back, Phillip twisted and turned as blows rained down on his ribs, side, elbows, and knees. He started to become dizzy, then as he sank into unconsciousness, he urinated and defecated on himself. He felt numb and could barely hear.

After arresting Phillip's co-defendants, Dignan and company took Phillip to the new Area 2 building, which had opened the year before. He was barely able to stand, but the detectives told him that if he didn't walk, they would "take him back to the spot and finish him off." As they entered the complex, a Black uniformed officer told him he should be given medical treatment, but Phillip was instead forced to walk up to the second floor, where he was handcuffed to an interrogation wall. Left alone, he vomited several times.

The sergeant in charge was Jack Byrne, who proudly dubbed himself Burge's "right-hand man." Byrne had supervised the arrests and was responsible for Phillip's being held for twelve hours rather than being rushed to the hospital. When Phillip was finally sent to the lockup, the keeper rejected him. He was transported to a nearby hospital, then taken by ambulance to the trauma unit of Cook County Hospital, where he remained for several days while being treated for multiple injuries, including blood around his penis.

Phillip, who was serving an eighteen-year sentence on the armed robbery and attempted murder charges, had been transported from prison pursuant to an order that appeared to have been authorized by the judge. We had named him as a witness well before the second trial began, but the defense complained that they did not have sufficient notice; further, that since his torture took place two years after Andrew Wilson's, it was not relevant to the pattern and practice claim against the City. We countered by arguing that the accepted way to show a pattern was, where possible, to present incidents both before and after the incident that was on trial, and that, like Willie Porch, Phillip fit our original pattern and practice definition: the torture of persons who were suspected of or charged with assaults on police officers. Aggravated that his clerk had issued the transport order without his knowledge, Duff barred Phillip from testifying.

Another battle was fought the next morning over whether OPS director David Fogel would be permitted to testify. We had subpoenaed Fogel and his file, and I greeted him outside the courtroom before the argument began. He was grim-faced and clutching a bulky envelope. I asked him if he had come to a decision about whether to reopen the Wilson investigation, as I had asked at his deposition, and he tersely said that he had decided not to. He also refused to share his file with me.

I laid out to Duff why Fogel's testimony was relevant to the continuation and ratification of the cover-up by the City's policymakers, including his purported lack of awareness of his agency's high-profile Wilson investigation and its "not sustained" finding, as well as his failure to reopen the investigation despite the Illinois Supreme Court's decision and the newly discovered evidence of a pattern of Burge-related torture. Fogel's testimony would thus give us another avenue to get before the jury the Supreme Court's decision and the proffer of other Burge victims, evidence that Duff seemed determined to block, no matter how relevant. I also urged Duff to order Fogel to turn over his file.

Maureen Murphy, who was taking a much more active role at the retrial, argued for the City that Fogel had not come on the scene until 1984, and therefore what he did or said was not relevant to the case. She carefully also argued that the file was not relevant because Fogel had testified at his deposition that it contained only six "unrelated" electric-shock cases. Duff sided with the City, ruling that Fogel did not have to testify or turn over the file. He also denied my request to question Fogel outside the jury's presence, in order to make the record on his refusal to reopen the investigation and to establish the contents of the file. (That file would not see the light of day for another sixteen years.)

Next, Andrew Wilson took the stand. As Andrew began to describe his torture, his voice fell, and Duff told John, "I would suggest that you try to make sure that your witness can be heard by everyone." When

Andrew started to describe the torture session that began with Burge coming back into the room with the black box, Andrew paused, took some deep breaths, and appeared to be fighting back tears. "Answer the question, please," Duff snapped.

"I am gonna answer. Just wait," Andrew retorted. He then described the electric shocking:

> Still it always go to your head. I don't care where he put it at. It goes to your head all the time. It always go to your head. And your teeth grinding, and pain in your head from the cranking it, cranking it.

Andrew recounted how the clips were attached to his ears, that he kept brushing them off, so the officers handcuffed him across the scalding radiator. At John's request, Andrew came down from the witness stand and got on his knees in front of the jury box to demonstrate what appeared to be a stationhouse crucifixion. At the close of the day, John asked Andrew about how it felt to talk about his torture:

> John: Mr. Wilson, earlier today, I was asking you questions about the period that Yucaitis and Burge electric-shocked you. And when I asked you the questions, you paused for a very long time. Can you tell me why you paused?
> Kunkle: Objection.
> Duff: Sustained.
> John: How does it feel to you today, Mr. Wilson, to talk about these defendants electric shocking you?
> Andrew: It affects me the same way any time I talk about it. I don't like talking about it.
> John: Well, how does it make you feel when you talk about it?
> Kunkle: Objection.
> Duff: Sustained.

The next Monday, Kunkle began his cross-examination. As in the first trial, Duff allowed Kunkle's questioning of Andrew about all manner of prejudicial matters that were tangentially relevant at best, including details about the killings of Fahey and O'Brien, other crimes that Andrew had been either convicted of or allegedly involved in, and the contents of his tortured confession. This ruling again brought into bold relief the contrast between how Duff treated evidence prejudicial to Andrew with evidence that discredited Burge. Duff's ruling made for an excruciating cross-examination that featured Andrew, at the prompting of his criminal defense lawyer, Alan Sincox, repeatedly taking the Fifth Amendment. At one point, Duff called a sidebar and accused Andrew of perjury.

As Kunkle's cross-examination was drawing to a close, public interest in the trial once again came to Duff's attention: "Evidently your handout has now added to it," Duff said, emphasizing the word "your." A man from the suburbs had heeded the leaflet's urging and written to Duff, enclosing the leaflet with a signed note that read, "Dear Judge Duff, it seems to me that you should know the charges being made against John [*sic*] Burge by the Citizens Alert." Looking at us, Duff asked, "Did any of you have anything to do with preparing this?" John responded, "No Judge, I didn't." Jeff and I remained silent.

Duff went on: "It is wrong to have anybody trying to write to influence any judge while a case is ongoing." Waving the leaflet, he continued, "It is nice, bright, and yellow, and reads very easily. . . . Some of my favorite words like 'blatant' and 'outrageous' were all in it."

"Commander, please take the stand." Our next witness was Jon Graham Burge. It would be the fifth separate time in the past nine months that I would question Burge; fifteen years would elapse before I got another opportunity. This time we had called Burge as an adverse witness so I could cross-examine him before Kunkle was able to lead him through their defense. The contrast between the treatment of Andrew and Burge could not have been starker. Judge Duff always referred to Burge as "Commander," almost reverently, while his contempt for Andrew had not diminished since he called him the "scum of the earth" during the first trial.

Our plan was to confront Burge's lies with evidence of other allegations of torture, such as that of Willie Porch, Michael Johnson, and Melvin Jones, without revealing that Burge was involved, as Duff had constrained. Using this court-imposed fiction, we hoped to impeach Burge's denials of knowledge, while showing that he did not act to stop the pattern of Area 2 torture and abuse, without crossing the ever-shifting line in the sand drawn by Duff. Even if Duff thwarted these questions, we would have a record on appeal that clearly demonstrated the error of Duff's rulings.

My opening question sought to do just that: "Sometime in 1979 you did become aware of allegations against your detectives at Area 2 with regard to Willie Porch, didn't you?" Duff sustained Kunkle's objection and also struck the question, giving the jury the signal that I was overstepping my bounds. As I continued down this path, Duff called for a sidebar. After some argument, he cut to his more pressing aggravation: "Evidently, to your full knowledge, people have come to this courtroom for the purpose of demonstration about the very issue and the point you are making now." I challenged his assertion, and Duff retorted:

> Are you telling me that you are not aware of the press release that went out from the committee that has said that people in this case have lined up and testified about Porch's torture and the judge won't let him testify? You are not aware of that?

I had been so focused on preparing to cross-examine Burge that I could honestly profess ignorance, but Duff was not buying my denials. He then recessed the jury. The argument raged on, with the restrictions on the Willie Porch evidence at the center, in open court for the better part of an hour. Clearly, Burge knew about Willie's and the others' allegations of torture, because he was a participant at the time and testified later about his and his detectives' roles in their arrest and interrogation. Duff accused me of "histrionics" when I said that I was trying to attack Burge's "palpable falsehood." To proceed as we sought to do, he said, would be "in total dereliction of the spirit of every ruling we have made up to this point." We then moved for a mistrial, and to sever the case against the City from the case against Burge:

> Mr. Taylor: What's happening here, Judge, is that we are in a situation where we can't prove our case against the City because Burge is in it and we can't prove our case against Burge because the City is in it. We can't mention facts that are true. We can't mention facts that have been previously testified to from the stand.

Duff cut off further argument, told me to sit down, to behave myself, and to be quiet. He then called for the jury, and I resumed the questioning by asking Burge about "Machine Gun" Joe Gorman, his role in the Willie Porch case, and his connection to the Hampton raid. Duff sustained Kunkle's and Murphy's objections, struck the questions, refused to permit me to be heard on the relevance of the questions, and once again threatened me with contempt. After sending the jury back to the jury room, he began an inquisition:

> I need to ask plaintiff's counsel and maybe some of their friends since they seem to be aware, you are in contact with people who are conducting a demonstration today. I don't want the jury to be walking out the doors and have somebody hand them materials that is going to force a mistrial. . . .

Who are the folks in the courtroom who are the leaders of this demonstration and protest. Can I speak to them?

Much to our surprise, Mariel Nanasi stood up and said, "I am. I was part of the demonstration." Duff had her give and spell her name, noted that she had been in the courtroom the past two weeks, asked her if she was a lawyer or law student, and then asked if she could "give [me] any kind of assurance on behalf of your committee that the jury would not get information that would create a mistrial." Mariel said that she would, and Duff told the marshals to accompany the jurors out of the building to lunch. Acting as a provocateur, Kunkle volunteered, "She's the same person who signed an affidavit on behalf of the counsel for the plaintiff as an employee of the People's Law Office during the first trial."

In fact, Mariel, who had attested to Duff's "scum of the earth" comment, was not officially part of our office. After graduating from law school, she had become deeply involved in organizing and educating around the trial and the emerging evidence of systemic torture. In that role she was working closely with us, in particular with Jeff. Together, Mariel and Mary Powers had spearheaded the Coalition to End Police Brutality and Torture, the group responsible for the demonstration. Given the repressive climate in the courtroom, we strove to be helpful to Mary and Mariel from a distance, hoping this would protect us from Duff's wrath. Needless to say, Mariel's spontaneous response to Duff's inquiry made us nervous.

Burge's examination resumed in the afternoon. I was able to establish that Mayor Byrne, during the manhunt, had come to Area 2 and personally questioned him about the investigation, what leads were being followed, and how long it might take. Burge told her that "everything that was humanly possible" was being done. He said he "definitely did not remember" her saying "Don't worry about the OPS complaints." I questioned him extensively about Donald White's interrogation, and he admitted to participating but denied any torture or brutality. I attacked his testimony that, after supposedly telling his men to handle Andrew Wilson "with kid gloves," he never entered the room where Andrew was being held to check on his condition; that this purported failure was contrary to his general practice; and that, in contrast, he had entered the room while Donald White and his brothers were being interrogated.

I moved on to Burge's knowledge of electric shock and whether he was aware of other allegations of its use at Area 2. Surprisingly, Duff overruled

Kunkle's objection, and Burge answered that he had been aware of such allegations on two other occasions. I intended to show that he did not report those instances, but Kunkle cut me off in mid-question, called a sidebar, and raised the specter of Melvin Jones and Michael Johnson. I argued that I was not intending to use their names or delve into the details of their torture, but Kunkle prevailed. Then, I picked up the alligator clips that Kunkle had used in his cross-examination of Andrew and asked Burge, "If you took these alligator clips, attached them to wires, attached those wires to a generator, and put it in a box, you would have the device that Andrew Wilson described, wouldn't you?" Kunkle objected, and Duff again went the extra mile for him: "Ladies and gentlemen of the jury, that is not a conclusion that the witness should be asked to draw. The objection is sustained, and you are instructed to disregard the question."

Bright and early the next day, Kunkle gave Duff a copy of an article and photo that appeared in that morning's *Chicago Tribune*. The article was about the demonstration, which, Kunkle elaborated, "took place during the day apparently yesterday at the south entrance to the building, the one that the Court instructed the jury to use." Pointing to the photo of Mariel Nanasi, Duff said, "And this little girl was here in the courtroom. You could prevent this from happening with any modicum of effort to instruct your people about the deleterious effect that this kind of activity could have on the trial."

Back before the jury, I continued to attempt to demonstrate a full-blown cover-up of Andrew Wilson's torture, combined with the total lack of any supervision, investigation, or discipline by Burge, his superior officers, the OPS, or State's Attorney Daley. Whenever the questioning returned to electric shock, the three-headed monster of Duff, Kunkle, and Murphy rose to blunt the effort. Nonetheless, I planned to finish my examination of Burge with one final series of electric-shock questions, concluding, as I had at the first trial, with "Did you throw the box off your boat into Lake Michigan?"

This time, instead of Burge's answering the question with a denial, Kunkle objected and asked the judge to admonish me. Duff called yet another sidebar, and I told the judge that Burge had answered the question at the first trial. Kunkle said that he "must have been asleep" if he had not objected at the time. Duff asked me my basis for asking the question. I cited an anonymous letter from Deep Badge. Duff said, "Let me see the letter," and I promised that I would bring it to court and make it part of the record. Duff denied that we had previously discussed the letters—which we had—and Kunkle said he would like to compare the handwriting on the letters "to some of the people." Duff ordered me to bring in the letter within twenty-four hours, and admonished me: "You have just behaved unethically and improperly in front of this jury."

Incredulously, I asked, as an officer of the court, "How can you say that when I tell you that I have a good-faith basis?"

"Because I don't believe it." Duff shot back. He then instructed the jury to disregard the final question "because it suggests a matter or basis of fact that there is no proof anywhere and it is to be disregarded totally." Bloodied but not defeated, I felt that I had just gone fifteen rounds with Burge, Kunkle, and Murphy, with Duff as a hopelessly biased referee.

A few days before, Judge Duff had signed an order to transport Donald White from Centralia. Murphy and Kunkle had objected, but Duff seemed to recognize that his testimony was highly relevant to our pattern and practice claims against the City. The day after Burge finished testifying, Kunkle and McCarthy deposed White in the judge's witness room during lunch and after court concluded. John put on the record that I had met with Donald within the past two weeks, and that he had agreed to testify on the condition that we facilitate his leaving the state—$270 for a U-Haul and $780 for one month's rent.

Donald detailed, for the first time under oath, his harrowing experience at police headquarters: the threats, the beatings, the suffocation with a bag, the screaming of the other detainees. He identified photographs of several of the officers who participated in his torture, including Burge, Hill, and O'Hara, but could not identify some of the others. He said that they looked like they "come from the Mafia. They was something like a little hit squad they bring out on stuff like that." He said that he had, until recently, told no one about his torture but his mother, and had convinced her, out of fear, not to mention his torture to the OPS when she reported the terrorization of her and her family—including putting guns up to his six- and eight-year-old brothers' heads—during the police search of her house. He recounted that he had recently confided in his mother-in-law, and she told him that he "would feel better if he told somebody the truth and got all of it off his mind. So when Mr. Taylor finally came to see me I just felt safe talking to him."

He continued to explain why he set the conditions of his testimony with me:

They not real policemen, they dirty policemen, and I told him that I fear for my life that I would not come here and testify the truth knowing that they would do me like they did the other boys, again.

He told of how the state's attorney's office put him up in a hotel, paid for his food, relocated his family to Aurora, Illinois, and paid for their moving, rent, and food. Kunkle produced the records of my visit with Donald, documenting that it was from 12:10 to 1:42 p.m. on July 3, 1989. Donald became impassioned as the deposition concluded:

> They beat my family, they beat me, they beat my brothers, they beat other people that came from around my house. They bluffed them from coming and telling the truth and they got a good bluff on them. I just got enough courage to come and tell my side of the story so people will really know they do beat people.

It was hard not to get excited about Donald's testimony. While the payment worried us, it was more than counterbalanced by all the money Kunkle's team had paid out during the criminal prosecution to Donald, his family, and friends for similar protections, money that appeared for all intents and purposes to be hush money. He was a powerful pattern and practice witness, showing that Burge and his men brutally tortured a number of men suspected of being involved in the police murders, and that they did it at police headquarters while the police superintendent, Brzeczek, was present on an adjacent floor, making it reasonable to conclude he could have heard the piercing screams and shouts that accompanied the torture.

Just as Donald White was about to take the stand, Murphy and Kunkle made a last-ditch effort to bar him. Murphy argued that Donald had not identified Brzeczek as being in the room when he was being tortured. Hence, she argued, the city's police policymaker did not have notice. This was wrong, as John argued, for several reasons. First, the law was clear that we did not have to show actual notice to the policymaker of each act of brutality. If that were required, then Willie Porch, Roy Brown, Walter Johnson, Paul Mike, and several other of our pattern and practice witnesses would have been barred. Additionally, basic rules of evidence provided that reasonable inferences could be drawn from circumstantial evidence, and it was reasonable to infer from that evidence that Brzeczek was aware of the torture going on in close proximity to him.

During the argument, Deep Badge's letters came up, and Duff asked me once again for the letters. I said that I would give them to him in his chambers but that I did not want to give them to Kunkle, in light of his threat to seek to identify the source. Duff threatened us with sanctions for not producing the letters and refused to take them *in camera*, saying, "If this [is a] person upon which so much presently depends, then everybody has a right to know what that police officer has seen and/or observed before such anonymous correspondence would be given credibility."

Later that day, Duff tersely announced his decision: "White will not be allowed to take the stand." Jeff stood and moved for a mistrial. "The more relevant the evidence gets, the closer it gets to the individual defendants, the closer it gets to proving the—" Duff cut Jeff off, called for the jury, and silenced him by saying "Don't say another word, sir, or I will hold you in contempt for obstructing the course of the trial."

Next, Jeff took on defendant Patrick O'Hara. Jeff had cross-examined untold numbers of law enforcement officers in his more than twenty years of trial experience. He had a confrontational style that was quite effective in exposing lying cops. Duff's sustaining of the defense's objections whenever we would confront a witness with prior inconsistent testimony was maddening, and Jeff told Duff so directly at one point in O'Hara's questioning: "I think that your rulings make using the depositions impossible. No matter how impeaching they are, the court finds a way to sustain the objection." Duff belittled Jeff's technique for impeaching O'Hara as "falling far short of skilled advocacy," and added that his "continued insistence on doing the wrong thing after instruction and admonition" was "improper behavior." Duff permitted Jeff to ask whether O'Hara had heard of "other allegations of beatings, pistols to the head, bags over the head, and electric shock." O'Hara answered that he had; Jeff asked when, and, surprisingly, Duff overruled Rubin's objection. But before O'Hara could answer, Rubin asked for a sidebar and told Duff that Jeff was going to elicit an answer that would violate "his prior orders." Duff responded, "If Mr. Haas misbehaves and he gets into a clear violation, I will declare a mistrial and I will prevent the plaintiff from continuing with the case in another trial." When Jeff repeated the question, Duff sustained the objection.

Our last two witnesses were Dr. Kirschner and Area 2 commander Milton Deas. Dr. Kirschner again strongly supported Andrew's burning and electric-shock claims, and again he was not permitted to testify as an expert on torture. Surprisingly, Kunkle, on cross-examination, brought out what we had been prevented from doing with Dr. Raba—that it was unlikely that Andrew's wounds were self-inflicted.

Deas once again defended Burge, saying that Burge's denial of wrong-doing had satisfied him and that he made no further inquiry, despite knowing that Andrew Wilson had suffered serious injuries and had been rejected from lockup. Later in his testimony, Deas admitted that it would have been important for him to have known about other allegations of electric shock that had been made against his men at Area 2, but I was blocked from showing him Michael Johnson's OPS complaint of electric shock or from asking him whether his opinion of Burge would have changed if he knew about other electric-shock allegations against him.

The next day, a propane tank blew up six floors below the courtroom, shattering a number of windows and starting a fire. After safety and order were restored, Duff told us that we were finished and must immediately rest our case. In order to make the record for appeal, we again offered, as a formality, the evidence of other torture victims: Melvin Jones, Michael Johnson, Anthony Holmes, and the others set forth in our pretrial proffer of evidence. To our amazement, Duff said, of the Melvin Jones evidence, that he had only "ruled on it specifically and narrowly on the grounds that it was offered—and, as a matter of fact, my certain knowledge is that there were areas of Mr. Jones's testimony that you could have put on as evidence that I didn't preclude nor did I discuss in any fashion."

I responded that we had "raised it again and again and again, and now you seem to indicate that it could have been admitted for certain purposes." With obvious relish for the Catch-22 he was presenting, Duff replied, "My purpose when I rule is not to teach or educate or take sides. There are areas, if you read my ruling carefully, that you could have put Mr. Jones on to testify about, and you chose not to put him on." Incredulous, I responded that we would call him as a witness on the spot before we rested. Duff refused to permit us to call Jones or to offer his prior testimony, declaring, "It's untimely, counsel. You have finished." Shortly thereafter, he called in the jury. John stood, dejected, and said, "Subject to the court's ruling, the plaintiff rests."

Kunkle, apparently fearing what Duff might now permit with regard to the Melvin Jones evidence, pulled Burge from his witness list. The City then called Brzeczek back to the stand. I asked Brzeczek about patterns of similar conduct, and Duff sustained the City's objection. I asked directly if he had ever heard of Melvin Jones, and the objection was likewise sustained. In response to Murphy's questioning, Brzeczek had said that there was no pattern or practice of abusing suspects who were accused of assaulting cops, but when I attempted to challenge that assertion during my cross-examination,

Duff again sustained the objection. In lawyers' parlance, Murphy had opened a door to a broad examination of a party-defendant, but Duff had slammed it shut.

At another sidebar, I moved for a mistrial because, as I said, Duff's blocking of all manner of relevant cross-examination "was becoming totally ridiculous." Duff responded that I was frustrated because I "was doing such a lousy job." I responded by moving for Duff to recuse himself because he was "totally, hopelessly involved in this case on the side of the defendants and so personally and hopelessly biased against me particularly. That comment shows it and your rulings show it."

That night, Duff summoned the court reporter from her suburban home to search for his "rulings" about Melvin Jones. The next morning, reading at length from his rambling remarks on the opening day of the retrial, he emphasized that, despite all his prior rulings, he had said at that time, "I am not going to preclude the possibility of the plaintiff developing the issue or the evidence in the liability area, even though I can't see it totally now." He went on reading: "However, at this stage, with a lot of thought, the only premise I can see that would allow the trial to go forward legitimately without error or without the possibility of a mistrial and without prejudice, which would be substantial, was to bifurcate it"—meaning that the trial would be split into two phases, with the first phase being limited to the defendants' liability, and the second, if the defendants were found by the jury to be liable, devoted to the amount of damages to be awarded. The Melvin Jones evidence would then be limited to the damages phase.

After his reading, Duff concluded, "I did not foreclose the possibility of Mr. Jones being put back in on the liability issue. The status of the record at the time was such that it couldn't have been, and I was never asked to rule further."

Jeff jumped to his feet:

Judge, every time we got near Melvin Jones in questioning any witness, they would raise prior rulings and you would sustain it. You would warn us. Now, in a self-serving manner with the only purpose to take away our record, because now the court recognizes that it was wrong to bar Melvin Jones, so you now say that you never ruled. Obviously the reason we didn't call Melvin Jones yet was because every time we even got close to Melvin Jones we almost got held in contempt of court. However, we'll proceed based on what you said today, and we'll assume that what was just said is the court's understanding and we'll proceed along those lines.

Patrick O'Hara, who had interrogated Andrew Wilson, was back on the stand, this time called by the defense. Jeff tried yet another approach in seeking to ask O'Hara about the Melvin Jones incident—that it was relevant to our claim that O'Hara and Burge had acted jointly as conspirators. At a heated exchange at sidebar, where arguments were supposed to be conducted in stage whispers so the jury could not overhear, Duff told Jeff to "stop it" in such loud tones that, soon after, while informing the jury that he had sustained the objection, he felt compelled to justify his outburst to the jurors.

Yucaitis followed O'Hara. He had transported Andrew to Area 2, had been implicated in the early-morning beating, and was Burge's main accomplice when Andrew was electric-shocked and burned on the radiator. He claimed that Burge had told him and his fellow transporters to handle Andrew "with special kindness," and said that Burge had assigned him to sit outside Andrew's interrogation room door to make sure that no one abused him. Like Burge, he also claimed that he never entered the room. Unfortunately, the jury at the first trial had absolved him and O'Hara of direct involvement in Andrew's torture, so Yucaitis's liability hinged on our showing him as a conspirator. Jeff asked him if he had "ever heard that anybody claimed that they had been beaten or electric-shocked." The judge sustained Rubin's objection and instructed the jury to disregard the question. A short time later Jeff asked, "Well, did you hear allegations from somebody named Melvin Jones that he had been shocked?" Duff snapped, "Objection sustained." Apparently, we had still not solved Duff's riddle. "I have had to rule on that more times than I should have had to, Mr. Haas. The jury is instructed to disregard the question. It is stricken from the record."

Donald White also was a topic of defense testimony. Duff had permitted the defense to bring out highly prejudicial evidence from a statement Donald had given while being interrogated at police headquarters. This evidence included that Andrew and Jackie Wilson had been planning to break their friend Edgar Hope out of the hospital just prior to the killings of Fahey and O'Brien, that Andrew had admitted to Anthony "Mertz" Williams that he had committed the murders, and that the guns were stashed at a beauty salon.

On July 26, detective Fred Hill took the stand. Once Duff had permitted the inclusion of the above evidence, we sought to complete the picture by showing that Donald was tortured by Hill, O'Hara, Burge, and their confederates into making the statement. If they denied the torture, we would have an avenue to call Donald as a rebuttal witness.

"Well, you participated in the bagging and beating of Donald White at police headquarters on February 12, 1982, didn't you?" I asked. Hill quickly answered, "I did not." Surprised by Kunkle's failure to object, I continued, "You took him into custody, did you not?" As Hill answered, "Yes," Kunkle jumped up and objected. At a sidebar, Kunkle claimed that he'd meant to object but couldn't get to his feet in time. He tossed in the fact that I had given White money to relocate. Duff seemed to be going our way, saying that Hill was subject to examination and impeachment on the issue. "If White has to take the stand to impeach him he can. If Mr. Kunkle wants to show that White talked about getting a thousand dollars, he may. There is no way I can stop, reasonably, legitimately, and from an evidentiary perspective, Mr. Taylor from asking this man who has just said he has never been accused of brutality." After Kunkle reargued his objection, Duff let Hill's denial stand but barred me from further inquiry.

My examination resumed, and at the next sidebar, Kunkle turned toward the jury and laughed scornfully at my argument. I took umbrage; Kunkle denied that he was facing the jury, and both McCarthy and Duff sprang to his defense. I told McCarthy that he "did not have to get involved in this garbage," and McCarthy repeated that Kunkle was not looking at the jury. This spectacle then spun further out of control:

McCarthy: I saw him, he didn't—
Taylor: You are lying.

McCarthy then challenged me to "step outside, and we will see who is lying." I asked Duff if he had heard that Hamiltonian challenge. Duff said that he had, but then put on his witness hat:

Duff: Mr. Taylor, you lied, excuse me sir. But Mr. Kunkle did snort. He did turn his head towards Mr. McCarthy. He has got his back to the jury. He is much too large to turn to the jury.

Once again, I moved for a mistrial and for recusal:

You have never said that anything that any of these other counsel have said was a lie, and it just goes to show that you are out for me—you are so totally personally embroiled in this case and against me that you are punishing my client because you don't like me.

After retorting that "most of the time" he liked me, Duff held me in contempt and fined me $500 for "calling the court a liar." I resumed my questioning and asked Hill if he was familiar with electric-shock devices or had heard talk about their use. "Objection sustained," Duff almost bellowed. "It's precisely in the nature of the last objection that I have already ruled on. You know it, Mr. Taylor. You have completed your examination. You have no more questions to ask. Mr. Kunkle, you may redirect."

Later that afternoon, I began my cross-examination of deputy superintendent Joseph McCarthy. A close friend of Mayor Byrne, McCarthy was acting as her eyes and ears at Area 2 during the manhunt. The slain officers, Fahey and O'Brien, were under McCarthy's command in the Gang Crimes Unit; nevertheless, he insisted on joining Burge as the co-leader of the raid to arrest Andrew Wilson, even though Burge later admitted that McCarthy was too personally involved to have done so. It also appeared that some of the unidentified officers who tortured Roy Brown, Paul Mike, and Walter Johnson were Gang Crimes officers. Kunkle had called to the stand McCarthy, whom he portrayed as an independent, high-ranking police official, primarily to deny having heard Burge tell Yucaitis and the other transporting officers that they would "get" Andrew at the station.

I endeavored to attack McCarthy's credibility by questioning him about these subjects in order to show his bias in favor of Burge and the City. The judge chided me in front of the jury, then called a sidebar, during which he shouted at me for trying to explain why the questions were permissible. Back before the jury, I started to explore McCarthy's failure to report Burge's comment or any other misconduct to Superintendent Brzeczek in his daily briefings. Before I could get the first few words of my question out, Murphy objected, and Duff shouted, "Objection sustained, objection sustained."

That finished my questioning, and the jury was sent home for the day. I attempted to make the record by saying that Duff had "screamed the last 'objection sustained' out at me." Duff responded that my questioning was "a deliberate attempt to evade at the very last minute of a long day an issue that you knew was totally thoroughly improper." I told Duff that the question was based on a document in evidence. After telling me I had the right to make a record for appeal, he added that I did not have "the right to put the court or the system in disrepute." He then escalated his threats:

> That's against the canons of ethics. And I am going to take this entire record when it's complete and examine it for that consideration. And if it is appropriate

I will ask for a criminal contempt charge to be brought against you or I will ask for the Attorney Registration and Disciplinary Committee to consider whether or not you should be disciplined by licensing and regulation.

Duff then rose, and gave a parting shot: "You are walking on the edge of disaster in your own behavior. Now you must behave, sir."

CHAPTER 7

The Fight
for Justice Broadens

Together with Mary Powers, Mariel Nanasi, and other allies, we had decided to open another front. With our help, Mary drafted a letter, on Citizens Alert letterhead, to OPS director David Fogel. Noting that there was much newly discovered evidence that was not being allowed before Duff's jury, the letter asked the OPS to open investigations into the allegations of torture made by Andrew Wilson, Donald White, and Melvin Jones and emphasized that "within a ten-day period, these three suspects were subjected to identical acts of torture and brutality by Burge and the same detectives." It further requested that the Chicago Police Board "conduct open hearings into patterns of torture by some members of the Chicago Police Department dating back at least sixteen years." The letter continued:

> A clear signal must be sent to other officers who may be prone to violence that such torture and abuse will not be tolerated in Chicago. We feel that it is the responsibility of OPS to uncover the deliberate repeated acts of torture of suspects in order to extract confessions, "solve" crimes, and/or inflict retribution.

The official sender of the letter was the Citywide Coalition Against Police Abuse, a group identified as including the Chicago Conference of Black Lawyers, Citizens Alert, the Chicago Committee to Defend the Bill of Rights, the Cabrini Green Citizens Alert Committee, the National Alliance Against Racist and Political Repression, the Committee to Investigate the Police, the Chicago Chapter of the National Lawyers Guild, and the Committee to End Police Abuse and Torture. As supporters, the letter also listed several prominent local African American leaders, including Conrad Worrill, Lu Palmer, and Randolph Stone.

The trial, now nearly two months after it had begun with jury selection, was winding to its conclusion. Duff asked for a list of our rebuttal witnesses, the witnesses we would call to contest various pieces of testimony presented by the defendants. Our list was highlighted by Melvin Jones, Donald White, Burge, Anthony "Satan" Holmes, Dr. Raba, and David Fogel. With regard to Melvin Jones, we again asked, alternatively, that we be permitted to reopen our case in chief to put him on the stand under the judge's recent reinterpretation of his prior rulings. I again sounded our theme that, given Duff's apparent change in position, we were open to the court's "suggestion" as to how the evidence was admissible. Duff refused to clarify his position, which he called "consistent and clear," and continued to speak in loquacious riddles. The trial, he waxed, was "like watching a sunset. Rays move and change through the course of a trial. Preparation assists, understanding assists. The standard rule by which the court has been making these rulings is clear."

The next afternoon, the topic of rebuttal witnesses was taken up again. Jeff pointed out that Melvin Jones was "the most important witness in the case." Duff agreed that Melvin's testimony was "very significant if true." After Duff said that the Jones issue was "complex," "delicate," "interesting," and "complicated," and once more alluded to the moving rays of light in a sunset, Jeff asked if he would "let us in on the riddle." Duff accused Jeff of having "continued, continued, and continued ad nauseam and ad infinitum," and then abruptly adjourned court for the weekend.

As the final week of the trial opened, Jeff began his cross-examination of Kunkle's star witness, jailhouse snitch extraordinaire, William Coleman. Coleman's purpose was to champion Kunkle's new defense strategy— self-infliction. Coleman, a British citizen, had a known history of crime and deception that spanned twenty years. He was represented by a former Cook County public defender, whose fee and expenses were being paid for by Kunkle and the City.

Coleman, aka Alfred Clarkson, had recently testified against Jackie Wilson, telling of an alleged plan to escape from Cook County Jail that Andrew had purportedly confided to him in 1987. According to Coleman, he had made passing reference to prosecutor Nick Trutenko, nearly two years after the alleged conversation, that Andrew had also mentioned that he had self-inflicted his torture wounds. Trutenko passed the information on to his former boss and co-counsel Bill Kunkle, and Coleman had been contacted as the second trial was about to begin. Kunkle visited Coleman twice in an Alexandria, Virginia, federal prison lockup. What emerged was a tall tale of self-infliction that Kunkle would much later admit he "wasn't crazy about."

We had vehemently objected to Coleman's testimony beforehand, but Duff blessed it in all its sensational and prejudicial completeness. It went like this: Days after Coleman was moved onto the same tier at Cook County Jail, Andrew Wilson befriended Coleman, who he erroneously thought was a member of the Irish Republican Army. Andrew began to tell him about his case and escape scheme, a plot designed so that Andrew could kill the witnesses against him at his retrial. He admitted that he had killed Fahey and O'Brien, and told Coleman that he had been tortured. When Andrew mentioned a hair dryer, Coleman laughed derisively. Andrew became upset but initiated a second conversation with Coleman later the same day.

According to Coleman, at this second meeting, Andrew asked him about his knowledge of torture. Coleman told him that when he was in custody in Hong Kong in 1970 for using stolen credit cards, he had been shown an interrogation room where clandestine British Special Branch agents tortured leaders of Mao's Red Guards in the 1960s. The interrogation room had a long table and chairs with leather straps. At his deposition, Coleman had said that the room contained field generators with hand cranks; perhaps because it mirrored what Andrew himself had described, Kunkle omitted that fact on his direct examination.

Coleman testified that he then told Andrew that his story was "bullshit" because a hair dryer would not transmit a shock, and that there would also be marks on his wrists caused by the electricity from the crank box hitting the handcuffs. Supposedly exposed as a fabricator by Coleman's expert knowledge, Andrew decided to come clean to this white stranger with a thick British accent, telling Coleman that he had burned himself on the red-hot radiator in order to create a basis for suppressing his confession after realizing he was in "deep shit." At his deposition, Coleman had at first testified that Andrew said that he had pushed his chest and arm across the radiator, which was in direct conflict with the up-and-down pattern of burns on Andrew's chest and the burns on Andrew's face and leg. Coleman realized his mistake and attempted to change this testimony later in his deposition. Kunkle avoided this problem in his trial questioning as well.

Continuing to follow Kunkle's lead, Coleman said that Andrew confided that the electric-shock part of his testimony came from other prisoners during intake at the jail. However, at his deposition, Coleman had testified that Andrew had said the electric-shock part of the story came later, gradually, after Andrew got on the cell block and talked to other prisoners and to his lawyers. A photo taken of Andrew at intake, showing clip marks on Andrew's nose and ear, accounted for this change in testimony, but it could not account for the fact that Barbara Steinberg, the public defender who represented Andrew at his early-morning bond hearing—before he ever got to the jail—testified that Andrew told her he had been electric shocked.

Coleman also testified that Andrew told him that he intended to use his torture testimony to get his confession suppressed at his retrial—also palpably false, as at the time of the purported conversation, the Illinois Supreme Court had already issued its finding that the confession was the product of torture and should not have been admitted as evidence at Andrew's original trial, a crucial fact that Andrew full well knew. For good measure, Coleman tossed in a couple of equally outlandish lies directed at Dale Coventry and at us—that Andrew claimed he had asked us to settle his case for short money so he could pay off a guard to get him guns for his escape, and that he had told his lawyers about the self-infliction and they had told him to keep his mouth shut.

Jeff started his cross-examination by attacking Coleman's credibility. In the mid-1980s Coleman's passport had been seized for alleged gun-running, and he was later arrested for having a false passport. Jeff then asked him whether he had a long history of forging and changing passports, starting in 1967 in Liverpool, with five convictions, but the judge sustained the objection under the rule that convictions over ten years old could not be used to impeach a witness. At a sidebar, Jeff argued that it was not offered to impeach Coleman but to show that he did not want to return to Britain due to a history of immigration problems and an immigration hold, and that his false testimony was offered with the hope that he would receive official help in avoiding that fate. Duff accused Jeff of obstruction and arrogance, told him to take his elbow off his bench, and threatened him with contempt. Back before the jury, Duff not only sustained Kunkle's objection, but also struck the prior questions and answers about passport fraud.

Jeff was able to bring out that Coleman had been awaiting trial on a cocaine possession charge and had escaped from Cook County Jail, shortly after his purported conversation with Andrew, by jumping out of the window of a jail bus after un-handcuffing himself with a paper clip. Coleman had threatened the prisoner to whom he was handcuffed with gang retaliation if he talked, and had been on the run for several months, using a false ID, before being apprehended in a Philadelphia bar. Jeff also established that Coleman was presently under indictment for mail fraud. Jeff was not permitted to bring out that he had killed a man in Ireland in 1972, taken the victim's wallet, and used his name as an alias before being apprehended and convicted of manslaughter, nor could he bring out several other crimes of fraud and deceit. We all had to suppress a smile when Coleman volunteered that his last job was "raising flowers."

In an exhaustive investigation of Coleman, our office had located an investigative British journalist named Gregory Miskiw, who had written an explosive exposé about Coleman's attempt to deceive him with fabrications for proposed stories in the *Daily Mirror*. We had listed Miskiw as a rebuttal witness, but after Coleman answered one question on the subject, Duff barred Jeff from questioning him further about Miskiw, saying that the topic was "collateral."

When Jeff revisited Coleman's Hong Kong story, Coleman said he told Andrew that Special Branch agents attached clips to the sensitive parts of the body, including the ears, nipples, genitals, and anus. Coleman said it was common knowledge in Britain that Special Branch agents tortured Chinese communists in the 1960s, but Duff sustained objections when Jeff sought to probe Coleman's dealings with the Special Branch and when he asked if it was also common knowledge that the US military tortured captives in nearby Vietnam.

Jeff attempted to attack Coleman's assertion that Andrew said he was going to use his claim of torture to suppress his confession at his upcoming retrial. This was tricky business because Duff had consistently barred any mention of the substance of the Illinois Supreme Court decision. And, once again, we were prevented from confronting an obvious lie.

Jeff also pointed out that Coleman had received a sweetheart deal from Kunkle's buddy Nick Trutenko—who dropped the cocaine charge and gave Coleman four years on the escape case—solely, supposedly, in exchange for his testimony against Jackie the previous month. He also established that Coleman had not told anyone about Andrew's remarkable admissions until he made a passing reference to Trutenko on the eve of Jackie's trial, some twenty months after Andrew had allegedly made them. In light of these facts, Coleman's denials of any favors, given or expected, for his testimony against Andrew a month after Jackie's trial rang hollow.

Kunkle's final witness was ASA Lawrence Hyman, who, in the morning hours of February 14, 1982, had told Burge to "get the jagoff out of here" when Andrew told him he had been tortured and refused to give a court-reported statement. Hyman denied this but was quite vulnerable on many fronts, most particularly on the question as to why he and Burge supposedly waited until 6:00 p.m. that night to take Andrew's court-reported statement if, as the defense claimed, Andrew had willingly given an oral confession to O'Hara in the early morning hours. According to Hyman, who remained at Area 2 from ten in the morning until after Andrew was dragged out by the wagon men that night, he neither heard nor saw anything amiss. He even went so far as to claim that he and Burge sat around with a friendly Andrew, drinking sodas, after Andrew gave his statement.

During Jeff's cross-examination, John approached the podium to suggest a question to Jeff. Duff reacted to this perfectly ordinary event by shouting, "Sit down, Mr. Stainthorp, sit down, Mr. Stainthorp!" Taken aback, John responded, "You have never done this to any of the defendants' lawyers. This is outrageous!" Jeff gathered himself and got Hyman to admit that the eight-hour delay was not good prosecutorial practice, and could have resulted in his losing the chance to get an all-important court-reported statement from Andrew.

As the cross-examination wound down, Jeff attempted to confront Hyman with the fact that he had not investigated Andrew's allegations of torture. Duff sustained the objections and sent the jury home for the day. He then accused Jeff of ignoring his rulings and of obstructing the course of the trial, and held him in contempt. Still smarting over Duff's treatment of him earlier in the afternoon, John headed to the back of the courtroom to put his files in his briefcase and interjected, over his shoulder, "That is an absurd ruling, Judge, absolutely absurd." Duff ordered John to come back to the table and to sit down, but John continued to pack to leave. "Judge, you have lost any, any pretense of impartiality in this case. You are obstructing the truth," shot back our voice of restraint and reason. Duff then made John a member of our exclusive club: "You are in contempt of court and the fine is $200." It had become, I told the judge as he headed off the bench, "too expensive to speak the truth."

It was on to our rebuttal case. We had flown Gregory Miskiw in from England, figuring, at the least, we could make a record for appeal. John had figured out that there were several separate rules of evidence that would permit Miskiw's testimony: to show Coleman's reputation for untruthfulness, his character, his motivation to lie, and other lies that he told. As John summarized it, Miskiw would show Coleman to be a "con man, a fabricator, and a billy liar." Duff permitted a limited voir dire. Miskiw recounted that, in January 1986, Coleman, calling himself Alfred Clarkson, had phoned Miskiw from Washington, DC, with a story about Queen Elizabeth's cousin, Lord Litchfield. According to Coleman, the Lord had been unceremoniously busted in DC for possession of $10,000 worth of cocaine. He also said that he had evidence that the South African tennis star Kevin Curran was a "sex pervert." After four or five phone conversations, Miskiw was convinced to fly to Washington to meet with Coleman and do further investigation. After about a dozen discussions with Coleman, he talked to local DC police, the FBI, and the Drug Enforcement Agency and determined that there was no truth to Coleman's story about Lord Litchfield. After talking to Curran, his former girlfriend, and the girlfriend's sister, he determined that Coleman had fabricated that "scandal" as well.

Miskiw then converted his story to an exposé of Coleman. He and his investigative team discovered that Coleman had cheated both his former girlfriend and his stepfather out of money, and that his family considered him the "blackest of the black sheep of the family." In Miskiw's opinion, Coleman was a "consummate liar, and he made up stories," and his reputation was that he was "regarded as a liar." Duff reserved his ruling for the moment.

We then argued that we should be allowed to call Coleman's lawyer to the stand to rebut Coleman's false claim that he did not know what his present charge was. In a written motion, we had suggested that the lawyer and Kunkle had the motive and opportunity, together, to induce Coleman to give that answer. Duff was incensed that we would imply such a thing about Kunkle, "a man of impeccable reputation," and about Coleman's lawyer, according to Duff "a man of high reputation" as well. He further said that our suggestions could be considered "scurrilous and libelous." He then questioned the lawyer in such a way as to absolve Coleman, Kunkle, and the lawyer of any whisper of wrongdoing.

Jeff established that Kunkle and the City already owed Coleman's lawyer approximately $5,000 for his services to date. After Duff repeatedly told Jeff to be quiet, I asked the judge for permission to leave. He said if I left I would not be permitted to return, so I sat down in protest. Duff again held us both in contempt and took a five-minute recess. When the smoke had cleared, Duff completely gutted our rebuttal case. No Melvin Jones, Donald White, or Anthony Holmes. No Fogel to rebut Brzeczek. No Burge to question about Jones and Holmes. No Raba or Kirschner to debunk Coleman's claims of self-infliction. No Doris Miller to rebut the defendants' claims that Andrew did not scream. No Frank Laverty to rebut the defendants' denials of a code of silence at Area 2. No Greg Miskiw or Coleman's lawyer. All we were left with was a cameo from Andrew.

Andrew denied telling Coleman that he was trying to suppress or, as Coleman put it, to "kick out" his statement at his retrial "because there was no reason to suppress the statement anymore." Kunkle objected, and Duff struck the explanation. John then told the judge at sidebar that he wanted to ask Andrew what he told Coleman the reason was for his case being reversed by the Illinois Supreme Court. Duff, maintaining his resolve to keep the real basis for the court's decision from the jury, told John, "If you ask that question and he gives that answer, I will declare a mistrial." John was extremely upset and said that the jury should hear the evidence. Duff responded, "Go ahead and do it. I will say it is in direct disobedience of my order and grant a mistrial if Mr. Kunkle so requests it."

Out went the jury, and Jeff said, quite correctly, that Duff was putting us in a "ridiculous, impossible situation." Jeff moved for a mistrial, Duff denied it, and upbraided the mild-mannered Stainthorp for "theatrics" when he smiled at Andrew, who remained on the witness stand. He then told John to take his hand off his head and get his elbow off the table. "Oh my Lord," John exclaimed, "the pettiness of the court is mind-boggling." Back before the jury, John was able to establish that Andrew never told Coleman he intended to make brutality allegations at a future suppression hearing, but nothing more. Duff denied us the right to call Dale Coventry to rebut Coleman's lies about him and Andrew. There would be no more witnesses. Duff then denied one final mistrial motion, and we were on to final arguments.

As we prepared for closings by reviewing the evidence, our certitude that there was no way this jury would bring back a verdict for Andrew gave way to a glimmer of hope that the proof we had managed to get before the jurors might carry the day, at least against the City. We had won some battles as to what instructions on the law the judge would tell the jury, but the one we'd lost—giving them a series of questions to answer concerning our pattern and practice claim against the City—would provide an insight into the fundamental questions that the evidence raised.

The Coalition had put out a call for people to attend closing arguments, so the courtroom was packed with supporters and members of the media. In my opening I emphasized the proof against the City. "In fact," I said, "I dare say that most, if not all, of the evidence that you heard in some way or another is relevant to that pattern and practice claim." I started with Willie Porch and his co-defendants, then discussed the "centerpiece" of our widespread pattern and practice claim—the numerous Black men who were tortured during the manhunt by officers from different police units; the mothers who saw their sons being beaten and their houses ransacked in front of their young children; the scores of complaints that attorney Ron Samuels had collected and reported to Brzeczek; and the resultant "hue and cry" in the Black community that Brzeczek himself had admitted.

The "crown jewel" of this pattern and practice, I continued, was the series of beatings and torture of Andrew Wilson at Area 2 by three different sets of Chicago police officers, including the Area 2 lieutenant in charge of the manhunt, with high-ranking police officials on the premises: officials who knew, as one police officer had admitted, that "every Chicago police officer had revenge and retaliation on their minds." I argued, acidly, that in spite of this obvious dynamic, Brzeczek, "this great defender of people's constitutional rights, this great safe-guarder against police violence, told us with a straight face that he had absolutely no concern that anything would happen to Andrew Wilson when he got the call that morning. Where had he been living, on the moon?"

I was also able to make reference to other instances of electric shock, as we had gotten admissions from both Burge and O'Hara that they had heard of other such allegations at Area 2, before Duff cut off our questioning. I read Burge's testimony verbatim, pointed out that Kunkle had gotten Burge to retract that admission during his subsequent questioning, that Duff had not permitted us to attack that obvious change, and that Kunkle had elected not to re-call Burge in his case. Surprisingly, Duff let me make this argument despite Kunkle's objections. I then pointed to Brzeczek's denial that he had heard anything about electric shock before the Andrew Wilson case and said, "Either Burge and O'Hara were covering up other allegations of electric shock like they are covering up here, or command personnel knew that Area 2 used electric shock and didn't do anything about it."

I also emphasized the police code of silence, dismantling the police officers' uniform testimony that the code was only something that they had "seen in the movies," when in fact they had reenacted it "time and time and time again as each of them took the witness stand." After decrying the top-to-bottom cover-up that was the signature of the City's ratification of the pattern and practice, I built to my conclusion:

> Nobody did anything until Andrew Wilson brought this lawsuit and put it
> squarely in your hands whether they are going to be allowed to continue to

do this kind of thing. The only way they will be told not to is by your verdict. Your verdict, ladies and gentlemen, will speak not only to what happened to Andrew Wilson, but it will also speak to what happened to Paul Mike and Walter Johnson and Mrs. Davis. . . . It will speak to what happened to Roy Brown. It will speak to what happened to all those people in those 120 lost complaints. It will speak to the people in the Black community on whom was foisted a reign of terror.

Playing off Coleman's unlikely claim that Andrew had said to him, "What do they know about torture in America?" I finished my argument:

That's what the defendants are banking on. They are saying, "What do you know about torture in America?" Well, you know a lot about torture in America in this city by these police defendants now. You have heard about it for eight weeks. You are here to judge it, to say whether it can go on in this country under this Constitution at this time or any other time, whether a police commander can remain to do his duty comfortable in the idea that he can torture again. Whether they can put bags over people's heads and beat them on the bottom of their feet, beat them in the testicles and hang them by their hands, that's what you are here to judge.

Maureen Murphy then gave only the second closing of her young career. Sticking closely to her script, she did a thorough job of attacking the credibility of each witness we had called to establish the pattern and practice. Highlighting contradictions in their testimony, no matter how insignificant or explainable, Murphy emphasized that they were gang members, or, in Ron Samuels's case, had been disciplined by the Attorney Registration & Disciplinary Commission, so they should not be believed. Duff would later tell Murphy, "For a second close, you should be proud of yourself."

Kunkle then rumbled up to the lectern, guns figuratively and literally at the ready. Knowing that Duff would give him latitude, he started by alluding to the fact that Andrew had asked for $10 million in his original *pro se* complaint yet would "rather stay down at Pontiac and watch TV" than attend the trial. He recited in detail each of Andrew's crimes, then, waving one of the guns, bombastically intoned, "Andrew Wilson is the kind of person who puts a gun at another human being's face or in the back of his head and says 'Give me your money or your life.'"

The main thrust of Kunkle's argument was to attack Andrew's credibility and character, using the latter to attack the former. He emphasized that despite the medical proof, the only evidence that tied Burge to the torture was Andrew's testimony, and that Andrew had the "motivation and opportunity to self-inflict those injuries and the motive and opportunity to exaggerate their consequences and how they were received." Perhaps not surprisingly, Kunkle played down Coleman's testimony, referring briefly to Coleman's claim that Andrew admitted that he burned himself on the radiator and tried to settle his case to buy guns to use in a jail escape attempt. Returning to his overarching theme, Kunkle again waved the gun, saying the defendants knew that Andrew "did it with the gun in his hand at the back of Fahey's neck." Jeff's objection to the gun waving was overruled by Duff.

Kunkle concluded with an emotional plea:

> Andrew Wilson has no regard whatever for the property, the Constitutional rights, or even the lives of his fellow citizens. Yet, on February 14, 1982, he discovered the United States Constitution when he needed a way out. On February 9, 1982, Fahey and O'Brien listened to a lone piper play "Amazing Grace" for Officer Doyle. Because of the choices that Andrew Wilson made, that lone piper played "Amazing Grace" two more times within a week.

At about 4:00 p.m., Jeff took the podium for his rebuttal. He quickly laid out what we felt was our easiest way home, given how effectively Duff, working in tandem with Kunkle, had protected Burge:

> All you need to find is if Ferro or Mulvaney [the wagon men] did it or other Chicago police officers did it, and they were acting pursuant to a policy to injure and beat persons who were suspects in police shooting cases, then you must find against the City.

After addressing a number of the defense lawyers' arguments, Jeff turned to the "miraculous Mr. Coleman," who we believed had become a liability to Kunkle's defense. Jeff called him a "professional scoundrel" and outlined the remarkable list of deceptions and criminality that Duff had permitted us to introduce—blackmail, passport fraud, money laundering, wire fraud for attempting to swindle farmers, escape, a deportation order, and cocaine possession; he was a man who, by his own admission, had a "file a foot thick" of allegations against him.

Jeff also debunked Coleman's—and Kunkle's—claim that Andrew came up with his electric-shock allegations in the jail, at the urging of other prisoners, using roach clips to leave the marks. Jeff pointed to Barbara Steinberg's testimony, the intake pictures, and the spark burn mark on Andrew's ear. With regard to the other injuries, Jeff asked, rhetorically, "Why would

Andrew make the statement, then mess himself up, hurt himself? Why wouldn't he just refuse to make the statement?"

Jeff closed his argument with two additional questions:

What happens when the police violate the law? Who is going to do something about that? Not the OPS, not Mr. Brzeczek, he is going to promote people. That's why it's important to you, because you are the only people who can do something. It's up to you.

After Duff read the instructions, the jury retired to eat dinner and deliberate. We were summoned back to the courtroom at about 8:30 that night. Duff told us that that the jury had sent out a question: "Please clarify the meaning of 'widespread' in Instruction No. 23–(1). The instruction set forth that "Plaintiff must prove the existence of the de facto policy, practice, or custom by: (1) showing a widespread practice of police misconduct." After some discussion, it was decided that a non-answer would be given: "You have received your instructions. Please continue to deliberate." At 10:00 p.m., the jury sent out another note: "We are stalled on two points of view and feel further deliberations tonight will be unproductive." Duff then sent the jury home for the weekend.

Exhausted by more than seven months of unrelenting trial-related stress, we did not know what to do with ourselves except to speculate and prepare for the worst. That the jury had asked a question about the pattern and practice so early in the deliberations, then said that they were split on "two points of view," made us think that they had already decided on the claims against Burge, Yucaitis, and O'Hara, most probably in their favor, and that the split was on the pattern and practice claim against the City, perhaps on whether the pattern and practice was sufficiently "widespread."

Duff summoned us again on Monday afternoon because the jury had sent out two more notes. The first said, "Given the instructions on Count 3 we cannot agree on a verdict on Count 3." Six minutes later, they added in a second message, "Although at this time we have not agreed on Count 3, we have agreed on a verdict on Counts 1 and 2." Kunkle asked that the judge receive those verdicts and instruct the jury to continue to deliberate on Count 3. Jeff, John, and I were in agreement that we did not want another hung jury, but we were opposed to the judge's taking a partial verdict. After much discussion, Duff told them simply to continue to deliberate.

That night, the jury sent out another note: "Further deliberations tonight will not be productive. We are experiencing brain drain." Duff then sent them home for the night. Late the next afternoon, at a little after 5:00 p.m., Duff inquired as to "whether further deliberations this evening would be fruitful?" In response the jury, in an oddly cheerful message, replied, "Further deliberations would, in fact, be peachy tonight. When and if we get hungry, we will let you know." That night the jury signaled that it had a complete verdict. Entering the courtroom, the foreman—the man whose car had been stolen during jury selection—handed over the verdicts to the clerk, who read them. As we feared, the jury cleared Burge on the torture claim and all three of the police defendants on the conspiracy claim. The foreman then read the jury's answers to the questions that were part of the verdict form:

> Do you find that Plaintiff's constitutional rights were violated while he was in police custody? Answer: *Yes.*
>
> Do you find that in 1982, the City of Chicago had a de facto policy, practice or custom whereby Chicago police officers were allowed to physically abuse persons suspected of injuring or killing another police officer? Answer: *Yes.*
>
> Do you find that plaintiff was subjected to excessive force as a direct and proximate result of this de facto policy, practice or custom?

We held our breath—could we actually have won on our claim against the City? What else could have caused the violation of Andrew's rights?

Answer: *No.*

The clerk continued reading:

> We the jury find that the plaintiff, Andrew Wilson, has suffered no actual damages and award Andrew Wilson actual damages in the amount of zero.

A Pyrrhic victory, we thought. Did the jury not understand, or was it sending a loud and clear message: the City had a de facto policy, pattern, and practice; Andrew was tortured, or at least abused; but there was no way that they would give him any money or hold a decorated commander of the Chicago Police Department responsible? We had lost in the legal sense, but our ordeal before Duff was finally coming to a close, and we would now be able to appeal the madness he had wrought to a more reasonable court.

CHAPTER 8

Out of the Court
and into the Streets

Two weeks after the confounding jury verdict, members of the City-wide Coalition Against Police Abuse attended a police board meeting in the auditorium at police headquarters. The Burge torture leaflet was handed out, and Mary Powers described the torture allegations to the board, likening Chicago to countries where torture was openly practiced. On behalf of the coalition, she again called for a broad investigation of the torture allegations, demanded that Burge be suspended, and requested public hearings on the torture allegations. Jeff and Mariel also spoke, forcefully supporting the call for his investigation and suspension, as did several community activists. Police board member Nancy Jefferson, a progressive leader from the west side of Chicago, supported the call for investigation and suspension but pointed out that the police board did not have the power to set those processes in motion.

Also in August 1989, Mayor Daley's Bridgeport neighborhood was the scene of a racist incident instigated by two white Chicago police officers. The officers picked up two Black youths, Calvin McClin and Joseph Weaver, near Comiskey Park; slapped them around; told them that they did not belong in that neighborhood; and dropped them off in Canaryville, the most racist section of Bridgeport, where they were chased and beaten by a gang of white racists. Only weeks later, Leonard Bannister, an unarmed, twenty-four-year-old Black man, was shot in the head and killed while he held his hands in the air. Jeff, our PLO partner Stan Willis, and I were retained to represent Calvin McClin, Joseph Weaver, and the Bannister family.

While the Andrew Wilson trials and verdicts had been largely ignored by the mainstream media, these newer cases drew widespread media attention and became a rallying point in the African American community. There was already resentment that, barely a year after Harold Washington's death, another Daley had ascended to the mayoral throne to serve out Harold's second term. Richie Daley had defeated interim mayor Eugene Sawyer, an African American, in the primary, and, a month later, he defeated Harold Washington Party candidate Tim Evans in the general election. Both elections were racially charged; Daley was videotaped as saying, in a speech to a white ethnic group, "You want a white mayor to sit down with everybody." The resentment was further fueled by reports that Black victims of police abuse had been told, "You don't have a Black mayor to protect you anymore."

In mid-September, the Citywide Coalition Against Police Abuse, which now counted twenty-nine organizations among its members, led a demonstration at police headquarters. The demonstration linked the current wave of police violence with the call to suspend Burge, and our PLO partner Michael Deutsch, who was present, told the press that since Harold Washington had died, "Cases of racist police acts are on the increase all over the city," and that the OPS was "whitewashing cases."

The same day, protesters and victims of police violence jammed a police board hearing. Bishop Turner, representing the Dr. King Movement, told Superintendent Martin, OPS Director Fogel, and the board that, since Mayor Daley had come into office, it was "open warfare on Black folks." Angry witnesses likened the brutality to that of apartheid South Africa and repeated the refrain that the Chicago Police Department was the "biggest gang in Chicago," paraphrasing Martin's own public proclamation that his department was the "baddest gang in town." When Mary Powers demanded, on behalf of a coalition of twenty-nine organizations, that Burge be immediately suspended, Martin responded, "Burge is still working. I have no reason to suspend him at this time."

The outcry led to police brutality hearings before the city council's police and fire committee, chaired by veteran African American machine politician and former Chicago police officer William Beavers. Embattled, Mayor Daley took the highly unusual step of appearing before the committee as its first "witness." He delivered a statement in which he called the issue of police brutality "crucial to the welfare of the City." After emphasizing that drugs and crime, along with gangs and drug dealers, were an "epidemic" in "some communities," he commended police superintendent LeRoy Martin for his "outstanding" administration of the department and stressed that, while he condemned police brutality, the vast majority of officers "served with distinction." He denied that brutality and racially motivated incidents were on the rise. Instead, according to Daley, "What is on the rise is irresponsible political rhetoric." All Chicagoans should not only deplore "what happened to those two kids in Canaryville" but also should reject the suggestion that "from now on kids who need help should run in fear from Chicago police officers."

Daley entertained no questions and left after several African American aldermen, including committee member Bobby Rush, made statements condemning police brutality. Rush, our client two decades earlier when he was the minister of defense of the Black Panther Party, denied that shining a light on egregious police violence was political in nature, and he reinforced that brutality, particularly by "repeater officers," was a longstanding problem within the department.

The hearing went on for five days in late September and early October, in front of packed galleries, with victims of police violence telling their stories. The mother of Stanley Howard was among the witnesses who testified; she recounted how her son, who was locked up on death row, had been tortured into confessing at Area 2 by suffocation with a typewriter cover and plastic bag placed over his head while he was punched and kicked. His attackers included Burge's disciple, sergeant John Byrne, and she had filed an OPS complaint on her son's behalf. Superintendent Martin and OPS Director Fogel testified at the hearing, and both grudgingly admitted that there was a police code of silence operating within the Chicago Police Department. Most of the committee's venom focused on Fogel rather than on Martin, and Fogel seemed to be the prime candidate for the role of "fall guy."

On a rainy, late October Saturday, as many as a thousand mostly Black demonstrators marched through Bridgeport and Canaryville, chanting "Fight the power" and "Racism must go," and carrying signs, among them "This is Chicago, not Johannesburg" and "Bridgeport—the real South Africa." Led by Lew Myers, attorney for Operation PUSH, and a group called 500 Black Men, the marchers were flanked by more than a hundred police officers. The Reverend Jesse Jackson Jr. addressed the crowd beforehand, announcing, "We have zero tolerance for police brutality. . . . We're here today to declare Chicago a free and open city." Along the route the marchers were met by a small group of white people carrying an Irish flag and yelling "white power," and by scattered racial epithets and profanities, as they traveled from the street corner in Canaryville where Calvin and Joe were dropped off and beaten; past Comiskey Park, where they were picked up by the officers; and by the Ninth District police station, where the officers were assigned.

On the heels of the march, a two-day People's Tribunal was held at

Northeastern Illinois University in Chicago. Organized by the Citywide Coalition Against Police Abuse and several campus organizations, the tribunal featured several Northeastern professors, a minister, and Margaret Burroughs, director of the African American DuSable Museum. Jeff and Mariel led the prosecutorial team, which presented as witnesses a dozen victims of police violence, including Calvin, Joe, and family members of three victims fatally shot by the police. In the coalition's ongoing efforts to link the unfolding police torture scandal with the recent wave of police brutality, John and Dr. Kirschner testified about the systematic use of torture techniques, and I testified as an expert on the history of police torture. We were aware that the tribunal had no official power—except, crucially, in the court of public opinion, where we continued to apply pressure.

Shortly after the conclusion of the second *Wilson* trial, OPS director David Fogel had called our office and talked to Jeff. He had a surprising request: Would we send him a box of what we considered to be the most important evidence in Andrew's case, including another copy of the Illinois Supreme Court's decision? During his testimony at the October police brutality hearings, Fogel, in response to a question from alderwoman Dorothy Tillman, had revealed that he was "taking another look" at the Andrew Wilson case. He said that documents "were coming over by the basketfuls" and that he "did see the injuries" on Andrew. Alderwoman Tillman then asked if there were a pattern of young men, such as Stanley Howard and others, "constantly complaining that there are plastic bags being put over their heads to force them into confessions." Fogel evaded the clumsily worded question, saying, "I don't have a bunch of complaints about people putting plastic things over suspects' faces" in a "particular district."

We would not learn the details of what Fogel had done with the materials we sent him until I deposed him in another police brutality case, nearly three years later. Fogel, who at first denied having told me he would not reopen the Andrew Wilson case, testified at a 1992 deposition that he reviewed the evidence we sent him and was particularly swayed by the Illinois Supreme Court decision, the enlargements of the photos of Andrew's injuries, and by a conversation he had with Dr. Kirschner, whom he rightly recognized to be a torture expert. This evidence caused Fogel to conclude that "probably something happened here." Sometime in the fall of 1989 Fogel approached a young, politically ambitious assistant US attorney, Andrea Davis, and requested that the Feds initiate a federal criminal prosecution. She told Fogel that the statute of limitations was an obstacle unless there had been a cover-up. Fogel responded that there had indeed been one.

He testified that he repeatedly called Andrea Davis to follow up but received no response. As a result, in early 1990—right before he was shown the door, as Mayor Daley's sacrificial lamb—Fogel made a game-changing decision: he reopened the OPS investigation in Andrew Wilson's case and appointed two highly intelligent and politically independent investigators, Francine Sanders and Michael Goldston, to pursue the reinvestigation.

Shortly after the police brutality hearings, where Fogel denied there was a pattern of baggings in any particular police district, the Illinois Appellate Court issued a landmark decision in the Gregory Banks case. Gregory and his co-defendant, David Bates, were arrested for murder in late October 1983 and taken to Area 2 Violent Crimes, newly relocated in a complex on 111th Street, for interrogation. Burge's midnight crew, led by Sergeant Byrne and detectives Peter Dignan and Charles Grunhard, obtained confessions to the crime from both men. Gregory Banks later alleged that he confessed after Byrne put a revolver in his mouth and Dignan took out a plastic bag, said they had "something special for niggers," and placed the bag over Banks's head while kicking and punching him, which exacerbated the terrifying sense he was being suffocated. David Bates independently described a similar harrowing experience, including repeated baggings, at the hands of Byrne and Grunhard.

At their trial, in 1985, Gregory and David had moved to suppress their confessions and sought to call Lee Holmes, who had alleged, in an OPS complaint, that he was "bagged" by Byrne and Dignan thirteen months before Gregory and David were tortured. The trial judge denied both the request to call Lee Holmes as a witness and their motions to suppress, and both men were convicted, largely on the basis of their confessions. The Illinois Appellate Court's decision, which granted Gregory a new trial, cautioned, "The trial judge must keep in mind that ours is an adversary criminal justice system, and there must not be any naiveté that it is otherwise. The stark realities of our adversary criminal justice system are such that what occurs within the confines of a police station during custodial interrogation when there is no attorney present is not always what the unsophisticated would expect."

The appeals court then made a powerful condemnation of racially motivated police torture:

We believe that this case is another reminder of the grave responsibility that trial judges have and must be willing to exercise when ruling on motions to suppress based on charges of police brutality and racial intimidation. If our constitutional rights and guarantees are to be in fact enjoyed equally by all our citizens, trial judges must ensure that those suspected of crimes do not relinquish their constitutional rights and guarantees solely because they become matched up against an uncaring or overzealous law enforcement officer who may be bent on obtaining a confession without regard to the suspect's constitutional rights and guarantees. In this regard, trial judges must bear in mind that while we no longer see cases involving the use of the rack and thumbscrew to obtain confessions, we are seeing cases, like the present case, involving punching, kicking and placing a plastic bag over a suspect's head to obtain confessions.

The court then took Gregory Banks's trial judge to task, in a statement that had wide application in the torture cases:

When trial judges do not courageously and forthrightly exercise their responsibility to suppress confessions obtained by such means, they pervert our criminal justice system as much as the few misguided law enforcement officers who obtain confessions in utter disregard of the rights guaranteed to every citizen—including criminal suspects—by our constitution. Moreover, trial judges must be most circumspect when it appears that a right guaranteed to every citizen by our Constitution may have been violated by police brutality or racial discrimination, for those affected are invariably the poorest, the weakest and the least educated, who are not sophisticated enough or do not have the resources to see and ensure that they are not denied the protections afforded by the rights and guarantees of our Constitution.

Gregory had made an OPS complaint, so the pattern of Area 2–related bagging complaints that Fogel had refused to recognize was, in fact, documented at the time of Gregory's testimony by OPS complaints in the cases of Andrew Wilson, Stanley Howard, Lee Holmes, Roy Brown, and Walter Johnson.

"House of Screams"

As Fogel was reopening the investigation in early 1990, investigative reporter John Conroy published a 20,000-word exposé, "House of Screams," in the *Chicago Reader*, an independent weekly similar to New York's *Village Voice*. At the suggestion of a friend, Conroy had attended the first day of Andrew's trial because he was working on a book on torture in democratic countries. He was aware of the torture of Irish Republican Army members by British soldiers and of Palestinians by Israeli military officers; the Andrew Wilson case, his friend suggested, offered a possible third example in the United States. After attending the two *Wilson* trials and conducting additional investigation and interviews, John wrote "House of Screams" with the hope it would generate a wide public response and prod the establishment media to seriously address the issue of police torture in Chicago.

Conroy's article offered a detailed recitation of much of the important testimony at the back-to-back trials; a depiction of the courtroom drama, hostility, and tedium; glimpses into the personalities and backgrounds of Andrew, Burge, Duff, the lawyers, and other witnesses; and an analysis of torture and its perpetrators.

While in the army, Conroy wrote, Burge was a drill instructor who volunteered twice to go to Vietnam, where his actions earned him two commendations for valor, both times for dragging wounded men back to safety amid enemy fire. He also was awarded the Bronze Star, the Vietnamese Cross of Gallantry, and a Purple Heart. As a twenty-four-year-old police officer, Patrolman Burge responded to a call of a "woman with a gun" and, when Burge arrived on the scene, the woman was pointing a .22-caliber Derringer at her own throat. After about an hour and a half of fielding her requests to return home and confer with a priest, Burge sensed that the distraught woman was likely to pull the trigger, so he made a move for the gun. She did pull the trigger, but Burge had managed to jam his thumb into the firing mechanism, so the gun did not fire. Conroy also noted that, seventeen years later, Burge was standing trial as a commander who "outranked 99 percent of the policemen in the city."

Relying on a 1988 pre-sentence report compiled by a social worker in Andrew Wilson's criminal case, Conroy contrasted Andrew's background with Burge's. Andrew was the third of nine children; his father worked as a machine operator and his mother worked as a waitress. They lived in a three-bedroom house on the far south side of Chicago, a house described as "neat, clean, and nicely furnished, with an electric organ and a small library." When Andrew was in first grade, he was diagnosed as "educable mentally handicapped." At the age of seven, he scored seventy-three on an IQ test, at age eleven he scored seventy-eight, and at age fifteen he scored seventy. The social worker concluded that Wilson was not diagnosed properly as a child, and that his low IQ scores were probably the result of a learning disability that was never identified or treated.

At eleven Andrew began to skip school and periodically to run away from home, sleeping in old cars in the neighborhood. According to his parents, they would "whup him . . . It didn't help. . . . We just couldn't control him." At thirteen he was sent to a school for children with behavioral problems. At fourteen he started stealing. He was committed to another special school, ran away after six weeks, and ended up in a juvenile detention center. At fifteen he was convicted of burglary, after which he spent time in a reformatory. Andrew was given a neurological exam, the results of which suggested an organic brain dysfunction. A reformatory doctor put him on tranquilizers for emotional disturbance and hyperactivity, and on an anticonvulsive medication used for treating seizure disorders. After about two years, his prescriptions were stopped. According to the social worker, Andrew "was never again given a neurological exam nor assessed for his need for anticonvulsive medication."

According to the social worker, Andrew had two daughters, born in 1971 and 1973. The girls' mother believed Andrew to be a good father and said he was very generous with his daughters. During Andrew's subsequent stays in prison, he took up knitting and crocheting, and his daughters, who were by then teenagers, said that their father had knitted them numerous scarves, hats, and headbands. "The girls reported that when they talk to him on the phone," Andrew "tries to teach us manners . . . wants us to be polite. . . . Dad always talks to us about school . . . how important school is, especially reading. . . . He tells us . . . 'Do good, and when you read in class, read for me.'" Both daughters were "bright and academically successful." Summarizing, the social worker called Andrew "an institutionalized person. Having spent much of his life since 1967 in institutions, he functions well in that setting. His ability to function in the community is severely limited. . . . Emotionally, he functions at an adolescent level. He has been impulsive and has been unable to accept delayed gratification. . . . he has learned not to work for what he has wanted; he chose, instead, to take it."

After delving into these contrasting personalities, Conroy set the stage for the trial:

In the public mind, Andrew Wilson was known only by the label "cop killer." So when opening arguments began on his civil suit in Judge Duff's court last February, the odds against him were more than considerable. He was a murderer. Burge was a war hero. Anarchy was suing order. The underclass was having a go at the establishment. In more than one sense it seemed to be a confrontation of black versus white.

Conroy went on to note that there was also "a case building against the city of Chicago." He found special significance in an explanation that one our witnesses, Mrs. Davis, gave on cross-examination—that she did not file an OPS complaint because she "thought that the police could do anything they wanted." After discussing the witnesses who were victimized during the manhunt, Conroy stated what had become obvious to him: "It often seemed there were two cultures in conflict in the courtroom. One was black, poor, given to violence, and often in trouble with the law. The other was white, respectable, given to violence, and in charge of enforcing the law."

Conroy tracked the Melvin Jones revelations, noting, with understatement, that Duff's rationale for barring the Jones evidence at the second trial was "hard to follow." He concluded that "the most amazing aspect of the second trial was not Judge Duff's rulings, but the detectives' revamped defense." He called William Coleman a "totally unbelievable witness to those who knew his record," adding, "but the jury did not know most of it." He recited Coleman's aliases: "Mark Krammer, Paul Roberts, Richard Hallaran, R. W. Stevenson, Doctor Roberts, W. Van der Vim, Peter Karl William, John Simmons, and Alfred Clarkson," noting that he had "served time in prisons in England, Ireland, Germany, Holland, Monaco, Hong Kong, and the United States" and had "been convicted of fraud, theft, perjury, manslaughter, and blackmail."

To everyone's surprise, Conroy wrote, the second trial's jury of six suburbanites deliberated for three days and then delivered a verdict that "on its face, made no sense." In an attempt at clarification, Conroy talked to the jury foreman, who, in a taped interview, gave what Conroy described as a "circuitous" explanation:

> He said that he believed the witnesses who testified that the police had run amok in their search for the killers of Fahey and O'Brien, and as a result he believed that there had been a policy of abuse. He did not, however, believe that Wilson was injured under that policy. He said he thought that if the detectives at Area 2 were able to abuse Wilson at will, knowing that no one in the department or the city would do anything about it, they would have abused him in such a way as to not leave any marks. Leaving marks, he said,

was the one way the public and the media could find out that Wilson was beaten. "If anything, I believe it was an emotional outburst by them, and that was the reason why he suffered his injuries. I don't think it necessarily had to be done under this policy."

Conroy then asked, "So you believed that Burge and his colleagues had tortured Wilson?" The foreman replied:

I'm not saying that. We believe that he did sustain these injuries from the police, some of the injuries, but there wasn't enough evidence to show that he got all of the injuries from the police. As to whether or not he was actually tortured, there is not enough evidence either. . . . We did agree that he got those injuries from someone, but as far as being specific as to who actually did the damage, there just wasn't enough evidence. . . . You know convicts, a lot of these guys are streetwise and they're pretty good at bullshitting."

"House of Screams" concluded with a disquisition on torture and torturers. From his observations in court and a post-trial interview with Burge, Conroy had found him "likeable." He cited a study of Nazi doctors that found torturers to be "quite normal people" and another study that concluded that Greek torturers were not "sadists. Torture was just part of their jobs." He cited to the literature that found that torturers dehumanized their victims, and that torture "becomes a method of controlling a community by intimidation, so in the end, the torturer's purpose is served no matter who the victim is or whether he or she is innocent or guilty." Conroy also offered as an explanation Nazi Adolf Eichmann's notorious defense--"I obeyed. Regardless of what I was ordered to do, I would have obeyed." Conroy then posited:

If one believes Wilson's description of the course of events, it follows that a fair number of policemen knew something strange was going on in that closed room, both that day and on others; perhaps they do not come forward because someone in charge sanctioned the operation.

"Why does the US attorney not investigate?" Conroy asked. He then proposed an answer:

Perhaps because no one believes it can happen here. Perhaps there is no investigation simply because, as other nations have found, torture is an intimate affair, something that happens among a few adults behind a closed door, something that is hard to prove afterward because the accused—often decorated soldiers who have served their country in a time of crisis—deny the allegations, and the victims are terrorists, alleged terrorists, associates of terrorists, associates of associates, subversives, dissidents, criminals, rioters, stone throwers, sympathizers, or relatives of the above.

CHAPTER 9

Fire Burge!

"House of Screams" fell on deaf ears when it came to the Chicago media. Michael Miner, the *Reader*'s media reporter, ran a follow-up piece entitled "Silent Screams," in which he quoted a *Sun Times* reporter's explanation for the paper's silence on the subject: "I don't know that the *Sun Times* follows up on projects in other publications" and that the *Sun Times* editors had pursued the story "sufficiently for their needs and tastes, or for the needs and tastes of our readers."

Miner reported that "House of Screams" had been read by the Midwest director of Amnesty International (AI), Marjorie Byler, who faxed it to AI's London headquarters. We had been sending her materials on Area 2 torture for the past year. Byler acknowledged that AI's acting US researcher had also reviewed the Area 2 torture file and had composed a letter to Illinois attorney general Neil Hartigan, in his position as the "highest law enforcement officer in the state." In "Silent Screams," Miner quoted Byler about why AI was getting involved:

> We define torture as the use of excessive force during interrogations carried out by official representatives of police forces, security forces or the military, usually with the collusion or some amount of awareness by the government. This is to separate it from police brutality, which is widespread, but which Amnesty doesn't work on.

Miner then observed, with evident cynicism, "As journalists we would define serious allegations of police torture as a big, big, local story. But it is a story that a newspaper might not want to touch."

Meanwhile, Francine Sanders—appointed, along with Michael Goldston, to reinvestigate the Andrew Wilson case—was taking her assignment very seriously. She tracked me down in late March 1990, and we began to supply her access to deposition and trial testimony and to answer questions about the evidence and the trials. Over the next few months,

John Stainthorp and I would have more than a dozen meetings and conversations with Sanders, and we hoped fervently that her work would not go for naught. A concerning factor, however, was Daley's appointment of a high-ranking assistant state's attorney named Gayle Shines, who had worked for Daley when he ran the state's attorney's office, to replace David Fogel as OPS director. This led us to fear that the new OPS investigation would likely see the same outcome as the original: "not sustained."

On the legal front, our appeal of the jury's confounding verdict was proceeding at a snail's pace. Judge Duff had messed up the final judgment order and had then unsuccessfully attempted to use his own error to prevent us from appealing. While this charade was unfolding, we decided, in June 1990, to file Deep Badge's letters in open court, so that the Court of Appeals could see that they in fact existed. We continued our search for more torture victims, and around this time we informed Francine Sanders about a prisoner who said that he had been bagged by Burge in October 1985. His name was Shadeed Mu'min, and Jeff interviewed him in prison.

Shadeed, a middle-aged African American man, told Jeff that he was arrested and placed in an interrogation room at Area 2. Both of his hands were cuffed so tightly to a ring in the wall that, after thirty minutes or so, his hands became numb. Burge then came into the room and asked him about a robbery. When Shadeed denied knowledge of the crime, Burge promised him that he would talk, and left. When Burge returned, Shadeed continued to deny knowledge. Burge became angry, said he was "a hard nigger to deal with," uncuffed him, and took him to his office down the hall. After calling him a "damn fool" for not talking, and threatening to "blow his Black fucking brains out," Burge pulled a long, silver-barreled .44 Magnum revolver out of a desk drawer and unloaded it—except, Shadeed thought, for one bullet. Burge spun the carriage, pointed the barrel at Shadeed's head, then slowly snapped the trigger three times. After the gun did not fire, Burge said, "You're damn lucky I didn't kill you."

Shadeed said that Burge, with increasing anger, then jumped up from behind his desk, grabbed a brown vinyl typewriter cover, and forced it over Shadeed's head, pushing the plastic into his face. Not able to breathe, Shadeed, thinking that he was going to die, passed out. Burge repeated this dry submarino two more times until Shadeed said he would sign a confession to the robbery. Burge, apparently having learned his lesson from the torture of Andrew Wilson, told Shadeed, "If you tell somebody, no one will believe you because there are no marks on you," and threatened that Shadeed would "get it even worse" than "what I did to you now" if he did not sign the confession when the assistant state's attorney came in the morning.

During the summer and fall, the activist struggle intensified. The Citywide Coalition Against Police Abuse circulated a petition to Mayor Daley and Superintendent Martin, and raised for the first time as one of its demands that the Chicago Police Department "pay reparations to the victims" of police torture.

Together with the Task Force to Prevent Police Violence, the coalition also led a demonstration at the Area 3 police station, on the southwest side of Chicago, where Burge was assigned as commander. According to the 10:00 o'clock news reports, hundreds of protesters marched on the street outside Burge's station, and video showed a line of police officers protecting the sealed red brick building. The news coverage was also quick to note that Burge had been cleared of torturing Andrew, and that the mounting allegations of torture "were not proven." One news report quoted Superintendent Martin as saying that he "[would] read a transcript from the *Wilson* trial."

The Task Force to Prevent Police Violence had emerged as a more radical offshoot of the coalition. Jeff, untethered at the moment from being a trial lawyer, and Mariel were the primary leaders of the group, predominantly composed of white activists, lawyers, and law students. Its attention was focused on pressuring the city council to hold a hearing on police torture. As a result of the group's lobbying, Marlene Carter, an African American alderwoman from the west side, introduced a resolution, cosponsored by twelve of her progressive colleagues, calling for hearings on torture by Jon Burge. Alderman Ed Burke, in an obvious attempt to bury the resolution, sent it to the council's rules committee.

Burke, collaborating with another powerful machine alderman, Richard Mell, attempted to quiet Alderwoman Carter by writing her a pointed letter asking that she "withhold any further action" because her resolution "not only questions the professionalism and integrity of various Chicago police officers, but also implicates fundamental issues relating to the operation of one of the city's most important departments." Carter, who had been consulting with Jeff and Mariel throughout this battle, shot back, "There is no place on the Chicago Police Department for a torturer, certainly not setting an example as Commander of Detectives." She then squarely raised the issue of racism: "I question if any of the persons making the allegations were white, whether there would be such reluctance to have public hearings." She followed up two days later with a press release demanding that "Alderman Mell stop condoning police torture."

In early fall, the task force upped the ante, staging a disruptive demonstration inside city council chambers while it was in session. About twenty demonstrators stood, blew whistles, and demanded that Burge be fired. The *Sun Times* reported that Mayor Daley "was angered that City Hall police responded slowly to the protest."

While the demand for Burge's firing swirled in the council chambers, OPS investigators Francine Sanders and Michael Goldston were completing their investigation and reports. On September 28, 1990, Goldston submitted his report to OPS chief administrator Gayle Shines. Goldston had created a computer database with fifty Area 2 victims, the majority of whom he had obtained from our court filings and transcripts, and performed what he called an "intersection study." While the great majority of the thirty victims whose information he had obtained from us were subjected to electric shock, baggings, or Russian roulette, he also obtained, from OPS files and other sources, information on an additional twenty victims subjected to other kinds of physical abuse by Area 2 officers. Goldston, tasked by his OPS bosses to address two specific questions, provided answers, supported by six appendices, that mirrored what we had been asserting for the past year.

In answer to the first question ("Determine if there was systematic abuse at Area 2 during this period") he found that, for the time period from 1973 to 1985:

> The preponderance of the evidence is that abuse did occur and that it was systematic. The time span involved covers more than ten years. The type of abuse described was not limited to the usual beating, but went into such esoteric areas as psychological techniques and planned torture. The evidence presented by some individuals convinced juries and appellate courts that personnel assigned to Area 2 engaged in methodical abuse.

His answer to the second question ("If so, determine the culpability, if any, of Area 2 Command personnel") would send shivers down the collective spine of the Chicago police brass, particularly of its superintendent:

> The number of incidents in which an Area 2 command member is identified as an accused can lead to only one conclusion. Particular command members were aware of the systematic abuse and perpetuated it either by actively participating in same or failing to take any action to bring it to an end.

On October 26, 1990, Francine Sanders tendered her report to Shines. Sanders had read and analyzed all of the voluminous testimony from the Wilson cases that we had supplied her, and her sixty-six-page report discussed this evidence in painstaking detail. She made findings, based on the "overwhelming body of evidence which supports the allegations," that administrative charges of excessive force should be sustained against Jon Burge and John Yucaitis, including that they "repeatedly administered electrical stimulation to Mr. [Andrew] Wilson's body in order to create pain" and that Burge "held Mr. Wilson, while handcuffed, against a hot radiator causing burns to Mr. Wilson's face, chest and thigh." She also recommended that charges be sustained against Burge, Yucaitis, and O'Hara for their "decision to ignore the wrongdoing," their "failure to take any action to stop" or report it, and for their failure to provide prompt medical attention.

A week later, unbeknownst to us, Administrator Shines surprisingly approved the reports in a strongly worded letter to Superintendent Martin accompanying the thick binder containing the OPS "Special Project." The project was presented in two sections: Sanders's report, *Analysis of Wilson Case*; and Goldston's report, *History of Allegations of Misconduct by Area 2 Personnel*. In her cover letter to Martin, Shines underscored that Goldston's assignment was to "determine if there was systematic abuse at Area 2 during this period, and, if so, determine the culpability, if any, of Area 2 command personnel." In conclusion, Shines told Martin—who had succeeded Milton Deas as the commander of Area 2 for the torture-filled year of 1983—that "both investigators have done a masterful job of marshaling the facts in this intensive and extensive project and their conclusions are compelling."

Just after the top-secret OPS report was tendered to Superintendent Martin, aldermen Richard Mell and Eddie Burke, unable to completely bury the demand for a hearing on police torture, came up with a new strategy: they scheduled the hearing for Christmas Eve, when the news media would be working with skeleton crews, and their news editors and the general public would be focused on Christmas cheer. In addition, the testimony would be heard by a subcommittee of Burke's finance committee rather than by the fire and police committee. Alderwoman Carter blasted Burke in the *Daily Defender* for setting the hearing when "no one would read it, hear it, or see it."

I was the first witness at the hearing. Assisted by Mariel Nanasi, I presented a raft of exhibits, including the black shock box, blowups of the photos of Andrew Wilson's injuries, and a twenty-one-page fact sheet that documented forty-three cases of torture and related interrogation abuse. Alderman Burke made it clear that the hearing would not go past noon, quipping, in a statement that brought laughter and some clapping from the press in attendance: "The distinguished members of the Fourth Estate would like to get out by noon and go back to their office parties." He introduced former Democratic machine judge Louis Garippo, who had been the judge in Anthony "Satan" Holmes's case in the early 1970s, as his "special counsel," and later informed allies of Alderwoman Carter that there would be no vote on her resolution, only a "majority report," prepared by the judge.

I went right to our fact sheet and cataloged the many allegations of electric shock, suffocation, Russian roulette, beatings with telephone books, hangings by the handcuffs, beatings on the genitals and the bottoms of the feet, and the repeated use of racial epithets against victims of color. Invoking Superintendent Martin's testimony from a few months before, "Where there's smoke there's fire," I condemned the police department and the state's attorney's office for not investigating or "seeing the pattern that was developing." I pointed out that Burge was consistently promoted: that "was the message" sent to Chicago police officers.

I told the committee that Area 2 torture was starting to garner international attention from Amnesty International and had been discussed at an international conference on torture in Brazil. When asked whether there was an open OPS reinvestigation of Andrew's torture, I showed my limited knowledge of its progress, and said, "I have no confidence that anything but a 'not sustained' will come, no matter what." I told the finance committee that, to date, its chairman, alderman Ed Burke, had authorized $750,000 in fees to Kunkle's and Devine's law firm for its work defending Burge in Andrew Wilson's case.

During my testimony, a man in attendance cried out, "Black people should not go to sleep. This is what happened to the Jews in Nazi Germany when Hitler was in charge. That is what they do with us."

Singling out Burge and his confederates, I offered more of a lawyer's closing argument than the testimony of a disinterested witness, saying that the police department "should not be promoting—which they are—should not be rewarding—which they are—but should be disciplining and removing them from its force. That is what we ask be done with Commander Burge and the others who are named repeatedly."

Dr. Kirschner was next. He testified to his finding, with a high degree of medical and scientific certainty, that "in fact Mr. Wilson was tortured at the time of his arrest and that he did receive the burns and electric shocks that he claims he had received." Alderman Burke tried to shut down his testimony, but the Black council members in attendance took up the questioning. Kirschner drew a parallel between torture and child abuse, in that child abuse by definition must be inflicted by the child's custodian while torture must be inflicted by a government official.

Alderwoman Carter then asked about a "Tucker Telephone." Dr. Kirschner, pointing to the black box sitting next to him, gave testimony that he had been barred by Judge Duff from presenting at Andrew's trials:

> This would be the equivalent to a Tucker Telephone. I say with a degree of embarrassment the Tucker Telephone is named after a physician at an Arkansas prison farm, who devised a device like this, and this has been used all around the world, where one uses a hand crank generator from a hand crank telephone to create an instrument for punishing prisoners.

Demonstrating by cranking the handle on the box, Dr. Kirschner continued:

> They would hook the prisoner up to the hand crank telephone, and if they wanted to punish him a little bit, they would make a local call like this, and if they wanted to punish him a lot, they would keep going like that.

The next witness was Alderman Danny Davis, a longtime progressive politician from Chicago's west side, who was mounting a grassroots campaign to challenge Richie Daley in the upcoming February primary election. Eloquent in the style of a southern Baptist preacher, Alderman Davis underscored the "clear relationship between brutality and racism" and called for the replacement of the OPS with a civilian review board, which, in his view, would go a long way to restoring the fractured relationship between communities of color and the police. He read excerpts from John Conroy's "House of Screams," including this chilling line: "Seven years after the crime, Andrew Wilson comes back to haunt the city, telling a tale of torture fit for some third world dictatorship."

Alderman Robert Shaw, an African American south side council member who had broken with the Daley machine on brutality issues, shed light on the way the torture scandal reflected the dawning era of mass incarceration, stating, "We need to look at the court system as it relates to black and Hispanic defendants. When black defendants go before these judges, some of these judges don't give a damn, and they go right on and just disregard their rights."

As the clock approached Burke's midday witching hour, Reverend Don Benedict gave the final witness presentation. The former chairman of the Chicago Ethics Board, Reverend Benedict offered an alternative to Alderwoman Carter's concerns about the timing of the hearing, finding it "most appropriate that this alleged flagrant use of force on the part of police, including torture and brutality, be brought to the public attention on the eve of the celebration of the birth of the prince of justice and peace." He hoped that the committee and the press "may have their hearts and minds made more sensitive because of the proximity of this most holy day."

Alderman Shaw, harboring far less confidence in the committee, moved that the minority be afforded counsel and the right to file a minority report, but Chairman Burke curtly tabled his request and adjourned the hearing.

Much to our own holiday cheer, Burke's plan to bury news of the hearing backfired. Whether it was the stark contrast between torture and Christmas, or just a slow news cycle, both the Christmas Eve TV news and the Christmas Day papers featured coverage of the hearing. Channel 9, the *Tribune*'s TV station, ran the most comprehensive piece, showing the photos of Andrew's injuries, mentioning the forty-three victims of torture on the fact sheet and the Illinois Supreme Court's decision in Andrew Wilson's case, and offering a sound bite of "Flynn Taylor" testifying that "these forms of incredibly barbaric police conduct should be stopped in this city in the year 1990 on Christmas Eve." Alderwoman Carter said, "We want something done. These are African American men who have suffered torture and abuse and no one is paying attention." Alderman Burke countered that the committee had no power to discipline Burge, who had the right to due process. Burge chimed in, during a reported phone interview, that the charges were "spurious."

In the Christmas Day *Sun Times*, city hall reporter Fran Spielman's piece emphasized mayoral candidate Danny Davis's call for a citizens' review board, recited the various alleged torture techniques discussed at the hearing, and added that I contended that the forty-three cases were only the "tip of the iceberg." She reported that Burge had not attended the hearing "on the advice of his attorney," repeated the "decorated Vietnam War veteran's" categorical denial of any wrongdoing, and voiced Burge's complaint that "the number of alleged victims goes up every time that idiot speaks." ("That idiot" being me.)

The next day, *Daily Defender* reporter Chinta Strausberg wrote, under the headline "Burge Denies Charges of Running a 'Horror Chamber,'" that Burge, after registering his claim that he "was innocent," had told her sarcastically that Flint Taylor "might know of 500 cases." Strausberg further reported that African American alderman John Steele was "calling on black officers who worked at Area 2 at the time of the alleged tortures to come forth and tell what they know." Steele condemned the CPD for promoting Burge "up the rank" and said that if he remained on the force, "the next promotion Burge will get will be police superintendent."

The public struggle got a major boost the next month as Amnesty International, after much prodding from the coalition and the task force, published a report, signed by its international secretary general, Ian Martin, entitled *Allegations of Police Torture in Illinois*. The report detailed the evidence of Andrew Wilson's torture and referred to the other allegations of Chicago police torture, the OPS's failure to sustain any of the allegations, and the Illinois Supreme Court's decision in Andrew's case. Most importantly, AI, for the first time in an official report, defined the allegations of "systematic" torture as setting forth violations of international human rights law and of the provisions of the United Nations Convention Against Torture:

> Amnesty International opposes the torture or other cruel, inhuman or degrading treatment or punishment of all prisoners without reservation. It calls on governments to implement the provisions of the United Nations Declaration on the Protection of All Persons from Torture and Other Cruel, Inhuman or Degrading Treatment or Punishment. This Declaration stipulates that governments are responsible for investigating torture allegations, instituting criminal proceedings in torture cases and compensating its victims.

As part of the report, AI included the letter it had sent nearly a year before, to the attorney general of Illinois and to the US attorney for the Northern District of Illinois, requesting an independent investigation. The report set forth that AI's letter had been ignored by the US attorney and was answered after three months by the Illinois first assistant attorney general, Joseph Claps. In his response, Claps, who would later become a Cook County criminal court judge, praised the OPS as an independent civilian investigative body and politely passed the buck to the Cook County state's attorney's office. Undeterred, AI concluded its report by stating that it had written to the Cook County state's attorney as well as the newly appointed

US attorney, and had "also called on the Chicago city authorities to insti-gate a full inquiry into the allegations."

The AI report was announced at a press conference orchestrated by the task force. The black shock box was displayed by task force co-chair Jennifer Modell, a law student who had worked in our office. She demon-strated how the box worked and condemned the "pattern and practice of racist brutality." Jeff showed the blowups of the photos of Andrew's ears, Mariel called out Daley for "doing nothing," and I discussed publicly for the first time how we had been contacted during the trial by Deep Badge. The *Southtown Economist* (where we had placed the ads Deep Badge had requested) ran my description in detail.

The press conference garnered widespread television and newspaper coverage, forcing Daley, after first issuing a "no comment" response, to speak publicly about the allegations of police torture. He was quoted as saying that the allegations were "false," and on-camera sound bites showed him saying it was "hard to believe" that AI and the task force were "con-demning an entire police department, federal prosecutors, the Justice Department, the State's Attorney, everybody." Kunkle came out of the woodwork to question the task force's "political motivation" for releas-ing the report during the mayoral election season and praised Burge as a "tough and effective cop." In his commentary on the evening news, Clar-ence Page, an African American reporter, spoke of the right of all citizens, even cop killers, to a fair trial, untainted by torture. Referring to the bête noire leaders of the era, he concluded that "only evil dictators like Saddam Hussein or Manuel Noriega would torture a confession out of somebody, or at least that is what many Americans like to tell the world."

Even with the increasing attention to the torture cases, the media coverage remained slanted and skeptical. John Stainthorp, Mary Johnson, Jennifer Modell, and alderwoman Marlene Carter appeared on a local CBS Sunday morning television talk show, *Common Ground*, that was moder-ated by Phil Ponce, a young colleague of Clarence Page. Ponce acknowl-edged that the AI report had "stunned some people in Chicago," then grilled the guests about Wilson, the cop killer, and posed a question he said people were asking: "Who cares?" John responded that "society should care" about electric shocking on the genitals, other forms of torture, and the violation of international law. Alderwoman Carter declared, "No one wants to talk about torture." Reminding Ponce and panelists that she was a proud daughter of a cop, she walked a fine line when asked about the task force's allegations that Chicago police torture and brutality was racist in nature. Alderwoman Carter pointed out that most of the brutalizers were white and most of the victims were "Black and Hispanic"; she then exhibited her political instincts, concluding that the situation was not about "Black and white" but about "right and wrong."

Riding this wave of publicity, representatives of the task force and the coalition met with Superintendent Martin and OPS Director Shines in Martin's office at police headquarters. Shines told the group that the OPS had finished its investigation and that she had sent the project to the superintendent, but Martin appeared to be unaware and asked Shines to look for it, then and there, on his desk. He promised to read it and make the OPS findings publicly available within two weeks.

Martin must have read the reports immediately after the meeting, because he shot a memo back to Shines. In his February 9, 1991, memo, he asked for "additional information and work on the project." Not surprisingly, given Goldston's condemnation of "command personnel" at Area 2, he showed the most skepticism about Goldston's methodology and findings. He asked to see Goldston's files; requested a detailed explanation of the spreadsheet appendices; inquired where Goldston discovered the names of the victims and why he thought them credible; and, in a mixed message, wrote, "I would suggest that we report 'only the facts' and leave editorial and/or personal comment out of this otherwise very well done draft."

He was more praising of Sanders's report, but, there too, complained about "detracting editorial comment." He also asked to see the physical evidence, the Illinois Supreme Court decision, and, with emphasis, asked for "some justification why in the face of several court cases this investigation appears to arrive at a different result!!" In conclusion, he asked to meet with Shines at her "earliest convenience."

The two white officers who, in September 1989, assaulted our clients Calvin McClin and Joseph Weaver, then dropped them in Canaryville to be chased and beaten, had been charged with official misconduct and battery. The case went to trial on April 1, 1991. When a police officer or public official is tried for a criminal offense in Cook County, very often the officer's lawyer elects to take a bench trial before a law-enforcement-friendly judge rather than running the risk of being convicted by a conscientious jury. The officers and their veteran Fraternal Order of Police (FOP) lawyer, Joe Roddy, had drawn judge Ralph Reyna, a former Cook County prosecutor with close ties to the FOP and the Daley machine. Normally a "hang 'em" judge when it came to poor defendants of color, Reyna acquitted the officers the next day.

The reaction was swift. Lew Myers, on behalf of 500 Black Men; the task force; the McClin and Weaver families; and our staff convened an angry press conference at our downtown office. Lew Myers declared that the judge's decision "perpetrates the perception that there can be no justice for the poor, the dispossessed and members of the black community." He called on Martin and Daley to move swiftly to fire the cops, and for the federal Department of Justice to bring criminal civil rights charges against the officers. Next, in late April, the task force and 500 Black Men led another march into Daley's Bridgeport neighborhood, this time starting at the Ninth District police station and passing by the mayor's house, braving a steady rain and racist taunts. Impelled by the acquittals; by the brutal, videotaped beating of Rodney King by the Los Angeles Police Department the previous month; and by the City of Chicago's continuing failure to suspend or fire Jon Burge, more than two hundred marchers were met by an equal number of men in blue, lining the march route. Calvin bravely stood in front of the police station and recounted his moment of terror: "The police knocked us around and dropped us off where they knew we'd get hurt, and a gang of white boys chased us and beat me up so bad I was in the hospital for a week." In a statement with wide applicability for Black youth then and now, Calvin continued, "I'll tell you one thing, the next time the police tell me to get in the car, I don't think I'll be so free to do so." On behalf of the task force, attorney Tim Lohraff spoke about the unraveling police torture scandal and slammed Daley for refusing to act while state's attorney.

The next week, OPS Director Shines responded to Superintendent Martin's letter demanding more information and explanation. Holding her investigators' ground, Shines attached a detailed "clarifying" memo from Michael Goldston, defining thirty-five terms used in his study. In these definitions, he discussed the interplay of the various factors that informed his conclusions that there was a pattern of police torture at Area 2, and that command staff were aware of, and participated in, the torture. He explicitly named as primary participants ("players," he called them) seven Area 2 actors, five of whom—Burge, Yucaitis, Byrne, Dignan, and Grunhard— had been independently identified by Deep Badge as Area 2 "asskickers."

Shines actively defended Francine Sanders and her findings, dismissing Martin's claim about editorial comments and asserting that Sanders's findings were "not inconsistent with prior decisions and reflect the unprecedented comprehensiveness of this investigation." She also informed Martin that the city's corporation counsel, Kelly Welsh, had reviewed the reports, at Martin's request, and had dismissed the possibility of criminal prosecutions because of the six-year statute of limitations. In so doing, he, like the federal prosecutors before him, willfully ignored the more recent allegations of torture, some of which were clearly within the statute; the concept of an ongoing criminal conspiracy to torture and cover-up; and the potential charges of police perjury and obstruction of justice in the *Wilson* civil proceedings.

Shines green-lighted Sanders to restart her investigation, which had been paused in the six months since her report was submitted. The next phase was to present Burge, Yucaitis, and O'Hara with the allegations and to take their statements. Shine presented the allegations in mid-May, but, instead of the officers giving statements, Kunkle intervened on their behalf and demanded a highly unusual alternative: he would file a document arguing why charges should not be sustained. Shines granted his request, and in July, Kunkle submitted a 125-page document that regurgitated the defense evidence and arguments he had presented at the trials.

At an early July press conference, the task force revealed details about the February meeting with Shines and Martin, speculated that the CPD was suppressing the report, and demanded that the "OPS release its findings on the allegations of torture against Burge and the City take action on these findings and immediately initiate proceedings to fire Burge."

The next week, Amnesty International increased the pressure on the City when it released its annual survey of human rights violations around the world. The survey, as the *Chicago Reader* reported, "singled out the Chicago Police Department" by "reporting allegations that between 1972 and 1984 officers at Area 2 headquarters on the south side 'had systematically tortured or otherwise ill-treated more than 20 people.'"

A veteran reporter named Phil Walters followed up with a piece on NBC Channel 5 that questioned whether the report was being "covered up." Superintendent Martin responded, on camera, "There is no cover-up, how can I cover it up, this thing is not going away." Phil included in his story the anonymous letters from Deep Badge, showing, for the first time in public, a close-up of them (shot in our conference room). As the camera zoomed in on one of the letters, Phil read aloud the phrase, "The common cord is Burge."

In mid-August, Mary Powers and several other coalition members met again with Martin at his office. He made another "two week" promise; in a follow-up letter, Mary Powers reminded him of the complaints she had filed two years before on behalf of Andrew Wilson, Melvin Jones, and Donald White, and also requested that the allegations of the forty other known Burge victims be investigated.

In late September, after Burge and his associates had signed Kunkle's document, Francine Sanders filed a twenty-eight-page *Supplemental Summary Report* that rebutted, point by point, each of Kunkle's main contentions. She emphasized that Andrew Wilson had "consistently told the same basic story," that "the accused have provided significantly inconsistent explanations for Wilson's injuries," and that Andrew's story was "consistent with the preponderance of medical opinion and physical evidence." Therefore, she recommended that "the findings presented in the primary report remain unchanged."

Two nights later, Area 3 detectives rounded up eleven young African American men, most of them juveniles, on a murder charge. The main officers involved had been part of Burge's midnight crew of "asskickers" at Area 2 and had been brought over to work for Burge when he became Area 3 commander in January 1988. One of the supervising sergeants that night was Jack Byrne, Burge's self-proclaimed "right-hand man," who had previously been a point man for the "asskickers." According to the arrested youth, they were subjected to an orchestrated night of terror that included electric shock and beatings to obtain confessions to the crime. The youngest arrestee was Marcus Wiggins, a tiny thirteen-year-old boy who was subjected to electric shock on his hands. Marcus signed a confession in which he falsely admitted that he served as a lookout during the murder.

Two weeks later, we filed a civil rights damages lawsuit on behalf of Gregory Banks, alleging that he was tortured by Byrne, Dignan, and Grunhard under the supervision of Burge; that he was wrongfully convicted on the basis of the confession that was tortured from him; and that Banks's torture was a product of the police department's pattern and practice of police torture under Burge's command. The night before the filing, we gave the story, complete with an interview with Gregory Banks, to Phil Walters at the local NBC affiliate. The piece played at the top of the 10:00 o'clock news. Anchor Ron Magers led with "a Chicago man is making charges that have rocked the Chicago Police Department. The man claims that police tortured and abused him for more than thirty hours, forcing him to confess to a crime he did not commit."

Greg then told of his torture: "They said, 'Well, we have something special for niggers,' then he took out a plastic bag." Gesturing with his hands, Greg continued, "and he put it over my head. I was scared. I thought they was trying to kill me . . . I knew they was trying to kill me." Phil Walters then talked about the other cases of torture, showed the black shock box, and repeated Superintendent Martin's claim that the OPS report was coming "soon." The piece then cut back to Greg, who said, "More so than anything, I want them to feel what it feels like to be in prison. I want them to see that, feel that." Walters soberly concluded, "There is no sign, however, that will happen. No criminal charges have ever been filed against any of the officers accused in any of the torture claims."

Around this time, we heard from a friend who worked for the OPS that Burge had threatened to "blow the People's Law Office away with a shotgun" if anything happened to him as a result of the OPS investigation. Our source told us, further, that the threat had been reported to someone in a command position within the department. Knowing Burge and his penchant for violence against those he did not like, we wrote a letter to Superintendent Martin detailing the threat, which we followed up by making a formal complaint against Burge. We had no illusions that our complaint would be seriously investigated, but we wanted to put the threat on the record and thereby compel Burge to respond to the charge.

The day after we filed the Gregory Banks lawsuit, Gayle Shines signed off on a formal "Recommendation for Separation" document and sent it to Martin for his approval. The recommendation cited numerous violations of police disciplinary rules, accused Burge of electric-shocking and burning Andrew on a radiator, of failing to report the mistreatment, and of failing to provide medical care. Similar accusations were made against Yucaitis, while O'Hara was not alleged to have participated in the torture itself. In layperson's terms, Shines was recommending that Burge and his confederates be fired for their roles in torturing Andrew Wilson.

While the recommendation sat on his desk, Superintendent Martin sent Goldston's report to the Police Foundation, an organization run by Herbert Williams, the former chief of the Newark Police Department and Martin's personal friend. After he received a response from Williams critical of Goldston's methodology, Martin sent a brief letter to Shines, saying, "As you know, I have various concerns about the conclusions contained in the report prepared by OPS investigator Michael Goldston. In light of the serious nature of those conclusions, I have hired the Police Foundation to review Mr. Goldston's report, and to advise me as to whether the methods

Mr. Goldston used and the materials he collected support the conclusions contained in his report." Martin would later admit that he was particularly angered by the implication that he sanctioned torture while a commander at Area 2.

At this time, we had several unrelated pattern, practice, and custom police brutality suits pending in federal court, including the McClin-Weaver case. As part of the discovery, we had, months before, sought to compel the City to produce the OPS Special Project reports as they applied to those cases. We argued that the reports were relevant to show a pattern and practice of uniformly failing to discipline cops who were repeatedly accused of abuse, including torture. Judge Milton Shadur agreed with us, and, on October 23, 1991, the City reluctantly gave us the OPS Special Project reports. We were blown away by Goldston's findings and Shine's unqualified approval, but the information came with a large caveat—it was covered by a protective order that barred us from publicly releasing it.

On October 25, 1991, Martin approved the administrative charges and sent them to the corporation counsel for his final review. Word leaked out shortly thereafter. Two weeks later, the corporation counsel's press secretary announced that the office had received a "request for action" from Martin and Shines and that its review "could take 30 days." Coalition members gathered that same day for a press conference outside the office of the City's top lawyer, on the sixth floor of city hall. Mary Powers declared that the request for action "should be sufficient to suspend Burge" adding, "We urge the City's counsel to act expediently on the case, regardless of the political fallout."

The very next day, Friday, November 9, 1991, it became official: "City Cop Commander Suspended," the *Sun Times* headlined in the Metro section, while the headline in the City section of the *Tribune* read, "Officers Face Dismissal on Charges of Torture."

CHAPTER 10

Burge on Trial Again

The fallout from the announcement of Burge's suspension and potential firing was immediate. The *Tribune* referred to Martin's move to suspend Burge as the "latest act in a drama that has occupied federal courtrooms, raucous City Council meetings and media reports for almost a decade." After contrasting the decorated war veteran with the "convicted cop killer," the *Trib* noted that the second *Wilson* jury "split its verdict," that it found a policy, but "did not find that Burge had tortured Wilson." John Dineen, head of the Fraternal Order of Police and a "good ol' boy" former detective, sounded a clarion call to the police union, declaring, "It seems to be an ongoing attempt to discredit police officers."

Syd Finley, executive secretary of the south side NAACP, told the *Defender* that although this was a "step in the right direction," it "by no means will be the final stroke to wipe out abuse against minorities." The *Defender* quoted a police board source as saying it was the first time in recent history that charges had been filed against an officer above the rank of sergeant. Well-connected gossip columnist Michael Sneed speculated that the decision to suspend Vietnam War hero Burge "came from City Hall—not Martin." Gayle Shines, she continued, "made the recommendation. Shines is this/close to Daley, who put her in the job—and whom she worked for when he was Cook County state's attorney."

Shines became a focal point of the pro-Burge attack. FOP leader Dineen railed at the nine-and-a-half-year delay in bringing charges against Burge and his associates, accusing Shines of succumbing to the "political atmosphere." Kunkle called the initiation of charges at such a late date "atrocious." Shines, as was her taciturn manner, gave a limited answer: "The investigation speaks for itself."

I called for the appointment of a special prosecutor. "How can the City prosecute Burge while at the same time defend him in the Wilson appeal and the Banks lawsuit?" I asked. The *Sun Times* quoted Albert

Maule, chairman of the police board, as saying that a special prosecutor had never been appointed in a police board case. Two days later, the City named Daniel Reidy, a well-respected former US prosecutor, to prosecute Burge, Yucaitis, and O'Hara. Meanwhile, Kunkle had switched hats in order to defend Burge before the police board, with the full approval of the lily-white FOP executive board, whose members' dues would pay for Kunkle's fees.

The hearing was set for Monday, November 25. The Friday before, NBC Channel 5 ran another Phil Walters exclusive that we had fed him— the torture of Shadeed Mu'min. Independent filmmakers Cindy Moran, Peter Kuttner, and Eric Scholl had embarked on a documentary weaving together the emerging torture scandal, the wave of police brutality in Chicago, and the task force's role in raising these issues. They had filmed Shadeed at Centralia Prison, where he was serving his robbery sentence, and we had supplied the footage to Phil Walters. Walters began his piece by stating, "Police watchdog groups claim that Burge is linked to dozens of cases of police brutality and want the police board to hear what people like Shadeed Mu'min have to say about Jon Burge." A calm man with a white goatee, Shadeed described how Burge said, "Oh, you tough," and repeatedly played Russian roulette by pointing a gun at Shadeed's head and pulling the trigger. "I knew that if it went off I would be through with it, it would have blew my head away," he said. He described how Burge, with "all this killer in his eyes," repeatedly placed a plastic typewriter cover over his face, causing him to pass out. The footage also showed Mariel Nanasi, who said it was "key" for other cases of torture to be admitted into evidence before the police board.

On the morning of the hearing, the task force mobilized for a demonstration. Carrying signs, each with the name of a different torture victim and how he was tortured, pickets marched in front of police headquarters. The *Tribune* ran a front-page article sympathetic to the "three highly decorated police officers" whose reputations "had been tarnished" by a "decade of investigations and courtroom battles." Reporter David Jackson, apparently succumbing to pressure from veteran reporters who were close to Burge, concluded the front-page section of his article with a quote from Burge: "When it is all over and we have been vindicated, then I'll be happy."

Continuing inside the paper, the next two columns of the article described in detail the killing of officers Fahey and O'Brien, Andrew Wilson's arrest, and the contents of his confession; a third column emphasized that "the attorneys for the officers introduced evidence indicating that some of Wilson's injuries were self-inflicted and others occurred when he was in the care of two squadron officers who drove him to lockup." In the final column, Jackson mentioned Dr. Kirschner's testimony, but interjected that the defense argued that the clip marks on Andrew's ears "were caused by Wilson himself when he found a roach clip on the prison floor and fixed it to his ear in an effort to simulate the marks of torture." Jackson concluded by quoting from an eleven-year-old prison diagnosis of Andrew that found him to be "aggressive, hostile, negativistic, uncooperative, anti-social, and a pathological liar."

Hearing officer Michael Berland, a former federal prosecutor, called the proceedings of the police board to order. Fifty people, the largest audience in police board history, packed the flag-draped hearing room on the second floor of police headquarters. Kunkle and his co-counsel, FOP lawyer Joe Roddy, aware that Special Prosecutor Reidy had just entered the case the week before, told Berland they were ready to proceed. Reidy asked for a continuance, which Berland granted, and a new hearing date was set for late January.

Reidy and his co-counsel, June Ghezzi, had imposed a de facto gag order on themselves. Our office assumed the role of spokesperson for the prosecution, as we had been assisting in their preparation. *Sun Times* reporter Charles Nicodemus quoted me as saying that Reidy had confided, in a "preliminary conversation," that he was going "to seek to present evidence of a pattern of brutality" that "would be based on more than 40 other cases." Kunkle told Nicodemus that he would oppose as "irrelevant" the introduction of any cases of torture other than Andrew Wilson's. The *Tribune* caught up with Mayor Daley after a speaking engagement and reported that he defended his administration's decision to seek the officers' dismissals, while offering a classic Daley non-answer as to why he had not pursued criminal charges in 1982: because "the accusations they faced involved violations of Police Department Regulations."

In mid-December I experienced déjà vu—another letter from a former Area 2 detective arrived, this time with a name, address, and phone number. The author introduced himself as detective William A. Parker Sr., a Chicago police officer who had served for thirty-two and a half years and retired in March 1990. The materials accompanying the letter made it clear that Parker was one of the first Black detectives to serve in the Chicago Police Department.

"Dear Mr. Flint," Parker began. "I am writing you this letter to break what has long been referred to as the code of silence within the Chicago Police Department and to let it be known publicly that I worked in the same unit (Area 2 Robbery) with Commander Jon Burge from September of 1972 to November of 1973 and during that time had an occasion to witness him commit an act of brutality." As I read the six-page, single-spaced letter, my anticipation and anxiety rose. Parker detailed what he called an "ongoing violation of my rights and privacy" while he had served as a police officer. He told of being an honest cop, attempting to prevent and report corruption, acts of brutality, and other injustices that he had witnessed over his career, and, as a result, suffering backlash for challenging the police code of silence.

He then summarized his story about Burge, which he said happened during the period he was assigned to work with Burge at Area 2 Robbery:

> On the day the incident occurred we were working the evening shift and I had remained in the office to catch up on some reports. That evening Burge and his partners brought an alleged offender in and took him to one of the interrogation rooms. As I continued typing my reports I heard a loud ghastly scream come from the room. My immediate instinct prompted me to run to the room. As I opened the door, I observed the offender, who was handcuffed to the steaming hot radiator whimpering and pleading for mercy to Burge and his partners.

Parker wrote that he was struck by the fact that he was the only detective who seemed to be at all alarmed by the scream, and everyone else just continued with their work as if nothing unusual had happened. He concluded, "I feel that the time is now that the truth be revealed with regard to Commander Jon Burge. I dread the thought of any human being having been subjected to an act of brutality and thereby finding themselves sentenced to a prison term based on the fact that they unwillingly submitted out of fear, anguish, and the pain inflicted upon them."

This seemed like a breakthrough—a former detective who had witnessed a Burge torture scene. We were also more than a bit skeptical and concerned that it might be a setup. I called Parker and made an appointment to meet with him in our office that Saturday morning. I convinced John to sit at his desk to provide some form of "security," but none was needed. Parker, a very large man, related his story to me in more detail. He added that the pants of the Black man handcuffed to the steaming radiator were open and down, and that there were two other detectives in the room along with Burge. When Parker entered the room, Burge had a "shocked" look on his face, and one of the other detectives took something from the desk next to Burge and put it on the floor. Parker said that he did not get a good look at the object, but later, when he heard mention of a black torture box, he concluded that such a box could have been the object taken from his view. After the object was placed on the floor, Parker continued, a sergeant entered the room and upbraided him for barging in on Burge's investigation. Shortly thereafter, Parker was transferred from Area 2. Parker's story was compelling and important, and I was inspired by his courage in coming forward. Unfortunately, it was too late for him to be a witness in Andrew Wilson's case, and the fact that he had been in conflict with the CPD throughout his career made him too risky for Special Prosecutor Reidy.

Meanwhile, Kunkle and the FOP were moving to lift the officers' suspensions. Arguing that the suspensions without pay violated their clients' due process rights, they sought an injunction in federal district court. They drew Judge Shadur, the same judge who had reviewed the Goldston and Sanders reports and ordered the City to turn them over to us. In a ruling from the bench, Judge Shadur denied the request to lift the suspensions. Undeterred, Kunkle immediately amended his complaint to ask Shadur to shut down the police board hearing altogether, arguing that the jury's verdict absolving the officers in our second trial barred the police board proceedings under the legal principle of res judicata ("a matter [previously] judged").

Less than a week before the hearing was scheduled to begin, Judge Shadur ruled that it would be a "serious distortion" of the legal process to bar the police board proceedings. This was so, he reasoned, because there was "highly material evidence" that had been excluded from the civil cases. Shadur concluded, "The public is entitled to a determination of whether, on the basis of all the evidence, these men are entitled to remain in a position of trust." We all breathed a sigh of relief: the Melvin Jones evidence had come home to roost.

That same day, a friendly source gave us a confidential memorandum from the Burge/O'Hara/Yucaitis (BOY) fund that was circulating at police roll calls and within the state's attorney's office. The fundraising committee was headed up by former police superintendent James O'Grady; a former deputy superintendent; and former chief of detectives William Hanhardt, who, Deep Badge had told us, was present when Donald White and his brothers were tortured at police headquarters. A long list of Burge's confederates, including Peter Dignan and Milton Deas, were listed as committee members.

The memo played on fears of a widespread persecution of rank-and-file officers by the OPS and described other "overwhelming repercussions," including that "the People's Law Office and other defense attorneys can continue their conspiracy with their convicted criminal clients and initiate factually baseless lawsuits." An insert from the FOP carried on the attack in more detail: "The People's Law Office are not, as their name might seem to imply, a public defender. They are a FOR PROFIT law firm." It accused us of being in the torture fight for the money: "That is what the PLO's malicious and continuing out of court prosecution of these officers is all about." The FOP was particularly rankled by our "continued display" of the "black box torture device that they themselves had built by a handyman at their offices."

Combined with the shotgun threat from Burge (quickly dismissed by a CPD investigator after Burge called it "ludicrous") this widely circulated smear job from the FOP and BOY fund made us, our law partners, and our families even more uncomfortable.

On January 21, the hearing was again delayed, this time for Hearing Officer Berland to consider several outstanding matters of evidence. Paramount among these issues was whether he would, in contrast to Judge Duff, permit Melvin Jones and other Burge victims to testify. In an about-face that would have seemed unimaginable only months before, the City, over Superintendent Martin's name, filed a brief that supported its motion to offer Melvin Jones and other Burge electric-shock victims as witnesses at the hearing. In support, the City admitted that "the testimony regarding similar acts" of "seven additional victims of torture tactics at Area 2 headquarters," whom they identified as Anthony Holmes, Melvin Jones, George Powell, Donald White, Shadeed Mu'min, Leroy Orange, and Lawrence Poree,

> sets forth detailed accounts of torturous treatment that are almost identical to the torture suffered by Andrew Wilson. The testimony reveals an astounding pattern or plan on the part of respondents [Burge, Yucaitis, and O'Hara] to torture certain suspects, often with substantial criminal records, into confessing to crimes or to condone such activity.

A few days later the Associated Press (AP) filed a story that was picked up by the *Oakland Tribune*. In the context of the upcoming hearing, it summarized the *Wilson* case, its aftermath, and the volatile run-up to the impending hearing. It quoted me as saying it was "very important that the police board ultimately know the full parameters of what went on here" and also printed the FOP's accusation that Gayle Shines was a "politically ambitious administrator" who had brought "baseless charges" to "grease her political career." According to the AP, the case was going to a hearing "amid charges of betrayal, cover-up, and racial division among police officers." On the theme of racial division, the AP asserted that "some black officers have broken the department's unwritten code of silence to speak out." The article then quoted Jerry Crawley, a twenty-four-year veteran of the CPD and the leader of Black Officers United for Justice and Equality, as saying, "Burge has a reputation among older African American officers of being a torturer."

As the pretrial maneuvers were playing out, we asked Judge Shadur to lift the protective order on the Goldston report. Reluctantly honoring the protective order, we had amended our complaint in Gregory Banks's case, which we filed under seal, to include Goldston's findings in our pattern and practice claim. Taking another tack, Jeff and Erica Thompson, a terrific lawyer who had recently joined our office, had issued a subpoena on the City to produce a copy of Goldston's report to use in their attempt to get torture victim David Bates a new trial. The nineteen year-old Bates was Greg's co-defendant and would, much later, receive an innocence pardon. His conviction rested almost completely on a confession that sergeant Jack Byrne, with the assistance of detectives Charles Grunhard and Robert Dwyer, had wrung out of him by subjecting him to dry submarino.

Judge Shadur granted our motion, and, on Friday, February 7, 1992, Jeff and I held a press conference on the OPS reports. The findings exploded in both the local and national media. The heretofore skeptical *Tribune* ran a banner front-page headline the next morning: "Thirteen Years of Cop Torture Alleged." The subhead read, "Daley and Martin Rip Internal Police Reports." The *Trib* gave me credit for obtaining the reports' release, and quoted me as saying that the City fought so hard to suppress the reports because they would "significantly impact future brutality suits against the police" by enabling victims to "contend that they were victimized by an unspoken department policy of torture."

The *Tribune* also caught up with Superintendent Martin at a lunch at Chicago's Urban League. He said it was an "outright lie" that police commanders knew about or condoned torture, and that he was "furious" about a finding that implicated him and his fellow commanders. Daley was asked about the findings by veteran reporter Dick Kay at a taping of WMAQ's "City Desk," and reacted in a similar manner, calling the fifty incidents of torture and abuse "only allegations," "stories," and "a lot of rumors." He told the press that it was "only one individual's report" and denied that the torture was systematic. Playing defense, later in the day Martin and the City released the October letter from Martin's buddy, Herbert Williams at the Police Foundation, challenging Goldston's methodology.

As the early edition of the *Tribune* was hitting the streets, task force spokesperson Tim Lohraff listened to the voice messages on his home phone. "You fucking liberal fruit," a message began. "I know where the fuck you are at. I'm going to come over there and fuck your pussy ass up, you understand? I'm going to torture your fucking pussy white liberal fucking ass. Understand that, you fucking punk ass motherfucker!" The next night the caller left another message, letting Tim know that he had his address, which he recited on the recording. Badly shaken, Tim headed for a friend's house to spend the night. (A task force leaflet had listed Tim's number. Later, we learned that, during the trials, Kunkle and Burge had obtained home addresses, phone numbers, and license plate numbers for John, Jeff, and me.)

But neither Daley, Martin, nor Burge's threat-spewing buddy could stop the media response to the release of the Goldston report. On the eve of the Rodney King trial, the front page of the *LA Times* led with "Police Officers and Commanders Engaged in 'Systematic' Torture and Abuse over a 13 Year Period." The article told of shocks from a black box to suspects' penises, testicles, and armpits; victims passing out after having plastic bags secured over their heads, stopping the flow of oxygen; guns with empty chambers being stuck into mouths and the trigger being pulled; hangings by handcuffs; beatings on the bottoms of the feet and testicles; and the fact that all the victims were Black or Latino while all the people doing the torturing were white. Quoted extensively in the article, I accused Martin of a "cover-up" and said, "The superintendent was the direct supervisor of the person responsible for the pattern of abuse."

Articles also appeared in the *Boston Globe*, the *Milwaukee Journal Sentinel*, both Houston papers, and the *Arizona Desert Sun*. Strangely absent was the "paper of record," the *New York Times*. The *Sun Times* gave the story less prominent play than the *Tribune*, but Charles Nicodemus referred to the report as a "ticking time bomb" that "exploded into view" when Judge Shadur ordered its release. The *Tribune* followed up with another front-page article that Sunday, accompanied by an editorial. Now decidedly less skeptical, reporter David Jackson relied on our fact sheet to describe Anthony Holmes as the first known Burge victim. Calling the Goldston report a "searing indictment," Jackson quoted former New York police superintendent Patrick Murphy as saying, "Smart chiefs, when they have a problem, send out a message, 'this will not be tolerated.'" Undeterred, Martin redoubled his resistance and issued a press release that called the report "flawed and unsubstantiated." Invoking his move to fire Burge, he told the *Tribune*, "Now someone is trying to turn it around and make me the heavy. I should be the hero."

The *Tribune's* editorial board was not buying it. Under the title, "Leads the Cops Don't Want to Follow," the board wrote, "There are too many allegations, some of them following chillingly similar patterns, for police or City Hall officials to continue to deny that the Chicago Police Department has a problem with brutality." While it was "extraordinary" for Martin to move to fire Burge, it was "all too ordinary for Martin and Mayor Richard Daley to pooh-pooh the report. Obfuscation and denial only perpetrate Chicago's ugly reputation for mean precincts."

The next day the police board hearing began, almost exactly ten years after the fact, with Andrew Wilson's testimony about his torture at the hands of Burge and his associates. For security reasons the hearing had been moved to the federal courthouse, and metal detectors and mandatory searches greeted the folks who attended. John had assisted Dan Reidy in preparing Andrew for his sixth live appearance as Burge's main accuser. "Cop Killer" dominated the headlines in both dailies for the next two days, and Kunkle told reporters, "We are showing how preposterous his story is." In reality, Andrew held up as well as could be expected, and Dr. Raba followed to bolster Andrew's testimony. This time he was permitted to invoke his extensive expertise as a jail doctor to dispute the defense's theory that Andrew's wounds were self-inflicted. The City's case was further strengthened by the testimony of Melvin Jones and Shadeed Mu'min, neither of whom knew Andrew or each other. They somberly described almost identical torture: electric shock from a box, racist threats, suffocation, and Russian roulette, administered by Burge himself. They were followed by Dr. Kirschner, who was permitted to testify as an expert on torture.

The City's presentation of its case reaffirmed what we had known— that our case would have been much more powerful if Judge Duff had not barred us from presenting some of our most compelling evidence before the jury.

The FOP fundraiser for Burge, O'Hara, and Yucaitis was held about two weeks into the police board hearings, on February 25, at the Teamsters Hall, just southwest of the downtown Loop. Upward of four thousand cops and prosecutors, at $20 a head, jammed into the hall, passing by about a hundred derisive demonstrators from the task force, the Malcolm X Grassroots Movement, Queer Nation, and the Coalition Against Bashing. The demonstrators were separated from the entering crowd by barricades and a contingent of decidedly unfriendly street cops, who no doubt would rather have been inside.

Outside, the demonstrators chanted provocative slogans through bullhorns—"Take the torture toys from the torture boys"—and waved colorful signs, including one that read, "Code of Silence Equals Racist Violence" and another that featured a pig-headed cop wearing a CPD hat with the message "Killer Kop Klub."

Inside, the angry law enforcement crowd, consisting almost entirely of white faces, ate pizza and drank beer while listening to a parade of speakers that culminated in speeches from the three embattled officers. Warming up the crowd, Dewey Stokes, national president of the FOP, called the hearings "lunacy" and warned that if Burge and company went down, similar charges would be brought "in every major city in the country." A clergyman read the names of the twenty-four officers who had been killed during the past decade, while bagpipes played. Burge closed his remarks with the old Yogi Berra truism, "It's not over till it's over," and, according to the *Tribune*, the "crowd went wild, cheering, stamping, yelling and giving Burge, Yucaitis, and O'Hara thunderous applause."

The next day a disappointingly low number of Chicagoans went to the polls to vote in the Democratic mayoral primary for Daley, Danny Davis, or former mayor Jane Byrne. Davis garnered 84 percent of the African American vote, but it was not nearly enough, and Daley was all but assured of continuing as mayor for another four years.

In the wake of the BOY fundraiser, Kunkle and the three officers enlisted a major ally in the Chicago media: iconic columnist Mike Royko. Independent, outspoken, and irreverent, Royko had made his bones skewering corrupt politicians, cops, and—first and foremost—the Daley Machine. Earlier in his career, he had written strongly critical columns about the Hampton raid and Hanrahan's role in it, and in the 1970s had published a best-seller, *Boss, Richard J. Daley of Chicago*, a book he was inspired to write by another iconic Chicago author, Studs Terkel.

In the early 1990s, however, Royko, now working for the *Tribune* (which he had previously hated), had taken a hard turn to the right. His column on the hearings, entitled "Facts Don't Add Up to Police Brutality," reflected this change of attitude as well as complete indifference to the emerging facts of systemic police torture and an official cover-up— issues the younger Royko would have taken delight in dissecting. Instead, he bemoaned the fact that Andrew was now the victim and the "bad guys" were "the cops who brought him in." He belittled the other torture victims as prison fabricators and dismissed the Amnesty International report as a successful "publicity stunt" orchestrated by Wilson's lawyers. He asked whether the prosecutions were about "racial politics," "huge legal fees that Wilson's lawyers might be seeking if they can get the cops booted," or "a social cause for protestors who are bored with holes in the ozone." Asserting that, as a journalist, he had exposed "far more cases of police brutality in Chicago than Amnesty International has," Royko wrote that he had "no doubt that Andrew had been abused" but "we don't know who did it and we'll never know." Hence, Royko concluded, the City "should let it go," and the protestors should "get a life." Our anger at the column was tinged with sadness at seeing that Royko, who counted Studs Terkel, Saul Alinsky, Leon Despres, and Nelson Algren among his early heroes and friends, had sunk to such know-nothing depths in the twilight of his illustrious career.

Kunkle and Roddy proceeded to present the defense testimony. While most was familiar, they added a few new wrinkles, the most prominent being yet another interpretation of the damning medical evidence, this time from a German pathologist named Werner Spitz. After conceding that Andrew's leg wound was a burn, Spitz contended that the wounds on Andrew's face and chest were scratches and abrasions that "could have been suffered from falling on the floor." Joe Roddy embellished this questionable testimony, telling reporters, "This doctor says that Dr. Kirschner is crazy," and that Spitz's testimony "put another nail in the lying coffin of Andrew Wilson."

Special prosecutor Dan Reidy, in his cross-examination of Burge and his men, was able to use some of the weapons we had developed but had not been permitted to utilize, including detective Patrick O'Hara's admission that Burge was a "hands-on" commander and Burge's concessions that he had called Andrew Wilson and Melvin Jones "human pieces of garbage."

Reidy also developed a new motivation for Burge's torture of Andrew: that Burge and his detectives were "embarrassed" by their failure to hold Andrew as a parole violator when they had arrested him for the robbery of a camera store two months prior to the fatal police shootings. In the meantime we informed the press of the most recent results of our continuing investigation, and Charles Nicodemus reported that "attorneys for the People's Law Office, which spearheaded the campaign to have Burge face brutality charges, said new information shows Burge and his detectives were accused of 72 incidents of torture from 1973 to 1991."

On March 19, 1992, Hearing Officer Berland heard closing arguments. Reidy argued that Burge and his men treated Andrew "like a piece of human garbage," when he was a "human being entitled to police protection rather than torture. . . . The police felt they were under siege. Four brothers had been killed. So the goal was to break that 'piece of garbage,' to make that 'piece of garbage' cooperate." Kunkle, in turn, forcefully attacked Andrew's credibility as "nil" and asserted that "the evidence stinks." With tears coming to his eyes and his voice wavering, Kunkle implored the decision makers "not to believe that son of a bitch."

With the conclusion of the six-week hearing, the testimony of the thirty-nine witnesses, along with two hundred exhibits, would be tendered to the nine police board members, who would review this extensive record and make a decision—sometime in the unspecified future.

The day after the Burge case was tendered, the police board issued its ruling in our other red-hot police case: the board fired the two white officers who had dropped off Calvin McClin and Joseph Weaver in Canaryville to be chased and beaten by a white racist gang. Two days after that, the *Tribune* ran a feature article headlined "Big Decisions Put Daley, Police Board on the Spot." In addition to considering the Burge case, the board was recommending three candidates to the mayor to replace the retiring LeRoy Martin as police superintendent. The *Tribune* reported that the four leading candidates were all CPD insider brass, three of whom were African Americans.

The article gave a rare inside look at how the political machine operated in these circumstances. The mayor would informally tell the board whom he or she favored among the applicants the board was considering. The board would then present its three finalists to the mayor to select the new superintendent. Daley, a short time later, chose deputy superintendent Matt Rodriguez, who was half Polish, half Puerto Rican, and all company man.

Turning to the disciplinary decisions of the police board in general, and the Burge case in particular, the *Tribune*, relying on police sources, reported that, in the rare cases the OPS was recommending dismissal, "the upper brass in the department would make phone calls to board members to tilt the decision away from dismissal." If the board did not dismiss Burge, Yucaitis, and O'Hara, it would "appear as though Daley's board exonerated them at the mayor's behest," whereas if they were fired, it would "enrage the police force as well as their sympathizers, a strong Daley constituency." Alderman Shaw predicted, "There's no question about it, the order will come from Daley." FOP mouthpiece John Dineen called the hearings a "kangaroo court,' and Eddie Burke offered cover for Daley, saying, "I don't think anyone wants to touch this with a ten foot pole. Nobody wants their fingerprints on it."

One of Eddie's surrogates, southwest side alderwoman Virginia Rugai, introduced a proposed ordinance aimed at preventing future Burge-like firing cases by imposing a two-year statute of limitations that would run from the time an OPS complaint was filed until the board made its final decision. She called the Burge prosecution ten years after the fact "insane," and Daley seemed to agree, saying, "It's a problem when you talk about going back ten or fifteen years."

On April 28, 1992, after a three-month trial, a predominantly white, suburban jury in Simi Valley, California, acquitted the gang of officers who had brutally beaten Rodney King, in spite of video that definitively showed the officers' wanton and excessive use of force on a defenseless Black man. Playing on racist and "law and order" themes, the officers' lawyers successfully portrayed King as the aggressor and the cops as defending against lawlessness. One of the defense lawyers summed it up: "These officers, these defendants, do not get paid to lose a street fight. They do not get paid to roll around in the dirt with the likes of Rodney Glen King."

The verdict sparked a six-day rebellion in South Central LA. Concern about what would happen in Chicago if Burge were exonerated began to be publicly discussed. When Matt Rodriguez appeared before city council a week later for his inauguration as LeRoy Martin's replacement as superintendent, he referred to the Burge case as a "no-win" situation and said that he was planning ahead for any negative reaction that might arise in the aftermath of the decision, which was reportedly expected "within the next two months." Following the King verdict, the *Tribune* reported that the board had initially decided to exonerate Burge on procedural grounds but had reconsidered in the wake of the LA rebellion.

In late June, the Illinois state legislature, in a nearly unanimous vote, passed a bill sponsored by a former Chicago cop and ardent Burge supporter, state senator Walter Dudycz, that placed a three-year statute of limitations on brutality complaints statewide. The only hope to derail its becoming law was to convince governor Jim Edgar, a moderate Republican, to veto the bill, a task Mary Powers and the coalition took on with urgent resolve.

Amid all this, police board officials announced that its members would need the summer to "plow through" all of the testimony. Jeff spoke for many of us when he surmised, "I don't think that the situation in LA makes them want to move very fast."

During the summer, *Sun Times* reporter Deborah Nelson had been investigating recent allegations of torture at Area 3, focusing on the allegations of electric shock made by the juvenile suspects just prior to Burge's suspension. The youngest of the victims, thirteen-year-old Marcus Wiggins, was represented by assistant public defender Julie Hull, who had filed a motion to suppress Marcus's confession on the basis that he had been tortured. Julie had obtained the Goldston report and the list of other torture victims from us and had included allegations about these other cases in her motion. In a Sunday front-page exclusive, headlined "3 Teens Say Police Used Shock Torture, 13 Year Old Charges Confession was Coerced," the *Sun Times* article detailed Marcus's chilling story.

Using the pseudonym "Mark," Deborah Nelson wrote, "Mark says they hooked him up to a box that sent jolts of electricity through his body." She quoted Mark's mother, who was barred from her son's interrogation, as saying that he told her the torture device looked like a cable box with black wires attached to paddles that were put on his hands. "It didn't happen," countered an implicated Area 3 detective, aptly named Michael Kill. "This is not Nazi Germany, 1933, where you torture people."

Nelson quoted attorney Julie Hull as saying, "Because detectives got away with doing this to adults, it was only a matter of time before they would do it to a child." The article pointed out that that allegation of torture by juveniles was "rare if not unprecedented." We had connected Julie with Dr. Kirschner, who agreed to testify for Marcus, and also with Dr. Antonio Martinez, a psychologist who specialized in the treatment of international victims of torture. Dr. Martinez had examined Marcus, and the article featured his photo, captioned with his finding that he "was convinced that police shocked Marcus to gain information." Martinez noted that Marcus "curls into a fetal position when discussing the questioning and shakes at the sight of the police and has nightmares a big man is chasing him." Daley, in keeping wth his prior stance about the Goldston report, told Fran Spielman, "It's one allegation. You cannot blanket all policemen."

Ten days later Julie Hull, armed with witnesses present and ready to testify, answered "ready to proceed" on her motion to suppress Marcus Wiggins's confession. The prosecutors sought a continuance, claiming that one of the alleged torturers was on vacation in Alaska. Juvenile judge Walter Williams was having none of it. "This is ridiculous," Williams, a well-respected African American judge, exclaimed from the bench. He denied the continuance request and granted Julie's motion to suppress when the prosecutors declined to proceed.

Throughout the summer, the Burge-inspired statute of limitations bill that had been rammed through the Illinois legislature sat on Governor Edgar's desk. Mary Powers and the coalition had mounted a letter-writing campaign, highlighting the possibility that the vagueness of the bill's language, if applied retroactively, could torpedo the pending police board proceedings and would also chill the pursuit of complex and politically controversial police brutality cases in the future. In response to the outcry, the *Sun Times* had editorialized against the bill. Finally, in September 1992, Edgar acted by invoking an amendatory veto. In so doing, he softened the bill, extending the statute of limitations to five years and specifying that the bill was not retroactive. Mary and the coalition declared the favorable compromise a "significant victory for the people"; State Senator Dudycz and FOP boss Dineen also accepted the amended legislation.

That fall, we filed our appellate brief in the *Wilson* case. We decided that we would not mount a frontal attack on Judge Duff's racist and unremittingly unfair rulings as a whole or his highly prejudicial comments, attitudes, and behavior. Instead, we constrained ourselves to his rulings—his permitting Kunkle to admit weeks of highly prejudicial and irrelevant evidence against Andrew; barring Melvin Jones and Donald White; limiting our attack on Coleman's credibility; barring journalist Miskiw; and rejecting our attempt to offer Dr. Kirschner as an expert on torture. As relief, we asked for a new trial against Burge, his cohorts, and the City.

In November, the *Southtown Economist*, which had been reporting on the Burge proceedings in great detail, quoted Alderman Shaw as saying he would seek an explanation for the "Burge delay" from police board officials at the upcoming budget hearings, complaining, "You could get a Supreme Court ruling faster." I raised concerns about the vacancy left by the death of Nancy Jefferson, our strongest ally on the board, an African American community activist who had died in October of cancer at the age of sixty-nine. Police board chairman Albert Maule responded that it was "very unlikely" that the decision would come before the end of the year, as the members had not yet completed their examination of the "four cartons of transcripts and exhibits."

Marcus Wiggins's mother, Carolyn Johnson, had retained us to file a lawsuit against her sons' abusers. Normally, we would have waited until the dismissal of Marcus's criminal case became final, but we decided, with Carolyn's encouragement, to file the suit in mid-January 1993. At a press conference, Marcus, his mother, Dr. Martinez, and Dr. Kirschner were available to the media. Marcus weighed at most sixty-five pounds soaking wet, and when we had talked with him about the case, he stuttered his responses, then curled up in a ball and sucked his thumb.

Legendary Chicago anchor Bill Kurtis introduced the story for CBS Channel 2. Marcus appeared, wearing a UCLA stocking cap, and I was quoted as saying that if the police board needed any more evidence to fire Burge, "This is a powerful straw that breaks the camel's back." Channel 2 reporter Jim Avila, with a touch of local cynicism, concluded the piece by saying, "Conventional wisdom is that the police board will wait until the coldest day in February" to make its decision.

NBC 5 reporter Phil Walters presented the most in-depth story. Marcus, looking down and speaking softly, told of "things being placed on his hand," feeling a burning sensation, shaking, and then passing out. Dr. Martinez appeared on camera to state that he was "totally convinced" Marcus was tortured, identifying his fear, nightmares, trembling, and other psychological reactions as markers of torture that were as clear as physical injuries would be. Dr. Kirschner told Phil Walters he found it compelling that over the years, the numerous allegations of torture were not random but rather all pointed toward Burge and his men, who were now at a different police station than when the allegations first began to mount against them. Thanks to Julie Hull, Phil was also able to interview a witness who was at Area 3 that night in 1991 when the juvenile suspects were rounded up and placed in a cage—similar to an animal cage, and adorned with African masks—because the ancient facility's lockup had been declared unfit in the 1950s. The witness, who was not charged, said he heard Marcus screaming, and when he saw Marcus pass by he looked "gone."

The *Sun Times*, identifying Marcus as the "Mark" in Deborah Nelson's earlier story, reported Marcus's description of his torture in more detail:

> They took me in a room, closed the door, and asked me to tell what happened. I told them I don't know, and they started hitting me and punching me. Then they brought in a box, it was silver, and they put it on my hands. They turned it on, I remember it burning my hands, and my head went back.

Kunkle, whom the City would soon retain to oppose us in Marcus's case, responded that his claims "were unfounded, as all the other charges have been," and that the case was a "nothing-burger" because Burge was not specifically named as one of the torturers. FOP mouthpiece John Dineen again attributed the lawsuit to our effort to "make money" and asserted that Burge had become "a red flag to wave anytime someone wants to make allegations about police brutality." They also accused us of trying to influence the police board; that charge, unlike the others, had more than a ring of truth.

It was a cold day in February when the police board announced its decision at chairman Albert Maule's downtown law office. After setting forth the facts it was relying on, the board opened its sixty-page decision with what bordered on an apology:

> The Board has every reason in the world to want to believe the Respondents and dismiss the testimony of Wilson, Jones and Mu'Min as the blatant mendacity of hardened criminals trying to extricate themselves from the sordid circumstances of their own making. We wish we could simply conclude that Wilson lied about having been physically abused at Area 2 to get out of his confession and spread the lie to his physicians, lawyers and jail-mates in order to buttress the credibility of his Motion to Suppress and give his fellow inmates a vehicle to suppress their own confessions. We wish we could reach that conclusion and end our opinion here, but we cannot.

The recitation of the facts tracked our evidence, relying in large part on the medical evidence and the testimony of Melvin Jones and Shadeed Mu'min. The board rejected the defense theories of "abrasions not burns," "self-infliction," and "the wagon men did it," and concluded that the injury to Andrew's leg was a burn inflicted at Area 2. Despite its detailed iteration of the evidence of electric shock, baggings, and Russian roulette, the board carefully avoided any use of the word "torture."

The board's ultimate determinations rivaled that of a divided Supreme Court opinion. In a 7–1 decision, it found that Burge "did, either alone or in concert with other police officers at Area 2 strike and/or kick and/or otherwise physically abuse or maltreat Andrew Wilson, and/or did cause or aggravate physical injury or injuries to the person of Andrew Wilson." The same majority voted that Burge was also guilty of failing to stop the brutality and to provide medical attention, and that he should be fired. Relying on Andrew's initially uncertain identification of Yucaitis at the 1982 motion to suppress hearing, the board voted 6–2 to find Yucaitis not guilty of the physical abuse allegations, whereas the board found him guilty of the failure to intervene and medical attention allegations by a reconfigured 6–2 vote. O'Hara was not charged with physical abuse, and was adjudged guilty of the failure to intervene and medical care allegations by the same 6–2 majority that found Yucaitis guilty. Both Yucaitis and O'Hara were given fifteen-month suspensions, which amounted to a "time served" sentence restoring them immediately to active duty. The same two board members—both persons of color—who dissented from the decision that found Yucaitis not guilty of the brutality charge also dissented from the fifteen-month sentences because they "believed a longer suspension was in order."

The board also recommended that the CPD videotape confessions in all murder cases, a call that the *Tribune* endorsed in an editorial.

The top half of the tabloid-format *Sun Times* featured a color photo of Burge's ruddy face with the two-inch-high headline, "Cop Loses Job Over Torture," and called the case "the most celebrated police brutality case in Chicago's recent history." The *Tribune*'s front-page story, under the headline "Police Board Fires Burge, Reinstates 2 Detectives," led with "Acting on one of the most divisive, long lasting, and heated controversies in the history of the Chicago Police Department, the Police Board voted Wednesday to dismiss Cmdr Jon Burge on charges that he tortured convicted cop-killer Andrew Wilson." Mayor Daley said he supported the board's decision, added that it was "clear" that the "police disciplinary system works," and opined that the decision would send a message that "could stop police brutality." Alderman Shaw called the decision "too lenient," said that Yucaitis and O'Hara should also have been fired, and called for criminal charges.

Board chairman Albert Maule and his vice chair, Brian Crowe, denied that they had caved to political pressure, but the *Tribune* reported that the police department was "poised for trouble" if Burge had been exonerated. All plainclothes officers were ordered to wear their uniforms and report for duty, and Maule was provided a police escort. Maule downplayed the systemic nature of the torture, saying it was "only three policemen out of 12,000, and not an indictment of the entire police force."

Alderman Burke criticized the ruling as "not good for police morale" and contended that Burge and his confederates "got a bad deal." A relative of slain officer Fahey described Burge as a "sacrificial lamb," offered to avoid an LA-style rebellion in Chicago. Kunkle and the FOP also rose to Burge's defense. An unscientific overnight call-in poll conducted by the *Sun Times* showed readers in support of Burge, 79 percent to 21 percent.

On the other side, spokespersons from a coalition of Black organizations, from the Afro American Patrolmen's League to the Chicago Conference of Black Lawyers, criticized the ruling and called for criminal indictments. Attorney Judith Scully said the board's "attempt to sanitize the acts of these terrorists in uniform is reprehensible." Jeff quoted Andrew Wilson as saying, from prison, that he was "very pleased that Burge was fired and received justice for torturing me. I'm upset that Yucaitis and another officer—not O'Hara—are not being fired." I called on the CPD to "clean house of all these people."

The police board decision was clearly a compromise, but its bottom line was vindication—to us, to our clients, and to our allies, for all the tireless work.

CHAPTER 11

A Parade and an Appeal

Another anonymous Burge associate called me directly after Burge got his walking papers. "Dan" said he had worked with Burge and that Burge often tortured suspects with electric shock, which he described in graphic detail. He also described Burge's shock box and said that he had gone along with the practice until Burge tortured a woman and some innocent suspects. Like Deep Badge, he added that Burge had thrown the box overboard from his boat. He also confided that he had talked to Phil Walters.

A few days later, "Dan" called again. He told me to meet him in thirty minutes at an Irish Pub in Old Town called O'Briens. Jeff and I hurried over to the well-known watering hole. It was 11:00 a.m., the place had just opened, and the bar was dark and nearly empty. We waited expectantly, but Dan never showed. Much later, I called Phil Walters, who confirmed that he had talked to Dan more than once, and that Dan, fortified by a few drinks, had agreed to tell his story on camera, with his face and voice distorted. But, according to Phil, Dan had gotten cold feet when the camera started to roll, ripped off the microphone, and fled the studio. When I asked Phil for Dan's contact information, Phil looked around on his paper-strewn and ashtray-littered desk for his notes, yet his search turned up nothing. I suspected that Phil, like all good reporters, might be protecting his source.

In the aftermath of the police board decision, the coalition of African American groups took their call to the February board meeting at police headquarters. Fifty-five demonstrators strong, they called for criminal charges. Chairman Maule's response—that the police board had no criminal powers—elicited such vociferous displeasure from the demonstrators that the board members picked up their papers and left the hearing room. The day before, the task force had led a demonstration in front of the OPS office, at which they emphasized the "systematic torture" finding of the

Goldston report. The action impelled the normally reclusive OPS director, Gayle Shines, to reveal publicly that Superintendent Rodriguez had asked her "a few months ago" to "take a look" at the allegations made by all fifty victims listed in the report. She said, "All of them are being reviewed, and some will be reopened." In a statement that would come back to haunt her, she estimated it would take "at least four to five weeks" to complete any new investigations.

That winter, with John's assistance, I argued another case before the US Supreme Court. Our client, Steven Buckley, together with Alejandro Hernandez and Rolando Cruz, had been wrongfully charged ten years before, by a politically motivated prosecutor, with raping and murdering eleven-year-old Jeanine Nicarico. After Steven spent three years in jail and his trial ended with a hung jury, the prosecution had dismissed his case. We responded by suing the police and prosecutors for conspiring to coerce false testimony, manufacturing phony boot-print evidence, and making false and prejudicial statements. These actions, we contended, violated Steven's right to a fair trial.

The prosecutors successfully invoked the doctrine of absolute prosecutorial immunity, and the US Supreme Court subsequently awarded us the seldom granted right to its review. As I began my argument, chief justice William Rehnquist fired the court's opening salvo, followed by a barrage of questions from justice Antonin Scalia that focused on an issue not directly discussed in the briefs. I was able to deflect Scalia's questions and turned the argument back to the question of immunity. Justices Sandra Day O'Connor, David Souter, and Byron "Whizzer" White then posed a series of questions that seemed to show little sympathy for our position. It was a "hot bench," as lawyers say, and the twenty minutes flew by with nary a friendly question.

The DuPage County prosecutors were represented by Jim Sotos. (Sotos would go on to face us as opposing counsel in numerous cases over the next two decades, as his office became one of the City's go-to law firms when the time came to defend Burge and his men on the taxpayers' dime.) As Sotos's presentation progressed, justice John Paul Stevens emerged as sympathetic to our cause.

A few months later, in what was heralded as an important civil rights decision, the Supreme Court ruled in our favor. Justice Stevens wrote the majority opinion that was joined by justices Harry Blackmun and

O'Connor, and, surprisingly, also by Scalia and Thomas. The thrust of this decision—which would subsequently provide the legal basis for suing prosecutors who participated in Burge's interrogations—was that the prosecutor in the *Buckley* case was acting like an investigating cop, rather than a prosecutor, when he allegedly fabricated the boot-print evidence.

As St. Patrick's Day approached, the task force caught wind of a rumor: the Fraternal Order of Police planned to honor Burge, Yucaitis, and O'Hara, as well as the two fired officers who had dropped off our clients in Canaryville, on the FOP's annual float in the south side St. Paddy's Day Parade. Burge supporters had requested that the float honor the five fired white cops, and the twenty-seven-member FOP executive committee, twenty-six of whom were white, unanimously embraced the idea. The parade, initiated in 1979 to support Richie Daley's political campaign for state's attorney, kicked off at 103rd and Western, near the bars where Burge bragged about his exploits after work, and traversed the predominantly white southwest side communities of Beverly and Mount Greenwood, where most Chicago cops and their families lived.

FOP President Dineen strongly supported the float, to be named "Travesties of Justice," which would feature the five disgraced officers waving from a double-decker bus decked out with supportive banners.

A front-page headline in the *Sun Times* announced the plan: "Parade Float Honors 5 Disciplined Cops, Planned Tribute Blasted as Racist." Syd Finley, head of the local NAACP, was quoted as saying, "I'm dumbstruck." Afro American Patrolmen's League president Pat Hill called the plan "an improper use of funds of the FOP, which represents many African American officers." James Compton, president of the Urban League, called on the FOP to reconsider: the float "sends a strong message that torture and other forms of police brutality will continue to plague Chicago's minority community." Stories about the parade float appeared in the *New York Times* and *Washington Post*, and an overnight *Sun Times* poll was evenly split on the question.

The parade committee quickly squelched the idea and disinvited the FOP, but the public fallout continued. The *Sun Times* devoted its colorful front page to the headline "It Won't Float," with photos of four Chicago police officers, accompanied by quotes from each. The two Black officers pictured called the float "polarizing" and welcomed its demise, while a white female officer supported it because the officers "got a raw deal." The

Southtown Economist, continuing its surprisingly honest coverage of the Burge case, ran an editorial that called the "acts of these five officers" a "disgrace to their uniforms," and the idea that they should be honored in a parade "an outrage."

Sun Times editorial board member and columnist Vernon Jarrett pulled no punches. He opined that "much damage has been done to the spiritual climate and national image of Chicago" and that "even experts can not accurately predict the damage that would be caused by the televised sight of parading white cops thumbing their noses at Chicago blacks while marching near the community that once stoned Martin Luther King." Calling out the powerful south side white politicians who had remained silent, Jarrett concluded: "If in Chicago we are defining the good and bad of police conduct based on the race of the cop and the victim, the forces of sanity had better sound the alarm and come together for the survival of this city. In a hurry."

Two white politicians did speak out, if only to reinforce their predictable stances. Daley, caught in a political whipsaw, attempted to balance the controversy over the float, which he reluctantly condemned, with the racially charged debates he was trying to defuse concerning affirmative action and city worker layoffs. Daley called for an "end to the political rhetoric" and to the "recent exploitation of racial tensions for political gain." Alderman Eddie Burke, a loyal marcher in the St. Paddy's Day parade, called the dispute "a tempest in a teapot," and said that it was "regrettable" that FOP was not going to participate.

Amid the furor, Burge, O'Hara, and Yucaitis filed appeals of the police board's decision in the circuit court of Cook County. They were not going down without a fight.

On April 17, 1993, a federal district court jury in Los Angeles brought some modicum of justice to Rodney King. After the 1992 acquittals and the rebellion that followed, the Department of Justice had indicted four of the beaters for criminal civil rights violations. The federal jury convicted the LAPD sergeant and patrol officer who were most centrally involved in King's videotaped beating, and Los Angeles was spared another uprising.

Six weeks later, John and I took the elevators to the top floor of the Dirksen Federal Building and entered the imposing courtroom of the Seventh Circuit Court of Appeals to argue that we should be granted a new trial in Andrew Wilson's case. It had been almost four years since the case was concluded in Duff's courtroom, and the tide had certainly shifted. Playing a bit fast and loose with the appellate rules, we had included the findings of the Goldston and Sanders OPS reports in our opening brief and attached the police board's decision to our reply brief, just in case the austere appellate court judges had not been following the news.

By Seventh Circuit rule, attorneys were not informed until the morning of the argument which three of the court's judges would hear their case. As we read the docket list, our hearts sank. We had drawn perhaps the three most conservative judges on the court: Frank Easterbrook, chief judge Richard Posner, and John Coffey. Two were from the Chicago School of Law and Economics and the third was an even more conservative former state court judge from Wisconsin. Certainly, under Chicago School theory, an illiterate and destitute prisoner stood little chance against Chicago's public fisc—but they couldn't be as bad as Judge Duff, and the show must go on.

A week prior, John and I had debated whether to pay our outstanding contempt fines, since we'd had no space left in our already cramped legal briefs to appeal them. I said no, as a matter of principle, but John, ever practical, won the debate, so we forked over the money to the district court. This proved to be a wise move, because, as soon as John began his argument, Chief Judge Posner interrupted. "Not to be petty, Mr. Stainthorp, but your opponents say that you were fined $100 by Judge Duff and never paid it."

John corrected the record and proceeded to lay out that it was a "hotly contested case where the trial judge had permitted, by his unbalanced and highly prejudicial rulings, the focus to be changed from a civil rights case to a retrial of the murder case." Coffey asked for the specific transcript page where Duff's prejudicial rulings had occurred, and John was ready with several from the myriad instances we had cited in our briefs. Judge Easterbrook, who loved to find obscure legal rationales to defeat cases with especially egregious fact patterns, asked John to identify where Duff "came closest to explaining why he let in this evidence." John, after doing so, quoted from a prior Seventh Circuit case that forbid a party from "lovingly parading" a litany of unfairly prejudicial evidence before the jury. When Coffey and Easterbrook challenged our argument that journalist Gregory Miskiw should have been permitted to give his opinions about William Coleman's credibility, John's tone rose as he described how Miskiw's testimony further discredited Coleman and his tale of self-infliction. John concluded that, given Duff's unbalanced rulings, it was "impossible for the jury to make a reasoned decision."

In my turn, I had ten minutes to argue why there needed to be a new trial against the City on the policy, pattern, and practice claim. I pointed to the inconsistent jury verdict, with its finding that the pattern and practice did not cause the violation of Andrew's constitutional rights, as evidence of the closeness of the case and the unfairness of the trial. Judge Easterbrook offered up a possible alternative rationale: that "the jury believed that Burge was a wild man so it didn't make any difference what the City's policy was. Burge was going to administer his penalty anyway." That's "not quite accurate," I responded, in an uncharacteristic understatement. "If Burge had been found liable, the proposition might be arguable, but that's not the situation here."

Judge Posner asked, "There is no evidence that Brzeczek knew about any of this stuff?" I argued that he knew about baggings and beatings during the manhunt—"torture, in his lingo and ours"—and that he responded not by demanding a stop to the rampant brutality but by enlisting his relatively few Black command officers to cool out the outraged Black community with a "public relations gambit." Easterbrook got me to chuckle, as he had John earlier, when he referred to the limited argument time: "Fortunately, we do not go on for nine weeks." I concluded: "Looking at the prejudice against the plaintiff, looking at the barring of significant causation evidence, and looking at the fundamentally unfair trial, particularly the impact that it had on Burge's liability, the jury's finding on causation must be reversed and there must be a new trial on causation against the City."

A young appellate lawyer, Ms. Gregg, argued for the City, and she was no match for Posner's and Easterbrook's sharp-tongued and often sarcastic queries. Posner challenged her on the City's contention that there was not a pattern and practice, and that Melvin Jones did not fit within it, saying, first, "Electric-shock technology was well established in Area 2. There was equipment. They must have talked about it. It begins to become a little unlikely that this was not widely known by the police department." Easterbrook then made the stunning declaration that "Tucker telephones were well established well outside of Area 2. You're not going to deny that?" Posner followed, "I find it very odd that if the department condoned the use of electric shock for non-police murders, you would think, a fortiori, it would condone its use for police murderers." Easterbrook sent Gregg back to her seat with an exchange about how many proven incidents would be sufficient to show a pattern, asking, with obvious scorn, "Do 100,000 people have to testify? Is ten too few?"

Kunkle then took the podium. He was no less prosecutorial than the last time we'd seen him, although his bluster had been toned down a bit. Chief Judge Posner repeatedly challenged him about the relevance of the dead officers' photos going to the jury. He then asked, "Did you deliver the opening statement in the second trial?" "Yes, I did," Kunkle responded with pride. Posner then recited Kunkle's words in a sing-song voice: "'What kind of due process Andrew Wilson gave the officers.' I don't understand that. When you ask the jury, rhetorically, what kind of due process it was when Andrew Wilson sentenced those officers to death, you are probing Andrew Wilson's mind? You have a theory of due process that you were investigating?" Kunkle chuckled, but Posner, leaning over the bench, moved in for the kill: "You wanted the jury to hate him?"

Kunkle paused. His lawyer's mind must have been struggling to keep his emotions at bay. It was a moment of "I made Andrew Wilson cry," but this wasn't a prison conference room, where he could embrace on the record his satisfied laugh, but a hall of the second highest court in the land. The pause seemed like an eternity, and the fate of our case could be hanging on his answer. "I probably did want the jury to hate him," Kunkle said, finally.

The rest of Kunkle's argument was anticlimactic: he denied that it was a close case, suggested that Andrew had been burned on a police headquarters radiator by the wagon men, and accused the police board of being "on a mission of political correctness." As Kunkle tried to explain away the board's decision, Posner curtly informed him, "Your time is up."

John then gave a five-minute rebuttal. Coffey, once again, with a disagreeable tone, attempted to challenge us. John told the court that we had "moved heaven and earth" to get the Melvin Jones evidence admitted, and "two minutes after we closed our case, the court said, 'You could have got that in.'" Looking up from my notes, I heard Posner and Easterbrook suppress a laugh. We left the courtroom with a guarded optimism that maybe, just maybe, some degree of judicial sanity might prevail.

The Seventh Circuit issued its unanimous decision that fall; Judge Posner authored the opinion. In his statement of facts, he referenced the findings of the Illinois Supreme Court and the police board, and even made note that, after the board's decision, "The Fraternal Order of Police was unsuccessful in its effort to enter a float in the most recent St. Patrick's Day parade honoring Burge and the other officers who were disciplined." The court agreed with us that "a mass of inflammatory evidence having little or no relevance to the issues in this trial (as distinct from Wilson's murder trial) was admitted, and the defendants' counsel was permitted to harp on it to the jury and thus turn the trial of the defendants into a trial of the plaintiff. . . . But even a murderer," Posner continued, "has a right to be free from torture and the correlative right to present his claim of torture to a jury that has not been whipped into a frenzy of hatred." Giving credence to the old lawyer's saw that you can't win an appeal at oral argument but only lose it, the court made a highly unusual reference to Kunkle's "come to Jesus" moment: "At the argument of the appeal, the lawyer for the officers—who had been the prosecutor at Wilson's criminal trials—acknowledged in answer to a question from the bench that he had tried to make the jury hate Wilson."

The court then turned to the Melvin Jones and Donald White evidence: Duff "kept out on grounds of relevance the plainly relevant testimony of Melvin Jones, who claimed to have been subjected to electroshock by Burge and other officers nine days before the interrogation of Wilson. If Burge had used an electroshock device on another suspect only a few days previously, this made it more likely (the operational meaning of "relevant") that he had used it on Wilson." He then explained why Jones's and White's testimony should have been admitted: "Although evidence of prior bad acts is inadmissible to prove a propensity to commit such acts, it is admissible for other purposes, including intent, opportunity, preparation, and plan. . . . Jones's evidence would have served all four of these purposes, White's all but the third (preparation); and, since Burge had denied under cross-examination that he had ever had or used an electroshock instrument, Jones's evidence could also have been used to impeach that denial."

After discussing Duff's most egregious missteps, the court announced its decision granting us a new trial against Burge, Yucaitis, and O'Hara:

> The plaintiff's case was strong, as evidenced by the decisions of the Supreme Court of Illinois and the Police Board of Chicago. The torrent of inflammatory evidence and argument that the judge allowed the jury to consider may well have been decisive. Evidence that the jury was in fact confused is found in its verdict, which declared that Wilson's rights had been violated but not by any of the individual defendants or even by the city's policy (as the jury found it to be) of authorizing the abuse of suspected cop killers. By whom then?

In our only loss thus far, the court upheld the rejection of Dr. Kirschner as an expert witness on torture: "If there is an objective body of scientific evidence concerning the effects of electroshock, it is unlikely that its sole possessor is a professed amateur in the subject." It did give the green light to journalist Miskiw's testimony in the unlikely event that Kunkle again tried to call "billy liar" Coleman to the stand.

The court affirmed that "a rational jury could have inferred from the frequency of the abuse, the number of officers involved in the torture of Wilson, and the number of complaints from the Black community, that Brzeczek knew that officers in Area 2 were prone to beat up suspected cop killers." It then detailed Brzeczek's knowledge and obvious failure to take corrective action—he "received many complaints from members of the Black community that officers in Area 2 Violent Crimes, were abusing suspects; such abuse was in fact common in Area 2." He "referred the complaints to the OPS, but it "had done nothing except lose a lot of the complaints." He had written State's Attorney Daley "that he would do nothing further" unless Daley "assured him that doing something would not interfere with the prosecution of Wilson" and that Brzeczek was "true to his word" when the letter was not answered, so he "did nothing further." He "downplayed the gravity of the problem in Area 2 in discussions with Black police officers" and then "even signed a commendation for Burge."

Then came a surprise and deeply disappointing ending, concerning Superintendent Brzeczek and our argument that the City should also be reinstated as a defendant for the CPD's policy and practice of torture and abuse:

> Brzeczek referred the complaints to the unit within the police department that is responsible for investigating police abuses. It was the plaintiff's responsibility to show that in doing this Brzeczek was not acting in good faith to extirpate the practice. That was not shown. At worst, the evidence suggests that Brzeczek did not respond quickly or effectively, as he should have done; that he was careless, maybe even grossly so given the volume of complaints. More was needed to show that he approved the practice. Failing to eliminate a practice cannot be equated to approving it. Otherwise every inept police chief in the country would be deemed to approve, and therefore become answerable in damages to all the victims of the misconduct of the officers under his command.

This part of the court's decision no doubt reflected the conservative political attitudes of the three judges and smacked of Easterbrook's "gotcha" judicial mentality. It also could have been a compromise to keep Coffey from dissenting from the decision. In any event, half a loaf, particularly the half that this threesome had awarded us, was decidedly better than none, and we embraced it as another hard-earned victory.

CHAPTER 12

The *Vigilante*, Aaron Patterson, and a Judgment against Burge

Around the time of the police board decision, I was discussing the case with a friendly neighbor over the backyard fence. He had been following the case in the news and was appalled by the idea that torture could be a trademark of Burge and the CPD. A college professor, he pulled out an innocuous-looking invitation to the Roosevelt University Faculty Boat Cruise party with a map of Burnham Harbor boat dock, where well-heeled Chicagoans kept their boats. He told me that when he went on the cruise, he discovered that Burge also docked his boat at Burnham Harbor, and, with a little amateur detective work, my professor friend located the boat, moored near the Children's Park, with its all-too-appropriate name, the *Vigilante*, prominent on the bow.

I also heard through the grapevine that Burge had been given a rousing going-away party by his many police buddies. He was headed to his Florida home, south of Tampa-St. Petersburg, located on a canal where he could dock the *Vigilante*. According to a caterer, the huge cake served at the party was adorned with a confectioner's depiction of the black shock box. Lawyers sometimes say that suspects "ate the evidence"; Burge and his Area 2 co-conspirators literally did so, rather than tossing it overboard this time.

Just after New Year's Day of 1994, I got a call from my close friend, the superlative death penalty lawyer Chick Hoffman. After working with the People's Law Office in the 1970s and 1980s, Chick had gone on to specialize in death cases. He sought to enlist me and my partners in representing a death row prisoner who alleged that several of Burge's detectives tortured him into falsely confessing to the double murder of an elderly couple on Chicago's south side. Time was running short, Chick told me, as the prisoner had lost his appeal in the Illinois Supreme Court, and that previous October, the US Supreme Court had refused to review his case. An execution date had been set; under Illinois law, he had six months to file a post-conviction challenge in the trial court. Not only would we be undertaking a gravely serious case, but we would also be entering a new legal arena.

Jan Susler volunteered to work with me. Long before, I had nicknamed her "Straight Ahead," for her uncompromising devotion to principle and indefatigable work ethic. The clock was ticking, and we had less than three months to file a comprehensive petition that raised every arguable issue in the hope that one of them would save our new client's life.

Aaron Patterson was no ordinary defendant. The son of a Chicago police lieutenant and a schoolteacher, Aaron, known on the streets as Ranger, prided himself on being the leader of the south side Apache Ranger gang and stood convicted of three gang-related attempted murders. However, he steadfastly maintained his innocence in the double murder case, saying it was "not his style" to stab his alleged victims or to victimize an elderly couple. Chick supplied us with Aaron's trial transcript, and from it we learned the details of his torture.

Aaron, on the run at the time, was captured in the spring of 1986 by Chicago police officers while he was hiding in an attic. He was turned over to Area 2 detectives, who told him they would have killed him if they had been the ones who arrested him. They transported him to Area 2—the new complex on 111th Street—where he was placed in an interrogation room. Late that night, after Aaron refused to cooperate, detective James Pienta, a longtime Burge associate, said he was "tired of this bullshit," and left the room. Pienta returned with a gray plastic typewriter cover, and when Aaron continued to deny his involvement in the crime, he was surrounded by Pienta and six other detectives. They handcuffed his hands behind his back, turned out the light, and began to hit Aaron in the chest. Next they pushed the plastic cover over his face and ears, and held it tightly for at least a minute. Like Anthony Holmes, Gregory Banks, and Andrew Wilson, Aaron experienced near-suffocation.

Pienta then threatened to "do something worse" to him if he did not cooperate. No stranger to the law, Aaron kept asking for an attorney while refusing to cooperate, so the detectives again turned off the light and put the plastic cover over his head. This time they held it tightly even longer, while emptying his lungs by punching him. The suffocation was unbearable, and Aaron stated that he would repeat "anything you say."

The detectives left the room to get an assistant state's attorney and were gone for about an hour. During that time Aaron, using a paper clip, scratched into the metal bench in the interview room the following outcry:

I lie about murders
Police threaten me with violence
Slapped and suffocated me with plastic
No lawyer or dad   No phone

He also scratched a second message on a door jamb:

Signed false statement to murders
Tonto on statement is the code word
Aaron

In the early morning hours, a "red haired" officer returned with an assistant state's attorney to take a written statement. Aaron asked the officer to leave the room, then told the assistant prosecutor he had nothing to say and wanted a lawyer. Aggravated, the prosecutor brought the red-haired officer back into the room. "You're fucking up," the officer said, then took out his revolver, put it on the table, and said, "We told you if you don't do what we tell you to, you're going to get something worse than before—it will have been a snap compared to what you will get." He also told Aaron that if he revealed the torture, "It's your word against ours." Later in the day, Aaron again agreed to make a statement in order to get phone calls to his family and an attorney; after the calls, he refused to sign a statement that a second prosecutor had handwritten, so he was further beaten. Aaron's twenty-four-hour ordeal finally ended with the detectives and prosecutors settling for an unsigned, handwritten statement that purported to describe the detectives' hypothesized version of the murders.

Jan and I, in frequent consultation with Chick, feverishly began to investigate. At the heart of our approach was that Aaron's series of public defenders was unconstitutionally ineffective because they did not properly obtain, develop, and present the evidence of Burge-related torture that we had been uncovering while Aaron's prosecution was proceeding in 1988 and 1989. As an alternative argument, we would contend that the evidence had been newly discovered since Aaron's 1988 motion to suppress hearing and 1989 trial, entitling him to a new hearing on that basis.

While I was reading Aaron's trial transcript, I noticed that the City had produced certain OPS files pursuant to a defense subpoena. Trial judge John Morrissey had looked at the files in camera and ruled they were not relevant. The files were missing from the court record, but a brief description of one case looked especially promising—the case of Mearon Diggins. The public defenders had made no effort to find Diggins, but we did, and he spoke with me on the phone from prison.

Contrary to the judge's ruling, Mearon's story was highly relevant. He told me that he was arrested for murder on October 9, 1985, and taken to Area 2, placed in an interview room, and handcuffed to a ring on the wall. He said that several detectives, including Pienta and others named by Aaron Patterson, were involved in questioning him and a friend named Terry. Mearon told me that during his two days of questioning, he was beaten on the legs and back with a flashlight by these detectives; that he could hear his friend Terry being beaten in the next room; and that he finally succumbed and gave a signed, written statement implicating himself in the crime. He was taken to Cook County Jail, where he complained of the brutality, and photos were taken of his legs, showing bruises. He said he also made an OPS complaint and was interviewed at the jail by investigators, but later, upon the advice of his defense counsel, he refused to further cooperate with the OPS, leading its investigator to "not sustain" his complaint.

As the filing deadline drew closer, Jan and I drove the one hundred miles down Interstate 55 to visit Aaron on Pontiac Penitentiary's death row. We had spoken with Aaron several times on the phone. He was very assertive, sometimes argumentative, and frequently shouted instructions. It was clear he would not be an easy client to deal with. Aaron was the subject of even tighter security than the average death-row prisoner due to a disciplinary violation. He was brought to our visit chained hand and foot, and we spoke to him, separated by a barrier, through a screen. He cut an imposing figure, tall, with what seemed to be a perpetual scowl; driven by a righteous anger, his intelligence and commitment to justice in his case shone through.

At one point during the discussion, Aaron told us something that would greatly strengthen his case: just before his September 1989 trial, he had seen the red-haired officer on the television news. It was Jon Burge. Aaron told his lawyer at the time, Brian Dosch, about his identification shortly thereafter.

I spoke to Dosch, who confirmed that Aaron had told him about his identification of Burge. Hardboiled and at times hard-drinking, Dosch said that he believed Aaron's claim of innocence and wanted to help. He was forthcoming about his failures in representing Aaron, including his last-minute decision not to call Aaron to the stand. He also told me that Dale Coventry had been his supervisor at the time of Aaron's trial, but Coventry did not share his extensive knowledge of the Burge evidence.

Dosch signed an affidavit, as did Coventry, and I compiled a statistical update on our investigation: nearly sixty Area 2 torture cases that featured Burge as either a participant or supervisor, including forty-six beatings; twenty-four baggings, three by typewriter covers; sixteen electric-shockings; and eight gun threats. I also documented several new cases that we had recently uncovered, including that of Patterson's unlikely co-defendant, Eric Caine. A member of a rival south side gang, Caine had been subjected to a beating and a painful torture technique known as "ear-cupping" by some of the same detectives who had tortured Aaron. After being threatened with "ending up like Aaron," Caine gave an improbable confession, falsely implicating himself and his gang rival in the double murder.

Armed with this new evidence, Jan and I drafted our lengthy post-conviction petition. Featuring the torture evidence as our centerpiece, we also called into question Aaron's original trial judge, Arthur Cieslik. A former lawyer for the City, in the early 1980s Cieslik had let off with a manslaughter conviction two cops who had brutally beaten a homeless Black man, Richard Ramey, to death. It was reported by Robert Cooley, an FBI snitch, that alderman Ed Burke had pressured Cieslik for an outright acquittal in the Ramey case, saying, "What's the big deal, it's only a nigger." Later, Cieslik had sent Burge torture survivor Leroy Orange to death row.

As we pointed out in our petition, Cieslik was "widely known for his racial and sexual intolerance" and had been censured for making a sexually offensive comment to an attorney. We further noted that Cieslik had referred to two African American public defenders, one of whom had represented Aaron at his motion to suppress hearing, as "Smiley" and "Laughing Boy." We also highlighted his denial from the bench of Aaron's suppression motion. Cieslik's rationale was a common refrain among Cook County judges whose rulings perpetuated the code of silence in the torture cases:

> In a murder case of this nature what possible benefit could be had by the police officer by abusing the defendant as he says he was abused—there is nothing to substantiate it. It is really his statement. And I do know that there are certain shortcomings of everybody in the performance of their duties. But

there are too many people that are involved in this particular case, too many people that fully understand what could happen if in fact somebody did get careless in the performance of his duties and abuses his authority and power.

As the clock ran out, our multitalented paralegal, Jose Berrios, raced down to the Criminal Courts Building to file our lengthy petition and set of exhibits. We needed to do additional investigation and file an amended petition, but the battle to save Aaron's life on the strength of the newly developed torture evidence had begun.

There were also new developments in Andrew Wilson's civil case. Mercifully, court rules provided for a new judge to be randomly selected when the court of appeals granted a new trial. This time we drew district judge James Holderman. Sometimes short-tempered and a bit erratic, Holderman was also considered to be smart, usually fair, and no friend of the City.

On the Burge firing front, circuit court judge Thomas J. O'Brien reluctantly upheld the police board's decision. Characterizing as "chameleon like" the City's change of positions—from its repeated denials, during our litigation, that Burge had committed any wrongdoing to the opposite position before the police board—he nonetheless rejected Kunkle's argument that the City was prevented by the legal principle of estoppel from taking the "diametrically opposed" position that it did before the board. He agreed with the Seventh Circuit that Melvin Jones's testimony was relevant, but cast severe doubt on Andrew Wilson's credibility, saying that he had a "quintessential motive for lying!" In the end, he accepted the police board's view of the evidence "with the most difficult restraint."

Just after Judge O'Brien issued his decision, the City morphed, in our opinion, from chameleon to snake. Counselors James McCarthy and Maureen Murphy were replaced by high-level City lawyers, who informed us that the City was changing its position with regard to its legal and financial responsibility for Burge's actions. It would continue to pay Kunkle and his co-counsel—the amount was approaching a cool million—but would no longer pay for any damages or settlement that Burge incurred going forward. This 180-degree turn was based on an argument that McCarthy and Murphy had expressly and repeatedly rejected on the record for the past eight years: that Burge was acting outside of his "scope of employment" when he tortured Andrew Wilson.

We fought back by moving that Judge Holderman restore the City as a defendant, under a state law theory of indemnification, and for a finding of liability against Burge, Yucaitis, and O'Hara. Our legal theory was another form of estoppel, one that sought to have the police board's finding that Burge physically abused Andrew accepted in our case without the necessity of a trial. That fall, the judicial gods looked kindly upon us, randomly reassigning Andrew's case to newly appointed federal judge Robert Gettleman, only days after his confirmation by the United States Senate. After graduating from Northwestern Law School, Gettleman had served as a law clerk for Seventh Circuit judge Luther Swygert, then worked as a practicing lawyer to expand the civil rights of persons with disabilities. Steady, sympathetic to victims of official misconduct, with a brilliant legal mind, he was the polar opposite of Judge Duff. He tackled the complex legal issues that the case now presented with the skill and courage that few judges, particularly rookies, would have the wherewithal to do.

Judge Gettleman first rejected a motion filed by the City to dismiss our new state law claim against it, then later addressed the question of whether estoppel principles made us winners against Burge, Yucaitis, O'Hara, and the City itself. The legal term for this was "summary judgment," and civil rights plaintiffs almost never prevailed on this pretrial maneuver, particularly when the grounds were that prior factual findings made by an administrative body precluded a public official from a trial on the issue that the findings addressed. Navigating a tangle of federal and Illinois state law precedents, Judge Gettleman, in a detailed written opinion, granted us summary judgment against the officers on the controlling factual questions of whether they had used excessive physical force, had failed to stop the use of that force, and had failed to provide medical care. Hence, he concluded, they had violated Andrew's constitutional rights and were thereby legally responsible for his injuries. He also ruled that Burge, Yucaitis, and O'Hara had acted within the scope of their employment as Chicago police officers when they tortured Andrew, thus making the City financially liable under state law for its officers' unconstitutional actions.

This turn of events made us strange bedfellows with Kunkle and company because our interests had converged—both our teams wanted the City to pay the damages that would flow from our now validated claims. Although we had some settlement discussions with Kunkle, it soon became clear that without the City's involvement and cooperation, we could not resolve the case. Judge Gettleman then endeavored to make an equitable settlement a reality and held periodic meetings with all of us in his chambers over the following months. At last, it appeared that we had arrived at an agreement with the City to pay approximately $1 million in damages and attorneys' fees to resolve the case, ten years after Andrew first filed it.

None of the funds would actually come Andrew's way; the family of one of the slain officers had filed a wrongful-death lawsuit against him and received a $6 million default judgment years before. We calculated that in our nine years of fighting the case, our office was due about $2 million in fees and costs for our work. With these factors in mind, we tentatively agreed to a division of the money: $900,000 to us and $100,000, through Andrew, to the slain officer's family.

Andrew's initial reaction to receiving nothing was an understandable one—he wanted to keep fighting, settlement be damned. John, using his considerable persuasive powers, convinced Andrew that this resolution was in all of our best interests. It was a significant victory after a decade of fighting.

We conveyed the good news to the judge and the opposing lawyers, but the City responded with a switch. First deputy City lawyer Larry Rosenthal had decided to withdraw the City's agreement to settle; instead, the City intended to contest its financial responsibility in another appeal to the Seventh Circuit. We knew better than to be surprised at anything the City did in the Burge cases, but resolution had felt so close, and yet was still so far away . . .

The End of the Nightstick

More than three years in the making, the film *The End of the Nightstick* aired nationally on public television in the summer of 1994. The title was taken from a statement made by NYPD lieutenant "Clubber" Williams in 1877 that continues to reflect prevalent police attitudes to this day: "There is more law at the end of a policeman's nightstick than in all the decisions of your Supreme Court."

The thrust of the hour-long piece by local filmmakers Eric Scholl, Cindy Moran, and Peter Kuttner was the torture cases and the task force's important role in bringing down Burge. Identifying Jeff and Mariel as the task force's leaders, the film tracked the group's role in organizing demonstrations and its use of militant tactics to confront Daley at his house, Burge's detectives at the police station, council members at city hall, and thousands of cops and prosecutors outside the FOP fundraiser. Footage was shown of the black shock box and its clips and crank, as an actor recited Andrew Wilson's testimony about how he was shocked by Burge during "fun time." Actors gave voice to descriptions of the torture suffered by the scores of men whose cases we had documented, in the men's own words, while the names of the tortured men and their testimony scrolled onscreen. Shadeed Mu'min, the only torture survivor to appear in person, told of how Burge suffocated him with a plastic typewriter cover.

In interviews a number of notable local African American activists condemned the systemic and racist nature of the brutality and likened it to apartheid. I helped narrate some of the factual and legal history behind the torture cases, adding that Daley was a "main player in the cover-up" of the torture. The film concluded with a screen shot of the front page of the February 1993 *Sun Times*, announcing that Burge had been fired.

Some critics faulted the film for having an agenda, overlooking the fact it had aired on a show called, quite openly, "Point of View." But Candice Russell of the Florida *Sun Sentinel*, grasped the filmmakers' aims in championing the work of the task force:

> It would be depressing if this film simply provided a voice of dissent. It is compelling viewing because it shows how various community groups coalesced behind a single goal—to oust Burge from his job and to put an end to his cruel tactics. It's empowering to see how much average citizens can do when faced with an implacable bureaucracy.

CHAPTER 13

The Marcus Wiggins Case

"They're Supposed to Serve and Protect, Right?"

W e had filed Marcus Wiggins's complaint almost three years
before, but the case had stalled. The roadblocks were cleared in
late 1995 after Marcus's criminal case was dismissed. In a related case,
a well-respected Black judge, Earl Strayhorn, had ruled that the "hor-
rendously oppressive atmosphere" at Burge's Area 3—including evidence
that Marcus and several other juveniles had been tortured and abused—
required the suppression of the confession of the alleged shooter.

Ever since OPS director Gayle Shines had publicly revealed, almost
three years before, that she had ordered the reopening of an undisclosed
number of torture investigations, we had pursued the files in those cases
through discovery demands in the Marcus Wiggins case. Finally, after
numerous phone calls, motions, and letters, we received three reopened
case files from the City: those of Gregory Banks, Phillip Adkins, and
Thomas Craft. The files revealed that the specially assigned African American investigators in those cases had recommended that sustained findings
be entered against John Byrne, Peter Dignan, and several other Area 2
detectives for brutality and for filing false reports. However, these proposed findings had not been approved by Shines, so no disciplinary action
had been taken.

Thus the Marcus Wiggins case gave us an avenue not only to question
the detectives who had interrogated Marcus but also to delve into the evidence we had uncovered since the *Wilson* trials. Two obvious candidates
for deposition were Peter Dignan and Mike Hoke.

Dignan was from a multigenerational police family, with a brother
also on the force, a great uncle described as a "legendary chief of detectives
in Chicago who was advanced to commissioner of police during the Al

Capone era," and an uncle who had served as a sergeant in the south side Woodlawn district.

Cocky, Dignan sauntered into his deposition wearing a Marines hat. I first questioned him about his background. A graduate of a south side Catholic school, he rose to the rank of corporal in the marines and spent thirteen months in Vietnam, eight or nine of them in daily combat. He rattled off the places where he had fought and the fact that he was wounded in the head and legs at Khe Sanh. He said he "had no idea" how many Vietnamese he had killed, using an M-16 rifle. He received a Purple Heart and several other military honors, and, for a time, was assigned to a prisoner of war detention camp at Duang Ha. He admitted to using military hand-crank field telephones, small enough to carry in a backpack, which were used to communicate with listening posts and observation towers.

Upon his return to Chicago, Dignan became a Chicago police officer and was assigned to the Third District, located on the south side at 75th and Maryland. There he met Jon Burge, and they became squad car partners and drinking buddies. Dignan made detective about a year after Burge and was assigned to Area 2 Homicide. He verified Deep Badge's assertions that Burge and his "asskickers" frequented the bars west of Area 2, along Western Avenue; praised those officers as excellent detectives; and denigrated Frank Laverty as only "fair" and "not that knowledgeable."

Knowing that Dignan, in particular, had been accused of using virulent racial slurs during his torture of Gregory Banks and another victim, Darrell Cannon, I asked him the following:

> Taylor: In any of your experiences, have you ever used the term "nigger"?
> Dignan: Yes.
> Taylor: How frequently have you used it?
> Dignan: You got to be kidding me. I have no idea.
> Taylor: Would you say more than ten times?
> Dignan: Yes.
> Taylor: More than a hundred times?
> Dignan: Probably.
> Taylor: Have you heard Jon Burge use the term "nigger" in your presence?
> Dignan: Yes.

The tension escalated as I asked about his involvement in torture on the Area 2 midnight crew. He denied, falsely, that there was a basement at Area 2 (where he was accused of torturing victims Alonzo Smith and

Stanley Wrice). He claimed that Gregory Banks's documented injuries came about when he tried to escape and that Phillip Adkins had suffered his during an auto accident. After Dignan denied that he had tortured several other victims, I asked him how many guns he owned, and his response surprised even me—he ticked off ten guns, including an Uzi submachine gun, a shotgun, and a litany of revolvers and automatic pistols.

Then the questioning turned personal. Dignan had gone off on a tirade when he had given his statements in the reopened OPS investigations. In the Adkins case, he had stated that the only reason he was being called down was "that the city, as is their practice, decided to pay the People's Law Office for this fallacious claim." When I challenged him, he called Adkins "a liar" and proclaimed, "You better believe that I said it." The war of words continued:

> Taylor: I want to know why you made this claim.
> Dignan: It was my belief at the time that you were looking for money and it's still my belief at this time that you're looking for money. I don't think what you're doing is right.

Dignan made no bones about his love and respect for Burge, whom he called "one of the best policemen I ever met"; Burge was, in Dignan's description, "extremely hardworking," an "effective interrogator" who got results. Dignan had worked on the BOY fundraising committee and confirmed that Burge's big boat was called the *Vigilante*. He was in regular contact with Burge and had traveled to Burge's home in Apollo Beach, Florida, the previous November to attend a football game in nearby Tampa Bay.

Two weeks before, I had deposed Mike Hoke. Hoke had been described in Deep Badge's second missive as a "weak link . . . he and Burge constantly were arguing and backstabbing each other." In his last letter, sent after we had filed our first list of Burge victims and had named Hoke in several cases, including Anthony "Satan" Holmes's, Deep Badge had gone into more detail:

> Another development is Mike Hoke was in the station looking for information. If you look at my first letter you will find that it was thought that he would not be on Burge's team. He was not the beating type but is a thoroughly humorless workaholic who stood up to Burge. He said he was named in your brief and you have your facts all wrong. Apparently he has done his homework and has paperwork to verify his non-involvement.

During the 1970s and 1980s, Hoke was on a career path parallel to Burge's. He became an Area 2 detective, then an Area 2 sergeant at about the same time as Burge, ascended first to lieutenant, then, in 1988, at the same time as Burge became the commander of Area 3, Hoke became the commander of the Vice Control Division. Soon after, their career paths sharply diverged; now, in July 1996, Hoke sat in the witness chair as an assistant deputy superintendent of police, in charge of the Internal Affairs division of the CPD.

Any hope that Hoke might come clean about Burge was quickly dashed by the power of the police code of silence. Not only was Hoke humorless, he was also defensive and hostile. After admitting that he was present for Anthony Holmes's arrest, he took himself out of Holmes's interrogation and then went the extra mile by asserting that he did not think Burge was present, either. Hoke was in Mexico on furlough when Andrew Wilson was tortured in February 1982 and was assigned to a different unit from Burge at Area 2 during the 1980s. He said he never saw Burge abuse anyone and that Burge was a "pretty good detective, a good police officer, a very good police officer." In answer to my question about conflicts with Burge, he said, "Not really, no." When asked if Burge was a friend, Hoke said, "We got along." Hoke had been on the *Vigilante* only once, as he had gotten violently seasick. He conceded that Burge's firing had caused him to change his opinion of Burge "somewhat."

Hoke testified that "House of Screams" author John Conroy had sent him the Deep Badge letters, but he had not responded to Conroy's request for an interview. He did give us a few nuggets—he said he had "probably" talked to Burge about the Deep Badge letters: "We probably discussed who wrote them." He also, unwittingly perhaps, gave some official authenticity to the letters, saying, "Whoever wrote the letters had to be familiar with whoever worked in Area 2, it had an awful lot of names in there." He also confirmed that the envelopes the letters came in were widely used by police personnel. Not surprisingly, he denied the existence of a police code of silence (the very one he was reenacting on the spot). He ducked my question as to whether Frank Laverty "did the right thing" by coming forward in the George Jones case, saying that he needed more facts to draw a conclusion, and he offered that Peter Dignan was "one of the nicest people I have ever met in my life."

The depositions in the Marcus Wiggins case also allowed for another investigation within the investigation—the cage in which suspects were held at Area 3. We had some photos that showed some black objects at the top of the cage. We had been told by Marcus and others that they were "scary-looking" African masks. The photos also showed a poster of a man behind bars, with the caption "Another Happy Ending" and two inscriptions: "Bonke's Bin" and "Vallandingham Memorial Cage." I asked each of the detectives who were defendants in the case about the masks, as shown in part in the photos, and they all gave the same answer: they did not know about any masks, and that the objects, even when the photos were blown up, appeared to be black smudges. (We would later obtain additional photos of the cage from the public defender that definitively showed the garish masks.)

Sergeant Bonke professed to have no knowledge of why the cage was called his "bin." Others admitted to a wide array of items being hung on or about the cage: a full-sized department-store mannequin; neckties (which could easily look like nooses if tied); and stuffed animals. The lieutenant in charge of the Area 3 Violent Crimes Unit admitted that all these items were "inappropriate" and claimed that he had taken them down when he noticed them. He also recounted why the cage was named after Detective Vallandingham—Vallandingham was in charge of a suspect who, supposedly without being pushed, went out of an open third-story window, landed three stories below, and, miraculously, lived to tell the tale. Unfortunately, the unnamed suspect in the Vallandingham case had, according to the lieutenant, been killed in a subsequent shooting.

Marcus Wiggins was subjected to two grueling days of questioning. Kunkle was on hand to represent Burge and Byrne, but two in-house City lawyers handled the questioning. It had been almost five years since Marcus was tortured, and he had gone from sixty-five pounds, at age thirteen, to a hundred fifty. He had been under Dr. Antonio Martinez's care for his PTSD for much of the time. At fifteen Marcus had become a father. In his brief life he had been shot in the head on three separate occasions and stabbed another time. The first shooting, when he was eight or nine, had contributed to his learning disability, and he stuttered badly when under stress. His mother had tried to get him away from the violence of their West Englewood neighborhood by moving, for a time, to Beloit, Wisconsin. Marcus had been chased and beaten on several occasions by Beloit gang members, was arrested several times, and had been in and out of school.

During our preparation, Marcus was very withdrawn and reverted to sucking his thumb. In the deposition, he often gave one-word answers, sometimes seemed confused, and stuttered repeatedly. John and I protected him as best we could with objections that sought to clear up confusion or to point out when Marcus did not understand the meaning of a word or phrase. Haltingly and in a very soft voice, Marcus told about how the police took him into custody at about 10:00 o'clock at night and put him in a red detective car, then moved him to another car, where a detective asked him where he lived. After he gave an address, the detective told him to "stop lying" and cracked him on the head with a long flashlight. When his mother, Carolyn Johnson, arrived on the scene and asked if she could go with him to the station, she was told an emphatic "no."

At Area 3, Marcus testified, he was taken into a closed interview room and handcuffed to a ring on the wall. A tall, blond, blue-eyed detective came into the room and asked Marcus what happened. Marcus said, "I don't know." The detective left and closed the door behind him. While sitting there alone, Marcus heard a young voice scream out ten or eleven times, "I didn't do nothing." After another detective briefly questioned him, the tall, blond detective reentered. When Marcus continued to deny knowledge of what happened, the detective called Marcus a liar and punched him four or five times in the chest. Marcus lost his breath and began to cry. The detective accused Marcus of shooting the victim and then left the room.

It was now about 1:15 in the morning. According to Marcus, the blond detective quickly returned, carrying a silver box about the size of a toaster. It had some black knobs on it, with wires coming out from it. Each wire had "a silver thing" attached to it. (Marcus drew a picture of the box for the City lawyers.) The blond detective unhandcuffed Marcus, put his hands on the table, and put the silver things, which had rubber on the top, on the back of Marcus's hands. Marcus asked, "What are you doing?" and the detective responded, "Shut up" and "Don't move." He turned some kind of switch, and Marcus heard a humming or whirring sound.

Stuttering, Marcus continued his testimony:

> My hands started burning, feeling like I was being burned. I was—I was shaking—and my—and my—jaws got tight and my eyes felt—they went blank. My whole body was shaking. I felt like I was spinning and I could just see light. It felt like my jaws was like—they was—I can't say the word. It felt like my jaw was sucking in.

Marcus's heart was pounding and his hands were sweaty. Then he passed out and fell face down on the table. When he came to, he was alone again, and the box was no longer in the room. He was taken into another room with detectives and a female assistant state's attorney present. Scared, drowsy, and "feeling terrible" from the torture, he was "ready to go home."

The City's lawyer pressed Marcus for more details:

Ms. Carey: Can you describe how you felt any further for me?
Marcus: I felt like I was going to die.

Carey asked again, "Can you describe how you felt any further for me?" Marcus lowered his head and helplessly shook his head "no," as if to ask, "What more do I need to say?"

In the room with the detectives and assistant state's attorney, Marcus signed a statement that put him at the scene of the crime with a crowd of juveniles when the victim was shot, a statement he later repudiated as false. He was placed in the cage for a while with a group of juveniles, some of whom would also be charged with the shooting. The next day he was taken to the juvenile detention center—"a jail for little kids," Marcus called it— where he remained for the next several months. The victim died the day after the shooting, so Marcus was charged with murder.

That ended his first day of testimony. We made sure that Marcus saw Dr. Martinez before the next session, a week later. During the second day of questioning, Marcus struggled his way through elaborating on his trauma, which Dr. Martinez had diagnosed as torture-related PTSD. He told of how his mother burst out crying when he described his torture to her. He described seeing Myron James, who had been rounded up with Marcus but not charged, and Myron said to Marcus that he heard him screaming. He told of recurring nightmares of white people chasing him and being tortured by having a stick shoved up his nose. He told of how he would run into his house whenever he saw the police. Marcus painfully admitted that he still sucked his thumb, which he did during one of the deposition breaks, and told of curling up in a ball at our office. As he tried to describe how his stutter had worsened since his torture, he began to stammer. When Carey asked him questions about the police department's illegal policies that we had alleged in his complaint, Marcus innocently responded, "They are supposed to serve—serve and protect, right?"

Two months later, the tall, blue-eyed detective marched into our conference room, flanked by City lawyers and several of his fellow Area 3 defendants. I was joined by a law student intern, Joey Mogul, who would later become a brilliant mainstay of our torture team. My first impression of the stiff, steely-eyed Burge disciple named Maslanka was that of an Aryan storm trooper, and over the two highly charged sessions he did little to dispel it.

Maslanka's testimony revealed that before becoming a police officer, he had been arrested on at least three occasions, once for aggravated battery and another time for battery. He was an expert in judo, ran three miles and did 125 push-ups daily, and had been accused of threatening to kill a precinct captain's wife.

Maslanka's loyalty to Burge was unquestioned. They were drinking buddies; he raised money for Burge's police board defense, attended the hearing in support, and commiserated with him. When Burge was cleaning out his desk after being suspended, Maslanka came down to give his friend support. After Burge moved to Florida, Maslanka stayed in touch, calling him at Christmas and taking a weekend road trip the previous November down to Burge's Apollo Beach home with several other former Area 2 detectives to watch Dave Wannstedt's Chicago Bears lose to the Tampa Bay Buccaneers.

Maslanka's version of events contrasted sharply from Marcus's. Maslanka depicted the events as a racially motivated, gang-related retaliation for an earlier shooting by a Latin gang, with Marcus a willing member of a group of juvenile gang wannabes who gathered around the victim as he was shot.

Marcus had been marched past the cage and left alone in a room for more than two hours. Then Detective Maslanka had conducted his interrogation of Marcus in a closed room, without Marcus's mother or a youth officer present. These facts had led the OPS to recommend a ten-day suspension for Maslanka, later reduced to a reprimand by superintendent Matt Rodriguez.

Maslanka admitted that he had not given Marcus any food or drink or taken him to the bathroom. He denied hitting or torturing Marcus, angrily denouncing the allegations as "lies." He claimed to have questioned Marcus in three relatively brief sessions from 1:00 to 1:30 in the morning, using nothing but a seasoned detective's skilled interrogation tactics. Ultimately, after Maslanka took a cigarette break and returned to the room, Marcus—who was not upset, crying, or stuttering at any time—admitted to sufficient involvement in the shooting to make him chargeable on an accountability theory. But as I continued to press Maslanka on the crucial details of his story, this seasoned detective, who had testified hundreds of times, asked for a break, saying, "I'm not thinking straight right now. The air conditioner is not on and I'm thirsty."

In light of Marcus's psychological and intellectual fragility, John and I could not imagine putting him through the rigors of a trial. The case was before Ruben Castillo, a direct and open-minded judge. At a conference in his chambers, Judge Castillo pointed out that there was an eyewitness who put Marcus at the scene of the crime, making our wrongful arrest and imprisonment claim highly problematic. He further counseled that while Marcus's torture was outrageous, Marcus might have credibility problems, given his fairly substantial arrest record and the lack of supporting eyewitnesses or physical evidence. Judge Castillo recommended a figure just north of $100,000, but the City steadfastly refused to go above its self-imposed ceiling of $100,000. With the trial date fast approaching, and with Marcus in no condition to go forward, we reluctantly agreed to accept $95,000 to resolve the case.

There was a hitch, however—before it would pay the settlement, the City wanted us to return the newly obtained OPS torture documents. In a letter to me, assistant corporation counsel Margaret Carey wrote: "You are apparently under the impression that these are 'plaintiff's documents'. This perception is incorrect, and these documents should be returned in compliance with your agreement."

We resisted this attempt to continue the cover-up, and the City finally relented and paid the money with the understanding that we would litigate the question of secrecy before Judge Castillo. The *Reader*, Citizens Alert, and the task force joined us in our fight to publicly release the documents, while the FOP intervened on the City's side. We were hopeful that Judge Castillo would stand against the forces of cover-up and secrecy, but the wheels of justice turn slowly, and we we were left to wait nearly a year for Judge Castillo's decision.

CHAPTER 14

Decisions, Decisions

After a hiatus of several years, journalist John Conroy returned to the investigation of torture, publishing "Town Without Pity" in the *Chicago Reader* in early 1996. His theme was encapsulated by the article's subtitle: "Torture: the courts know about it, the media know about it, and chances are, you know about it. So why aren't we doing anything about it?"

"Burge's fall from grace has been well publicized and is known at some level by millions of people in the Chicago area and around the country," Conroy wrote. "That torture was administered by certain Area Two policemen is not a wild claim made by some lunatic and radical fringe; it is a fact known to well-established, well-meaning, and well-off members of the community." But, Conroy continued, "there is something strangely absent here, namely the victims of Burge and his fellow detectives." After referring to Andrew Wilson's case, Conroy asked, "What about the 58 other claims made thus far and the uncounted others that haven't surfaced? Why is there no chorus calling for justice for Madison Hobley, for instance?"

He then told Madison's story. A college graduate with no prior criminal record, Madison Hobley was on death row for the arson-murder of seven people, including his wife and fifteen-month-old son. The single most damning piece of evidence against Madison was an alleged confession that was tortured from him by several Area 2 detectives under the supervision of sergeant John Byrne. At his trial, Madison had testified that he was suffocated with a typewriter cover, poked in the throat with pressure applied to his Adam's apple, punched in the ribs and chest, and kicked in the groin and shins. Madison also testified that his handcuffs were applied so tightly that he experienced extreme pain in his wrists; that detective Robert Dwyer called him a "skinny little nigger"; and that Detective James Lotito taunted him with a remark about Black people liking pork chops. Despite this torture, Madison maintained that he did not confess.

Photographs showed scrapes on Madison's wrists and a bruise on his chest, but Dwyer testified that the wrist wounds were self-inflicted, and he was never asked to explain the chest bruise. Dwyer said that Madison had willingly made an oral confession but claimed that his notes got wet when he spilled coffee on them—so he threw them away. Lotito's notes, in contrast, showed that Madison had denied committing the crime. Conroy concluded:

> And so there is no contemporaneous record of a confession—no notes taken by detectives, no handwritten admission of guilt from a penitent suspect, no statement typed by detectives and signed by Hobley, no formal transcription typed by a court reporter and witnessed by an assistant state's attorney. All we have is the word of the policemen involved. And any serious student of the Area Two cases would put little faith in the word of Dwyer, Lotito, McWeeny, and a small group of their immediate colleagues. Under oath, those detectives have told tales that appear to be contradicted by physical evidence.

The cases Conroy documented not only gave names and faces to a number of additional torture survivors but also focused on Burge's underlings: Byrne, Dignan, Dwyer, Lotito, and McWeeny. Conroy discussed how McWeeny, operating in tandem with Burge and his "asskickers," played the classic "good cop" role in case after case, appearing on the heels of the torture to promise relief from the bad guys and leniency if the victim cooperated and confessed. (The cases of Melvin Jones, Aaron Patterson, and Stanley Howard were prime examples of McWeeny's tactics in action.)

Conroy also profiled our office's lonely pursuit of torture victims:

> The list put together by Flint Taylor and his colleagues at the People's Law Office was not the result of 58 phone calls from other defense attorneys, public defenders, and former assistant state's attorneys, each recalling an Area Two case they had handled in the past. Taylor's list has grown largely because the victim he was led to by the anonymous police officer knew of two other electric shock victims, and those men knew of still others, and eventually word traveled around various jailhouses that Taylor and his colleagues were trying to document torture at Area Two. The People's Law Office was then able to track the victims down, locate their lawyers, and pull court records in which some of the men described what they had been through.

The legal community, Conroy noted, "with a few exceptions, was of no help at all and has demonstrated extraordinarily little concern." Casting the net of complicity more widely and specifically, he wrote:

The judiciary might have been less blind if a single policeman had come forward. A policeman might have come forward if pressure had been brought by prosecutors. Prosecutors and politicians might have shown more interest if the media were on the case. The media might have been on the case if the public had demonstrated significant outrage or if individual reporters had felt some kinship with the victims. . . . In all likelihood, Hobley and the others on death row will be executed with the enthusiastic and uninformed consent of the citizens of Illinois.

We were determined to defy Conroy's chilling conclusion. Tim Lohraff, a veteran of the criminal courts as a public defender as well as a mainstay of the task force, had joined our office. We found several alternative suspects in Aaron Patterson's case, including one who had access to the victims' home, told a witness he planned to rob them, and was now in prison for another multiple-stabbing case. Tim visited him in prison in the hope of convincing him to come clean, but he would only hint at possible involvement. Another potential suspect, Michael Arbuckle, told of being arrested by Burge and another officer, placed in an office, and questioned about the murders. According to Michael, his interrogators said that they "really wanted to get Aaron Patterson"; after he refused to cooperate, they threatened him with the death penalty and electrocution. He signed an affidavit recounting his interrogation.

Armed with these witnesses and several others who supplied us with further evidence pointing away from Aaron; an ever-increasing list of torture victims; and a powerful affidavit from Dr. Antonio Martinez, who had examined Aaron on four occasions, we filed, in November 1996, an amended post-conviction petition for Aaron Patterson. It ran to 120 pages, not counting exhibits. With this filing, two and a half years after the first, we had accomplished two important things: first, we had delayed Aaron's execution, and second, we had created a compelling record for our inevitable appeal to the Illinois Supreme Court.

The State moved quickly to dismiss our petition without an evidentiary hearing only a few weeks after we had filed it. Aaron's trial judge, John Morrissey, also viewed our efforts with contempt; he denied our petition from the bench, finding that "any nexus between Area 2 Chicago Police Department Headquarters' alleged systematic torture of people and Aaron Patterson is tenuous at best."

The following May, Judge Castillo, showing his characteristic judicial courage, announced his decision on the OPS documents that the City and the FOP had fought to keep under wraps. He ruled that they should be released, because the public "has a right to know whether allegations of police torture are appropriately investigated and resolved by the City of Chicago." Castillo wrote:

> In essence, this Court concludes that the allegations of police misconduct in the disputed documents before the Court must receive public exposure in order to insure that the significant public interest is served. As Martin Luther King, Jr. stated in his now famous letter from the Birmingham County Jail in April of 1963: "Like a boil that can never be cured as long as it is covered up but must be opened with all its pus-flowing ugliness to the natural medicines of air and light, injustice must likewise be exposed, with all of the tension its exposing creates, to the light of human conscience and the air of national opinion before it can be cured."

Three weeks later, we were back before the Seventh Circuit Court of Appeals, this time to argue that the City was responsible for paying the judgment that Judge Gettleman had entered against Burge in Andrew Wilson's case. Under the rules of procedure, we would have the same troika of judges—Posner, Easterbrook, and Coffey—as we had on the prior *Wilson* appeal. This time John argued the case solo. The court did not wait long to rule, issuing its opinion in mid-July. Written by Posner, the decision characterized the City's main contention—that Burge was not acting in the scope of employment as a Chicago police officer—as "bordering on the frivolous." Burge, "when he tortured Wilson," "was not pursuing a frolic of his own. He was enforcing the criminal law of Illinois overzealously by extracting confessions from criminal suspects by improper means. He was, as it were, too loyal an employee. He was acting squarely within the scope of his employment." One of the highest federal courts in the land expressly called Burge's torture by its name, and held the two-faced City of Chicago civilly responsible for Burge's crimes. The amount of public money expended by this time—a million to Kunkle, now a million to us, half a million to the lawyers who prosecuted Burge before the police board, and $100,000 to the family of one of the slain officers, via Andrew—would be only a drop in the bucket, as the torture cases continued to unfold over the next twenty years.

That fall, New York City was the scene of an egregious case of police torture. Abner Louima, a Haitian security guard, was wrongly identified as having punched an NYPD officer and taken to the 70th Precinct. At the precinct, two of the arresting officers took him, handcuffed, into the bathroom, where they beat him, kicked him in the groin, then took a broken broomstick and rammed it six inches into his rectum. The officers then removed the broomstick and taunted Abner with the feces-covered stick. He suffered serious injuries to his penis and rectum and was left bleeding on the floor of a cell.

Abner Louima's torture caused widespread outrage. US congressman John Conyers, a ranking member of the House Judiciary Committee, convened a hearing a few months later in New York City. I was asked to represent the PLO and the National Lawyers Guild as a witness at the hearing, and I focused on torture and police brutality in Chicago and linked it to the Louima case, police torture in New Orleans, and systemic brutality at the hands of law enforcement across the country. It was the first time we were able to discuss Chicago police torture in an official national forum. I began:

> For the past ten years in Chicago, we have devoted a great deal of our time and energy to uncovering, exposing, and fighting against systemic patterns and practices of police brutality within the Chicago Police Department, and brought to light evidence which establishes that Chicago was, from 1972 to 1991, the police torture "capital" of the United States.

After pointing out that Burge had been fired, and that the Goldston report had found there to be "systematic" torture at Area 2, I brought the cover-up to the present:

> The police superintendent rejected the findings of the Goldston report and attempted to suppress it; no criminal prosecutions have been instituted; no independent investigation has been conducted; no officer, other than Burge, has been disciplined for any of the 65 documented cases; several of Burge's closest henchmen have been promoted, commended and allowed to retire with full benefits; and ten men remain on death row as a result of confessions tortured from them by Burge and his men.

In late July 1998, I was shocked to hear on the radio, while on vacation and out for a run, that two young boys, aged seven and eight, had been charged with the sexual assault and murder of an eleven-year-old girl named Ryan Harris in the poverty-ravaged south side Englewood community. Supposedly, the seven-year-old had confessed to a detective named James Cassidy, who was well-known for eliciting purported "confessions" from Black children. Cassidy obtained juvenile murder charges against the boys and they were locked up in a maximum-security juvenile mental hospital on the west side of Chicago. The case was sensationalized in the media, with the racist stereotype of the Black child predator, popularized by the Clinton administration, running rampant. The seven-year-old was represented by the public defenders' office, while Eugene Pincham, who had returned to legal practice after years on the bench, along with his young associate, Andre Grant, and civil rights attorney Lew Myers, represented the eight-year-old boy.

Three weeks later, in juvenile court, a public hearing was convened to determine whether there was probable cause to bring the boys to trial and an "urgent necessity" to continue to hold them in custody. While the boys played with crayons and the press created a "circus like atmosphere," an overzealous prosecutor named Michael Oppenheimer and his partner quoted from the Bible, admonishing the boys that they "shalt not kill," and accused them of committing a "very brutal," "shocking," and "violent murder." The judge ruled in favor of a trial but released the boys on home monitoring.

In a few weeks, the crime lab returned its results: adult sperm was found on the underpants that had been stuffed in the murdered girl's mouth. As the boys in custody were incapable of ejaculating, the state's attorney's office reluctantly dismissed the charges against the little boys. Soon after, the seven-year-old's public defender contacted us to bring a civil rights suit on behalf of the little boy and his mother. We eagerly agreed, and Jan Susler and I set out to draft a complaint.

Earlier, in 1997, John and I had become counsel in another extremely high-profile civil rights case. From the dirt-poor, predominantly African American suburb of Ford Heights, the Ford Heights Four had been railroaded on rape and murder charges twenty years before. The Four had been charged, on the basis of coerced evidence, with abducting a young white couple from a neighboring, affluent, and overwhelmingly white town and taking them to a housing project in Ford Heights, where they supposedly raped the young woman and murdered both victims. Two of the four had been sentenced to death, while our client, Kenneth Adams, was sentenced to seventy-five years in prison.

The Ford Heights Four had been exonerated after a group of students, working with Northwestern journalism professor David Protess, identified the actual killers, obtained a jailhouse confession from one of them, and confirmed via DNA tests that those men were the real killers. The legal team assembled to pursue the civil case that followed was remarkable—superstar

Wyoming lawyer Gerry Spence (best known for never losing a case), together with local counsel Peter King and Bill Jones, represented Dennis Williams. Dennis, who served his sentence on death row, was the respected leader of the Ford Heights Four, and courageously fought for their freedom in the courts and in the media, from beginning to end. Northwestern Law professor Lawrence Marshall, a leader in the legal battle to end the death penalty, together with Matt Kennelly, a top-notch criminal defense lawyer, represented Willie Raines; and Mark Ter Molen, from the high-powered downtown law firm of Mayer Brown, represented Verneal Jimerson. We, as mentioned, were representing Kenneth Adams.

In preparation for his deposition, Kenny and I, together with several others from the legal team and an expert psychologist, traveled deep into Klan country to visit Menard, the maximum-security prison where Kenny and his co-defendants had served the majority of their time. Upon entering the grounds, we first headed up a hill that overlooked the prison and the adjacent Mississippi River. Kenny described having been brought up there directly after being transported to Menard, looking down, and thinking, as a young man just out of high school, that this was where he was going to spend the rest of his life. We next walked to the decrepit death-row structure. Dark, small, and draped in cobwebs, its cells were tiny, set in a row. We sought out Dennis Williams's former cell, which I believe was number nine, and took photos. We then descended the hill to the main prison, to Kenny's cell, on the fourth tier of the main cell-house. Kenny pointed to the target on the wall near his cell, where the guards fired ear-splitting gunshots to quell prison disturbances. After that, we walked down the four flights of stairs that Kenny had been forced to descend, unaided, while in excruciating pain from kidney stones that required surgery. The experience was extremely emotional, and my respect for Kenny and the Ford Heights Four was redoubled.

The battle against the death penalty was heating up, and Aaron Patterson's case got a big boost when *Chicago Tribune* reporter Steve Mills published an in-depth feature article. Together with Maurice Possley and Ken Armstrong, Mills was working on a series of articles on wrongful-conviction death penalty cases. Featuring Aaron's case on the front page of the *Tribune* was a big deal, both for us and for the evolution of the Death Row Ten movement, initiated by tortured prisoners on death row and supported by radical Chicago activists from the Campaign to End the Death Penalty.

In addition to interviewing Aaron and his mother, Mills published an exclusive interview with Marva Hall, a young woman who had testified against Aaron at his trial. "Hall now recants the statement and her testimony," Mills wrote. "She said police and prosecutors forced her to implicate Patterson, taking an incident that occurred before the Sanchez murders, when she did in fact see Patterson, and fitting it to the investigation. She said Assistant State's Attorney Hynes coached her testimony and threatened to jail her if she did not testify." The article then quoted Marva Hall, whom Mills had tracked down in Alabama with our assistance:

> "I lied on that [witness] stand. They made me say things that wasn't true," said Hall, tears welling in her eyes. "I know that I did wrong getting up on that stand. But it let nothing happen to me."

In a death row phone interview, Aaron acknowledged his history as the leader of the violent Apache Ranger gang, and Mills quoted him as saying:

> I'm telling you, as God is my witness, I didn't have nothing to do with that case. Yes, I did some things. But I didn't do this.

We continued our pursuit of the reopened OPS torture files that had not been produced in the *Wiggins* case. Our vehicle this time was the police brutality case of Marco Santiago. The case was in front of federal judge David Coar, and our relevancy argument was once again premised on the City's continuing failure to discipline Burge's men for their systemic acts of torture and cover-up. After much obfuscation and delay by the City, we had finally obtained a forty-page draft report of the reinvestigation of the case of Darrell Cannon, written by OPS investigator Veronica Tillman-Messenger, recommending that electric-shock and mock-execution allegations be sustained against John Byrne and Peter Dignan. We also obtained a report from Tillman's colleague Leutie Lawrence, recommending that allegations be sustained against Byrne and other Area 2 detectives for torturing death-row prisoner Stanley Howard, as well as the aborted Shadeed Mu'min file. The documents did not indicate that OPS director Shines had taken any action during the intervening five years, once the sustained findings had been tendered to her; and, shockingly, the reports were accompanied by a one-page memo from Tom Needham, a top assistant to newly installed police superintendent Terry Hillard, summarily dismissing all of the charges.

We decided again to utilize the two-pronged approach that had been successful in publicizing the newly obtained evidence in the *Hampton* and *Wilson* cases. I drafted a motion seeking further documents—the final Darrell Cannon report, the Melvin Jones file—and requesting that Judge Coar compel the City to produce OPS Director Shines, Assistant Needham, Superintendent Tillman, and investigator Leutie Lawrence for depositions. To the motion, I attached the Darrell Cannon and Stanley Howard reports, which the City had marked "confidential," and Needham's memo—and tipped off reporter Steve Mills about its filing.

A few days before the motion was to be argued before Judge Coar, the front-page headline of the *Tribune* read: "Brutality Probe Haunts City, Cops Go Unpunished Despite OPS Findings Suspects Were Tortured." Steve Mills's lede succinctly laid out the continuing cover-up:

> Amid allegations that officers working for Chicago Police Cmdr. Jon Burge had physically abused suspects, city investigators in the early 1990s quietly reopened nine controversial brutality cases, reversing earlier rulings and determining some detectives had tortured suspects. But that, according to documents, is where the investigations stopped. In spite of findings that torture and brutality occurred, the cases languished and no one was disciplined. Then, last year, a top police official decided to simply shelve the investigations. He said they were too old to pursue.

Mills linked the OPS investigators' findings in the Darrell Cannon and Stanley Howard reports to the victims' ongoing criminal cases and the death penalty:

> Moreover, the findings were kept secret from the lawyers for the alleged brutality victims, some of whom say that they are critical to appeals, and might help keep their clients from being executed or prove their innocence.

Mills also highlighted the torture-related death penalty case of Ronald Kitchen, who alleged that he was beaten and tortured by Burge and his detectives. His lawyer, Dick Cunningham, a close ally of ours, was quoted as saying, "It makes the case that there was a pattern and practice by Burge and his underlings of doing these things."

At the motion hearing, an impatient Judge Coar made short shrift of the City's excuses that the public officials were "too busy" to sit for depositions, and that additional documents could not be found. The *Trib*'s headline said it all: "City Told to Produce in Torture Suit, Judge Orders Police Files

Scoured, Probers Deposed." Buoyed by Judge Coar's response but mindful not to upset him, I gave a relatively measured statement to the *Trib*: "That those results were not followed by any disciplinary action seemed to reaffirm our feeling that there's something seriously wrong both with the investigations of the torture and the city's ability to produce the materials."

The next day the historically conservative *Tribune* ran a powerful editorial. Titled "Probing Burge," the editorial led with "Former Chicago police Lt. Jon Burge has left behind a dishonorable and potentially lethal legacy." Acknowledging that "activists are fighting to have the cases of 10 Death Row inmates reviewed in the hope of getting them new trials or freedom," the editorial board segued to the broader struggle against the death penalty:

> Given the recent exoneration of Anthony Porter, who was wrongly convicted of a 1982 double murder, and the growing outcry for a moratorium on the death penalty in Illinois, these new accusations against Burge should sound an alarm. In most cases the confessions were the main or only evidence against those convicted.

The editorial also took a shot at Mayor Daley for attempting to discredit the Goldston report years before, and then continued:

> The link between Burge and the 10 death penalty cases no longer can be ignored as if it is some bizarre coincidence. The Chicago Police Department and the Cook County state's attorney's office already have proven they are not capable of thoroughly investigating these cases.

Next, the board called for an independent investigation:

> Considering what is at stake, the U.S. Justice Department or the Illinois attorney general's office should open an independent investigation into allegations of misconduct by Burge. . . . Now is the time to determine whether there was a pattern of brutality by police or others that put innocent people on Death Row.

The cover-up scandal clearly touched a nerve. A few days later, with city hall reporter Fran Spielman in the audience, notepad in hand, Mayor Daley felt compelled to tell a class of graduating Chicago police recruits to "exercise restraint—even when provoked." Spielman also cornered Superintendent Hillard and quizzed him about Needham's memo dismissing the charges: "Hillard said he's 'seeking out' officers still on the force who may have participated with fired Detective Cmdr. Jon Burge in the alleged torture of suspects during the 1980s. But, barring 'new evidence,' it's time to close the book on the Burge era." Spielman quoted Hillard as saying, "I have to move ahead. This is something that happened 12, 15 years ago. I can't continually go back and look at old cases." Hillard's standing behind Needham was not surprising, given that Needham's father was a former deputy superintendent, close to the Daley family and to Hillard, while Needham was himself a former assistant state's attorney who had prosecuted a number of Burge torture victims.

The City mounted a personal attack against us, claiming that we had publicly filed documents and testimony that its lawyers had unilaterally marked as confidential. We countered by arguing that Judge Castillo's prior order in *Wiggins* was a clear precedent for the public filing. We not only continued to argue for the missing documents but also sought an order requiring that Superintendent Hillard sit for a deposition on the subject of his role in quashing the re-investigations.

These issues were set to be argued in April. Two weeks before the hearing I deposed the stone-faced former OPS director Gayle Shines. Long pauses between questions and answers and claims that she did not understand the question dominated the long and exhausting interrogation. It was hard to understand how this Daley loyalist and former supervisor in his state's attorney's office had approved and praised the Goldston report, only then to sit on the reinvestigation findings for nearly five years. Her cold feet had to be the result of official pressure from Daley himself, from Dignan's people, or from other unknown police powerbrokers, but Shines was not about to illuminate us.

In the run-up to the April hearing, Steve Mills published another article in the *Tribune*: "Claims, Probes of Cop Brutality Getting New Life." He first noted that judge Milton Shadur had once again taken a strong stance, this time granting a hearing in the habeas case of death-row prisoner Andrew Maxwell. Mills quoted Judge Shadur's finding that "it is now common knowledge that in the early- to mid-1980s, Chicago Police Cmdr. Jon Burge and many officers working under him regularly engaged in the physical abuse and torture of prisoners to extract confessions." Mills then articulated what we had been saying for years:

The charges against Burge involve players at the heart of the political establishment in Chicago and Cook County. Mayor Richard M. Daley was state's attorney, and Devine, now the state's attorney, was his first assistant, when some of these cases were prosecuted. In addition, some of the prosecutors who handled the cases during the initial investigation or at trial are now among Devine's top aides.

Mills also reminded his readers that Devine, as Kunkle's law partner, had been involved in representing Burge while in private practice. He then gave me the floor:

> Lawyer G. Flint Taylor, who has been pursuing Burge and the torture allegations for more than a decade, maintains that the conflict for Devine is readily apparent. "It makes it clear that there has to be an independent investigation, unconnected to the state's attorney's office and Chicago police," he said.

Not to be outdone by Mills, Charles Nicodemus of the *Sun Times* covered Shines's testimony under the headline, "Ex-Official Acknowledges Sitting on Torture Cases." Nicodemus wrote, "In a deposition filed Wednesday, the former head of the agency assigned to investigate police misconduct has admitted that for three years she sat on two 'sustained' allegations of torture by cops, then resigned without ever acting on the cases." The article continued:

> The alleged torture during the 1980s was performed on two suspects, Darrell Cannon and Stanley Howard, later convicted of murder. The deposition disclosed that the records of the OPS investigations had been kept in boxes in Shines' office for three years before she resigned, and that she had left no instructions for her successor on how to handle the cases. Taylor's questions disclosed that attorneys for Cannon and Howard had subpoenaed the records during appeals of their murder convictions, but had been told no such records could be found.

When we appeared at the April hearing, the City had hired a big-time private defense firm, Hinshaw and Culbertson. Judge Coar was not welcoming. Over objections from the City lawyers, Coar said, "There is no doubt in my mind" that we had a right to question Hillard. "Discovery with respect to the superintendent must go forward."

Two weeks later Jeff and I traveled to the downtown offices of Hinshaw and Culbertson to depose Superintendent Hillard. An African American "lifer," who many felt was a powerless public relations front man for Chicago's entrenched police and political forces, Hillard had become a police officer in 1968, served as a bodyguard for mayor Jane

Byrne, then worked for a short period of time on mayor Harold Washington's security detail.

Hillard acknowledged knowing Peter Dignan, who had been promoted to lieutenant with Mayor Daley's approval and without having to go through the regular procedures—a "meritorious" promotion, they called it. Dignan was a "hard working" detective; when I asked if he knew that there had been at least ten complaints of torture and excessive force against Dignan, Hillard responded, "That's new to me Mr. Flint . . . Mr. Taylor." Hillard testified that Needham did not consult him prior to his jettisoning of the OPS cases, and that he had first learned of it from the *Tribune*. Nonetheless, he fully supported Needham's decision because he trusted him and "had to back him up." He grudgingly admitted that if a case of electric shock, mock execution, or bagging were sustained, the officer should be fired; but he refused to apply that conclusion to Dignan. Despite the City's prior admission that its own police board witness, Melvin Jones, was tortured by Burge in the presence of detective Robert Flood—who was still active on the force—Hillard would not commit to opening a Melvin Jones OPS investigation or to reopening the suspended torture investigation of the City's other star witness, Shadeed Mu'min.

Judge Coar continued to rule for us, declaring that the files and depositions in question were public record and sanctioning the City for its obstructionist conduct. He even ordered that the City pay us for the time we had expended to obtain the documents. The City, desperate to put an end to our quest, offered our client, Marco Santiago, a generous settlement, together with substantial attorneys' fees. It was an offer we could not turn down.

CHAPTER 15

And It Seemed Like
They Blew My Brains Out

Darrell Cannon grew up in the Woodlawn neighborhood on the south side of Chicago, the youngest of four children in a working-class family. As a teenager, he was affiliated with the south side's most powerful street gang, the Blackstone Rangers. After a stint in juvenile prison, he became a favorite of the Stones' leader, Jeff Fort, and in 1969 earned the permanent enmity of the Chicago Police Department by engaging in a shootout with some Gang Crimes officers and escaping to tell the tale. The next year, Darrell was on his way to a maximum-security prison on a murder conviction.

In the early 1980s, the Illinois parole system still sometimes released first-time offenders convicted of murder after a reasonable amount of time served, and, in 1983, Darrell, as one of the last beneficiaries of this system, was returned to the streets and to the Stones (now known as the El Rukns). Only months later, he was entangled in another murder case, as the alleged driver of the car in which a south side drug dealer was shot and killed in the backseat by an El Rukns leader.

Byrne's and Dignan's midnight crew of asskickers, having long memories and a personal relationship with the Gang Crimes officer who had shot it out with Darrell in 1969, sprang into action. Together with a contingent of Area 2 detectives, they rousted Darrell and his female partner out of bed, terrorized them, and transported Darrell to Area 2. When Darrell refused to cooperate, they threw him in the backseat of Byrne's and Dignan's unmarked detective car, loaded a shotgun into the trunk, and headed southeast, ostensibly to the spot in the Altgeld Gardens housing complex where the victim's body had been found. Instead, they headed south on Torrence Avenue, stopped for breakfast at a local greasy spoon at 103rd Street with Darrell double-cuffed in the backseat, then drove almost three miles farther south, past the Wisconsin Steelworks, to a tube-like viaduct that led off the road to the east.

Darrell later described the ensuing events to my daughter, Kate, when she was filming her documentary *America Never Was America to Me*:

> They drove me to a site that I call the torture area, where there's a big huge pipe you drive through and come out on the other side. There's a river, and they went up this hill, and the railroad tracks was right there. They turned the car around. They parked there. They got me out. And they told me, they said, "Nigger, look around," and I looked around and it was an isolated area. They told me nobody would hear or know anything about what has happened to me. And then that's when they started to ask me about the murder.

Byrne, Dignan, and Grunhard went to work:

> My, my, my arms was handcuffed behind me. And Sergeant Byrne got on the bumper. Now, what I remember about that day was there was a fine mist rain, real fine. . . . They tried to hold me on each side while Byrne held the handcuffs from behind and they would let me go and that would make my arms come up behind me. But, they wasn't successful in doing that. Byrne almost slipped off the bumper.

Next, they turned to mock execution:

> So then they went and they opened the trunk of the detective car. Dignan got out a shotgun and he told me, he said, "Nigger, look." And he showed me the shotgun shell. He said, "Now, listen, nigger," then turned around and I thought he was puttin' the shell up in the shotgun because it sounded like that to me. Then he turned back around and he said, "Nigga, you gone tell us what we want to hear."

When Darrell replied "no," he would not cooperate, Dignan continued the attack:

> This is when he shoved the shotgun in my mouth. And when he shoved it in my mouth, he kept saying, "You gonna tell me what I wanna hear, you gonna tell me what I wanna hear?" And when I refused to do so, one of the other ones told him, "Pull the trigger, blow that nigger's head off." And he pulled the trigger. They did this on three separate occasions. And the third time they did it, it seemed like when I heard the trigger click, that the back of my brains was being blown out. That's what my mind was telling me.

Unsuccessful, the torturers escalated their tactics:

They took me around to the passenger's side, the back seat, on the passenger's side of the car. And it was Byrne that took an automatic and put it to my head and told me, "Don't move." And they redid the handcuffs and then, at that point, they made me sit down, in the backseat of the car.

Darrell described the struggle that ensued:

They had pulled my pants and my shorts down and it was Grunhard, had went around to the other side of the back door, opened the door and he came in, and they made me sit down, and my hands was up in the air, and he grabbed them after I sat down, he grabbed them, and so they pulled me back, made me lay down. And he had to handcuff my hands so I couldn't rise back up.

It was now Sergeant Byrne's turn:

And it was Byrne that first used the electric cattle prod on me. And at that time . . . he . . . he stuck it to my testicles. And I remember trying to kick him. . . . Dignan was trying to step on one of my feet, Byrne was trying to step on the other one. And they kept shocking me with the cattle prod, telling me that they knew what had happened, and they wanted me to confirm it. . . . And I refused to answer and they kept shocking me with that cattle prod.

Finally, Darrell agreed to cooperate:

I don't think we was there very long, but I know that to me, it seemed like a long time. It ended up me telling them that "Ok, I'll tell you anything you want to hear. Anything." To get them to stop doing that.

They loaded Darrell back into the car and headed to the auto pound to have Darrell identify the crime car. At the pound, he said, "I'm not telling you nothing," and, with McWeeny looking on, "They put the cattle prod in my mouth that time, on my mouth. On my lips and shocked me again." This time they had broken Darrell for good:

We ended up at the station, I think that was sometime after three . . . I remember seeing children coming from school. And I eventually ended up seeing a state's attorney and signing a confession implicating myself in a crime I had nothing to do with. And they locked me up downstairs in a basement that night. And the next morning I went to court.

He also described the torturers' sadistically racist pleasure:

> There's no doubt in my mind that in my case racism played a huge role in what happened to me, because they enjoyed this. You know, this wasn't something that was sickening to them. . . . No. They enjoyed it. They laughed. They smiled.

Darrell's case was assigned to Thomas J. Maloney, a thoroughly corrupt judge who would later do fifteen years for fixing cases. To make matters worse, Darrell had become the poster boy for the "law and order" political attack being waged by Daley, then state's attorney, against the parole board for releasing violent reoffenders, and Darrell stood no chance of prevailing on his motion to suppress his confession. Maloney denied the motion, a jury convicted Darrell, and he was sentenced to life in prison.

While serving his sentence, Darrell assumed a leadership role and was often relied upon by prison authorities to negotiate truces between warring prison gangs. Darrell's criminal case had been reversed by the appellate court because the prosecutor was found to have exercised his peremptory jury challenges in a racially discriminatory manner. When the case returned to the trial court, it was at first assigned to a judge who was formerly an Area 2 detective, then ended up with judge John Morrissey, who had later denied Aaron Patterson's petition. At the retrial, in 1993 and 1994, Darrell's lawyer, Anita Carrothers, tried to get Morrissey to consider the vast amount of newly discovered evidence we had unearthed and documented, including evidence that officers Byrne, Dignan, and Grunhard had been accused in numerous other torture cases. OPS investigator Veronica Tillman-Messenger was called to the stand, but Judge Morrissey barred her from revealing the findings of her reinvestigation or from producing her file. Tillman-Messenger was permitted to reveal one remarkable fact: based on Darrell's descriptions, she had located the diner, a place known as the Purple Steer, and the torture site.

With his tortured confession presented at the retrial, Darrell was once again convicted, and resentenced to life. Fortunately, Darrell's subsequent appeal was assigned to a very competent and motivated young appellate defender, Frank Ralph, who went to work marshaling and analyzing all the torture evidence that Anita Carrothers had entered into the trial record, for the purposes of the appeal. He argued in a persuasive brief that Darrell was entitled to a new motion to suppress hearing, where he could challenge the admissibility of his confession with the newly uncovered evidence.

Darrell's appeal was assigned to a three-judge panel that included Warren Wolfson, a superb former criminal defense lawyer, who had represented one of the survivors of the murderous Fred Hampton raid. Wolfson wrote a unanimous and precedent-setting opinion, released the week before Thanksgiving 1997. The decision overturned Judge Morrissey's ruling and ordered that Darrell be granted the right to a completely new torture hearing. Relying on the prior decisions in Andrew Wilson's and Gregory Banks's cases, the court held that the other torture allegations lodged against detectives Dignan and Byrne were relevant to show their motive, plan, intent, and course of conduct, and to impeach their denials. Wolfson wrote:

> No citation of authority is required for the proposition that in a civilized society torture by police officers is an unacceptable means of obtaining confessions from suspects. The use of a defendant's coerced confession as substantive evidence of his guilt never is harmless error.

Judge Wolfson and the court also rejected the State's argument that the torture methods employed in the other cases in which Byrne and Dignan were accused were too dissimilar to be admissible:

> To say, as the State does, that there is a qualitative distinction between shocking one suspect's genitals with a cattle prod and beating another with a flashlight, or inserting a shotgun in a suspect's mouth as opposed to a handgun, is to trivialize established principles for decent law enforcement. Under that view, accepted standards descend to banality. Minor differences in technique do not alter the nature of the torturer's work.

At this juncture Darrell began to reach out from his maximum-security cell at Menard for lawyers to handle his hearing. As he later related, "I got in touch with Flint after seeing a special on TV about the Fred Hampton case. . . . I told him up front that I don't have any money. But I'm thankful to God that something struck him that caused him to take my case." What struck me, Tim, and Joey was the strength of Darrell's case and the opportunity that Judge Wolfson's decision offered us to continue to advance in the torture wars.

Around this time, in 1998, the Illinois Department of Corrections opened the first supermax ("super-maximum-security") prison, in rural Tamms, Illinois. Tamms was located southeast of St. Louis, closer to Memphis than to Chicago. Apparently as punishment for his having won a significant legal victory, Darrell was one of the first prisoners transferred to Tamms. There, he and 250 other men were subjected to another form of torture, premised on extreme sensory deprivation. Tamms would be Darrell's "home" for most of the next nine years.

Darrell graphically described the routine dehumanization:

> Supermax is that anytime you step out your cell where the officers have to escort you, you gonna first get naked. Totally naked in front of the two officers. And they pull the cell front, the front of your cell has a little slot. They will open the slot up. You will pass out each item of your clothes to them. They will shake it down, hold it out there, and once you naked they'll tell you open your mouth, your tongue, raise your tongue, put your hands over your hair. And then they'll tell you to turn around, bend over, and spread your cheeks, if you refuse to do any of these things they have what is called the Orange Crush. Which are especially big, country-fed officers that suit up in orange outfits that has bullet-proof vests, knee-guards, chin, helmet, the whole works. And they will come in and force you to do these things if you don't do them voluntarily.

He recounted his daily struggle to stay sane:

> It was total solitary confinement. There were times I would wake up shaking. It would be my system trying to go haywire. I would have to get up off that concrete bed and go to the sink and run some cold water and wait until the sink fills up and then throw the water all over me, and I would have to talk to myself and say, "Hey, look. Do not break. You can't let this happen." I would walk the floor in circles. And I may do that for two hours straight. Saturday night was dedicated to all the old songs. "Blue Moon." "Stand By Me" . . . all those old songs I could think of. I would try to remember the words. I would sing just loud enough where I could hear myself.

In July 1998, we traveled back to the Criminal Courts Building at 26th and California to begin Darrell's hearing before judge John Morrissey, no fan of ours. Our hearing team included Larry Marshall, from Northwestern Law School, and Tom Geraghty, an experienced criminal defense attorney and the longtime director of Northwestern's Bluhm Legal Clinic.

Darrell, tall and almost gaunt, had been brought up from Tamms for the long-anticipated hearing. We were armed with Judge Wolfson's decision, the OPS reinvestigation findings, and expert opinions from doctors Kirschner and Martinez, both of whom had interviewed and evaluated Darrell. Our first witness was Dr. Martinez. In the preceding few years he had also evaluated Aaron Patterson, Marcus Wiggins, and Stanley

Howard for torture-related posttraumatic stress symptoms, using personal interviews and the Hopkins Symptoms Checklist, a widely used, validated screening tool developed to evaluate torture victims from Vietnam and Cambodia. Martinez testified that there was a recognized psychiatric field of torture care and treatment that relied heavily on the existence of post-traumatic stress symptoms. He also gave a detailed analysis of the symptomatology that he had observed in the Chicago police torture survivors and equated it to what he had seen in other torture victims he had treated from around the world. In addition, Dr. Martinez defined the forms of torture used by Burge and his confederates in internationally accepted terms, and he opined that Darrell and the other Chicago survivors exhibited post-traumatic stress symptoms that were caused by their torture.

He described how Darrell's symptoms of PTSD increased in score on the Hopkins checklist from his first session to the second, a common phenomenon called revictimization. He recounted that when Darrell talked about the mock execution he was "visibly upset, trembling, and sweating." Martinez recounted how he came to Darrell's second interview with a small toy device that made a clicking sound, similar to that of a trigger's being pulled, and covertly clicked it when they reached the shotgun part of Darrell's story. Darrell "began to tremble out of control. I had to stop the interview and do breathing exercises with him in order to calm him down." This "startle response" was "very typical of survivors of torture." He described a similar reaction when Darrell described the electric shock—trembling, Darrell "could not hold his tears and at one moment he stopped talking because he was blocking the material from consciousness." Quoting from the Diagnostic and Statistical Manual of Mental Disorders (DSM-IV), Dr. Martinez's diagnosis, given the presence of numerous psychological markers, including terror and racist dehumanization, was "post-traumatic stress disorder in remission," with the accompanying finding, reached with a "reasonable degree of clinical certainty," that "Mr. Cannon was indeed tortured by Area 2 police officers."

Judge Morrissey's skepticism was palpable. After veteran Gang Crimes prosecutor Dave Kelly (a former colleague of Tom Needham) finished his cross-examination, Morrissey adjourned for the day without hearing from our second witness, Dr. Kirschner. It was only mid-July, but in all too typical 26th Street fashion, the next day Morrissey continued the hearing to the fall. Darrell was returned to Tamms, and we had to acknowledge that as long as we were saddled with Morrissey, a third appeal was almost a foregone conclusion.

During this time, Mariel Nanasi, Jan Susler, and I were litigating a case against the City for its sexual and domestic violence policies and practices. We learned that a potential witness in that case was Doris Byrd—one of the individuals listed by Deep Badge, years before, as a potential "weak link." Prior to Darrell Cannon's hearing, I deposed Sergeant Byrd at Mariel's downtown office. Asking background questions, I focused on the early and mid-1980s, when she was working as a detective at Area 2 under Burge. Byrd, a middle-aged African American woman, dressed out in her white sergeant's shirt, quickly became apprehensive and responded, "Wait a minute—I didn't know that I was giving a deposition on Burge." The young Hinshaw and Culbertson lawyer representing the City seemed unaware of where I was headed, and reassured her, "Don't worry, I'm going to object on the basis of relevance." I asked, "Did you ever hear that Burge or any of those people that worked with him in interrogating suspects at Area 2 had used devices such as electric shock devices?" She paused, then answered, "I read in the newspapers just like you and every other citizen of Chicago." I pressed on: "Other than that, during the time you were working at Area 2, did you ever hear that Burge used any of those kinds of devices?" The pause was longer, but her aggravated response was the same: "I read the newspapers just like you." I tried several more variations. After a particularly long pause, she looked away and said, "No."

She then threatened to leave, maintaining that she had "been brought here under false pretenses." "Was Burge a racist?" I asked, after she had returned to her seat. Following another pause and a long objection from the newly alert young lawyer, Byrd spat out, "I don't know." What was Dignan's reputation? "I don't know." Did you ever hear that they used typewriter covers or plastic bags? "I read it in the newspapers." Again, the same series of evasive non-answers followed, as I pressed the bagging question. When I asked her about Andrew Wilson's case, the City lawyer instructed her not to answer any more questions about Burge and Area 2. After the deposition concluded, Mariel, now working as a private police brutality lawyer, after having been a public defender for several years, agreed that Byrd knew a great deal more than she was willing to admit. We had just seen a very reluctant version of the CPD's code of silence in action.

We also tried to keep up the pressure in the public and political arenas. Chicago police officers had recently shot and killed two unarmed African

Americans: LaTanya Haggerty, who was holding a cell phone; and Robert Russ, a former Northwestern football player. People were protesting in the streets, and Bobby Rush had organized an eight-person delegation to meet with US attorney general Janet Reno and the assistant head of the Justice Department's Civil Rights Division, Bill Lan Lee. Our goal was to urge the division to undertake a pattern and practice investigation in Chicago, in order to obtain a court-approved consent decree that would institute fundamental reform within the department. My role in the delegation was to talk about these racist, unconstitutional practices, the ongoing cover-up, and to link them to the Burge torture scandal, while fellow delegate Eugene Pincham dramatically urged criminal prosecutions in the Haggerty and Russ cases. Attorney General Reno seemed receptive to our presentation, and the meeting was reported on by the Washington bureaus of the *Tribune* and *Sun Times*. Bobby Rush told reporters that if the Feds did not intervene, he thought "all hell would break loose," but he added that "there is a perception in Chicago that the Justice Department is reluctant to do its job simply because of the perception of the coziness between the Clinton Administration and the Daleys." Truer words were never spoken; this coziness held sway regardless of who the president happened to be, Democrat or Republican.

Rush and his congressional colleague Danny Davis followed up the next Saturday with a hearing convened by the Congressional Black Caucus's Task Force on Police Brutality at the Quinn Chapel AME Church on South Wabash Avenue. I was asked to testify, along with a long list of activists, politicians, brutality victims, and their family members. I rushed into the church, my mind on my presentation, and was warmly greeted by a vaguely familiar woman who was working security. She smiled, called me by name, and said that I should talk to her about Jon Burge. I said, "Sure," and stuck her card in my pocket. After I finished my testimony, I headed home and pulled her card out of my pocket. Doris Byrd, Sergeant of Police, it read.

In the fall, Darrell Cannon's hearing reconvened with two days of testimony from three of the five OPS investigators who had made the various findings of torture and abuse. Tim Lohraff and I shared the questioning. Judge Morrissey signaled early on that he was not going to consider their testimony, but, unlike judges Perry and Duff, he did let us make the record. Michael Goldston detailed his findings that there was "systematic abuse" at Area 2, that command members were aware of and participated in the abuse, and that officers Dignan and Byrne were among the main "players" in this torture. OPS investigators Robert Cosey and Leutie Lawrence explained the basis for sustained recommendations against Dignan and Byrne in the cases of Gregory Banks, Stanley Howard, Phillip Adkins, and Thomas Craft. Morrissey astounded us by making his own gratuitous finding that OPS investigator Lawrence, a middle-aged African American woman with a schoolteacher-like demeanor, was, in his estimation, not credible. After we protested this finding, Morrissey continued the hearing to early November.

When we reconvened, we ended the first phase of our proof with two of our star witnesses—Dr. Robert Kirschner and OPS investigator Veronica Tillman-Messenger. Dr. Kirschner, now with an additional ten years of torture-related experience, testified as an expert in "the field of the methodology and evaluation of cases of torture." He drew on his extensive experience in evaluating and documenting two hundred torture cases worldwide, particularly ones in which electric shock, simulated suffocation ("dry submarino"), and mock executions were employed; his extensive writing, consulting, and lecturing; his leading role in drafting and presenting the *United Nations Manual on the Effective Investigation and Documentation of Torture*; his experience in evaluating patterns and practices of torture in Israel, Turkey, Czechoslavakia, and several Central and South American countries; and his evaluation of several Chicago police torture survivors and their cases, including Darrell's. He testified that electric shock torture was used by the US military in Vietnam, and that cattle prods, like the one used to shock Darrell, were routinely used to torture people around the world. Kirschner then offered his most damning opinion: that there was a "pattern and practice of torture at Area 2," which "featured electric shock . . . dry submarino and mock executions."

Tillman-Messenger, a young Black woman, followed Kirschner. She first talked about her preliminary findings that Lee Holmes was suffocated with a plastic bag and beaten with a rubber hose in September 1982. She also revealed that during her preliminary Shadeed Mu'min investigation, she obtained a document showing that Burge possessed, at the time he tortured Mu'min, a registered, silver .44 Magnum revolver, the same unusual weapon that Mu'min said Burge had used to threaten him.

Tillman-Messenger then set forth in detail her exhaustive reinvestigation of Darrell Cannon's case—talking to Darrell and other witnesses; finding the torture site and the breakfast diner; reading the trial transcripts;

reviewing the weapons inventory sheet that made lie of Dignan's denial that he had a shotgun; the statements of Darrell's initial lawyer, who was now a judge, and of Darrell's sister, that Darrell had told them the details of his torture soon after it happened and had drawn a sketch of the torture; and the denials and feigned lapses of memory by Dignan and his pals. She testified that her direct supervisor, Carmen Christia, had approved her recommended findings, which she matter-of-factly listed from her fifty-six-page draft report: Byrne had called Darrell's partner a "bitch" and Darrell a "nigger," put his gun to Darrell's head, and electric-shocked him on the testicles and penis; Dignan had cracked Darrell on the knee with his flashlight, and repeatedly shoved a shotgun into his mouth; and Dignan and Grunhard lifted Darrell up by his handcuffs.

It was the first time Darrell had heard Tillman-Messenger detail her investigation and set forth her findings, and he quite rightfully felt that she had vindicated him. However, it would mean little, at least in the short run, if we could not somehow find a way to get Judge Morrissey removed from the case.

CHAPTER 16

Those Idiots from
the People's Law Office

In 1999, as the Aaron Patterson case, the work on behalf of the Death Row Ten, and the Campaign to End the Death Penalty were all marching forward, our legal team settled the Ford Heights Four case for a record-setting $36 million. We also filed a major civil rights lawsuit on behalf of the falsely accused little boy, Romarr Gipson, and his mother, Shannon. In the press release that accompanied the filing, we underscored that the unconstitutional abuse by detective James Cassidy and his fellow Area 1 detectives was part of a city-wide practice of condoning coerced confessions. The case was assigned to an excellent federal judge (and former law school classmate of mine), Joan Humphrey Lefkow.

In late April, we met with state's attorney Richard Devine. Devine was publicly on the defensive because of the recent exoneration of a falsely accused man, Anthony Porter—bringing the exonerations from Illinois's death row to ten—and the mounting evidence of police torture that raised serious questions about the roles played by Devine's former boss, Richie Daley, Devine himself, and many of his assistant prosecutors in sending potentially innocent torture survivors to death row.

State representative Connie Howard, a well-respected progressive Democrat, who was outspoken in her opposition to the death penalty, had been instrumental in setting up the meeting, with the help of activists from Aaron's defense committee and the Campaign to End the Death Penalty. Given Devine's conflict of interest and record of intransigence, we were reluctant but agreed to attend in order to present Aaron's case. Our distrust was heightened when Devine barred Aaron's mother, JoAnn, a moving force on Aaron's committee, at the last minute. The meeting lasted about an hour, during which Representative Howard and I made impassioned arguments about Aaron's innocence and the systematic torture that put him on death row, and urged Devine to join us in asking the Illinois Supreme Court for a new evidentiary hearing in Aaron's case. Devine listened politely but clearly was not about to do anything to help us. His response was that he needed to see "new evidence"—in spite of what we had shown him, in writing and in person. I called for new hearings for all the men on death row and also told Steve Mills, who reported on the meeting, that Devine had a conflict of interest because his law firm had defended Burge in Andrew Wilson's case.

With little hope that Devine would do the right thing, we moved to supplement the record in the Illinois Supreme Court with the newly obtained OPS torture documents, and filed our reply brief. In fashioning our reply, Tim, Joey, and I faced a legal dilemma: Devine's lawyers had used Andrew Wilson's Supreme Court decision against us in Aaron's case, arguing that the *Wilson* decision meant that a showing of physical injury was required in order to win a coerced-confession case. To rebut this, we traced the history of Western torture, from Ancient Greece and Rome to the present, and specifically tracked the avowed purpose and intent of torture: to extract confessions and other information without leaving physical injury.

We quoted the United Nations Special Rapporteur on Torture, reporting on torture in Mexico, Venezuela, and Chile:

> Detainees were routinely tortured in ways that would leave no marks, with attempted suffocation by plastic bags and electric shock being commonly utilized by interrogators for that purpose. In reference to these torture techniques, the Special Rapporteur found that "infliction of torture is an offense that must be prosecuted by itself, independently of the physical harm caused to the victim. There are, for example, methods of torture that leave no after-effects but are no less effective for the torturer's purposes," and "the absence of marks on the body consistent with allegations of torture should not necessarily be treated by the prosecutors and judges as proof that the torture did not occur."

Devine countered with a move designed to delay Aaron's case. He asked the Supreme Court to put Aaron's case on hold while Darrell Cannon's case was pending before Judge Morrissey—as well as two other death row torture cases—because "the issue of systematic coercion . . . has been put in play," and "this seems to be a central issue in all of these cases."

It did not take a genius to see that Devine and his crew wanted to put these cases on the slow track to nowhere. Dick Cunningham, who was litigating Ronald Kitchen's case before the Supreme Court, and I vociferously opposed Devine's maneuver. "Why not give us each an evidentiary hearing right now?" Dick asked.

A few days later, the *Tribune* weighed in with an editorial, "Torture Charges Demand Full Probe." The editorial board, recognizing our position and, pointing to Morrissey's prior decisions in Aaron and Darrell's cases, wrote, "Given Morrissey's record on these types of cases, defense attorneys are understandably concerned about his impartiality in the Cannon case—and about Devine's noncommittal offer that he might reconsider the other three cases based on that ruling. . . . The three men deserve a full review of their cases and of their allegations of coerced confessions by the police," conducted "by an independent judicial panel."

A small contingent of Patterson supporters rallied across from the Supreme Court's Chicago office. JoAnn Patterson spoke out for her son: "My purpose here is to show my resistance to the state. I want a thorough investigation into my son's case." The court agreed, denied Devine's motion, and set arguments on the three appeals for mid-September 1999.

Just prior to the argument, the Campaign to End the Death Penalty staged the latest and largest in a series of marches and demonstrations, in front of the Chicago courthouse. Earlier in the year, a key demonstration in front of police headquarters had featured the mothers of three of the Death Row Ten: JoAnn Patterson; Louva Bell, Ronald Kitchen's mother; and Jenette Johnson, Stanley Howard's mother. The rally had culminated with the reading of a statement from Stanley, calling for the public to keep the pressure on:

> Me, I'll work for justice in here. You, you work for justice out there. If not, these people are actually gonna kill us. It's gonna be a party or it's gonna be a funeral. It's that simple.

A bus filled with demonstrators traveled down Interstate 55—Route 66, to old-timers—to the capital of Springfield, to bear witness to the historic presentations.

It was exciting to envision a young Abraham Lincoln arguing before the court in this very chamber, a century and a half earlier. The presence of news cameras brought the staid old chamber into the present, thanks to a motion by reporter Carol Marin, who was now working for CBS and *60 Minutes 2*.

The court had set two days for the arguments on behalf of Aaron Patterson, Ronald Kitchen, and fellow Death Row Ten member Derrick King. I went first; to be followed by Dick Cunningham, representing Ronald

Kitchen; and Tom Geraghty, representing Derrick King. I hammered home the remarkable record of systemic torture, including the newly obtained OPS findings, and described the many instances of baggings, Russian roulette, and racially motivated beatings as the unique "fingerprints" that made the other acts of similar Area 2 torture relevant to Aaron's case.

Assistant state's attorney Carol Gaines, appearing on behalf of Devine and his office, countered by arguing that the court had consistently held there must be some evidence showing that an arrestee had suffered injury. I was ready; I read a passage from an opinion written by US Supreme Court justice Harry Blackmun that I had posted on my office wall:

> The Court today puts to rest the seriously misguided view that the pain inflicted by excessive force is actionable under the Eighth Amendment only when coupled by "significant injury," that is, injury that requires medical attention or leaves permanent marks.

I recited Blackmun's daunting list of torture tactics that did not cause "significant" physical injury, with added emphasis on those that were trademarks of Burge and his men:

> In other words, the constitutional prohibition against cruel and unusual punishments then might not constrain prison officials from lashing prisoners with leather straps, whipping them with rubber hoses, beating them with naked fists, shocking them with electric currents, asphyxiating them short of death, intentionally exposing them to undue hot and cold, or forcibly injecting them with psychosis-inducing drugs.

That evening, the Supreme Court arguments, the Burge torture scandal, and the Death Row Ten dominated Chicago's 10:00 o'clock news. On Channel 2, co-anchor Lester Holt threw the ball to Carol Marin, who traced the long history of the torture scandal, linking it to Aaron Patterson's case and the Death Row Ten. She interviewed Aaron's parents; not only did they maintain their son's innocence, but Aaron's father, police lieutenant Ray Patterson, also noted that there was no physical evidence tying his son to the murders.

Carol, honoring me as Burge's longtime "nemesis," surprised me with a candid question:

> Carol: Your critics say that Flint Taylor will do anything, you are a lefty, anti-establishment, cop-hating lawyer. Is there some truth in that?

Taylor: I intensely dislike police who frame people, who put people on death row who are innocent. I hate what police do when they abuse the law, and I feel that when they abuse the law they should be brought to justice just like other people.

Two months later, *60 Minutes 2* aired Carol Marin's expanded piece on national television. Anchor Dan Rather introduced the fifteen-minute segment: "Using electric shock, suffocation, and beatings are at the center of Carol Marin's report tonight. Hanging in the balance—the lives of ten men on death row in Illinois." Carol led with Melvin Jones, who quoted Burge telling him, after he asked for a lawyer, "You only have two rights in here, to confess and to get your ass kicked." He related how Burge touched the radiator with the torture device, causing a spark, then shocked him on his leg and groin. Carol recounted Andrew Wilson's story and our role in it, and showed the black shock box and the Deep Badge letters. She interviewed Dr. Kirschner, who shot down a straw-man argument Carol raised (a line of reasoning popular in the public arena), saying that, no, Burge and his men were not driven to torture because of a rising crime rate but because no one in authority told them not to.

Burge had refused to talk on the record, but John Byrne, whom Carol called Burge's "right-hand man," appeared on camera to defend Burge, whom he called a lifelong friend from the days of grammar school football. According to Byrne, now heavyset, with graying hair and beard, Burge was "an honest and upstanding citizen" who "wanted to do the right thing— doing his job as effectively as he can, within the bounds of law, he's not a stupid man." Surprisingly, Carol described Byrne as a "highly decorated officer," when, in fact, he had resigned to avoid the OPS reinvestigations focused on him and Dignan.

More surprisingly, Carol identified Byrne as a supervisor of Aaron Patterson's interrogation, who was in and out of the room while Aaron was being questioned. This was news to us. Byrne went on to say that Aaron's allegations were lies, "did not square" with what he observed, and that Aaron was "guilty, without a doubt." Unwittingly, Byrne—whom our evidence showed to be a lying, serial torturer, and who was joined at the hip to Burge—had placed himself squarely into Aaron's case.

Carol replayed the evasive responses from Devine and reported that Daley would not talk, despite his having been state's attorney when Aaron and his Death Row Ten brothers were tortured and sentenced. She turned to Dr. Kirschner to drive home another fundamental point: "No one should be tortured," whether innocent or guilty. Melvin Jones reemphasized this point, saying, "I was a prime candidate, but I also could be innocent."

Carol closed the piece by returning to the death penalty:

> Since the death penalty was put back on the books in the US, for every man Illinois has executed, it has set another man free on the basis of new evidence or the reevaluation of the old. Twelve men have been put to death, and another twelve have walked off death row because prosecutors had the wrong man.

As we awaited the Supreme Court's decision in Aaron's case, we got an early holiday present. Chick Hoffman called to say, tongue in cheek, that he had chanced upon a transcript from a Morrissey case he thought we might be interested in. The year before, the defendant in a murder case, an African American man named Edward Smith, had made a pro se request for DNA testing. Morrissey detested the recently enacted law giving defendants a limited right to seek testing in cases that arose in 1997 and thereafter. Morrissey had responded:

> I mean how far are we going to go? Are we going to review cases around the Civil War? I mean this is ridiculous, I will tell you one thing, folks, if you guys confess error in DNA, I am going to have Mr. Devine come down here . . . if you think I am going to have Cunningham and those idiots from the People's Law Office come in here and say release my prisoner, uh-uh, that's not going to work.

I wrote to Darrell Cannon, informing him of the news and asking his opinion as to whether we should move to remove Morrissey—a decision the judge himself would have to make, in the end. Darrell let us know, in no uncertain terms, that he was in favor, so we did, in mid-January 2000. In a *Tribune* piece Steve Mills quoted Morrissey's "idiots" comment to expose him as a grossly unfair, pro-prosecution jurist:

> Morrissey has presided over some of Chicago's most serious and contentious criminal cases, including three in which a defendant was sentenced to death. . . . In the past year, Morrissey has seen one Death Row prisoner freed after he ridiculed his requests for DNA tests, expressed misgivings about his own guilty verdict in another murder trial, and been accused in a pending murder case of withholding from defense attorneys evidence that could undermine a key witness' credibility. Since November 1997, Morrissey has

been reversed by higher courts at least nine times for errors he committed, forcing new trials, sentencings or hearings.

The next week, when we appeared before Morrissey to argue our motion, he was on his best behavior. Referring to his "intemperate remarks" in an "unrelated matter several years ago," he said, "I offer to recuse myself at this time." We accepted his offer, and with little further ado, Judge Morrissey thanked us and transferred Darrell's case to chief judge Thomas Fitzgerald for reassignment.

Three days later Tim and I were ushered into Judge Fitzgerald's chambers to discuss the judicial reassignment. Cases were normally reassigned randomly by computer, but Fitz, as Judge Fitzgerald was known around the courthouse, presented us with a proposal. Speculating that the case was going to be a "real burden," time-wise, to whomever it was assigned, he suggested that he take the case off the computer and select a judge whose court calendar might be open to accommodating the case, with the caveat that each side would have the right to challenge two of his suggestions. If that process did not yield a judge agreeable to both sides, Fitz would then turn to the computer for the assignment.

The proposal sounded good to us, and the assistant state's attorney agreed. Fitz selected judge Lawrence Fox and gave his reasons:

> I think he has a wonderful background, both as a public defender and as a teacher, and has been an outstanding judge who has had no connection with the prosecutor's office and he has the time to devote to this case.

I thanked Fitz, and we all shared a fervent hope that the tide had turned, not only in Darrell's case but perhaps in other torture cases as well: the chief judge had—albeit in typical Cook County backroom style—paid deference to, at the very least, the appearance of justice in the most important torture case pending in the criminal courts of Cook County.

Ronald "Doc" Satchel, Fred Hampton, and Bobby Rush, with poster of Bobby Seale, 1969

The PLO, 1976: Jeff Haas, Peter Schmiedel, myself, Charles "Chick" Hoffman, Dennis Cunningham, Pat Murray, Pat Handlin

Friday, August 4, 1978   Volume 7, No. 44   CHICAGO'S FREE WEEKLY

Why don't Jeff Haas and Flint Taylor just give up?

Above: Jeff Haas
and I at the former
Chicago BPP
headquarters, 1978

Pat and I discuss
the *Saxner* case,
1978

Jeff Haas, Bill
Hampton,
Fannie Mae
Clark, and Clark
siblings, 1983

PLO client Maxine Smith, the first
woman jailhouse lawyer, *Al Qalam*, 1981

Chicago Tribune, February 5, 1983

Wilsons found guilty in slaying of 2 cops

By Marianne Taylor

ANDREW AND Jackie Wilson were found guilty Friday of murdering Chicago police officers William P. Fahey and Richard J. O'Brien, who had stopped the Wilson brothers' car Feb. 9, 1982, on a South Side street.

The same jury that convicted Andrew, 30, and Jackie, 22, agreed Friday afternoon that the men are eligible under state law to be considered for the death penalty.

On Monday the panel will begin hearing evidence to determine whether it will sentence the two men to the electric chair.

After more than five hours of deliberation, the jurors filed into Judge John J. Crowley's courtroom Friday morning, their faces taut and not looking at the two defendants, who were scanning the jurors' faces for clues to their decision.

AS THE CRIMINAL Court clerk intoned the verdict, "guilty" for each count of murder and armed robbery, the slain officers' families, who sat in two rows near the jury, began to cry.

Jackie and Andrew Wilson

"I think Richard is finally resting," said Laverne O'Brien, Officer O'Brien's mother.

"There is no equation," added Patricia Fahey, Fahey's widow, "but at least I know now it wasn't all in vain."

The two policemen had stopped the

Continued on page 6, col. 2

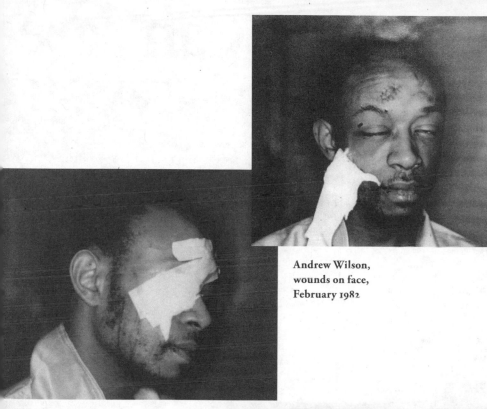

Andrew Wilson,
wounds on face,
February 1982

Chick Hoffman and I
on the steps of the
US Supreme Court after
the *Saxner* argument,
October 16, 1985

Victory in Klan case

By LEWIS COHEN
Special to the Guardian

WINSTON-SALEM, N.C.—It was a far cry from full justice, but it was a victory nonetheless.

On June 7, a North Carolina jury held eight people responsible for the wrongful death of Michael Nathan, a 32-year-old doctor slain with four other anti-Klan activists by Ku Klux Klan and Nazi party members in Greensboro, N.C., Nov. 3, 1979. The jury ordered three Nazis, two Klansmen, two police officers and a police informant to pay Nathan's widow, Martha Nathan, $355,000 in damages. The jury also held two Klansmen and two Nazis liable for assault and battery against Nathan, Dr. Paul Bermanzohn and Tom Clark. Bermanzohn, still partially paralyzed from head wounds, was awarded $38,360. Clark, who had been shot in the back several times, was awarded $1500.

FINALLY, A GUILTY PARTY

The case had been brought by the families of the Communist Workers Party (CWP) activists who were killed and eight of the 10 people injured at the Nov. 1979 anti-Klan demonstration against 62 defendants including FBI agents, 36 officials of the city of Greensboro and members of the Nazi and Klan caravan that attacked the demonstration.

For the first time, after two previous trials, someone has been held responsible for the

Klan and Nazi members prepare to shoot Greensboro protesters in 1979. Five leftists were killed but last week the jury cited only one 'wrongful death.'

between the CWP and the Nazis and KKK.

The suit charged that federal agents and the Greensboro police conspired with the Nazis and Klansmen to violate the civil rights of

frontation was imminent.

The verdict was not a complete victory for the plaintiffs, however. The jury did not find a conspiracy and none of the six Black plaintiffs

Top: *Guardian*, June 1985

Bottom: PLO staff, 1986: Jan Susler, Jose Berrios, Jeff Haas, Peter Schmiedel, Jani Hoft, Michael Deutsch, myself, Rosie Velez, Jill Inglis, Stan Willis, John Stainthorp

Chicago Lawyer

Volume 10 Number 4   *An Independent Monthly*   April 1987 $2.50

Why
Comerford
Must Go

EDITORIAL
— PAGE 8

GEORGE JONES GETS EVEN

Chicago Lawyer, April 1987

Aaron Patterson's etchings,
made in 1986 with a paper clip
on a metal bench, documenting
his torture by Chicago police

Excerpts of the letters received from "Deep Badge"

Mr. Flint Taylor:

I understand you all are representing Andrew Wilson in his civil action against several police officers for brutality.

Check the following:

Several witnesses including the White's were severely beaten at 1121 S State St in front of the Chief of Detectives, the Superintendent of Police and the State's Attorneys.

Mayor Byrne and States Attorney Daley were aware of the actions of the detectives. ASA Angarola told both of them and condoned the actions.

Several of the officers named in the suit ⋯

⋯ rials

Mr. Taylor:

Your ad in the newspaper was a little to obvious. Before I tell you anymore I need to know if anyone will ever see these letters.

Would you place another ad in the personal column and answer the following questions.

Address the ad to **TY**

1. Will the letters ever be shown to anyone other than you and the other attorney's in your law firm? Yes or no.

2. Will the letters ever be referred to in court or in depositions? Yes or no.

⋯ have learned something that will blow the lid off of your case. You

⋯ accused of using this devices. I

ST.

Mr. Taylor:

As I have said previously I do not want to be involved in this affair. That is why I asked for the reassurance that these letters would be kept private. I do not wish to be shunned like Officer Laverty has been since he co-operated with you.

The following points should be made.

Burge hates black people and is an ego maniac. He would do antyhing to furthur himself.

Almost all of the detectives and police officers involved know the Wilson's did the murders but they do not approve of the beatings and torture. No one wants to see the Wilson's get any money but they would like to see the families of the police officers get any funds that the Wilson's get. McKenna and O'Hare did nothing at all. They have never been involved in those type of activities.

I advise you to immediately interview a Melvin Jones who is in the Cook County Jail on a murder charge. He is being re-tried in Markham. When you speak with him compare the dates from 1982 and you will see why it is important. You will also find that the States Attorney knew that he was complaining and that is why his charges were dropped then. That decision was made in the top levels at 26th and California.

There is something else but I am not quite sure of the facts if you need it contact me by the same means.

TY

Det Pat O'hare and ⋯ client. Your client was beat after he ⋯ off.
In return for this information I ask that youtreat those subjects who were not involved with leniency. In the future you will hear from me only if I feel that I won't be disclosed ever. Do not leave this letter or the other in the file-take them home. That way they won't be available for reproduction or subpeona. TY

Andrew Wilson's civil trial team: myself, Jeff Haas, and John Stainthorp, *Chicago Lawyer*, 1990

CHICAGO SUN-TIMES   METRO   JAN. 14, 1993

With Marcus Wiggins, *Chicago Sun Times*, January 14, 1993

Three of the Ford Heights Four: Verneal Jimerson, Dennis Williams, and Kenneth Adams, 1999

Demonstrating Duane Jensen's shock box while testifying on behalf of Leroy Orange at governor George Ryan's Clemency and Pardon Hearings, October 2002

Aaron Patterson, his mother, JoAnn, and I upon Aaron's pardon from death row, *Chicago Tribune*, January 10, 2003

With Iberia Hampton and Francis Hampton, December 4, 2006

Andrew Wilson,
Chicago Reader, 2007

With Leroy Orange as the city council approved a $19.8 million settlement for him and the three other pardoned torture survivors. Pictured: myself, Joey Mogul, Leroy Orange, Sage Smith, and Mort Smith, *Chicago Tribune*, January 2008

PULL HIS PENSION

City needs to find way to stop paying ex-cop accused of torture

The quicker the city can pull the pension of former Chicago Police Lt. Jon Burge, the better. At least that would deliver a small measure of justice in the slippery case that has left a lasting stain on the Police Department. After reliving the details in a searing Tuesday, aldermen were incensed at the thought of Burge, now retired in Florida, receiving his $3,500 pension every month. One or another vowed to pursue any and all legal avenues — including a possible perjury prosecution — to cut off Burge's pension. Godspeed.

Tuesday's six-hour hearing turned up all the old laundry. Aldermen watched videotapes of victims telling how Burge and his thugs at Area 2 administered electric shocks to their genitals, smothered them with plastic bags and typewriter covers, beat them and handcuffed them to hot radiators until they confessed to crimes they did not commit.

They also watched a videotape of

in 2004 for a federal civil case. He took the Fifth when asked what he did to the people he arrested. He took the Fifth when asked whether he dumped a crude shock machine into Lake Michigan from his boat. The one question he answered directly was whether he received a

Never convicted of a crime, Burge sits in the Florida sun and collects his pension.

city pension.

Aldermen fumed at the millions the city has spent defending civil suits brought by alleged victims, some of whom were on Death Row when their convictions were overturned. The city paid $2.04 million in Burge-related legal fees in 2006 alone and an additional $399,416 in

port by special prosecutors last year that concluded that yes, there was evidence of police torture in the 1970s and 1980s. The state's attorney at the time was Richard M. Daley.

Twenty years later, Daley is mayor, and the statute of limitations on Burge's alleged police abuse is long up. Never convicted of a crime, Burge sits in the Florida sun and collects his pension. For now.

Smarting from barroom brawls involving off-duty police officers and the subsequent resignation of Police Supt. Phil Cline, the city is taking action to restore public confidence. The mayor last week severed the Office of Professional Standards from the Police Department and appointed an outsider from Los Angeles as its independent watchdog.

The unresolved Burge case eats at our sense of justice, taking a terrible toll on the public trust. Aggressively seeking new legal avenues to bring it to some degree of

JEFF SZUC—SPECIAL TO THE SUN-TIMES

Feds catch up with Burge

Notorious ex-Chicago commander charged with lying about torture

By Steve Mills and Jeff Coen
TRIBUNE REPORTERS

More than three decades after allegations surfaced that Chicago police detectives routinely tortured murder suspects, retired Cmdr. Jon Burge was arrested Tuesday at his Florida home on charges that he testified falsely about the brutality.

The perjury and obstruction of justice counts against Burge mark the first criminal charges in the long-running scandal. But a dozen or more officers once under Burge's command who have denied under oath taking part in the alleged torture could be in legal peril as well.

The indictment of the 60-year-old Burge breathes new life into a scandal that has had a stubborn hold on the Police Department and the city and involves claims of abuse—elec-

tric shock, Russian roulette and suffocation with bags and typewriter covers. The allegations continue to figure prominently in the appeals of dozens of inmates.

Much of the scandal grew out of some of the most brutal crimes. Andrew Wilson was allegedly tortured after his arrest for the murder of two Chicago police officers in 1982. Madison Hobley made similar allegations after he was charged in a 1987 arson that killed his wife, young child and five others. Hobley was sentenced to Death Row, but was pardoned and set free by Gov. George Ryan.

The allegations also raised ques-

Please turn to Page 23

More inside

John Kass presses Mayor Daley about his memories of Jon Burge. PAGE 2

Darrell Cannon (from left), Anthony Holmes, Gregory Banks and David Bates, who say they were tortured by former Chicago Police Cmdr. Jon Burge and fellow officers in the 1980s, attend a news conference at Rainbow/PUSH Coalition in Chicago on Tuesday after Burge was indicted on obstruction of justice and perjury charges. ZBIGNIEW BZDAK/TRIBUNE

Burge

Top: *Chicago Sun Times* cartoon of Jon Burge on the *Vigilante*, July 25, 2007
Bottom: *Chicago Tribune*, October 21, 2008

Michael Tillman
is freed.
Pictured: myself,
Sarah Gelsomino,
Michael Tillman,
Joey Mogul,
Ben Elson,
January 14, 2010

Chicago Sun Times,
June 29, 2010

Jon Burge arrives at the federal building Monday morning. He could face up to 45 years in prison. | RICH HEIN~SUN-TIMES

GUILTY

Ex-cop Jon Burge convicted
of lying about torture

PAGES 14-15, EDITORIAL ON PAGE 18

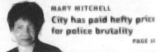

MARY MITCHELL
City has paid hefty price
for police brutality

PAGE 11

With Locke Bowman and
Ronald Kitchen at press conference to announce the filing
of Ronald Kitchen's civil suit,
Chicago Tribune, June 2010

Jon Burge in prison,
May 10, 2011

Richie Daley, 2011

Chicago Sun Times,
August 10, 2011

BE IT RESOLVED, That we, the Mayor and members of the City Council of the City of Chicago, on behalf of all Chicagoans:

(1) acknowledge and condemn, as evil and reprehensible, any and all acts of torture and abuse inflicted upon the Burge victims; and

(2) apologize to the Burge victims for these horrific and inexcusable acts; and

(3) express our most solemn regrets to the families of the Burge victims for any and all harm that they suffered as a consequence of the ordeal that their loved ones were subjected to; and

(4) remember these past events, to ensure that this sad chapter in our City's history is never forgotten; and

(5) reaffirm our City's commitment to righting the wrongs of the past, and in so doing, reassure Chicago's residents that such wrongs will not be repeated in the future; and

BE IT FURTHER RESOLVED, That a suitable copy of this resolution be presented to Chicago Torture Justice Memorials, as a sign of our respect for their work and of our concern about this important matter.

_____
MAYOR

_____
CITY CLERK

Excerpt from the final Reparations Ordinance, May 4, 2015

Saturday, June 23, 2018 | *The Hardest-Working Paper in America* | ☼ 79°/62° For

CHICAGO SUN ★TI

$1 CITY/BURBS $2 ELSEWHERE | **LATE SPORTS FINAL**

Jackie Wilson walks with his attorneys Friday after his release, saying he is "happy to be a member of society again." COLIN BOYLE/SUN-TIMES

WILSON WALKS

Twice convicted in double cop-killing but granted new trial, Jackie Wilson is given bond in ruling called 'disgraceful' by FOP chief RACHEL HINTON AND ANDY GRIMM REPORT, PAGE 8

Jackie Wilson is freed, *Chicago Sun Times*, June 23, 2018
(pictured: myself, Jackie Wilson, Elliot Slosar)

CHAPTER 17

A Landmark Victory, a Plea, and a Tragedy

I n April we proceeded with the second stage of the hearing—calling other torture victims of the detectives who had tortured Darrell. Judge Fox was not overly friendly, and we clashed when he limited our witnesses to those who had been tortured by Byrne, Dignan, Grunhard, and McWeeny—Darrell's cast of abusers—with Burge excluded. Our team, which Darrell dubbed "Dream Team 2," in a nod to O. J. Simpson's legal team, had been joined by a firecracker of a young lawyer from Northwestern named Cathryn Stewart.

Our first two witnesses were our former clients Gregory Banks and David Bates. Their testimony was made even more compelling by the fact that their torture at the hands of Byrne, Dignan, and fellow midnight-shift detectives was visited upon them less than a week before Darrell was tortured by the same cast of characters. Greg related once more how Dignan had announced the terrifying dry submarino torture with the line "We have something special for niggers." He surprised all of us by adding, on cross-examination, one detail for the first time—that Burge was outside the room at some point during his interrogation.

Next, we called Alonzo Smith to the stand. A Vietnam veteran, married with four children, Alonzo had been employed as a Chicago Transit Authority bus driver for the ten years previous to his January 1983 arrest. He was not one of the midnight crew's typical victims, and it appeared that he might have been targeted in an attempt to get him to implicate an African American police officer who had been arrested in a nasty murder case.

Alonzo voluntarily reported to the "House of Screams" for questioning on a cold January morning; he would not regain his freedom for nearly twenty years. A large and friendly man, Alonzo told the court that, at about 10:00 p.m., Dignan told him they were "going to have a talk," and took him down the back stairs to the first floor, where Dignan retrieved a key and disappeared out a door to the parking lot. When Dignan returned, he had a twisted plastic bag in his hand. He unlocked a door to the basement and led Alonzo, handcuffed, down the stairs, with Byrne trailing behind them. Past a big boiler, they directed him to an armless swivel chair, with a light bulb hanging from the ceiling. Either Byrne or Dignan turned on the light by pulling the attached string, and Alonzo observed an old white refrigerator with a large handle nearby and a drain in the floor.

After Dignan conferred with someone—Burge?—in the stairwell behind Alonzo, the torture began. Dignan returned, said he was "tired of fucking around," that Alonzo was lying, and that he "wanted the truth." When Alonzo said that his denials were the truth, Dignan responded that they "had all night." Using a rubber nightstick that he pulled out of a bag, he smashed Alonzo in his groin, and Byrne followed up by kicking Alonzo in the stomach. Kicks, punches, and nightstick strikes to the thighs, calves, and hands followed as Alonzo, with his hands cuffed behind the back of the chair, twisted in pain. "Is there anything you want to tell us now?" Dignan asked. When Alonzo said no, Dignan said, "This is round one."

Dignan then grabbed the plastic bag, forced it over Alonzo's head, and secured it with a large rubber band that he stretched around the bottom of the bag and Alonzo's neck. The bag was tight and, as Alonzo described it, "Every time I breathed, the bag would come into my mouth." Byrne and Dignan pummeled him on his body while he gasped for air, and the next thing he remembered was waking up on the floor, face down, still cuffed behind his back, with the bag no longer on his head.

After Byrne and Dignan pulled Alonzo back into the chair, and Alonzo continued to withhold his cooperation, Dignan declared, "Round two." The bagging and beating was repeated, with the same result: Alonzo passed out and came to on the floor. This time, Alonzo concluded, he must have been shaking or squirming, because either Byrne or Dignan asked if he "was doing a new nigger dance."

Back in the chair, he again refused to cooperate. When they started to bag him once more, Alonzo testified that, upon seeing blood from his mouth in the bag, "It freaked me out. I said to them, 'Hey I've had enough of this, what do you want me to say? What do you want from me?'" Broken, Alonzo was taken back upstairs, where Byrne and Dignan summoned a felony review prosecutor, who, with Dignan's assistance, led him through a confession that Alonzo would later claim, credibly, was constructed by his interrogators and placed in his mouth. We also called Phillip Adkins, who had been beaten to the point of losing control of his bodily functions; and Melvin Jones, who told his painful story for the fifth time. We decided that we did not need to call Darrell to the stand, subjecting him to another round of intense cross-examination, because Judge Wolfson's decision had mandated a hearing in which newly discovered evidence—that is, evidence not available to Darrell and his lawyer at the time of his 1984 motion to suppress—was to be heard. To complete our case, we offered Darrell's prior motion to suppress testimony, along with the prior testimony of fifteen additional victims of Burge, Byrne, Dignan, and fellow detectives, and sixty documentary exhibits that included medical affidavits, OPS files and statements, and a stipulation from OPS investigator Francine Sanders.

The assistant state's attorneys objected to nearly all of our evidence, particularly the testimony of the OPS witnesses, the testimony of doctors Martinez and Kirschner, and the testimony of all of the torture victims who were not tortured specifically by Byrne or Dignan. Judge Fox decided that he would determine these issues before requiring the State to proceed.

Meanwhile, Darrell's case had garnered national and international exposure, thanks to an English journalist named Sasha Abramsky. Writing for the London *Independent* and *Mother Jones*, Abramsky had interviewed and photographed Darrell in Cook County Jail; caught up with former police superintendent Richard Brzeczek; talked to Tim and me; and traveled to Florida in search of Burge. He succeeded in getting Brzeczek, now a defense lawyer, to make admissions that he had consciously withheld a decade earlier, in the three separate times I had cross-examined him during Andrew Wilson's case. According to Abramsky, Brzeczek now claimed that, when he had learned of Andrew's torture, he "gave the local commanders 'one of the great chewing-outs of a lifetime.' He wanted both suspects to be given a quick ticket to death row, and was irate that defence lawyers might now have grounds to challenge such a sentence."

Abramsky reported that Burge, who had quietly begun to collect his police pension, was doing freelance security and had recently landed a major security contract at the National Association of Programming and Television Executives Convention. His description of Burge was vivid: "Decorated war hero and police commander though he was, the redheaded Burge, with his heavy jowls and cocky sneer, was slated to take the blame for all of the violence and brutality and disregard for due process that had permeated Areas Two and Three for a quarter of a century under the purposely blind eye of Chicago's political machine."

The depiction of Burge's adopted home was also striking:

> More than 1,500 miles from the rough streets of inner-city Chicago is the genteel little town of Apollo Beach, Florida, perched just north of Cockroach Bay on an inlet feeding into the Gulf of Mexico. . . . The houses in Apollo Beach are almost all bungalows, painted pretty pinks and yellows and sky-blues, with grass lawns and carefully trimmed squat sabal palm trees. Yet, despite the suburban façade, this is also a place where people come to escape the gaze of a world that doesn't understand them.

Burge did not answer Abramsky's letters, and when Abramsky knocked on the door of Burge's large bungalow—a sterile-looking place with pink wooden shutters, a red-tile roof, and a swimming pool inside a glass solarium at the rear of the building—Burge ordered him off his land and threatened to call the sheriff. When Abramsky phoned, Burge shouted, "You're causing me great personal angst and anxiety. . . . I've done nothing wrong and I don't need to talk to you or anyone else."

According to Brzeczek, the police justification was "Yeah, we know he did it, but we have to circumvent these goofy rules of due process, either by lying or fabricating evidence, whatever it takes to convict this person . . . It's OK, because he's going to do the time for all the crimes he didn't get caught for." Abramsky, with an apt literary reference, concluded, "But fitting people up is one thing, systematic torture another; and Burge's detractors claim to find echoes of Kurtz—in Conrad's *Heart of Darkness*—in his apparent transformation from champion of law and order to lawless bully who seemed to revel in his power to inflict injury on those he had within his clutches. At the very least, his fall from grace reads like an unusually disturbing cautionary tale."

In August, the Illinois Supreme Court issued its long-awaited opinion in Aaron Patterson's case. As we read through the lengthy decision, our optimism diminished as the court rejected, one after another, each argument we had raised. They even rejected our argument that Aaron's lawyers at the motion to suppress, at trial, and on appeal had been unconstitutionally ineffective because they had not uncovered or effectively presented the newly discovered evidence of a pattern and practice of torture.

But the court had opted to save the good news for last. Relying on the constitutional principle of fundamental fairness, the court held that Aaron was entitled to an evidentiary hearing on the question of newly discovered torture evidence. Rejecting the State's reliance on the court's prior decisions in the cases of Andrew Wilson, Madison Hobley, and Leroy Orange, the court modified its physical injury rule:

> The fact that the defendant has suffered a physical injury is only one of many factors to consider when determining whether evidence of prior allegations of police brutality are admissible. The question of relevancy is a determination to be made by the trial court after a consideration of, inter alia, the defendant's allegations of torture and their similarity to the prior allegations.

The court detailed our newly discovered evidence, including the sixty incidents of torture implicating Burge and the detectives who tortured Aaron Patterson; the Goldston and Sanders OPS reports; and several judicial and administrative decisions, and evaluated their relevance in light of the appellate decisions in the *Cannon* and *Banks* cases and the Seventh Circuit's decision in Andrew's case. The court found that the sixty incidents, some of which were contained in our proffer of evidence in Andrew's case, were not too remote in time:

> A series of incidents spanning several years can be relevant to establishing a claim of a pattern and practice of torture. Consequently, we believe that the claims detailed in the proffer should be considered new evidence, but only if defendant can establish the later discovery of other torture allegations linking defendant's claims to those contained in the proffer.

In conclusion, the court found that all this evidence was relevant and should be considered by the trial court:

> After reviewing the new evidence relied upon by defendant, we believe that it is material and that, as pleaded, would likely change the result upon retrial. In particular, we note that defendant has consistently claimed that he was tortured. In fact, he made this claim during his first court appearance. Moreover, defendant's claims are now and have always been strikingly similar to other claims involving the use of a typewriter cover to simulate suffocation. Additionally, defendant describes the use of a gun as a threat and beatings that do not leave physical evidence. Further, the officers that defendant alleges were involved in his case are officers that are identified in other allegations of torture. Finally, defendant's allegations are consistent with the OPS findings that

torture, as alleged by defendant, was systemic and methodical at Area 2 under the command of Burge.

The court, relying on this brand-new decision in *Patterson*, also ordered a new evidentiary hearing in Derrick King's case and reinstated the post-conviction petition of Ronald Kitchen. In addition, the court ruled on several other death penalty cases. This battery of decisions came in the wake of Republican governor George Ryan's granting of a moratorium on executions six months before. The next day, the front page of the *Tribune* read: "Justices Reject 6 Death Sentences—2 Inmates Get New Hearings on Police Brutality Charges." Investigative reporter Ken Armstrong wrote:

> In a release of opinions that highlighted nearly every problem plaguing the state's criminal justice system, the Illinois Supreme Court reversed or remanded six death penalty cases Thursday, ordering new trials, sentencings, briefs or hearings based on allegations of torture by police, cheating by prosecutors and ineptitude by defense attorneys. . . . Two of the court's opinions focused on long-standing charges that Chicago police in one South Side area, working under since-fired Cmdr. Jon Burge, systematically tortured suspects to obtain confessions. After reciting the substantial evidence supporting those claims, the Illinois Supreme Court ordered that Death Row inmates Aaron Patterson and Derrick King be granted hearings to present evidence of their allegations.

In a sentence that must have sent chills up and down Richard Devine's spine, Armstrong continued, "If their claims are found credible, Patterson and King could be awarded new trials and might go free because in each man's original trial, the centerpiece of the prosecution's case was the defendant's confession."

That same week, the district court judge in Buffalo, New York, finalized the settlement terms in the Attica civil rights lawsuit that PLO partners Michael Deutsch and Dennis Cunningham, along with New York lawyers Liz Fink and Danny Meyers, had fiercely litigated for a quarter of a century. It was originally a class action suit on behalf of more than 1,500 Attica prisoners (or their families) who were killed, tortured, or otherwise brutalized by the New York State Police and prison guards during the September 13, 1971, assault and massacre. They had won liability against two Attica prison officials, and later, in a damages trial, won a $4 million verdict for Frank "Big Black" Smith, a prison leader who had been mercilessly tortured. The State appealed, and the Second Circuit Court of Appeals reversed the verdicts, ruling that there needed to be individual trials—a practical and financial impossibility. So the settlement was brokered: $8 million to be divided among the prisoners, and $4 million to the legal team. It was the largest prisoner settlement in US history and marked a victory in a case that rivaled the *Hampton* and CPD torture cases in length and in historical significance.

Meanwhile, in Darrell Cannon's hearing, Judge Fox had taken a relatively even hand with his rulings on our evidence. Devine and company seemed troubled by the level playing field and the prospect of their now discredited star witnesses having to take the stand for our cross-examination. Reporter John Conroy had stayed on the case, and, in two *Reader* articles, had exploded the myth of Dignan as hero cop. Conroy had revealed that Dignan's version of the shootout with an alleged drug dealer—which brought him national attention and a handshake with President Clinton as one of the country's "Top Cops"—was riddled with lies, including the story that Dignan had dragged a fellow cop to safety. Conroy established that Dignan might have shot and killed the alleged drug dealer after he was disarmed and lay on the floor, dying. Conroy had also detailed, to quote the Illinois Attorney Registration and Disciplinary Commission, John Byrne's "fraud, dishonesty, deceit and misrepresentation" in his second career as a lawyer, which included ripping off and deceiving a Chicago firefighter, a former police partner, and his law partners.

The prosecutors, with Devine's blessing, approached us to see if we might be open to resolving the case with a plea to a lesser charge. On our side of the fence, Darrell had learned from his mother that she had terminal cancer, and she very much wanted to see him a free man before she died. The State's offer was a plea to conspiracy to commit murder, and a forty-year sentence. At the time, under Illinois law, a prisoner earned one day of "good time" for each day served, so the offer, in reality, was a reduction from a natural life sentence to twenty years—and, having already served seventeen, Darrell would have less than three years left to serve. Darrell asked his mother if she thought she could survive that long and she gamely said, yes, she could, so Darrell reluctantly agreed to accept the offer—thereby abandoning the hearing on police torture that was proceeding to its climax. On January 19, 2001, Judge Fox accepted Darrell's plea and sentenced him to forty years.

Steve Mills, in that Sunday's *Tribune*, conveyed the mixed message under the headline "Convicted Killer Drops Claim of Cop Torture to Win Freedom." I gave the deal a positive spin: "The potential of what could have happened is what drove the state and Devine to give us this remarkable deal," I was quoted as saying. "If you're a judge in another one of these cases, you have to recognize the significance of what the state did here." Darrell, in a jailhouse interview, articulated the other side: "They knew I could win. . . . [otherwise] there's no way they would take back a natural life sentence." Devine's spokesman blamed Judge Fox's rulings for the need to strike a deal, while liberal *Tribune* columnist Eric Zorn, a dogged critic of the death penalty, summed it up as follows: "Let there be no mistaking what happened Friday in the Darrell Cannon case. Cook County State's Atty. Dick Devine ran away and hid yet again from the disgraceful police-torture scandal—a scandal that becomes increasingly scandalous with every new such evasion."

No longer inhibited by the possibility of perjury or the crucible of cross-examination, Dignan sought out a sympathetic police reporter. The *Sun Times* headline was an attention-grabber: "Silent No More, Cop Lashes Back." The torture "didn't happen, it didn't happen," the article quoted Dignan, whom they described as a police lieutenant decorated for heroism. He went on to claim that Burge was fired by a "kangaroo court."

In the *Reader*, John Conroy published another major article, this one focused on Darrell's hearing and the ramifications of the plea deal and its significance to the torture scandal and the fate of the Death Row Ten. "What Price Freedom?" asked the headline. "Darrell Cannon has accepted a plea bargain that will spare him a lifetime in prison. But there's a catch: the police officers he's accused of torture won't be forced to testify."

Conroy highlighted the importance of the hearing:

The hearing Judge Wolfson ordered became vastly important, not just to Cannon, who was serving a sentence of natural life, but to other Area Two victims as well. . . . If the judge suppressed Cannon's confession because he believed it had been extracted by force, could other judges go on ignoring similar claims of torture? "Who will the judge believe?" was the question of the moment.

Alas, we will never know.

Conroy told of a letter Darrell wrote him just before he agreed to the deal:

His father and grandmother had died while he was in prison and he had not been allowed to attend their funerals, and he hoped his mother would die at peace, seeing her son a free man. While he had nothing but praise for his lawyers, he feared the deal would result in Dignan and Byrne never being exposed.

Conroy quoted me, elaborating on Devine's reason for offering the deal:

Flint Taylor called the state's offer an admission of "fear of the power of the evidence in front of a judge they can't control." Up to now, Taylor said, Devine had fought every Area Two case and had never admitted that torture occurred. Suddenly, faced with the first case that would get anything resembling a full judicial hearing, the state was willing to chop 30 to 40 years off the sentence of an El Rukn general convicted of two murders. "You don't do that," Taylor said, "unless you are looking down the barrel of a gun."

Conroy recognized that "the other judges at 26th Street handling Area Two cases cannot help but note that the state ran scared in Cannon's case." However, Conroy worried, "There seems little to stop Devine's office from plea-bargaining its way through the Area Two cases one by one. Eleven men on death row allege that they were tortured at Area Two. Innocent though some of them may be, what sort of deal might they be willing to make in exchange for their lives?"

Aaron Patterson's case had been returned from the Illinois Supreme Court to the trial court for a hearing, and the chief judge, heeding the back-room precedent we had established in Darrell's case, sent the case to judge Michael Toomin, a judicially ambitious former public defender. In Illinois, the petitioner-defendant in post-conviction proceedings is permitted limited pre-hearing discovery, so we summoned John Byrne to testify about the many allegations of torture against him, his short career as a lawyer, and his revelation in Carol Marin's *60 Minutes 2* special that he was involved in Aaron's interrogation. We were lawyered up, with Joey Mogul and Cathryn Stewart sitting with me. We had expected that Dick Cunningham would also attend. Fearless, dedicated, and a true "lawyer for the damned," in the tradition of Clarence Darrow, Dick represented Ronald Kitchen, Alonzo Smith, and several other death row prisoners, including Ronald Jones, who had recently been exonerated on the basis of DNA testing.

I deposed Burge's self-proclaimed "right-hand man" at our Milwaukee Avenue office. Byrne was less overtly hostile and decidedly more talkative than Dignan or Burge. Like Dignan, he was a product of the US Marine Corps, where he got training in electronics, but he was only active for a year and never left the States. A psychology major at Loyola University, he spent his early days as a Chicago police officer at the Grand Crossing

Station in West Englewood with Burge, Dignan, and several other Area 2 detectives. He attempted to project an attitude of racial tolerance, claiming to have been partnered with Aaron's father, Ray, at Grand Crossing in one of the CPD's first integrated squad cars. He professed that he tried to avoid using racial epithets, but admitted to using the "n-word" on occasion. When asked if Jon Burge was a racist, Byrne at first ducked the question, saying that he "couldn't get into [Burge's] head," before offering that Burge had "Black friends on the job." Until Byrne came to Area 2, he was a detective in another south side area, and did not have a record of alleged brutality, except in one high-profile, racially charged case. It was easy to see Byrne, in contrast to Dignan and Burge, as a follower, someone who aimed to please his boss and childhood friend.

When the questioning turned to the numerous allegations of torture lodged against him and Dignan at Area 2, and the sustained findings in several of those cases, Byrne's mood changed as he tried to explain away the testimony of Gregory Banks, David Bates, Darrell Cannon, Phillip Adkins, Stanley Howard, and Alonzo Smith. Faced with Alonzo's detailed and accurate description of Area 2's basement, Byrne denied having ever visited it. However, he admitted knowledge of the secret torture site where, as Darrell testified, Byrne and Dignan had taken him. Byrne said that while he was a sergeant in the Fourth District, just before he was reassigned to Area 2, he would often drive up and down Torrence Avenue, past the viaduct that led to the water, by some railroad tracks. He said that he sometimes saw people going in there to fish, and that he "drove the squad in probably at various times." We looked at each other with some amazement—Byrne had admitted visiting the remote torture site that Darrell had described and OPS investigator Tillman-Messenger had located.

Byrne attempted to minimize his statement to Carol Marin, saying, "I believe I told Carol Marin that I may have gone into the room once or twice, but I had no involvement with [Aaron]." He volunteered, in testimony sure to alienate Aaron further from his father, that he had run into Ray Patterson a few days before Aaron was arrested for the double murder, and quoted Ray as saying, "I know he's my son, John, but I want you to be careful. He's known to carry a gun. I don't want you or your detectives to get hurt if you find him." Byrne said, "I thanked him. I thought it took a lot of balls for him to say that about his son." As a finishing touch, he added that while Aaron was on the lam, Ray had called him with a tip as to where his son might be hiding.

Like Dignan, he had visited Burge in Florida; rather than a Bears-Bucs game, Byrne and his family, accompanied by Burge, journeyed several hours north to Orlando to visit Disney World. Byrne also confirmed that Burge's boat, which he visited several times, was named the *Vigilante*, and that Deep Badge's letters had caused quite a stir at Area 2 when they became known. He became sullen, almost morose, when I began to question him about his disbarment. Yet he did, ultimately, admit to the accuracy of all eleven charges of attorney misconduct that formed the basis of his disbarment.

As I left the deposition, I was told my wife, Pat, was on the line. She was very upset, and told me the unthinkable: while we were examining John Byrne, our friend and colleague Dick Cunningham was stabbed to death by his twenty-seven-year-old son, Jesse. A brilliant young man, Jesse suffered from schizophrenia and sometimes became violent when he did not take his medication. He had recently been released from the hospital. Dick had decided to stay at home with his son, rather than coming to the deposition, and was making lunch when Jesse grabbed a knife and mortally wounded him. As he was bleeding to death, Dick managed to tell the police officers who responded, "Don't hurt my son, he's sick," and "He needs a good lawyer. Call Chick Hoffman."

Pat was also Dick's longtime friend; they had shared an office in the early 1980s in the appeals division of the public defenders' office. Devastated, Chick and Pat went to visit Jesse at the 18th District lockup, with the intent of counseling him not to give a statement to the police. They found him completely out of it, uncomprehending of what he had done. He had already given a statement to the police.

We were all deeply saddened by the tragedy. In addition to his son, Dick left two daughters and his wife, Maria, herself a staunch death penalty opponent.

Later that year, in an eight-part series, *Tribune* reporter Ken Armstrong captured the essence of Dick Cunningham: what he meant to us, and what he meant to his death row clients and their loved ones.

> He walked some of our criminal justice system's darkest halls—through police stations where suspects are tortured and courts where judges don't care and prisons where inmates are executed in front of witnesses who sit in a room where the floor slopes from back to front so that any vomit will flow toward a drain and can be easily hosed away.
>
> He offered lessons on living and dying to men on Death Row. Don't leave this world with your middle finger extended, he told one man about to

be executed. Don't give them that to remember you by. To others, he said, paint, read, write, learn, hope. Live a life that is worth saving, a life that will be missed.

He appealed for more than 20 Death Row inmates in his career. They had killed more than 50 men, women and children.

In his office, in the back of his home, Cunningham kept trial transcripts on the floor and prayers on the walls. "Where there is hatred, let me sow love; where there is injury, pardon." That was the prayer on the wall he saw most, the one facing his desk.

He fought as hard as any lawyer in Illinois for an end to the death penalty. . . . But what set Cunningham apart was his ability to relate. Wherever he looked as a lawyer and saw hurt and misfortune, he could probably superimpose his own life. He was an alcoholic and his son was mentally ill. Demons surrounded Cunningham at home and at work, allowing him to empathize but refusing him escape.

Armstrong's profile also captured how the news swept down Pontiac Penitentiary's death row, from Aaron Patterson to Ronald Kitchen to numerous other clients and friends:

Louva Bell, Kitchen's mother, would call Cunningham at night, crying. She kept seeing her son strapped onto a gurney. "It's going to be all right Louva," Cunningham would tell her. "We're going to get Ronnie out of there." When she heard about Cunningham's death, her world caved in. "Who's going to be there now for me and Ronnie?" she thought.

Through our collective grief, there was only one answer: we had to collectively step up and continue the work to which Dick Cunningham had so selflessly dedicated his life.

CHAPTER 18

Special Prosecutors, Clemencies, and Pardons

Since 2000, a group of lawyers and activists had been planning a political and legal offensive aimed at obtaining what we had been advocating for almost a decade: an independent prosecutor to investigate and prosecute Burge and his crew for their conspiratorial crimes. Lawyers included Locke Bowman from the MacArthur Justice Center; Randolph Stone, the former Cook County Public Defender and current director of the Mandel Legal Aid Clinic; Clyde Murphy, former deputy director of the NAACP Legal Defense Fund and current legal director of the Committee for Civil Rights Under Law; Frank Ralph, who had won Darrell Cannon's appeal; Stan Willis, formerly our PLO partner, representing the National Conference of Black Lawyers; Larry Kennon of the Cook County Bar Association; former appellate court judge Eugene Pincham; and Joey Mogul and me from the People's Law Office. The activist organizations and leaders included Mary Powers and Citizens Alert; Mary L. Johnson, who, as the mother of Michael Johnson, represented the torture survivors; Reverend Jesse Jackson and the Rainbow/PUSH Coalition; Amnesty International; the National Lawyers Guild; the Justice Coalition for Greater Chicago; the Campaign to End the Death Penalty; the Illinois Coalition Against the Death Penalty; the Afro American Patrolmen's League; and the Chicago Council of Lawyers.

On April 6, 2001, the group filed a petition, drafted by Locke and Randolph, before the chief judge of the criminal court, Paul Biebel, requesting the appointment of an independent special prosecutor. The petition relied on the legal conflict that affected Devine and, by extension, his entire office, and asked for an independent prosecutor "to investigate any and all wrongdoing arising out of abuse of suspects by police officers under the command of Jon Burge . . . from 1973 until the present." Because the statute of limitations had run out on the torture itself, the petition focused on two crimes that survived: obstruction of justice and conspiracy to obstruct justice. Of the steady stream of false denials offered by Burge and his men in each and every torture case, the petition stated, "There is no innocent explanation for the consistency of such lies in each and every case. The inescapable conclusion was that the officers in each of these cases conspired together to obstruct justice by agreeing that all should tell the same lie." Paramount in this conspiracy, the petition claimed, were John Byrne's categorical denials of torturing Darrell Cannon, Gregory Banks, Lee Holmes, and Alonzo Smith when I had questioned Byrne under oath only a few months before.

Mary Powers, representing the citizens; Mary L. Johnson, representing the victims; and Larry Kennon of the Cook County Bar Association were the named petitioners. Speaking for the group, I told the media: "In New York, the police officers who tortured Abner Louima are behind bars, in Houston, officers who tortured defendants are behind bars, but in Chicago, those officers are on their pensions, or their vacations, or on their boats."

Devine responded with a vengeance. He denied a conflict of interest and went further to claim that the evidence did not support conspiracy or obstruction indictments—and, if it did, that the statute of limitations barred those claims in the same way as it barred the investigation of the underlying torture crimes. He also belittled the petitioners' argument that the public interest would be strongly advanced by an independent investigation, asserting, "It would be unethical for a prosecutor to undertake investigations on time-barred crimes merely because the investigations might clarify the historical record or satisfy public demand."

While Devine was fighting his removal in court, his brain trust devised a plan to offer individual plea deals to those members of the Death Row Ten who had been granted new hearings. According to one assistant prosecutor, it was because they had gotten their "butt kicked" in Darrell Cannon's case. Devine's office contacted us and Tom Geraghty to explore deals for Aaron Patterson and Derrick King. They hinted at a Cannon-like deal of five years for Aaron but started with a much less favorable one, natural life, for Derrick King.

Aaron had told us in no uncertain terms that he would not plead guilty to crimes he did not commit and would settle for nothing less than either immediate release or a new trial. We communicated that position to Devine's lieutenant, Bob Milan, and awaited a response. Meanwhile, though, news of the deal leaked to the press. In the *Tribune*, Steve Mills wrote:

> In a stunning turnabout, Cook County State's Atty. Richard Devine has begun to discuss deals with a handful of Death Row inmates who have long-standing claims they were tortured to confess by Chicago Police Cmdr. Jon Burge and his detectives, according to sources close to the cases. The deals would give the convicted murderers who once faced execution a chance at freedom. But in exchange, the inmates would have to drop their claims of torture and plead guilty—even though some insist they are innocent.

The *Tribune* followed up with an editorial, "What Not to Sweep under Rugs." Calling Devine's move "breathtakingly irresponsible," the editorial called for an all-or-nothing approach: "If these men are innocent, they are innocent. If they are guilty and concocting tales about false confessions, they should serve full sentences. What is important is that their allegations—and all the Burge-related allegations—are fully aired and investigated." The *Tribune* once again pointed to Devine's conflict of interest, and his close connection during the 1980s to then State's Attorney Daley, as among the "compelling reasons to call for a sweeping, independent investigation of these claims."

As vital as it was to see the bigger picture, our chief concern was the life of our client. The offer in Aaron's case was enticing, given the current alternative was death. But before we could have a final discussion with Aaron, Steve Mills reported Aaron's decision in the next day's *Tribune*: "Death Row Deal Rejected—Inmate Says No to Devine's Offer." Steve quoted Aaron in a telephone interview from death row:

> I'm pretty much certain they know now I didn't do it, but they're trying to wiggle their way out of it. But I'm not so frantic that I just want to get out. If you're innocent, you've got to make your stand.

As upset as we might have been, it was ultimately Aaron's decision to make, and he had made it. We couldn't argue with that.

A week later, John Conroy published "A Hell of a Deal," a feature article in the *Reader*. He discussed in depth the legal and political positions of the parties in the battle for a special prosecutor, pointing out that the last time such a petition had been successful was in 1970 in the Fred Hampton case. He analyzed Devine's position with regard to the deals obtained in Darrell Cannon's case and those that were floated to Aaron and several other death row prisoners. Conroy noted that the scope of an independent investigation could be very broad:

> Burge served as a supervisor in Area Two, Area Three, and Bomb and Arson, and thus the actions of a fair number of detectives could come under the microscope. At least three detectives who served under Burge at Area Two later moved to Area One and have been accused of framing suspects there, and it may be that Burge alumni also took their practices to Areas Four and Five, to various district stations, and to special units like Narcotics and Organized Crime.

Conroy analyzed Devine's position and concluded that he was "in something of a corner," because he "has no good answer for the question 'Was there torture at Area Two?'"

> If his response is no, then he must be asked, "If the state's attorney's office has never investigated the policemen, how can you say there was no torture? If the only government bodies that have investigated it—the Police Board and the Office of Professional Standards—concluded that the police were guilty, how can you unequivocally say they are not?"
>
> If he says, "Yes, there was torture at Area Two," then he admits not only that he knows the police committed Class X felonies and got away with it but that he is putting those officers on the stand knowing they are liars, knowing they may be framing innocent men.
>
> If Devine says, "I don't know if there was torture at Area Two," then he must acknowledge that his star witnesses might be Class X felons obstructing justice every time they take the stand, but that he doesn't want to know and doesn't want anyone else to know, though such willing ignorance could result in the deaths of a dozen men.

Given Aaron's public call to action, we continued to move forward in his case before Judge Michael Toomin. Stan Willis, Tom Geraghty, Cathryn Stewart Crawford, and Frank Ralph had all joined our defense team, and we focused on the two issues we had won in the Illinois Supreme Court. The broader issue was, of course, whether Aaron's confession was coerced by torture, yet we had gained entry on a narrower issue as well—whether Aaron's trial counsel, Brian Dosch, had been unconstitutionally ineffective when, based on an erroneous interpretation of the law, he decided not to call Aaron to the stand during his 1989 trial. If we won on either of these issues, Aaron would get a new trial.

Judge Toomin set a hearing on the Dosch issue for the week before Christmas 2001. Dosch would be the only witness. In preparation, I spoke with Dosch, who told me that after several discussions with one of Devine's prosecutors, he was now prepared to offer additional reasons why he had decided not to call Aaron to the stand. These reasons, unlike the one he had originally sworn to—an erroneous interpretation of the law—were legally permissible, and therefore did not amount to ineffective assistance of counsel. He confided that the prosecutor had told him his reputation would be tarnished if the judge found him ineffective, and that it would torpedo any chance he might have of becoming a judge. Pointedly, the prosecutor had asked Dosch, "Don't you want to clean yourself up in front of the Supreme Court in case you are going to become a judge?"

Dosch had flipped us, to use lawyer's jargon. This put me in the unenviable position of having to confront Dosch, a veteran public defender, in front of a judge who was, himself, a former public defender. On the stand, Dosch admitted that he was upset by a recent news article that said the hearing was to determine if he had "so badly bungled the case that Aaron Patterson would get a new trial." However, he denied being pressured by the prosecutors or that he was interested in becoming a judge. Toomin cut off my attempts to further challenge Dosch's flip-flop. The judge ruled that he believed Dosch's change of testimony, and found that Dosch had not been ineffective when he declined to call Aaron to the stand in 1989.

Afterward we obtained a list of lawyers who had applied to become judges around the time that Dosch was denying interest on the stand, and, lo and behold, on that list was none other than Brian Boru Dosch.

On April 24, 2002, we gathered in Chief Judge Biebel's courtroom at 26th and California to receive his decision on the petition for a special prosecutor. We knew little about Judge Biebel, who had recently been appointed to the post, except that during his previous career he had been a Cook County assistant state's attorney, and later, the acting Cook County public defender. He was polite, intelligent, and thorough, but, given the sordid history of the Cook County criminal courts when it came to police torture, we were not overly optimistic.

Judge Biebel read his eight-page decision from the bench. He focused on Devine's conflict of interest, based on documentation that we had obtained in Andrew Wilson's case. This documentation, Biebel noted, established that Devine's law firm had received almost a million dollars for representing Burge in the *Wilson* case, that Devine himself had appeared before Judge Duff on Burge's behalf on at least one occasion, and had billed for about twenty-five hours of work during the case. This, Biebel concluded, provided the basis for the disqualification of Devine and the entire Cook County state's attorney's office and necessitated "the appointment of a special prosecutor to investigate the facts alleged by petitioners and to determine if any prosecutions are warranted."

We all shared a silent cheer. However, Judge Biebel's final words would have profound ramifications for the pursuit of criminal charges that we had worked toward for the past thirteen years: "This court therefore appoints retired Illinois appellate court justice Edward J. Egan as special state's attorney and Robert D. Boyle as assistant special state's attorney."

The *Tribune*, calling the "Burge matter" a potential "political hand grenade," was quick to embrace the decision in an editorial entitled, "A Look into the House of Torture."

> It has been two decades since the infamous interrogation of Andrew Wilson, two decades in which at least 66 people have come forward to claim that they, too, were tortured by Burge or his associates while they were in police custody. Two decades in which no one has known the full story of what went on under Burge's command, whether anyone committed a criminal offense while wearing a police uniform, whether anyone tried to cover it up.
>
> Now, finally, that will end.

For our part, the sense of relief had turned to deep concern as soon as Judge Biebel named Egan and Boyle as the special prosecutors. While neither of them had worked for Devine or Richie Daley, both were former high-level Cook County assistant prosecutors who had served during the reign of Daley's dad, Richard the First. Boyle was involved as a criminal division chief at the time of Fred Hampton's murder and the prosecution that followed of the Panther raid survivors; and Egan, as an appellate judge, had written the decision denying Andrew Wilson's second criminal appeal. These old-school prosecutors were, without a doubt, longtime Democratic machine operatives. Before the ink was dry on Judge Biebel's order, the City's chief lawyer had reassured her assistants that the special prosecutors would treat the City and the police department well—they would not turn their investigation into an "unfocused witch-hunt" sought by the "PLO and their ilk."

The lawyers and activists on the Special Prosecutor Committee quickly conceived of a two-pronged strategy to lessen the impact of the Egan and Boyle appointment. I would fully cooperate with Egan and Boyle, supplying them with all the evidence we had collected over the years; at the same time, the committee would urge them to hire independent African

American lawyers and investigators as lead attorneys and other assistants.

Petitioner Larry Kennon, a veteran civil rights lawyer who had served as an assistant state's attorney during Egan's and Boyle's tenure, made the first contact. We had collectively decided to recommend William Hooks, a former Marine Corps prosecutor and previous chair of the Cook County Bar Association, and an experienced investigator named John Smith. In a letter sent shortly after the appointment, Larry laid out the committee's priorities:

> Given the strong and longstanding community concern and interest in this issue, our committee feels that it is imperative that there be equal representation from the community at all levels of the Special Prosecutor's team, including lead attorneys, staff attorneys, investigators, and other staff persons. We stand ready to play an important role in recommending and providing persons who have been committed to the fight for justice for the citizenry of the City of Chicago as candidates for those jobs.

Larry then recommended Hooks and Smith. Judge Eugene Pincham, Locke Bowman, and Randolph Stone followed up by meeting with Egan and Boyle, who maintained they would strongly consider Hooks. Instead, without further consultation, they hired a well-connected African American lawyer named Donald Hubert, who had previously represented the City of Chicago in police cases. The precedent was set: we would have a one-way, adversarial relationship with Egan and Boyle, who would pay no more than lip service to Chicago's Black community, the survivors of police torture, and the committee that was acting in their interest.

Back in the criminal courts of Cook County, Devine had given us an opening by asking Judge Biebel to clarify whether his order also disqualified Devine's office from representing the State in the numerous torture cases, including Aaron Patterson's, that were pending before Biebel's criminal court judges. Devine argued that it did not, asserting that the order should only apply to him personally in those cases, and informed the judge that he was appointing one of his top assistants in his stead.

After several meetings with a battery of lawyers representing each of the Death Row Ten defendants with post-conviction cases pending at 26th Street and subject to Devine's motion to clarify, we hammered out a strategy to disqualify not only the entire state's attorney's office but also the entire Cook County criminal court bench, and move the cases out of Cook County. The *Chicago Law Bulletin* described our effort as that of a "group of disparate lawyers" from a "scrappy public interest law firm, law school legal clinics, big corporate law firms, and government funded public defenders offices," who had "ganged up" in the death row torture cases.

With assistance from Joey, Michael, and our staff, I spearheaded the investigation into the backgrounds of more than three hundred assistant state's attorneys and judges of Cook County. Drawing on our fifteen years' worth of accumulated collective knowledge, I documented the extensive and complex interrelationships and deep involvements of many of these actors in the torture cases, aided by a data systems program developed by the lawyers for death row prisoner Andrew Maxwell.

There was little that could shock us about Daley, Devine, and their cast of assistant prosecutors. We knew from painful experience that the scandal could not have gone on for so long without their active participation, quiet cooperation, and blind acquiescence. We also knew that this involvement, like that of Burge and his men, was fueled by a code of silence and by racism, individual and systemic. This was underscored by the recent revelations of a former prosecutor, who admitted that in the 1970s criminal court prosecutors ran a contest called "nigger by the pound": convicted defendants were weighed, tabulations made, and yearly commendations awarded to the prosecutors with the greatest collective weight of convictees.

Nonetheless, the interconnections we uncovered were shocking, even to us. I wrote in the petition:

One hundred and ninety-three ASAs, including sixty-seven supervisors and Chiefs, and two State's Attorneys, have been directly involved or otherwise significantly connected to the torture cases since the first allegations arose almost thirty years ago. Among this group of one hundred and ninety-three ASAs, there are forty-one Felony Review ASAs who took statements from defendants who alleged that they were tortured or otherwise physically abused by Burge and his men, and one hundred and fifty-four more, including Daley, Devine, and their Chiefs and Deputies, who have been involved in the prosecution or appeal of these cases, the defense of Burge and his associates, who have been witnesses for the State or Burge, and/or who directly supervised one or more of the interrogations and prosecutions in question.

Further, the analysis demonstrated:

The command structure of the SAO [state's attorney's office] in the early 1980s—State's Attorney Daley, First Assistant Devine, First Deputy Kunkle, the Chiefs of Criminal Prosecutions, the Felony Trial Division and the Municipal Division, and the supervisors of the Felony Review Unit—all have had substantial involvement in some aspect of the torture cases. Additionally, several of the successors to these posts were also directly involved in these cases and all of them were veterans of the Felony Trial Division, had served in the Felony Review Unit when the tainted statements were taken by their colleagues, and/or had served as supervisors and trial assistants in the courtrooms where the allegations of torture were repeatedly raised and successfully resisted.

The evidence detailed in the accompanying judges' petition was equally, if not more startling:

There are sixty-one judges assigned to the Felony Courts of Cook County, including six presiding judges, forty-one of whom are former Assistant States Attorneys and thirty-eight of whom served in the SAO Felony Trial Section, the Felony Review Unit and/or as supervisors during the period it is alleged that statements coerced by acts of brutality and torture were obtained or relied upon in criminal prosecutions.

Four of these forty-one are also former Chicago police detectives or officers.

In addition to the forty-one former ASAs, there are four felony court judges who are former Assistant Corporation Counsel, three of whom defended police officers, including Area 2 detectives, in civil cases;

Additionally, there are two who were formerly Assistant Attorney Generals, one was previously counsel for a City agency; one who worked for another law enforcement agency; and one who is a former Chicago police officer.

This is a total of fifty of the sixty-one felony court judges.

Moreover,

At least eighteen of these judges had material involvement in the torture cases, either by obtaining the allegedly coerced statements, by approving charges based on them in Felony Review, by using the confessions—and the testimony of Jon Burge and other Area 2 supervisors and detectives—as trial prosecutors, and/or by participating in Burge's defense as lawyers or witnesses. Others were high ranking supervisors in the SAO who approved the charges, oversaw the prosecutions or helped to develop policy which resisted any investigation into these claims of coerced confessions caused by police wrongdoing.

In the fall of 2002, the struggle against the death penalty was moving ahead at an almost frantic pace. The most pressing goal was to convince outgoing governor George Ryan, who was not seeking reelection amid allegations of political illegalities, to grant clemencies by commuting, to life in prison, the sentences of all of the more than 160 men and women on Illinois's death row before Ryan would leave office in mid-January of 2003. The idea to file blanket clemency petitions on behalf of all death row prisoners had been conceived more than a year earlier by Chick Hoffman, his colleagues at the Office of the State Appellate Defender (OSAD), and Northwestern Law's Larry Marshall. The massive legal effort that followed was implemented by lawyers at OSAD, the MacArthur Justice Center, and the law schools of Northwestern, DePaul, and Chicago-Kent. Rob Warden, now the director of Northwestern's Center on Wrongful Convictions, played an important role on the political front; the Campaign to End the Death Penalty, the Coalition Against the Death Penalty, the Committee for Justice for Death Row Families of Illinois, the Aaron Patterson Defense Committee, and family members of death row prisoners circulated petitions and held regular vigils and demonstrations, press conferences, and forums, including the "Live from Death Row" gatherings at the Hothouse jazz club, during which Aaron Patterson, Stanley Howard, and others addressed the crowd from death row.

In October, at Devine's insistence, the Illinois Prisoner Review Board held a series of highly publicized clemency hearings. One hundred forty-two cases were heard over nine days. Devine's forces had lined up family members of the victims of the often heinous crimes to testify. At one point in the proceedings, Devine and a large group of his assistants, wearing yellow ribbons in support of the crime victims, staged a press conference at which Devine railed against clemency for two torture survivors. Ignoring the pending disqualification motion pending before Judge Biebel, a battery of veteran assistant state's attorneys argued the cases with bloodthirsty passion, while Chick Hoffman and a team of defense lawyers argued for mercy.

At the hearings, the defense's collective strategy was to highlight the death row torture cases, the question of innocence in those cases, and the numerous moral, political, and legal reasons that Illinois's death penalty was blatantly unfair, discriminatory, and unconscionable. This counterattack would be waged by expert testimony, as well as in the individual cases that were being heard by the board. Abby Mann, an Academy Award–winning writer and filmmaker, was on hand to film the proceedings, as an ally who had taken a filmmaker's interest in the fight against the death penalty and the torture scandal.

Prior to the hearings, in the *Tribune* Steve Mills publicized the innocence strategy and laid out some of Governor Ryan's options: "How Ryan will handle the cases is unclear. He could commute some of the sentences.

Or, as he recently suggested, he might issue a blanket commutation for Death Row prisoners, a process that would not weed out cases of potential innocence." In a direct quote, Ryan's spokesman Dennis Culloton added, "The Governor is aware that there are a few cases out there where lawyers are actively pursuing appeals to prove actual innocence. That is a thing that deeply concerns him. Those cases are definitely in the mix in some way, and depending on where those cases are when the Prisoner Review Board is done with its work, we'll have to factor it into the review."

The first day of the Prisoner Review Board hearings, Cathyrn Stewart Crawford spoke on behalf of Leroy Orange; Tom Geraghty and Joey Mogul spoke on behalf of Ronald Kitchen. They presented several experts, including one on false confessions and another on mental disabilities. Larry Marshall of Northwestern testified as a highly respected death penalty expert and called out the proponents of capital punishment: "For all these people who are telling you that the system is foolproof, that the system works, the news is, it doesn't. When is the law enforcement community going to start to be humbled by the experience here?"

The Northwestern team had asked me to testify about the Death Row Ten and the pattern and practice of torture that led to their wrongful convictions. Communicating through his defense committee, Aaron Patterson had objected to my appearing because I would not be focusing solely on the innocence cases, but Joey and I decided that my testimony was important to the broader campaign for clemency and did not conflict with Aaron's own innocence claim.

As the lead witness in Leroy Orange's case, I brought the black shock box with me. The emotionally charged room was packed with the media and their cameras, and the family members of the victims and the defendants. I demonstrated how the box worked, saying, "You then attach these wires to the ears, fingers, the arms, and the genitals and crank." I tracked the history of the police torture cases, the numerous favorable judicial findings, and the expert opinions of Dr. Kirschner, who had died of cancer a month earlier, and Dr. Martinez.

The national media was paying attention. The *New York Times* wrote, "The much anticipated hearings turned the theoretical national argument over capital punishment into a vivid real life drama." I linked the death penalty to the Death Row Ten and police torture: "Whether [the Death Row Ten] are guilty or innocent," I said, their convictions and sentences "are irrevocably tainted" and "they all have the right to be free of a conviction that was based on a confession that was tortured from them." Tom and Cathryn had arranged for CNN to conduct an exclusive interview with Leroy Orange, introduced to a national audience as an innocent man who was tortured with electric shock, confessed to crimes he did not commit, and had served nineteen years on death row. Speaking softly, Leroy said that although he wanted a pardon, he would settle for his life being spared: "I suppose I would basically beg for my life . . . so I could stay alive to fight my case."

Aaron Patterson must have been watching from his cell. Unbeknownst to us, he sent a letter to Judge Toomin, asserting that we had betrayed his claim of innocence by advocating for clemency, and demanding that my fellow PLO lawyers and I be removed from his case. Judge Toomin reluctantly agreed to bring Aaron up from Menard's death row for a conference, and, after a spirited discussion, Aaron withdrew his demand to remove us.

As the holidays approached, Aaron announced a hunger strike. His Defense Committee pressed Governor Ryan for a meeting, and the governor's people reached out to us for a letter detailing the case for Aaron's torture-related innocence. Keeping Ryan's well-known enmity for Devine in mind, we emphasized his conflict of interest and that of his office, his bias, and his deep involvement in the scandal.

Around this time, another plan came to fruition. It was a presentation for the governor and his wife of *The Exonerated*, a powerful theatrical event in which actors performed the true stories of exonerated death row prisoners. The cast included Hollywood star and longtime activist Danny Glover. At the play's end, Mrs. Ryan was in tears, and all of us in attendance were buoyed by its impact.

Still, the governor's intentions were up in the air. A group of activists including Robin Hobley, Madison Hobley's sister and a leader of the Committee for Justice for Death Row Families of Illinois; JoAnn Patterson; Chick Hoffman; Jane Bohman and Bill Ryan from Coalition Against the Death Penalty; and Alice Kim from the Campaign to End the Death Penalty arranged a meeting with the governor, in order that he could come face to face with the families of the men and women on death row, just as he had already done with the crime victims' families. The meeting took place on January 3, 2003, at Old St. Mary's Catholic Church, on South Michigan Avenue, and the gathering humanized the prisoners on death row to Ryan, a once conservative Republican, who was deeply affected.

Robin Hobley told the media assembled outside the church, "This meeting is about clemency for everyone on death row and to stop the death penalty. We're not trying to let out people who are killers, but there are people who are on death row who are innocent. Madison is one of those. It's time for Madison to come home."

The governor, clearly struggling with the historic choice that lay before him, soberly told the press, "I was here strictly to listen and to understand their pain, and there was a lot of it. . . . Now I have to make the decision and I'll do that before I leave office."

Less than a week before Ryan was to leave office, Larry Marshall told us that the governor and his people were worried about Aaron Patterson's volatile and unpredictable behavior and wanted us to send Ryan a letter to reassure him, with specifics, that Aaron would be a model citizen if released. We quickly delivered a glowing letter, emphasizing Aaron's strong mother, his intelligence, education, and community contacts. After that, there was nothing to do but wait.

CHAPTER 19

Free at Last

On January 10, 2003, we gathered at DePaul Law School with nervous anticipation. That morning, both the *Tribune* and the *Washington Post* had published that Ryan was planning to announce some innocence pardons, but specifics had not been confirmed. JoAnn Patterson, Robin Hobley, and other death row family members sat in the front of the auditorium, along with activists, law students, and a phalanx of local, national, and international media. Just before Governor Ryan appeared, copies of his speech were distributed. JoAnn scanned the eighteen-page document and, upon seeing Aaron's name, started to shake. She said, "Now that I read this, everything is really just fine." Robin Hobley burst into tears and said, "I don't believe what I'm reading. . . . It seems just like Christmas and New Year's and a birthday all wrapped up into one."

Veteran death penalty attorney Andrea Lyon —one of Madison Hobley's lawyers and the head of DePaul's Center for Justice in Capital Cases— introduced the governor. Ryan began his speech by saying that when he had started his term almost four years before, the death penalty was "not on his radar." He then listed those men who had been exonerated from Illinois's death row—among them Anthony Porter, the Ford Heights Four, and Rolando Cruz—now thirteen in all. He pointed out that two-thirds of the men on death row were African American and thirty-five of them had been convicted by all-white juries. He talked about the proliferation of jailhouse snitches and incompetent lawyers, then detailed Madison Hobley's torture and the case for his innocence. Next he turned to Stanley Howard, then to Aaron, who, Ryan said, "was tortured by Area 2 Violent Crimes detectives under the direct supervision and with the participation of Commander Burge." He finished by describing the case of Leroy Orange. All four men, he emphasized, were tortured by Burge and his men: Leroy by electric shock; the other three by baggings and beatings. He then condemned the entire Illinois "justice" system:

The catalog of horrors was hard to believe . . . If I hadn't reviewed the cases myself, I wouldn't believe it. What I can't understand is why the courts can't find a way to act in the interests of justice. Here we have four more men who were wrongfully convicted and sentenced to die for crimes they did not commit. We have evidence from four men, who did not know each other, all getting beaten and tortured and convicted on the basis of the confessions they allegedly provided. They are perfect examples of what is so terribly broken about our system.

Stating that a "manifest injustice" had occurred, Ryan declared, "I believe these men are innocent." He then alluded to Abraham Lincoln's speech upon pardoning a Union soldier:

Today I shall be a friend to Madison Hobley, Stanley Howard, Aaron Patterson, and Leroy Orange. Today I am pardoning them for crimes for which they were wrongfully prosecuted and sentenced to die.

As Aaron walked down Pontiac's death row to his freedom, his fellow prisoners broke out in cheers and shouted pleas that he advocate for them with the governor. Stanley Howard and a deeply disappointed Ronald Kitchen remained in their cells: Howard, because he was serving another sentence; and Kitchen, despite a strong case for innocence made on his behalf by the Campaign to End the Death Penalty. As he walked out, Aaron told the assembled media that he was "that angry Black man that you all talk about all the time"; he did not intend to just "thank God" and say he wanted to spend time with his family, but intended to continue the fight for his imprisoned brothers and sisters.

Governor Ryan's announcement concerning clemencies was scheduled for 2:00 p.m. the next day at Northwestern Law School's Lincoln Hall, the venue where I had haltingly introduced Fred Hampton nearly thirty-five years before. The early edition of the Sunday *Tribune* had hit the newsstand with the front-page headline "Decision Day" and beneath it a large color photo of Aaron, flanked by JoAnn, Frank Ralph, and me, as Aaron addressed the media in the Pontiac parking lot. Inside were large color photos of Madison Hobley and Leroy Orange and stories about their first hours of freedom. In his statements, Devine condemned the pardons as "outrageous and unconscionable," vowing that he would try to undo Ryan's decision.

As I made my way to the second historic gathering in two days, I got an urgent call that all hell was breaking loose at Northwestern Law. Aaron was threatening to disrupt the speech if he did not get an audience with the governor, at which he could advocate for the release of one of his death row comrades. A quick intervention brought him to reason, and Aaron and I were led upstairs to a room overlooking Lake Michigan, where Governor Ryan was putting the final touches on his speech. The governor, in his booming voice, greeted Aaron and waved him over to speak privately. After their discussion, Aaron, who had not slept since his release, seemed much calmer and assured us that he would not disrupt the proceedings.

The governor's speech showed the remarkable transformation of a politician who, as a state senator, had voted to reinstate the Illinois death penalty twenty years before, and had still considered it fair and just when he became governor. He lauded the dedicated work of Larry Marshall and Northwestern journalism professor David Protess of the Medill Innocence Project, and told of a call from Nelson Mandela:

> The other day, I received a call from former South African president Nelson Mandela, who reminded me that the United States sets the example for justice and fairness for the rest of the world. Today the United States is not in league with most of our major allies: Europe, South Africa, Canada, Mexico, most of South and Central America. These countries rejected the death penalty. We are partners in death with several third world countries. Even Russia called a moratorium.

Calling the death penalty a "human rights issue," the governor quoted South African Bishop Desmond Tutu and repeated the famous words of Supreme Court justice Harry Blackmun, in the landmark dissenting opinion in which Blackmun first declared his opposition to the death penalty: "From this day forward I no longer shall tinker with the machinery of death." To thunderous applause, Ryan changed the debate on the death penalty forever:

> Because our three-year study has found only more questions about the fairness of the sentencing, because of our spectacular failure to reform the system, because we have seen justice delayed for countless death row inmates with potentially meritorious claims, and because the Illinois death penalty is arbitrary and capricious and therefore immoral, I can no longer tinker with the machinery of death.
>
> The legislature couldn't reform it; lawmakers won't repeal it.
>
> But I will not stand for it. I must act.
>
> Our capital system is haunted by the demon of error—error in determining guilt, and who among the guilty deserves to die.

> Because of all of these reasons, today I am commuting the sentences of all death row inmates.

CNN covered Ryan's speech live. Reporter Jeff Flock did a lengthy live interview with a highly energized Aaron and me. Angry and eloquent, Aaron fielded some difficult questions from Flock, who seemed skeptical of the governor's blanket commutations. Asked about the families of crime victims, Aaron said that he wanted to meet with them, to let them know that the men on death row were redeemable, that many had turned their lives around, and that while some were gulity, others were not. As for the commutations, Aaron described the experience of serving life without parole in a six-by-twelve cell as the death penalty on "an installment plan."

Flock posed a question to me that echoed a point raised by some liberal critics of mass commutations. Citing pro–death penalty national polls, he asked, "Are you concerned that the backlash against this unprecedented and dramatic action by the governor is going to set you back?" I countered with optimism. "I certainly hope not. I think that people are open-minded out there." I recounted what had happened when we had stopped to eat with Aaron the night before, his first meal as a newly free man. "What did the waitress say, what did a customer say? They said, 'Congratulations, Aaron. I used to to be for the death penalty but too many innocent people have been executed. Now I'm against the death penalty.' This is a truck stop in Dwight, Illinois. I think that what the governor did will resonate across the entire country."

Aaron finished the interview with a flourish, repeating the names of several of the innocent men left on death row, including Ronald Kitchen, and threw down a challenge: "I'll tell you one thing, I will meet with Richard Daley this week and by Thursday I will meet with Dick Devine. He has a whole lot to say. I would like to meet with him one on one."

Our whirlwind tour took us next not to Daley and Devine but to Oprah Winfrey's Harpo Studios. Aaron, Leroy Orange, and Madison Hobley were brought on stage to join Governor Ryan. After Ryan shook the men's hands, he told Oprah and the audience, "The only evidence that there was against these people was obtained through brutal beatings, electrocutions and suffocations. I wouldn't have done it if I didn't think they were innocent." When Oprah asked the men if they felt free, Leroy responded by saying, "I feel physically free but mentally, spiritually, I don't care for the accusations that this man [Ryan] did the wrong thing. In spite of the statistics, it appears as if people are saying some are innocent, but kill them all and we'll get the right one."

The concerted efforts to link the torture struggle to the death penalty, starting with Aaron's case and championed by the Death Row Ten and dedicated activist organizations, were bolstered not only by the innocence pardons themselves but also by how the pardons, commutations, and police torture were publicly connected in the aftermath of Ryan's historic decision. The *Sun Times* sent a reporter from the *Tampa Tribune* to Burge's home in an unsuccessful attempt to get his comment and reported, under the headline "Pardons Put Burge on Hot Seat," that "a woman who answered his door Friday morning said he was out of town and did not know when he would be back." Carol Marin, in a *Sun Times* opinion piece entitled "Code of Silence Got Us to Where We Are on the Death Penalty," also focused on Burge and the torture scandal. Marin likened the police code of silence to that of the Mafia: "The Mob is known for omertà, a code of silence, but it has got nothing on Cook County when it comes to disciplined refusal to talk about the awful truth." After specifically calling out Daley, Devine, and the Chicago Police Department, she concluded:

> No one who had the power wanted to perform the politically thankless task of telling the public what virtually no one wanted to hear, that the system we count on to right terrible wrongs had on too many occasions betrayed them. That, by the way, included George Ryan. Until now.

Aaron also appeared at a press conference with congressman Bobby Rush and Leroy Orange to criticize the pace of the special prosecutor's investigation. Rush said that it was "overdue for Burge and his henchmen to be brought before the judicial system of this state." The eighty-year-old Egan was spending the winter in Florida, but his partner, Bob Boyle, reacted with displeasure, calling the criticism "surprising" and "unwarranted," invoking the "massive undertaking" of the investigation. Our relationship with the special prosecutors had further deteriorated; not only had they ignored our requests for transparency and an independent staff, but we were also disturbed by their approach to our clients and the other men who had been tortured. Instead of treating the torture survivors as witnesses for the prosecution and protecting them, Egan and Boyle approached them as adversarial witnesses, seeking to put them under oath and taking long and often hostile sworn statements from them. It appeared that they were trying to discredit the men's stories, while the clock was steadily ticking down on the statute of limitations for perjury, obstruction of justice, and conspiracy charges against Burge and his henchmen.

Aaron continued to hammer away at the death penalty. He and I appeared as witnesses at a congressional hearing convened by Congressman Rush at the federal courthouse a few days after the press conference, and Aaron was prominently present that same week when state representative Art Turner introduced a long-shot bill to abolish the death penalty. Paraphrasing Fred Hampton's famous lines, Aaron emphasized, "I hope I don't have to take a Bible and hit them over the head with it. But sometimes they need a rude awakening."

In April, Judge Biebel ruled on our motions to disqualify Devine's office and the entire Cook County bench from the ongoing criminal post-conviction cases. Biebel first ruled that Devine's office must be disqualified from the criminal cases, but, in a compromise move, he appointed attorney general Lisa Madigan and her office—rather than independent lawyers, as we had urged—to replace Devine. As for the judge disqualification portion of our motion, Biebel had been very skeptical, almost openly hostile, in defense of his judges when Michael Deutsch and Cathryn Stewart Crawford had made their arguments before him back in December. Clearly, he was not about to extend his conflict-of-interest rationale to the criminal courts of Cook County, appearances of impropriety be damned.

In a curious turn of what seemed to be circular logic, Judge Biebel concluded:

> This court agrees that public confidence in the judiciary is of significant importance. However, the court disagrees that removing the cases from the judiciary of Cook County is the best way to foster such confidence. The best remedy for any perceived lack of faith is to allow the judges of this jurisdiction to preside over these cases with diligence and impartiality as they have been sworn to do.

In the aftermath of the pardons, we were preparing a major civil rights lawsuit for damages to be brought on Aaron's behalf, as were the lawyers for the other three pardoned men. With the filing near, Locke Bowman and Randolph Stone published an opinion piece in the *Tribune* on the one-year anniversary of the appointment of Egan and Boyle, appropriately titled "Special Prosecutors Need to Be More Aggressive." Citing the "powerful investigative tools" at the prosecutors' command, from subpoena power to the granting of immunity in order to compel truthful testimony, they wrote,

"If the special prosecutor is pursuing these investigative strategies, there have been no signs of it. If he is not, then he risks muffing an important, historic opportunity to do justice. This case calls for an aggressive no-nonsense prosecutor and an independent and aggressive staff that is representative of the community that demanded and obtained his appointment."

Egan and Boyle responded by granting Steve Mills an exclusive interview in the *Tribune*. Stated Egan, "We believe something happened. You'd have to be a chump not to, but whether I can say as a prosecutor that I can prove somebody guilty beyond a reasonable doubt, that's an entirely different matter." They claimed to be in the process of reviewing a million pages of documents, to have impaneled a grand jury and, in a dubious assertion, to have received some cooperation from police witnesses. They said that they hoped to finish by the end of the year, claimed to be looking at eighty-four cases, and promised a report if they did not bring charges. Mills pointed out that the investigation had cost county taxpayers almost a million dollars to date, and quoted me as saying, "I guess the proof is in the pudding. There's obviously, and we've known for many years, a pattern of torture. The question now is to get beyond that and to hold people responsible."

Aaron's complaint and our fight for justice for the torture victims got another boost, just as we were about to file. Longtime Chicago news anchor Bill Kurtis was now the host of *Investigative Reports*, a long-running show on the Arts & Entertainment network. Kurtis interviewed Joey Mogul, Aaron, and me, as well as wrongful convictions experts Richard Leo and Northwestern professor Steve Drizin, for an hour-long piece called "False Confessions." In the piece, Kurtis presented three very different in-custody scenarios from across the country: the interrogations of a juvenile named Michael Crowe; a farmworker named Oliverio Martinez; and Aaron.

After Kurtis described Burge's interrogations as "medieval" and akin to an "inquisition," Aaron told of his near-suffocation and of Burge putting his gun on the table "like a Wild West show, saying, more or less, we're in the murder game now." A "red alert really went up then that I may not ever make it out of here," so, after Burge left the room, Aaron took a paper clip and scratched into the metal bench that Burge "slapped and suffocated me with plastic." As Aaron explained, "This is my dying declaration—that I would let somebody know after the fact that it was no accident if I got killed in the police station. So I wanted to leave some kind of message."

Joey explained that "the only piece of incriminating evidence against him was his coerced confession by torture. There was no physical or forensic evidence linking Aaron to this crime." I recounted how we had unpeeled the cover-up, then, when Kurtis noted, "Stories coming out of this one police station were too strange to be made up," I emphasized "the fact that these people did not know each other, they had no real reason or opportunity to get together and talk about this. If you were going to make up a case, why would you make up one that seemed so outlandish; why would you come up with a typewriter cover; why would you come up with a black box with electric shock?" Interviewed while walking along the lakefront, Aaron summed up his feelings about Burge and his "asskickers": "Oh, yeah. Every single one of them should go to jail, and I am going to take an active role in seeing them go to jail, lose their jobs, and feel some of the things we felt over these last seventeen years."

Our complaint on Aaron's behalf was not quite so dramatic, but, for the first time in a legal pleading, it laid out in nearly complete detail the conspiracy to torture, the conspiracy to maliciously prosecute, the conspiracy to cover up, the police code of silence, and the pattern and practice of systemic torture. It named as defendants almost all the conspirators—including Burge and his cabal; the prosecutors who wrote out Aaron's statement; former superintendents LeRoy Martin and Terry Hillard; former OPS director Gayle Shines; and Hillard's assistant, Thomas Needham—and the City of Chicago. We also named Devine, alleging that his conflict of interest, defamatory public statements about Aaron, and role in keeping Aaron in prison made him an active co-conspirator.

One conspirator was conspicuously missing, however: Richie Daley. Aaron wanted to name him in the worst way, but we were concerned about prosecutorial immunity and wanted to take Daley's deposition first, then, armed with the added factual detail that we hoped to develop, name him in an amended complaint. After some intense discussions, Aaron reluctantly agreed to accept our advice.

In late June, Aaron and his legal team—Stan Willis, his associate Demitrus Evans, Michael Deutsch, Joey Mogul, and I—announced the filing at a press conference. Aaron declared that he was "a living witness of terrorism in Chicago," and that "we hold each one of these individuals responsible for holding me hostage on death row for seventeen years, including our mayor, gangster Richard Daley. And I'm putting that emphasis on 'gangster.'" Aaron also referred to former superintendent Brzeczek's 1982 letter to then State's Attorney Daley, an important fact that we had intentionally omitted from our complaint. I told the press we would be asking for $2 million for each year Aaron was on death row and $1 million for his non–death row years; the headline in both daily papers was predictable: "Freed Death Row Inmate Files $30 Million Suit."

A few weeks later, Aaron was present when newly elected Illinois governor Rod Blagojevich signed a bill that provided for videotaping station-house interrogations in homicide cases. Videotaping, a major thrust of Bill Kurtis's *Investigative Reports* piece, had originally been opposed by the FOP and other law enforcement officials, which had caused the governor to equivocate; as a result, the bill had been watered down in order to obtain the governor's approval. Blagojevich noted that videotaping murder interrogations would "help restore the public's trust in a justice system that has seen thirteen people released from death row and four pardoned based on innocence." Steve Drizin spoke cautiously, saying that while it was a "good first step, the big question is whether the courts will allow the exceptions to swallow the rule."

The bill was sponsored by state senator Barack Obama, who, we noted, had not spoken out against police torture or otherwise come to our support during his previous six years in the state senate. The next day, Obama, who was disliked by much of the south side's Black community because of his unsuccessful bid to unseat Bobby Rush, appeared together with Aaron in a large *Tribune* photo. A year later, Obama would be electrifying the Democratic National Convention with his keynote speech as the junior senator from Illinois, while Aaron would be on his way back to prison.

CHAPTER 20

Freedom Denied

In early August 2003, John Conroy published another major investigative article, "Deaf to the Screams." In this 12,000-word expose, subtitled "The next state's attorney to investigate police torture in Chicago will be the first," Conroy exhaustively examined all of the known evidence about the state's attorneys' role in what Conroy called "well known" and "savage torture." "Among the many mysteries surrounding the torture cases," he wrote, "one question looms large. Where were the prosecutors? Could a torture ring exist for nearly two decades without anyone in the state's attorney's office noticing? Did state's attorneys look the other way in Cook County? Did their office know—or have good reason to suspect—that torture was deployed under Jon Burge's command?"

Conroy tracked the damning trail of complicity, uncovered in the *Wilson* cases and in numerous cases after that, from Richie Daley and felony review supervisor Larry Hyman to Dick Devine. He highlighted the interrelationship of the police, prosecutors, and criminal court judges, using our statistics, observing that the "network has periodically shown itself in amazing ways." As an example, John pointed to Stanley Howard's case: Stanley was tortured by Area 2's midnight crew into confessing to a six-month-old murder after being arrested for the armed robbery of a former Area 2 lieutenant. He was represented by an appointed public defender before a criminal court judge, both of whom had previously worked as detectives with the lieutenant at Area 2. Not surprisingly, the judge rejected Stanley's claims of torture, and, after the jury convicted Stanley of murder on the basis of his tortured confession, sentenced him to death.

Conroy turned to former superintendent Richard Brzeczek for an analysis from someone who had previously called the shots from the inside:

> Put it this way—I have never heard in my career in the police department, nor have I had it brought to my attention since I left the police department, that somebody from felony review reported that a prisoner was claiming

abuse. I see a lot of incestual activity going on between felony review and the detective division. The state's attorneys, instead of examining the situation and looking at it objectively, they basically take the police officer's word for it, rubber-stamp it, and bang, that's it. In felony review you have young assistants with limited experience, and you've got older, experienced detectives, and I think the assistants are intimidated. They both have the same objective in mind, putting people in jail.

Darrell Cannon's plea agreement had him due to be released on parole in August. As we learned, however, the Prisoner Review Board was refusing to approve his release, claiming that his plea in the 1983 torture case established a violation of his 1971 parole. Darrell had raised this potential problem with us before he had agreed to plead guilty, and, in turn, we had raised it with the prosecutors who had offered us the plea deal. The lead prosecutor assured us that the 1971 case "was over," and both sides informed the court that our shared intent was for Darrell to be released in August 2003. Now, Devine's office was telling us they had no power to override a vindictive Prisoner Review Board that was refusing to release Darrell.

We devised a plan to file a post-conviction petition, claiming that Tim, Cathryn, Frank, and I were ineffective for not discovering and informing Darrell about the very real possibility that the Prisoner Review Board might refuse to release him because of his 1971 parole hold. Locke and Chick filed the post-conviction petition in front of Judge Fox in the fall. The prosecutors did not oppose it but, instead, moved to vacate Darrell's 1983 conviction:

> At the time of the plea, the People believed that Cannon would be released in August of 2003. After extensive review, the People have determined that there is only one option available that honors the intent of the parties at the time of the plea. This option is a drastic step to take on Cannon's behalf but the People feel obligated to honor the intent of the parties. The only option available is to dismiss the substantive case. In doing so the People have fulfilled their obligation to honor a "gentlemen's agreement" struck in 2001 and have taken the only step that they can to give him the benefit that he bargained for.

On this basis, Judge Fox vacated Darrell's plea agreement and dismissed his 1983 murder case. Next was a parole revocation hearing that the Prisoner Review Board set for August 2004, a year after Darrell's scheduled release.

Governor Ryan's pardons and the lawsuits that followed gave us a fruitful avenue for seeking additional evidence of the pattern and practice of police torture. Andrea Lyon, together with Loevy and Loevy, an up-and-coming Chicago civil rights law firm, had filed suit on behalf of Madison Hobley, and Loevy and Loevy filed on behalf of Stanley Howard later in 2003. Tom Geraghty and Cathryn Stewart Crawford had asked us to collaborate with them in drafting a suit on behalf of Leroy Orange and, in early 2004, we filed on his behalf.

Leroy and his half-brother, Leonard Kidd, had been subjected to thirteen brutal hours of torture at the hands of Burge and his henchmen. Their interrogation demonstrated not only how Burge and his men worked when they were torturing more than one suspect, but also how integral the felony review prosecutor was to the process.

Leroy and Leonard were arrested in January 1984 for a south side murder and arson that had left four people, including several children, dead. They were taken to an interrogation room at the new Area 2 complex by several of Burge's trusted detectives, including Flood, McGuire, and McWeeny. Another member of the interrogation team was Leonard Bajenski, who had cut his teeth as a patrolman with Burge, Dignan, and Byrne at the 3rd District in the early 1970s.

When Leroy denied knowledge of the murders, Burge's detectives turned out the light, told him he was going to talk, and forced a bag over his head. A second bagging followed, this time with the interrogation room door open and Burge on the scene, and the dry submarino was accompanied by punches to the chest when Leroy attempted to hold his breath.

Meanwhile, in a nearby room, Leonard Kidd was interrogated by the same team of detectives, who shuttled from room to room. According to Leonard, Bajenski hit him twice on the head, a bag was placed over his head, and the detectives kept telling him that he was "going to tell them what they want to know about the murders." Leonard was repeatedly hit on the back of the head; his head hit the table twice, opening a cut that bled on the table. The detectives called Leonard "nigger" and threatened to "kill his Black ass." Later, Burge brought a black box in a bag into the room. Leonard's pants were pulled down, he tried to scuffle, and several of the detectives, including Flood and Bajenski, jumped on top of him. They hooked the wires up to his "nuts" and electric shocked him on his genitals.

Leroy was brought to Leonard's interrogation room, where he saw his half-brother looking beaten and bruised and as though he had been crying. Leroy told him, "Just tell them I did it and they'll leave you alone." After they returned Leroy to his room, one of the detectives demanded, "So tell me what happened." Thinking he could prevent the interrogation team from further brutalizing Leonard and him, Leroy responded, "You want somebody said he done it, okay, I done it, but I don't have a story for you." This did not satisfy his interrogators, who insisted that Leroy take them to the murder weapon.

Burge then summoned assistant state's attorney Dennis Dernbach to Area 2. Dernbach, who would later be elevated to the position of Cook County criminal court judge, was then the supervisor of state's attorney Richie Daley's felony review unit, and no stranger to allegations of torture, having defended the State in the case of Alonzo Smith. Dernbach would be at Area 2 for the final six hours of the interrogations of Leroy Orange and Leonard Kidd. After being briefed by Burge, Dernbach sought to get a written statement from the bloodied Leonard Kidd. Leonard defied the detectives' instructions to say that he had not been mistreated and told the stocky prosecutor that the detectives "had been kicking his ass." According to Leonard, a red-faced Dernbach responded, "He ain't ready," and walked out of the room, leaving Leonard for the detectives to visit further abuse upon him.

Leroy, unable to deliver the murder weapon, resisted repeating the story that the detectives were trying to feed him. His interrogators became more agitated and summoned Burge, swearing and cursing, to the interrogation room. Accusing Leroy of "bullshitting," Burge demanded his cooperation. Repeatedly calling him "nigger," Burge then supervised a brutal session of electric shocking that began with a shiny object being rubbed across Leroy's handcuffed and outstretched arm, causing an extremely painful shock. Burge was standing in front of Leroy, with four others from his interrogation team in the room, and continued spewing threats and racial epithets.

The detectives then pulled Leroy's pants down; he felt something sharp, then was jolted by three or four shocks on his buttocks. During the shocking Leroy was in full view of the interrogation room door. Held around the neck and body, Leroy struggled to stop the shocking and tried to wiggle away. While struggling, he briefly saw a dark box and wires with a generator or transformer in it near the desk on the floor. The detectives next shocked the back of his scrotum, and he felt excruciating pain.

Leroy then felt one of his torturers trying to "stick something in my butt," but Leroy jerked away. Next he felt his anus being lubricated and the shocking device "inside his butt." He experienced an electric shock that was almost unbearably painful, and affected his bowel muscles for months afterward. Leroy later described how he felt after this ordeal ended: "I felt like a rape victim. I was ashamed, I just wanted to cover my—put my pants back on and just sit there."

Leroy had repeatedly screamed out in pain. Dernbach, who was sitting in the open work space into which the interrogation rooms opened, was within earshot of Leroy's screams but later claimed to have heard nothing. At various times Dernbach entered Leroy's room to show him photos. At one point, soon after the shocking session, Leroy described a prosecutor who looked like Dernbach entering the room, expecting to take his statement. When Leroy instead tried to tell him about his torture, the prosecutor said, "Bullshit, just as I thought," and walked out of the room. After he left, Bajenski approached Leroy from behind, grabbed his testicles, and said, "We can go through this again all night if you want to."

Dernbach then re-entered the room, and Bajenski remained, staring at him. Burge returned and said of Dernbach, "I know how this guy works. Just go along with him and everything is going to be fine." Dernbach first went over some written questions and the photos with Leroy, then left the room and returned with a court reporter. At about 3:50 a.m., with Bajenski still present, Dernbach led Leroy, completely broken, into reciting to the court reporter the false confession that they fed to him. It would be the sole evidence that sent Leroy Orange to death row and cost him nineteen years of his life.

Just after we filed Leroy's amended complaint, CBS's *60 Minutes 2*, followed by Seymour Hersh in the *New Yorker*, exposed a shocking military torture scandal at the Abu Ghraib prison in Iraq. After the US invaded Iraq in March 2003, the US military and intelligence services had converted Saddam Hussein's torture chamber to one of their own. The lead photo in Hersh's expose was of an Iraqi prisoner, fully hooded from head to foot, standing barefoot on a box with electrical wires attached to his hands. A series of sexually degrading and dehumanizing photos taken by the US military torturers was circulated from computer to computer for amusement.

The parallels between the dehumanizing and racist torture as described by Hersh and that practiced by Vietnam-schooled Burge, Dignan, and their confederates were impossible to miss. In response, John Conroy explicitly drew some of those parallels in a new piece, "Torturer's Logic," based on his 2000 book, *Unspeakable Acts, Ordinary People*:

> In Chicago it all has a familiar ring. The interrogations during Jon Burge's years at Areas Two and Three had glee (Burge called it "fun time"), women

(albeit in peripheral roles and as bystanders), photographs (of the results, but not of the work in progress), sexual debasement (cattle prods to the rectum and genitals), the city's attempt to suppress reports (ultimately released by order of federal judges), and the denial of a police superintendent that he had read—or even heard of—the department's own report on the torture ("I don't know nothing about the Goldston report," Terry Hillard said in a 1999 deposition).

Conroy debunked the "few bad apples" defense and emphasized the prosecutorial role in the continuing scandal:

> In Chicago the detectives who tortured suspects under Burge's command were only a few among many, but the few become many when you consider the coconspirators. Many detectives who did not participate but knew about the torture said nothing. And scores of assistant state's attorneys participated: Felony review ASAs took confessions despite evidence that suspects had been "softened." Trial prosecutors pressed for execution on the basis of tainted confessions. Appeal prosecutors seemed to have raised not a whimper of dissent as they filed more than a hundred briefs that named the same set of detectives as perpetrators. Above it all reigned Richard Daley, Cecil Partee, Jack O'Malley, and Dick Devine, the county's successive chief prosecutors, none of them willing to investigate despite evidence that something was seriously wrong.

In his book, Conroy analyzed cases of torture by the Israelis of Palestinians; by the British of Irish Republican prisoners in Northern Ireland; and by Burge and company in the Andrew Wilson case. He drew on this analysis to discuss the mentality of the torturer:

> What is absolutely forbidden in the eyes of the civilian is conceivably normal behavior in war with a foreign enemy or war on crime at home. Soldiers (or police officers) feel they occupy the high moral ground. Each knows he's on the front line of a noble war keeping the nation (or the city) safe from those who would destroy it. The behavior that so shocks civilians is something he saw yesterday and will see again tomorrow. The victims are . . . whoever the out group happens to be.

The collective strategy in the lawsuits filed on behalf of the four pardoned men was basically threefold: seek documentation that had not yet been unearthed; search for favorable witnesses and record their stories; and question under oath all of the close to fifty detectives, supervisors, police brass, and prosecutors who were central to the systemic torture and its cover-up.

Early on, it became apparent that the teams of high-powered private law-yers retained by the City and County at taxpayers' expense would fight us tooth and nail, just as Kunkle's and Devine's law firm had done. Ironically, among the first documents that Madison Hobley's lawyer Kurt Feuer and I unearthed were two emails between the top City lawyer, Mara Georges, and her top aides, discussing a suggestion by Daley's chief of staff that the City cut Burge loose and no longer defend him at taxpayer expense. It was obvious that this suggestion had been rejected, most likely by Daley himself, and the firm that was responsible for turning over the emails was fired by Georges.

As our examination of box after box of City documents continued, Joey came across a highly relevant packet: the torture file of former OPS Director Fogel, which he had downplayed and the City had refused to produce during the second *Wilson* trial. The file showed that in 1984 and 1985 Fogel was communicating with his supervisors and with then police superintendent Fred Rice about cases of electric-shock torture at Area 2; that they had accumulated a number of cases, including those of Andrew Wilson, Darrell Cannon, and Leroy Orange; and that they had identi-fied eleven other unrelated cases of electric shock from several other police districts. The file also reflected that the OPS investigation was cut short rather than pursued further.

It soon became apparent that Burge, Byrne, and the other Area 2 defendants in the four cases did not intend to testify. The previous Novem-ber, Burge and his City-financed lawyers had made what would prove to be a monumental mistake—Burge had denied, in writing and under oath, that he had tortured anyone, or had witnessed or supervised any torture. In the meantime his team had changed their strategy, and sought for Judge Gottschall, the judge in Aaron Patterson's case, to delay their obli-gation to answer interrogatories or give depositions until after the special prosecutors concluded their investigation, which had no end in sight. We opposed the delay, and the judge ordered them to answer. In the summer of 2004, Burge, Byrne, and the other Area 2 detectives all filed interroga-tory answers in which they asserted, under oath, their Fifth Amendment rights in response to all questions about torture, frame-ups, and cover-ups.

Our next move was to make each of these men sit for a videotaped deposition at which they would repeatedly assert their Fifth Amendment right in response to each and every detailed question that we would ask them. Unlike in criminal cases, the US Supreme Court had decided that the invocation of the Fifth Amendment could be used against a civil defendant, and we intended to play these videos for the jury if the cases went to trial.

Our first target was Jon Burge. We wanted him on video, both for the civil cases and for Darrell Cannon's parole revocation hearing, scheduled for late August. We talked the Prisoner Review Board into issuing a subpoena for Burge, but it was not enforceable without a court order from a Florida judge. So we headed to Hillsborough County Court in Tampa to seek a court order. Mort Smith, my trusted investigator and, in this instance, also my personal bodyguard, joined the trip. Mort and I had been conducting investigations together since the late 1990s, when we traveled to rural Arkansas to locate a key witness in the Ford Heights Four case. Mort was not only a highly skilled investigator but also cut an imposing figure—six foot two, 225 pounds, and trained in the martial arts.

The dark, cavernous courtroom of the Florida judge known locally as "Dirty Harry" was almost deserted when Mort and I entered. We waited while the judge gave a thirty-second airing to each of numerous bond hearings he conducted via video from the local jail. Burge made his entrance, flanked by a local lawyer retained by the City of Chicago, and the judge's clerk called our case. It was the first time I had met Burge face to face since the 1992 police board hearings. His reddish hair had turned white, but he still carried himself with a cocky arrogance, and, if looks could kill, I wouldn't have lived to tell the tale. His self-assurance toned down substantially, however, when "Dirty Harry" told Burge and his ill-prepared lawyer that he was "dubious" about their argument that our subpoena was not enforceable in Florida. The judge wanted them to return to the courtroom in a few days for his final decision. Burge's lawyers then agreed that he would come to Chicago to be deposed on September 1, 2004, for use both at Darrell Cannon's hearing and in the four civil cases.

Our excitement at the successful trip was tempered by some very sobering news. Aaron Patterson had been arrested on a drug-running and weapons charge during a federal sting operation. According to a federal source, as reported by the *Tribune*, the arrests "capped a five-month investigation that included undercover heroin and marijuana sales. During the probe, Patterson asked a federal agent for several types of guns, a law enforcement source said, including a MAC-10 submachine gun with a silencer."

Aaron's mother, JoAnn, and his criminal defense lawyer, Tommy Brewer, were dubious of the charges. Brewer pointed out that Aaron was "a millionaire in waiting" and had been incredibly active in speaking out against the death penalty and police torture, and had even made an unsuccessful run for the state legislature. Aaron had been living with JoAnn and had an infant child. JoAnn defended her son with a passion, as she had always done, but the Feds had collected a massive amount of wiretap and surveillance evidence, some of which showed that Aaron was allegedly conspiring under his unsuspecting mother's roof.

We would not, and could not, represent Aaron in his criminal case, but it certainly impacted our efforts in the civil case. We had begun settlement discussions with the City, and Aaron's arrest on serious federal charges further complicated the already sensitive negotiations. It would no doubt prejudice him in the eyes of our judge—practically overnight, Aaron had morphed from a wrongfully convicted torture survivor who had reformed his previous gang-banger ways to an alleged gun-running, heroin-distributing gang boss who had run a con on the public and used his wonderful mother's house as a base for his conspiracy.

On the morning of August 27, 2004, Locke Bowman, Chick Hoffman, Frank Ralph, and I were ushered into a large room at Stateville Prison in Joliet, Illinois, to represent Darrell Cannon at the Prisoner Review Board's parole revocation hearing. The *Tribune*'s Steve Mills was also on hand to cover the proceedings. Our strategy was simple: to put on a mini-torture hearing in order to show there was no competent evidence that supported Darrell's involvement in the 1983 murder. It was a three-person panel, with the liberal, at least by the unabashedly pro–law enforcement standards of the board, Jorge Montes sitting as the chair.

Darrell testified first. He admitted to driving the car when the 1983 murder took place but denied any pre-knowledge of or involvement in the crime. He then told the story of his mock execution and electric shocking. We then brought Byrne, Dignan, and McWeeny to the stand. Dignan, proudly wearing a Fraternal Order of Police shirt, invoked the Fifth in response to a set of questions similar to those he had answered with false denials at his 1996 deposition in the Marcus Wiggins case. Byrne followed suit, invoking the Fifth rather than denying, as he had in March 2001, that he had tortured Darrell Cannon, Gregory Banks, and the other men who had accused him. After McWeeny did the same, I briefly questioned former superintendent LeRoy Martin in order to establish that Burge had been fired after Martin had signed off on the charges.

The hearing was then continued for ten days so we could question Burge and present an edited version of the video to the panel. Steve Mills's story the next day was headlined "Burge's Men Take the Fifth," and explained that "Cannon was supposed to be set free in 2003. Officials, however, have refused to release him, saying he is in violation of his parole for a 1971 murder conviction for which he was sentenced to 100 to 200 years in prison." Mills also highlighted that "with attorney Flint Taylor questioning them, McWeeny took the 5th 38 times, Dignan 23 times and Byrne 33 times, even in response to such seemingly simple questions as whether Burge was their commander. Most of the questions, however, centered on whether they had ever taken part in or witnessed the torture of murder suspects at the Area 2 police station, the now-infamous precinct at the center of torture allegations."

On September 1, Burge appeared in Chicago for his consolidated deposition, held in his lawyers' downtown offices. Burge was smuggled in through a back entrance in order to avoid angry demonstrators chanting "Jail Burge," the assembled media, and three process servers who were attempting to subpoena Burge to testify before the special prosecutors' grand jury. I questioned Burge for nearly four hours in the super-charged atmosphere, followed by two of Madison Hobley's lawyers. He repeatedly invoked the Fifth Amendment in response to each and every question, except for admitting that he had owned a boat named the *Vigilante*, and that he was still receiving his yearly police pension of $30,000.

The media was not permitted inside the deposition room, but they gave the event extensive coverage nonetheless. TV cameras caught Burge looking like a Mafia Don, hiding his face from the cameras, as he was driven into the parking garage in the basement of the lawyers' offices. Afterward, at an impromptu press conference, we briefed the media, told them that the number of documented torture cases was now at 108, and said that the City should stop defending Burge. I said that the City "should step forward and admit the torture that was committed by him" and asked why Burge was "being allowed to take the 5th and obstruct justice." I once again accused Daley and Devine of "covering up," a charge that Daley's veteran mouthpiece, Jackie Heard, claimed was "absolutely absurd." In an emotional moment, I described our long-running pursuit of Burge: "We feel that we have finally in some way brought to the stand and brought to public questioning a police criminal, a criminal we felt we had to hunt down, not unlike a Nazi war criminal."

The next week, Darrell Cannon's hearing reconvened, this time in Chicago. The main event was the showing of the Burge video, and after the hearing concluded, excerpts of the video were featured on the TV news. A few days later, Prisoner Review Board Chairman Montes released the board's four-page decision. While Montes acknowledged that he was "inclined to believe" that Darrell confessed under torture, the board's decision dismissed the torture evidence as irrelevant to its determination, and instead relied on Darrell's concession that he was at the scene of the crime and drove the getaway car, together with the 1983 grand jury testimony of a witness—later recanted as false and coerced—that Darrell supplied the gun for the shooting. Locke Bowman condemned the decision, pointing out that the grand jury testimony was not only coerced and recanted, but was also the "rankest hearsay" and not subjected to cross-examination. I said, angrily, "There was an agreement for him to get out. They should honor that." But the board had not, and it appeared that Darrell would remain locked up at Tamms for the indefinite future.

CHAPTER 21

An Open Secret

M ort and I, together with our dedicated court reporter Carmella Fagan, had been on the investigation trail of torture survivors since April 2004. Our first stop had been the state prison in Dixon, Illinois, where three of Burge's earliest victims—Anthony "Satan" Holmes, Lawrence Poree, and Edward James—were all still doing time. It had been fifteen years since Jeff Haas and I had talked to these men during the *Wilson* trials, and Mort, Carm, and I did not know what to expect.

Dixon was a medium-security prison, so our investigative team was permitted to take court-reported statements from each of the men. At about two in the afternoon the guards delivered Anthony to our conference room. A big man, now fifty-seven years old and hopeful of making parole after thirty years in prison, he spoke slowly and quietly. He retold his story for the first time in fifteen years: how he was arrested in the early morning hours of May 29, 1973, in front of his terrified wife and small children, how the detectives pointed their guns at his kids, and how Burge threw him to the ground and stepped on his neck. He recounted how he was bagged, heard the cranking of Burge's shock box, and was repeatedly electric-shocked until he passed out, again and again. He told of a "white shirt" supervisor who came into the room, had a laugh with his torturers, and left him for another round of torture. He described his torment:

> It felt like a thousand needles going through my body. And then, after that, it just feel like, you know . . . it feel like something just burning me from the inside, and I shook, I gritted I hollered, then I passed out . . . I come to, and I thought I was dead because they was lifting me off the floor and trying to pump air into me, all I could see was blackness and I said, "This is it, I'm gone."

I conducted a photo lineup, showing Anthony the photos of four Area 2 detectives, and he unhesitatingly picked Burge out of the group as the person he remembered orchestrating his torture, repeatedly saying, "You're going to talk, 'nigger,'" and standing over him each time he came to. Anthony then also identified John Yucaitis's photo as another of the main participants in his torture.

Anthony thanked us for listening to his story and was taken back to his cell. Shortly, Edward James was brought into the room. Edward had been arrested in Memphis in 1979 for a Chicago armed robbery, and Burge, then a sergeant, flew down to Memphis with two Area 2 detectives to bring Edward and one of his co-defendants back to Chicago on an extradition warrant. As Edward told us, when he objected, Burge told him: "Nigger, is you crazy? Now we come down here on a plane and we plan on going back the same way, but if you keep talking this shit about not going back and make us have to rent a car, you going back in the trunk." Edward stopped objecting and they headed to the airport.

According to Edward, the plane was late, so the detectives bought them drinks at the airport bar, and Burge carried on, talking about how they would get them to talk when they got back to the "horror chamber in Chicago," where they used techniques like "squeezing people's nuts." Once at Area 2, Edward refused to confess to the robbery, so Burge repeatedly punched him flush in the mouth, and two detectives joined in. When Edward, hoping to be heard on the street below, screamed loudly, Burge choked him to shut him up. The next day, when Edward was brought to court, he told the chief judge, to no avail, that he had been brutalized. Edward steadfastly maintained, at the time and to us in 2004, that he never admitted to the crime, but Burge, despite having no notes, testified at Edward's trial that he had confessed. Edward was convicted and was serving out a sixty-year sentence when we talked to him.

At about six o'clock, Lawrence Poree, hunched over and moving very slowly, was brought in to talk to us. He told us that he would be celebrating his sixty-fifth birthday the next day, and that he was suffering from terminal lung cancer. He had spent almost forty-one of his adult years behind bars. Lawrence told his story about Burge: when Lawrence was released from the penitentiary in 1973, Burge, Hoke, and two other detectives from Area 2 Robbery, having heard that Lawrence and some associates had formed a robbery gang known as the Black Disciples, rounded them up for a "get-to-know-you session." Afterward, Burge and his boys, angered by the fact that Lawrence had used an alias, administered what Poree called the "third degree"—kicking him down a flight of stairs—and an "ass whipping" that was topped off with Burge showing him the black box and how it worked.

The next time, Burge and his confederates were looking for one of the gang's alleged leaders, Anthony "Satan" Holmes, who was wanted for murder. They kicked in Lawrence's door on the pretext of unpaid traffic tickets, dragged him to the second floor of the House of Screams, and grilled him about Anthony's whereabouts. When Lawrence remained tight-lipped, they put a loose-fitting paper bag over his head and beat him with phone books. Next, they doused his legs with water and "hit him with the rod" on his thigh, causing him to "jump straight up" and "tingle all over." Later, when he dozed off from exhaustion, they used firecrackers to roust him.

Lawrence told of how he and his associates were harassed during his longest stint on the streets, from 1976 to 1979. Burge brought him in and "flashed his big ol' silver gun"—it was "a cannon, a big piece"—and that he aimed to "get all of you together at one time and blow you all away." He was reintroduced to Area 2's horror chamber in August 1979. After being beaten in the police van under the watchful eye of a Black supervisor, Lawrence was subjected to what he called a "round robin, musical chairs" beating, with Burge saying, "Don't mark him up" while kicking him in his back. He was hit in the head with a pistol, then shocked on the arms and legs. It was "a hell of a feeling" and he bit his tongue and the side of his mouth. He, like Anthony Holmes and Edward James, identified Burge's and Yucaitis's photos, and when I asked him if he had any doubt that it was Burge, he said, "No, no, no, bless his soul, no, no doubt in my mind." He pulled up his sleeve and showed us marks on his arm that he said remained, some twenty-five years later, from his shocking. When I asked if he had told his lawyer about his torture, he said he had, but got the standard response of the 1970s: "Ain't nobody going to believe that."

A few weeks later, Mort and I traveled to northwestern Indiana to interview a Black former detective who had worked with Dignan in the Area 2 Homicide Division in the 1970s. We were investigating the wrongful conviction case of Paul Terry, who had spent twenty-seven years in the penitentiary for a murder he did not commit. Paul did not allege torture, and Burge was on a short hiatus from Area 2 when the crime was committed in 1976, so our intended focus was on the facts of the case and Dignan's role in it.

The detective, Melvin Duncan, had left the Chicago Police Department in the late 1970s for a job in the insurance field. He opened up to us briefly. Duncan had no love for Dignan, whom he called a racist, and described a case in which Dignan, while questioning a Black victim beaten by four whites, treated the Black man as though he were the perpetrator.

When the topic turned to Burge, Duncan told us that the Area 2 Robbery and Homicide Divisions shared the second floor at Area 2 during the 1970s, that they sometimes worked cases together, and that from time to time he had heard "loud and unusual noises" coming from the Robbery offices. He then carefully told us that he saw a "dark wooden box" on a table in the Robbery offices on one occasion. He seemed reluctant to directly identify it as Burge's torture box, so he described it in a roundabout way:

> As a child, my father had made a homemade electrical device with prongs, wires, and a crank, and demonstrated it by giving little shocks to my brother and me. When I first saw the box, the first thing that hit my mind was that this box could be used to give electrical shocks like my father's device did.

Duncan added that while working at Area 2, he had "heard that certain Area 2 robbery detectives had used an electrical box and cattle prods on people to get confessions from them."

This was powerful new evidence: a former Area 2 detective corroborated the existence of Burge's shock box and Dignan and Byrne's cattle prod. Initially, though, Duncan was reluctant to get involved, but after some pleading we were able to convince him to go on the record. He signed an affadavit, and we had another important building block in our still-evolving case of systemic torture.

Our next stop was Danville, a medium-security prison in rural southeastern Illinois, about 150 miles south of Chicago, to take a statement from George Powell. With us was my nephew Scott, who was interning in our office for the summer. George, a barber by trade, was doing a short sentence for drug possession and was due to be released in less than two weeks. Quiet and withdrawn, he told us that he had previously served twenty years on a 1979 murder and kidnaping conviction based on a false confession that was tortured from him by Burge, then a sergeant, and several of his detectives. They arrested George, told him, "You're a pretty boy, we're going to mess your face up," and took him to an Area 2 interrogation room, where they produced a Sears and Roebuck plastic bag and forced it over his head. They pulled the drawstrings tightly around his neck, and he shouted, "I can't breathe, I can't breathe" so loudly that they took the bag off for a moment.

He then caught a glimpse of the electric-shock device that the detectives had brought into the room. He called it a "cattle prod" that looked like a police nightstick. George became more animated as he described his torture:

They put the bag back over my head and they started asking me questions. And the next thing I know, they started hitting me with shocks, you know throughout my body. And I couldn't breathe, plus the cuffs was tight, and I'm like getting dizzy, so I'm trying to bite a hole in the bag. And one of the officers, I don't know who because I had the bag over my head, hit me in the mouth, busted my lip.

George said that the torture, led by Burge, went on "for hours," with the shocks being administered all over his body, from his chest to his testicles, until he agreed to recite the story they were feeding him—that he was present for the murders and had a minor role in the kidnaping. He was taken to another police station where the felony review state's attorney asked him only if he had "been treated fairly *here* today."

George's lawyer was Earl Washington, who later also represented Leroy Orange and Leonard Kidd. Washington skated on the thin ice of incompetence and conflict of interest in those and other cases. When George told Washington about the torture, Washington said that the coerced statement was "one of the best things in the case. . . . Let it come on in as evidence." Washington also said that the judge would "think negative" about George, that he was "trying to hide something" if they tried to suppress his confession on the grounds of police torture.

That summer we took statements from three additional Area 2 torture survivors, two of whom were previously unknown to us. We found Rodney Mastin in a Racine, Wisconsin, flophouse. Several years before, in jail in Whiteville, Tennessee, Rodney had seen a TV piece on the Burge torture cases by Geraldo Rivera and had gotten in touch with me through David Protess.

We had marked the beginning of Burge's reign of terror from Anthony Holmes's May 1973 arrest, but Rodney told me that he and three of his teenage friends had been brutalized by Burge and company in August 1972, only a few months after Burge had made detective and was transferred to Area 2. Rodney told of his arrest, as a nineteen-year-old, at his parents' house by the "red haired, red faced" Burge and another "real slender" detective, who had "thin lips, pale skin, short hair, and piercing eyes that looked straight through your eyes." Rodney's brother, a Chicago cop, lived upstairs at the time. The arrest was for home invasion and the brutal beating of a nine-year-old white boy in a racially changing neighborhood.

When Rodney and his friend, Philip Moore, were taken into Area 2, they were led past an open door, where they saw seventeen-year-old Lindsey

Smith, beaten so badly about the face that he was almost unrecognizable. Burge took Rodney to a separate room and questioned him while walking around the table where Rodney was seated. When Rodney did not cooperate, Burge punched him in the head, face, and chest, knocked him to the floor, kicked him in the groin, then slammed him back into the chair. At one point Burge threw an ashtray, hitting Rodney in the back of the head.

Rodney then gave a written statement admitting to participating in the high-profile crime, as did the other three teenagers who had also been rounded up and brutally beaten. When called to testify at the motion to suppress the young men's confessions, Burge denied any wrongdoing. This was the first known time that he perjured himself when asked about torture at Area 2. After the judge denied the motion, Rodney and his co-defendants all pled guilty to reduced charges and received sentences ranging from six to nine years.

George Powell had mentioned another arrestee in the 1979 kidnap/murder case by the nickname "Gbaba," and we had figured out the man's real name, Ollie Hammonds. Ollie had been picked up by Burge and one of his detectives, George Basile, in an attempt to turn him into a witness against their main targets. When Ollie did not agree to cooperate and testify before the grand jury, Burge orchestrated a sixty-hour torture session that ended with Ollie refusing to testify and his being charged with the crimes. He spent another month in jail before the case was dismissed for lack of evidence. Ollie had gone on to lead a prison-free life, so we took his statement at our offices on Milwaukee Avenue.

Ollie told us that, after a series of beatings by Burge, Basile, and two other Area 2 detectives, Burge and Basile produced the black shock box. Burge asked Ollie if he "knew what this did to a man's dick," then nodded to Basile, who touched together the two wires coming from the box. The wires created a spark and the two detectives then set the box on a table and left. They later moved Ollie to a cell, where he was deprived of food and water. Over the next two days, Burge and Basile visited him periodically and subjected him to further beatings.

That fall, Mort, Carm, and I also took statements from three of the four African American detectives who had worked the four-to-midnight shift under Burge in the early and mid-1980s, what we considered the apex of the two-decade reign of torture. These detectives were finishing their shifts and writing up their reports when Sergeant Byrne and his midnight crew of "ass-kickers" were starting their work. I was most interested in looking up Doris

Byrd, to see if her evasiveness and subsequent refusal to go on the record five years before had softened, now that she was retired.

First, we traveled to the suburb of Evergreen Park to talk to Sammy Lacey, now a lawyer. When Lacey came to Area 2 in 1981 he was partnered with Doris Byrd. He told us that during the 1980s, police personnel working at the Fifth District station, on the first floor of Area 2, asked him, "What are they doing to people up there on midnights?" Lacey averred that Jon Burge was often present at Area 2 when Lacey left work at midnight, and "if there was any questioning, he was there." He said that he was present at police headquarters when Donald White was brought there as a suspect in the Fahey and O'Brien murders, and that he was left downstairs in an empty office with African American commander Milton Deas, while Burge and chief of detectives William Hanhardt took Donald to another floor.

Lacey said he heard that strange things were going on at Area 3, after Burge was transferred there as the commander in January 1988, and that a lot of confessions were being obtained. Lacey further stated that Burge did not permit Black detectives to work the midnight shift or to investigate homicides, and that when Area 2 commander LeRoy Martin was notified of this scheme, Burge found out and subsequently berated the Black detectives the next day. He also confided that he was sent to the north side during the Wilson manhunt, and that when he went by Area 2 to drop off his overtime vouchers, on the day the Wilson brothers were being tortured, he heard screaming coming from the second floor.

Former detective Walter Young told us that while he was assigned to Area 2, in its basement he saw a box-like object with what appeared to be a crank, and that after hearing stories and conversations from other Area 2 detectives he concluded that the box he saw might have been the electrical box said to have been used on certain people brought into the area. Young said that he overheard references to the Vietnamese and to Vietnam; that suspects could be made to talk if the same basic techniques were used as in Vietnam; that the term "Vietnam special" or "Vietnam treatment" was used; and that, based on seeing the box and overhearing conversations, he later concluded that the "Vietnam treatment" probably referred to the use of electric shock.

Young said that while walking past an interview room, he heard unusual noises, saw Burge exit the room, and saw an African American suspect sitting on the floor, handcuffed to a ring on the wall. Young further stated that Burge had a reputation of being forceful in his investigations; that during the manhunt for the killers of officers Fahey and O'Brien in

February 1982, Young overheard conversations from detectives that force was being used on suspects; and that he heard Area 2 detectives say that a phone book would sometimes help people refresh their memories, phone books don't leave marks, and plastic bags help to cushion the phone book. Young also concluded, from the way he and his fellow African American detectives were treated by Jon Burge, that Burge was a racist.

Now we ventured to the far south side to renew acquaintances with retired police sergeant Doris Byrd. Feisty as ever, she was not initially of a mind to speak on the record, but Mort and I were able to convince her to talk. She told us that when she had first made detective, she had been assigned on a few occasions to work with Dignan, but he had refused to accept the assignment because she was a Black woman. She also told how the Black detectives all worked together and were given the "non-newsworthy, in-custody, known but flown, and ghost offender cases," while the "A-Team," as she called Burge's and Byrne's midnight crew, got "all the newsworthy and high-profile cases."

She also gave us an inside view of the code of silence. She revealed that shortly after detective Frank Laverty came forward during the George Jones trial to expose the existence of secret street files, Burge had pointed a gun at the back of Laverty's head as he left the main detectives' room at Area 2 and said "bang." She also said that after Deep Badge named her as a possible "weak link," a police captain who was a friend of Dignan's called her to tell her that Dignan was worried about her testifying against him. She pointed out that the department had "squashed" Laverty's career.

Byrd also told us that during the Wilson manhunt she observed an African American man attached to a hot Area 2 radiator. She said it was her understanding that Burge was given a mandate by Mayor Byrne to do anything he had to do, including using torture techniques, to solve the murders of Fahey and O'Brien. She was also involved in the arrest and initial questioning of Gregory Banks, who would not give them a statement. After the midnight crew took over Greg's interrogation, he was "singing like a bird." She said that she understood that his cooperation was obtained by torture.

Byrd said that she would often remain on duty after 1:00 a.m. and on occasion would hear screaming and other unusual noises coming from interview rooms. Byrd further recounted that she was told by individuals interrogated at Area 2 that detectives had physically abused them with telephone books, plastic bags, and an electric shock box. She said that "the black box was running rampantly through the little unit up there"; that she heard about it both from detectives and suspects; and that this kind of abuse was linked to Burge, Byrne, Dignan, and the midnight shift.

The month before, Mort had spoken with Rodney Mastin's brother Barry, a former Area 2 general assignments detective who worked on the first floor of Area 2 from 1972 to 1977. He told Mort it was an "open secret" that certain white detectives tortured and abused suspects on the second floor. He said that suspects were often brought through the back door and held incommunicado for several days. He also heard that a suspect was held out the window by his ankles during an interrogation, accidentally dropped, and charged with attempted escape. I asked Doris Byrd if she agreed that torture by electric shock, baggings, and beatings was "an open secret" at Area 2. Without hesitation, she concurred that it was, saying it was well known that Burge and his subordinates used torture to obtain confessions.

All the Black detectives agreed that Burge was a racist. They told similar stories of segregation and discrimination in assignments and in performance ratings, and of recrimination from Burge on the one occasion when they complained to commander LeRoy Martin. Doris Byrd added, "It was going around that Burge was in the Klan."

In addition, Madison Hobley's lawyers had obtained a videotaped sworn statement from Eileen Pryweller, the sister of Area 2 detective Robert Dwyer. Dwyer was deeply involved in the torture of Madison, and his sister's statement illuminated this pervasive racism from a third perspective. Pryweller told Mort and lawyers Kurt Feuer and Andrea Lyon that she'd had a conversation with her brother and Burge at her brother's house in January 1987. During that conversation, Burge and Dwyer described how they dealt with "niggers" during interrogations, stating that they'd "give them hell," "beat the shit out of them, throw them against walls, burn them against the radiator, smother them, poke them with objects, [and] do something to some guys' testicles." She recounted that her brother said, "This skinny little nigger boy, I got him by just torturing him, smothering him," while Burge laughed. They made it clear that they were talking about Madison Hobley. She continued that Burge seemed proud of his torture tactics, that he and Dwyer were "full of hate," that Burge "described some techniques that he had that no one could even fathom," and that Dwyer said he could "make anyone confess to anything." She stated that after the special prosecutor began his investigation in 2002, Dwyer, from whom she was estranged, brought up the 1987 conversation at a family wedding, in a way that she perceived to be a threat.

CHAPTER 22

The Daley Show

Richie Daley's shadow had hovered over the torture scandal, the death penalty, and wrongful convictions for nearly twenty-five years, and our office's entanglements with his family went back even further. Although we harbored strong suspicions at the time, we had never uncovered any evidence that Richie's father, the legendary mayor Richard J. Daley, was directly involved in the cover-up of the assassination of Fred Hampton. The trail ran cold at his anointed successor, state's attorney Edward Hanrahan. Such was not the case with Richie and the police torture scandal, and we were determined to make him answer under oath for his role in it.

I had met with Richie Daley in person only once, about twenty years before, when Jeff Haas and I were seeking the prosecution of cops who had shot and killed a mentally disturbed man. Daley was a small man with shifty eyes, sitting behind a large desk in his office at the Cook County state's attorney's office. Belying his reputation as an advocate for the mentally ill, the meeting did not go well.

Daley and I continued to lock horns in the media. In the late spring of 2004, I deposed superintendent Terry Hillard in the case of the little boys who had been falsely accused of raping and murdering Ryan Harris in 1998. Hillard admitted under oath that he was aware that his detectives were interrogating the boys but did not question the detectives about their conduct or intervene to stop the coercive interrogation and arrests that followed. We made the deposition transcript available to Maurice Possley of the *Tribune*, who asked Daley about it. Invoking his previous experience as state's attorney, Daley told Possley that Hillard's failure to act was "good management," while I countered by saying that Hillard's conduct "amounted to his approval of the false arrest and malicious prosecution of the boys." The *Trib*'s headline read, "Daley Backs Hillard Over Harris Inquiry."

That July, we filed notices of deposition for Daley, Devine, and several other high-ranking officials in the four pardoned plaintiffs' cases. With regard to Daley, his lawyers with the Dykema firm, Terrence Burns and Dan Noland, who also represented the City, responded with an emphatic "no," in a letter claiming that Daley was "a busy public official"; that his testimony was not relevant; and that we were causing "annoyance, embarrassment, oppression, or undue burden or expense." We fired back, and so did they, demanding that we withdraw Daley's name, which we were not about to do. After we had several frustrating conferences with Burns and Noland, they brought the question to court by filing a short motion to bar the depositions we were seeking.

We responded with guns blazing, arguing in a lengthy pleading that

> in this unique set of cases, where high public officials, including former police superintendents and the State's Attorney of Cook County are named both as policymakers and co-conspirator Defendants in a notorious thirty year pattern and practice of torture, cover-up, and code of silence, the public record, as well as the discovery obtained in this case, fully supports the depositions of Daley and his fellow policymakers, because it demonstrates, at various times and in various ways, their active participation, ratification, condoning, acquiescence in, and actual knowledge of this continuing pattern and practice.

We then documented the evidence of Daley's involvement that we had gathered over the previous fifteen years. We attached fifty exhibits, and the complete document was so voluminous that Joey and I toted copies of it to court in two bankers' boxes. Strategically, we had also supplied the media with copies of the motion. CBS 2's Dave Savini struck first, with a special investigative report entitled "Torture Investigation—Memo to Daley" that ran at the top of the six o'clock news. Anchor Antonio Mora opened the piece:

> Attorneys for four death row inmates say a memo warning of the alleged actions of former police commander Jon Burge had been sent to Mayor Richard M. Daley back when he was a prosecutor and tonight they say that memo was simply ignored.

Reporter Dave Savini continued, over video of Daley: "Mayor Daley was State's Attorney of Cook County when at least sixty-nine alleged torture cases arose during a time when former police commander Jon Burge and Burge's alleged right-hand man John Byrne were accused of torturing murder suspects." The segment cut to a photo of a battered Andrew Wilson, then to our cranking black box. Savini said, "Again and again, men have claimed that they were coerced through abuses into confessing." He then cut to me, saying that Daley "is the one who refused to prosecute Burge and investigate torture that he was specifically presented with by police superintendent Richard Brzeczek in 1982."

Savini returned to Daley's deposition, weaving together the story we had set forth in the document we had just filed in court: "What did Daley know, and what didn't he know? Those are the kinds of questions plaintiff's attorney Taylor wants to ask the mayor on a sworn deposition." As Savini thumbed through our three-inch-thick pleading, he quoted me as saying that "the City just recently turned over fourteen more cases of alleged electric shock torture, cases kept confidential for nearly twenty years." I reappeared onscreen with another shot aimed directly at Daley's bow: "Mayor Daley, and previously State's Attorney Daley, had notice of the serious and systematic nature of the torture as far back as twenty years ago and chose to do nothing about it."

The powerful piece closed with footage of Daley, our video clips of Burge, Byrne, and several other Area 2 detectives taking the Fifth, and, finally, posters of the Death Row Ten, as Savini concluded: "Daley has said little about the highly publicized and embarrassing civil case against the city, which now stands at at least 120 cases of alleged torture, the alleged torture team of officers are now taking the Fifth, and the cost to taxpayers to defend the allegations is in the millions, a number that is sure to rise as the legal fight builds."

We also got featured billing on TV 5's ten o'clock news, with a young and earnest Don Lemon reporting to veteran anchor Warner Saunders. Referring to our filed pleading, Lemon stated: "At the bottom of these documents are two questions [for Daley], Did you know about torture claims and what did you do?" He then turned to me, and I elaborated:

> There is a significant body of evidence that shows that Mayor Daley, both when he was state's attorney of Cook County and now as mayor, dealt with the torture evidence, was aware of the torture allegations and evidence, and did not do what we would expect a prosecutor or a mayor to do.

Lemon then linked Daley to the newly uncovered electric-shock allegations: "Among the documents filed today are at least fourteen new torture claims from secret documents made public today for the first time, and date back to the time when Daley was at the state's attorney's office. There are familiar allegations of electrical shock, cattle prods put in arrestees' mouths and on their testicles, and the use of electrical wires, nooses, and even stun guns."

I addressed the new revelations: "One of the major questions is, 'Why did so many different officers in so many different places in the city have access to electric shock devices that they could use?'"

Although all four of the pardoned plaintiffs were seeking Daley's deposition, Judge Gottschall, the judge in Aaron Patterson's case, had been selected to decide the Daley question. This would have seemed a favorable choice, as Gottschall had a solid liberal reputation, and, the previous spring, she had written a strong decision denying the motions to dismiss brought by all the defendants, including Devine, whom we had sued in Aaron's case.

Lamentably, the fallout from Aaron's arrest was strong in the federal courthouse. Aaron had given what we considered an ill-advised interview to the *Tribune* from his cell in the Metropolitan Correctional Center shortly after his arrest. He put forward a defense that he was engaging in a "double sting," designed to expose the informant and agents who were allegedly entrapping him, but the government's tape-recorded evidence, as detailed in the article, was not so forgiving. So, when we gathered in Judge Gottschall's courtroom in December 2004, it was not surprising that she was disinclined to permit Aaron's lawyers to depose the "busy city official" named Daley, regardless of the history of his involvement that we had brought before her. The judge denied our request "without prejudice," saying that we could refile a "more specific" motion "at any time"—a motion that did not focus on the "entire history" of the policy, pattern, and practice claims but rather specifically delineated the "subject matters" upon which questioning was sought, and what we "hoped to get from the mayor's deposition."

Round one went to Daley, but his role in the scandal was now squarely in the public eye.

CHAPTER 23

Broadening the Struggle against Police Torture

In early 2005, we located Tony Thompson outside of Phoenix, Arizona, where he was working as an assistant warehouse parts manager. Tony and his brother Timothy had been arrested in 1979, together with Willie Porch. Tony had never given a statement about his interrogation. Mort and I met him at a videographer's office on North 48th Street in Phoenix and took his statement. Tony told how he was arrested for armed robbery and shooting at a cop, taken to Area 2, and interrogated by Burge and "Machine Gun" Joe Gorman. Burge led the charge, calling him "nigger" and "Black son of a bitch," saying, "God had diarrhea when he created you motherfuckers." Gorman bragged about killing Fred Hampton. They hit Tony with a flashlight and telephone book, knocked him out of his chair, and then kicked and punched him. He was bleeding profusely, so they took him to the hospital, where he received eight to ten stitches to his face and eyelid.

Burge and Gorman then brought Tony back to Area 2 and resumed their interrogation. His face was swollen beyond recognition. They threatened to pick up his pregnant girlfriend and beat her up, and they told Willie in Tony's presence that before it was over Willie was going to look "like Puff Face here." Gorman then called for someone to get the "nigger box," and, laughing, they poked Tony in the chest and genitals with the wires that came out of the box, shocking him and causing him to urinate on himself and pass out. They doused him with water, and after he came to, they shocked him a few more times for "fucking up" their night. He felt "excruciating pain," and soon thereafter Tony Thompson relented and gave them a confession. His lawyer convinced him to take a plea rather than raise the subject of his torture in court, so Tony pleaded to twenty years in prison. While in prison, he had educated himself and earned an associate's degree, and he had stayed out of prison, with one six-month exception, since his release in 1989.

Two weeks later, Mort and I were on the road again, this time to Northern Florida to see a prisoner named Eric Smith at the Florida State Prison at Starke. Starke was home to Florida's death row, holding most of Florida's 372 death row prisoners. Florida, which gave the prisoner the "choice" of electrocution or lethal injection, was third in the country, after Texas and Alabama, in the number of prisoners facing execution. Eric was doing eight years for credit card fraud and failing to report as a sex offender. He was brought down to the little interview room chained hand and foot, and told us that the whole prison was on constant lockdown.

On New Year's Day 1983, Eric had been arrested on a rape-murder charge and taken to several district police stations, then to Area 2, where he was interrogated in the early morning hours by Dignan and two other detectives. When he maintained that he did not commit the rape or murder, Dignan called him a liar and beat him on the ribs, back, and genitals with a rubber-encased lead pipe.

After Eric passed out, the torture began again. After he woke up a second time, he found himself naked and handcuffed on the floor of a different room. This time he was shocked with a dark object that looked like a broomstick with metal prongs on one end. As he told us about being shocked on the back and genitals, he broke down and cried, saying that he still has "nightmares about this shit," and had told the prison psychiatrist about it. Maneuvering around the shackles on his hands, Eric pulled out a small piece of paper, on which he had drawn a diagram of the torture device.

The detectives threatened to kill him, and shocked him again. After that, as Eric told us:

> I got tired of being shocked, you know. They said, "Who did it? You're going to tell us what we want, now." And I said, "Just don't shock me no more, man. I'll tell you what you want to know."

Eric then broke down again, in the interview. After two mistrials, he gave up and pleaded guilty to spare his mother further grief. He was given a twenty-eight-year sentence and branded a sex offender, despite his unwavering insistence, which he passionately maintained to us, that he was innocent.

While we were on the road, John Conroy was continuing to investigate and write about the torture scandal, this time exploring our theory that Burge had learned the specific electric-shock techniques while assigned as a military police sergeant to the Dong Tam prisoner of war camp in Vietnam's

Mekong Delta in 1968 and 1969. Conroy's investigation focused on tracking down Vietnam veterans who had worked on that base as MPs in the Ninth Military Police Company at the same time as Burge.

His *Reader* cover story, "Tools of Torture," began with an excerpt from my examination of Burge during the 1989 *Wilson* trial:

> Q. While you were in Vietnam on that base camp did you ever hear of any torture that went on in that POW compound?
> A. No, sir, I didn't.
> Q. Never had any discussions about that that whole time you were there, is that right?
> A. No. I was in the US Army, counselor.

Conroy then advanced the theory connecting Vietnam and Chicago police torture:

> [Andrew] Wilson said Burge wired him up to a black box and turned a crank that generated an electric shock. This technique bore a striking resemblance to what American troops in Vietnam called "the Bell telephone hour"— shocking prisoners by means of a hand-cranked army field phone.

After repeating Burge's assertion that he "had never heard of field phone interrogations" and stating that Burge "bristled at the suggestion that Americans in Vietnam had conducted them," Conroy wrote, "Burge's peers from the Ninth Military Police Company, however, remember such torture in considerable detail."

> According to Edwin Freeman, the company commander during part of Burge's tour, the interrogation rooms at Dong Tam were adjacent to the POW compound and 20 steps from the MP command post. Prisoners were questioned individually in one of five interrogation rooms, and MPs escorted them back and forth. Freeman says the compound could hold 300 prisoners and at times was full. Given the statistics in the available Ninth Infantry operational reports, it's likely that several thousand prisoners were moved back and forth between the compound and the interrogation room during Burge's tour of duty. Would a man praised by his superiors in Korea for his "attention to detail" and "extra effort," who would go on to become such a resourceful detective, not notice his fellow MPs moving handcuffed detainees—the enemy—back and forth, perhaps a hundred trips or more on some days? Would he not know that prisoners were being interrogated 20 steps from the MP command post?

Conroy recounted that both officers and enlisted men who had served in the Ninth as company commander, executive officer, lieutenant, and sergeant all told him that they had "heard of or witnessed field phone interrogations. These men, some outranking Burge and others beneath him, told stories set both at outlying firebases and at Dong Tam."

Several of the Ninth MP veterans told how the field telephone torture was commonly employed as retribution for the ambushing of US soldiers and to get "fast information." One veteran described a US Military Intelligence torture scene he had witnessed:

> They would take them in and they had a kind of large tent, and they would tie them up to the poles right in the center there, their hands behind them and their feet strapped to the pole. And they would give them treatment, and it was not uncommon for them to rig up a field telephone and put one [wire] around a finger and the other around the scrotum and start cranking. And they would eventually tell you what you wanted to know . . . [Was it painful?] Oh, hell yes, it's painful. I mean, you can hold the two wires and barely crank it and get a jolt. The more you crank the higher the voltage, and it's DC voltage, so that's more intense shock.

The electric shocks were commonly applied to the testicles and nipples, and in the scheme of the atrocities committed in the name of the United States government, this was, according to one veteran, "on the lower end of the list of things that probably was used."

Like the torture at Area 2, it was an open secret, protected by the military's version of the code of silence:

> So if some MP got it in his head to report the incident, what would happen to him? It would probably be swept under the rug, and he would either be sent to another duty station or put on shit duty the rest of the time—KP, picking up cigarette butts—anything they can think of that can keep him quiet and keep him in a certain place.

Conroy then circled back to Area 2. Drawing on the statements that Mort, Carm, and I had recently taken, he talked about the torture of Anthony Holmes and related the stories of torture and the shock box that the Black detectives told us. He closed his piece by quoting detective Walter Young:

> He said he had seen a hand-cranked device in the basement of Area Two but didn't know what it was at the time. He wasn't told the specifics of the

techniques then in use, he said, but he heard them referred to as the "Vietnam special" or the "Vietnamese treatment."

As the July date for Aaron Patterson's criminal trial approached, he became more and more disruptive during court proceedings. A clinical psychologist testified in support of a request by Aaron's criminal defense team that he be declared incompetent to stand trial: "He is suspicious of others and tends to be hostile in his relations with others," the psychologist testified. He "thinks he is alone in the world and has no one to take care of him but himself," and is "on the edge" of being suicidal. He also testified that Aaron was suffering from PTSD as a result of his torture.

Judge Pallmeyer, a patient and liberal judge, gave Aaron second, third, and fourth chances, but he continued to escalate his disruptive conduct. Moments into jury selection, after one of Aaron's lawyers complained that he was interfering with his work, Aaron shouted, "I'm not interfering with my lawyers. I don't have any lawyers here." When three deputy marshals moved in to forcibly remove him from the courtroom, Aaron fell on top of the defense table, his body limp, and ended up on the floor, screaming and cursing.

Back in the courtroom, Aaron once again erupted. As the court of appeals later described it, Aaron interrupted the cross-examination of a witness and yelled at his lawyers to

> "get off [his] case." He accused the defense attorneys of setting him up for a fall, then stood up, knocked one of his attorneys to the ground, grabbed the other attorney by his necktie, and threw him to the ground as well. Both attorneys were in a tangle in the corner and one limped around afterwards.

Aaron was forcibly removed once again. The next day, over the government's objection, Judge Pallmeyer permitted Aaron to return to the courtroom, shackled, to testify on his own behalf. He condemned the proceedings as a "legal lynching," and, as tensions in the courtroom escalated, the government asked its first cross-examination question:

> Mr. Patterson, you testified you were the leader of the Apache Rangers street gang before you went to prison, is that correct?

Aaron responded: "You said, 'Do I know who The Three Stooges were?'" He then answered his own question: "Daley, Devine, and Fitzgerald."

(Patrick Fitzgerald was the US attorney prosecuting Aaron.) Removed from the courtroom once again, Aaron was convicted the next day, and Judge Pallmeyer later sentenced him to thirty years in federal prison.

In June, special prosecutors Egan and Boyle had told the *Chicago Law Bulletin* that they could "see the light in the end of the tunnel" and that "It's a safe guess" their investigation would conclude within the year: "We will issue a report." Boyle declined to say whether they would seek indictments and implied that they were not getting full cooperation from some of Burge's victims. The *Law Bulletin* reported that "the case has ballooned into a far-reaching probe of claims by 135 people that they were victims of police torture between 1973 and 1991" and that it had cost county taxpayers $4.2 million to date, running $150,000 a month. The article also recounted that Boyle had been found civilly liable in Wisconsin, along with Democratic machine politician Morgan Murphy, for "fraud, racketeering, mail fraud, and theft."

As much as we'd maintained a cautious and measured public face, these latest public pronouncements only added to our deep frustration with special prosecutors Egan and Boyle and their investigation. They had retaliated against me the previous year for voicing concerns, on behalf of all the survivors' lawyers, that, by persisting in taking detailed statements from our clients under oath despite having their sworn testimony in prior proceedings, their investigation was tilted against the victims of torture and toward Burge and his men. In a letter, Egan and Boyle castigated me and ended with a threat: "If you or any other lawyers see fit not to cooperate with us, the responsibility for what happens after that will be yours and those lawyers. Justice will be ill served by your unreasonable interference in our investigation."

Our distrust escalated when filmmaker Abby Mann informed us of an interview he and his wife Myrna had conducted with Egan and Boyle, which Abby had surreptitiously recorded. Swearing us to secrecy, Abby, who was deeply disturbed by the conversation, gave us a copy of the tape. Egan could be heard saying that a retired judge, as well as Egan's own nephew, a former Area 2 detective, had told him "what a great, hard worker" Burge was: "That's what I've heard from everybody, what a hard worker Burge was." Egan also told Mann that his detective nephew, while working at Area 2, had participated in the arrest of Gregory Banks.

Anti-torture activists were as frustrated as we were by the delays. Drawing on our collective experience in dealing with the international aspects of torture, several of us—Joey Mogul, Stan Willis, Locke Bowman, and I, together with activists Bernardine Dohrn, Susan Gzesch, and torture survivor David Bates—decided to raise the issue of Chicago police torture to the international community as a human rights issue. First, we petitioned the Inter-American Commission for Human Rights (IACHR), which was part of the Organization of American States. Stan, backed by the National Conference of Black Lawyers and Congressman Danny Davis, put out the public call for an IACHR hearing at a Washington, DC, press conference, and we made a formal request on behalf of forty-four human rights and civil rights organizations in an August 2005 letter to the IACHR, signed by Locke. After the IACHR granted the request, we all traveled to Washington that October to testify before the commission, made up of representatives from Antigua, Chile, and Paraguay. Our goal was to convince the commission to open an investigation, come to Chicago to question witnesses, and issue a report. Short of that, we hoped to bring national and international attention to the subject of Chicago police torture.

An emotional David Bates told the commission, "We have officials in Chicago who could deal with it, but they don't want to deal with it. It's a shame we have to come to Washington, DC, to get people from different countries to deal with it." Stan Willis added, "This is probably the most documented case of abuse in the history of the republic. Everybody knows about it, but nobody has stepped forward to punish those responsible."

Immediately prior to the hearing, I told the Washington bureau reporters that Daley was Cook County state's attorney when at least fifty-five of the torture cases took place, and repeated what was becoming a familiar refrain: "He was aware of torture from the beginning, and he did nothing about it." In a typical Daley non-response, the Associated Press reported, "A spokeswoman for Daley's office said the mayor was in Poland and unavailable for comment."

CHAPTER 24

The Tale of Two Reports

Our relationship with Aaron Patterson was growing more tumultuous. Joey, with the help of Ben Elson—a former Ella Baker fellow at the Center for Constitutional Rights, who had joined our office the previous summer—had taken on the responsibility of preparing Aaron for his deposition. All of us were trying to keep track of Aaron's ever-changing positions concerning settlement. This deteriorating state of affairs was complicated by an attempt by Madison Hobley's lawyers to leverage the fact that Madison was the only one of the four plaintiffs not presently behind bars into what we felt was an unfair split of any negotiated settlement. (Leroy Orange had been returned to jail for a minor drug offense, Aaron was about to begin serving his thirty-year term, and Stanley Howard continued to be locked up on his unrelated sentence.)

Joey and I were reporting back to magistrate judge Michael Mason on the subject of settlement negotiations, and Mason's own frustrations with the constantly moving goalposts added to the drama. At one point, Mason had gone to the jail himself, in an unsuccessful attempt to determine Aaron's settlement position in person. At one of several meetings the magistrate conducted with Joey and me, I engaged in a heated confrontation with Mason that culminated in a jaw-dropping exchange of "fuck yous" and my ejection, baseball rhubarb style, from his chambers, while Joey remained, trying to calm the waters. Even more remarkable was the aftermath, or absence thereof—I did not end up in jail or sanctioned for my impulsive conduct, apparently because Judge Mason recognized that the profane flare-up was a product of forces beyond our control.

In early January 2006, Michael Deutsch, Joey, and I returned to the Metropolitan Correctional Center on Van Buren Street to make a final attempt to get Aaron's written approval to a minimum joint settlement amount and to a proposed percentage split of the joint settlement, if one were reached. As a team we had decided that if he would not cooperate, we would withdraw as his lawyers.

While waiting for Aaron to arrive in the visiting area, we ran into former assistant state's attorney turned defense lawyer Larry Hyman. Hyman, the ASA who had taken Andrew and Jackie Wilson's tortured statements, volunteered that he was embroiled in a legal battle with the special prosecutors over his appearance before the Special Grand Jury, at which he had taken the Fifth Amendment. This was news to us, and, as far as we could tell, not publicly known.

The meeting with Aaron that followed did not go well. With deep regret but undeniable relief, we informed him that our eleven-year roller-coaster ride as his lawyers was at its end.

Special prosecutors Egan and Boyle missed their end-of-year deadline and were sending out mixed signals, publicly and privately, about whether they were going to charge Burge or any of his men. Meanwhile, in March 2006, I deposed Sergeant Thomas Ferry, another Burge associate listed by Deep Badge as a "weak link." According to Deep Badge, Ferry, who was a witness in an unrelated wrongful conviction case, was "dumped" (that is, unceremoniously transferred) out of Area 2 by Burge, only months after Burge took over the Violent Crimes Unit in the early 1980s. Ferry, a veteran of Area 2, confirmed that Burge had banished him to another assignment without cause. When I asked Ferry about torture at Area 2, he said that he had "heard rumors and comments about Burge's reputation for mistreating people" that "probably came from other detectives who were working there and didn't particularly like what he might have been doing." He refused to be more specific, claiming not to remember if the mistreatment included electroshock or suffocation. His answers and demeanor reminded me of Doris Byrd's deposition years before. After Ferry died two years later, a close relative confided that Area 2 detectives were "pressured to break arms if necessary to close a case," that Ferry was "outraged" by the "culture" at Area 2, and that he was "harassed" and "threatened." And, the relative added, "all the allegations [against Burge] were true."

In late April, on the fourth anniversary of the the special prosecutors' appointment, the investigation was thrust into the spotlight as local television stations reported on a public demonstration demanding that they conclude their investigation and issue indictments. Reverend Calvin Morris, leader of the broad-based Community Renewal Society, called for the release of the promised report, saying, "Justice requires it," while Darby Tillis, an exonerated death row prisoner and a fixture in the fight against capital punishment, put it more bluntly: "What are we waiting on? We know that Jon Burge is guilty!"

Days later, the focus intensified when Egan and Boyle filed a short motion before Judge Biebel that requested he permit them to make public "the names of all police officers and assistant state's attorneys we have subpoenaed before the grand jury and all steps we have taken to enforce those subpoenas," and for the report to include "certain excerpts of grand jury testimony from a certain individual." The motion implied that the report would be forthcoming early the next week.

The next Tuesday, Judge Biebel's courtroom was packed with lawyers, activists, and concerned community members, with David Bates representing the torture survivors. The lawyers representing Burge, Byrne, and numerous other Area 2 officers had filed a motion asking Judge Biebel to keep the long-awaited report secret, kindling more consternation and rage. The proceedings were somewhat anticlimactic, as Judge Biebel delayed the release of the report while the issue of secrecy was briefed. David Bates, Locke, and I spoke to the media outside the courtroom, with David saying, "We want the police officers—everyone involved in this—names exposed. None hidden." Locke was equally impassioned: "We are talking about torture that is reverberating and affecting lives today. This torture has sent people to prison who are languishing there, as we speak, as a result of confessions they gave under torture."

Our attention was also focused on the United Nations Convention Against Torture (UNCAT). The previous fall, the Midwest Coalition for Human Rights had submitted to UNCAT a formal letter entitled "Issues Regarding United States' Second Periodic Report." The letter called attention to the numerous survivors who were imprisoned as a result of confessions tortured from them:

> Despite the fact that the Convention Against Torture prohibits the use of "any statement which is established to have been made as a result of torture [as] evidence in any proceedings," (Article 15) dozens of individuals have been charged, convicted and imprisoned for crimes they confessed to as a result of torture, and many of these individuals continue to languish in prison despite continued claims of innocence. Questions of guilt or innocence aside, the use of evidence obtained through torture is clearly in violation of the Convention Against Torture.

The MCHR, on behalf of all the petitioning groups, also "[urged] the Committee to address the question of racial discrimination with the U.S. Government concerning these cases":

> The Convention Against Torture clearly prohibits the intentional infliction of "severe pain or suffering, whether physical or mental . . . for any reason based on discrimination of any kind." (Article 1(1)). The victims of the torture detailed above were all African-American, which suggests that race was a factor in the use of torture by Chicago police. Recognizing the ubiquity of racial prejudice and discrimination in American society, including in the United States legal system, we have reason to believe that the race of the victims has also contributed to the government's failure to rectify the situation.

So, as we awaited the release of the special prosecutors' report, in early May, Joey and Susan Gzesch, a local attorney and MCHR leader, traveled to Geneva, Switzerland, to address the UNCAT and to present supporting documentation concerning the Burge torture scandal.

Chicago's local NPR station described the historic events:

> Human rights representatives from Chicago and elsewhere spoke this morning at the United Nations in Geneva, Switzerland. They were there to discuss US compliance with the UN's rules against torture. Longstanding allegations against Chicago police officers were part of the presentation. The UN gets these reports on torture every three or four years. But Chicago was included today for the first time.

Susan Gzesch then spoke:

> The fact that there's international focus and attention on human rights problems in the United States by a United Nations body creates a significant, what you might call blowback, effect that local officials are going to have to pay attention to.

That same day, the Black Caucus of the Chicago City Council held a press conference at City Hall to demand that the special prosecutor's report be released. Alderwoman Freddrenna Lyle, representing the Sixth Ward on the south side, spoke strongly in support of the release of the report, for indictments, and for closure: "There is still this belief in our community that we allowed Black people to be tortured by Chicago Police and did nothing. This belief will be there until we put closure to it." Alderwoman Lyle, who had represented torture survivor Alfonzo Pinex, continued:

We want that report released for the same reason Holocaust victims want Nazi soldiers found and prosecuted: to feel there is justice in this world. . . . If there are allegations of torture in that report, we want the people prosecuted. . . . If there are allegations about any state's attorney, I want their name in the paper so when they try to become a judge, we can say, "Wait a minute. This is the guy who participated when they were torturing people."

Alderwoman Toni Preckwinkle pointed out that suppressing the report "would make it appear as if there's an effort to sweep under the rug, to cover up, to protect illicit, illegal activity on the part of our police officers who pledge to serve and protect us, and that's disgraceful."

On May 9, journalist Amy Goodman addressed Chicago police torture on her fearless national radio and television show *Democracy Now!* Interviewing torture survivor David Bates, reporter John Conroy, and me, she tied together the current local and international aspects of the scandal, linking it to the other overarching US torture issues that were also presented to the UN Commission Against Torture—military prisons Abu Ghraib and Guantánamo:

> Extraordinary rendition. Overseas prisons. Abu Ghraib. Guantánamo Bay. Practices and places that have become synonymous with the abuse of detainees in US custody are getting renewed attention at the United Nations this week, where the UN Committee Against Torture is holding hearings on U.S. compliance with its international obligations. But there is one name expected to arise this week that few people in this country will have heard about—and it's the one that's closest to home.
>
> It's called Area 2. And for nearly two decades beginning in 1971, it was the epicenter for what has been described as the systematic torture of dozens of African-American males by Chicago police officers. In total, more than 135 people say they were subjected to abuse including having guns forced into their mouths, bags placed over their heads, and electric shocks inflicted to their genitals. Four men have been released from death row after government investigators concluded torture led to their wrongful convictions.
>
> Yet the case around Area 2 is nowhere near a resolution—to date, not one Chicago police officer has been charged with any crime. The most prominent officer, former police commander Jon Burge, was dismissed in the early 1990s. He retired to Florida where he continues to collect a pension. Today, a special prosecutor is now in the fourth year of an investigation. Just last week, a group of Chicago police officers won a court ruling to delay the release of the prosecutor's preliminary report.

Amy then introduced us:

David Bates, one of dozens of men to come forward with allegations of abuse at the hands of the Chicago police.

Flint Taylor, an attorney with the People's Law Office in Chicago, which he helped found in the late 1960s. He has represented many of the torture victims and was directly involved in spearheading the special prosecutor's investigation.

John Conroy, a journalist and author, who has covered the case for over a decade. He has written several articles for the *Chicago Reader*, and is the author of the book *Unspeakable Acts, Ordinary People: The Dynamics of Torture*.

She turned to me for "the scope of the story." I traced the history, from Burge in Vietnam to Daley and the appointment of the special prosecutors, which I attributed to a culmination of community outrage. Amy turned to David, who briefly described his torture and then cut to the chase:

The torture has never been resolved. No one has ever owned up to the torture. So we have hundreds of individuals who have psychologically been warped, been destroyed. . . . We're talking about a city. We're talking about a state. We're talking about legislators, who have not looked into the issue of torture, and I say it's a shame. I say it's time for the legislators and mayor and individuals who had firsthand knowledge of it to come clean with it and bring these individuals to justice.

Amy then made the connection between the torture and the death row cases:

Flint Taylor, I remember years ago with an especially active group of mothers, mothers in Chicago of men on death row, who kept raising the issue of this police commander, Burge, and saying that their sons had been tortured, that one had engraved in a metal bench in the police station, "I am tortured, I'm forced to confess," something like that. What about this? What about death row cases, where men ended up on death row?

I elaborated:

That's been a major, major piece of this whole struggle against police torture. In the early and mid-'90s, the movement against police torture and for human rights came together with the anti–death penalty movement here in Chicago and raised a very strong set of voices, some of whom you've just mentioned. There were at least ten to twelve people on death row here in

Illinois who alleged and had evidence to show that Burge and his men had tortured them into giving confessions, one of whom was Aaron Patterson, whom you just mentioned, who during a break in one of his torture sessions etched in a bench that he had been suffocated with a bag and was being tortured. That later came out.

Ultimately, due to the combination of the factors, and articles that John wrote, and speaking out by David and others in the community, and the work of various lawyers, Governor Ryan looked at all of these cases, and as you know, he not only commuted the sentences of all of those on death row, some 160-odd people, but he looked specifically at four cases of torture by Burge and others and found that those individuals were innocent, that they had been tortured into giving false confessions, and he gave full innocence pardons to those four individuals. That's Aaron Patterson, Stanley Howard, Madison Hobley, and Leroy Orange.

Amy then turned to John Conroy, asking, "How has this taken so long to come out, though it has come out in parts over the years and in certain communities is well-known?" John responded:

Well, it hasn't taken that long to be out. It was out in 1990, when we did the story in the *Chicago Reader*, the first story, and we've done more than 100,000 words since. And I think that what's dragged on, the reason why it's dragged on—I differ with the estimable Mr. Taylor here on this—is that there is no community outrage. People don't care. As in every society in which people are tortured, there's a torturable class in Chicago. It's African American men, most of them with criminal records. And they're just beyond the pale of our compassion. We just don't care.

And that's why it's taken fifteen years for you probably to do this program and many others now interested in this report, when the information has been out there for a very long time. The *New York Times*, I think it's covered this twice: once, when the men were pardoned; and once, when there was a float in the St. Patrick's Day parade that was going to honor four of the officers who had been accused, and the float never came to be in the parade, but there was a controversy about it. So, that shows you, I think, the level of concern in the United States about this issue.

When I spoke next, I reemphasized that prosecutions were required:

There are continuing criminal violations here, and if the special prosecutor won't do anything about them, then Fitzgerald, who is the US Attorney here and who, of course, has made his name in the Valerie Plame case and has already indicted Daley's people in a wide-ranging truck scandal, he has to open his investigation into federal RICO or racketeering charges, as well as obstruction of justice and perjury.

I brought it back to the international arena:

And so, perhaps there's not enough public outrage here, but the international community is looking at it in a very strong way, and to hear Chicago put in the same breath with Guantánamo and Abu Ghraib is something that—if that doesn't wake up the powers that be here in the city of Chicago and that doesn't wake up the US Attorney's office and that doesn't, in fact, put on the carpet the state's attorney of Cook County and the mayor of the city of Chicago, I don't know what will.

Three days later, on May 12, Judge Biebel heard arguments on the question of the secrecy of the special prosecutor's report. The courtroom was packed and the judge had to tell the spectators not to cheer for our arguments. Locke, Larry Kennon, and I argued for its release. Surprisingly, so did the City's lawyer Terry Burns. One of the cops' lawyers, veteran FOP attorney Joe Roddy, invoking the secrecy of the grand jury, urged Biebel not to cave to the "hysteria." The judge, perhaps showing his hand, replied, "Don't you think I should be entitled to know what are the results of four years of work here?" He then set May 19 for his ruling.

On May 19, coincidentally, UNCAT chairman Fernando Marino Menendez, on behalf of the ten-person committee, announced the "Conclusions and Recommendations of the UN Committee Against Torture." The UN's report criticized US torture at Abu Ghraib, called for the shutting down of the prison at Guantánamo, and, in another important accomplishment for all of us, found:

The Committee notes the limited investigation and lack of prosecution in respect to the allegations of torture perpetrated in Areas 2 and 3 of the Chicago Police Department (article 12).

The State party should promptly, thoroughly and impartially investigate all allegations of acts of torture or cruel, inhuman or degrading treatment or punishment by law enforcement personnel and bring perpetrators to justice, in order to fulfill its obligations under article 12 of the Convention.

Later that day, Judge Biebel issued his ruling that the long-awaited special prosecutors' report should be made public. In a strongly worded, nineteen-page decision, Biebel wrote that the torture scandal was "an open sore on the civic body of Chicago that has festered for many years."

Therefore, "this Court opts on the side of public disclosure and finds the public's right to be informed of the results of this exhaustive investigation outweighs the privacy rights of the individual officers."

As it turned out, not only the cops' lawyers were opposing disclosure of the special prosecutors' report; an unnamed former prosecutor was also seeking suppression of the report. This prosecutor had appealed to the Illinois Supreme Court the decision permitting Egan to publicly name him in the report. Based on our prior conversation with former ASA Larry Hyman, I knew that Hyman was the "John Doe" who had appealed, and at our after-court press conference I outed him to the press. As the Associated Press reported:

> While the name of the former prosecutor who filed the appeal with the Supreme Court was kept under seal, attorney Flint Taylor of the People's Law Office, which has battled the police in court for decades, told reporters he believed he knew the attorney's name. He said the attorney volunteered in a conversation with him that he had taken the Fifth Amendment before a grand jury when asked about the alleged police torture of 1982 murder suspect Andrew Wilson.

I linked Hyman's secrecy to Daley:

> Taylor said it was possible the former prosecutor didn't want to answer questions to protect his boss at the time, Chicago Mayor Richard M. Daley, who was then Cook County state's attorney. He said the man might have spoken with Daley about the *Wilson* case when it was fresh.

I gave the press the 1982 letters from Dr. Raba to former superintendent Brzeczek and from Brzeczek to Daley, and the press treated them as newly revealed evidence:

> Taylor released a February 1982 letter from Dr. John M. Raba, medical director of Cermak (prison) health services, to then-police Superintendent Richard J. Brzeczek, saying that Wilson had been brought in two nights earlier with bruises, swelling and abrasions on his head as well as a battered right eye and burns on his thigh. Taylor released a second letter dated eight days later from Brzeczek to Daley, saying he had opened an internal investigation but seeking instructions on what else he should do.

The *Sun Times* elaborated on my comments, reporting, "Taylor says that Daley did nothing" in response to Brzeczek's letter. After declining to publish

Hyman's name—a precaution followed by all the media except the *Chicago Law Bulletin*—*Sun Times* reporter Abdon Pallasch repeated in more detail my conversation with Hyman, and ended his article by again quoting me: "Taylor said that when police took Wilson to 'Doe,' Wilson told 'Doe' the police had tortured him and 'Doe' told the police, 'Get this [expletive] out of here.'"

Channel 2's Mike Parker tracked down Brzeczek, who was more than willing to discuss his letter to Daley on camera:

> This one has lingered for over a quarter of a century. To what effect? I think to undermine the confidence that people have in the police department.

Parker's piece continued: "Brzeczek says that in 1982 when he ran the department, he got a letter from the Cook County Jail's chief physician. In it, the doctor describes injuries suffered in custody by cop killer suspect Andrew Wilson. He says Wilson was 'cuffed to a radiator and pushed into it,' and that he was given 'electric shocks' to his mouth and genitals." Brzeczek then told Parker:

> I was livid when I got the letter because the whole world was watching.

Parker continued: "Brzeczek wrote to then state's attorney Richard M. Daley, seeking his direction on proceeding with an investigation. 'I will forbear from taking any steps until I hear from you,' Brzeczek said. Daley never wrote, never called." Brzeczek then declared to Parker:

> I think he was more concerned with making political decisions as to what would be appropriate for his political career, rather than the appropriate legal decision.

Once again, the press had to report, "Mayor Daley was unavailable for questions Friday. The city law office said he could not comment because of pending civil lawsuits by those who claim they were tortured by Burge and some of his officers."

Channel 7's Charles Thomas quoted my assertion that "Doe" could be a "critical link" to Daley, who was state's attorney when fifty-five victims "were tortured," and gave voice to our prospective strategy: "The public interest lawyers said they are willing to wait another month, if necessary, to hear the findings of the four-year-long investigation. They want the . . . report in hand when they go to federal court to press civil lawsuits and seek criminal charges against those responsible for committing or covering up alleged police torture."

Perhaps the *Tribune* best captured our fighting spirit:

"There have been roadblocks at every turn," said Flint Taylor, a lawyer representing one of Burge's alleged victims. "There were roadblocks before the special prosecutor was appointed," Taylor said. "There were roadblocks to firing Burge. There will be other roadblocks. But we intend to roll over all of those roadblocks."

CHAPTER 25

Beyond All Reasonable Doubt

"Electric shocks. Suffocation. Beatings. Chokings. Intimidation with weapons. A whole Inquisition's worth of coercive sadism. So what else is new?" wrote the *Tribune*'s Eric Zorn. Answering his own question, he continued:

> Well, one thing new is that the four-year, $7 million probe is not only the most comprehensive to date by far, it's also the first to employ a grand jury with subpoena powers. Another is that special prosecutors Edward Egan and Robert Boyle reportedly have identified nearly 200 torture victims—more than twice the number previously known to Flint Taylor, the People's Law Office attorney who is at the forefront of this issue.

Reading the tea leaves, Zorn wrote, "All signs are that the report will explosively confirm previous assessments. If so, that bombshell will destroy the wall of denial and dismissal that Mayor Richard M. Daley and Cook County State's Atty. Dick Devine have stood behind since the early 1980s, when Daley was state's attorney, Devine was his top deputy and the torture allegations were coming to light."

Looking more hopefully at Chicago's body politic than John Conroy had, Zorn concluded: "Will citizens be angry? I hope so. This mess has cost them tens of millions of dollars in legal and settlement fees, put innocent people in prison and trampled on the Constitution. Freelance justice got us into this mess in the first place. Only real justice can get us out."

Conroy was also staying on the case. He confirmed that Assistant State's Attorney "Doe" was Larry Hyman and identified him as the most likely candidate while discussing what was publicly known about "Doe's" case, including that "Doe" had originally been held in contempt for refusing to appear before the special prosecutors' grand jury, that the Illinois Supreme Court had ordered him to testify, that he had done so, and that he was now back before the Supreme Court trying to keep the report—and the fact that he had taken the Fifth—secret.

Building on our theory, Conroy wrote:

> Of the many assistant state's attorneys whom the special prosecutor might have wished to talk to, Hyman would be high on the list. Pushing him still higher would be the fact that Hyman could testify about what he'd told his bosses—State's Attorney Richard M. Daley and First Assistant State's Attorney Dick Devine—about the treatment of Andrew Wilson. Naturally those preparing to prosecute Wilson knew of his allegations of torture. Hyman might be able to explain what Daley and Devine knew, when they knew it, and perhaps what they chose to do—or not do—about it.

The next Thursday, Conroy and the *Reader* ran a huge pictorial spread called "The Police Torture Scandal, a Who's Who." In full color, accompanied by thumbnail descriptions of their roles in the scandal, were a dozen of the principals, including Burge, Dignan, Byrne, Daley, Hyman, Devine, Brzeczek, Martin, and Hillard. Courtesy of one of our court filings, Conroy listed twenty-six officers who had taken the Fifth in the depositions we had taken in the civil torture cases. The final picture was of US attorney Patrick Fitzgerald, looking stern and pointing his finger, with the following caption:

> Victims' lawyers don't expect the special prosecutor's report to contain indictments. They speculate that Egan will say that the statute of limitations precludes state charges, and that the prosecutors' job was made extremely difficult when so many witnesses—police officers, former prosecutors, and perhaps even sitting judges and active prosecutors—took the Fifth rather than testify before the grand jury. But Egan's report may provide the pry bar needed to get new trials. It may also lead to federal prosecutions for civil rights violations, violations of the RICO statute, and possibly perjury. The key audience for the report, after an investment of four years and millions of dollars, may be the U.S. attorney, the person who can make a case for prosecutions on the federal level.

On July 18, 2006, I got a phone call from Bob Boyle. A relatively friendly man, Boyle was decidedly less hostile to me than Egan. He told me that he thought I "would really like the report." When we got a copy of it early the next day, his prediction could not have been further from the truth.

Blaming the statute of limitations, the report confirmed that there would be no indictments. Of the 148 cases the special prosecutors investigated, they determined that there were only three—Andrew Wilson, Phillip

Adkins, and Alfonzo Pinex—where the evidence was strong enough to prove guilt beyond a reasonable doubt. They conceded that there were "many other cases" in which the special prosecutors "believed" that the persons, including Melvin Jones, Shadeed Mu'min, and Michael Johnson, were "abused," but "proof beyond a reasonable doubt was absent." The closest they came to finding that the torture was systemic was to say that "Burge, the commander of the Violent Crimes Section of Detective Areas 2 and 3," was "guilty [of] abus[ing] persons with impunity," and that it therefore "necessarily follows that a number of those serving under his command recognized that if their commander could abuse persons with impunity, so could they."

The special prosecutors also found "that no meaningful police investigation was conducted, nor any police witness questioned either in the Wilson case, or in the Michael Johnson electric-shock case, which occurred a few months after Wilson, and had glaring similarities to the Wilson allegations." Again focusing on Andrew Wilson's case, they concluded that former ASA Hyman gave "false testimony" when "he denied that Andrew Wilson told him he had been tortured by detectives under the command of Jon Burge." They also criticized then prosecutor Bill Kunkle—a Republican, a political distinction worth noting—but only for changing his explanation for Andrew's injuries:

> In four separate hearings, Judge Kunkle took four separate positions—no explanation; no burns; self-inflicted burns; and last, self-inflicted burns or alternatively, burns caused by the wagon men. When we questioned Judge Kunkle, we sought some explanation of the seeming inconsistencies in the positions he had taken. He invoked the attorney-client privilege. Our hopes that Judge Kunkle . . . would shed some light on the question were dashed.

Daley, Devine, and former superintendent LeRoy Martin escaped any responsibility for the scandal, while the report attacked the credibility of the four men pardoned by former governor George Ryan—also a Republican. As former superintendent Brzeczek, another political outsider, had predicted, the special prosecutors, acting their part in the Democratic machine, placed the supervisory blame squarely and almost exclusively on Brzeczek's shoulders. Specifically, they found the following:

- that something should have been done about the disgrace and embarrassment at Area 2 twenty-four years ago by the Chicago Police Superintendent.
- that our judgment is that this investigation we have conducted would never have been necessary if Richard Brzeczek had done his sworn

non-delegable duty on reception of Dr. Raba's letter.

• that if action had been taken against Jon Burge at the time of the Andrew Wilson case, or even shortly thereafter, the appointment of the Special Prosecutors would not have been necessary.

• that this action should have included, at the very least, the Superintendent's removal of Burge from any investigative command and a complete shake-up at detective Area 2.

Egan and Boyle then addressed an overflow crowd of media at a press conference as disjointed as their report. Pressed by reporters, they made several statements that to some degree bolstered their findings. Boyle said that, of the 148 cases they investigated, they believed that "abuse" occurred in approximately half. The report did not specifically mention Byrne or Dignan, but Boyle offered that the allegations "seemed to center on a crew known as the Midnight Crew" and that "there are a number of officers who seem to predominate relative to the number of allegations that are made, allegations that we have said that we think happened. It centers basically around eight to twelve policemen out of a unit of forty-four." Boyle said that a copy of the report had been delivered to US Attorney Fitzgerald, but also noted, pointedly, that the Feds had on two prior occasions—one of which was in 1989 when we, and later OPS director Fogel, had approached them—declined to prosecute.

Conspicuously absent was any characterization of the "abuse" as torture, or that it was systemic—or, as OPS investigator Goldston had found fifteen years before, "systematic." Boyle conceded to the crowd of reporters that he was comfortable with using the word *torture*, but when he was asked if he thought the abuse was "systematic," he answered, "We think we can prove there were three cases beyond a reasonable doubt. There are a considerable number of other cases where we may think so but doubt we could prove it." When pressed by reporters to say anything critical of Daley's conduct, Boyle dismissed our now widely accepted contention that Daley knew about the torture, saying that Daley "relied on the judgment of others." He grudgingly conceded that there was a "bit of a slide" in Daley's office at the time of Andrew Wilson's case, that "more hands-on judgment" was called for than Daley provided, and that "we accept Mayor Daley's explanation, but would not have done it the way that he did."

We had convened at Northwestern Law School's Bluhm Legal Clinic to conduct our own press conference. Locke began: "It's deeply puzzling to us that Richard Brzeczek could be so strongly condemned for failing to take action when the state's attorney of Cook County, now the mayor of the City of Chicago, was equally aware of the torture." I followed: "Daley and Devine are ultimately culpable. What did they do to stop the torture? Nothing." Larry Kennon said, "Four years and seven million dollars and there's not enough evidence to prosecute anybody? That's what I am calling a cover-up because of political clout."

David Bates lowered his head into his hands, and, his voice cracking with emotion, said,

> We understood what Egan was going to do—he was going to continue to keep stuff covered up. We didn't look for a remedy here. I am at a loss for words to look at this fucking report and to hear that torture existed but that there is no way we can deal with it.

Mary Johnson, Michael Johnson's mother, observed that there was no justice because "people just don't care." She said, "Guess what? My son is Black. Guess what? His mother is poor. We are the minority." While she had "no idea" whether Burge would ever go to prison, she made a prediction, one shared by many: "But I know if there's a hell, he's going."

That evening Brzeczek and I appeared on WTTW's *Chicago Tonight*, hosted by Carol Marin. Carol first let Brzeczek rebut the report's condemnation of his role, which he did with gusto. The report's purpose was to "cover up" and to "scapegoat" him, Brzeczek declared. She asked him if torture at Area 2 was an "open secret" in the department, and Brzeczek pleaded ignorance prior to receiving Dr. Raba's letter. When she asked if Burge was a "rogue cop," Brzeczek pointed out that he was a lieutenant and that his detectives did not want to speak out for fear of being ostracized, as Frank Laverty was, for speaking out about the street files cases. Brzeczek said, knowing what he knew now, "Yes, [I] could have done more," but maintained that by sending the letter to Daley, he "did everything he could do that was appropriate."

Carol then turned to me. I rebutted the special prosecutor's invocation of the statute of limitations, pointing to the numerous ongoing "serious crimes." After cutting Brzeczek a bit too much slack, I shifted the focus to Daley and Devine, and told her that, despite the special prosecutor's implication of closure, "No way we are done."

Carol then asked me about reparations. I emphasized, "There [have] to be reparations. Nothing is being done for the men with serious PTSD or other psychological problems." I then added, "There must be federal indictments. There must be new hearings for the men in prison." Referencing "community outrage" and the growing number of identified torture victims, I said it was time for the City to step up—"Twenty million to defend Burge but nary a cent for his victims."

The news of the report and its failure to condemn Daley's role dominated local newspaper headlines and TV news reports, and was also covered in places as far away as Scotland, China, and Qatar. Although the Special Prosecutor's Report never used the term *torture*, these headlines and reports did:

> *Chicago Tribune*: REPORT: COPS USED TORTURE, Mayor Is Untouched, but Ex-Police Chief Is Berated
> *Chicago Sun Times*: SUSPECTS TORTURED, COPS CAN'T BE CHARGED
> *Chicago Defender*: A DAMN SHAME Chicago Police Torture Report Substantiates Massive Abuse of Black Men, but No Charges Will Be Filed
> *Tribune Red Eye*: Bombshell Report: TORTURE COP UNTOUCHABLE, Guns to Suspects' Mouths, Electric Shocks, Burns and Beatings . . . Probe Ends Without Charges
> *Chicago Crusader*: BURGE GETS AWAY WITH TORTURE

The *New York Times* was characteristically more restrained in its national section headline: "Inquiry Finds Police Abuse, but Says Law Bars Trial." The article quoted Boyle as saying that he "wished" they could have indicted in the three cases that they had cited for criminal conduct beyond a reasonable doubt, and quoted me as saying, "Something as serious as police torture, there shouldn't be a statute of limitations . . . It's like murder." The *Times* underscored that Daley and Devine had escaped criticism, noting that the "political implications were clear," and continued:

> Prisoners who have alleged torture and their lawyers said they were profoundly disappointed with the report and that Mr. Daley and Mr. Devine should face federal indictment along with former Commander Jon Burge, whom they accuse of overseeing torture, and some officers under his command at what are known as Detective Areas 2 and 3. They cited at least 20 recent instances of court testimony by police officers, prosecutors and other officials that they said constituted continuing criminal behavior that would justify charges of obstruction of justice, perjury, racketeering and civil rights violations.

Larry Kennon captured our collective attitude: "Somebody needs to go to jail. Burge needs to go to jail. His henchmen need to go to jail. The mayor should be indicted for covering up."

Back home, the numerous articles focused on the report's language, Egan's and Boyle's press conference, the reactions of our clients and our team, and Daley's and Devine's escape from responsibility. The *Tribune's* editorial "Getting Away with Torture" was sweeping in its condemnation: "Prosecution would have been possible in some cases. And short of prosecution, if anyone in authority had spoken out, the torture techniques that went on for years in the hidden corners of Chicago police facilities could have been stopped. No one did. No one stopped it. Those who could have apparently didn't care enough to try. That is Chicago's shame."

The *Sun Times's* editorial board was frustrated but suggested some possible solutions: "Fortunately a tenacious federal prosecutor is just what we have in Patrick Fitzgerald. His office is reviewing the report and we trust he will do what he can." They also suggested a novel, if underwhelming, approach to Daley's, Devine's, and Kunkle's misconduct: disbarment as attorneys.

We had made Anthony Holmes available for an interview with the *Sun Times*, and it was powerful. In a piece entitled "It Felt Like a Thousand Needles All at One Time," *Sun Times* reporter Stephan Esposito wrote:

> Thirty-three years later the bare wires twisted into his leg iron, the little black box and the sickening grinding sound of a hand crank are all distinct in Anthony Holmes' mind. And in his nightmares, Holmes sees burly Jon Burge, with wavy slicked-back hair, grinning as the infamous Chicago police commander administers electric shocks. "It felt like a thousand needles all at one time," Holmes said.

Anthony showed "no surprise" when he learned that Burge would not be charged: "You think that they are going to charge Burge with something and let him pull everyone else down? That's why they ain't going to let it happen."

The *Southtown Economist* also ran the Esposito article, together with a guest column from veteran conservative radio talk show host Eddie Schwartz, "Recalling Jon Burge, Grade School Patrol Boy and Electrical Whiz." Growing up with "Johnny Burge" in the racially changing Jeffrey Manor community on Chicago's far southeast side, Schwartz became buddies with Burge in junior high school. According to Schwartz, "Jon commanded an impressive understanding of sound, electricity and things mechanical." When they "engineered" a class play, Burge "produced a collection of headphones, telephones, wiring and control boxes to provide an intercom system to coordinate the lighting and sound." Schwartz "vividly remembered" Burge "showing me a telephone control box that contained a little crank that generated voltage to ring a bell for a closed-circuit phone system. It was 1960 and Jon was already a 'junior lineman.'"

Our focus on Daley, Devine, and the whitewashing nature of the report was taken up by several columnists. John Kass, a libertarian version of Mike Royko, with no love for the Democratic machine, wrote a column describing "a tortuous path to not blaming Daley." He quoted Brzeczek: "When they appointed Democratic sycophants to investigate this, I said they'd blame me, and they did. I'm not a Daley guy. This whole thing is about covering Daley's ass." I followed, saying, "I'm not absolving Brzeczek, he was superintendent when Jon Burge was active. But he at least passed on the information about Burge to Daley, and Daley, as state's attorney, did nothing. . . . The man who should be blamed is Daley." Kass concluded, "So a white paper was required, to put a political lid on things . . . along with some whitewash."

Black leaders also aimed their wrath at Daley. Alderman Howard Brookins called Daley's failure to launch an investigation of Burge during the 1980s a "potential bombshell" that could "turn into a lightning rod" in the Black community during the upcoming mayoral primary. Daley's "inaction could galvanize large numbers of people in the African-American community against him— even more so than the corruption," referring to the recent federal conviction of Daley's former patronage chief and three others in what was known as the "Hired Truck Scandal." Reverend Jesse Jackson asserted, "If people knew then what we know now, Daley would never have been elected mayor in the first place."

Eric Zorn was both lamenting and sarcastic in his critique in the *Tribune*. "Dude, where are my adjectives? Where's my 'appalling'? My 'unconscionable'? My 'malignant'? My 'degrading and offensive'?" He pointed out that the special prosecutors did not use the word "torture" during their lengthy press conference until the question-and-answer period, when Channel 7 reporter Charles Thomas "goaded" Boyle into it. Zorn concluded, "Without the language of anger, regret and even shame to surround the voluminous facts, the stain remains."

State's Attorney Devine, praised in the report for some modest reforms he had recently implemented, offered a prosecutorial defense of sorts, saying that claims of systemic Area 2 torture had not "crystallized" at the time of the Brzeczek letter, and it was not "unexpected" that defendants in a high-profile murder case would later claim their confessions had been coerced. "We cannot undo the past," Devine was quoted as saying. "We can only commit ourselves to doing all in our power to prevent such abuses from happening in the future." Kunkle was unavailable for comment, as was Daley, this time in San Francisco. Longtime Democratic operative David Axelrod attempted to defend Daley, saying with a straight face, "If the mayor runs for reelection, he'll run on the record of a mayor who has done more than any other to reform police practices to try to prevent the kinds of abuses described here."

From a close reading of the report and listening to the special prosecutors' press conference, we learned that Egan and Boyle had taken some form of statements from Daley, Devine, former mayor Byrne, and Kunkle. We quickly drew up a subpoena for those statements, as well as for Brzeczek's testimony before the grand jury. While we were waiting for the documents, Daley returned to town and broke his silence—at an unrelated press conference. City Hall reporter Fran Spielman pressed the issue, and Daley responded with a rambling self-defense and apologia:

> Do you think I would sit by, let anyone say that police brutality takes place, I know about it, that I had knowledge of it and I would allow it? Then you don't know my public career. You don't know what I stand for. I'm proud of my public service as state senator, state's attorney and mayor of the city of Chicago. I would not allow anything like this. One incident is too many. Though the report does not allege any misconduct or cover-up within the state's attorney's office, I know that there are those who will seek to play politics and draw inferences that aren't there. My emphasis is and will continue to be on making sure we are doing everything possible to ensure that the horrendous abuses of two and three decades ago never happen again.

On the one hand, he blamed Brzeczek and the police department; on the other, he said that he would "take responsibility and apologize to anyone" for "this shameful episode in our history." He said that the pattern of torture documented by the special prosecutor "fundamentally undermines our system of justice and destroys public confidence," but also minimized the significance of Dr. Raba's letter, saying that it "suggested, but did not charge, abuse," and blamed his own failure to prosecute Burge on Andrew Wilson's non-cooperation.

The *Sun Times* played Daley's statements to the hilt, with a full front-page headline, "IT WILL NEVER HAPPEN AGAIN," next to a color photo of the mayor. The accompanying article, by Fran Spielman, quoted Daley at length, as did to a lesser extent the *New York Times*, which omitted Daley's apology offer but noted that I had subpoenaed Daley's statement to the special prosecutors. The *Times* quoted me as saying, "Daley is therefore ultimately responsible for Burge having tortured all of our clients. This case has to be investigated and prosecuted under federal statutes."

The *Tribune*, reporting on our subpoena, followed a day later with a front-page banner headline, "Daley in the Crosshairs," and also quoted US representative Luis Gutierrez, who blasted Daley for his roles in the torture and hired truck scandals:

> The essence of his message is, "You know me, trust me, I have a record, but the hiring incident isn't part of my record. Jon Burge isn't part of my record. The scandals of contracting, those aren't part of my record." Every time there's an issue, "That's not part of my record. Judge me on the totality of who I am," and that's what he says. This is the totality of who he is.

Forced once again to respond to the torture scandal, Daley mustered up some righteous indignation, "You better believe it. [I'm] very proud of when I was state's attorney of Cook County, very proud. I've got a good record there."

A few days later we received the subpoenaed statements given by Daley, Devine, Kunkle, Brzeczek, and Jane Byrne. Brzeczek had given lengthy sworn testimony on two occasions in 2005, whereas Daley, Devine, and Byrne had given short statements in early 2006, when the investigation was being wrapped up, that were neither transcribed nor recorded. Boyle had not put down in writing what Daley had told him until ten days after the brief interview. In Boyle's poorly worded, two-page memo, constructed from memory, he wrote, "Daley assumes that the letter directed to him by Superintendent Brzeczek, with the enclosed letter from Dr. Raba, was directed to his first assistant, Richard Devine. He also assumes that he was advised that the letter and its enclosure was reviewed by his first assistant, was probably discussed with Mr. Daley by Mr. Devine." Devine's similarly brief interview confirmed that the letter was discussed with Daley.

Apparently satisfied, the special prosecutors had announced that the report was complete and ready for release in late April, but the delay requested by former ASA Hyman and the cops had given us the opportunity to hammer away at Daley and Devine. This apparently motivated Egan and Boyle, in June, to cover their asses. First, they called Kunkle, then Daley and Devine, to give more detailed explanations—this time transcribed—about the Brzeczek letter. This time Daley was accompanied by his attorneys, corporation counsel Mara Georges and Dykema lawyer Terry Burns, and both the questions and answers were appalling.

We called a press conference to distribute copies of Daley's transcript and to discuss its contents. The *Trib's* headline, "Attorney Slams Daley Interview," accurately captured my outrage. I emphasized that Daley's statement had been taken after the report was initially finalized, raising "serious questions about the integrity of this investigation." I compared Egan's and Boyle's questioning to Chicago-style sandlot ball: "They weren't just softball questions, they were 16-inch softball questions." According to the *Trib*, I "highlighted how Daley, in the interview, acknowledged that he must have received a critical 1982 letter from a Cook County Jail doctor about the alleged torture of Andrew Wilson, and shows that City Corporation Counsel Mara Georges interrupted the Mayor's answer, telling him, 'Just if you remember.' 'I don't remember today,' Daley then said."

Reporting that "Daley said he couldn't recall in answer to more than 20 questions during the interview," the *Tribune* printed a number of noteworthy passages:

> The transcript shows sometimes long and rambling questions or comments by Egan and his deputy, Robert Boyle, followed by usually brief responses from Daley. Noting that Wilson was in such bad shape—apparently after being beaten by police—that officers at the lockup would not let him in, Boyle posed his question this way: "I assume that nobody ever brought that to your attention?" "No," Daley answered.

Noting that "Boyle sounds almost apologetic in raising the question of whether the police killings that led to Wilson's arrest put pressure on law enforcement authorities," the article continued:

> "And this may be an unfair question," Boyle began. "But in the normal course of events, I assume that the [William] Fahey and [Richard] O'Brien killing was a somewhat heightened case. And it's difficult, we've all been in law enforcement, and it's difficult to characterize a terrible event like that, so I don't know how to characterize it." Boyle's question continues for four more lines in the transcript. Daley's answer was brief: "Yes. It was known as a heater case."

The article pointed out, "The tone of the Daley interview was markedly different from excerpts of the special prosecutor's aggressive questioning of Brzeczek contained in the 290-page report released last week," and described my reaction: "Taylor told reporters he was shocked at the questions that were not asked. 'There were no follow-up questions, there were no questions about what [Daley] knew.'"

Egan fired back, claiming that the investigation was not complete in June, when Daley and Devine were reinterviewed: "This has been an ongoing investigation, and we were not completely finished. As a matter of fact, we are still doing work." He asserted that they went after Brzeczek because "we had evidence that Brzeczek had done something wrong. By his own admission, he had sat silently by for over 20 years that he knew these police officers had brutalized Andrew Wilson. And a man was sentenced to death, and he remained mute." Above all, Egan saved his personal venom for me: "Flint Taylor's interest is money. He is a legal huckster, and I have no respect for him."

That same day, three south side alderpersons—Dorothy Tillman, Howard Brookins, and Arenda Troutman—announced that they were introducing a resolution into city council to end the city's financing of Burge's defense and to discontinue his police pension. "We intend to tell Mr. Burge, 'You can no longer sit in Florida and enjoy your life on the taxpayers' money," said Tillman. "The motto of the Chicago Police Department is to serve and protect. I'm sure Chicago doesn't want to be the city that says, 'To Serve and Torture.'" Stating that her outrage reflected that of the Black community she and her fellow alderpersons represented, she continued:

> What he did to our men was no less than what was done in Nazi Germany. The statute of limitations did not run out in Nazi Germany. People are still chasing the people . . . But, when it comes to the black people in this country, there's always a statute of limitations. There was a statute of limitations on Emmett Till. There's a statute of limitations for reparations. And now you're saying there's a statute of limitations in terms of Commander Burge.

Journalist Salim Muwakkil, writing for *In These Times*, expanded on the theme of racism in an analytical piece that week. Writing that "racial bias is systematic in policing institutions because they were structurally designed to contain rather than serve the black community," Muwakkil linked the assassination of Fred Hampton to the police torture scandal, pointing to the recent defeat in city council of a resolution to name a street in Fred's honor:

> When the Fraternal Order of Police (FOP) mobilized opposition to a bill naming one Chicago block in honor of the late Fred Hampton, the legislation

died, despite vigorous support from African-American activists and politicians. Hampton, a Black Panther killed by police in an infamous 1969 raid, was popular among many in the black community because he aggressively challenged police brutality. Hampton's brazen assassination confirmed his complaint and transformed him into an international martyr. But the FOP said Hampton advocated cop killing and the bill for an honorific street died without any support from the city's white aldermen.

Muwakkil contended that the special prosecutors' report was "not completely worthless" because "it provides additional evidence of the criminal justice system's racial biases. All of the torture targets were black men. These biases are deeply rooted; the nation's first police departments in the South evolved from the organized slave patrols. The police had a dual duty: law-and-order and maintenance of the racial hierarchy." His analysis continued:

> For most of U.S. history, African-Americans were denied access to the nation's cultural and economic capital. Police forces were the "thin blue line" that enforced those barriers. This job of racial containment has been white America's mandate to the police and, for the most part, they have faithfully performed their duty. . . . African Americans remain victims of a disparate proportion of police abuse because so many wind up in the criminal justice system. This high ratio of black inmates is largely a function of poverty and their participation in the underground economy.

Hence, he concluded, we must do more than "tinker around the edges" of this systemic racism: "Without a serious program designed to help repair this damage, debilitating symptoms soon will overwhelm us and police torturers may seem like the least of our problems."

The next Monday, Egan and Boyle appeared before the Litigation Subcommittee of the Cook County Board of Commissioners—the body that had approved their fees each month for the past four and a half years. Several county commissioners expressed their frustration at the failure to bring charges, and commissioner Mike Quigley grilled them on giving Daley a pass. In response, Boyle went farther than they had in the report in evaluating Daley's conduct: "We think something more should have been done. Clearly you respond. You don't fail to respond . . . that was a complete mistake."

Two days later we held a press conference to release Boyle's memo that recorded his interview of former mayor Jane Byrne and the transcript of

Devine's June interview. Byrne's interview revealed that she visited with Jon Burge on three occasions during the Wilson manhunt; that, citing "problems in the community," she endorsed the door-to-door search in Black neighborhoods; and that she had a celebratory dinner with Brzeczek after the Wilson brothers were apprehended. The Associated Press quoted me:

> Taylor said he was stunned that Byrne would take a direct role in the manhunt, which he said could have influenced the case and should have been pursued further by the special prosecutors. "That statement in itself was a shocker," Taylor said. "There was no effort to put her under oath" and investigate her role further. Taylor said the special prosecutors had demonstrated a lack of follow-up throughout their investigation and said federal prosecutors should now investigate what he sees as a cover-up that is still under way.

The *Tribune* published Devine's admission that he, Daley, and Kunkle saw the Brzeczek letter:

> "I don't have a specific date that I became aware, but my general recollection is that relatively soon after it was received, either the state's attorney [Daley] or the chief deputy showed me the letter, and I had an opportunity to look at it," Devine told the special prosecutors on June 15.

As the *Tribune* recounted, Devine "told the special prosecutors the allegations were not shocking in light of the charges against Wilson"; that he, Daley, and Kunkle suspected that Brzeczek had political motives; and that Devine also said to Egan and Boyle:

> I mean, there was not a context at that time of, "Gee, there had been 50 charges or 50 claims against this particular officer, so there better be a heads-up." I didn't know Jon Burge from a load of hay at the time, and I'm sure the state's attorney didn't either.

I minced no words in the *Tribune* piece: "We think that this was evidence of a crime of obstruction of justice by the now-mayor and the now-state's attorney. There would not have been 100 more victims of torture if they had acted then."

Three days later, another bombshell hit. *Sun Times* reporters had delved into Special Prosecutor Egan's family tree and discovered what Abby Mann had told us off the record—that Egan's nephew was one of the Area 2 detectives who had arrested Gregory Banks in 1982. They had also found out much more: Edward Egan's father, grandfather, three uncles, two brothers, and two nephews were Chicago police lieutenants, captains, sergeants, and detectives, and Egan's uncle was killed in the line of duty, guarding the home of former Chicago police superintendent Charles Fitzmorris in 1921.

In a feature article titled "Torture Report and Family Ties: Top Investigator had Nephew on Burge's staff," the *Sun Times* reported Egan's claim that he had told Judge Biebel and Locke Bowman about his nephew years before, but neither remembered it. Locke said, "Looking back at what a sharply disappointingly bad job was done . . . I can't imagine I was told." Madison Hobley's lawyer Kurt Feuer also sounded off: "We have been saying, 'We have a biased, cover-your-ass report.' The question was: Why?" The *Sun Times* captured my amazed responses to the scope of Egan's police ties:

> Attorney Flint Taylor interrupted a reading of Egan's relatives on the force with "Get out!" and "Cut it out!"

Local television stations picked up the story. Mary Powers told Channel 7, "People aren't surprised because it's kind of the Chicago way, you know. Cover-up is the name of the game here" and Larry Kennon said, "The African American community is very, very, very, very upset." Mike Parker of Channel 2 first showed video of me, claiming that "the chickens have come home to roost on the investigation" and that Egan's conflict of interest should have led to his refusing the special prosecutor assignment. He then cut to Egan, leveling an absurd and slanderous attack on me: "Mr. Taylor gets 75 percent of his income from suing policemen and municipalities. I've described him as a legal huckster." Egan added, "The most dangerous position to be in in the justice system is between Flint Taylor and a television camera."

The *Sun Times* continued the discussion of Egan's family ties the next day, reporting that "legal experts call the revelations 'distressing' and a conflict of interest." The article quoted me as it continued:

> It was an "open secret" in the '80s that Burge's "midnight crew" of detectives used torture devices such as the bags they allegedly put over [Gregory] Banks' head, along with punches and kicks to extract confessions from suspects, Taylor said. Another detective, Doris Byrd, who worked the evening shift with Egan's nephew, testified she heard screams coming from the interrogation rooms.

"What does that say about Edward Egan's nephew?" I asked. "Wouldn't he have known? . . . [William] Egan apparently was not brought before the grand jury. Would Egan's nephew, like 40 other Area 2 detectives, have taken the Fifth Amendment?"

A week later, with Abby Mann's blessing, I released to the *Sun Times* the tape of his 2002 conversation with Judge Egan. Not only did Egan quote, on the tape, a retired judge saying that Burge was "personable" and "hardworking," but he also quoted his Area 2 nephew as telling him "what a great, hard worker—that's what I've heard from everybody—what a hard worker Burge was." I said that Egan was using his nephew "as a character witness for Burge. Six months into it, he has already formed an opinion, through his nephew and a retired judge, that was pro-Burge, that was sympathetic to Burge." Abby Mann told the *Sun Times*, "Egan was talking in such complimentary terms about Burge and we had heard so many frightening things about him. [Egan] was quite gracious, quite eloquent. But what he said about Burge was quite disturbing."

CHAPTER 26

The Art of the No Deal

W e were pursuing a police practices expert witness who could put the massive conspiracy and cover-up in perspective. Our first choice was Tony Bouza, who was retired from a distinguished—and maverick—career that included stints as the commander of detectives in the Bronx and as police chief of Minneapolis. Recently he had published *Police Unbound: Corruption, Abuse and Heroism by the Boys in Blue*, his third book.

In the summer of 2006, John Stainthorp and I visited Tony at his vacation home on Cape Cod. Tony was a gregarious, larger-than-life figure, who readily agreed to serve as our expert. His opinions strongly supported our case against the City. He concluded that there was a racially motivated pattern and practice of torture under Burge's supervision; a systemic code of silence; that Daley, Brzeczek, Devine, Martin, Hillard, and others had knowledge of the systemic and racist torture; and that they condoned, encouraged, and were complicit in it. It was a powerful assessment, coming from a former high-ranking police official.

Later that summer, reporter John Conroy sent me a disturbing note: "I recently received an anonymous letter, addressed to me, in peculiar handwritten block letters, at the *Reader*. It was dated 7/24/06, postmarked 7/27/06 in Chicago, and it carried this typed, single paragraph with no signature or closing." It read:

> You and Mr. Taylor have cost the taxpayers of Cook County over seven million dollars and have also caused the death of a fine individual in George Karl. I hope that the two of you find satisfaction in carrying your personal vendetta against Jon Burge to the extreme position you have. I do not.

The letter to Conroy, sent only days after the release of the special prosecutors' report referenced the suicide of Area 2 detective George Karl, one of the officers who had transported Andrew Wilson to Area 2. Until now we had not known that, the previous December, an intoxicated Karl had put the barrel of a loaded shotgun into his mouth and pulled the trigger. John and I were left to wonder if Karl might have been Deep Badge, or perhaps one of the other pseudonymous individuals—"Dan," or Phil Walters's skittish source.

We continued taking depositions of survivors and torturers alike; renewed settlement discussions in the Leroy Orange, Madison Hobley, and Stanley Howard cases; drafted a community-supported shadow report to expose the special prosecutors' report as a whitewash and serve as a tool in seeking federal charges; persisted in pursuing freedom for Darrell Cannon; and kept up the chase for the ever-elusive Richard M. Daley.

The on-again, off-again settlement negotiations and mediation with the City had been transferred to the veteran federal court judge Marvin Aspen, who had been hearing the Hobley case. We enlisted Sam Tenenbaum, a clinical professor at Northwestern's Bluhm Legal Clinic, to be the point man for the negotiations because of his long-standing relationship with Judge Aspen. During several sessions in the judge's chambers over the summer and fall of 2006, Judge Aspen made sure that Corporation Counsel Mara Georges was in the negotiations loop. The magic number for the joint settlement seemed to be around $15 million, but it was left to the lawyers to work out the final split among the three plaintiffs. This was no small task, and Joey and I battled long and hard with the Loevy firm for Leroy to receive his fair share.

Finally, in late October, we reached an agreement among the lawyers, and Sam informed Judge Aspen that we would accept $14.8 million, a number the judge had told Sam he thought the City would accept. Aspen called back and told Sam that the City would agree to the $14.8 million, but had some additional nonmonetary conditions they were requiring as part of the deal.

When we gathered in Judge Aspen's chambers a few days later, we learned that the stipulations were all about Daley:

- We would not file amended complaints naming Mayor Daley as a defendant, as I had publicly threatened to do, in a civil rights, obstruction of justice, and racketeering conspiracy (RICO) claim in our lawsuits and we would not seek a finding of liability and damages against Daley for his alleged conspiratorial actions while serving as the Cook County State's Attorney;

- We would not pursue the deposition of Richard M. Daley in our remaining claims against Richard Devine and other Cook County officials despite

Mayor Daley's role as State's Attorney during the critical time when most of the torture under Burge's command occurred;

- We would not criticize Mayor Daley in any public statements we made in connection with the settlement;

- The agreement to settle and its terms would be held confidential at the City's request, including from other counsel in the cases—including the attorneys for the individual City defendants—for a limited period of time.

These additional terms would preclude us from pursuing Daley in our remaining claims against Cook County State's Attorney Devine. They also posed a dilemma that had arisen in the past and would recur throughout the next decade of litigation—that of the financial and liberty interests of our clients versus the greater social and political issues at stake. Of course, when these interests come into conflict, lawyers must always serve their clients' interests, and we would do so here. It was of some consolation that we had filed a similar lawsuit on behalf of Darrell Cannon after the state dismissed his murder case, and we had made sure we could pursue Daley in that case.

Judge Aspen was elated when we told him that we agreed to the City's terms. Now it was only a matter of drawing up the paperwork, or so we thought, and Judge Aspen passed on the news about the secret deal to Judge Holderman, who was hearing Leroy Orange's case. It was quite an accomplishment, and Judge Aspen was rightly pleased and no doubt proud of his success in navigating the numerous minefields. For his part, Judge Holderman also welcomed the news that a hotly contested, politically sensitive case against the City would be removed from his docket.

Darrell remained at Tamms supermax prison. At his urging we had filed suit against the Prisoner Review Board back in 2005, and later that year the attorney general's office had moved to dismiss this case. The attorney general then made a settlement offer: Darrell would be released on parole in two years, subject to five years on parole after that. He had agonized over the offer—his mother, whose dying wish was to see Darrell a free man, had died two years prior—but he ultimately agreed, in late 2005. The entire series of events must have seemed a cruel déjà vu, as the attorney general then reneged on the deal, claiming that the deal did not have the PRB's approval. We had returned to court to enforce the settlement, recounting in our motion the litany of offenses perpetrated against Darrell and concluding:

Sadly, psychic torture is now being applied as a supplement to the physical abuse that initiated Mr. Cannon's nightmare. The PRB should not be allowed to toy with Mr. Cannon's life by retracting their offered settlement after Mr. Cannon had already accepted it. This Court should not permit such a perpetuation of injustice.

The case had been transferred to judge James Henry, who seemed receptive to our cries of injustice. He held a hearing, at which I testified about the history of Darrell's case. Although he decided that the settlement was not legally binding because the PRB had not approved it, he also ruled that the PRB's September 2004 decision denying Darrell parole had violated his rights because it was based on evidence that was the product of torture and not subjected to cross-examination. He therefore reversed that decision and ordered that the PRB promptly hold a new hearing, limited to evidence not so tainted. We were confident that the PRB could produce no such evidence, and were grateful to Judge Henry, but there would be no rejoicing until Darrell actually walked out of prison.

The next week, we lost two dear comrades—David Saxner and Frank Laverty. David, only fifty-eight, died suddenly of a heart attack while out for a walk on Thanksgiving Day. After his release from prison thirty years before, he had worked closely with Michael, Jeff, Jan, and others at the office, fighting for prisoners' rights and, in particular, for the release of long-term prisoners repeatedly denied parole. Aviva Futorian, president of the Long Term Prisoner Policy Project, estimated that David had directly or indirectly gained release for as many as one hundred prisoners.

Frank Laverty died a few days later, following a long battle with lung cancer. After he had testified for us in the George Jones case and other street files cases during the 1980s, Frank became our consultant and expert witness on all things Area 2. Most recently, he had given us a lengthy opinion in some wrongful conviction cases, demonstrating how Dignan and his Area 2 cohorts must have kept a secret street file, now missing, in which were buried reports that would have exonerated our clients. The City had insisted on deposing Frank, who was so weak from the cancer that he could only testify for an hour at a time.

Frank's obituary in the *Tribune* quoted Jeff Haas and Peter Schmiedel, who lauded Frank's courage in coming forward to save George Jones's life. I had the honor of eulogizing Frank at his memorial service and invoked the legendary cop who broke the NYPD's code of silence: "He was Frank

Serpico without the glamor. He was a great detective, but instead of being honored by the department, he was castigated because he had the courage to expose police wrongdoing."

The *Reader*'s cover featured a photo of Frank with the simple headline "The Good Cop." John Conroy led off his story by quoting from Deep Badge's first letter: "As I have said previously I do not want to be involved in this affair. . . . I do not wish to be shunned like Officer Laverty has been." Conroy had located George Jones, who was living in a Chicago suburb, working in public relations. He had lived in different places over the years and said that he avoided the city because he feared policemen with long memories. George said that Frank Laverty had been in his thoughts ever since his criminal trial. "That took more guts than anything—to come forward and say, 'Hey this isn't right,' to go against the entire department, and to go through the hell that he went through afterward. . . . I know his life was never the same again. How do you say 'Thank you' enough?"

Conroy ended his *Reader* piece with a quote from Frank:

> I don't bear them any animosity because I'm way ahead of that game, I would never trust them, or not look over my shoulder, but I don't have any grudges against them. And what would have happened if I'd kept going down the road that they traveled? I'd be up there taking the Fifth Amendment because I'd looked the other way one too many times.
>
> In retrospect, I'd rather be me than any of them.

As of December the settlement papers for the three death penalty damages cases had not been finalized. The City was stalling, and we brought it to Judge Aspen's attention. He received assurances from the City that indicated the settlement papers would be coming shortly. A week later, Judge Aspen stayed all depositions and discovery in the three cases and told the City that he expected the final papers to be presented to him right after New Year's Day. City attorney Terry Burns raised no objection, but the next week he presented Judge Aspen with a New Year's surprise: a new "issue," on which he sought the judge's guidance. He would not tell Judge Aspen what the "issue" was, but said its only effect would be on the timing of the presentation of the settlement to city council and payment of the money.

We surmised that Daley wanted to delay the settlement until after the February mayoral primary. But the City was not only playing us; they were also misleading Judge Aspen and failed to produce the settlement papers during January. Finally, on February 1, 2007, Judge Aspen, himself a former assistant corporation counsel, summoned Terry Burns and corporation counsel Mara Georges to his chambers for a private meeting, after which he ordered all of us to appear in open court two weeks later to discuss what the hell was going on. When we appeared before him, the normally calm and collected senior judge was clearly disgusted by the City's conduct. He recited the history of the settlement negotiations, absolved Burns from acting in bad faith, but condemned the City's conduct as "unprecedented" in his three decades of judicial experience. He stated that the City was now reasserting the "issue" to further delay signing the written settlement agreement.

Outraged, we confronted Burns and demanded that he identify the mysterious "issue." He refused, and also refused to give us a date by which the City would sign the settlement agreement or to tell us whether the City intended to honor their agreement to settle. Judge Aspen terminated the hearing and dissolved the stay of discovery in Madison Hobley's case. We then moved to implement a two-part strategy to force the City to comply.

Back at our office we put the final touches on a motion to amend our complaint to add Daley and Jane Byrne in Darrell Cannon's case. We based the motion, which needed the court's approval, on newly obtained evidence, including the findings in the special prosecutors' report; Daley's admissions in response to the report; and Daley's, Devine's, Jane Byrne's, and Kunkle's statements to the special prosecutors. The proposed amendment sought to join Daley and his conduct, both as state's attorney and as mayor, to the continuing conspiracy to torture and cover up. Former mayor Byrne was added for her role in encouraging the lawless Wilson manhunt, and the claims against Devine were expanded to include his primary role with Daley in the refusal to prosecute Burge after receiving the letter from former superintendent Brzeczek.

We not only alleged a civil rights conspiracy but also sought to hold Daley and company civilly liable for violations of the Racketeering Influenced and Corrupt Organizations (RICO) Act, a sweeping law that was usually employed by federal prosecutors to pursue the Mob and Black and Latinx street gangs. The seventy-three-page complaint presented a litany of conspiracy and obstruction of justice that spanned from 1973 to the present. It itemized more than 350 acts in furtherance of this racially motivated conspiracy, including hundreds of separate occasions when the dozens of co-conspirators—from Daley and Devine to Burge, Dignan, and John Byrne—allegedly committed perjury when they denied knowledge or participation in the pattern and practice of torture.

The proposed complaint alleged, in part:

From 1973 to the present, these Defendants and their co-conspirators conspired to conduct and/or to participate directly in the conduct of the affairs of
the City of Chicago, its Police Department, and/or the Cook County State's
Attorney's Office through a pattern of racketeering activity which includes
the systemic torture and abuse of more than 100 African-American suspects,
including Plaintiff, in order to obtain and use their confessions and other
inculpatory evidence against them in wrongful prosecutions without regard
to their guilt or innocence; the wholesale obstruction of State and Federal
Courts by use of this tortured and coerced evidence, as well as wholesale
perjury, in order to obtain, continue, and maintain the charging, conviction
and imprisonment of the tortured and abused suspects, including Plaintiff,
without regard to their guilt or innocence; the wholesale obstruction of State
and Federal Courts and investigations by suppressing and destroying exculpatory evidence of torture, abuse and cover-up from the Plaintiff and numerous
other criminal defendants who were victims of torture and abuse; and the
wholesale obstruction of State and Federal courts and Federal and State prosecutors to cover up the torture, perjury, and fraudulently obtained convictions
and imprisonment of Plaintiff and numerous other victims, and to prevent
the victims of this torture and wrongful prosecution from discovering and
developing exculpatory evidence of a pattern and practice of torture.

The media took note, focusing, as we had hoped, on His Honor.
The *Sun Times* headlined "Burge Foes Target Daley," and the *Tribune*'s
read "Inmate Wants Daley on Cop Torture Suit." Jane Byrne declined to
comment but Daley was dismissive: "Mayors get sued every day. Myself,
Harold Washington, Gene Sawyer, Jane Byrne—all of us historically have
all been sued." (Maybe so, but not for being an accessory to torture and
obstruction of justice.)

The second part of our strategy was to make public, in detail, the
heretofore secret settlement negotiations. We felt that Judge Aspen's public
airing out of the City's legal team gave us cover, and, in a motion that
we filed a few days later, we blasted the City for its "egregious bad faith."
The media covered the motion, which called for enforcement of the settlement and for sanctions against the City, quoting extensively from our
recitation of the negotiations and repeating our accusation of bad faith. It
was less than a week before the election, and Daley spoke up on the City's
behalf, telling the *Tribune* that he was never presented with an agreement.
He added, "A lot of people want to settle things. Lawyers want to settle

because of fees. . . . Everybody wants to settle, and there are always proposed settlements."

I responded in disbelief, saying that Daley's lawyers—Mara Georges and Terry Burns—would not be able to deny that the agreement had been reached if they were to testify at the hearing we had requested as part of our motion. "I defy them to say that under oath. If they say that under oath, then perjury is the only recourse." Madison Hobley told reporters that he was disappointed, as he planned on using some of the money to move his mother, who was battling emphysema, to a warmer climate. "Sadly it doesn't seem like I can get on with the rest of my free life," he said.

The *Sun Times* castigated Daley and the City in an editorial—playing on the title of Donald Trump's book—called "The Art of the No Deal":

> Was someone in City Hall trying to drag things out so the bad publicity from the case wouldn't bite the mayor until after next week's mayoral election? According to a memo filed by lawyers for the plaintiffs, the settlement was contingent on Daley not being named as a defendant in the case, deposed or publicly criticized. Plaintiffs' attorney Flint Taylor told Channel 7 he would have been willing to wait until after the election to finalize the agreement.
>
> When as esteemed a judge as Aspen issues the kind of rebuke he did, many Chicagoans will think there's good reason to believe something is amiss in the handling of this matter. With accusations by other plaintiffs pending against Burge, whose methods allegedly included electric shock and suffocation, it is imperative to clear up all legal questions and let justice have its day.

It was hard to believe that Daley's denial was for political reasons, on the eve of the election. His most serious challenger had withdrawn in November, and whatever slim hope remained for an upset was dashed when Barack Obama, the junior senator from Illinois, gave Daley a full-throated endorsement. Obama said that he had made his decision to endorse Daley months before, despite his concerns about the ongoing federal investigation that had uncovered contract fraud and illegal hiring practices. Without once mentioning police torture, Obama said, "I think you want to look at the whole record of this administration of the last several years, and I think the city overall has moved in a positive direction." There was some speculation of a quid pro quo, with Richie and his brother Bill Daley supporting Obama's presidential candidacy—announced just two weeks later, in Springfield—in exchange for his endorsement. Long-shot mayoral candidate William "Doc" Walls asserted that Obama "did the citizens of

Chicago a great disservice because he basically condoned everything Daley has done."

Judge Aspen gave the City a month to answer our motion, but magistrate Geraldine Soat Brown was not about to wait. Whether she got a signal from Judge Aspen or was acting on her own, she chose the next day to issue her decision on the long-delayed motion to depose Daley. In a written decision, she ordered that he would have to submit to a deposition. Pointing to the Brzeczek letter, she said that the facts "support a conclusion that Mr. Daley may have information about the activities of Burge and other police officers, about who in the city and police administration knew about those activities, and about whether any action was taken on the basis of such knowledge."

We were elated. Madison Hobley's lawyer Kurt Feuer told the media, "We always felt we had the right to depose the guy, and it kept getting put off and put off and put off. So I guess, at this stage of the game, the judges are finally getting as fed up as we are with the City's antics." He extemporized a question for the mayor: "Why, when faced with documented injuries that clearly indicated torture above and beyond a beating—this guy had alligator clips burned into his earlobes—did Daley apparently kick the issue down the line to a very junior associate and never follow up on it?"

The next day—the Friday before the Tuesday election—City Hall reporter Fran Spielman was once again up in Daley's grill, asking him about the deposition at an appearance at police headquarters. With characteristic doublespeak, Daley said, "If they require me to be deposed, I have no problems with that. That's all I have to say." Then he continued, referencing his statement to the special prosecutors: "I answered all those questions. Why are you trying to [get] me to answer the question differently from last time? I answered the question. You know what the answer was."

Carol Marin devoted her Sunday *Sun Times* column to the twin issues that had been thrust into the spotlight during the week. Relying on a document we gave her, she laid out the City's blatant hypocrisy:

> Let's be clear.
>> Were Black suspects tortured at the hands of former Chicago police commander Jon Burge and his all-white band of detectives?
>> Yes.
>> How do we know?
>> The city said so.
>> The very same Law Department that has spent at least $10 million of

our tax money defending these cops, and is still defending them to this very day, is the same Law Department that confirmed the torture.

Back in 1992 as it was preparing to suddenly fire Burge right after spending a million bucks defending him, the city's lawyer detailed seven cases of suspects being tortured, "spitting blood," "pants pulled down . . . electroshocks," and threats to a prisoner to "blow his Black head off."

The city's attorney back then called it an "astounding pattern" of conduct by Burge and his boys.

The only thing that remains astounding today is that the city is still fighting what it long ago admitted was true. And should have settled. And apologized for.

CHAPTER 27

Hearings, Hearings, and More Hearings

As predicted, Daley won easily, with 71 percent of the vote. Nevertheless, the legal, political, and grassroots pressure on him continued unabated. Daley had entered the City into a high-stakes attempt to bring the 2016 Olympic Games to Chicago and had organized a high-powered group of financers to back the effort. Opposition to the plan included an organization called Black People Against Police Torture (BPAPT), started by Stan Willis, Larry Kennon, and Pat Hill in the wake of the special prosecutors' report. BPAPT was focused on obtaining justice, including reparations, for the torture survivors—and on stopping the Olympics from coming to Chicago, which it viewed as an egregious misuse of public funds in the face of police torture.

BPAPT held community-based town halls and delivered a large packet of torture-related documents to the US Olympic Committee's national headquarters in Colorado Springs. In February 2007, BPAPT brought Olympic hero John Carlos—who, together with fellow sprinter Tommie Smith, had raised his gloved fist in a Black Power salute from the the the victory stand at the 1968 Olympics—to speak against Chicago's Olympic effort. Stan, Pat Hill, and I appeared with John at a press conference where he spoke out against bringing the Games to Chicago:

> I want the mayor to get off his fanny and address this issue. He was the state's attorney when this torture was taking place. The mayor needs to step up to the plate and get this thing resolved. It's not even just about the Olympics coming to Chicago. It's for Chicago too. These individuals who tortured shed a bad light on many good police officers that they have in the city.

Pat Hill, herself a former track star who had nearly qualified for the 1968 Games, put the Olympics in context with torture:

The Olympics is an honor. It represents peace, humanity, and good sportsmanship. You dishonor the spirit of the Olympics by bringing it to the torture capital of the Western world. You should not honor this city with the Olympics until this city comes to terms with this part of the past.

The next month, the Olympic Committee came to Chicago, as guests of the mayor, for an early-morning visit to Washington Park on Chicago's south side, the proposed site of the Games. Met by a late snowfall and a group of hardy BPAPT members demanding to speak with the committee, Daley and his guests never even got off the bus.

At the end of March, the police department released two videos of its cops beating down defenseless Chicago citizens. In the first, a diminutive white bartender named Karolina Obrycka, working at the Shortstop Inn, was beaten by a drunken off-duty cop twice her size, named Anthony Abbate. The second video showed another drunken off-duty cop whaling on several downtown businessmen at the Jefferson Tap, breaking four ribs of one and sending another into surgery to reconstruct his face. On-duty cops and their supervisors, in a textbook display of the code of silence, had attempted to cover up these crimes. Once released, the videos were viewed around the world. Police superintendent Phil Cline—who, back in 1986 when he was a lieutenant, had succeeded Burge as the commander of Area 2's Violent Crimes Unit—said he was "sickened and embarrassed" by the Abbate tape, and that Abbate had "tarnished our image worse than anybody else in the history of the department."

Two *Sun Times* reporters begged to differ. Monroe Anderson—a veteran African American reporter, whose thirty-five years of experience included having been beaten while covering the "police riot" during the 1968 Democratic Convention—wrote, in response to Superintendent Cline:

> Well, I wouldn't say that. With the possible exception of the '68 police riot, that dishonor belongs to Jon Graham Burge. Behind closed doors and with no cameras rolling, Cmdr. Burge and his boys tortured more than 100 black men over two decades. Like all

officers on the scene, then-State's Attorney Richard M. Daley and his deputy, Dick Devine, failed to hear and chose not to see the savagery at play. That impairment in the justice system set the stage, creating the atmosphere that encouraged the police performances at the Shortstop Inn and Jefferson Tap.

Carol Marin connected Burge with several other brutal cops recently in the news, while emphasizing the same overriding theme:

> Daley, who was the Cook County state's attorney for many of the years when Burge and his gang were brutalizing suspects, has yet to have a candid conversation with the public or the courts about how it could have happened under his and other public officials' watch. Not a single solitary police officer, prosecutor or judge has ever come forward to testify about what Burge did to make his cases. Make no mistake, a number of them knew.

Daley, as ever, was unavailable, this time somewhere in Europe, but upon the mayor's return a few days later, Superintendent Cline tendered his resignation.

We had not abandoned our campaign to expose the special prosecutors' report as a whitewash, and this latest public police crisis gave us more impetus to complete a shadow report we had been drafting. (I had churned out a twenty-thousand-word screed in the fall of 2006 and turned it over to Rob Warden and Locke to edit.) Rob, Joey, Locke, and I, with the help of Mary Powers and several other lawyers and activists, amassed a list of 212 organizations and individuals as signatories to our "Report on the Failure of Special Prosecutors Edward J. Egan and Robert D. Boyle to Fairly Investigate Systemic Police Torture in Chicago." We released our report at a press conference on April 24, 2007. The fifty-page, fact-intensive document began with the words of Anthony Holmes:

> [Burge] put some handcuffs on my ankles, then he took one wire and put it on my ankles, he took the other wire and put it behind my back, on the handcuffs behind my back. Then after that, when he—then he went and got a plastic bag, put it over my head, and he told me, don't bite through it. I thought, man, you ain't fixing to put this on my head, so I bit through it. So he went and got another bag and put it on my head and he twisted it. When he twisted it, it cut my air off and I started shaking, but I'm still breathing because I'm still trying to suck it in where I could bite this one, but I couldn't because the other bag was there and kept me from biting through it. So then he hit me with the voltage. When he hit me with the voltage, that's when I started gritting, crying, hollering. . . . It feel like a thousand needles going through my body. And then after that, it just feel like, you know—it feel like something just burning me from the inside, and, um, I shook, I gritted, I hollered, then I passed out.

In our summary of findings, we wrote that the special prosecutors:

- Did not bring criminal charges against members of the Chicago Police Department despite the apparent existence of numerous provable offenses within the statute of limitations.

- Ignored the failure of former Cook County State's Attorney Richard M. Daley, state's attorney Richard A. Devine, and various other high-ranking officials to investigate and prosecute police officers who engaged in a documented pattern of torture and wrongful prosecution of torture victims.

- Did not document the systemic and racist nature of the torture and did not brand it as such in accordance with the international definition of torture.

- Unfairly evaluated the credibility of the alleged torturers and of their victims and unfairly attempted to discredit torture victims who had pending civil or criminal cases.

- Conducted an investigation that was hopelessly flawed and calculated to obfuscate the truth about the torture scandal.

- Ignored a wealth of evidence establishing that there was a widespread and continuing cover-up of the torture scandal—a conspiracy of silence—implicating high officials of the City of Chicago, the Chicago Police Department, and the Cook County State's Attorney's Office.

- Failed to document the role of judges of the Criminal Division of the Cook County Circuit Court in the torture scandal.

- Had appearances of conflict of interest and bias in favor of those whom they had been appointed to investigate.

We detailed numerous indictable offenses against Burge, Byrne, McWeeny, and four of their co-conspirators that—contrary to what the special prosecutors' had asserted—were not barred by the statute of limitations. Our conclusion pulled no punches:

> The record strongly suggests that the Special Prosecutors' investigation and resultant Report, which cost the taxpayers of Cook County $7 million, were driven, at least in part, by pro-law-enforcement bias and conflict of interest, were riddled with omissions, inconsistencies, half-truths and misrepresentations, and reflect shoddy investigation and questionable prosecutorial tactics and strategies. The Report also failed to address the systemic and racist nature of the dehumanizing physical and psychological abuse, or to identify it as torture, in accordance with the international

definition. Additionally, the record suggests that the investigation was neither designed nor intended to develop evidence in support of indictments for crimes not barred by the statute of limitations but rather was designed to avoid embarrassing City, County, CPD, and SAO officials responsible for the torture scandal and cover-up, and protecting the City from civil liability.

In our call to action, we requested that:

- The Cook County Board hold a public hearing to investigate the squandering of public resources by the Special Prosecutors on an investigation that appears to have been flawed by design.

- The U.S. Attorney for the Northern District of Illinois and U.S. Department of Justice conduct an independent investigation into all of the criminal conduct implicated by the evidence outlined above.

- The City of Chicago and the County of Cook establish a fund to provide compensation and treatment for the more than one hundred victims of torture who may be barred from obtaining relief by the statute of limitations.

- The City of Chicago stop spending public funds to defend the torturers in civil cases.

- The Illinois Attorney General agree to new criminal court hearings for persons behind bars who were convicted in whole or in part on the basis of confessions obtained by Burge and his subordinates.

- The Special Prosecutors make public all transcripts, documents, and other materials gathered during their investigation.

- The U.S. Congress, the United Nations Convention Against Torture (CAT), and the Inter-American Commission for Human Rights continue to monitor the City, County and U.S. Government's responses to the above demands.

The report closed as it had started, with the words of Anthony Holmes:

The last time before they brought the statement in and had me to talk to them, I come to, and I thought I was dead then because they was lifting me off the floor trying to pump air into me because I wasn't breathing. I remember that. I thought I was dead because all I could see was blackness and I said, man, this is it. I'm gone. When I looked up, they brought me back. I said, man, I'm on a seesaw, here we go again. I can't take no more of this. They did it again. So they asked me some questions, I answered them. I answered more questions. Then I said, man, I ain't going through this no more. So I said, I ain't saying nothing else. So then they put me back through it again, and the last time, I thought that was it. That was it.

The ad hoc Committee against Police Torture circulated our report, with specifically tailored cover letters, to congressman John Conyers, the Inter-American Commission for Human Rights, US attorney Patrick Fitzgerald, Illinois attorney general Lisa Madigan, the Cook County Board of Commissioners, and each and every member of the Chicago City Council. The letter to the City Council included the demand that it "establish with the county a fund to provide compensation and treatment for Burge survivors who were barred from obtaining relief by the statute of limitations."

The next week, Locke, Chick, and I were at Stateville Prison to represent Darrell Cannon, who had been brought up from Tamms, at his long-delayed parole revocation hearing, ordered by Judge Henry five months before. The Prisoner Review Board had done all it could to delay the hearing and would not inform us in advance whether they had developed any new "evidence," so we were still in suspense when the hearing began. Reluctantly, board chairman Jorge Montes conceded that they had nothing new, so that evening Darrell walked out of Stateville a free man, finally, four years after he was scheduled to be released under the original deal.

Enforcement of the settlement agreement with the City had been placed on an indefinite hold; Judge Aspen had recused himself because he might have to testify about the secret mediation if a hearing were to be held on our enforcement motion. He transferred the motion to Judge Holderman, who, understandably, wanted the issue resolved without the spectacle of the former chief judge (Aspen) testifying against the corporation counsel in front of the current chief judge (himself). At the same time, the City's appeal of the order to depose Daley was sitting on Judge Aspen's desk, in limbo.

Joey and I had decided, even before we released the "shadow report," that we needed to lobby the progressive city council members who seemed ready to open another avenue of protest against the City's actions. We drafted a letter to these alderpeople, signed on behalf of our collective clients by Locke and Sam Tenenbaum from Northwestern, Jon Loevy and Kurt Feuer from the Loevy firm, Andrea Lyon from DePaul, and by us, together with a proposed resolution to introduce into the council. With twenty-seven WHEREAS clauses that told the torture and settlement story, our RESOLVED clause stated that the "Corporation Counsel is hereby instructed to either honor the settlement which it allegedly agreed to in November of 2006, or, alternatively, to appear before the City Council at a hearing to fully explain why it refused to sign the settlement papers and present this alleged agreement to City Council for approval and to further explain why the alleged agreement is not in the best interests of the Citizens of the City of Chicago."

In late May, a majority of the council members—twenty-six to be exact—resolved that it did "hereby call upon the Committee for Police and Fire to invite Special State's Attorneys Edward Egan and Robert Boyle along with Superintendent Phillip Cline to hearings to discuss the Special State's Attorneys findings published in their Report." The chairman of the Fire and Police Committee, Ike Carrothers, a staunch Daley ally, agreed to hold the hearing, in July, and alderperson Toni Preckwinkle, the sponsor of the resolution, told the *Tribune* that the signers were "very anxious to hear from the special [prosecutors] about their methods of investigation and their findings." The *Trib* turned to Daley himself for a response to the hearing:

> "That's up to them," Daley said. "They can look into anything they want." Daley has said he would never have allowed abuse to continue if he had been aware of it. And he said Wednesday he has nothing to fear from hearings on the topic. "I was not the mayor or [police] superintendent during all of that time," said Daley, who as state's attorney was the county's top prosecutor.

Daley was also feeling the heat from the widely shown police beating videotapes and the revitalized cries for a true citizens' review board. He moved to defuse the policing crisis and blunt the movement for citizens' review using the same maneuver his father had used in 1974, when he created OPS—he presented city council with an ordinance that created a successor police disciplinary agency, this time called the Independent Police Review Authority. IPRA would have a new home and subpoena power, with some final decision making moved from the police superintendent to the mayor. This "compromise" seemed acceptable to the majority of the council, but the coalition seeking fundamental reform was far from satisfied.

We made our last stand at a June hearing before the Fire and Police Committee. Joining on behalf of the People's Law Office with Citizens Alert, the MacArthur Foundation, the Public Defenders' Office, the ACLU, and numerous other community organizations and individuals, I raised "our strong objections to the police disciplinary ordinance proposed by the mayor and his corporation counsel's office." I continued:

> I am afraid that a review of the creation and performance of the Office of Professional Standards over the past thirty-five years leads to the inescapable conclusion that hasty passage of the Mayor's ordinance will doom us in the future to an equally inadequate and ineffectual police disciplinary system as that which we have suffered with since OPS was created in 1974. Like the present system, the Mayor's ordinance provides for a disciplinary agency that continues to be far from truly independent, but rather continues to be controlled politically by the mayor, with the Fraternal Order of Police vested with de facto veto power through its contract, and with the superintendent still empowered with the right to overturn the sustained findings of the agency.

Unfortunately, the die was cast (or, in Chicago parlance, the fix was in). The ordinance was adopted by the council with a few minor amendments, dooming those most affected by police violence and the police code of silence to another version of business as usual when they attempted to complain about police abuse.

Days later the Cook County Board of Commissioners held a hearing on police torture and the special prosecutors' report. Joey had taken the lead, working primarily through commissioner Earlean Collins and her administrative assistant. Collins, a Democrat representing the west side of Chicago and some of the western suburbs, was the first African American woman to have served in the Illinois State Senate. She chaired the hearing, with the mayor's brother, commissioner John Daley, in attendance. Torture survivors Madison Hobley, David Bates, Darrell Cannon, and Anthony Holmes, along with Joey and me, were among the witnesses who either testified or presented written statements. Cook County clerk David Orr, quoting our report, called for federal prosecutions; an expert on treating survivors of torture for psychological trauma also testified. Special prosecutors Egan and Boyle, despite being county officials paid by the county commissioners, declined the board's invitation to appear.

Joey and I filed exhibits with the board that we had compiled over the years, including a laundry list of prosecutable crimes. We also offered several proposed resolutions we had drafted: supporting a federal investigation and prosecutions, as well as new hearings for the torture survivors who remained in prison; and recommending that the Illinois State Legislature and Congress pass legislation, without a statute of limitations, "expressly proscribing the crime of torture" as defined by the UN Committee Against Torture.

The board president, Democrat Todd Stroger—son of political powerhouse John Stroger—and liberal Evanston commissioner Larry Suffredin both spoke out in support. Stroger commented, "I think that there are a lot of people who are concerned that something of that nature could go on and there would be no one who was prosecuted for it," while Suffredin blasted Egan's and Boyle's report: "Right now what's happened is we've taken a terrible situation and we've actually made it worse because this report doesn't satisfy anybody's understanding of really what happened and who was responsible, and how it was allowed to go on." A few weeks later the board passed our resolutions.

The third summer hearing, before the city council's Fire and Police Committee, was set for the last week in July. Only days before, thirteen members of the council had signed a resolution, sponsored by Black Caucus stalwarts Ed Smith and Howard Brookins, which cited our up-to-date figures—$10 million in attorneys' fees paid for Burge's defense—as it excoriated the corporation counsel for "a serious breach of fiduciary duty to the taxpaying public," and exhorted her to

> cease and desist the continuing accumulation of attorneys' fees in defense of Jon Burge and the other officers who participated with him in these heinous and indefensible acts and instruct the legal counsel representing the City to fashion a settlement with all Burge Plaintiffs. Furthermore we appeal to our colleagues on the Finance Committee to deny any more payments to outside legal counsel and swiftly approve a settlement in all outstanding cases that will end this shameful chapter in this city's history.

The resolution was sent to the Finance Committee and its chairman, our powerful adversary Ed Burke, for a September hearing.

Meanwhile, in planning for the July hearing, Joey and I decided that we would broaden our presentations to address the questions of settlement, defense fees, and Burge's pension, even though those were not among the stated topics to be considered. Once again, special prosecutors Egan and Boyle did not show up, but the eight-person committee was joined by eighteen other city council members, most of whom were our allies. The police department sent the first deputy superintendent, Dana Starks, to promote the proposition that Burge and his men were "rogue cops," a fallacy that all too many of the council members in attendance, including some of our allies, embraced. Starks also put forward the city's stock argument to justify the continued financing of Burge's defense—that the Seventh Circuit had mandated this result in its second *Wilson* decision, a dubious argument on its face.

I came armed with a large posterboard exhibit that showed the current defense fees figures—$10,348,000 and counting—as well as calculations of the pension money that had been paid to Burge and his crew, about $2 million a year and $16 million to date. I had also found a city ordinance that gave the mayor and the city council the authority to cut off defense payments to any officer who had committed a crime, and argued that the special prosecutors' findings of "beyond a reasonable doubt," as applied to Burge and several members of his crew, brought them within the purview of the ordinance. Apply the ordinance, I argued, and "let Burge sue them" if he chose to do so.

Councilwoman Sandi Jackson lauded our work and invoked the photographic images of torture from Abu Ghraib, but, not surprisingly, Ed Burke took me on, pointing out that the mandate to hire outside lawyers to defend Burge and company came before Daley was mayor, and before he, Burke, was chairman of the Finance Committee. I fired back that those decisions were made before the evidence of a pattern and practice of torture had come to light, and said, "You and I both know that you can stop it at any time." The issue of the global $14.8 million settlement agreement had become even more urgent because Judge Holderman had recently declined to hold a hearing, instead ruling that there was no enforceable settlement because the corporation counsel's office had not presented the agreement to the city council for its required approval. I urged the council to call in Mara Georges to speak to why it had not been presented, and alderman Bob Fioretti promised, "We will have this body ask our corporation counsel to resolve these cases." As good as that sounded, we all knew that Mara Georges got her marching orders from her patron and boss, the mayor, and, as with everything else, Daley would make the ultimate call.

We then showed a fifteen-minute video called *Jon Burge and His Victims*. It consisted of excerpts from Anthony Holmes's deposition, describing his electric-shocking and bagging; from Darrell Cannon's description, provided during an appearance at Rainbow/PUSH shortly after his release, of his mock execution; and Madison Hobley's testimony, given at the Cook County Board hearing, describing how he was bagged, beaten, and racially degraded. The last five minutes of the tape were devoted to my questioning of Burge at his 2004 deposition, where he took the Fifth Amendment in response to questions about the torture of Anthony Holmes, Andrew

Wilson, and Leroy Orange; whether he committed perjury; whether there was a pattern and practice of torture at Area 2; and even whether the City was paying for his lawyers.

The next witness was former Area 2 detective Bill Parker, who related the story he had told me fifteen years before—how, back in 1973, he heard an excruciating scream, walked in on Burge and two other white detectives torturing a whimpering Black man chained to a radiator, and was told by a supervisor to leave. Alderman Ed Smith, seemingly oblivious to what might have happened to a Black detective who broke the code of silence in 1973, grilled Parker on why he had not reported the event to anyone at the time.

Joey focused her testimony on the findings of the UN Committee Against Torture, the demand for the Feds to prosecute Burge, and the bill introduced by congressman Danny Davis to make torture a federal crime without a statute of limitations. DePaul Law School human rights professor Len Cavise explained why the statute of limitations was not a bar to prosecutions. Attorney Julie Hull and Carolyn Johnson, Marcus Wiggins's mother, talked about Marcus's case; and Mary L. Johnson, Michael Johnson's mother, spoke about her son's torture.

The official condemnation of the pattern of torture throughout the hearing was resounding:

> Chairman Ike Carrothers: "No doubt" there were "atrocities";
> Alderman Tom Allen: "It was a serial torture operation that ran out of Area 2;" "a scurrilous history of torture";
> Alderman Ed Smith: "The worst disgrace I have ever seen"; "atrocities that were condoned and acquiesced in";
> Alderman Joe Moore: "Must bring those who committed these heinous crimes to justice";
> Alderwoman Jackson: "Obscene and outrageous";
> Congressman Davis: "Illegal, immoral and repugnant activities";
> Alderman Beale: "There is a hole in our system";
> Alderman Ed Burke: "An embarrassment to our city, an embarrassment to law enforcement."

Noteworthy, however, was the official avoidance of directly calling out the racism of the CPD. Perhaps alderman Tom Allen, who, as a former public defender, had operated in the belly of the beast, came the closest to identifying one of the root causes: he said that the torture was "part of the societal problem"; that "for us to blame the police superintendent or anyone else without sharing the blame with everybody universally I don't believe is fair."

The media gave full coverage to the hearing, and our video was aired on television and radio. Fran Spielman's piece, which ran in the *Tribune* next to a photo of Burge taking the Fifth, led by saying: "Chicago aldermen on Tuesday relived the nightmare of police torture by former Lt. Jon Burge—and came away more determined than ever to cut off $2 million in annual pension payments to Burge and his Area 2 cohorts and their $10 million legal defense." She invoked the video:

> Aldermen also watched Burge repeatedly take the Fifth Amendment during a 2004 deposition when asked what he did to those offenders—and whether he tossed the device used to shock suspects into submission over the deck of his private boat and into Lake Michigan. The only question Burge answered directly was whether he received a city pension. His answer: "yes"—roughly $2,500 a month.

The *Sun Times* also topped its editorial page with the headline "PULL HIS PENSION" and a cartoon by Jeff Szuc that depicted Burge on his boat, drink in hand, sporting a police hat and sunglasses. After pointing out that Daley was state's attorney when much of the torture took place, the *Sun Times* continued, "Twenty years later Daley is Mayor, the statute of limitations on Burge's abuse is long up, and he sits in the Florida sun collecting his pension, for now." The editorial concluded thus:

> The unresolved Burge case eats at our sense of justice, taking a terrible toll on the public trust. Aggressively seeking new legal avenues to bring it to some degree of closure is one small step toward resolving the past.

CHAPTER 28

The Feds
Come Marching In

Shortly after the special prosecutors delivered their report to the US attorneys' office in the summer of 2006, Locke and I spoke with Stan Willis. Stan had a cordial relationship with Sergio Acosta, head of General Crimes Division and coordinator of criminal civil rights prosecutions in Patrick Fitzgerald's office. We agreed that Stan would reach out to Sergio and request a meeting at which we would attempt to gauge how serious the Feds were and, assuming that they were indeed serious, discuss how we could assist them. Sergio conveyed our request to Fitzgerald and his first assistant, and they said we should go ahead and meet, as long as they received assurance that we would not publicize our meeting—such as, one of them said, pulling a "publicity stunt" by going downstairs in the federal building and holding a press conference after we met. It was an assurance Stan readily gave.

We met with Sergio in the fall, and, despite the long history of local and federal prosecutors' refusal to prosecute Burge and his confederates, we came away from the meeting with the feeling that this time it might be different. Unlike with Egan and Boyle, we were treated with respect. We also knew of Fitzgerald's reputation, gained in part from his prosecution, while Department of Justice special counsel, of vice president Dick Cheney's chief of staff, Scooter Libby, for perjury and obstruction of justice. We agreed to help find and present torture survivors who were potential witnesses, and also to make our considerable array of evidence available. Over the next year we had quietly done so, keeping our knowledge of the investigation close to the vest, as promised, while Sergio and his team—most notably Jeff Kramer, Barry Miller, and several top-of-the-line FBI agents—pursued an aggressive investigation of Burge for perjury and obstruction of justice. From their point of view, the torture scandal had reached a "critical mass," and their investigation offered the last chance to bring Burge to justice. Fitzgerald, like his team, took the positive findings of the special prosecutors very seriously and fully supported the investigation.

The federal investigation focused on proving that Burge had perjured himself and obstructed the federal courts when he denied under oath, in November 2003, in the Madison Hobley civil case, that he participated in, directed, or witnessed any acts of torture. Directly after he made the denial, the lawyers representing him, Byrne, Dignan, and all the other involved officers advised them to take the Fifth Amendment, which they had done in the parade of depositions we had taken over the next three years. However, in another burst of arrogance, Dignan and many of the other officers—Burge excepted—had done an about-face after they escaped indictment by the special prosecutors and came in, one by one, to waive their Fifth Amendment rights and to deny, under oath, any and all torture. This gave me another shot at Byrne, Dignan, McWeeny, and company. At the outset of each deposition, I inquired if the witness truly wanted to testify, given the possibility that the Feds might be investigating. The answer was invariably "yes," and their false denials flowed thereafter.

I was particularly focused on getting denials from Byrne and Dignan, which I accomplished in six tension-packed videotaped sessions. The Feds now had five years to prosecute them for this false testimony, and we strongly advocated that they do so. Unfortunately, in our view, Sergio Acosta and Jeff Kramer seemed almost exclusively focused on Burge, whose statute of limitations would expire in November 2008.

We decided to persist in publicly playing up the obscene contradiction of the City's continuing to pay Burge's lawyers many millions while reneging on its deal to compensate the torture victims. I had floated a figure of at least $20 million as projected total fees to be paid in pinstripe patronage if the City continued to stonewall on the settlement and we went to trial. I came up with the idea of creating a complete statistical projection of verdicts and corresponding fees in the five pending cases—adding Darrell Cannon's and Aaron Patterson's cases to the mix—to be presented at the upcoming Finance Committee hearing. I contacted an old friend, Steve Whitman, a well-respected epidemiologist and a veteran of the social justice movement, who enthusiastically took on the task.

Based on the detailed numbers we supplied him, Steve's mathematically detailed conclusions were surprising even to us. If all five cases went to trial, there was a 3 percent chance that the City would win all five.

Using a potential range of recovery of $500,000 to $2 million for each year of incarceration, and factoring in additional defense fees, Steve projected that the City stood to expend, in addition to what it had already spent, between $16,000,000 (if it won all five cases) and $195,000,000 (if it lost all five). The numbers were breathtaking.

We released the numbers to the *Sun Times* the Sunday before the scheduled September hearing. "Burge Suits Could Cost City $195 Mil." was a real Sunday morning attention-grabber. Reporter Abdon Pallasch, who had also broken the story about Special Prosecutor Egan's police relatives, got Daley to give him a weekend quote:

> Every lawyer wants more money. It's all about money. Sure you have to settle but you have to have a reasonable settlement. You would take $300 million? That's why lawyers sue everybody.

The day before the Wednesday hearing, the *Sun Times* followed with another editorial: "Stop the Financial Torture, Settle Burge Lawsuits Now." Repeating the shocking projected expenses and the City's refusal to honor the settlement, the editorial concluded, "Aside from the economics of settling, these victims deserve justice. And even though nobody wants to pay another dime in defense of Burge, taxpayers are on the losing end no matter what the outcome." That same day, council members Bob Fioretti, Pat Dowell, Toni Preckwinkle, Howard Brookins, Ed Smith, and Joe Moore, armed with Steve Whitman's financial report, again demanded at City Hall that the Burge cases be settled, with Preckwinkle calling the scandal "one of the most disgraceful episodes in Chicago history." Corporation counsel Mara Georges was "unavailable for comment," but Daley's press secretary, Jacquelyn Heard, told reporters, "Stay tuned . . . Mara will have something interesting to say at tomorrow's Finance Committee meeting."

Daley and Georges were feeling the heat; the hearing was shaping up to be eventful, to say the least. We had Steve Whitman prepared to testify, and Joey and I rushed down to council chambers just in time to hear Mara Georges make her presentation. In what Fran Spielman called a "bombshell," Georges told the world what the City's "issue" was: she had learned last fall that the Feds were reinvestigating Madison Hobley's murder/arson case to determine whether Madison had committed any federal crimes. She claimed that first assistant US attorney Gary Shapiro had released her from the secrecy agreement just in time for the hearing. She also disclosed that only the day before, Judge Aspen had reconvened settlement talks and put "a proposal on the table." She then offered up this nonsense:

> We have been attempting to settle all of the cases and to do it as a package. I have heard the aldermen loud and clear. The aldermen have said to me time and time again that they desire to get these cases settled. I have heard what they've told me and I've been operating in good faith to satisfy their wishes.

Livid, I confronted Georges in the hallway behind council chambers and challenged both the truth and the timing of her revelations. She did not deign to respond as she brushed past me and Joey. I turned to the press, who were nearby, and blasted the City:

> What kind of an investigation could it be? He's been pardoned for those crimes on the basis of innocence. What's the federal crime? How could he be investigated? This is just a smear tactic to try to influence the negotiations. It's the lowest kind of trying to renegotiate a situation. Why does she bring this out into the public eye at a time when she looks particularly bad because she and the city and the mayor haven't honored a settlement agreement they made many months ago?

Over the objection of several of our supporters, alderman Ed Smith scuttled the hearing, explaining, "I think they're gonna settle." Feeling betrayed both by the City and by Madison Hobley's lawyers—who must have known about the reinvestigation—Joey and I headed back to our office. Later that day, however, Abdon Pallasch, who covered the federal courthouse, called with good news: US Attorney Fitzgerald, apparently angered by Georges's antics, released a highly unusual press statement that publicly declared what we already knew—the Feds were actively investigating Burge and his cohorts. Less than a week prior, several city council members had delivered a letter to Fitzgerald's office and held a joint press conference with us, calling for prosecutions, and the mounting pressure seemed to be paying dividends.

Fitzgerald's statement put the investigation on the public record:

> The United States Attorney's Office is conducting an active criminal investigation into allegations of perjury, false statements and obstruction of justice by officers who served in the Chicago Police Department in the 1980s, in relation to currently pending federal civil lawsuits in which persons in Chicago Police Department custody during those years allege they were abused.

At an unrelated press conference that same day, Fitzgerald elaborated:

We're not going to prejudge what will happen. We're not going to predict whether there will be charges or anything beyond that, but we do want to make clear that we're very, very serious about this investigation.

Fitzgerald's statements were encouraging because they publicly demonstrated his personal commitment to the investigation and asserted that the focus was broader than Burge.

That weekend, Chicago's police scandals once again went national, as Michael Robinson of the Associated Press filed a widely published story, "Chicago Cops Awash in Scandal," which exposed a murder plot within the Special Operations Section of the CPD. Robinson began: "Videotapes of angry officers savagely beating civilians and charges that a murder plot was hatched within an elite special operations unit have Chicago's troubled police department reeling again. Adding to the department's woes is word from federal prosecutors that they are investigating claims that homicide detectives tortured suspects into confessing to murders that landed them on death row in the 1980s."

The Special Operations Section was a gang of completely out-of-control officers, whose rampant brutality in Chicago's housing projects had been exposed by attorney Craig Futterman of the University of Chicago's Mandel Legal Clinic and independent investigative journalist Jamie Kalven. In the AP piece, Futterman took aim at police discipline, saying, "If they investigated crimes the way they investigate complaints against police officers they would never close a case." The FOP's president attempted to minimize the problem while also blaming the messenger: "I subscribe to the few-bad-apples theory. It is also due to the attention that the few bad apples are getting from the media."

It was true that the City, at Judge Aspen's request, had returned to the mediation table just prior to Mara Georges's appearance at city council, and Aspen had made a proposal that included two new elements: the Madison Hobley complication and the City's new requirement that Aaron Patterson's case be included in the group package. After a time without counsel, Aaron had retained a politically connected lawyer with little experience in civil rights cases, who envisioned a big payday. Including Aaron, the total settlement package was increased to $19.8 million, with the final $4.8 million to be paid by the City's excess insurance carrier. Unfortunately, despite the urgings of our city council allies, Darrell Cannon's case was not included. This was because, in 1988, Darrell—represented by a real estate lawyer who had been appointed for him—had reluctantly accepted a torture settlement of $3,000.

Mara Georges's claim about the federal investigation of Madison Hobley's criminal case had been confirmed by Fitzgerald, and the City was not about to make a large payout to him while an investigation was hanging over his head. His lawyers were not overly concerned and agreed to a contingency in the settlement agreement: Madison would get $1 million now, with the remainder to be paid if he wasn't charged by January 2009.

Just before Thanksgiving, we received the sad news that Andrew Wilson had died in prison, after serving twenty-five years of his double life sentence. John and I had stayed in touch with Andrew over the years, and we had received letters from him only a month or two before. We were anticipating that he would be a star witness for the Feds, and his death might deal a serious blow to their investigation. John Conroy was the first reporter to learn of Andrew's death, and the *Reader* three days later carried a front-page story. On the cover was a photo of Andrew with the title "The Persistence of Andrew Wilson." In a well-deserved tribute, Conroy wrote that Andrew "will long be remembered not only for his crime but for his pivotal role in what followed—the exposure of torture within the police department. And he may yet have a role to play from beyond the grave." Conroy explained, "The Federal Rules of Evidence prohibit the use of testimony from someone who cannot be cross-examined by a lawyer representing the accused, but there's an exception. According to rule 804(b)(1), testimony given at another proceeding at which the accused had a similar opportunity and motive to question the witness is admissible if the witness is 'unavailable by death.'"

Conroy recounted once again the long history of Andrew's case, noting that it was pivotal because it had "uncovered a torture ring," and that "another prisoner in Wilson's position might not have raised his voice. He was a cop killer—most people wouldn't believe he'd been tortured, and many who did wouldn't care. But Wilson testified under oath six times about what had happened to him." Conroy quoted John Stainthorp to conclude this unusual eulogy:

> I was always amazed that every time he told it he would have the details absolutely correct. And sometimes I would get something a little wrong and he would correct me, and this is without reading anything. I mean he had no way

of refreshing his recollection. And he would have all the details correct and it would always be the same account.

Stainthorp told of a visit about a year before, almost a quarter century after Wilson was tortured.

He still cried when he talked about it, and it still made him furious that he cried. Obviously for Andrew it was important to be strong. One thing about torture is that it makes you weak and it makes you know that you are weak.

The daily press briefly noted Andrew's death days later, with the headline acknowledging the importance of the "cop killer": "Pivotal Figure in Chicago Police Torture Case Dies in Prison." The *Tribune* reported further that a spokesman for the Department of Corrections said that "Wilson had been in the hospital for some time and died of complications associated with a long-standing medical condition.".

Sadly, the retrospective on Andrew Wilson was to be John Conroy's last as a staff writer for the *Reader*, as huge editorial cuts were sweeping across local and national newsrooms. Conroy's work was heralded both in Chicago and in the *New York Times*, which published an article titled "Muckraking Pays, Just Not in Profits." The article cited Conroy's leading role in exposing and chronicling the torture scandal and quoted Aaron Patterson's mother JoAnn, in an email to Conroy: "My son, Aaron Patterson, tortured by the Chicago Police Department, would not be alive today, I believe, without your articles about police torture in the City of Chicago. You documented and wrote the realization of police torture, of which we will never forget. You helped save my son's life for which I thank you." Eighteen years of critical investigative reporting and powerful writing had been terminated, and the leading journalistic voice for justice in the torture cases no longer had a job.

After much back and forth, the settlement with the City was scheduled to be presented to the city council's Finance Committee on Monday, December 10, and, if approved, to the full council two days later. Capitalizing on Daley's absence, this time on a junket to Italy, the City released news of the tentative settlement on Friday afternoon—the traditional time to bury news. The attempt was unsuccessful, as the media focused on the settlement and the torture scandal over the next few days. The City had also released the division of the settlement money: $7.5 million to Madison

Hobley, with $6.5 million contingent; $5.5 million to Leroy Orange; $5 million to Aaron Patterson; $1.8 million to Stanley Howard.

NBC Channel 5 led the news with the specter of Burge: "His name has dogged the city and its police department for years. It was there, like a scab that refused to heal, whenever there were allegations of police brutality or police mistreatment of suspects." City council member Toni Preckwinkle spoke out in support:

> Failure to settle these cases when there was no argument anymore that there was torture by Area 2 detectives made the city look like it was unwilling to acknowledge, apologize and make restitution. For me, it meant we weren't holding the Police Department and ourselves accountable for the bad conduct that went on. It reflected badly on us as a city. Settling promptly is a fiscally responsible thing to do, in addition to being morally right. My concern is, there may be some outstanding cases that are yet to be dealt with, but it's a great step forward.

Alderman Ed Smith said that he was "euphoric" but added that Burge must be prosecuted and should no longer be living "off the fat of the land" on his pension. Kurt Feuer decried how long it took to reach the settlement, and I emphasized its significance, telling the *New York Times*, "It speaks volumes about the seriousness of the systematic torture, abuse and cover-up that went on in the city of Chicago for decades." I also underscored to Channel 5 what remained to be accomplished, including "hearings for the twenty-five to thirty Black men imprisoned after allegedly being tortured into confessing to crimes they didn't commit" and "indictments and prosecutions of Burge and his men for obstruction of justice, perjury, and conspiracy."

A Sunday *Sun Times* editorial continued the coverage, calling once again for Burge to be prosecuted and to have his pension pulled. Steve Mills wrote a major piece in the *Tribune* that put Daley back in the crosshairs: "The fallout from the police torture scandal not only has cost Daley politically, it also has had mounting financial consequences for city taxpayers." Mills continued, "Besides Daley, the torture issue touches the current state's attorney, Richard Devine, whose office defended against numerous appeals in which torture was a central claim. It has even been raised among the many candidates seeking to succeed Devine, suggesting the scandal is not losing steam in spite of its age."

On Monday, the city council's Finance Committee approved the settlement, and we awaited the formality of approval by the full council to follow, two days later. Mayor Daley, back in town, responded to media inquiries by saying that the cases were "very, very complicated," involving torture allegations over a number of years, and that when a lawsuit is filed, "you settle it." He added that he hoped the settlement signaled "an end of that type of error we had."

In keeping with the star-crossed history of what was billed as "one of the largest settlements in the city's history," another roadblock arose just as it was about to be presented to the full council. According to Mara Georges, Aaron Patterson's lawyer had failed to produce a signed power of attorney from Aaron that gave the lawyer the authority to settle, and Stanley Howard had also raised an issue at the last minute. Many council members were exasperated; Jon Loevy, Stanley's lawyer, called the issue a "red herring." Aaron Patterson's lawyer, Frank Avila Jr., living up to his reputation of being a loose cannon, threatened to raise his demand to $10 million if the settlement were not approved that day. Daley cavalierly said, "That's how life is," and the *Sun Times* headlined the bad news, "Police Torture Victims Deal Falls Apart."

In reality, all sides wanted the settlement to happen. Frank Avila drove to the federal prison in Kentucky to get Aaron's signature, and Judge Aspen intervened to facilitate Stanley Howard's agreement. So, just after New Year's 2008, the settlement was scheduled to be considered once again by the full council.

Adding to the drama was a looming conflict over how to split the attorneys' share of Aaron Patterson's settlement. Frank Avila, displaying remarkable chutzpah and greed, claimed that he was entitled to the entire 33 percent retainer that Aaron had signed with him. Our position, grounded solidly both in the law and basic fairness, was that the fee should be divided proportionately, according to the amount of time expended by each of the lawyers. We also wanted the dispute resolved by Judge Gottschall, who had heard Aaron's case and was in the best position to determine the relative merits of the attorneys' claims.

Two days before the settlement was to be considered by the city council, Avila filed a frivolous lawsuit in the circuit court of Cook County, accusing us of extortion and breach of contract, and told the press that our claim to a share of the fees was "ridiculous." Referring to our decade-plus of work on Aaron's behalf, I countered, saying, "Our work got Aaron a torture hearing before the Illinois Supreme Court, an innocence pardon from the governor, and a $5 million settlement. I guess no good deed goes unpunished."

So it was with both anticipation and concern that Joey, Leroy Orange, and I went to city council chambers on January 9, 2008—one day short of five years from the day that Governor Ryan had pardoned Leroy, Aaron, Madison, and Stanley. We had asked Mort Smith to come with us to act as a de facto bodyguard—to protect us not from Burge's people but from Avila's. As the discussion of the settlement began, Mayor Daley, who was presiding over the proceedings, left the chamber.

Numerous council members spoke emotionally. Alderman Smith began by giving thanks "to the members of the council who pushed the issue, and thanks to Governor Ryan who got them off death row. It's a black eye on Chicago. Let's hope this never happens again." He later added that it was "a disgrace" that "Jon Burge is still walking around in Florida, spending the city's money."

Alderwoman Leslie Hairston apologized to the four men: "For the lies that you had to encounter, and the deceptions and the denials and the cover-ups in getting to the truth, I want to recognize you for that." She added, "We still have many Jon Burges running around in each of our police districts—particularly in my neck of the woods, and that has to stop. I'm hoping that today is the first step."

Alderman Brookins sounded the same theme: "This city still owes an apology to these people, who spent years in prison and some on death row, who were tortured in ways that put Abu Ghraib and Guantánamo Bay to shame. On behalf of the city council and the corporation counsel, we apologize to all of you."

Afterward, as we rode down in the elevator, an Avila operative threatened Leroy Orange and me. He moved to attack us, but Darrell Cannon, who had attended the proceedings as a spectator, intervened to protect us from harm.

The next day, a color photo of Leroy, Mort, Joey, myself, and Sage Smith—a former prisoner who worked at Northwestern as a paralegal—ran at the top of the *Tribune*'s Metro section over a bold headline, "DISGRACE COSTS MILLIONS." CBS Channel 2 called the discussion "emotional and cathartic" and reminded viewers that "the four plaintiffs were part of a story that made international headlines in January 2003 when then governor George Ryan pardoned them and commuted the sentences of every death row inmate in the state in a stinging rebuke of capital punishment." JoAnn Patterson called the settlement "blood money" and said, "The money doesn't make me feel better, it doesn't give me closure."

After the council session adjourned, Daley said it was "galling to every-body" that Burge was still receiving his pension, but sought to dispel the notion that the City could remedy the situation. He explained that Mara Georges had researched the issue extensively and was unable to "find a via-ble cause of action" against Burge. Fran Spielman quoted the mayor and, as ever, took the opportunity to remind her readers of Daley's role in the torture scandal: "'Now, this tragic chapter in our city's history is closed. At the same time, we must learn from this experience,' said Mayor Daley, who served as state's attorney during much of Burge's alleged reign of terror."

CHAPTER 29

The Worm Turns

I n early February 2008, voters went to the polls in the Democratic primary to choose among six candidates for Cook County state's attorney. After twelve years of refusing to investigate or prosecute Burge and his men, or to admit that the men pardoned by Governor Ryan (or any other tortured prisoner) were wrongfully convicted, Dick Devine retired to a professorship at Loyola Law School, where he taught a class on the death penalty. I had deposed him before he left office, and although he admitted that he, Daley, and Kunkle discussed the Brzeczek letter, he persisted in saying that he did not believe torture had occurred.

The two reform candidates, Howard Brookins and Larry Suffredin, both of whom raised police torture and brutality in their campaigns, split the Black and liberal vote, permitting Devine's deputy, Anita Alvarez, to squeak by with a 26 percent plurality of the vote. So it would be law and order/mass incarceration business as usual in Cook County, as it had been since Daley was elected state's attorney in 1980.

In June, Carol Marin, who had excellent federal sources, and police reporter Frank Main broke a *Sun Times* story about the federal investigation: "Retired Cops Subpoenaed, Alleged Torture Probe into Burge Ramping Up," the headline read. Several Area 2 detectives had been subpoenaed to testify secretly on June 19, they reported. The *Sun Times* followed with an editorial urging a "thorough probe" by Fitzgerald's "crack team" of prosecutors who "seem, at times, to be the only ones around here who can figure out how to prosecute certain bad guys, whether it's crooked cops or political players trading city jobs for campaign work." According to the editorial board,

> But for all Fitzgerald's efforts, his investigation might be going nowhere were it not for the principled people who shoved an unpopular issue uphill for many years. People such as journalist John Conroy, who wrote detailed and damning stories about police torture for the Chicago *Reader*, long before it

became a hot issue. People such as Ald. Ed Smith, who has been strident in his criticism in the City Council. People such as the attorneys at the People's Law Office, who have been tough advocates for the men whose liberties were violated in the shadows of police interrogation rooms.

Fitzgerald's team had added Betsy Biffl, an accomplished civil rights prosecutor from the Justice Department, and had empaneled a special grand jury that had been periodically hearing evidence since June 2007. The case was at a critical point, as the statute of limitations on Burge's perjury and obstruction was due to expire in less than less than five months, in November 2008, and that prized witness—a Burge confederate willing to testify that he or she witnessed an act of torture—had yet to appear. In June, each of the subpoenaed detective witnesses appeared, one at a time, before the grand jury, with FOP attorney Joe Roddy as their lawyer. They were each given a use-immunity letter, guaranteeing that their testimony could not be used against them. Nonetheless, one after the other, each of them honored the police code of silence, and saw no evil, heard no evil, and spoke no evil.

On July, 3, 2008, the final detective was called into the jury room. Unlike the others, he had retained his own private lawyer. US Attorney Fitzgerald was present and reminded the witness that he could be charged with perjury if he lied. This piece of legal verbiage was more bluff than anything else, as the prosecutors had little or nothing on this detective except for his involvement in the alleged beating of Alfonzo Pinex in 1985.

Sergio Acosta began the questioning. The witness identified himself as Michael McDermott, a retired sergeant with the Chicago Police Department. Unlike the others, McDermott's attorney had required that the prosecutors take him before the chief judge for the grant of immunity before he testified. After preliminary questions, Sergio asked why he had sought immunity. To the surprise of all the prosecutors in the room, McDermott said, "I witnessed an abusive act by Jon Burge." He said that the act occurred in Burge's office at the new Area 2 in the 1980s, and the victim was Shadeed Mu'min. Corroborating Shadeed's story in detail, McDermott swore that Burge had pointed his gun at Shadeed, that McDermott had seen him put what appeared to be a plastic bag or typewriter cover over Shadeed's head, that he did not think Shadeed was able to breathe, and that he was sure Burge was seeking to coerce a confession from Shadeed. He further testified that Shadeed was seated, that it was a "one sided" confrontation, and that the only time Shadeed struggled was when the bag was put over his head. He also admitted that he had lied to the OPS about Shadeed, and that he had pushed Alfonzo Pinex. It was a watershed moment for the Feds.

As we did not know what was going on in front of the grand jury, we continued to pursue similar evidence and discovery in Darrell's case. In late August, we took the deposition of Diane Panos, a divorce lawyer who had shared office space with Frank Laverty when he became a lawyer in his later life. Frank had told me before he died that Panos had confided in him that she'd had a conversation with Burge that would be of interest.

I had called Ms. Panos just after Frank's death, in December 2006, and she had reluctantly talked to me. She told me that she had dated a longtime friend and coworker of Burge, that she had spent time in the bars with him and Burge, and that Burge talked about "what actually happened" at Area 2. I asked her if she would give a statement to me or the US attorney, and she said she would have to think about it.

I hadn't heard from her in the ensuing year and a half. I had given Sergio Acosta and Jeff Kramer the memo I had written after my conversation with her, but the strict secrecy provisions protecting grand jury proceedings prevented them from telling me what measures, if any, they had taken to obtain her testimony.

The tension in our fourth-floor conference room was intense as the deposition began. Ms. Panos was angry at me for making her go on the public record and afraid of the repercussions she might face from Burge and the police department. I first asked her if she had talked to the FBI and testified before the grand jury, and she admitted that she had. She was emotional and reluctant at the same time, as I tiptoed into the substance of her testimony. She testified that her boyfriend at the time, a cop who had worked with Burge, introduced her to Burge in a bar frequented by cops. Burge was red-faced, with watery eyes, and appeared drunk. He gave her his card, which she had kept. This was sometime in the late 1980s, and, as an aspiring lawyer, she told Burge she was contemplating criminal defense as a possible career.

According to Panos, Burge then went off, calling African American defendants "dogs" and their lawyers "low-lifes"; he said that criminal defendants had no Fourth, Fifth, or Sixth Amendment rights and that coerced confessions were acceptable because if the suspect did not commit the crime for which he was being interrogated, he had committed some other crime. She also said that Burge told her the Wilson brothers were beaten, and that they got what they deserved. She felt intimidated, and then, after breaking down and crying, described "vile and vulgar" remarks Burge had made of an explicit sexual nature, which understandably still caused her pain and anguish.

Two weeks later, Michael McDermott appeared at our offices for his deposition. He admitted that he had recently appeared before the federal grand jury and gave a vague answer hinting that he had been granted immunity. He did not reveal that he was scheduled to reappear for further questioning a week later. McDermott invoked the Fifth Amendment when I asked him whether he was the unknown officer whom Shadeed Mu'min saw in the doorway of Burge's office, and whether he witnessed Burge point a gun at Shadeed and put a plastic typewriter cover over his head. We could only surmise as to whether he was granted immunity, and, if he was, what he had told the special grand jury under that grant.

In early October, Ben Elson, who had become a trusted member of our torture litigation team, journeyed south to prepare two important witnesses in Darrell Cannon's civil case. Rodney Benson, who, along with Stanley Wrice and Lee Holmes, was tortured by officers Byrne and Dignan in September 1982, was serving a fourteen-year sentence in a state prison located in St. Joseph, Missouri. At his deposition, Rodney testified that he was picked up for a violent rape of a white woman, taken to Area 2, interrogated, and, after he denied involvement in the crime, beaten on the body and groin with a flashlight and a black piece of rubber with tape on both ends. After he continued to deny involvement in the crime, Rodney was hit on his groin, back, chest, stomach, and knee by Byrne and was threatened with hanging by Dignan. They told him that they had hung other "niggers" and threatened to kill him if they ever saw him in a white neighborhood. The beating stopped only after Rodney confessed.

Two days later Ben drove six hours to Menard Penitentiary in southern Illinois, where he met with Michael Tillman. A short and stocky man, Michael had suffered greatly while imprisoned for more than two decades. He was serving a life sentence for the brutal murder, aggravated kidnaping, and sexual assault of Betty Howard. Ben and Michael went over his case in great detail, and Ben was convinced that Michael was innocent of the crime. At his deposition, the soft-spoken Michael described being tortured over a three-day period by a team of Area 2 officers, headed up by Byrne and Dignan. The torture began when Dignan and another detective hand-cuffed Michael to a ring on the wall in an interrogation room and smacked him on the head. Two Black detectives, Hines and Patton, then entered the room. Hines struck Michael in the head and violently punched him in the stomach, causing him to vomit on his clothes and on the floor of the interrogation room.

Hines and Patton then drove Michael to a secluded location near some railroad tracks, where Hines forced him to his knees, put a gun to his head, and threatened to kill him "like you killed that woman." Then, back in an interview room, Hines hit him on his back and cracked him on the head with a telephone book, causing his nose to gush blood all over his pants, shirt, and the interrogation room floor. His interrogators made him clean up his blood with paper towels.

Later, Dignan and John Yucaitis, another of Area 2's midnight crew of "asskickers," rejoined the brutal and bloody interrogation. In a crude form of waterboarding, they pushed their thumbs against Michael's ears, forcing his head back so they could pour 7-Up into his nose. They followed by repeatedly placing a plastic bag over Michael's head, subjecting him to the terrifying sensation of suffocation. Dignan also cracked Michael on the leg with his metal flashlight.

In a nearby interrogation room, Steven Bell was also being physically abused and tortured while being interrogated about the Howard murder. After Steven denied involvement in the crime, Dignan, Yucaitis, and Byrne, after telling him that his "Black brothers"—detectives Hines and Patton—had left, repeatedly hit Steven on the head with a telephone book, repeatedly kicked him in the ribs, and repeatedly punched him in the face and forehead.

Ben returned from the trip with a mission to convince Joey and me to file a last-ditch post-conviction petition on Michael Tillman's behalf. But the most pressing task was to find torture survivor Melvin Jones so he could give a deposition and be interviewed by the Feds.

Ben and I had previously found Melvin, addicted, hanging out with a street vendor named Shim Shine, and living on the street at 75th and Stony Island. This time, we found him in Jackson Park Hospital, a dingy place, on what appeared to be his deathbed. Shim Shine told us that Melvin had AIDS. Melvin was barely conscious but seemed to recognize us. I consulted with Steve Whitman, our epidemiologist friend, who worked at Mt. Sinai Hospital. Steve worked closely with a network of progressive doctors who treated AIDS patients, and he advised us that Melvin needed to be immediately transferred to an AIDS treatment center.

A physician at Jackson Park confirmed the diagnosis: "Full-blown AIDS, meningitis and encephalitis infection of the brain, dementia, and noncompliant with medication." Thankfully, and perhaps at our urging, Jackson Park was sending Melvin to Kendrick Hospital on the north side for twenty-one days of IV antibiotics and further evaluation, but the doctor, who had just started to see Melvin a few days before, was not optimistic. He also said, not surprisingly, that Melvin was not competent to testify.

When Ben and I, decked out in hazmat suits, visited Melvin a while later at Kendrick Hospital, he seemed a little better, and we gained some hope that another of the key witnesses against Burge would not pass away.

In the middle of the health crisis with Melvin, I received an early morning call from assistant US attorney Jeff Kramer. After swearing me to secrecy, Kramer told me the news: an arrest warrant had been issued for Jon Burge on the charges of perjury and obstruction of justice, and US marshals were on their way to Burge's Apollo Beach house to slap the cuffs on him!

Burge was taken to the federal lockup in Tampa, then before US magistrate judge Thomas B. McCoun III and served with a copy of the indictment, which alleged that Burge "was present for, and at times participated in, the torture and physical abuse of a person being questioned on one or more occasions," that Burge "was aware that detectives he was supervising engaged in torture and physical abuse of a person being questioned on one or more occasions," and that, by lying under oath in November 2003 when asked if he had ever used, or was aware of the use of, torture techniques during questioning, he had committed the federal crimes of obstruction of justice and perjury.

Burge told the judge that he regularly traveled to Las Vegas for tradeshows, where he worked as a security consultant, most recently for the world's largest jewelry show. The judge restricted Burge's travel to Florida and Chicago, ordered that he relinquish the five guns he owned, and set bond at $250,000, which Burge made by posting his house. He limped out of court and told the assembled media, including *Sun Times* reporter Natasha Korecki, "I'm old. I'm hurting. Please leave me alone."

Back in Chicago, US Attorney Fitzgerald and his team held a press conference to announce the indictment. Borrowing one of my lines, Fitzgerald said, "If people commit multiple crimes and you can't prosecute them for one, there's nothing wrong with prosecuting for another. If Al Capone went down for taxes, that was better than him going down for nothing." Fitzgerald emphasized that the "investigation [was] continuing," adding:

The charges should serve as a warning to officers who worked for Burge and if their lifeline is to hang on a perceived code of silence, they may be hanging on air. Anyone who thinks that they can safely lie in a grand jury, relying upon an unspoken conspiracy of silence, is taking a great risk.

Anthony Holmes, Gregory Banks, Darrell Cannon, David Bates, and I went to Rainbow/PUSH for a press conference to discuss this historic event. Each of the survivors gave his reaction to Burge's arrest.

Darrell Cannon: "The man who has been skating for so long, riding in his boat, catching fish . . . now he's in jail killing roaches, and that's where he belongs."

Gregory Banks: "This is hard—it's real hard. . . . It's a great day for me and America. I'm glad to be an American."

Anthony Holmes: "It pleases me to see that Burge got locked up—and I hope they give him as much time as he gave all of us."

David Bates: "It's probably one of the very first times in history that I'm proud to be an American. I feel a part of the system. I feel a part of the justice. This is how we are going to be made whole. This is the start of something big."

I urged that the tortured men who languished in prison deserved new trials and said that Melvin Jones was a perfect example of why "the claim for reparations is one of moral and political righteousness. If you're gonna pay $1.25 million a year in pensions to Burge and his men," I continued, "you should pay some money to the men who were victimized, regardless of whether or not you have a legal obligation to do so."

Once again, Chicago police torture was national news. The *New York Times* noted that Burge could face up to twenty years in jail and a $250,000 fine, and quoted Fitzgerald as saying, "There is no place for torture and abuse in a police station. No person is above the law, and nobody—even a suspected murderer—is beneath its protection." Locally, city hall reporter Fran Spielman had confronted Daley just after the indictments became public, and the headline said it all: "Daley Accepts No Responsibility for Burge Torture Cases." Daley told her, "I was very proud of my role as prosecutor. I was not the mayor. I was not the police chief. I did not promote this man in the '80s." As Egan and Boyle had done two years earlier, he pointed the finger at Brzeczek: "He was the head of the police department. The police department cleared Burge and they promoted him in the '80s. I was not the mayor then." Daley did concede that he was pleased that a "20-year-long" federal investigation of Burge had "finally" culminated in an indictment. However, he said, "Anything could happen again. You try to do a lot of prevention but individuals could do something outrageous any time."

The *Sun Times* editorialized, "It Was a Good Day for Justice," and Carol Marin wrote in her column that "outrage lies at the heart of Burge charges." I had told her about Melvin Jones's dire medical condition, and she focused on his case, which she knew well from her *60 Minutes 2* interview with him nine years earlier. "Justice for Melvin Jones is coming late," she wrote. "Jones is dying. In and out of consciousness, according to his lawyers, it's possible he doesn't yet know the big news that broke Tuesday." Carol had reached Burge's right-hand man, John Byrne, who told her, "I feel bad for Jon." "I don't," Carol wrote. "I feel sorry for Melvin Jones. A thug and crook, you bet. Even he admitted police had a good reason to question him. 'I'm a prime candidate,' he told me. 'But I also could be innocent.'"

Eric Zorn published a column entitled, "Why the Torture 'Whitewash' May Turn Out to Be an Industrial Strength Disinfectant." Giving credit to our "shadow report," Zorn wrote,

> The grounds for the charges were spelled out in a widely disseminated April 2007 rebuttal, signed by scores of concerned activists, to the special prosecutors. One of the authors of the rebuttal, attorney Flint Taylor, said he not only brought this perjury-rap opportunity to the attention of special prosecutors Edward Egan and Robert Boyle during the course of their investigation, but he also supplied them with the necessary documentary evidence.

Their refusal to indict, Zorn continued, "now looks like a boon to those who have long waited for the alleged police thugs to be brought to justice." As Zorn explained it, after the special prosecutors had seemingly sounded an "all-clear," the detectives we deposed had abandoned their earlier strategy of taking the Fifth and went on the record to deny that torture had occurred. Up to a dozen officers had thus perjured themselves. "Hence," Zorn concluded, "the Special Prosecutors' 'whitewash' may turn out to have been a powerful cleansing agent after all."

Daley's continued placement at the center of the scandal must have been eating away at him, and he let loose the day after Fran Spielman shamed him in her article. Spielman had pointed to his promise in 2006 to apologize, after the special prosecutors' report was released, and his about-face now that Burge was indicted. She quoted a sneering, laughing Daley:

The best way is to say, "Okay. I apologize to everybody for whatever happened to anybody in the city of Chicago." So, I apologize to everybody. Whatever happened to them in the city of Chicago in the past, I apologize. I didn't do it, but somebody else did it. Your editorial was bad. I apologize. Your article about the mayor, I apologize. I need an apology from you because you wrote a bad editorial. . . . But I was not the mayor. I was not the police chief. I did not promote him. You know that. But you've never written that and you're afraid to. I understand.

The negative fallout was immediate, and Daley's press secretary was compelled to rehabilitate his remarks, in a statement to Spielman:

The Mayor's flippant tone Thursday—and Taylor's response—prompted mayoral press secretary Jacquelyn Heard to try to clarify Daley's remarks. "Mayor Daley has, on more than one occasion expressed regret for what were clearly horrific acts and a regrettable time in our city's history," she said. "His remarks today reflect his frustration that those sentiments are routinely lost in the media with certain key points. Namely the fact that it wasn't until he became mayor that Burge was fired."

CHAPTER 30

Exonerations

urge was back in town the next Monday to plead not guilty to the
charges. A crowd of demonstrators gathered outside Dirksen Federal
Courthouse, chanting, "Jon Burge should do time." A fired-up Darrell
Cannon addressed the demonstrators, saying that he couldn't wait "to see
that buzzard face a judge," and I promised, "We will not rest until Burge's
cohorts are indicted as well."

Judge Joan Lefkow's courtroom was only a few floors up from where
Burge had first testified in Andrew Wilson's case, two decades earlier.
The overflow crowd heard Judge Lefkow politely tell Burge "Good morning." One of Burge's lawyers, former assistant state's attorney Rick Bueke,
entered a not-guilty plea on Burge's behalf. The judge set a preliminary
trial date of May 11, 2009, and US marshals whisked Burge out of the
courthouse through a tunnel in order to avoid the demonstrators.

Newsweek had taken notice of Chicago's torture scandal, and Darrell and
I sat down with a reporter to discuss his case. The day after Burge entered
his plea, the *Newsweek* article went up as an exclusive online. The reporter
quoted Darrell: "I felt like I was on fire. I screamed so hard I was hoarse.
The guys who tortured me—it was Burge who trained them." Describing
Darrell as "a soft-spoken man in a brown suit and tie," the article evoked an
appearance we made the Saturday after Burge was arrested: "People stood in
line to shake Darrell's hand, hug him and tell their own stories, some with
tears in their eyes." The reporter also captured the anger that continued
to burn within Darrell, an anger I had unsuccessfully tried to tamp down
when we spoke in public:

> During an interview with NEWSWEEK, Cannon said he still suffers night-
> mares remembering the torture. He said he still harbors "hatred for the
> detectives who tortured me and the judges who covered it up." His lawyer
> asked Cannon if he wanted to reconsider using the word "hatred" in his
> comments with NEWSWEEK. "No," said Cannon quietly, as he shook his

head. "I do feel hatred. I hate the very air that they breathe."

On December 4 the FOP made an announcement: their lily-white board had voted to finance Burge's criminal defense. My reaction was captured in both the *Tribune* and the *Sun Times*: "I think it's outrageous that the FOP is going to spend another million dollars to defend a known torturer after they defended him 15 years ago when he was fired. It continues a sordid and racist history of the FOP of defending police torture in the city." FOP president Mark Donahue claimed that we had fueled a "media hysteria" that "has caused Jon Burge to be the 'poster child' of alleged police torture in this city for an entire generation."

Just in time to meet the January 2009 deadline, Madison Hobley received news that the Feds were no longer investigating him, and he therefore would be receiving the $6.5 million due him under the 2008 settlement agreement. On another front, Stan Willis, Pat Hill, and Black People Against Police Torture scored a major victory. They had been campaigning for a commission that would revisit the cases of those Area 2 torture survivors who were still imprisoned, holding town hall meetings to discuss the issue and transporting busloads of people to Springfield to lobby for legislation that would establish such a commission. Stan had drafted a proposed bill in conjunction with state senator Kwame Raoul, who had sponsored it in the senate. In January it passed the senate, and newly elected governor Pat Quinn would sign it into law later in the year. The bill provided for an eight-person commission, known as the Torture Inquiry and Relief Commission (TIRC), that would accept petitions from Burge-related torture survivors, conduct investigations, and—if a majority of the commission concluded, by a preponderance of evidence, that the petitioner was entitled to judicial review—send the case to a Cook County judge for an evidentiary hearing to determine whether the petitioner's confession was a product of torture or physical abuse. If so, a new trial would follow.

State Senator Raoul spoke out upon the bill's passage:

> The City of Chicago currently faces allegations which undermine the core principles of the Chicago Police Department. Those who have the duty to serve and protect the citizens of Chicago must protect the human rights of those Chicagoans who fall into their custody. The actions of Jon Burge and officers under his command are appalling. It is my hope that this legislation will create a path towards relief for victims that were subject to vicious human rights abuses.

We had turned our attention to the case of Victor Safford, one of the prisoners spared the death penalty by Governor Ryan's clemencies. Victor, arrested under the name Cortez Brown, had converted to Islam, and his case had been taken up by the Nation of Islam. Locke and the PLO had been enlisted to represent Victor on a post-conviction petition, and we assembled our team, which had been joined by a smart and dynamic young lawyer, Sarah Gelsomino.

Judge Clayton Crane set us for a May evidentiary hearing. Victor had been beaten at Area 3 Detective Division, in 1990, into confessing to two separate murders. His interrogators included Detective Maslanka, who was implicated in the torture of Marcus Wiggins. John Byrne was one of the supervising sergeants, and Burge was commander. Several years earlier, when Burge was promoted to commander and subsequently transferred to Area 3, he had been joined by trusted confederates, including Byrne and Maslanka.

Our plan was to submit a wealth of prior torture testimony on paper, to call Victor and two other torture victims live, and also to call these former Area 3 officers as witnesses. Given the ongoing federal investigation, all of them had retreated to invoking the Fifth Amendment. With Burge in Florida, I had to make another visit to "Dirty Harry" to seek his judicial blessing for Burge's return to Chicago. This time Burge's lawyers had not come down to represent him. Burge, who now walked with a cane, told the judge that he was heavily medicated for a back problem and intended to take the Fifth Amendment if returned to Chicago to testify. Becoming animated, he added, "Your Honor, Mr. Taylor has been suing me and members of the Chicago Police Department for over thirty years. My personal feeling is this is strictly for harassment."

"Dirty Harry" opined that he would not require Burge to return to Chicago, despite the fact that Judge Crane had certified him to be a material witness. I packed up my briefcase and opened one of the heavy wooden double doors to leave the empty courtroom. At that instant, Burge opened the other door to come back in, and our eyes met. He said nothing, but I felt a chill down my spine as he pushed past me.

Our presentation went according to plan. Victor testified, and Marcus Wiggins was one of our witnesses. It was the first time I had seen Marcus in almost fifteen years. He was now a sturdy-looking, soft-spoken thirty-one-year-old man. On the stand, Marcus haltingly described how, as a tiny thirteen-year-old, he was tortured with electric shock by Maslanka and gave a statement inculpating himself in a crime he did not commit.

Byrne, just months before, had been all too willing to tell the *Tribune* that he never tortured anyone, but he and his brethren all invoked their Fifth Amendment rights. The attorney general's lawyers presented their case: the two assistant state's attorneys who had taken Victor's statements in 1990 testified that he showed no signs of abuse, did not complain, and, in fact, when asked, said that he was treated well by the detectives.

Judge Crane wasted little time before issuing his ruling. Speaking from the bench, the judge found that while he had some reservations about Victor's credibility, he was swayed by the "staggering" and "damning" evidence that the detectives under Byrne's supervision and Burge's command had similarly tortured other interrogation suspects. He vacated one of Victor's murder convictions and ordered a new trial, without the coerced confession. Judge Crane's ruling, a first of its kind by a Cook County Criminal Court judge in a torture case, set into motion a series of prosecutorial and judicial decisions that resulted in Victor's subsequently gaining his freedom.

On June 25, 2009, I was witness to one of the most emotional events of my then twenty-two years of involvement in the torture struggle. Jonathan Jackson, Reverend Jesse Jackson's son and a moving force in Rainbow/ PUSH, had taken an active interest in the torture cases since Darrell's release two years before. He had arranged for Darrell, Greg Banks, and Anthony Holmes, together with Johnnie Savory, who was wrongfully convicted of murder at the age of fourteen and had spent nearly thirty years in prison, to give a group interview to CNN's Don Lemon. They each related their stories with deep emotion, and Greg burst into tears as Johnnie told of his suffering. Lemon seemed truly moved, and the piece would be groundbreaking. Then Lemon's cell phone rang, and he hastily left without finishing the interviews. Michael Jackson, "The King of Pop," had died, and this remarkable story also died with him.

In early July, more than six years after his bid for a pardon had been rejected by governor George Ryan, Ronald Kitchen, a Burge torture survivor and former death row prisoner, and his co-defendant, Marvin Reeves, were exonerated after a long legal struggle championed by Tom Geraghty and Carolyn Frazier of Northwestern's Bluhm Legal Clinic. The lawyers had uncovered a wealth of evidence favorable to Ronald and Marvin that had been suppressed by the police and prosecutors, in violation of their constitutional rights to due process of law. The attorney general's office agreed to dismiss the cases and, a short time later, awarded the men certificates of innocence.

Ben Elson had succeeded in convincing Joey and me to take on Michael Tillman's case, and we had started compiling a post-conviction petition that raised both torture and innocence. The case against Michael hinged on the fact that he was painting an apartment in the same building where Betty Howard was raped and murdered. He had allegedly made some inculpatory oral statements under torture, and a hair that supposedly bore similarities to Michael's was found in Betty Howard's bathroom. Michael's original co-defendant, Steven Bell, had been assisting Michael with the painting. Subsequently, items taken from Howard's apartment were traced to a third man, unconnected to Michael and Steven, and the third man's fingerprint was found at the murder scene. Rather than admitting a mistake and releasing Tillman and Bell, the prosecutors charged the man as a third participant.

The case was assigned to Cook County judge Kenneth Gillis, a Republican with a reputation for fairness. Both Michael and Steven had moved to suppress their confessions because the statements were tortured and beaten out of them by Dignan, Byrne, and their fellow midnight "asskickers." The hearing was held in November 1986, more than two years before evidence of systemic torture had begun to emerge in Andrew Wilson's case. It was a "heater" case, and, in the absence of corroborating evidence of torture, Judge Gillis was not prepared to acknowledge that Michael and Steven were believable and that the Area 2 cabal was lying. He denied their motions and permitted the evidence to be admitted. Michael and Bell then waived their right to jury trials and instead agreed for Judge Gillis to decide their fate.

After hearing the evidence, Gillis rendered a split verdict. He acquitted Steven Bell on the basis of his documented alibi. Unfortunately, Michael's alibi put him in the building where the crime took place, so Gillis found him guilty as charged. He spared Michael the death penalty, sentencing him instead to natural life plus forty-five years. On appeal, his case was reversed, but at retrial he was not allowed to challenge his confession on the basis of the newly uncovered evidence of systemic torture, and he was again convicted, this time by a jury. The appellate court upheld Michael's conviction in 1999. Without funds to hire a lawyer, Michael had not filed a post-conviction petition within the applicable time limits. Several other lawyers had subsequently looked at his case, but had been stymied by these procedural hurdles.

Undeterred, we filed our petition for post-conviction relief on July 21, 2009. Our facts were compelling: Byrne, Dignan, and the midnight crew were at the center of the torture; Burge's fingerprints were all over the case as the lieutenant in charge; there was virtually no evidence against Michael except for his tortured admissions; and there was a compelling alternative suspect, unconnected to Michael, who was linked to the crime by physical and fingerprint evidence and had recently been implicated in an earlier rape and murder through DNA tests. We argued that fundamental fairness, newly discovered evidence, the fraudulent concealment of evidence, and Michael's obvious innocence required that the procedural hurdles be relaxed so that Michael could have a just determination of his claims of torture and innocence. In summary, we concluded:

> While the evidence of systemic torture and abuse by Burge, Byrne, and their men continues to emerge, and court and administrative findings and decisions continue to mount, Petitioner and others like him, who have claimed for years that their convictions rest on tortured evidence, remain in prison. The travesty of justice in Petitioner's individual case must be corrected.

Michael's petition, crafted by Ben, Sarah, Joey, Locke, and me, was to be heard by judge Vincent Gaughan, who was known to be a wild card. We had no idea what to expect.

Burge's prosecution was moving slowly ahead. Jeff Kramer had left the US attorney's office shortly after Burge's indictment was announced and had been replaced by David Weisman, an excellent prosecutor who had previously been a straight-shooting FBI agent. When Kramer told me he was leaving, he made a sobering prediction—that the US attorney's office was exclusively focused on the "big fish," Jon Burge, and that I should not expect prosecutions of his underlings.

In October, a year after Burge had been charged, his lawyers asked Judge Lefkow for another continuance of his trial date. In private they told the judge that Burge was suffering from prostate cancer that required surgery. I expressed a healthy skepticism that was shared by many, telling the Sun Times, "It makes one wonder if their motivation is to avoid trial altogether and never give the victims of torture a day in court." In response, one of Burge's lawyers dismissed my suggestion, saying "Flint Taylor doesn't know what he's talking about in this particular matter." Judge Lefkow, in deference to Burge's medical problems, continued the trial to April 2010.

We now had a new adversary in Michael Tillman's case. State's attorney Anita Alvarez and attorney general Lisa Madigan tried to pull a fast one by requesting that Chief Judge Biebel return the adjudication of the torture cases to the state's attorneys' office, six years after Biebel had disqualified Devine's office on the basis of conflict of interest. Joey, Locke, and I opposed the AG's motion, and Judge Biebel found that Devine's conflict continued to infect the SAO even though Devine himself had retired. This time, Judge Biebel appointed former judge Stuart Nudelman as a special prosecutor. Nudelman had been a public defender before he took the bench, and was thought to be relatively sympathetic to the rights of criminal defendants. As his staff, he had tapped several young lawyers.

Nudelman's appointment paid immediate dividends in Michael's case. Instead of reactively opposing our petition, the special prosecutor team closely examined our evidence and took our claims of torture and innocence seriously. Just before the Christmas holidays, they agreed not only that they would forego arguing that the petition was untimely, but also that they would not oppose the granting of the motion. After some back and forth, the special prosecutors filed a remarkable statement of facts and legal conclusions that supported granting our petition and awarding Michael a new trial. The special prosecutors' statement included admissions that we would be able to "produce uncontrovertible evidence to show the deprivation of [Michael's] constitutional rights" and that "findings of a pattern and practice of abuse at Area 2" was "of such conclusive character that it would probably change the result on re-trial."

Judge Gaughan granted our petition, and the special prosecutors, accompanied by former judge Nudelman, dismissed Michael Tillman's case. Betty Howard's daughter was present at the hearing, and, after the dismissal, she left the court sobbing, "They let him go." Michael and I attempted to offer our condolences, but her boyfriend, in a reference to Michael's torture, told a reporter, "I would have done more than that to him."

It was twenty-three and a half years since Michael had been a free man, so a few hours later we celebrated at a west side restaurant with his mother, Winter, and his sister, Elizabeth. The exoneration was big news, with Michael and me smiling broadly on the front page of the *Tribune* under a banner headline that proclaimed, "ALLEGED POLICE TORTURE VICTIM GOES FREE." Channel 7 reporter Ben Bradley recorded Michael's joyous walk to freedom and his reunion with his mother and sister. Bradley reported, correctly, "Those who handle these wrongful conviction cases say it was the first time anyone affiliated with the Cook County state's attorney's office has ever admitted in open court that there was systematic torture of suspects by Chicago police officers."

The next month Michael was granted a certificate of innocence. The path was now clear for Michael and Ronald Kitchen to sue everyone from Burge to Daley for their torture, wrongful convictions, and decades in prison.

CHAPTER 31

Burge in the Dock

The Burge trial had been continued once more, this time to late May 2010. The prosecution's trial team—Betsy Biffl, David Weisman, and April Perry—reached out to us to locate Melvin Jones as they made final trial preparations. After we had found him close to death in 2008, Melvin had lived with his sister, who had helped nurse him back to relative stability until he suffered an aneurysm a year later. He had returned to the streets, where Ben and I found him, homeless, but he was game for yet another trip to the witness stand.

Judge Lefkow had issued several important pretrial decisions that favored the prosecution. In the first she ruled that Andrew Wilson's prior testimony, although legally hearsay, could be read to the jury because he had been subjected to extensive cross-examination by Burge's lawyers at the time. Subsequently the judge ruled that the same legal rationale did not apply to two of Burge's key witnesses, also deceased—detectives John Yucaitis and Patrick O'Hara—because the government did not have the opportunity to cross-examine them, and because the testimony was not sufficiently trustworthy.

A few weeks before jury selection was to begin, the *Sun Times* ran a front-page article revealing that the government was bringing new police witnesses before the grand jury as part of their investigation into several of Burge's confederates. The story received significant follow-up coverage, including an interview with me, and Burge's counsel seized on the publicity to move, once again, to transfer the trial out of Chicago, alleging that the People's Law Office was in effect part of the prosecution's team. They compounded this attack by subpoenaing me for our financial settlement documents for the past twenty years, purportedly to use in arguing that the survivors and their lawyers had fabricated the torture claims to make money. The judge denied the change of venue motion and, after Michael Deutsch and I appeared in court, quashed the subpoena.

Jury selection began on May 24, 2010, and the media was in high gear. Carol Marin was covering both for the *Sun Times* and Channel 5. John Conroy had been contracted by the local public radio station to attend the trial and write a daily blog, and I would make frequent on-air reports to Cliff Kelly, the "governor of talk radio," with a wide listenership among Chicago's Black community. Amy Goodman previewed the trial on *Democracy Now!*; in dialogue with her, I put the case in a national perspective, calling out the failures of the Obama administration to address torture under the previous regime:

> We sit here in Chicago actually prosecuting a torturer. That hasn't happened nationally. The administration hasn't seen fit to even give serious investigation to people like Dick Cheney and Karl Rove and those who tortured across the world in our name. And in the same way that the conscience of this country cannot be cleansed without proper prosecutions of those who approved and participated in torture in Guantánamo and Abu Ghraib and places like that, the conscience of the city of Chicago cannot be cleansed until there's a complete dealing with all of the issues of torture, starting with the mayor, on all the way down, and starting with the men behind bars and starting with all the men that need to be prosecuted. . . . What we're dealing with here is a microcosm of what's going on and isn't going on nationally, in terms of prosecutions, in terms of restorative justice, in terms of dealing with the victims and the survivors of torture, and compelling the court system and the powers that be to deal responsibly and thoroughly and in a just manner with the whole scope of torture as an issue, both nationally and locally.

Jury selection was fascinating. The government was awarded six peremptory challenges, while Burge's team was given ten. Individual voir dire of each juror, outside the presence of the other panel members, was conducted by the judge. John Conroy described the voir dire in a blog post:

> It was striking how little some knew about the accusations. The first potential juror questioned said she'd first heard of the charges "about a year ago" and thought Burge had been accused of torturing two suspects. An attractive middle-aged white woman said she thought the case involved "stuff that happened in the 1970s." Others, however, said they knew quite a bit. One African-American minced no words, saying she'd been reading about it for years and had heard a broadcast of a man talking about "his balls being squeezed." (The judge excused her shortly thereafter.) The woman who thought the case involved 1970s cases came across initially as a fairly neutral juror. Then in response to a question from Judge Joan Lefkow about police officers she

indicated that she thought there was a racial aspect in law enforcement. Her husband, she said, was a polite, respectful, well-educated black man, but if he was driving with a taillight out he would get a traffic ticket no matter what he said, while if she was driving the same car she wouldn't.

After two days, both sides exercised their peremptory challenges. Of the remaining venire, nine were African American: six potential jurors and three potential alternates. Burge's lawyers exercised seven of their challenges to excuse all the Black potential jurors and one of the three potential alternates. The government challenged these strikes as racially discriminatory, and after Burge's counsel offered their allegedly nondiscriminatory reasons, the government continued to contest the challenges to one of the Black potential jurors and one Black potential alternate. Judge Lefkow, in a carefully considered decision, found the reasons given by Burge's counsel to be pretextual and granted the government's challenges. Hence, the twelve-person jury included one African American juror and one Hispanic juror, a man who had unsuccessfully applied to become a Chicago police officer.

Betsy Biffl, in the government's opening statement, calmly asserted that Area 2 "had a dirty little secret. Hear no evil, see no evil, speak no evil could have been the motto of Area 2." She was thorough and persuasive as she laid out the government's evidence, revealing that Michael McDermott would testify under a grant of immunity regarding one of the five torture incidents upon which the government had chosen to rest its proof, and concluding that this evidence established beyond a reasonable doubt that Burge was guilty of perjury and obstruction of justice. While we were not part of the prosecution's team, it was clear that the government's case was built in large part on evidence we had developed over the past twenty years.

Former Cook County assistant state's attorney William Gamboney argued for defendant Burge. Demonstrating that the defense's pursuit of a jury devoid of African Americans was part of a broader strategy, Gamboney stridently appealed to law and order, emphasizing the criminal backgrounds and alleged gang affiliations of several of the survivor witnesses, whom, he said, he was "certain" the jury was "not going to like." Dodging frequent sustained government objections, he emphasized that Burge was a decorated Vietnam veteran, that Burge had risen quickly through department ranks due to "efficient, legal, hard, and often heroic work," and that Burge "did not torture anybody." In a preview of things to come, Burge wiped away a tear during Gamboney's histrionic presentation.

Anthony Holmes was the government's first witness. Although exhausted from sleepless nights anticipating his first face-to-face confrontation with the man who, thirty-eight years before, sent what felt like "a thousand needles" coursing through his body, Anthony withstood a withering cross-examination by Rick Bueke. The attack-dog approach taken by Bueke and his co-counsel was more suited for a prosecutor in the rough-and-tumble Cook County courts; it seemed decidedly out of place in a federal courtroom, presided over by a calm and collected judge who almost always firmly sustained the government's objections when Bueke and company repeatedly crossed the line.

One of the next witnesses was Anthony's lawyer back in 1973, the now powerful county commissioner Larry Suffredin. Rob Warden had put me in touch with Larry two years earlier. Larry had recounted to me that Anthony, whom he described as very believable, had told him about his torture shortly after it had occurred. I had passed Larry on to the Feds, and his trial testimony corroborated Anthony's.

Melvin Jones was the next survivor to take the stand. He was definitely showing the physical and mental wear-and-tear of his illnesses and alcoholism, and he spoke slowly. Melvin repeated his harrowing testimony, including how Burge threatened to "blow [his] Black brains out" and that he would have him crawling on the floor "like Satan and Cochise." Melvin's lawyer at the time, Cassandra Watson, followed. She was as reluctant now as she had been twenty years earlier, and this made her testimony even more believable. Remarkably, the defense did not bring out that she was a former Black Panther before she became a lawyer.

When court resumed the next week, portions of Andrew Wilson's direct and cross-examinations from his civil rights trials and the police board proceedings were read from the stand by a young white FBI agent. This testimony ranged from his descriptions of his torture to his invocation of the Fifth Amendment when asked questions relevant to the killings of officers Fahey and O'Brien. The government bolstered Andrew's testimony with several live witnesses who had previously testified to Andrew's injuries at our trials and before the police board. Dale Coventry, Andrew's long-ago public defender, identified the photos of Andrew's injuries, including the marks on his ears, and the government introduced these powerful photos into evidence through Coventry's testimony. The government also called the emergency room nurse who, along with an emergency room doctor, had attempted to treat Andrew at the hospital, only to be thwarted by Mulvaney, one of the wagon men, who was pointing his gun at the floor and "advising" Andrew to refuse treatment.

The government also called Dr. Raba. An extremely credible witness, Raba told the jury of being called to the jail by a doctor who was disturbed by Andrew's "unique" injuries. He described examining Andrew with a flashlight in his jail cell, seeing unmistakable evidence of burns, and hearing Andrew describe being electric-shocked. He said he was so distressed by his examination that he wrote a letter to Superintendent Brzeczek, detailing what he saw and heard, and demanding a complete investigation. He was not permitted to testify that Brzeczek sent his letter to Daley, but he did say that soon after he sent the letter, he received a call from the very powerful chairman of the Cook County Board, George Dunne, advising him not to get involved.

The government then called Doris Byrd and Sammy Lacey to the stand. From these African American former detectives, the jury learned that there was an "A-Team," which included several of Burge's accomplices, including Byrne and Dignan; that the A-Team worked the midnight shift; that they obtained confessions at a much higher rate than other detectives; and that Lacey had heard screams coming from Area 2 while Andrew was being held there and saw "footprints" on the clothes of Gregory Banks after the A-Team had interrogated him.

Diane Panos told the jury about her barroom conversation with Burge, minus his vulgar sexual harassment, which the judge had barred. The government had located the sister of one of Burge's girlfriends, Darlene Lopez, who had partied on Burge's boat on several occasions. She produced photos of her and her sister on the boat, and told the jury of Burge's boastful talk about one suspect being locked in the trunk of a car and about another who was beaten with a baseball bat while handcuffed.

The government next presented the fourth torture case, and our fourth client-witness, Gregory Banks. In October 1983, Gregory was arrested for murder and taken to Area 2 by Burge and two detectives under his command. He testified that Byrne and Dignan, after pointing a gun at his head and saying that they had "something special for niggers," put a bag over his head, then beat him on the body while his air supply was cut off. He also testified that although Burge did not participate in the torture, he looked into the room on two occasions. Greg, who became emotional when he talked about his torture, had a difficult time on cross-examination. He started to become upset when pressed about his previous drug habit, his prior street gang membership, and his criminal record for burglaries. At one point he refused to answer further questions about his signed, court-reported statement, until ordered to do so by the judge.

Joey and I felt terrible for Greg personally, and about his testimony. Fortunately, the government was able to substantially rehabilitate his testimony when it called as its next witnesses the defense lawyer to whom Greg had reported his torture at the time, and the doctor who had treated Greg at the jail. The doctor testified that he found Greg's injuries consistent with his being beaten and inconsistent with the defense's theory—that he had received the injuries falling down a flight of stairs.

The government chose to end its case with the 1985 torture of Shadeed Mu'min. While Shadeed was a convicted armed robber, he had no gang affiliation, did not know any of the other victim-witnesses, and, even more significantly, the government had Michael McDermott's testimony. However, when brought before the judge a few weeks before the trial for reimmunization, McDermott had publicly stated outside the courtroom that he thought Burge should not be prosecuted at this late date, and his lawyer hinted that McDermott might try to minimize the harm he could do to his former boss. Soon after assistant US attorney April Perry started McDermott's direct examination, it became obvious that McDermott, quickly declared a hostile witness on the government's motion, was going to attempt to walk a tightrope between an outright repudiation of his grand jury testimony and the almost certain perjury charge that would follow, and the damning grand jury testimony itself.

On direct examination, McDermott volunteered a tale of alleged intimidation at the grand jury by US Attorney Fitzgerald, who, he said, appeared as he was about to enter the grand jury room and whispered to him that if he did not tell the whole truth, he could be indicted not only for perjury but also for obstruction of justice. McDermott professed a concern for his family and a fear that he would lose his current job with the state's attorney's office, and his police pension, if he did not testify against Burge. Asserting that he had thought long and hard since his grand jury testimony, he said that Burge briefly pointed his gun in Shadeed's direction; that he saw what he now termed a twenty-second "scuffle" between Burge and Shadeed; that Burge put a piece of plastic in front of Shadeed's face, rather than over his head; that Shadeed did not appear to be intimidated or have his breathing cut off; that he was only "guessing" when he said that Burge was seeking to coerce a confession; and that Burge could have been using the plastic because Shadeed might have been spitting or holding drugs in his mouth. McDermott said, now, that Burge's conduct was "inappropriate" rather than abusive, and it was for the jury to decide whether it was a crime or not. "We're tussling with people every week," McDermott said. "You don't understand. This is nothing." Perry aggressively and repeatedly impeached McDermott with his grand jury testimony; in response he most often said either that he had "misspoken" or that he was only "guessing" when he had testified more affirmatively.

For the first part of his cross-examination, Rick Bueke treated McDermott as if he were Burge's own witness, bringing out what a dedicated and conscientious boss Burge was, that McDermott respected him, and how crime-infested and gang-dominated the far south side of Chicago was in the 1980s. In an ironic twist, Bueke's questioning even brought out, in violation of an agreed *in limine* order, that Burge had been terminated from the force. Bueke then shifted gears, attacking McDermott's credibility, bringing out that McDermott had admitted to the grand jury that he had pushed Alfonzo Pinex and had lied about it under oath at Alfonzo's motion to suppress hearing, as well as having denied witnessing any abuse of Shadeed Mu'min when he gave a statement to the OPS in 1993.

On redirect examination, Perry again impeached McDermott with additional grand jury testimony that bolstered the version of events he had told there, and further put the lie to his transparent attempt to repudiate it. When McDermott attempted to chastise the government for waiting twenty years to prosecute Burge, Perry asked, "Sir, isn't it true the reason that these cases were not brought earlier is because people like you did not come forward earlier?"

Perry also turned the tables on McDermott's claim of fear and intimidation:

Perry: Now, you testified on cross-examination regarding what you say Pat Fitzgerald told you before the grand jury, is that correct?
McDermott: Yes.
Perry: And during that incident, even as you recount it, Pat Fitzgerald didn't use any bad language with you, did he?
McDermott: No.
Perry: He didn't scream at you, did he?
McDermott: No.
Perry: He didn't physically touch you in any way, did he?
McDermott: No.
Perry: He certainly didn't point a gun in your direction, did he?

McDermott: That's correct.

Perry: He certainly didn't put a bag over your head, did he, sir?

McDermott: That's correct.

Perry: He didn't make you feel in any way that you were going to be physically assaulted, is that correct?

McDermott: It was worse, he was threatening my family.

Perry: Sir, he was threatening your family by telling you that you had to tell the truth?

Since the beginning of June, the Burge trial had been playing second fiddle to the sensational corruption trial of former Illinois governor Rod Blagojevich, but McDermott's testimony returned it to the front page and the top of the TV news. On Channel 5, I told Carol Marin, "What you saw today was the code of silence back at work." I suggested that McDermott was trying to protect himself while not hurting Burge, but had failed at both, and that "his words under oath to the grand jury belied how he tried to reinterpret them today."

Privately, we were much less sure of how McDermott's testimony had played with the jury. *Sun Times* columnist Marc Brown captured the nervousness we all felt:

> I can't say just how much harm McDermott did to the prosecution's overall case, but if anyone on the jury was hoping for a white knight police officer to step up and provide the eyewitness testimony that would tie together the rest of the evidence from less credible sources, well, that just didn't happen. Either way, though, he came across as someone for whom the truth is a moving object depending on what his audience wants to hear and what best suits his current purposes. And in that situation, juries often choose to nullify whatever that witness has to say.

Shadeed Mu'min, now sixty-six years old and living in Ohio, then took the stand. He testified that Burge, who was seeking a confession, removed his .44 Magnum revolver from a drawer, placed it at Shadeed's head on several occasions, and simulated Russian roulette. He testified that Burge placed a plastic typewriter cover over his face on three occasions, cutting off his air supply and causing him to pass out. He also described the actions of a Burge "associate," who, he said, assisted Burge by holding him down, and who may have been McDermott.

Shadeed remained calm, even dispassionate, during his cross-examination, and his story was corroborated by the introduction of records—initially produced to us well after Shadeed had first identified Burge's unusual police weapon—documenting that Burge had registered a .44 Magnum revolver with the secretary of state prior to Shadeed's torture.

The government then rested its case, having put on the stand more than thirty witnesses. The defense moved for a judgment of acquittal. Not surprisingly, Judge Lefkow denied the motion, so it was on to the defense's case.

Burge's original witness list included mayor Richard M. Daley, presumably to recount why he had not prosecuted Burge twenty-eight years before, but it had become obvious that Daley was not going to testify. During the government's case, former police superintendent LeRoy Martin, nine of Burge's listed police witnesses, and former assistant state's attorney Larry Hyman had all appeared before Judge Lefkow to inform her that they intended to invoke the Fifth Amendment if Burge's lawyers called them to the stand. Burge's counsel challenged their right to do so; the government informed the court of the status of its ongoing investigation, and Judge Lefkow conducted closed-door proceedings with the witnesses and their attorneys.

She then ruled that the vulnerability of Hyman and the police witnesses to indictment for perjury, obstruction of justice, and a third undisclosed offense was not "fanciful," and that they were therefore entitled to assert the Fifth, but did not decide Superintendent Martin's claim because the defense informed her that he would be called only if the government were to present certain witnesses. Curiously, Byrne and Dignan, both of whom had been directly named by Greg Banks and had been regular attendees at the trial, were not on Burge's list of witnesses.

As a result, Burge's lawyers presented the testimony of none of the fifteen white officers most directly involved in the five torture cases presented by the government. Instead, his defense called the assistant state's attorneys involved in taking the statements from Anthony Holmes, Gregory Banks, and Shadeed Mu'min; the state's attorney's court reporter who transcribed Andrew Wilson's statement; and an assistant state's attorney present at Area 2 during part of the day while Andrew was being tortured. Their testimony unintentionally reaffirmed that the systemic torture could not have continued without the cooperation and silence of the Cook County state's attorney's office.

All these witnesses conceded that they worked with the police. The court reporter, Michael Hartnett, admitted on cross-examination that he had told the grand jury that he "didn't give a damn" about Andrew and that he was "surprised to see him alive." Hartnett also admitted that he sometimes took statements from bloody suspects and asserted that it wasn't his job to do anything about it. Additionally, he conceded that it was standard procedure to include questions concerning voluntariness in the court-reported statement, but there were no such questions and answers in the confessions of Andrew Wilson and his brother Jackie.

While the defense had consistently played up the fact that several sergeants and commanders at Area 2 were Black, it ended up calling only one Black officer to the stand, an elderly former sergeant, who testified that he caught a glimpse of Andrew at Area 2 and that he did not look injured. Unfortunately for Burge, the former sergeant also described him as a "hands-on" detective-supervisor. Surprisingly, the defense brought out, through one of Egan's and Boyle's assistants, that the special prosecutor's office had investigated Burge for torture allegations for several years and had conducted hundreds of interviews. However, the government lawyers did not seize the opportunity to argue that the defense had opened the door to a subject that had been previously barred, which might have permitted them to introduce the findings of the special prosecutor—particularly that Burge had abused Andrew and obstructed justice beyond a reasonable doubt.

One of the more surprising defense witnesses was Dr. Michael Baden, a preeminent forensic pathologist with an impressive resume that featured the investigation and analysis of injuries and deaths of prisoners. Baden was serving as an expert witness for us in an unrelated wrongful conviction case. He was ferried to and from the courtroom by John Byrne, who was acting as Burge's gofer. Baden contested the treating diagnoses of Dr. Raba and the emergency room nurse that the marks on Andrew's face and chest were burns, and the opinions of Dr. Kirschner that the burns on Andrew's chest, face, and leg were consistent with the ribs of the steam radiator and the mark on one of Andrew's ears was a spark burn mark. Dr. Baden also asserted that if Andrew had been shocked, he would expect to see evidence of burning at the shocking points. He concluded that the facial injuries were not burns and had been suffered by Andrew prior to his arrest, and he also doubted that the leg burn had been inflicted during the interrogation.

Betsy Biffl conducted a very effective cross-examination, raising some jurors' eyebrows when she brought out that Baden was paid $27,000 for about fifty hours of work, viewing photos and reading testimony. She contrasted the viewing of photos nearly thirty years after the fact with the diagnoses of a treating nurse and doctor, impeached Baden with a prior admission from Burge that he saw no injuries on Andrew's face and chest when Andrew was arrested, and brought out more details from Dr. Kirschner's prior opinion. She also emphasized Baden's grudging admissions that the leg injury was a burn, and that the marks on the ears were puncture injuries consistent with alligator clips; brought out that there was also a puncture wound on Andrew's nose; and raised questions about the basis of Baden's opinions concerning electrical burns.

Directly after Dr. Baden's testimony, the defense announced that it intended to call Burge the next morning. Judge Lefkow called Burge to the bench, admonished him that he was not required to testify, and inquired as to how he was holding up. "Marvelously," Burge replied sarcastically.

The courtroom was packed to overflow the next morning. Among the spectators was US Attorney Fitzgerald. Burge's testimony was limited by orders obtained by both sides: on direct examination, the defense was permitted to put on only limited evidence concerning Burge's decorated background, including his awards as a military police sergeant while serving in Vietnam, thereby precluding the government's going into the area of his gaining knowledge of electric-shock torture while serving there.

Attorney Marc Martin led Burge through his background. Burge brazenly testified that he had "retired" in 1997 rather than that he was fired. He then recounted, in vivid detail, his version of each of the five cases in which he was accused of torture. He described Anthony Holmes as a physically imposing former prison "barn boss" and a leader in a pursued robbery gang, then told how he and Yucaitis convinced Anthony, in less than an hour, to admit voluntarily to a murder and to knowledge of a string of armed robberies, and to name a host of participants in the robberies, by using what Superintendent Brzeczek later described in a commendation as "skillful interrogation." According to Burge, his only contact with Melvin Jones was when he entered the interrogation room to tell him that they would bring him to justice if it took "a year or ten years."

Burge's testimony then turned to Andrew Wilson's case. As he described his role in leading the small army of detectives assigned to investigate the police murders, how he worked around the clock for five days on the investigation and manhunt, and how he led a team of officers to make Andrew's pre-dawn arrest, Burge appeared to break down in tears, saying this was "very much" an emotional topic for him. I was not convinced, remembering that Burge had testified extensively about Andrew's case in five separate proceedings between 1982 and 2004 without so much as a sniffle. Burge testified that he told the officers transporting Andrew back to Area 2 to handle him with "kid gloves," then never entered the room where Andrew was being held for the entire fourteen hours that Andrew was in his custody.

Burge denied any involvement in the interrogation of Gregory Banks, and attention then turned to McDermott and Shadeed Mu'min. Burge testified that when McDermott brought Shadeed into his office, he took his revolver, which he admitted was a .44 Magnum, out of its holster and locked it in his desk drawer. He denied that he had a plastic object in his hand or placed it on or over Shadeed's face. Next, he admitted that Darlene Lopez had been on his boat but denied making any admissions to her. He claimed no specific recollection of Diane Panos but asserted that he would not have mentioned the *Wilson* case to her, as he was being sued by Andrew for $10 million at the time she testified he made the admission.

David Weisman cross-examined Burge. Normally calm and collected, he flashed with anger and passion as he challenged and impeached Burge's presentation. Weisman highlighted the implausibility that Burge, the "hands-on" supervisor who often monitored interrogations from the doorway and who had purportedly found it necessary to tell his detectives to handle Andrew with "kid gloves," never entered Andrew's interview room or observed his interrogation—despite the fact that the investigation was the most important of Burge's career. When confronted with McDermott's testimony concerning the plastic, Burge volunteered that McDermott looked "terribly distraught and under great pressure at the time he testified." Weisman shot back, "That's because there's a big code of silence within the Chicago Police Department, isn't there?" Burge, flustered, denied knowledge of a code, and, in an obvious reference to the public statement I had made a few days before, stated that he had only heard of the code "from a bottom-feeding lawyer."

The government seized on Burge's answers regarding the code of silence as well as firearm maintenance, arguing that Weisman should now be permitted to confront Burge with Doris Byrd's testimony, previously barred, that Burge had pointed a gun at Frank Laverty's back and said, "Bang." When court resumed on Monday morning, the court permitted Weisman to inquire about the incident, which Burge predictably denied. Weisman proceded to focus on a statement Burge had volunteered on cross-examination the previous week—that he "lied to suspects all the time"—to make Burge squirm. Burge first denied having made the statement, then, when confronted with his prior testimony, tried, with little success, to explain it away. Weisman then brought out that Burge had named his boat the *Vigilante.* According to Burge this was not because he prided himself on taking the law into his own hands, as Weisman suggested, but rather, as Burge claimed on redirect examination, because it was the only name on a computer-generated list he had not heard of previously. Weisman closed his examination with a series of questions, obviously intended to describe Burge himself:

> Weisman: In your experience, sophisticated criminals are sometimes diffi-
> cult to catch, isn't that true?
> Burge: I never met a sophisticated criminal.
> Weisman: Well, sir, you would agree with me that sometimes it takes a long
> time to bring a criminal to justice, wouldn't you?
> Burge: Sometimes it takes a long time to find them. Sometimes it takes a
> long time to develop enough evidence to bring them to the bar of justice, yes.
> Weisman: No further questions.

Due to the limitations imposed by both parties and by the judge, and the tactical and strategic decisions made by the government, Burge was not confronted with the following: any of the 105 other documented cases of torture of Black suspects that he allegedly either supervised or participated in; the reign of terror in the Black community that he commanded during the manhunt for the Wilson brothers; the fact that Jackie Wilson had also been abused at Area 2 the same morning that Andrew had been tortured; the racial epithets that so frequently accompanied Burge's torture; racial and sexual comments he made and actions he took, outside the five torture cases presented; the connection between his service in Vietnam and torture; the fact that Burge was fired rather than "retired"; and the finding by the special prosecutor, beyond a reasonable doubt, that Burge had tortured Andrew Wilson. Nonetheless, the image of a courageous and intelligent law enforcement officer with an almost photographic memory, as projected by the self-assured Burge on direct examination, was thrown into serious question by Weisman's cross-examination. By the time Burge had completed his testimony, the central question as to whether he was a liar, both on the stand and in his interrogatory answers, stood in bold relief.

The next witness called by the defense was jailhouse snitch Ricky Shaw. In keeping with the court's prior orders, Shaw's testimony was limited to any alleged involvement of the five victims in a purported plan to fabricate torture claims. Shaw, clad in an orange prison jumpsuit, told of a plan, supposedly hatched in prison—long after all the victims who testified in the case had already reported their torture—to fabricate abuse claims against Burge and other Area 2 detectives. Specifically, Shaw testified that he had been told of the plan by Melvin Jones, who had confided in him even though they were members of rival gangs. Shaw said that Jones told him that "he had lawyers and everybody trying to get on the case and there were others who were dying to get on it and that there were movie deals and book deals," as well as a civil suit. Shaw's cross-examination revealed a long history of supplying false and fabricated stories to law enforcement authorities, and the fact that when he first reported this alleged plan to authorities in 1992, he never mentioned Melvin Jones.

In his blog, John Conroy dissected the highly suspect testimony:

> Melvin Jones is featured in no movie, no book exists with Melvin as the hero, and when the two alleged prison pals got to talking in 1987, Jones couldn't have filed a civil suit if he'd wanted to—the statute of limitations had expired. (Jones, who is now homeless, has never sued anyone for the torture. When he testified earlier in this trial he said he'd didn't know a Ricky Shaw.) Flint Taylor, a founder of the People's Law Office, which represented cop killer Andrew Wilson in his 1989 civil suit against Burge and the city, said in an interview last night that not only was Jones no cause célèbre, he was a complete unknown. "In 1989, we thought the only torture case was Andrew Wilson," Taylor said. "We probably still wouldn't know about Melvin Jones if it weren't for the anonymous cop."

A few days later, we filed into the packed courtroom for closing arguments. Weisman gave the government's opening closing. He began by telling the jury that the case was about more than just perjury and obstruction of justice, that it was about the use of electric shock, suffocations, mock executions, and radiator burning on five suspects over a twelve-year period from 1973 until 1985. Weisman took the jury through each of the five cases, arguing that the torture did not stop because Burge was "above the law"; that he "lied about what happened then" and "is lying now"; and that "he never envisioned these four weeks when his conduct would be exposed in its full brutality." According to Conroy, Weisman was like "a guided missile, politely boring in."

Rick Bueke closed for the defense. Although the defense had been barred from arguing jury nullification—whereupon members of a jury disregard either the evidence presented or the instructions of the judge, in order to reach a verdict based upon their own consciences—or that it was permissible for Burge to torture because the US government had tortured in Abu Ghraib and Guantánamo, Bueke's argument, which occasioned a large number of sustained objections, was clearly designed to suggest those propositions; to racially inflame the predominantly white jury; and to wrap Burge in the mantle of effective and necessary law enforcement. Ignoring the "reasonable doubt" standard that most defense lawyers emphasize in their closing arguments, Bueke stressed the purported conspiracy among the victims, as assisted by our office, and intoned that Andrew Wilson, whom he called "Mr. Wonderful," was "somewhere in the darkest, dingiest corner of hell, laughing hysterically at how he has manipulated this system." In 1973, Bueke asserted, Anthony Holmes's "calling was to turn the street into a crime-infested, drug-infested, gun-infested cesspool." Bueke mocked the torture survivors as "poor, poor victims." Shadeed Mu'min was a "rat" and "a psychopathic armed robber trying to play the system," and Gregory Banks was "a serial burglar," a "pathological liar," and an "addict." Bueke's venom reached a peak when he said that representing Burge was the highlight of his legal career. Of Burge and his asskickers, Bueke argued:

> They were honorable true heroes. They were the only people that the south side of the city had to stand for them in the face of the Anthony Holmes of the world, and especially the Andrew Wilsons of the world. . . . Evil still lurks, these monsters are all over the south side, they are all out there just like they were then.

Putting his arm on Burge's shoulder, he concluded, "I don't know if that will ever change, but I do know that people would be better off if this gentleman was still there."

April Perry, who had earned her trial chops when she aggressively handled McDermott's attempt to repudiate his grand jury testimony, gave the government's rebuttal. She came out swinging. "They can get up there and scream and curse all they want and talk about who is and who is not going to hell . . . but it is not evidence," Perry argued. Addressing the victims' numerous convictions, she argued, "So what? What does that have to do with this case?" Instead, she said, the case was about what happened to the victims. How was it, she asked, that of all their crimes, they all independently chose one case in which to assert they were tortured, and that one case, for each victim, involved Burge. She deconstructed Bueke's claim that the five victims had engaged in a decades-long conspiracy and told the jury that it was not for them to decide whether the victims were bad people. "We did not pick these victims. The defendant picked them. He believed no one would ever believe their word against his." Perry closed by urging the jury not to stand by, as other "good men" had done for decades while the torture continued. "You have seen the evil, you have heard the evil, and now we ask you to speak the truth," she concluded.

We all headed to the elevators afterward. I had another chance encounter with Burge, who mouthed "Fuck you" to me as the elevator doors closed. Burge then retired to Cavanaugh's, across the street from the courthouse, to await the jury's verdict. Sitting alone, next to an open sidewalk window, belting down vodka, Burge spotted a former prosecutor who was friends with Michael McDermott and had made Burge's acquaintance while attending the trial. Burge called the former prosecutor over and asked him whether he thought the jury would "believe that bunch of niggers."

CHAPTER 32

A Modicum of Justice

It was a nerve-wracking weekend as the jury deliberated. The Sunday *New York Times* ran an article that called Burge an "effective witness." It did put the upcoming verdict in perspective, quoting Francine Sanders, the OPS investigator who recommended that Burge be fired twenty years earlier, as saying, "No matter which way the verdict goes, there's no happy ending here for anyone. This case is not about Jon Burge. It's about a system, a culture, a sickness in human nature that allows things like this to happen."

The word came on Monday, June 28, 2010, at about 3:00 p.m. that the jury had reached its verdict. Apprehensive as we headed downtown, we were a few minutes late and were standing outside the courtroom in a long line when the jury filed into the jury box. The courtroom hushed as the verdict was read: guilty on all three counts—two counts of obstruction of justice and one count of perjury. Inside, the response was muted, but outside a cheer broke out.

US Attorney Fitzgerald held a post-verdict press conference, followed by our own. Fitzgerald said he was "gratified" by the verdict but "sad" that it took so long, and reasserted that the investigation of Burge's crew was ongoing. I said we were "very elated that this jury, with only one Black person, spoke loudly and clearly. . . . Finally, twenty-five years after this evidence came to light, there is some modicum of justice in this case."

Locke proclaimed,

It's a theme in our nation's civil rights history that corrupt, bigoted, or inept state systems that can't deal with their own problems require the intervention of the federal authorities. This is another example. Most of the prosecutors and judges at 26th Street are deeply entrenched with the police and the status quo. It doesn't surprise me that in the end it took the US Attorney's Office and the US Department of Justice to do what the state authorities should have done thirty years ago.

Banner headlines in both dailies the next day trumpeted "Guilty," and editorials praising the verdict quickly followed. Burge's bond was raised to $450,000, which was secured by his brother's house, and Burge was permitted to return to Florida to await his sentencing. While Burge faced a maximum of forty-five years, a former federal prosecutor familiar with federal sentencing guidelines predicted a more likely sentence of eight to ten years. The pension board subsequently continued its hearing on whether to revoke Burge's police pension until after his sentencing, articulating the determinative issue to be whether Burge was convicted for crimes committed in connection with his employment.

I told CBS 2 that I thought ten years would be a fair sentence and told ABC 7 that Melvin Jones was "one of the men who has made the city better by testifying both on Burge's firing case and now his prosecution. The city needs to compensate the victims and create a fund for the victims of police torture."

Several jurors spoke to the press. As reported by the *Sun Times*, thirty-one-year-old Gary Dollinger said what "sent [him] over the top" was the testimony of Michael McDermott. "Mike McDermott was pretty compelling. He may have wavered from his grand jury testimony, but you could tell he was scared. He didn't recant it to say there was no brutality." Dollinger recounted, "Of all of the victims, Andrew Wilson was huge. There's the leg burns. There's the clips on his ears. I could think maybe he got a clip in prison and scratched his ear, but that would be like a Martian landing on Earth. What are the odds?" With regard to the victims' criminal backgrounds, Dollinger said, "What some of these people had done was despicable. In some ways that made this decision harder." He asserted that the deliberations were always civil, with no one injecting race or personal factors, and that "everyone seemed fair and impartial." Despite his firm belief in Burge's guilt, Dollinger said he was moved by the defense arguments about Burge's heroic service in Vietnam and other contributions he made to society. "I believe he was guilty, but frankly if I was sentencing, I don't know. It was brutal on the South Side. I hate to see them lock him up and throw away the key. He served the city well for a period of time."

Rachel Thielmann, a twenty-eight-year-old makeup artist, said Burge did not seem believable on the stand: "The way he kept saying 'no,' it didn't seem believable to me, like he didn't want to be there." She found the testimony of the four victims to be stronger, saying, "They had nothing to win and nothing to lose."

Several of the torture survivors were asked for their reactions. As reported by John Conroy on his blog, Melvin Jones was "flabbergasted" by the verdict:

> I jumped around and some things like that, but the main thing was that I got justice, something I have been wanting for twenty-eight years. I wasn't an angel, but I didn't deserve the suffering he put me through. Everyone I turned to thought I was crying wolf. I just kept hoping and praying he would have his day, and today is his day.

Anthony Holmes, who was working two jobs, doing maintenance in a clothing manufacturer's warehouse and delivering bundles of the *Chicago Tribune* to stores, told Conroy:

> It's like a new life. It won't stop the nightmares I've been having, but now he is going to have some of his own. . . . It's been a long time coming. I thought they [the jury] were going to let us down. I figured he would just win again. But we got people who believe in us now.

Gregory Banks, who was studying to become an alcohol and drug counselor, voiced similar relief and added, "I am still looking for them to get the two men who tortured me."

Conroy also reported the police reaction, which was mixed. The former Afro American Patrolmen's League president, Howard Saffold, hailed the verdict, as did an unnamed former police commander, who also questioned the role of higher-placed police officials in the torture scandal. Several former colleagues of Burge, including John Byrne, defended him. Byrne blamed the "liberal" media and Judge Lefkow for the verdict, and asserted that "people lie all the time in interrogatories, depositions, and trials in civil matters on both sides of a suit, and they are not prosecuted for perjury. Even witnesses for the prosecution and defense lie in criminal trials with impunity." Daley remained silent until he was questioned about the verdict a few days later. He responded reluctantly, claiming, "We did everything possible in that time. After you look back you could change a lot of things," adding that he regretted "a lot of things in my life—just not that."

Striking while the iron was hot, the next day we, together with Locke and Northwestern, filed a civil rights damages suit on behalf of Ronald Kitchen, naming Daley, former superintendent LeRoy Martin, Burge, and others in a torture and wrongful conviction conspiracy.

Only months after Burge took over as commander of Area 3 in 1988, he had led the investigation into a quintuple murder case. Not having success in solving the high-profile crime, Burge, Byrne, and their detectives focused on a couple of small-time drug dealers: Ronald Kitchen and Marvin Reeves. Ronald alleged that he was picked up at night, taken to Area 3, and subjected to sixteen hours of sleep deprivation and physical torture that forced him to give a false confession that was fed to him by one of his torturers. As he described it to my daughter, Kate:

I was taken to 39th and California. They slammed my head into the lockers. From there I was taken into a side room and I was being questioned. I asked him can I call my lawyer. [One of the detectives] actually picked the phone up and hit me upside the head with the receiver and asked me do I hear it ringing. [Detective] Michael Kill and Burge come in and that's when the kicks and the punches and the knees and the slaps and the hits all started. They took me to [a] side room. That's when I was introduced to another detective and he introduced me to the blackjack and the telephone book. . . . He put the book on my head and he used the nightstick, that blackjack, and he whacked the hell out of that telephone book while it was on your head. And just whack it. And you have no defense because your hands are handcuffed behind your back so your defense mechanism is gone. And then he had me stand up and placed that blackjack between my legs and that wall and just grind on my groins with that.

Ronald also described the racism he experienced:

To constantly be called a nigger by a white person, it's already a racist word. That word has very powerful hatred towards it. And to be called that and to be beaten at the same time as being called that, we can't help but to realize this is what this is. . . . Racism played a big part in that.

We also sued the assistant state's attorney who took Ronald's statement because, as Ronald told it, the ASA facilitated the continuation of his torture by sending him back to the torturers when Ronald did not fully cooperate, and by collaborating with Detective Kill in feeding Ronald the false story. Ronald's testicles were badly injured by the torture, but his confession was nonetheless admitted against him at trial. He was convicted, sent to death row, and served twenty-one years, until Tom Geraghty, Carolyn Frazier, and their students at Northwestern had obtained his freedom a year before.

The very same day, congressman Danny Davis announced that he was introducing into Congress an anti-torture bill that Joey and I had drafted.

The bill made torture, as defined by the UN Convention Against Torture, committed by law enforcement officers a federal crime that carried a maximum ten-year sentence, unless the torture resulted in death. Importantly, it also provided that the crime did not have a statute of limitations. I had asked Danny, a staunch ally since the assassination of Fred Hampton, to introduce the bill, and he readily agreed. Announcing the bill, Congressman Davis said:

> Jon Burge was convicted of obstruction of justice and perjury because these were the only charges for which he could be charged because the statute of limitations had run out on the torture and brutality allegations. As a result of these circumstances, I am introducing today legislation which is designed to provide a criminal penalty for torture committed by law enforcement officers and others acting under color of law. Had this bill been in effect, former Chicago Police Detective Jon Burge would be guilty of torture and not just perjury.

Three weeks later we filed a conspiracy and pattern and practice case against Daley and company on behalf of Michael Tillman. To date, Daley had avoided being named as a defendant, except for our unsuccessful attempt to join him in Darrell Cannon's case, and had eluded sitting for a deposition when the City finally settled the four death row torture cases. Now, with the Ronald Kitchen suit and this one, we had opened two new fronts to continue our pursuit and had drawn two good federal judges to hear these very similar cases.

Just after New Year's 2011, the motions Burge had filed seeking judgment of acquittal, arrest of judgment, and for a new trial were denied, as was a highly suspect motion to recuse Judge Lefkow. His sentencing hearing was set for January 20, 2011.

The Federal Probation Office, in its pre-sentence report, had treated the case as a simple conviction for perjury and obstruction of justice in a civil proceeding because the false and obstructive answers "were not made to law enforcement officials involved in a criminal investigation or prosecution, nor were the answers presented to a criminal grand jury." Hence, it found, under federal sentencing guidelines, that the recommended sentence should be fifteen to twenty-one months. The government filed a lengthy objection to the pre-sentence report, arguing that the probation office should have applied the guidelines in a way that would have permitted application of the harsher civil rights guidelines, and thereby would have enhanced Burge's sentence tenfold.

In support, the government first argued that Burge's obstructive conduct "included obstructing a criminal investigation"—namely, the investigation of the Cook County special prosecutor—and because his lying in the Madison Hobley interrogatories was an extension of his continued false denials in numerous other cases since the 1970s, which "infected numerous criminal prosecutions in which Burge participated, and has called into question many other criminal prosecutions, as well as the criminal justice system that allowed his conduct to go unchecked." Noting that he continued his perjurious course of conduct while testifying at trial, the government concluded:

> The defendant was an organizer or leader of a criminal activity that involved 5 or more participants or was otherwise extensive. Specifically, defendant was the Commander of Area 2 Violent Crimes. At trial, evidence was presented that he supervised several other officers who engaged in torture, including: Peter Dignan, John Byrne, Charles Grunhard, John Yucaitis, and other unidentified officers.

In a written decision, Judge Lefkow rejected the government's arguments. Pointing out that Burge took the Fifth Amendment rather than lying before the special prosecutor's grand jury, she rejected the government's argument that Burge's conduct was "connected to" or "threatened" the special prosecutor's investigation. She also rejected the government's argument that Burge's prior perjury in denying torture was relevant conduct, because it had occurred between fourteen and twenty-one years before the "instant offense" (that is, the offense under discussion at trial) and was not committed during the commission of the instant offense or as part of Burge's attempt to avoid responsibility for the instant offense.

As part of the sentencing process, Judge Lefkow received a large number of letters and a community petition, circulated by the Illinois Coalition Against Torture, with more than a thousand signatures. More than thirty letters submitted by Burge and his lawyers were given to the press the night before the hearing. Nineteen were from fellow police officers, including letters from a former CPD deputy chief, three former commanders, and ten officers who had worked under Burge, including John Byrne, who argued to the court that Burge "was no racist."

On the eve of the two-day sentencing hearing, Judge Lefkow announced that she would employ one sentencing enhancement—that Burge took the stand at trial and committed further perjury—and consequently raised the recommended sentence range to twenty-one to twenty-seven months.

The government called as its first witness Anthony Holmes. Reading from a statement that Joey had helped him prepare, he began: "Burge electric-shocked me and suffocated me and he forced me to confess to a murder I did not do. And I had to accept that I was in the penitentiary for something I didn't do." Anthony continued:

> I still have nightmares. I wake up in a cold sweat. I still fear that I am going back to jail for this again. I see myself falling in a deep hole and no one helping me get out. I felt helpless and hopeless when it happened and when I dream I feel like I'm in that room again, screaming for help and no one comes to help me. I can never expect when I will have the dream. I just lay down at night and then I wake up and the bed is soaked.

Anthony recalled, "I remember looking around the room at the other officers and I thought one of them would say that was enough, but they never did." He concluded, "Let him suffer like we suffered. If it had been one of us, we would get the maximum without [anyone] batting an eye."

Melvin Jones gave a more muted statement in which he also described Burge's fellow officers looking the other way while the torture proceeded. Next, the government called former Area 2 detective Sammy Lacey. Lacey recounted the well-known reputation of Burge's midnight "asskickers" for torture and abuse, described Burge's racist treatment of the few Black detectives who worked under his command, and revealed the special relationship between the "asskickers" and the assistant state's attorneys who took the confessions obtained by the midnight crew.

The government then called Howard Saffold, one of the original leaders of the Afro American Patrolmen's League and a close ally. Saffold talked expansively about his experiences with police racism, brutality, and the police code of silence, both on the job and organizationally with the AAPL, from the mid 1960s to the present. He characterized Area 2 as "the pits" and Burge as a "cancer."

University of Chicago professor Adam Green followed. As with Saffold, we had also suggested Green as a witness. Professor Green, whose specialty was the history of Black Chicago, noted that at the height of Burge's torture, Chicago was America's "most segregated city," with extremely high poverty and jobless rates in much of the Black community. He described how the white mainstream media had dismissed the allegations of torture, leading to further distrust of the police and its disciplinary process among the Black community. He compared the torture scandal to the

1969 murders of Fred Hampton and Mark Clark, the beating of Rodney King by the LAPD in the early 1990s, and the LA Ramparts scandal, but concluded that the longstanding and systematic torture in Chicago was "unprecedented" and a "singular chapter" of "horror."

Green underscored the importance of considering the purpose and intent of torture: it is not only intended to achieve a practical result, a confession, or the compliance of those detained, but it is also meant "to establish a sense of supremacy, a kind of total control, by one human being over another." Its psychological aspects, he continued, rest on a capacity to assert to the captive person, "You are alone, and you are in my power." Torture, he testified, "deeply demoralizes" the community and "undercuts its humanity."

The defense countered by calling Burge's sister-in-law, his brother Jeff, and Michael Fahey, brother of slain officer William Fahey. Fahey talked about Burge's key role in the Wilson murder investigation and described Burge as an "inspiration" and "hero" to his family. Burge's brother asserted that Burge was not a racist because he was appointed as commander, the youngest in the history of the Chicago Police Department, by a Black superintendent (Fred Rice), who was a personal friend, and Burge's appointment was approved by mayor Harold Washington. He detailed a long list of Burge's health problems, including an "aggressive" form of prostate cancer, for which he faced surgery in April, and told the judge that "almost any sentence will be a death sentence."

Burge then addressed the court. He said that the Chicago Police Department "meant everything" to him, and that he was "deeply sorry" that this case brought "disrepute" to the department. He said the charge that he was a racist "deeply disturbed" him, that he worked a high-crime area, and that "race did not matter" to him. He said that there was "nothing further from the truth" than the charge that he framed innocent people. He asserted that he had been the "target of lawyers," vilified, and compared to Al Capone. He declared himself "a broken man," but made no admission of wrongdoing.

After the hearing's conclusion, Judge Lefkow called Burge to the podium and spoke to him directly:

> You're here today having been convicted by a jury of two counts of obstruction of justice and one count of perjury in connection with making false statements in interrogatories served on you in a lawsuit filed against you in this court. That lawsuit made allegations that individuals under your supervision or command had tortured the plaintiff to confess to a crime he claims he did not commit. You denied any knowledge of torture of the plaintiff or of any other torture

or abuse having occurred under your direction or command. You denied it in answers to the interrogatories, and you maintained that denial under oath in this courtroom where you testified in your own defense. Unfortunately for you the jury did not believe you, and I must agree that I did not either.

The judge then addressed the factors she was required to consider in rendering her sentence:

I have read letters and statements from many individuals who were not called to testify at trial but wanted to be heard. Those statements describe brutality at your hands or those under your supervision or command, some even more appalling than the torture the witnesses here have testified about. One remarkable thing about the statements was how many came from outside the Chicago area. These people say they had to leave Chicago because they were terrified that the police would do this to them again. One statement from a prisoner, however, will probably haunt me the longest. This man reports that he has been in prison for 30 years. He stated he was 17 when he was arrested while walking down the street and brutally tortured until he confessed to a murder. He said, I had the body of a man; but was a child inside. He remains in prison for a crime he insists he did not commit, being abandoned by family and friends who trusted that the police would not have charged him had he not done the crime. The grandmother who stood by him died while he is in prison, a graying, middle-aged adult. Imagine the loss.

Judge Lefkow addressed the credibility of the victims and the nature of the crime. After saying that she found Anthony's statement "particularly moving," she declared:

Now when I hear your attorney implying that if someone did the crime, no harm, no foul, they deserved it, I am frankly shocked. Even if counsel only means to say that none of these people can be believed because they are criminals, the mountain of evidence to the contrary completely belies that position. So what does all of this have to do with the crimes of conviction, you ask? It demonstrates at the very least a serious lack of respect for the due process of law and your unwillingness to acknowledge the truth in the face of all of this evidence.

Judge Lefkow next addressed the responsibility that public officials bore:

The freedom that we treasure most of all in this country is the right to live free of governmental abuse of power. . . . For that reason those of us who are entrusted with governmental power take an oath upon entering office that we will uphold the law. For the police it means to protect the safety of the people so they may go about their lives peaceably and productively as they see fit, and to use their abilities and resources to identify those who commit crimes that threaten that safety. It is obvious that officers who do this important work must operate within the bounds of the law.

She then addressed the harm to the criminal justice system that Burge's widespread conduct caused:

> When a confession is coerced, the truth of the confession is called into question. When this becomes widespread, as one can infer from the accounts that have been presented here in this court, the administration of justice is undermined irreparably. How can one trust that justice will be served when the justice system has been so defiled? This is why the crimes of obstructing justice and perjury, and even more so when it is about matters relating to the duties of one's office, are serious offenses.

Judge Lefkow next addressed Burge's rationale for lying in the *Hobley* lawsuit:

> I have also asked myself in practical terms why you would not have asserted your privilege against self-incrimination as you did in the same time frame before the special investigator? I infer that you must have reckoned that doing so would result in an adverse inference against you in the civil suit, bringing the house of cards of denial down around you, further damaging your reputation as a decorated police officer and commander, exposing your long history of misconduct, and undermining your long history of denial that these events occurred.

She also addressed the police code of silence as embodied in police perjury:

> Yet too many times I have seen officers sit in the witness box to my right and give implausible testimony to defend themselves or a fellow officer against accusations of wrongdoing. Each time I see it, I feel pain because the office they hold has been diminished.

Judge Lefkow, who had kept much of the evidence of Burge's racial animus out of the trial, chose not to render an opinion as to whether Burge was a racist, stating:

> There are those who believe you are deeply racist, and there are those who believe you could not possibly have tortured suspects. I doubt that my

opinion or what happens here will change anyone's views. You are the person you are, neither all good, nor all evil, just like the rest of us.

In a statement that implicated former state's attorneys Richard M. Daley and Richard Devine, as well as a series of Chicago police superintendents, the judge condemned the "dismal failure" of police and prosecutorial leadership to act:

Perhaps the praise, publicity, and commendations you received for solving these awful crimes was seductive and may have led you down this path. On your behalf how I wish that there had not been such a dismal failure of leadership in the department that it came to this. As one commentator wrote, if the first time—I'm paraphrasing—if the first time this happened your commander had said, you do that again, and you'll be guarding the parking lot at 35th and State, then you might have enjoyed your retirement without this prosecution over your head, without the reality that you will be going to prison in your declining years, when your health is compromised as it is. If others, such as the United States attorney and the state's attorney, had given heed long ago, so much pain could have been avoided.

Judge Lefkow then rendered her sentence:

I am charged with the unhappy duty of imposing a sentence. The sentencing guidelines counsel that a sentence of 21 to 27 months is a starting point for me. I am now prepared to impose a sentence. Pursuant to the Sentencing Reform Act of 1984, it is the judgment of the court that the defendant Jon Burge is hereby committed to the custody of the Bureau of Prisons to be imprisoned for a term of 54 months on Counts 1, 2, and 3, all to run concurrently. Upon release from prison you shall be placed on supervised release for a term of three years. The term consists of three years on each of Counts 1, 2, and 3, all terms to run concurrently. You must then immediately report upon your release with drug testing and alcohol treatment.

Front-page headlines highlighted the sentence, with the *Sun Times* trumpeting "Burge's Turn for Prison." Reaction was mixed, as several torture survivors and community activists protested that the sentence was too short and was a "complete injustice." US Attorney Fitzgerald, acknowledging the frustration of many, stated, "Justice should have come sooner, but justice delayed isn't justice completely denied." After pointing a finger at Daley, I called it "a significant step in the process to bring some justice to all of those people who were tortured, and to get not only Burge, but all of the people who tortured our clients and all of the others, to bring all of them to justice." Anthony Holmes struck a similarly forward-looking note: "Now, finally, I feel that people will begin to believe . . . for all these years, nobody listened to what I had to say because they didn't believe me, but now it's all going to come to the light."

CHAPTER 33

Daley the Defendant

Only days after Burge was sentenced, the police pension board rendered its decision. Composed of four former or active police officers and four civilians, the board voted four to four, as the four men in blue adopted Burge's argument that his felony convictions—for lying about his activities while a cop—were not performed "relating to or arising out of or in connection with" his police duties as required by law. Since the vote was whether to rescind his pension rather than to grant it, a majority was required, so the tie went to Burge. Burge would continue to receive $3,000 a month, with yearly cost-of-living increases, while he served his sentence and beyond. I told the *Tribune*, "To say that he should still be paid is mind-boggling. It is a total slap in the face to the entire city."

That Sunday, I opened the *Sun Times* to a photo of myself atop a 2,700-word story by AP national writer Sharon Cohen. The story told the long history of the torture struggle, primarily through my eyes, episode by episode, starting with Deep Badge and the anonymous letters. Cohen quoted me as saying that the twenty-one-year odyssey in pursuit of the evidence was "just like peeling an onion." I made a point to reiterate that Daley's refusal to act in Andrew Wilson's case was responsible for a decade of torture, and then addressed the concept of "selective torture": "What proves the lie to anyone who says it's OK to torture the cop killer but it's not OK to torture innocent people is, how do you know which is which?"

Former OPS investigator Francine Sanders talked about the "grim duty" of investigating Andrew's torture: "While you're satisfied you've gotten to the truth, the truth is horrific." John Conroy said that it wasn't a "one man show": "Not only were there other police, but state's attorneys and judges who looked the other way and ignored these obvious truths of what people were saying." When Cohen's narrative reached Burge's conviction and sentencing, she quoted Ronald Kitchen:

This is not going to make up for what was taken from me. I did 13 years on death row, then eight more years. I missed my kids growing up. My daughter doesn't know me. My sons, they're hurting. And I'm hurting. The things we were fighting for we didn't get, but something is better than nothing.

Ten days later, the *Sun Times*, focusing on the nineteen Burge torture survivors who remained in prison, editorialized, "By means of evidentiary hearings or some other judicial undertaking, each of these cases must be re-examined. We can't take the chance that even one innocent man remains behind bars simply because incriminating statements were beaten out of him. A confession extracted through torture is never a harmless error, and a conviction based even in part on such a confession cannot be allowed to stand."

The same day, Illinois attorney general Lisa Madigan announced she was filing suit against Burge and the pension board to immediately revoke his pension: "Jon Burge forfeited his right to a public pension when he lied about his knowledge of and participation in the torture and physical abuse of suspects," Madigan said. "It's this type of criminal conduct by a public servant that our pension forfeiture laws were designed to discourage. The public should never have to pay for the retirement of a corrupt public official." The *Sun Times* concurred, writing that Burge "lied under oath about ugly and sordid matters—physically torturing suspects—that had absolutely everything to do with his official police duties. If he is not stripped of his pension, it will be a legal and moral outrage."

Two years before, the Illinois Coalition Against the Death Penalty had hired a former labor organizer named Jeremy Schroeder, who brought a tremendous amount of energy and organizational skills to a thirty-year campaign that had stalled while Rod Blagojevich was governor. Jeremy was joined by an impressive group of activists and politicians, including Jeanne Bishop, whose sister and brother-in-law had been brutally murdered; Randy Steidl, a former death row prisoner and current client of ours; African American politicians Karen Yarborough and Kwame Raoul; and old hand Rob Warden, director of Northwestern's Center on Wrongful Convictions. Chick Hoffman and his team had continued to expertly argue appeals for those sent to death row in the years following Governor Ryan's 2003 clemencies.

Thanks to these forces, just after New Year's 2011, a lame-duck session of the Illinois State Legislature considered a bill to abolish the death penalty. There was no hope that the incoming Illinois House would pass the bill, so it was now or never. Kwame Raoul had the votes in the senate, so the pressure was on Karen Yarborough and her allies in the House to get sixty votes. Randy Steidl, a white working-class man from downstate Paris, Illinois, who had spent twelve years on death row for crimes he did not commit, lobbied eloquently and passionately and had a profound impact on some of the more conservative members of the House. Nonetheless, Chick Hoffman called me, dejected, on the afternoon of January 6, and said the bill had fallen short by one vote.

In "what seemed to be a miraculous turn of events," as later described by Rob Warden, two representatives, one Democrat and one Republican, changed their votes to yes, and the bill passed the house. The bill easily passed in the senate, but the task was far from over. Governor Pat Quinn had sixty days to sign the bill, veto it, or let it pass into law without acting. While a progressive on many issues, Quinn was far from an abolitionist, and he had seen New Mexico governor Bill Richardson go down in defeat after he signed a bill that abolished the death penalty in his state. Quinn, a Roman Catholic, said he would "follow his conscience." He visited Barack Obama, who, like Quinn, was on record as supporting the death penalty for heinous crimes. Revered abolitionist Sister Helen Prejean came to talk to Quinn, and Chick Hoffman had the honor of briefing her. Former governor James Thompson, who had signed the current death penalty law, headed up an impressive list of public officials urging Quinn to sign the bill; the law enforcement opposition was headed up by attorney general Lisa Madigan and Cook County state's attorney Anita Alvarez. On March 9, 2011, Governor Quinn, citing inspiration from the Bible, signed the bill into law, making Illinois the sixteenth state to abolish the death penalty.

In late February, John and I went to trial in a sixty-year-old police torture case. In January 1952, twenty-year-old Oscar Walden was arrested by Chicago police for the rape of a fifty-year-old white woman. He was taken to the station and tortured by a brutal detective who threatened to hang him, lynching style, with a rope. Oscar, who had never before been arrested, gave a false confession, and the police obtained the rape victim's identification by parading Oscar before her and compelling him to apologize. He was convicted and sentenced to seventy-five years in the penitentiary for a crime he did not commit.

Oscar continued to protest his innocence from his prison cell, and, with the help of renowned civil rights attorney George Leighton, was released on parole fourteen years later. After almost four decades, in January 2003, governor George Ryan granted Oscar an innocence pardon, which paved the way for us to bring a damages case in federal court. Since all the police and prosecutors involved, as well as the rape victim, were long deceased, we were compelled to sue the City as the sole defendant, under a theory that its police department had a pattern and practice, predating Oscar's arrest, of torturing Black suspects accused of raping white women.

The City fought the case tooth and nail, retaining the private law firm of Andrew Hale and Associates, an office that had already cost the City's taxpayers tens of millions of dollars in "pinstripe patronage," defending a series of torture and wrongful conviction cases.

To prove our case, John and I relied on a mosaic of musty documents, reports, and studies, and the testimony of the ninety-nine-year-old George Leighton. We had developed evidence that the CPD used torture techniques back in the 1920s, dubbed "the fourth degree"; that its officers had used electric shock in the 1940s and 1950s; and that the CPD had a torture chamber at one of its stations. We also introduced a report that documented the wrongful convictions of Black men for the rape of white women in Illinois.

Andrew Hale argued that Oscar was guilty, and presented the 1952 criminal trial testimony of the rape victim, the police officers, and prosecutors. Hale and his co-counsel, Avi Kamionski, repeatedly drew the wrath of trial judge Ruben Castillo by making unfairly prejudicial arguments before the jury and tendering to the jury highly prejudicial evidence about the rape that the judge had specifically barred.

In closing arguments I emphasized the racist nature of Oscar's torture and wrongful conviction. An aspiring musician at the time of his arrest, Oscar testified that he had played Billie Holiday's "Strange Fruit," so I recited some of the song's lyrics to the jury:

Southern trees bear strange fruit
Blood on the leaves and blood at the root
Black bodies swinging in the southern breeze
Strange fruit hanging from the poplar trees

The jury was not persuaded, perhaps because Oscar, now eighty, was repeatedly tripped up on the stand and tried to extemporize explanations for contradictions in his story that had arisen over the decades. In addition, the blatant misconduct of Hale and Kamionski no doubt influenced the jury. Months later, a disgusted Judge Castillo granted us a new trial on the specific grounds of Hale's and Kamionski's misconduct. The City then quietly settled the case for a shade under $1 million.

On March 16, the very day that Jon Burge entered the Federal Corrections Complex in Butner, North Carolina, Aaron Patterson's co-defendant Eric Caine, who had also been tortured and suffered a broken eardrum from a technique called "ear cupping," was exonerated. It had always seemed an injustice within an injustice that Eric remained in prison long after Aaron had been pardoned in 2003, and Russell Ainsworth of Loevy and Loevy had fought long and hard for Eric's freedom. Judge William Hooks, former chair of the Cook County Bar Association and now a criminal court judge, had granted Eric a new trial based on the overwhelming evidence of a "pattern and practice of torture," and the special prosecutors, under Stuart Nudelman, had dismissed Eric's case. A few months later Eric would obtain a certificate of innocence.

We had opened up a new avenue for discovery, thanks to the Michael Tillman and Ronald Kitchen civil cases, and deposing Burge was at the top of our to-do list. I moved for an order from Judge Pallmeyer, who had been assigned to Michael Tillman's case; Burge's lawyers resisted, but, thankfully, the judge ordered that the deposition proceed—and that it be videotaped. So in May, Joey and I traveled to North Carolina to once again depose Burge.

Burge entered the small prison conference room dressed in brown prison garb and made his animosity toward me clear. FCC Butner had the reputation of being somewhat of a "country club" that housed prisoners convicted of high-profile white-collar crimes, including the notorious Bernie Madoff, but Burge nonetheless complained about the quality of the food and the lack of adequate medical care. Once the camera was turned on, he proceeded to assert his Fifth Amendment right to all questions about torture that Joey and I posed.

After we left the prison three hours later, I reflected on the significance of what I had just observed. Bearing witness to Burge's imprisonment—even if it was not for his systemic torture—and capturing it on videotape was an important event. Burge was behind bars, while the torture survivors who had courageously testified against Burge were free.

Two weeks later, we convened the deposition of Michael Kill, a main participant, along with Burge, in the brutal torture of Ronald Kitchen. A wiry man with a gangster-like voice, Kill, who was an actor on the side, decided to eschew the safety of the Fifth Amendment and repeatedly gave jaw-dropping answers, accompanied by exaggerated facial expressions. When I asked him how many times he had used the "n-word" during interrogations, he gestured toward videographer Rick Kosberg: "More times than he's got tape on that machine." When I pressed for an estimate, he sat back in his chair and said, "How about a million times, for starters?" He informed me that I did not understand "these people," that "it's like trying to explain physics to my grandson, who's three months old—you're not there, you haven't been there, you don't understand it, okay?"

Kill testified that he had been accused of abuse "about nine hundred times," and when asked whether he used the "n-word" while interrogating Ronald, he responded that he "was not going to make him feel like the King of England." When I accused him of "covering for Burge," Kill responded that he "was not sending love letters to that muttonhead."

Daley also remained at the top of our agenda. In May, amid glowing media retrospectives, he had handed over the mayoral reins to Rahm Emanuel. Earlier in the spring we had endured another legal setback when the judge in Ronald Kitchen's case dismissed our claims against Daley. We were now 0 for 4 in chasing Daley in our torture cases; we had chosen not to sue him in the Aaron Patterson and Leroy Orange cases, and judge Amy St. Eve had recently rejected our request to bring Daley into Darrell Cannon's case. But in late July we got some great news—Judge Pallmeyer, in a landmark decision, had upheld our right to include Daley in Michael Tillman's case.

Judge Pallmeyer's lengthy decision was an affirmation of our long battle to put Daley in the legal crosshairs. She summarized our conspiracy allegations against Daley and the high-ranking police officials:

> Former Mayor and State's Attorney Richard M. Daley and former Chicago Police Superintendent LeRoy Martin refused and failed to investigate a pattern of torture carried out at Area 2 prior to Plaintiff's arrest, proximately causing Plaintiff's torture and wrongful conviction. Plaintiff claims that Daley, Martin, former Chicago Police Superintendent Terry Hillard, former aide to the Chicago Police Superintendent, Thomas Needham, and former Office of Professional Standards Director Gayle Shines all conspired to suppress evidence of police torture that Plaintiff claims would have been exculpatory.

The judge further detailed our allegations against Daley:

Plaintiff alleges that as Mayor and State's Attorney, Defendant Richard Daley had personal knowledge of the alleged abuses perpetrated by Burge and other Defendants at Area 2, Plaintiff asserts that, had Daley and Martin investigated the allegations of abuse at Area 2 prior to his arrest, he would not have been tortured and would not have been wrongfully convicted. Plaintiff further alleges that as a result of a conspiracy between Daley, Martin, Hillard, Needham, Shines, and others to suppress information about torture at Area 2, "Plaintiff's wrongful prosecution was continued, his exoneration was delayed and his imprisonment lasted far longer than it otherwise would have." According to Plaintiff, between 1989 and 1992, Daley and Martin were given "additional actual notice that Burge was the leader of a group of Chicago detectives that systematically tortured and abused African American suspects" through an Amnesty International report and public hearings. Plaintiff alleges that in 1996, despite his knowledge that findings of torture and abuse had been made against Defendant Dignan, Daley promoted Dignan to lieutenant. Plaintiff also alleges that Daley, against the advice of his senior advisers, "personally insisted" throughout his tenure that the City of Chicago continue to finance the defense of Burge, Byrne, Dignan, and other Area 2 detectives, despite his personal knowledge that Burge committed acts of torture.

Based on these allegations, which we had extensively documented over the years, she held that we had sufficiently pleaded four interrelated civil rights and state law conspiracies, including two that were racially motivated, against Daley and all the other defendants:

[Tillman's] allegations suggest that Plaintiff's torture was more than just an isolated incident, and suggest, further, that the suppression of the truth about what occurred at Area 2 was the result of coordinated efforts that continued for some time. . . . As discussed above, the Defendant Officers are alleged to have participated directly in the torture, as did Burge; [Assistant State's Attorney] Frenzer allegedly did so as well, by attempting to take a statement when he knew the torture was ongoing; Martin and Daley are said to have undermined and obstructed findings of torture; Shines allegedly suppressed findings of torture; and Plaintiff claims that Needham and Hillard continued to suppress findings and undermine investigations into torture at Area 2 after they took office. Plaintiff has listed a litany of actions at Area 2 furthering and concealing the abuse that took place there . . . and has also provided specific allegations regarding acts of torture performed on this Plaintiff and on others. These allegations are sufficient to allege a [Section] 1983 conspiracy.

Judge Pallmeyer continued: "[Michael Tillman] has alleged that all or nearly all of the victims of the alleged conspiracy were members of the same class, and that racial epithets were commonly used during the course of this torture. Those allegations lend sufficient credence to Plaintiff's claims at the pleading stage." Finally, the judge also upheld Michael's state-law conspiracy claim, restating Daley's role in the alleged conspiracy in broad and powerful terms: "The allegations are the same—that Defendant Officers, Burge, and Frenzer participated in the torture itself and that Daley, Hillard, Martin, Needham, and Shines covered up and suppressed evidence of that pattern and practice of torture of which Plaintiff was a victim."

We served Daley's lawyers a notice of deposition for September 8. They countered by accusing Judge Pallmeyer of making a "mistake of law," and asked her to reconsider her decision. A couple days later—after I tipped her off—Carol Marin led off the ten o'clock news with an exclusive: "If all goes according to the plan of attorney Flint Taylor, former Mayor Richard Daley, on September 8, will raise his right hand and be sworn as a witness. At that point, and for the first time, Taylor will get to question the former mayor about what he knew and when he knew it, regarding the torture of 110 African-American men by a small band of white Chicago police officers."

As Carol also worked for the *Sun Times*, the paper's front page the next morning, August 10, 2011, featured big white capital letters on a black background: "DALEY THE DEFENDANT." AP reporter Karen Hawkins quoted me as saying, "It's the first time that a federal judge has acknowledged that Daley was part of a conspiracy to cover up the torture. We're hopeful she won't back down from that position."

That same morning Fran Spielman confronted a second Chicago mayor about the torture scandal. Writing that Emanuel "walked a political tightrope Wednesday on the explosive police torture allegations that continue to surround convicted former Chicago Police Commander Jon Burge," she quoted Emanuel as defending the City's "obligation" to defend Burge and Daley on the taxpayers' dime, while supporting Attorney General Madigan's effort to strip Burge of his pension. Turning back to Daley, according to Spielman, "sources close to Daley" said that Richie's deposition was "not a done deal."

In response, I took on the new mayor for the first time, accusing him of adopting the Daley administration's "head in the sand line." "It's totally established that Burge tortured these people, yet the defense goes on," I said. "[Emanuel] doesn't need to do that. . . . Not only should he resolve these cases so taxpayers can compensate the victims rather than the torturers. He should apologize to the African-American community and to the victims for this pattern of torture."

Emanuel quickly got defensive, refused to apologize, and said, "I answered one question. Some people say, 'This pulls Rahm into it' . . . [Daley's] allowed to have the cost of his legal defense . . . That's it. I'm not part of it."

The *Sun Times* editorial board focused on the issues of settlement and attorneys' fees:

> Too bad federal Judge Elaine Bucklo is not the mayor of Chicago. Maybe then the city would get out of the business of fighting no-win lawsuits brought by the alleged victims of former police torture meister Jon Burge. In March, during a hearing in a suit brought by former prison inmate Ronald Kitchen, who was wrongly convicted of murder, Bucklo looked around her courtroom at a slew of attorneys for the city and marveled:
>
> "There's an awful lot of you . . . Does this make sense? I don't understand why this case, why you don't settle. [Kitchen] was declared innocent. Burge is in jail. Have you tried to settle this?"

Emanuel, no doubt reading the *Sun Times* as well as the political tea leaves, spoke about the settlement question a few days later. "TIME WE END IT, Mayor Says He's 'Working Toward' Settling Burge Torture Cases," read the banner headline, with photos of Emanuel and Burge side by side. It remained to be seen if Emanuel was serious, seeking to calm the political waters, or both.

Fran Spielman's sources were spot on. Days before Daley's scheduled deposition, we received a nasty letter from Terry Burns—once again wearing two hats, as lawyer for Daley and for the City—that refused to produce Daley and urged us to withdraw our notice of deposition. We fired back in both the legal and public forums. We wrote what is known as a Local Rule 37.2 letter, perfecting our right to move in court for an order to compel Daley's appearance, and I called Carol Marin to update her. Carol and her longtime producer, Don Moseley, once again made Daley's intransigence a leading news item. We also convinced a reluctant Michael Tillman to sit with me for an interview. His powerful words were broadcast on the ten o'clock news and quoted in Carol's column, "Time for Daley to Talk about Brutality":

I was hit with the fist, the phone book, I had a plastic bag placed over my head repeatedly, I had a gun put to my head while I was on my knees. I had a 7-Up poured down my nose. I was hit in the leg with a flashlight. I felt like a slave, tied to a tree, that couldn't do nothing 'cause I was always bound.

We also provided Carol an interview that Ben and I had done with Michael's trial judge, Kenneth Gillis, a week before. Gillis was one of the few "good" criminal court judges, and my wife Pat had gotten to know and respect him when she was a public defender assigned to his courtroom in the late '80s. Gillis told us that if he knew then what he knew now, he would have believed Michael and Steven Bell had been tortured by Byrne and Dignan, would not have permitted their confessions to be admitted into evidence, and, in an excerpt that Carol quoted, said he was "ashamed" that he had convicted Michael.

The next morning, Michael and I talked to a Channel 7 news crew. Michael made it clear that he wanted to hold Emanuel to his promise to "end it," and described what he wanted from Daley:

> We can end it. All he has to do is man up, take his weight, just like he made everyone else take his weight. I want him to admit what he did, and I want him to change what he did to people that are still incarcerated.

Two months later, Judge Pallmeyer denied Daley's motion to reconsider her July ruling, holding that while Daley was protected by the doctrine of prosecutorial immunity from liability for his actions while state's attorney, we had " sufficiently alleged that Daley, as mayor, participated in a conspiracy that included the concealment of exculpatory evidence." Carol Marin and Don Moseley featured Michael talking about what he had lost by being wrongfully convicted:

> I had a little girl eight years old teaching me how to use a phone, show me how to use a microwave. Do you know what that's like? I lost my sister who passed away while I was incarcerated for something I didn't do. I lost my kids, but they came back.

WBEZ radio asked Michael about Daley. He responded bluntly: "This been going on before they gave me a case. Once you became the mayor, you knew about it when you were the state's attorney. Why didn't you stop it then? You just let it prolong, prolong, prolong." I told the media that I was issuing another notice for Daley to appear, and gave an even longer view of the history: "The Daleys have been above the law since Richard J. Daley became mayor. That's half a century ago. Now maybe a Daley can be held accountable for something outrageous."

A few days later, Locke, his MacArthur Justice Center associate Alexa Van Brunt, and I opened up another front against Daley. Back in 2004, twenty-one-year-old David Koschman and several of his suburban friends got into a verbal altercation on Chicago's Division Street with a group of four drunken revelers. Koschman, five foot five and 125 pounds, got "mouthy," and a six foot three, 230-pound ex–football player punched him in the face. Koschman was knocked unconscious and fell backward to the ground, where the back of his head crashed against the pavement. The ex–football player fled with one of his friends, while Koschman was rushed to the hospital, where he remained unconscious in critical condition.

The ex–football player, it turned out, was R. J. Vanecko, a nephew of Richie Daley. The mayor was informed of the incident shortly after it occurred. Vanecko and his friends were coming from a Daley family engagement party honoring Daley's niece, Kathleen. An investigation was started, but shortly thereafter, the commander and lieutenant in charge of the investigation were informed that the unknown assailant might be the mayor's nephew. "Holy crap," one of them exclaimed, and the investigation stopped in its tracks.

David Koschman lay unconscious in the hospital for twelve days, his mother Nanci at his side, until she was compelled to make the agonizing decision to remove David from life support. His death was reclassified as a homicide and the investigation reactivated. Koschman's friends were interviewed, and they accurately described the assailant as the biggest of the group. Vanecko's friends and two bystanders were also interviewed, and Vanecko subsequently appeared at the police station with a high-powered criminal defense lawyer retained by the mayor's brother, and remained silent.

Despite compelling evidence that Vanecko threw the killer punch, and that Koschman, while perhaps verbally combative, did not pose a physical threat, the Chicago Police Department, with the concurrence of the head of the Cook County state's attorney's Felony Review Unit, decided not to charge Vanecko. They based this decision, reviewed by then Cook County state's attorney Richard Devine and his top assistants, on purported iden-tification problems and a theory of self-defense. Police superintendent Phil Cline announced the decision and its dubious basis to the media in late May 2004.

The case had lain dormant for almost seven years until Carol Marin and two *Sun Times* investigative reporters, Tim Novak and Chris Fusco, began their own investigation and put the case on the front page of the *Sun Times*, again and again. Carol asked if I would be interested in representing Nanci Koschman, David's mother, in bringing a lawsuit, but I was skeptical about the statute of limitations. I told Carol I would talk to Locke about petitioning for a Cook County special prosecutor to reinvestigate.

We decided to make the move. Locke and his associate Alexa drafted the petition, which we filed on November 8, 2011. Our emphasis was on a full and independent investigation into the official cover-up and the roles played by the CPD, the SAO, and the Daley family. The petition was assigned to judge Michael Toomin, who had presided over Aaron Patterson's case after it had been returned from the Illinois Supreme Court in 2000.

In January 2012, the Human Relations Committee of the Chicago City Council, chaired by alderman Joe Moore, held a hearing on a resolution proposed by the Illinois Coalition Against Torture (ICAT) declaring Chicago a "torture-free zone." The resolution was backed by a petition signed by 3,500 persons. Debra Erenberg, Amnesty International's regional director for the Midwest, while recognizing that the resolution was largely symbolic, emphasized that it was an important step toward justice. Referring to the upcoming G8 and NATO summits, she said, "In May, Nobel laureates, including some victims of torture, will come to Chicago. If the measure passes, the whole world will see that Chicago is a fitting host for these beacons of human rights." Testifying at the hearing, Mary L. Johnson, torture victim Michael Johnson's mother, urged that the resolution be used as a lever for action: "They say at the end of the pledge, 'Justice for all.' So we're pleading with you, please help us get that justice that we've never had."

The city council voted 45 to 0 to pass the resolution, making Chicago the first city in the US to formally oppose all forms of torture.

After Judge Pallmeyer had rejected their motion to reconsider in November 2011, Terry Burns and Daley resorted to stalling tactics to delay Daley's questioning. The recent death of Daley's wife, Maggie, provided a legitimate excuse. Then Burns orchestrated several frustrating conferences during which he unsuccessfully attempted to set unreasonable limitations on our questioning. Finally, in April 2012, we raised the question of the delaying tactics before Judge Pallmeyer. This impelled another of Daley's lawyers to announce publicly that Daley had agreed to testify, but he continued to hedge on the date and the scope of the questioning.

Judge Pallmeyer was satisfied for the moment, but I was not. I told the courtroom scribes, after the proceedings, "We've been frustrated over the last seven months. . . . They say the devil is in the details. Certainly, we don't believe there is any reason to limit the scope."

During this seven-month period, the Cook County state's attorney's office had taken a pretrial appeal to the Seventh Circuit Court of Appeals as to whether Judge Pallmeyer was correct in denying prosecutorial immunity from suit to the Cook County felony review prosecutor who participated in Michael Tillman's interrogation. While the appeal was pending, we participated in a mediation process with lawyers working for the Seventh Circuit and attorneys from the SAO. Former alderwoman Toni Preckwinkle was now the elected president of the Cook County Board of Commissioners, and Cook County commissioner Larry Suffredin was a ranking member of the county board's Litigation Committee, so we were hopeful that we might reach a settlement agreement with the County. In April, we agreed to settle with the County for $600,000, and the county board of commissioners approved it in May. "I want to commend President Preckwinkle and the County Board for fairly and reasonably reaching this rather small but important part of the case," I said.

Mayor Emanuel had replaced Mara Georges as the City's corporation counsel with a high-powered former corporate lawyer, Steve Patton, with a wealth of experience negotiating billion-dollar settlements as a partner at Kirkland Ellis. Early on, Patton had reached out to me to talk about settling the Michael Tillman and Ronald Kitchen cases. In consultation with Locke, Ben, and Joey, I had several conversations with Patton, who, while personable, relished playing hardball.

What Patton may have sensed, but did not know for certain, was that both Michael and Ronald wanted to end their revictimization, in court and in the media, by settling their cases. This was particularly true of Michael, who was scheduled to sit for his deposition in the near future. As Ben and I prepared him for his testimony, the sessions were excruciating for him as he painfully told us of his torture, of suffering through two trials, and of the emotional and physical trauma and abuse that he suffered while serving twenty-three and a half years in maximum-security prisons. We accelerated talks with Patton, and, after some back and forth, agreed to a $5,375,000 settlement with the City; unfortunately it did not also honor my request for an apology from the mayor. Steve Patton said that he would offer Ronald Kitchen a similar amount, but Ronald and Locke were not ready to accept and felt that we could up the ante if we continued with discovery.

On July 23, 2012, exactly twenty-six years after Michael endured three days of torture, the city council's Finance Committee approved the agreement, and two days later the full council sealed the approval. Michael was profoundly relieved that the ordeal was over and refused all requests for interviews. We released a statement on his behalf in which he addressed Daley's culpability: "If he had done what he should have, I would not have been tortured, lived with the fear of the death penalty, or sent to prison. To me, this settlement proves that Daley, Jon Burge, and Burge's torture crew did me terribly wrong."

Once more, we called on Mayor Emanuel to apologize, a demand I had publicly renewed in a *Sun Times* op-ed the month before: "Such an apology, sincerely offered during Torture Awareness Month, would be of real significance to the survivors of Chicago police torture, their families, and Chicago's African-American community, who were so brutally abused, lied to, and then rudely mocked." But no apology was forthcoming, as I noted in a follow-up article posted on my *Huffington Post* blog: "Mayor Emanuel Stands Mum as the Chicago City Council Approves Tillman Torture Settlement."

In our discovery work on Ronald Kitchen's case, we learned that a relative of one of the Mexican American victims had mentioned that the victim's husband, Pedro Sepulveda, was originally a suspect, and had been abused by the investigating detectives. Our trusted paralegal, Alberto Rodriguez, and I headed out to West Englewood, not far from where Alberto grew up, to follow this lead.

Alberto was no ordinary paralegal, to say the least. As a kid in the '70s, he was a member of the Latin Souls street gang, and later, after becoming educated about the colonialization of his native Puerto Rico, he had affiliated with the FALN, a revolutionary Puerto Rican organization that was waging armed struggle in the United States. He was arrested in 1983 for seditious conspiracy and was convicted after taking, along with his fellow defendants, a prisoner-of-war position in his federal trial. He spent the next fifteen years in federal prison, mostly in Lewisburg, until he was released in 1999, along with most of his co-defendants, thanks to the tireless efforts of Jan Susler and many others in the Puerto Rican independence movement. Shortly thereafter, we hired him and he joined

Lourdes Arias, our office manager since the 1990s, to form the heart and soul of our staff.

Pedro Sepulveda was now dead, but just after he was interrogated by detective Michael Kill at Area 3, he had told his mother, sister, and brother he had been brutalized. We located Pedro's sister, who told us Pedro had recounted to the family that he had been beaten and kicked in the chest and testicles, had his head pushed into a toilet, and was also bagged by his Area 3 interrogator. He had shown his mother the bruises, and she had taken him to the hospital. Pedro's sister took us to her mother's house, and she confirmed the story. Of the more than 110 cases of Burge-related torture we had documented, this was the first case of a Latinx victim; all the other torture survivors whose cases we had documented were African American.

After Burge had entered prison, the Feds had continued their investigation, with Byrne and Dignan the main targets. The statute of limitations would run out on these primary Burge accomplices in November 2012, five years after they had last denied, falsely and under oath, torturing Darrell Cannon, Michael Tillman, Greg Banks, and others. In the meantime they had retreated to the Fifth Amendment as they saw their boss and role model indicted, convicted, and imprisoned.

As the deadline approached, US attorney Patrick Fitzgerald and all the dedicated assistants who had shepherded the case through Burge's sentencing were long gone, but the assistant who had taken over seemed serious about making indictments happen. Unfortunately, the assistant was overruled by the acting US attorney, Gary Shapiro, who was not as committed to going beyond Burge as Fitzgerald had professed to be, and the Feds had not been successful in flipping an Area 2 officer against Byrne and Dignan as they had with McDermott in Burge's case. They let the statute run out, fulfilling Jeff Kramer's prediction, years before, that Burge would be their big and only fish.

CHAPTER 34

On What Planet . . .

On January 14, 2013, our team—Locke, Ben, Joey, Darrell, Chick, Michael, and I—walked into the large courtroom on the top floor of the federal courthouse to argue our appeal in Darrell Cannon's civil case.

Much had happened since we had filed our complaint more than seven years before. The City had argued that we were barred from bringing our case because Darrell had previously sued Byrne and Dignan for his torture, in the mid-1980s, and had settled it for $3,000. We had based our case on the theory that the original settlement, which Darrell had reluctantly accepted, was a product of police department fraud and cover-up that were not exposed until after he accepted the settlement. This argument had been previously accepted by the Seventh Circuit in a Milwaukee police shooting case, *Bell v. Milwaukee*, in which the court upheld a "redo" of the case, which had been settled for a pittance, after an egregious police cover-up was brought to light. Judge Amy St. Eve, a highly intelligent, conservative jurist, had initially denied the City's motion to dismiss our case, but five years later, after we had done an enormous amount of additional work, and the taxpayer-funded City lawyers had billed $1.5 million in fees, she had reversed her field and deemed the cover-up irrelevant to the issue of fraud. Darrell knew he had been tortured, she said; therefore, he had not been deceived and was not entitled to anything more than his scant original $3,000, of which he had netted a grand total of $1,247 after the court-appointed lawyer had taken his cut.

Nationally noted antitorture lawyer Joe Margolies, with assistance from Ben, Locke, and me, had drafted a powerful brief, setting forth the police cover-up and the central roles played by Burge, Byrne, and Dignan and demonstrating that the official fraud in our case was even more egregious than that in *Bell v. Milwaukee*. Darrell had asked me to argue for our side, and I was prepared for just about anything. The three-judge Seventh Circuit panel was made up of judge Ilana Rovner, who had the well-deserved reputation of being a liberal with a big heart, and two conservative judges: Sarah Barker, formerly the US attorney for the Southern District of Indiana, and Kenneth Ripple. Rovner had served as a district court judge in the 1990s, and we had developed a friendly and mutually respectful relationship.

My argument went well, and the City's lawyer, Justin Houppert, stepped to the podium. Judge Rovner addressed Houppert:

> And before you even introduce yourself, I want to start you off because it seems to me that the City has misread *Bell*. In both *Bell* and this case the determinative fact is not what the plaintiffs knew but what the plaintiffs could not prove because of the cover-up. In each case the plaintiff or the plaintiff's surviving representative knew the officers engaged in wrongful conduct and in each case the extensive cover-ups prevented them from proving it.

After Houppert offered a response, Judge Rovner continued:

> Look, if a defendant destroys evidence of wrongdoing and the plaintiff knows that the defendant destroyed that evidence, does that knowledge preclude the plaintiff from later claiming fraud in the inducement of a settlement? If so, does that mean that the more successfully you lie, you cheat, you commit fraud, in litigation, the greater your reward for forcing a small settlement?

Calling the City's "no fraud" argument "unavailing . . . to be kind," Judge Rovner summarized the facts in the record:

> These officers take a man with a prior murder conviction. Then they lie, then they torture him into making a statement that leads to a second murder conviction, then they lie about it, then they destroy evidence, then they engage in this incredibly lengthy cover-up with other city officials. You've got to help me. On what planet does he have a meaningful redress in the courts under those circumstances. . . . You would have us enforce a settlement procured by defendants who so rigged the deck that no plaintiff could have proven a legitimate claim and that to me seems to be the bottom line here.

Judge Rovner then dismantled the City's argument that Darrell's lawyer was required to ask the defendants during his initial case if they had tortured other suspects:

> That astonishes me, that argument because, in other words, he is supposed to have asked in discovery, "By the way, have these officers tortured anyone else? Is the City helping these officers cover up other criminal acts?"

Judge Sarah Barker then suggested, "Where it's completely futile, because of corruption basically, you've deprived him of access to the courts, haven't you?" Judge Rovner then returned to the City's argument that Darrell should have further questioned the police conspirators:

> Judge Rovner: So why is Burge in prison right now? Why, bottom line, why do you think he is in prison right now? What was it that put him in prison right now?
> Houppert: He was convicted of committing perjury for denying acts of torture, yes.
> Judge Rovner: Exactly.

Judge Rovner then addressed the question of the settlement's unconscionability:

> At the time he settled, there was no way for him to even begin to prove his case for torture, much less prove the cover-up. . . . He's in prison for murder, based on the confession that he now alleges, and indeed alleged from the very beginning, was the result of torture, his bargaining position was absolutely non-existent in those circumstances, and it was non-existent because the defendants obtained that condition through a confession that was given under torture and then covered up the torture, and that to me is the bottom line here.

Judge Rovner, calling it "a miracle" that the truth had come out, underscored the symmetry between Darrell's case and the *Bell* decision:

> Under *Bell,* the plaintiff, it seems to me, has shown exactly what [he] needed to show, and any other result would mean that defendants could engage in a decade-long cover-up with impunity. . . . It seems to me that if the defendants successfully suppressed the truth in an effort to force an unfavorable settlement out of the plaintiff, they should not be rewarded for the success of their scheme when the truth eventually comes out.

As the City's argument concluded, Judge Barker addressed the paltry settlement given to Darrell in 1988:

> Given all the things you know now and all the corruption that came to light, and the facts that have settled out in a different way than anybody understood or would admit at the time the settlement agreement was entered into, don't you think that it's a thin reed on which you're attempting to hang your resolution to say, given all of that, $3,000 is a fair settlement?

In the many dozens of arguments before the Seventh Circuit and the US and Illinois Supreme Courts that we had made over the past forty years, we had never seen a court so strongly take a side. We tried to curb our enthusiasm, but the impact of the court's reaction was not lost on the City. A few days later, I got a call from Jim Sotos, an old adversary, who was representing Burge, Byrne, and Dignan on the appeal but had been spared the indignity of arguing the case. He said that Steve Patton wanted to convey a settlement demand if we were willing to talk. This was a total sea change—the City had never offered a nickel during the previous seven years. We said we were open to talking, and Patton offered Darrell $1.1 million.

It was certainly tempting, and we thought we could probably move the City to $1.5 or $2 million if we engaged further. Joey, Ben, Locke, and I met with Darrell to discuss our options. In light of Judge Rovner's responses, I advocated strongly for holding out until the decision was rendered. My thinking was twofold: the decision would be significant in furthering the ongoing battle for the torture survivors, and it would put us in an even better bargaining position. My co-counsel were less confident, but Darrell, who was now working with CeaseFire to prevent gang violence on the south side, agreed that we should play it out for the time being. I communicated our decision to Patton.

I tipped off Carol Marin about the argument, and she presented a ten o'clock investigative exclusive. Introduced as NBC 5's political editor, Carol characterized the argument as an "extraordinary tongue lashing" and featured a photo of Judge Rovner over excerpts from the audiotape, including one of our favorite clips: "They lie about it. Then they destroy evidence and then they engage in this lengthy cover-up with other city officials." After playing the exchange between Houppert and Judge Rovner that included the indignant judge saying, "On what planet," Carol cut to Darrell, saying, "If I had known then what I know now there is no way on God's green earth I would have settled for $3,000, but full justice can never be given to me because of what I've lost in those twenty-four years."

Anchor Marion Brooks closed Carol's piece—which she had introduced by stating that the case "might cost the City millions"—with the acknowledgment that both Dignan and Byrne "adamantly deny they tortured any suspect" and Byrne's claim that "Darrell Cannon is a two-time convicted murderer who never deserved the $3,000 and doesn't deserve another payday at taxpayer expense."

A few months after Michael Tillman's case was settled, Ronald Kitchen had urged us to aggressively pursue a negotiated resolution in his case. I contacted Steve Patton and reminded him that he had told me he was willing to offer Ronald what he had offered Michael. Patton told me the offer was no longer on the table, so we had no choice but to continue to conduct discovery in Ronald's case. We once again sought to depose Daley. After several fruitless months of negotiations with Terry Burns and company, we filed yet another motion, in February 2013, to compel Daley's testimony.

On April 1, the Seventh Circuit issued a unanimous decision that, in spite of April Fool's Day, was no joke. A three-judge panel that included Judge Rovner upheld Burge's perjury and obstruction of justice conviction. The opinion was written by judge Ann Williams, the only African American judge in the history of the Seventh Circuit. Introducing the decision, Judge Williams wrote:

> Former Chicago Police Commander Jon Burge presided over an interrogation regime where suspects were suffocated with plastic bags, electrocuted until they lost consciousness, held down against radiators, and had loaded guns pointed at their heads during rounds of Russian roulette. The use of this kind of torture was designed to inflict pain and instill fear while leaving minimal marks. When Burge was asked about these practices in civil interrogatories served on him years later, he lied and denied any knowledge of, or participation in, torture of suspects in police custody. But the jury heard overwhelming evidence to contradict that assertion and convicted Burge for obstruction of justice and perjury.

In the court's decision, Judge Williams summarized the "horrific" evidence the government had introduced against Burge at trial:

> At trial, the government called multiple witnesses to testify about the methods of torture and abuse used by Burge and others at Area 2 in order to establish that Burge lied when he answered the interrogatories in the *Hobley* case. . . . The witnesses at trial detailed a record of decades of abuse that is unquestionably horrific. The witnesses described how they were suffocated with plastic bags, electrocuted with homemade devices attached to their genitals, beaten, and had guns forced into their mouths during questioning. Burge denied all allegations of abuse, but other witnesses stated that he bragged in the 1980s about how suspects were beaten in order to extract confessions. Another witness testified that Burge told her that he did not care if those tortured were innocent or guilty, because as he saw it, every suspect had surely committed some other offense anyway.

The court then found that the evidence Burge had lied was "overwhelming" and that he had received a fair trial. It was another important victory and seemed to bode well for Darrell's appeal.

Locke had taken over as "point man" in the Ronald Kitchen negotiations, and during the summer we worked out a deal: the City would pay Ronald $6.1 million and his former co-defendant, Marvin Reeves, a like amount. City council approved the settlement in September 2013.

After being confronted once again by Fran Spielman, Mayor Emanuel finally offered an impromptu apology:

> I am sorry this happened. Let us all now move on. This is a dark chapter on the history of the city of Chicago. I want to build a future for the city. . . . But, we have to close the books on this. We have to reconcile our past. . . . Yes, there has been a settlement. And I do believe that this is a way of saying all of us are sorry about what happened . . . and closing that stain on the city's reputation.

Cook County board president Toni Preckwinkle praised the mayor for his apology, saying it was "long overdue and entirely appropriate." She also acknowledged the role that county prosecutors had played in the torture conspiracy, and added:

> You've got to 'fess up and acknowledge the difficult, problematic parts of your own history if you're ever going to make any progress forward. Denial gets you nowhere. Refusing to acknowledge those reprehensible parts of our national or local history is self-destructive in the long run.

I praised Emanuel's actions, saying, "It's important that he has acknowledged that it is a dark stain on the history of the city and he's sorry for it. That is certainly a step forward from what Mayor Daley refused to do." But, I continued, the apology was not enough. I suggested, for the first time, that the City should establish a $20 million fund—equal to the amount already spent to defend Burge and his cohorts—to compensate torture victims who were not able to sue because of the cover-up. A few days later, Steve Patton publicly rejected the demand for compensation, stating, "It would be very difficult to justify spending taxpayer dollars to settle a claim that's barred."

At the same time, the battle around the Torture Inquiry and Relief Commission (TIRC) had once again come to the fore. Among TIRC's members were Rob Warden of Northwestern and human rights lawyer Len

Cavise; the director was David Thomas, a well-respected criminal defense lawyer who had campaigned for its creation. David, like Rob and Len, brought a keen understanding of the operations of Burge's cabal of torturers to his work at the TIRC.

In its two years of existence, the TIRC had referred sixteen cases to the criminal courts for evidentiary hearings. Consequently, state's attorney Anita Alvarez, the FOP, and their reactionary allies despised the TIRC and wanted to destroy it. They had been able to temporarily stop its funding in late 2012 and early 2013, but community outrage, led by Black People Against Police Torture, had successfully obtained its reinstatement. In May 2013, the TIRC had recommended an evidentiary hearing in the high-profile case of Andrew Wilson's brother, Jackie.

Seizing on governor Pat Quinn's vulnerability in the upcoming 2014 primary election, Alvarez forged an unholy alliance with him, designed to depose director David Thomas and reconfigure the TIRC board with more pro–law enforcement members. Alvarez and her allies seized on the fact that TIRC had not informed the crime victims' families in Jackie's case and another high-profile case, as required by the TIRC statute.

A hearing was held September 25. We were there to support David, together with several torture survivors, their families, and antitorture activists on one side of the room, and the crime victims' families, wearing yellow ribbons, and representatives of the SAO, the FOP, and the Police Memorial Foundation on the other. Former superintendent Phil Cline, who had succeeded Burge as Area 2 Violent Crimes commander, was prominent among the torture deniers in attendance, as was disgraced Burge attorney Andrew Hale.

After nearly ninety minutes of discussion in private session, the TIRC board announced that David Thomas had "resigned," following a 5–4 vote, with the three new Quinn appointments toeing the governor's line to force the resignation. Soon thereafter, the new board withdrew its decision in Jackie Wilson's case, pending formal notification of the Fahey and O'Brien families and further investigation.

CHAPTER 35

Reparations Now!

In October 2013, aldermen Howard Brookins and "Proco" Joe Moreno introduced into the Chicago City Council an ordinance calling for reparations for Burge torture survivors. The ordinance was a product of more than thirty years of advocacy, following the first call in 1989. Since then, the concept—and the labeling—had received little attention until being resurrected by Stan Willis and BPAPT in 2006. Subsequently BPAPT incorporated the demand for reparations into proposed legislation, the Illinois Reparations for Police Torture Victims Act, which focused on the Burge victims still in prison and the long-term trauma inflicted by torture on its victims and their families. The proposed act called for the establishment of a Center for Torture Victims and Families to provide psychological and psychiatric treatment and vocational assistance. While the antitorture movement had long recognized that Chicago police torture was overtly and fundamentally racist both in design and effect, the direct, aggressive linking of Chicago police torture to the brutality of slavery through the concept of reparations—similar to the link forged over the previous decade with torture historically and internationally—was an important step toward affording torture survivors acknowledgment of the scope of their suffering, as well as remedies. In 2008 the demand for reparations for Chicago torture victims was reasserted to the UN Committee on the Elimination of Racial Discrimination (CERD) in a report and at a CERD hearing.

There was no response from the powers that be. In late 2012, the demand was again taken up, this time by the Chicago Torture Justice Memorials (CTJM). Founded in June 2011 by a group of artists, educators, lawyers, and activists, under the leadership of Joey and anti–death penalty activist Alice Kim, CTJM sought to memorialize the Chicago police torture cases and the struggle for justice. In a public call for people to submit proposals for the memorials, CTJM announced as its intention "to honor the survivors of torture, their family members, and the African American communities affected by the torture." Throughout the previous year, CTJM had conducted roundtables, workshops, readings, performances, a film festival, and other educational events focused on the police torture scandal. A fall exhibit at a local art gallery, entitled "Opening the Black Box, the Charge Is Torture," featured seventy-five torture-related proposals submitted by artists, educators, architects, and activists as ways to memorialize Chicago police torture.

Later in the year, Joey drafted the original Reparations Ordinance. After much discussion, CTJM decided that the relief for victims should continue to be called "reparations," despite the term's potential to alienate some of the politicians whose support CTJM was seeking. As was later explained to the *Washington Post* by CTJM leader Mariame Kaba, the term "reparations" reflected the fact that this was compensation meant to make amends for abuse at the hands of the state, and underscored that race and bias were central: "The racial component of this is an essential part of the torture itself . . . the victims were subject to repeated racial epithets. The . . . box that was used to electrocute them was called the 'n——' box."

Joey redrafted the ordinance, relying on reparations legislation passed in other countries; further input from torture survivors, their family members, and the affected community; and international models adopted in Chile, Argentina, and South Africa. It now called for an official apology, compensation to the survivors, tuition-free education at the City Colleges of Chicago for all torture survivors and their families, and a center on Chicago's south side that would provide psychological counseling, healthcare services, and vocational training to those affected by law enforcement torture and abuse. The ordinance also called for the establishment of a fund of at least $20 million to finance these reparations, required that the Chicago Public Schools teach students about the torture cases, and mandated that the City sponsor the construction of public memorials for torture victims.

In December 2013, Stanley Wrice, who was tortured by Byrne and Dignan in the garage at old Area 2 in September of 1982, was exonerated after an evidentiary hearing. This capped a long legal struggle during which the special prosecutors' office had taken the untenable position that the admission of a tortured confession into evidence was "harmless error" and did not require the granting of a new trial. Northwestern professor David Protess, now the director of the Chicago Innocence Project, had taken up

Stanley's cause, and in 2012 the Illinois Supreme Court had granted Stanley a new hearing. Represented by defense lawyers Jennifer Bonjean and Heidi Lambros, Stanley described his torture at the mandated hearing; Byrne and Dignan took the Fifth; and the trial judge, finding that Byrne and Dignan committed perjury at Stanley's 1983 trial, granted him a new trial with the confession barred. Denied the only "evidence," the special prosecutor reluctantly dismissed Stanley's case in time for him to be home for Christmas after more than thirty years in jail.

After aldermen Brookins and Moreno introduced the Reparations Ordinance, Joey, Alice Kim, Northwestern professor Martha Biondi, several other CTJM members, and I took on the task of meeting with numerous members of the city council to explain the ordinance and, one by one, obtain the members' endorsements. Two of the enlisted aldermen, Joe Moore and Roderick Sawyer, joined Moreno and Brookins as our de facto political consultants. A hearing on the ordinance was scheduled for March 2014 before the council's Finance Committee, chaired by the powerful (and pro–law enforcement) Ed Burke, but it was postponed days beforehand, because of the indictment of Alderman Brookins's chief of staff.

In early February 2014, Daley dodged another bullet, this time in the David Koschman case. Judge Toomin had granted our motion and appointed Dan Webb, a former US attorney, as special prosecutor. Webb had indicted Daley's nephew R. J. Vanecko for manslaughter; Vanecko had pleaded guilty in January, paving the way for Webb to issue a report declaring that Daley and his family had not exercised any "undue influence." Webb had afforded Richie the same courtesy that Egan and Boyle had afforded him—a deferential interview, the contents of which would remain secret. Webb's report was critical of some of the main police and prosecutorial officers, but, again echoing Egan and Boyle, none of the offenders were charged.

In April 2014, Amnesty International joined the reparations coalition spearheaded by CTJM and declared its support for the Reparations Ordinance. In its Global Campaign Against Torture, AI featured Darrell, and during its national convention took the lead in organizing a march, a demonstration, and a vigil in downtown Chicago. Each of the participants carried a black flag, designed by CTJM members, emblazoned with the name of one of the known Burge torture survivors. Addressing the crowd, Darrell declared, "People power is gonna keep this issue alive." Joey rejoined, "It can be passed, should be passed, and will be passed," and I followed with "This scandal will not end until all the men receive reparations for the torture." As the names of the survivors were read aloud, the corresponding flags were presented in a line facing City Hall.

It was now sixteen months since Judge Rovner had roasted the City at Darrell's argument, and I had lost many a night's sleep worrying why the decision was taking so long. We had ascertained that Judge Rovner was writing the decision, which had bolstered our confidence. Then, on May 27, 2014, Judge Rovner handed down the Seventh Circuit's decision.

It was unanimous, and a shocker. Judge Rovner set the tone in her opening paragraph:

> This appeal casts a harsh light on some of the darkest corners of life in Chicago. The plaintiff, at the time of the events giving rise to this suit, was a general in the El Rukn street gang, out on parole for a murder conviction, when he became embroiled in a second murder. Among the defendants are several disgraced police officers, including the infamous Jon Burge, a man whose name evokes shame and disgust in the City of Chicago.

She then reversed her field on everything she had so forcefully advocated at the argument, rejecting fraud, unconscionability, and the similarities to *Bell v. Milwaukee*, while holding that the 1988 settlement agreement that Darrell's appointed lawyer had convinced him to sign was so broad that it also prevented Darrell from suing for the twenty-four years of wrongful imprisonment he had subsequently suffered. Now, Judge Rovner, speaking for the panel, downplayed the evidence of cover-up and the City's role in it, and, in conclusion, blamed the victim, as she did throughout, and washed the panel's hands of the matter:

> This case casts a pall of shame over the City of Chicago: on the police officers who abused the position of power entrusted to them, on the initial trial judge who was later imprisoned for accepting bribes to fix murder cases, on City officials who turned a blind eye to (and in some instances actively concealed) the claims of scores of African-American men that they were being bizarrely and horrifically abused at Area 2, and last but not least on Cannon himself, who was a convicted murderer out on parole when, by his own admission, he drove a car for his fellow El Rukn general as a murder was committed in the back seat, and then helped dispose of the body and conceal the crime. It is difficult to conceive of a just outcome given the appalling actions by almost everyone associated with these events, but the law regarding the finality of settlements governs the result.

Our worst nightmare was realized. How did this come to be, we asked each other. Did the other two judges refuse to go along with Rovner? If so, why didn't she dissent rather than write such a hateful decision? Did she have a change of heart after looking in more detail at Darrell's past? Was the court unwilling to apply its own groundbreaking precedent? Was Judge Rovner's initial plan to compel the City to settle by forcefully attacking its case, and when we did not accept its offer, she took the easy way out? Or did some outside political power put his finger on the scales?

Whatever the answer—and to this day, we have not discovered it—we were devastated and angry, and felt a sense of betrayal, though we had learned long ago that the courts were not our friends when it came to unpopular clients and racially charged cases. To his credit, Darrell did not second-guess our collective decision. We fired off a motion, petitioning the entire Seventh Circuit bench to rehear the case:

> This is a case of exceptional importance. It asks the Court to decide whether an acknowledged victim of the Burge torture scandal is bound by the settlement he entered into before the nature of the scandal could have been known outside the conspiratorial circle. The Panel held that the defendants are entitled to the benefit of their ill-gotten settlement, though it acknowledges what no one can fairly deny: that they hid the truth from the world for decades. Moreover, the decision of the Panel cannot be squared with this Court's landmark decision in *Bell v. City of Milwaukee*. It also does violence to all fair principles of summary judgment law, as the Panel distorts and otherwise takes crucial facts in the light most favorable to the defendant torturers rather than their victim, Darrell Cannon. Additionally, its holding that the settlement was not unconscionable flies in the face of all principles of equity and fundamental fairness. Most fundamentally, the Panel impermissibly holds that Mr. Cannon is not worthy of just compensation because he is a former gang member who had a prior conviction for murder.

We compared Judge Rovner's statements at the argument with those in her decision, and, in conclusion, we invoked international law:

> This is without question, an exceptional case of national and international importance, as it is now the subject of Amnesty International's Global Campaign Against Torture, and implicates Article 14 of the Convention Against Torture (CAT) under which the United States is obligated to "ensure in its legal system that the victim of an act of torture obtains redress and has an

enforceable right to fair and adequate compensation including the means for as full rehabilitation as possible."

The court, in an unusual order, directed the City to respond to our petition and "to focus on whether defendants' actions violated Cannon's constitutional rights by impeding or depriving him of meaningful access to the courts." This gave us a small glimmer of hope, but shortly after the City responded, the court denied our petition in an unsigned one-sentence order. A silver lining to this patently unfair result was that both Darrell and I were motivated to fight even harder for reparations.

In July, the Illinois Supreme Court issued a decision that rekindled community outrage. After the Police Pension Board had decided, in a 4–4 vote, that Burge could continue to collect his police pension despite his conviction, attorney general Lisa Madigan challenged the board's split decision by bringing suit in Cook County Chancery Court. The case was dismissed by the chancery judge, but the appellate court had reversed the decision, holding that the attorney general had legal standing to challenge the board's determination. Now, in a 4–3 decision, written by justice Ann Burke (alderman Ed Burke's wife), the Supreme Court reversed the appellate court in a technical ruling that guaranteed Burge the right to continue to collect his pension, which at that time had reached a total of nearly $700,000.

In the *Tribune,* Anthony Holmes condemned the decision as "crazy," while adding, "The sad part about it is they don't even think about us." I placed the decision in the context of reparations:

> G. Flint Taylor, an attorney who has battled Burge in court for more than a quarter century, contrasted how the ruling preserves Burge's pension—which records show totaled $48,502 last year—while many of his victims continue to struggle financially. "Some of them have no jobs and they've received no compensation from the city, yet Burge continues to get his compensation," Taylor said. "I find that to be an outrageous miscarriage of justice."

The *Tribune,* in an editorial, declared:

> The outrage is official. Ex-Chicago police Cmdr. Jon Burge gets to keep drawing money from the taxpayers. Burge's actions disgraced his badge, his department and his profession. . . . He'll be out of prison in less than a year. Thanks to his allies on the pension board, the taxpayers will be paying for Burge's crimes for a lot longer than he will.

In October 2014, Burge was released to a halfway house after serving three and a half years of his four-and-a-half-year sentence. Capitalizing on the outrage fostered by Burge's release, CTJM held a press conference at which torture survivors, other CTJM members, and Joey and I called for the city council's Finance Committee to resume plans to hold a hearing on the Reparations Ordinance. We contrasted Burge's release with his police pension intact to the plight of the survivors, who had not received "one red cent." Anthony spoke about the need for counseling:

> I need some help. I still have nightmares. If they can help vets who came back from Vietnam, then they can help me. All of us are like that. Every last one of us. You might not see it, but people come home, their wife do something stupid and they end up killing them or they might hurt them. Or they might just kill themselves because of the pressure we've been under for all of these years.

In discussing the political implications, Fran Spielman gave me the floor:

> Plaintiffs' attorney Flint Taylor then issued a thinly veiled political warning to Emanuel, who has been trying to rebuild his image with African-American voters who helped put him in office, but abandoned him in droves when he closed a record 50 Chicago Public Schools.
>
> "There's definitely a political downside for the mayor if he doesn't step forward and step forward quickly," said Taylor, who noted that the $20 million in reparations would be equal to the amount Chicago taxpayers have spent to defend Burge, his cohorts and former Mayor Richard M. Daley, who served as state's attorney during Burge's torture spree.
>
> "We've heard from [Chicago Teachers Union president and mayoral challenger] Karen Lewis. With a majority of the aldermen on board for this ordinance, the powers that be in this city should take it seriously. If they don't, they're going to have to answer for that at the polls."

The *Sun Times* and NBC TV 5 both editorialized in favor of reparations. Fran Spielman also reported that Emanuel again apologized for Burge's "disgraceful" misdeeds, and, later, that Emanuel was "riding the fence" on reparations and its proposed financial component:

> "As we get ready for what we have to do from a financial standpoint, there must be some way to address those whose statute of limitations has run out. But that doesn't mean there's only one way to do it." The mayor was asked whether that answer should be construed as a "yes, no or maybe." With trademark sarcasm, he replied, "I don't know. You've got all three answers."

Also that fall, CTJM worked with the Midwest Coalition for Human Rights to submit a brief to the UN Convention Against Torture, urging the committee to recommend that the US government support reparations, which, as the brief pointed out, were guaranteed under Article 14 of the UNCAT. CTJM and members of the antitorture group We Charge Genocide, including an inspiring young leader named Page May, traveled to Geneva to appear before UNCAT, where they pressed the issue of reparations and staged a dramatic silent protest to highlight ongoing racist police violence in Chicago. A few weeks later, UNCAT again formally recognized Chicago police torture under Jon Burge and the necessity for compensation to the survivors:

> With regard to the acts of torture committed by CPD Commander Jon Burge and others under his command between 1972 and 1991, the Committee . . . remains concerned that, despite the fact that Jon Burge was convicted for perjury and obstruction of justice, no Chicago police officer has been convicted for these acts of torture for reasons including the statute of limitations expiring. While noting that several victims were ultimately exonerated of the underlying crimes, the vast majority of those tortured—most of them African Americans—have received no compensation for the extensive injuries suffered.

UNCAT then specifically urged that the "state party" should "provide redress for CPD torture survivors by supporting the passage of the Ordinance entitled Reparations for the Chicago Police Torture Survivors."

Joey and I, together with Darrell, Anthony, fellow torture survivor Mark Clements, and several mothers of imprisoned torture survivors, continued to speak out in support of reparations. In December 2014, AI, CTJM, Project NIA, and We Charge Genocide led a five-mile march from police headquarters to the mayor's office, where the marchers delivered petitions signed by more than 45,000 people and held a peaceful teach-in outside his office. The effort also included a Twitter "power hour" directed at the mayor.

In January 2015 Joey and I obtained an order from judge Erica Reddick to depose Jon Burge in Alonzo Smith's post-conviction case. Alonzo had been released on parole more than a decade before, but his petition, filed by our close friend and colleague Dick Cunningham before his tragic death in 2001, had languished in the public defender's office until Joey had convinced the head of the post-conviction section to pass the case to us. The case was originally in front of one of the most pro-police judges at 26th Street, but when she took a leave of absence for health reasons, Judge Biebel had reassigned the case to Judge Reddick. An African American former public defender, Erica Reddick had been instrumental in winning freedom for Alton Logan, who had been wrongfully convicted at the hand of Jon Burge. Subsequent to her order, I would have yet another confrontation with the ex-convict police commander, this time in early February, to question him about his active role in supervising the torture of Alonzo in the basement of old Area 2.

Burge's deposition was set for Monday, February 9, at 11:00 a.m. in downtown Tampa. Burge had been served, but I was worried that he would not show up and we would not be able to enforce the subpoena. The Friday beforehand, Kris Klutter, who, together with Alexis Pegues formed a terrific PLO paralegal team, buzzed me over the office intercom. He was incredulous as he told me that someone who said he was Jon Burge was on the phone. Thinking it was Chick Hoffman, pulling my leg, I picked up. The voice on the other end of the line was unmistakable—it was Burge, without a doubt. He sounded weak, and pleaded with me to change the location of the deposition because he could not walk the block from where he thought he would have to park, owing to various physical ailments, including emphysema. For a fleeting moment I felt sorry for him, but I wasn't inclined to change the location at the last moment. When I told him so, the real Burge emerged, and he snarled that he just might not show up. As it turned out, there was an indoor garage attached to the court reporter's office, so he would only have to walk a few yards. I called him back with the information, and it seemed to satisfy him.

I caught an early-morning flight to Tampa that Monday, but the aircraft was returned to the gate with mechanical failure. The next flight would not arrive in Tampa until 1:00 p.m. I called the special prosecutor, who had traveled to Tampa the night before, and Burge's parole officer, explaining that he was required to wait, but received no assurances. Once the plane landed, I rushed to the court reporter's office to face an angry Burge. I apologized and then began what I represented as a very short deposition, focused on Alonzo Smith's case. After Burge took the Fifth to my first question, he rose slowly and headed for the door, saying, "Good day, nice meeting you" to the special prosecutor, the court reporter, and videographer. I stood and with raised voice told him that he could not leave, that I would call the judge, who would order him to return if he left and would report him to his parole officer. He sat back down and asserted the Fifth to my questions for the next forty-five minutes. My final question was about Jackie Wilson. When I stated that I had not asked about Jackie at Burge's 2011 deposition at FCC Butner, his animosity again came to the fore: "I'll exercise my Fifth Amendment rights," he snarled, "even though I would like to call you a liar."

As the February 2015 mayoral primary election approached, the campaign for reparations redoubled its efforts. CTJM now had a majority of the fifty Chicago aldermen committed as sponsors, and a significant number of other politicians, aldermanic candidates, and community organizations had come aboard, as had Jesus "Chuy" Garcia, Emanuel's main opponent in the race for mayor.

On Valentine's Day the reparations movement held a downtown rally in the historic Chicago Temple, attended by a large, multiracial, and multi-generational crowd. CTJM distributed a leaflet listing which politicians had announced support for the ordinance and highlighting those who had not done so, with particular emphasis on Mayor Emanuel. Many attendees wore black T-shirts, designed and distributed by CTJM, featuring the City of Chicago flag with a fifth star, black in color, added to represent the torture survivors. Joey was the MC, and a long list of speakers, from torture survivors and their mothers to progressive politicians, addressed the crowd, with several emphasizing the demand for the long-postponed hearing on the ordinance. Other coalition actions included a light show in front of the mayor's house that spelled out "Reparations Now," community teach-ins, a sing-in at City Hall, church presentations, and demonstrations on the subway and outside mayoral debates.

A few days after the rally, corporation counsel Steve Patton called me to suggest a post–primary election meeting with CTJM representatives, at which the City would present its plan for reparations. Patton repeated his previous position that the City was not inclined to provide any financial compensation to the survivors. I told him that compensation was a non-negotiable demand, but CTJM decided to accept Patton's invitation in order to learn what the City had planned and to advocate for the complete reparations package.

The CTJM negotiation team was comprised of Joey and me; Dorothy Burge from BPAPT (no relation to Jon); three CTJM members, including Martha Biondi; and two representatives from Amnesty International. On the other side of the table, Patton headed up a group that included deputies from his office and representatives from the mayor's legislative, legal, and human relations departments. The first meeting was convened shortly after Emanuel had suffered an unanticipated setback in the mayoral primary—he had not won a majority of the vote and was therefore required to face Chuy Garcia in an early April runoff.

While the negotiations were ongoing, Alderman Burke—in response to a public announcement from the reparations coalition that it planned to disrupt the next Finance Committee meeting if no hearing date had been announced—set a hearing on the ordinance for the week after the April runoff election.

We continued to meet with Patton and his team throughout March and early April. Even though nonfinancial issues were at the forefront of the discussions, the CTJM team firmly maintained its position that financial compensation was a required part of the legislation. At first Patton's corporate lawyer approach offended several of our nonlawyer team members, but an initial guardedness and occasional hostility was gradually replaced by a mutual spirit of cooperation. Both sides recognized the other's good faith and worked out the parameters of the nonfinancial issues. Compensation to the survivors was discussed hesitantly at first, and as the April 14 hearing date approached, CTJM and its negotiating team reluctantly agreed, internally, upon a bottom line of $100,000 per survivor. Based on an estimated total of 120 potential survivors, CTJM set its total financial demand at $12 million. The City responded with an offer in the range of $2 to $3 million.

Another difficult decision was to remove the families of the deceased survivors from eligibility for financial compensation. We calculated that the actual number of eligible living survivors would likely be in the range of fifty to sixty, making the bottom line of $100,000 per survivor more feasible from a total pool of $5 to $6 million. The City had reluctantly raised its "final" offer to $5 million, and Patton had told me that the City would go no higher.

On April 7, a week before the scheduled hearing, Rahm Emanuel, dubbed "Mayor of the 1%" by writer Kari Lyderson, beat Chuy Garcia in the hotly contested mayoral election. Steve Patton and I exchanged cell phone numbers as I headed to Boston to speak about police torture at Harvard Law School and Patton headed south to Florida for a long post-election weekend.

After I spoke at the law school, I drove to the neighborhood where I'd grown up to explore my old stomping grounds. When I returned to the car, I saw that I had a missed call from Steve Patton. I called him back, and after we exchanged pleasantries, he raised the City's offer to $5.5 million. I told him that I would convey the offer to Joey and CTJM and get back to him. A few CTJM members were reluctant to agree, but Joey and I were convinced that this was the top offer. Joey polled as many survivors as she could reach, and they were all in agreement with us, so I informed Patton that we had a deal.

At the April 14 hearing, held in the City Hall chamber packed with hundreds of reparations supporters, the agreement between the City and CTJM, formalized as a Resolution and Amended Ordinance, was supported with testimony from numerous witnesses. Joey and Steve Patton detailed the Resolution and Amended Ordinance, and their presentations were followed by supporting testimony from Darrell, Anthony, Amnesty International USA's executive director Steve Hawkins, Dorothy Burge, and me.

The Finance Committee unanimously voiced its approval for the legislation, which provided for financial compensation to the living survivors in the total amount of $5.5 million; it also provided for nonfinancial reparations to the living survivors and their immediate families, as well as to the immediate families of the deceased survivors. These nonfinancial reparations included psychological counseling at a dedicated community center, free education at the City Colleges, an official apology, the teaching of the torture scandal in the Chicago Public Schools, job training, and a public memorial.

Outside, Darrell told the Associated Press: "For those of us who have been fighting and struggling to set a landmark, this is a landmark. This is the moment. What we do here will not be undone. People across the country will talk about Chicago." Joey and I issued a joint statement, a bit more cautious. We called the passage and implementation "historic" and said it "will go a long way to remove the longstanding stain of police torture from the conscience of the city." Martha Biondi, an integral CTJM member and negotiator, told the *Tribune* that she hoped the reparations ordinance would "inform the national conversation" about police treatment of people of color as well as police accountability, and that the ordinance's provision for a permanent memorial would "offer a lasting image of the scandal in the city." I added that the city's apology was "doubly important given the fact that Burge refused to take responsibility for what he has done."

The *Tribune* also featured Patton's statement at the hearing, where he said, "We do this not because it's legally required, because it's not. We do this because we believe it's the right thing to do, both for the victims and their families and for the city." Mayor Emanuel was quoted as saying, "Today, we stand together as a city to try and right those wrongs, and to bring this dark chapter of Chicago's history to a close."

The reaction to the reparations package was overwhelmingly positive, although there was some criticism that the financial compensation was not enough. The *Sun Times*, in a lengthy editorial entitled "A Big Step toward Justice for Police Torture Victims," wrote:

> When crimes of heinous proportions are committed, it is not possible to fully compensate the victims. But it is possible to make a generous and enlightened effort at atonement, and that's what Mayor Rahm Emanuel and the City Council did Tuesday by agreeing to create a $5.5 million reparations fund for victims tortured by former Chicago Police Cmdr. Jon Burge. The agreement even includes a remarkable commitment to educate the public and future Chicago generations about Burge's reign of terror. . . . The commitment to education is especially important. The only way to ward off a future Jon Burge—a future brute in any walk of life, really—is to teach the lessons to be drawn from the horrors of the past.

CHAPTER 36

Never Before
in America

The Resolution and Amended Ordinance was to be introduced into the full council the following day and voted on in a special meeting in early May. I was sitting in the gallery the next day in order to make sure everything went according to plan, when I saw colleague and friend Craig Futterman. I asked him why he was there, and he replied that it was because the council was slated to approve a multimillion-dollar settlement for the family of a young man who had been slain by the Chicago police. The victim's name was Laquan McDonald, and Craig said that he and independent journalist Jamie Kalven were investigating a high-level cover-up in the case.

Two days later, I was on the train to Milwaukee, preparing to take a deposition in a case in which a Burge-like cop had led a squad of officers who had body cavity–searched dozens of Black men on the streets of Milwaukee. My cell phone rang, and it was Fran Spielman. She matter-of-factly told me that Burge had given a statement about reparations to Chicago police officer and wannabe author Martin Preib, and that Preib had posted it on his out-of-control cop blog. When she told me what Burge had said, I became angry—or "outraged," as Fran later wrote in a piece titled "Disgraced Chicago Cop Jon Burge Breaks Silence, Condemns $5.5 Million Reparations Fund." Burge, Fran said, specifically called out Darrell, Anthony, and me, saying that he found it "hard to believe" that Chicago's "political leadership" could "even contemplate giving reparations to human vermin" like the "guilty vicious criminals" he tried to take off the streets, and that I and others with a "radical political agenda" had been "working to free guilty, vicious criminals for years by filing specious lawsuits," and "grow rich because the city of Chicago is afraid to defend the lawsuits filed by these human vultures."

Spontaneously, I denounced Burge as a "convicted perjurer and liar" and pointed out that recently, Burge had once again taken the Fifth

Amendment rather than "tell these lies and commit this perjury under oath and run the risk of going back to jail where he truly belongs to spend the rest of his life." I said that I stood "ready to go anywhere, any time, any place to place him under oath and to ask him point-blank whether he tortured Anthony Holmes and whether he was responsible for the torture of Darrell Cannon and 115 to 120 other African-American men about whom we have documented proof that he and his co-conspirators tortured."

I wasn't finished, and went on to tell Fran:

He is clearly a serial human rights violator who has committed racist crimes against humanity too numerous to count. And this attack on the men who have so bravely stood up to him—and who a jury and a federal judge relied upon to send him to the penitentiary—only underscores how disgraceful and cowardly his unsworn statements—slandering me, my fellow lawyers and these clients—are.

I also addressed Burge's claim that we were "money-grubbers":

We have been committed to this for over two and a half decades—not to make money, but because we are firmly committed to exposing racist crimes against humanity. And the people who have joined with us include Amnesty International and a wide range of other organizations who see his crimes for what they are. He says the truth will come out. The truth has come out.

Fran quoted a "livid" Darrell as saying:

He talks about families [of crime victims]. What about all of our families who suffered while he was running free and rampant throughout the black community? And if I'm such a vermin or whatever he called me, look at my record since I've been home. Not one time have I had a negative encounter with the Police Department other than a traffic ticket.

An "equally incensed" Anthony told Fran:

He accuses us, but when you ask him to comment on what he did to us, he takes the Fifth. . . . The city is trying to help us because he put us in this position. If he hadn't, we wouldn't need no help. All of us are mentally unstable. We're not ourselves. He's trying to cover up for himself and saying he did everything right. He didn't do everything right. He tortured us. He's saying what he did to us was justified to get information. We can't stand torture. That's how he broke all of us. I was a gang-banger out on the street. True enough. But I didn't deserve what he did to me.

On May 6, 2015, alderman "Proco" Joe Moreno presented the Resolution and Amended Ordinance to the full city council. During his presentation, Moreno read each of the attending survivors' names, and each person stood. The council members then spontaneously faced the standing men, and, in a moment of high emotion, applauded them. After several other aldermen spoke, Mayor Emanuel officially apologized on behalf of the City:

This is another step but an essential step in righting a wrong, removing a stain on the reputation of this great city. Chicago finally will confront its past and come to terms with it and recognize when something wrong was done and be able to be strong enough to say something was wrong.

Addressing the torture survivors and their families, the mayor continued:

I want to thank you for your persistence. I want to thank you for never giving in and never giving up and allowing the city to join you on that journey to come face to face with the past and be honest enough and strong enough to say when we are wrong and try to make right what we've done wrong. This stain cannot be removed from the history of our city. But it can be used as a lesson of what not to do and the responsibility that all of us have.

The council then unanimously adopted the Resolution and Amended Ordinance. The resolution invoked a "sincere hope" that "the process of repair, renewal and reconciliation that we affirm today will help to restore the trust of all Chicagoans in the decency and fairness of their municipal and county governments, including their law enforcement agencies." Further, the resolution acknowledged respect for the work of CTJM and resolved that:

We, the Mayor and Members of the City Council of the City of Chicago, on behalf of all Chicagoans—

(1) acknowledge and condemn, as evil and reprehensible, any and all acts of torture and abuse inflicted upon the Burge victims; and

(2) apologize to the Burge victims for these horrific and inexcusable acts; and

(3) express our most solemn regrets to the families of the Burge victims for any and all harm that they suffered as a consequence of the ordeal that their loved ones were subjected to; and

(4) remember these past events, to ensure that this sad chapter in our City's history is never forgotten; and

(5) reaffirm our City's commitment to righting the wrongs of the past, and in so doing, reassure Chicago's residents that such wrongs will not be repeated in the future.

After the ceremony, we all traveled across the street to the Chicago Temple for a celebration with the survivors, their families, CTJM members, and other friends and loved ones. A documentary crew was interviewing the men, and the mood was joyful. Darrell summed it up in a quote to the *Guardian*:

> This is something that sets a precedent that has never been done in the history of America. Reparations given to black men tortured by white detectives. It's historic.

Pursuant to the terms of the ordinance, Joey and I compiled a list of living claimants for financial compensation and gave it to Corporation Counsel Patton for the City's review. There were 119 men on the most recent list of Burge torture survivors that we had compiled over the decades, and we used that list as the starting point for our submission. Deceased survivors were eliminated, some survivors chose not to pursue reparations for various reasons, ten had been officially exonerated and already received multimillion-dollar settlements, and others could not be located, and thus the final list contained forty-eight names. We presented documentation in support of the claimants and met with Patton and his deputy, Jenny Notz, on several occasions during the summer to informally advocate for the men on our list. Patton and Notz accepted all but six of the claims as "credible" and thereby eligible for reparations.

In response to the public notice provision in the ordinance, fifty additional persons made claims to an independent third-party administrator, Daniel Coyne, a professor at Chicago-Kent College of Law. After evaluating those claims Coyne presented to the City and CTJM eleven additional claimants he determined to be eligible. The City ultimately accepted seven of those claims, one of the claimants withdrew, and the City contested the other three.

The disputed cases were to be resolved by an arbitrator who would be jointly selected by the City and us. We proposed two former jurists for whom we had great respect: former federal magistrate Nan Nolan and former US district court judge David Coar. The city rejected Nolan but agreed to Judge Coar. Coar had grown up during the 1950s in the "Dynamite Hill" section of Birmingham, Alabama, so named because it was regularly the target of Klan bombings during the civil rights movement, and had worked for the NAACP Legal Defense Fund as a young lawyer.

Judge Coar was tasked with deciding whether the nine contested claimants were entitled to compensation, based on paper submissions and oral presentations. The ordinance further mandated that he was to consider factors including under what circumstances the claim was first made or reported to someone, the consistency of the claim over time, and any credible affirmative proof rebutting the claim. However, we convinced Patton and Notz that denials by Burge or any of his associates who had, on some other occasion, invoked the Fifth Amendment in response to questions about police torture could not be considered. We also obtained the City's agreement that Judge Coar should employ a flexible standard of proof, greater than "probable cause" but less than "a preponderance of the evidence."

We were also getting ready for a hearing in Alonzo Smith's case. Martin Preib's incendiary posting of Burge's statement on reparations had really fired me up, so I drafted a subpoena for all of Preib's communications with Burge and Dignan. Preib showed up in Judge Reddick's courtroom, a tall cop wearing a replica Chicago Cubs game shirt with "FOP" insignia replacing that of the Cubs, carrying three hundred pages of emails. After reviewing the documents in her chambers, Judge Reddick gave us about fifteen pages she deemed relevant.

It appeared from the documents tendered to us that Preib was working on a book to serve as an apologia for Burge and his "asskickers," and Burge and Dignan were spearheading this disingenuous effort. Their private writings were chilling. Dignan wrote in 2012: "Flint Taylor is a low life rat and has been for as long as I've known, but don't let the bastard fool you, he covers his tracks well. Maybe we can turn up something." He bemoaned the fact that he had known a gang crimes cop who "hated [Darrell] Cannon and would have killed his ass on sight, but alas he's gone."

Burge carried the vicious attacks one step further in a series of emails, saying that Jeff Haas "was a bigger snake than Taylor" and that John Conroy and Hobley attorney Andrea Lyon were also "snakes." Our former colleague Mariel Nanasi was a "bitch," and "as bad as Haas and Taylor." He regaled Preib with a story about how he'd had Jeff arrested for unpaid traffic tickets while he was visiting a client at Area 2, and suggested that Preib explore the possibility of having Anthony Holmes arrested at a reparations rally for a forty-year-old murder.

In July, Joey and I conducted a three-day hearing before Judge Reddick in Alonzo Smith's case. We supplemented Alonzo's powerful testimony (see chapter 17) detailing how Dignan and Byrne suffocated him in the basement of Area 2 with the testimony of Darrell Cannon, Greg

Banks, and Stanley Wrice, who were also survivors of Dignan and Byrne. After showing a video of Burge taking the Fifth, we called Dignan, then Byrne, to the stand. However bold in their emails and in statements to the press, they once again took the Fifth, after swearing to tell the truth.

As part of the evidence we presented an affidavit obtained from a Chicago librarian that shed further light on Dignan's racism and disregard for the truth. The librarian had told me, after a chance meeting in 2013, that, in 1965, she was a high school student at the Academy of Our Lady and became acquainted with Dignan, who was attending Mendel Catholic High School. She said she would ride around with Dignan and two of his friends in Dignan's Triumph TR4 and drink beer. Dignan and his friends called themselves the "Fernwood Boys," after their changing neighborhood. During these ride-arounds, Dignan and his buddies would engage in racist talk about "nigs," "niggas," and "jigaboos." On several occasions in the summer of 1966, the librarian stated, "Dignan stopped the car, and the boys jumped out and beat up blacks and hippies who were walking in the neighborhood." She was "horrified" but never told anyone, she said. She further recounted that she reconnected with Dignan in 1969, after he returned from Vietnam and joined the CPD; that they smoked dope he bragged he had taken from an arrestee; and that he boasted that, in exchange for a $100 bribe, he would let people he arrested for gun possession go.

About two weeks later, while awaiting Judge Reddick's decision, we got some welcome news in another torture post-conviction case. Fearing the death penalty, Shawn Whirl had pleaded guilty to the murder of a cab driver back in the early 1990s and had languished in prison ever since. He maintained that he did not commit the crime, and that he had been tortured into confessing by an Area 2 detective named James Pienta. Ben Elson from our office and Tara Thompson from the University of Chicago's Exoneration Project took on the case and enlisted me to work with them in challenging Shawn's confession in his post-conviction case. The judge, Jorge Alonzo, a former Cook County public defender, had at first denied us the right to an evidentiary hearing but had reversed his field. We had conducted the hearing in January 2014.

The hearing presented several obstacles not present in Alonzo Smith's case. Most significantly, the torture Shawn alleged—repeated scratching, with a key, over an open wound on his leg—had happened several years after Burge left Area 2. Additionally, in the cases that implicated Pienta with Burge, Pienta was not a main actor. We nonetheless focused on Burge and his legacy, and Pienta's prior working relationship with Burge in the 1970s and the first half of the 1980s. We had called Anthony Holmes as a witness because Pienta was involved with Burge in his arrest, and torture survivor Mearon Diggins, who also implicated Pienta. Pienta took the Fifth and we showed the video of Burge doing the same. We felt that the hearing had gone well, but Judge Alonzo, who would soon be appointed to a federal judgeship by President Obama, was not about to take the risk of finding that Shawn was tortured and granting him a new trial. Instead, relying on discrepancies in Shawn's testimony and the fact that Burge was no longer working at Area 2 at the time of Shawn's torture, Judge Alonzo denied our petition.

We had appealed to the Illinois Appellate Court, and I had argued the case in January 2015. The three judges gave assistant special prosecutor Brian Stefanich an exceptionally hard time, but with the Darrell Cannon experience fresh in my mind, I was not about to celebrate yet. However, when the unanimous decision came down that August, we were able to savor a hard-earned victory. Appellate judge Mary Anne Mason, married to magistrate Michael Mason, wrote the unanimous decision. For the court, she found that Judge Alonzo's findings of fact were "clearly erroneous" and that he used the wrong legal standard. Judge Mason, who had apparently not held my altercation with her husband a decade earlier against Shawn, dismantled Judge Alonzo's findings concerning Shawn's lack of credibility, finding that "the fact that some of the details of his testimony are slightly different now has marginal relevance to the central issue at the evidentiary hearing, i.e., whether the new evidence of a pattern and practice of abusive tactics employed by Pienta, had it been presented at the suppression hearing, would likely have produced a different outcome."

Turning to the torture evidence we presented at the hearing, Judge Mason wrote, "We believe all of this evidence supports a finding that Pienta was directly involved in a pattern of torture at Area 2." This evidence was not too remote in time, the court held, and Burge's absence from Area 2 was not determinative either:

> The evidence clearly establishes a long history, going back to at least 1973, of Pienta's involvement in abusing suspects in order to obtain confessions. The only evidence of change appears to be that the methods became less brutal over time and more care was taken to avoid causing detectable injuries. Pienta continued to work in violent crimes at Area 2 after Burge was transferred. There is no basis to assume Pienta's use of physical force to obtain confessions ceased simply because Burge was transferred to Area 3 while Pienta remained at Area 2. And, as Whirl points out, Burge's transfer to Area 3 was

a promotion and, thus, his departure would not dissuade officers like Pienta from continuing to "solve" cases by means of coerced confessions.

This set an important precedent for other torture defendants, as did the court's determination that "we believe Pienta's invocation of his fifth amendment rights is significant and a negative inference should have been drawn" from it. Finally, the court found that we met the legal standard that the outcome of Shawn's original suppression hearing would probably have been different if the pattern and practice evidence had been available and presented at that time, that "indeed, it is impossible to conceive of how the State could prevail at a new suppression hearing with the officer alleged to have coerced a suspect's confession invoking his privilege against self-incrimination." For good measure, Judge Mason, in a clear signal to all concerned, added, "Without Whirl's confession, the State's case was nonexistent."

The *Sun Times* hailed the decision in an editorial as "a big step forward in investigating police torture claims," and wrote:

> This case highlights another important issue: In many other cases like Whirl's, torture is alleged by a Burge underling. Unfortunately, a Cook County judge ruled after Whirl's case was already under way that the torture commission can't investigate cases in which Burge did not personally abuse a suspect. A bill introduced by state Sen. Iris Martinez and state Sen. Kwame Raoul would fix that—making it clear the commission can investigate police torture wherever it finds it. The bill has passed the Illinois Senate, but is stalled in the House. The House should pass it and the governor should sign it.

Two months later, the special prosecutor reluctantly dismissed Shawn's case and he walked out of prison a free man, twenty-five years after he was tortured into confessing.

In September 2015, Alonzo Smith, Joey, and I returned to Judge Reddick's courtroom to hear her announce her decision from the bench. Her decision was straightforward: she found that the physical abuse endured by Alonzo, Darrell Cannon, Greg Banks, and Stanley Wrice was accurately described as "torture"; that the evidence demonstrating the pattern and practice was "staggering"; that Alonzo's confession had been physically coerced from him; and that he had been deprived of a fair trial. Consequently, she overturned Alonzo's conviction and soon thereafter the special prosecutor dismissed his case, fourteen years after he had been released on parole.

On October 13, Shubra Ohri, a committed young lawyer who had joined our office while playing a supportive role in the reparations movement, Sarah Gelsomino and I filed a lawsuit on behalf of three clients against a team of narcotics officers and the City of Chicago, challenging the unconstitutional police practices that had allegedly occurred for a decade and a half at Homan Square. An "off the books" police detention center, the activities at Homan Square had been exposed over the previous six months in a series of articles by investigative reporter Spencer Ackerman in the *Guardian*. Dubbed a "secret black site" by the newspaper and located in the sprawling former Sears warehouse on Chicago's west side, Homan Square was the hub of clandestine police intelligence-gathering activities. At least ten thousand people, the vast majority of whom were Black and Latinx, had been taken to Homan Square over the previous fifteen years. They were held incommunicado and shackled in windowless rooms and cells for hours while they were interrogated for information. On numerous occasions, as documented by the *Guardian*, the detainees were subjected to physical abuse that, on at least one occasion, included anal rape. If the interrogation did not yield sufficient information, the victim would be sent to the nearby district police station, where he or she would be charged with a drug or gun offense.

Our three clients alleged that they had been taken to Homan Square on trumped-up drug charges, strip-searched, physically threatened, subjected to racial slurs, and denied the right to speak with a lawyer. When they were unable to provide the information sought by the police interrogators, they were charged with the sale of heroin and spent fifteen months in jail until an exasperated judge, citing the inexplicable contradictions in the officers' stories, dismissed the case midtrial. In our complaint, we linked Homan Square to the pattern and practice of racist torture during the Burge era, and the *Guardian* quoted me by way of explanation:

> Taylor, who is representing the three men in the latest Homan Square suit, said he saw an indirect link to Burge-era torture in the facility's intelligence-gathering operation: "It's just one method they use to terrorize a community that is black and people of color. If you take a look at what happened to all of these guys, it does fit into torture under the United Nations definition. First of all, there's sensory deprivation, and in some cases there is physical violence. There's the deprivation of food, drink, bathrooms, the racial epithets during an interrogation. It's to get information. So, yes, it's torture."

CHAPTER 37

Coming Full Circle

Any anticipated restoration of trust from the Black community that Mayor Emanuel had hoped to glean from the reparations ordinance and his apology was dashed just before Thanksgiving 2015, when the City's suppression of the police video that captured the wanton killing of Laquan McDonald by CPD officers finally came to light. This was the case that Craig Futterman and Jamie Kalven had been quietly investigating. The video made a complete lie out of the police version of events, showing a nonthreatening young Black man, shot down in a fusillade of sixteen shots from a white police officer's gun. Public release of the video shook the City and its power structure, leading to mass protests, the firing of the Chicago police superintendent and the head of the police disciplinary agency, repeated calls for the resignation of Mayor Emanuel and Cook County state's attorney Anita Alvarez, and a Department of Justice pattern and practice investigation of the CPD. In response, Emanuel publicly admitted to a police code of silence and appointed a task force to conduct a wide-ranging investigation into the patterns and practices of police misconduct we had been documenting for the past twenty-five years. The mayor attempted to proffer his role in approving torture reparations as a defense against the calls for his resignation.

On the heels of the Laquan McDonald revelations, Judge Coar conducted hearings on the nine reparations claims that the City had contended were not credible. Joey and I presented the cases at mini-hearings on behalf of seven of the claimants and other lawyers presented on behalf of two. Survivors appeared in person in four of the cases. Shortly thereafter, Judge Coar rendered his final written decisions, accepting eight of these claims as credible. Thus the final total of recipients stood at fifty-seven, and included Darrell Cannon and Anthony Holmes. As several recipients were to receive partial shares because they had previously received small settlements, each of the fifty-seven was guaranteed a total of $100,000 in compensation.

On January 4, 2016, the City began to issue reparations checks to the entitled survivors. Fran Spielman linked the police torture scandal to the Laquan McDonald case in a feature article:

> When the City Council agreed last spring to make Chicago the nation's first major city to pay reparations, there were high hopes that the $100,000 checks to individual torture victims would restore public trust between citizens and police in the African-American community so undermined by the convicted former Area 2 commander and his cohorts.
>
> But damage done by the police dashcam video that showed white police officer Jason Van Dyke pumping 16 shots into the body of 17-year-old Laquan McDonald, who was black, has added a new and equally ugly chapter in the history of the Chicago Police Department.

Fran also quoted my assessment:

> Reparations, although an historic accomplishment that recognizes that racist violence by the police is not a recent phenomenon, but rather spans many decades, cannot heal the city without fundamental, systemic changes within the Chicago Police Department, the Cook County State's attorney's office and the Cook County criminal justice system.

A few weeks later, an excellent young lawyer from Loevy and Loevy, Elliot Slosar, and I were in the courtroom of judge Nicholas Ford, a former Burge-era assistant state's attorney, on Jackie Wilson's case. That previous May, the Torture Inquiry and Relief Commission, after an exhaustive reinvestigation, had sent Jackie's case back to the criminal courts for a hearing on his torture claim. Elliot and I had volunteered to represent Jackie at the hearing, so here I was, twenty-eight years after we had begun to represent Andrew, taking on the case again, this time for his brother, in a criminal courtroom one floor up from where Jackie and his brother had been tried and convicted in the early 1980s.

It was hard to imagine a worse judge to be in front of in such an important, high-profile case. Not only was Ford a former prosecutor, but he had also taken a confession from a man who alleged that he had been tortured at Area 3 by one of Burge's underlings. This seemed a guaranteed ticket to remove him from the case, as Ford was a potential witness on the issue central to Jackie's hearing: whether he had been tortured into giving a confession as part of the pattern and practice of torture under Burge's command. Furthermore, Ford, after ascending to the bench, had been soundly rebuked by the appellate court for denying post-conviction relief to the man whose confession he took as a prosecutor.

We gathered all the information we could find about Ford—his close relationship with the FOP, the fact he was Facebook "friends" with several of Burge's henchmen and Burge's lawyer—combined with the obvious conflict he had as a potential witness, and composed a lengthy motion to recuse him that we brought before Chief Criminal Court Judge Biebel.

We were hopeful that Biebel would once again do the right thing, as he had so many times in the past. Unfortunately, Judge Biebel was retiring and wasn't about to grant our motion on the way out the door. As a result, we had to ask Ford to remove himself.

Appearing before Ford brought on a lawyer's version of post-traumatic stress—memories of J. Sam Perry and Brian Barnett Duff flooded back to me, as Judge Ford berated me repeatedly for having the temerity to raise his conflict and bias. He accused me of being "the sort of person that comes into court and will say anything because that's what you just did." He claimed that I was trying to "sew him into some bag of conspiracy." Prodded by comments from the assistant special prosecutor, he agreed that our motion was "a show" and "bordered on ridiculousness."

We were outraged and contacted a supportive member of the *Sun Times* editorial board, who was taken aback by Judge Ford's bias and conflict of interest. Shortly, an editorial entitled, "Change Judges in Case of Burge-Era Torture Claim" appeared in the *Sun Times:*

> A judge should not preside over a case in which he has such close ties or in which he might be a witness. Ford seems to have had trouble with that concept in the past, having been rebuked by appellate justices for presiding as a judge on cases in which he had earlier been a prosecutor. When Wilson and others first complained of police torture, no one believed such things could go on. It's taken decades, but we now know the tragic extent of physical pain that Burge and his detectives inflicted on African-American suspects. What we don't know is whether any of the men remaining in prison are innocent. It's time for a process that for so long has been mired in obfuscation and denial to be clear and aboveboard. Ford should take himself off the case.

Seeming oblivious to the editorial, Ford denied our motion the day after the editorial appeared in December 2015, setting the case for a January 2016 status date. I started preparing a petition to Cook County chief judge Tim Evans. At the status, Ford made us wait in his courtroom for several hours until he called us into his chambers for an off-the-record discussion that quickly degenerated.

I demanded that we return to the courtroom and that he make his comments on the record. Ford conceded, and continued his personal attacks in the courtroom for half an hour. He grilled us on how we obtained his publicly available Facebook page, threatened us with contempt, and, in a loud and angry voice, attempted to argue why he was not a witness. He sank to a new low when he accused me of being "on crack." Then, when the special prosecutor claimed that there was "absolutely no basis" for our already defeated motion, he responded, "I would agree with you completely if it wasn't for the fact that, and I didn't see it until I got home that night, somehow, someone, someone went to the *Sun Times* and told them that I was duty bound to recuse myself on this case." He accused me of "manipulating the system" and "manipulating him," and we went toe to toe on the evidence of torture central to Jackie Wilson's case, before he delivered what he obviously perceived as a coup de grace:

> I've never been involved. You created a Burge case where no Burge case exists. You went to the *Sun Times* and said Ford is on the Burge case. You have done it again and again. Whenever you don't get your way, like a little child, in the court, stomping his feet, that's what you are.

Then came the real jaw-dropper:

> I am recusing myself on this case, not because I have a conflict whatsoever. This is what you wanted. I know that. So you are going to get your wish.

Had Ford felt the pressure from the *Sun Times* editorial? Had Chief Judge Evans, a former Harold Washington alderman, given him the word? Whatever the answer, it was a breakthrough worthy of celebration.

The case was sent for assignment to the newly appointed chief judge of the criminal courts, LeRoy Martin Jr., who had been appointed by Judge Evans to succeed Biebel. Martin was the son of former police superintendent LeRoy Martin, but he had the reputation of being fair and respectful to all parties. Rather than run the risk of drawing another tainted judge, Martin assigned the case to William Hooks, an independent and outspoken African American judge, who had found there to be a pattern and practice of torture in the post-conviction case of Eric Caine, Aaron Patterson's co-defendant, several years earlier.

Soon thereafter we asked Judge Hooks for an order to once again depose Burge, this time with a focus on Jackie Wilson's case. Judge Hooks obliged, and I was once again off to Tampa. I rushed into the court reporter's waiting room at high noon and was surprised by Burge, sitting in a wheelchair, with oxygen tubes in his nose. His brother and caretaker wheeled him into the conference room, the videographer started to record, and I began to question Burge for the ninth time in twenty-eight years.

Burge displayed three separate medications, said he was on a heavy dosage of morphine, then answered a few preliminary questions before retreating to the Fifth Amendment. This time the FOP, rather than the City, was paying for his lawyer. He conceded that he was still receiving his pension but would not reveal how much. I turned to the Wilson manhunt, the torture of Donald White and his brothers, and Jackie's case. When I asked Burge about the arrest of the White brothers, Burge bristled and accused me of lying about the evidence:

> Burge: I am going to have to exert my Fifth Amendment right, but it really bothers me when you're sitting there stating falsehoods and you know better.
> Taylor: Well, let me make clear for the record that I have a good-faith basis based on the testimony of Frank Laverty before he passed away that this is what, in fact, happened at 84th and Carpenter on or about February 12th of 1982. If you would like to testify in substance as to Laverty's role in the arrest of the White brothers and others at that address, feel free to do so. Otherwise, don't make the assertions that I don't have any basis for what I'm saying. Everything that I'm asking you about I have a good-faith basis based on prior testimony and statements of officers or persons who alleged that they were tortured. Would you like to further testify about Frank Laverty's role?
> Burge: I would love to, but I can't.

After I ran Burge through the torture of Jackie Wilson, I placed Burge's statement, as posted on Preib's blog, and his emails to Preib in front of him. He referred to his own emails as "garbage," and then I read him a portion of what he wrote about me.

> Taylor: And in the next page you're quoted as saying that myself and others at Northwestern are "working to free guilty, vicious criminals" . . . is that your statement?
> Burge: I exercise my Fifth Amendment right.
> Taylor: You find that humorous?
> Burge: I certainly do.

His smirk set me off and I continued:

Taylor: Do you have any evidence that myself or others have grown rich based on our work in fighting to free innocent people and to deal with human rights violations and torture under your command?
Burge: I exercise my Fifth Amendment but you are dressing much better . . . that was an attempt at humor, sir.

I turned to the most recent racist statement of his that had come to our attention. The year before, I had confronted him with a statement he made at a bar to a friend, who asked him, in 1983, how his day was. The man had given us an affidavit in 2013 that Burge answered, "Not bad for dealing with dead niggers all day." This time it was his 2010 question to a former prosecutor, after his own trial, asking whether he thought the jury would "believe all those niggers."

My capstone was to ask about Richie Daley. Over time, a couple of witnesses had told us that Daley and Burge had communicated about the *Wilson* case, and that Burge resented Daley for not standing behind him when he was fired a decade later. So I plunged right in:

Taylor: Did you have any communication with Richie Daley when he was state's attorney about the torture and abuse of Andrew Wilson?
Burge: I exercise my Fifth Amendment.
Taylor: And you seem to be chuckling. Is that because you think it's funny that I would ask you that whether Richie Daley was involved or had any knowledge?
Burge: I think it's very stupid, sir.
Taylor: And why is that?
Burge: I exercise my Fifth Amendment right.
Taylor: You did have some sort of relationship with Richie Daley, didn't you?
Burge: I exercise my Fifth Amendment right.
Taylor: Do you have an opinion as to Richie Daley's involvement or lack of involvement with regard to the allegations of police torture in Area 2?
Burge: I exercise my Fifth Amendment right.

As I was gathering my things to leave, Burge spoke. "You know, you're full of crap," he said, "but you are very inventive. You should write a novel." No need to write a novel, I thought, with so much factual material to work with. "It's all in the record," I said, then, sensing that it might be my last and only chance to see if he might talk about Richie, I asked him again about Daley. "He wouldn't know me if he was sitting right next to me," Burge snorted.

It looked like Burge would take his knowledge of Daley's role in the torture scandal to the grave.

Coming back from Tampa, I was met at Chicago's Midway Airport by documentarian James Sorrels, who had been filming significant events and interviews in the torture saga for several years. On the long subway ride to the office, James interviewed me about the deposition and my latest confrontation with Burge. I surprised myself when I said that I did not want Burge to physically suffer, but quickly added that I "hate what he had done, hate that he continues to deny, hate that he intended to leave as a legacy further lies and perjury in some kind of book."

Before traveling to Florida for Burge's deposition, I had gone back to the old Area 2, to take photos of the interview room where Andrew Wilson was tortured and the basement where Byrne and Dignan bagged and beat Alonzo Smith. It was my first time in the basement, and, despite the cobwebs, it was essentially unchanged from Alonzo's description of it from thirty years before. The stairs, the boiler, the drain, the sink, and the electrical outlet for the refrigerator were all there, and it was chilling to picture Alonzo sitting in a chair by the boiler, then falling to the floor, passed out, with a bag over his head. In another little room there was an old typewriter, no doubt used, with a plastic cover, by the detectives in the 1980s. Under the typewriter was a moldy photo of a smiling Richie Daley.

In May 2016, we were able to apply the concept of reparations in a case that Michael Deutsch, Ben Elson, and I were working on in Little Rock. Eugene Ellison was an elderly African American man who was fatally shot down in his apartment by a Little Rock police officer who claimed that Mr. Ellison was threatening her with his cane. Our trial team was made up of myself and California lawyers Mike Laux and Doris Chen, and on the eve of the trial the defense lawyers made a settlement offer that would be the largest obtained in a Little Rock police case. Our clients were Mr. Ellison's two sons, Spencer and Troy, remarkable men and tremendous clients. They suggested that we seek, in addition to the money, other nonfinancial relief, and we decided to ask for an official apology from Little Rock's city manager and for a memorial. The City agreed, and that fall, the city manager offered the apology at a beautiful ceremony during which an inscribed park bench was dedicated to Eugene Ellison.

In late June, I headed back to Florida, this time to a location halfway between Tampa and Orlando, to depose Thomas McKenna, an Area 2 detective who was a main participant in Jackie Wilson's interrogation. Like Burge, McKenna repeatedly invoked his Fifth Amendment right. On the trip back to the airport, I received some very sad news from a *Sun Times* reporter. Old friend and comrade Mary Powers had passed away at the age of ninety-three. Mary had embarked on seventy years of activism in 1946, fighting for gay and lesbian rights. She had brought Dr. Martin Luther King to her North Shore hometown of Winnetka to speak on the village green in 1965. She had toured Fred Hampton's apartment while we were gathering evidence and became a staunch advocate for justice in the *Hampton* case. She had been on the front lines in the struggle against police torture and for police accountability for decades. As I told the *Sun Times*, "She was just a wonderful soldier in the struggle for justice. She was not only there in court and on the streets but meeting with superintendents."

Much had happened since the release of the video of the police murder of Laquan McDonald one year before. Locke Bowman and I had joined forces, this time with MacArthur attorneys Sheila Bedi and Vanessa Del Valle, to obtain the appointment of a special prosecutor in the McDonald case. Cook County state's attorney Anita Alvarez, who had played a key role in suppressing the video, was soundly defeated in the March Democratic primary by Kim Foxx, an African American reform candidate, who also easily won the general election. The mayor's Task Force on Police Accountability had released a scathing report, but an aggressive US Department of Justice investigation by the Obama administration's Civil Rights Division was put in serious jeopardy by the election of white supremacist Donald Trump.

The *Sun Times* published a long article titled, "Has There Been Enough Change a Year after McDonald Video Release?" The piece quoted Johnae Strong, an organizer with Black Youth Project 100, who was arrested at a protest after the video's release: "'Things have definitely changed in terms of the popular framing of the issue,' but police continue 'harassing, violating, assaulting and murdering people' with impunity. 'We have a long way to go. I don't believe real accountability has happened.'"

FOP lawyer Dan Herbert, who was representing Jason Van Dyke, the officer charged with murdering Laquan, tried to spin the events in the opposite direction: "At the end of the day, there has to be law enforcement and order in the streets. Officers need to have the ability to do their jobs. What we have now is, if somebody makes a mistake, they will be indicted criminally."

I was given an opportunity to offer my analysis in detail:

> Flint Taylor, a veteran civil-rights lawyer, says there remains "a tremendous amount of unfinished business." Chicago has seen many police scandals come and go over the decades. Summerdale. Fred Hampton. Jon Burge. The release of the video of McDonald's death, Taylor says, ranks right up there with the lowest moments in the department's history. "It was a very profound moment," he says. "It exposed for all to see the racist police violence and the code of silence and cover-ups that have been endemic for the [nearly] 50 years I've been involved in these issues."
>
> Still, Taylor views many of the changes of the past year with skepticism. He noted that the new police superintendent, Eddie Johnson, came from within the department ranks, meaning the department has not been led by a "true outside reformer" since O. W. Wilson was top cop in the 1960s. . . .
>
> The future of police reform, he says, will hinge greatly on whether a "powerful citizen review aspect to the disciplinary system" is allowed to emerge from the ruins of the ineffectual, old Independent Police Review Authority.
>
> Taylor predicts that Trump's new attorney general, Jeff Sessions, will dismantle the civil-rights efforts of the Justice Department. He and officials with the American Civil Liberties Union of Illinois said they hoped the federal civil-rights probe would lead to a consent decree between the feds and the police, as happened in many other cities during President Barack Obama's administration.

Just before Christmas 2016, preeminent New Orleans civil rights attorney Mary Howell shared the important news that the City of New Orleans had agreed to settle seventeen cases that arose in the aftermath of Hurricane Katrina, in 2005. I had first worked with Mary in the early 1980s, when she asked me to come down to New Orleans to help her and her law partner litigate a high-profile civil rights case in which four Black citizens had been shot and killed by police, and others tortured, in the course of an NOPD investigation into the killing of a white police officer. The Algiers case, as it was known locally, bore striking similarities to the Hampton and Clark murders (one of the Algiers victims was slain in her bathtub) and, as became clearer to me over time, to the Wilson manhunt and other Chicago torture cases as well. Over the decades Mary's path and mine had often intersected in our work against racist police violence and other systemic civil rights violations.

Mary was a leading advocate in many of the Hurricane Katrina cases, and we had talked from time to time about the possibility of settlement in light of reparations in Chicago and the settlement in Little Rock. The cases, many of which happened on Danziger Bridge—locals were shot in the back, some fatally, in a display of extremely violent, racist, and deadly police conduct—were representative of the official lawlessness that reigned in NOLA before, during, and after the storm. Mayor Mitch Landrieu announced the $13.3 million settlement at a press conference after a prayer meeting with the victims and families. He hugged the mother of one of the slain victims and issued an emotional apology, saying that he wanted to express "how intensely sorry I am to the members of these families and to the people of the city of New Orleans for the actions that were taken during that fateful time, when these individuals were looking for people to protect and serve, and they got the exact opposite."

Two weeks later, the City of Chicago revealed that the City had agreed to settle Shawn Whirl's civil case for $4 million.

Alonzo Smith's exoneration had reset the statute of limitations, so we had filed a civil rights torture and wrongful conviction case on his behalf in the spring of 2016. It was patterned after the Michael Tillman case, with Daley named, along with Burge, Byrne, and Dignan, as some of the main defendants. The case had been assigned to Judge St. Eve, who had unceremoniously dismissed Darrell Cannon's case several years earlier, after rejecting our efforts to join Daley as a defendant and to depose him. This time, however, she followed Judge Pallmeyer's decision in Michael Tillman's case and denied Daley's motion to dismiss. Once again, we served Daley with notice for a deposition, slated for early January 2017. This would be our fifth try over twelve years.

Daley had retired to a professorship at the University of Chicago, then became "of counsel" for the high-powered firm Katten Muchin, where he served as an international lobbyist. In January 2014, the media reported that, on a flight from Arizona, Daley had taken ill and was rushed to the intensive care unit of Northwestern Hospital, where he spent more than a week. The details were kept secret, but the media quoted "sources" as reporting that Daley had "stroke like symptoms," a "stroke like seizure," and a "small stroke."

In April 2015, Daley gave his first public interview since his reported stroke. He was "back to work" at the law firm. He was keeping his health issues private, the article noted, and remained out of the public eye until August 2016, when he appeared with members of his law firm at a public event.

Without any response from Daley or his lawyers—once again, Terry Burns and his colleagues at Dykema—we issued a second notice, for February 2017. In response to the judge's order denying their motions to dismiss, all of the defendants, including Daley, were required to file answers to the detailed factual allegations we had made in our complaint. Burge, Byrne, and Dignan all once again pleaded the Fifth, but Daley and his lawyers broke their silence by denying almost all of our allegations, save for some of the documented statements he had made in the media about the Goldston report. The denials were not under oath.

In mid-February, Daley and Burns put up a new obstacle to Daley's deposition. Joey and I were sworn to secrecy by Judge St. Eve after a visibly nervous Burns asked that she do so. Her order on the court record read simply, "Daley defendants' motion regarding Mr. Daley's deposition shall be filed, under seal, by 3/17/17. Status hearing as to plaintiff and Daley defendants only set for 3/22/17 at 8:30 a.m." On March 17, the court record read: "MOTION by Defendant Richard M Daley for extension of time to File a Motion for Protective Order; Motion for Entry of a HIPAA/Attorneys' Eyes Only Protective Order." (Protective orders are a device often used by lawyers seeking to prevent the taking of depositions, and it was a motion that Daley's lawyers had filed in the past when seeking to shield Daley from questioning. HIPAA [Health Insurance Portability and Accountability Act] orders are used to protect sensitive medical and mental health records.)

Five days later we were back in court, discussing the Daley motion in a private sidebar conference. The court record reflected only the bare bones of that day's proceedings:

> MINUTE entry before the Honorable Amy J. St. Eve: Status hearing as to plaintiff and Daley defendants only held on 3/22/2017. Defendant Daley's motion for entry of a HIPAA/Attorneys' eyes only protective order is granted without prejudice. SEALED MOTION by Defendant Richard M. Daley for Protective Order (Burns, Terrence) (Entered: 03/22/2017).

Both the *Tribune* and the *Sun Times* had figured out that something was afoot—in no small measure because Burns had made some comments in open court, and had attached a transcript of the February 15 court appearance and emails from Joey to a publicly filed motion. The *Tribune's* headline read, "Undisclosed Medical Issue for Ex-Mayor Daley Raised in Burge-Related Federal Lawsuit," and reporter Jason Meisner filled in some of the details:

> [Alonzo] Smith's lawyers had originally asked that the deposition take place in January. But last month, one of Daley's attorneys, Terrence Burns, told U.S. District Judge Amy St. Eve there was "an issue relative to (Daley's) medical

condition" that could affect the deposition. Burns asked the judge for permission to file detailed medical records concerning the former mayor under seal and for a protective order that made any such records "for attorneys' eyes only," according to a transcript of the Feb. 15 hearing.

Meisner also referred to the emails to give further clarity about the secret proceedings:

People's Law Office attorney Joey Mogul wrote in a March 13 email to Daley's attorneys that they may need to hire an expert to review "any conclusions Mr. Daley sets forth with respect to his mental health and competency to answer questions at a deposition or in this litigation" court records show.

In early April, a mum Daley appeared on a cold and damp day at the Chicago White Sox home opener, and shortly thereafter Judge St. Eve issued an order concerning our proposed expert, whose specialties were strokes and geriatric mental health: "Status hearing as to the Daley defendant held on 4/4/17. Daley's motion for protective order is entered and continued. Plaintiff shall disclose his expert to defense counsel and the Court by 4/14/17." Later that spring, Judge St. Eve issued an order concerning the medical records: "Status hearing held on 5/15/17. Defendant Daley's continued motion for protective order is entered and continued. Defendant Daley is to turn over materials as stated in court by 5/26/17."

During the spring and summer, two important parts of the Reparations Ordinance were implemented. After much planning, in late May, the Chicago Torture Justice Center opened in the Englewood Neighborhood Health Clinic, at 63rd Street and Lowe Avenue. The staff announced that the Center "will provide individual and group therapy to anyone who feels they need healing services or legal assistance resulting from police misconduct. There is no criteria to qualify for those services and anyone who feels they have a case of police brutality is welcome to walk in." In the *Tribune* Darrell, who had been working as an outreach coordinator for the center, retold his story of torture and said, "Our door is open to anyone who feels like egregious wrong has been done to them."

In late August, just before the public school year was to begin, the second important reparations development was announced. Darrell and Anthony joined Chicago Public Schools CEO Forrest Claypool at the CPS Central Office with, of all people, police superintendent Eddie Johnson, to announce the implementation of a curriculum to educate CPS students about the torture crimes. The *Sun Times* covered the announcement, its headline quipping, "Reading, Writing and Torture: CPS Kids to Learn about Jon Burge Cases." Superintendent Johnson, to the chagrin of many, attempted to hijack the announcement, but did include another apology in his remarks:

> On behalf of [the] Chicago Police Department, I want to apologize to Darrell Cannon and Anthony Holmes for what they went through. But I think it's important to know that that Chicago Police Department does not exist anymore and it will not exist.

Janice Jackson, chief education officer for CPS, added, "The curriculum was developed with input from victims, police officers and CPS officials, and revised after a pilot curriculum was tested at six CPS schools last year." She released lesson plans showing that the curriculum was "heavy on group discussions on topics like the nature of police work, constitutional rights, students' attitudes about police, designing an ideal department." The *Sun Times* article also quoted the reprehensible Martin Preib, whom it characterized as the spokesman for the FOP, saying, "Until the full review of the wrongful conviction movement is completed, the FOP does not believe the Burge mythology should be codified into public school curriculum."

Preib and his reactionary pals were unable to block the curriculum, and during the CPS's second semester, Darrell Cannon, Greg Banks, Anthony Holmes, and several other torture survivors spoke at more than fifty Chicago Public Schools. Joey and I were also asked to speak on several occasions. Darrell, who has to calm his stomach with Pepto Bismol each time before he speaks, was brought to tears as he received hundreds of letters from eighth and tenth graders moved by his presentations. Students at Walsh Elementary School, where I spoke, sent me scores of letters and several sketches, including one titled "Flint Taylor A Man Who took a Stand."

Jackie Wilson's hearing was scheduled for mid-July. The special prosecutors, feeling the pressure from FOP and other right-wing political forces, were resisting our efforts with uncommon belligerence. One of the assistants, Andrew Levine, had taken our victories in the Alonzo Smith and Shawn Whirl cases personally, and had mounted ad hominem attacks on me on several occasions. During one courtroom encounter, Levine, apparently angered by the unintentional mispronunciation of his name, went completely off the rails while Judge Hooks was in his chambers. Moving menacingly toward our table, Levine shouted at me, "You haven't done an ethical thing in twenty years." The judge's burly bailiff quickly appeared to quell any further abuse. Levine was notably absent the next few times we appeared in court.

Judge Hooks had permitted the special prosecutors to depose Jackie. He was transported up from Menard for the deposition, and I met him for the first time. Dressed in a black-and-white striped prison uniform that harked back to prison chain gangs, Jackie met with Elliot and me first in the judge's lockup, and later, accompanied by John Stainthorp—a welcome addition to our defense team—at the jail. Jackie was friendly, talkative, and outgoing, in contrast to his brother Andrew. Issues arose, though, in the special prosecutors' objectionable questioning of Jackie at his deposition, and at the last minute, Judge Hooks continued the hearing until the end of the year.

The Daley saga continued. In September, Judge St. Eve had held an in-chambers evidentiary hearing on Daley's motion for a protective order, then had denied his motion "without prejudice." She had given Daley's lawyers the right to file a second motion, based on all that had transpired over the preceding nine months, and they had done so just before Christmas.

On January 24, 2018, after yet another secret hearing, Judge St. Eve ruled on Daley's renewed motion for a protective order concerning his deposition. The public record said simply: "Defendant Daley's motion for protective order is granted in part and denied in part as stated at the hearing. The parties are directed to meet and confer." Later in the year, Judge St. Eve, in another public order, shed more light on the subject, revealing that Daley had been deposed and that he would also be required to answer numerous requests to admit facts.

So, fourteen years after we first sought to depose him, I questioned Daley in several ninety-minute sessions during the spring of 2018. The content of the deposition, however, remains shrouded in court-ordered secrecy, leaving to speculation—given his age and medical condition, combined with his highly selective memory and his skilled propensity for obfuscation, which he had demonstrated time and again throughout his political career—how (or if) he answered my questions. Hopefully, the final Daley chapter will not remain indefinitely hidden from public view.

CHAPTER 38

Wilson Walks

Two days after Christmas 2017, Judge Hooks convened Jackie Wilson's hearing. With cameras recording the proceedings, I outlined the "mountain of evidence" that supported the "horrific" pattern and practice of torture, while Elliot detailed the terrorizing manhunt in February 1982 that culminated in the torture of Andrew and his brother Jackie. Judge Hooks, in sharp contrast to Judge Duff nearly thirty years before, seemed receptive to our arguments and grilled special prosecutor Mike O'Rourke about our pattern and practice evidence, forcing O'Rourke to admit that there were at least seventy credible cases of torture. The judge then cut to the quick concerning the special prosecutors' conduct:

> In many cases your position as a special prosecutor has lined up precisely with the people who defend people, particularly the police officers involved in this case . . . I have not seen aggressive action towards those that may have caused these actions, and that includes Lieutenant Burge. That includes anyone that's tied to him in these cases. All I have seen is defending . . . quite honestly, based on what I've seen, I don't know why we even appointed a special prosecutor. Rather than public funds being expended, perhaps those police officers should have paid for the bill.

We opened our case by presenting evidence from Donald White, Doris Miller, and Anthony Williams. Donald and Anthony had been hauled in and tortured by Burge and his men a few nights before Andrew and Jackie were arrested; Doris Miller, a postal worker, was arrested as a possible "accessory to murder" and held in the room next to Andrew. Tensions rose when former felony review prosecutor Larry Hyman, accompanied by his own lawyer, took the stand and asserted the Fifth Amendment to my questions about his involvement in the interrogations of Jackie and Andrew. Judge Hooks was skeptical of Hyman's right to do so, but his lawyer maintained that his client remained in jeopardy of criminal prosecution, and Judge Hooks reluctantly permitted him to assert the Fifth.

Jackie then took the stand. In response to Elliot's questioning, Jackie, for the first time in complete detail, described how he was electric-shocked, beaten on the head with a book, punched, kicked, stomped, and threatened with a revolver by Burge and his interrogating detectives. The *Tribune* depicted his testimony:

> Nearly 36 years after two Chicago police officers were shot to death on the South Side, the graying inmate serving life in prison for the crime took the stand in Cook County court and gave an account that has grown familiar in recent decades—that officers including disgraced former Cmdr. Jon Burge had tortured him into confessing. Burge was not in court, but Jackie Wilson, wearing a gray-and-black striped jumpsuit, repeatedly picked up a black-and-white picture of the former officer as he emphatically and sometimes tearfully alleged that officers beat him, kicked him in the groin, put a gun in his mouth and gave him electric shocks. Believing he would be killed if he didn't confess . . . Wilson, now 57, said he would have confessed to shooting the president if the detectives had asked him. "I told them, 'Game over . . . whatever you want me to say, I'm gonna say it,'" he said. "I wanted it to stop."

When O'Rourke objected to our describing Jackie's abuse as "torture," I cited the UN Convention Against Torture definition, and Jackie pointed at him and asked angrily, "What would you call it?" After the hearing adjourned, the brother of slain officer William Fahey, still committed to the FOP's unbending and racist defense of Jon Burge, responded to a question from a *Tribune* reporter about Jackie's testimony by saying, "What is he going to say? He's a [expletive] cop killer."

When the hearing reconvened on January 16, our plan was to call former Area 2 detectives Doris Byrd and Sammy Lacey, to be followed by the videotaped depositions of Burge and interrogating detective Thomas McKenna. The *Tribune* article about Jackie's hearing had reawakened the FOP and its vice president, Martin Preib, and they put out a call to convene the FOP's monthly general membership meeting in Judge Hooks's courtroom:

> Flint Taylor of the People's Law Office is claiming Wilson was the victim of police abuse. The FOP rejects this claim. The families of Fahey and O'Brien have endured several trials and hearings over the last three decades as Taylor has worked to get Wilson set free. All members are strongly encouraged to attend.

As I approached the courthouse at 26th and California, I saw at least a dozen police cars parked in the area. Going up in the elevator, I pictured a courtroom packed with armed FOP members, so I decided to ask the judge to order the cops to check their weapons. As I waded through the overflow crowd of hostile officers, I saw that Judge Hooks had beaten me to the punch—a handwritten order was tacked on the courtroom door, mandating that all arms be checked on the first floor.

Sammy Lacey, who was to be our first witness, told John, Elliot, and me outside the courtroom that he feared for his family and was not going to testify. It was one thing to testify against Jon Burge, he said, but quite another to testify on behalf of Jackie Wilson. We cajoled Sammy, then invoked the power of the subpoena, and he reluctantly walked down the aisle to take the witness stand. With some prodding, he told the judge about Burge's "asskickers," the racism that permeated Area 2 under Burge's command, and how he heard screaming coming from the second floor of Area 2 on the morning of February 14, 1982. The judge was most attentive and seemed to take offense when O'Rourke objected to Sammy's testimony about the racial make-up of the "asskickers":

> Mr. O'Rourke: The racial background. That's irrelevant, Judge . . .
> Judge Hooks: You are saying that the racial makeup of the particular unit that has caused us all to be here is not relevant? Overruled counsel, please, overruled.

After he completed his testimony, Sammy stepped down and motioned the courtroom bailiff to escort him through the FOP gauntlet to the elevator. The FOP audience left shortly thereafter. Despite our repeated pleas, Doris Byrd had previously told us in no uncertain terms that she did not intend to get involved again and would not honor our subpoena. The former sergeant's prior testimony was read by Christian Snow, a student intern we would later hire as an associate, including Byrd's saying that torture was an "open secret" at Area 2 under Burge, with the black box "running rampant." We followed this testimony with the videos of Burge and Detective McKenna taking the Fifth.

Next, Jackie was cross-examined by O'Rourke. The *Sun Times* headlined its article, over a picture of Jackie in his striped prison garb, "Burge and Nemesis Flint Taylor Spar in Video Depositions in Jackie Wilson Case," and summarized Jackie's cross-examination:

Wiping his eyes, Wilson, 57, took issue with Special Prosecutor Michael O'Rourke skipping steps in Wilson's account of the abuse when O'Rourke jumped from Wilson being clubbed with a phone book directly to being hooked up to an electroshock box. "They beat me over the head with dictionaries, a telephone book, put guns in my mouth. Then they brought in the electric shock," Wilson said, his face pained. "It's just upsetting, judge, I'm reliving things."

The special prosecutors' approach, in their case, was to return to 1982, before the evidence of systemic torture had come to light, ignoring that unrebuttable evidence and mercilessly attacking Jackie as a liar. Since almost all their witnesses were either on the Fifth Amendment or had been previously found to be perjurers, they focused on two perceived weaknesses in Jackie's story: that in his 1982 motion to suppress testimony he had not mentioned that he was electric-shocked, or that Burge was involved in his torture. To emphasize these points, they called Jackie's 1982 trial attorney, Richard Kling, to the stand in an effort to demonstrate that Jackie had never told him these important facts. I drew the assignment of cross-examining Kling, and my task was made much easier when he professed to have no specific recollection of what Jackie did or did not tell him in 1982. Kling became our witness when I elicited that he had included all the other aspects of Jackie's torture in his written motion, and that when Kling had interviewed Donald White almost twenty years later, Donald said he had recently been visited by Detective McKenna and threatened.

The special prosecutors' only other live witness was Michael Hartnett, the court reporter who had taken Jackie's and Andrew's confessions in 1982. On direct examination, he told of a compliant and cooperative Jackie, who showed no visible injuries and voluntarily smiled for his photo after giving his statement. Elliot quickly exposed Hartnett on cross-examination. Hartnett was not an independent court reporter but worked for the state's attorney's office. He was friendly with Burge and his lawyer, was surprised that Burge and his men had not killed Andrew and Jackie, and "did not give a damn" about what the police did to Jackie prior to obtaining his statement. ASA Larry Hyman had not asked Jackie or Andrew if they had been abused or coerced, which was a highly unusual omission, but Hartnett did not mention this failure to Hyman. In the past, Hartnett had recorded statements from bloodied suspects but did not consider it his job to do anything about it, so he remained mum. This was the case with Andrew, whom Hartnett observed with facial injuries when taking his statement. And, as important,

Hartnett was not present when Jackie and Andrew were interrogated. By the time Elliot finished, Hartnett had been exposed as a hopelessly biased and uncaring participant in the cover-up of Jackie's and Andrew's torture.

The final day of evidence was February 16, 2018. Bill Hampton, Fred's older brother, had died the week before, and the judge excused me for a few hours to speak at Bill's funeral. Fred's entire nuclear family was now gone, as his mother, Iberia, had died in the fall of 2016 and his sister, Dolores, in the summer of 2017. Before I left, I re-raised an issue that had loomed throughout the hearing: the special prosecutors' close connection to Burge, his confederates, and their lawyers, in particular Andrew Hale. I pointed out that former assistant special prosecutor Brian Stefanich, previously lead counsel on Jackie's case, had jumped ship to join Hale's firm and had filed his appearance as counsel for Burge, Byrne, and Dignan in Alonzo Smith's civil case. Judge Hooks, who was a stickler for ethics and had previously ordered the special prosecutors to present their monthly bills for attorneys' fees for his approval, was disturbed by this revelation. As the *Tribune* described it:

> O'Rourke defended Stefanich's move, saying he believed that "the interests" of the special prosecutors and the defendants in the lawsuit "are aligned." That drew a murmur from spectators in the courtroom, and Hooks raised his eyebrows and leaned back in his seat on the bench. "After hundreds of thousands of dollars of taxpayers' [money has] been spent . . . you're stating that convicted federal felon Jon Burge's interests are aligned with the special prosecutors' interest in this matter before this court?" Hooks asked.

After O'Rourke told Judge Hooks he was talking only about the lawsuit that Stefanich joined, Hooks called Stefanich's representation of Burge in the lawsuit "a very big complication" and sounded the same theme he had previously articulated: "What's special about the special state's attorneys?" The *Tribune* also quoted me:

> Stefanich could not be reached Friday for comment, but attorney G. Flint Taylor, who represents Wilson, later scoffed at O'Rourke's explanation."You can parse it in this case and that case and any case you want, but that is not the role of the special prosecutor," he told the *Tribune*. "It should be to do justice. . . . They're supposed to bring an independent eye to this."

Amid the furor, the special prosecutors rested their case. The highlight of our rebuttal was a passage from Andrew's 1988 deposition that undercut the special prosecutors' argument that Jackie's testimony about electric shock was a "recent fabrication," first added in 2010. The passage revealed that, according to Andrew, Jackie told him he was electric-shocked the day after the torture, while they were being held together in the courtroom bullpen. This corroborated Jackie's testimony that he had told Andrew—and lawyer Richard Kling—shortly after the torture occurred. We also offered transcripts from the 1982 motion to suppress hearings that showed that Burge did not testify in Jackie's case, only in Andrew's portion of the hearing, when Jackie was not in the courtroom, thus explaining why Jackie had not named Burge as one of his torturers. We also offered the testimony of Diane Panos, who said that Burge boasted about beating the Wilson brothers (plural), and of Burge's barroom acquaintance Kenneth Caddick, who recounted how Burge's bartender girlfriend had turned Burge's face red by asking him to tell how he had tortured the Wilsons, while she mimed cranking a box.

Apparently concerned about the outcome and enraged by the judge's highly publicized denunciation of their conduct, the special prosecutors retained a high-profile lawyer, Lance Northcutt, to intervene on their behalf in an attempt to remove Judge Hooks for bias. Northcutt told the *Tribune*, "The cynical ploy by certain attorneys in this case to suggest improper conduct on the part of the Office of the Special Prosecutor is as offensive as it is false." Judge Hooks was not pleased and referred to the potential conflict that was exacerbated by former special prosecutor Stefanich joining Andrew Hale's firm by saying, "That smelled really bad. . . . It becomes a suspect situation at this point, to be quite honest with you." I told the *Tribune*, "These men have stretched out this case for two years. Any other case, they would have agreed to a new trial . . . [but] they're in bed with the Fraternal Order of Police."

Off the record, Northcutt threatened to delay the hearing further by appealing the recusal issue to the Illinois Supreme Court if Hooks refused to remove himself. While the motion had little or no chance of success, the possible delay deeply concerned us, so we reluctantly agreed to back off on the possible conflict of interest if Northcutt agreed to withdraw his motion. A skeptical Judge Hooks accepted this compromise after the special prosecutors explained their position. Northcutt withdrew his motion, and the judge set April 5 for closing arguments.

We drafted and filed a one-hundred-page statement of facts that set forth our evidence. The *Sun Times* described the scene at the closing arguments: "A half-dozen relatives of Fahey and O'Brien, some wearing 'Police Lives Matter' T-shirts, sat in the tiny gallery. Across the aisle sat Darrell Cannon, who was released from prison after his confession to a 1983 murder—obtained by Burge subordinates who shocked Cannon with a cattle prod—was thrown out by a judge a decade ago." Elliot and I divided our time, with Elliot focusing on Jackie's and Andrew's torture, while I detailed our pattern and practice evidence. Elliot argued:

> Here the vigilantes with badges broke the law, the interrogation methods they used to coerce an involuntary statement from Jackie Wilson broke the law. Jon Burge was bouncing between torture chambers like the conductor of an orchestra, but the only sounds that were coming out were screams.

The new assistant special prosecutor, formerly a prosecutor in Ireland, sounded the same tired theme of fabrication: "[Jackie's] lying. He wants to be Andrew. He wants to have you pull the wool over your eyes and for you to believe that he is Andrew and what was perpetrated on his brother . . . was perpetrated on him as well." In our rebuttal argument, I suggested that Richard Kling's failure to include electric shock in Jackie's motion to suppress might have been a legal strategy to avoid the wrath of a hostile judge, who would not be disposed to believing what, at that point, would have seemed an outlandish claim. I concluded by debunking the absurd proposition that Jackie, alone, was not tortured:

> Tony Thompson was tortured because he was shooting at police, but not Jackie Wilson? Roy Brown was tortured in the manhunt because he supposedly knew something about the killing of the police, but Jackie Wilson wasn't? Walter Johnson supposedly knew something about the killings of police. He was tortured, but Jackie Wilson wasn't? Donald White had a gun put in his mouth and a bag put over his head and was hung out of a window because they thought he committed the murders until they didn't have an identification to back them up. He was tortured, but Jackie Wilson wasn't? . . . Anthony Williams. They thought he had something to do with the crimes. He was tortured, but Jackie Wilson wasn't? By the same men, O'Hara, McKenna, Hill, and Burge. Lamont and Walter White . . . Dwight Anthony. Derrick Martin. He was beaten and tortured, but Jackie wasn't? And Andrew Wilson, everybody agrees that he was brutally tortured because they thought he was the shooter, but they thought that Jackie was involved too. Andrew Wilson was tortured, but Jackie wasn't?
>
> I have nothing further, Judge.

After another round of briefing, we gathered in Judge Hooks's courtroom on June 14, 2018, for his reading of his decision. As we were entering
the courthouse, we saw a copy of that morning's *Sun Times*. The editors had
devoted a full page to a letter written by William Fahey's daughter, Erin, who
was four years old when her father was killed. The headline above a photo of
Jackie read, "Alleged Torture of Jackie Wilson Doesn't Diminish His Guilt
in Cops' Murders." Relying on evidence from Jackie's tortured confession
and the testimony of discredited witnesses, Erin Fahey (with, we suspected,
the assistance of the FOP and the special prosecutors), argued in essence that
Judge Hooks should ignore the evidence of torture because Jackie was guilty:
"The bottom line here is that justice in this case has already been served. To
grant Wilson a third trial will only serve as an injustice to these fallen police
officers, their families, the two juries that convicted him and, ultimately, to
the truth."

In spite of the *Sun Times*' apparent capitulation to the FOP and its
continuing defense of police torture, we entered Judge Hooks's courtroom
convinced that this emotional eleventh-hour plea would not change his
decision. The judge announced that his decision was 119 pages long and
he intended to read the entire document from the bench. In the company
of portraits of Sojourner Truth, Ida B. Wells, Frederick Douglass, Dred
Scott, and Thurgood Marshall, Judge Hooks read for almost four hours,
painstakingly setting forth the factual and legal bases for his decision.
Relying in large part on our evidence and analysis, he adopted verbatim
270 of our proposed factual findings. He assailed the credibility of the
state's witnesses and underscored the importance of Burge, McKenna, and
Hyman asserting the Fifth Amendment. On the issue of Jackie's credibility, he found:

> Jackie's claims and credibility are not unassailable. Ordinarily, adding an
> allegation as significant as police using a device to give electric shocks, when
> not included in an original motion to suppress, would be reason to doubt.
> The State labels Jackie's addition of this allegation "a fantastic story." Such
> an allegation should be a fantastic story. But pattern and practice evidence
> shows shocking suspects was common. And each witness in a position to
> deny it invoked the Fifth Amendment. Those considerations take the "story"
> out of the realm of fiction.

After invoking the case of the Scottsboro Boys and the importance of
the right to due process of law, Judge Hooks concluded his disquisition:

So, in short, all rights matter. The rights of the good; the bad; and the ugly all count. Who is good, who is bad, and who is ugly is not the job of this Court. However, there is more than enough to surmise that what happened in the investigation and interrogation of Jackie Wilson was not good—instead, very bad and ugly. The conduct of those involved in this most serious of investigations, which involved attempting to discover and ethically prosecute the murderer or murderers of two Chicago police officers required more. Much more was required of the Chicago Police Department, the office of the Cook County State's Attorney, our courts, the private and public defense bar and, indeed, our federal government. In this matter, as well as dozens of related cases, too many postconviction tribunals and the Torture Commission have been forced to conduct post-mortem examinations of the torture and death of nothing less than our constitution at the hands of Jon Burge and his crew. The abhorrence of basic rights of suspects by Mr. Burge and his underlings has been costly to the taxpayers, the wrongfully convicted, and worst of all, the dozens of victims and their families who have suffered untold grief—in many cases, a 30-plus year horror story.

Judge Hooks then spoke directly to Jackie:

Use of a physically coerced confession as substantive evidence of guilt is never harmless error no matter how strong the case against a particular defendant may otherwise be. Since such a confession was used against Jackie Wilson to obtain his conviction, he is entitled to a new trial where that confession may not be used. Based on the foregoing, the Court hereby vacates the convictions in the instant matters and grants Petitioner, Jackie Wilson's, petition for a new trial. IT IS SO ORDERED.

We were elated, and, for Jackie, the elation was mixed with shock. I told the assembled media, "It was a courageous decision. It was the right decision, and it's a decision that I think not only speaks to Jackie Wilson but to all of the victims of police torture under the regime of Jon Burge." The FOP condemned the decision and Special Prosecutor O'Rourke promised an appeal and a retrial. We fired back, calling on the County to stop financing this FOP-directed boondoggle, and, citing to the absence of any credible evidence that Jackie participated in the murders, informed Judge Hooks that we would be seeking Jackie's release on bond. The judge set the bond hearing for the next week.

Elliot and John immediately began to draft the bail motion, while I had a conversation with a member of the *Sun Times* editorial board. That weekend, the *Sun Times* published a full-page editorial: "Lessons of the

Jackie Wilson Murder Trial Saga." Praising Judge Hooks's decision, the editors wrote:

> The blame for this endless travesty lies not with the judge, or with Wilson's defense attorneys. The blame lies with a crew of rogue officers who once had so little respect for our criminal justice system that they beat confessions out of suspects. Now those bad confessions, transparently worthless, continue to haunt. The simple hard truth is that Jackie Wilson, whatever the character of the man, has yet to receive a fully fair trial. And our disgust is with the original sin of police torture.

While we had issue with the concept of "rogue cops" and wished that the board had called out the County for its continuing financial support for the special prosecutors, it was as much as we could expect at this point in the case.

Six days later we were back in court because the special prosecutors were attempting to continue the bond hearing. Their motion angered me, not only because they were once more attempting to delay the proceedings, but also because they had again attacked Jackie and referred to the case as a "capital case." Of course, the death penalty had been abolished seven years before, and Jackie had been acquitted of a death sentence back in 1983, when there was capital punishment. I opened our opposition before Judge Hooks by calling out these transgressions, saying that the special prosecutors were acting "in my view like prosecutors in the Jim Crow South." The special prosecutors loudly objected, and Judge Hooks admonished me. Not satisfied, they persisted in condemning my comments, with the Irish attorney saying, "I regard what Mr. Taylor said as being an accusation of racism, and I think it's absolutely outrageous." This prompted the judge to say, "Have you heard what happened in this case? Toughen up . . . counsel." The *Tribune* captured the import of my comments: "Given the racial history of the Burge accusations, the Jim Crow reference was all the more fraught. Scores of African-American men have alleged that Burge, who is white, and detectives working under him tortured or abused them during the 1970s and '80s."

Judge Hooks denied the special prosecutors' motion, so we were back the next day to argue for bond. The thrust of our argument was that the prosecutors had no case after the coerced confession was suppressed from evidence. The state's key witness, Tyrone Sims, had previously testified that Jackie had stood by in shock while Andrew shot the two officers, and another "witness" was "peripatetic felon" and "billy liar" William Coleman, who claimed that Jackie had admitted to the murders several years after the fact. Elliot, who took the lead in arguing our case for bond, had a surprise in store—an affidavit from another State's witness, Dewayne Hardin, obtained only weeks before. Hardin had previously testified that he had seen Jackie and Andrew drive away from the scene of the shooting "smiling." In his affidavit, Hardin repudiated this testimony, saying that he was ill from diabetes, had been "bothered by conscience" for the past thirty-six years, and wanted to "reveal the truth." He corroborated Sims, saying that Jackie appeared to be in a "state of shock" and "did not do anything to assist Andrew in the shooting." He said that Jackie was not smiling as they drove away but had "a scared expression on his face" and continued to look like he was in shock. Hardin asserted that he was pressured by ASAs Kunkle and Angarola to tell a false story because they knew if he "told the truth, Jackie Wilson would likely not be convicted." Hardin said that he feared for his life if he told the truth, that Burge "terrorized" him, and that he believed that Area 2 asskicker Fred Hill had tried to kill him. It was a bombshell to be sure, and after I followed Elliot to dismantle Coleman, the special prosecutors' case against Jackie lay in shambles.

The judge prepared a seven-page written order overnight, and, once again, demonstrated uncommon judicial courage. He found in his decision that

> the hearing revealed that the State is still viewing this case under a constitu-tionally tortured view of what evidence will be allowed at a new trial. The State essentially expects the Court to view the matters at issue through the lens of a court sitting in 1982 or 1988 without considering the revelations that have come to light over the last three decades. Statutory authority gov-erns the parameters of a bond hearing and sets forth the burdens the State must meet to deny a defendant bond. The State utterly failed to meet its burdens in spite of its lengthy and overtime attempts.

Referring to the special prosecutors' case as a "a collection of jailhouse snitches, correctional officers, and persons who allege they observed Wilson and his brother Andrew at the time of the incident" and noting that "after years of preparation and substantial public expenditure . . . the State, with at least three Special Prosecutors in court, could not say if any witness is still alive or available to participate in a new trial," Judge Hooks pro-nounced his decision:

> Jackie Wilson stands before the Court as a senior citizen even though his age is short of 65. His 36 years in IDOC have aged him far beyond his

chronological age. In the totality of the circumstances, this Court does not find Wilson to be a danger to the community or a flight risk. The State has failed to provide just and proper cause for Mr. Wilson's continued incarceration as a pretrial condition while the retrial of his case is pending. Accordingly, Jackie Wilson is ordered to be released forthwith in the most minimal time period required for the Cook County Jail and Illinois Department of Corrections to comply with this order with all dispatch. This bond will be without the necessity of a monetary amount.

At 4:00 p.m. on June 22, 2018, Jackie walked arm and arm with Elliot and me out of the gates of Cook County Jail and addressed the gathering of cameras and reporters. The *Tribune* and *Sun Times* recounted Jackie's first public words:

"Being a victim of one of a number of Jon Burge's brutalities . . . " he said as his voice trailed off and he sighed heavily. "Oh Lord, it's just, it's been a rocky ride. [I'm] happy to be a member of society again after 36 years of incarceration for a crime I didn't commit . . . I'd just like to move forward with my life barring any further complications and I'd like to make my contribution to society."

The *Sun Times* front-page banner headline said it all: WILSON WALKS.

Epilogue

After thirty-one years of fighting against police torture, I took a moment to look back. The *Wilson* cases had come full circle, from our struggle to fight and win Andrew's case to using the evidence uncovered in that case and in those that followed to free Jackie, decades later. Collectively, we had accomplished numerous exonerations; obtained more than $40,000,000 in settlements, verdicts, and reparations for more than sixty torture survivors; played an important role in Jon Burge's firing and conviction; and contributed to the ultimately successful struggle to abolish the death penalty in Illinois. As important, we had joined with many others over those three decades—courageous torture survivors, dedicated citizens and activists, families of torture victims, fellow attorneys, political allies, and intrepid reporters—to use our roles as lawyers to help change the narrative. Together, we changed the story from the solitary cries of an unheeded, convicted "cop killer" in 1982 to the accepted truth, locally and internationally, that there was a racist pattern and practice of police torture that reigned for more than twenty years in Chicago; encouraged, condoned, and covered up in the highest halls of power, from police superintendents, state's attorneys, and judges to the all-powerful Daley machine.

The cost of the torture scandal, and the wallets of our opposing counsel, continues to grow. According to public records, which I have obtained and updated each year since 2005, the scandal had cost city, county, and state taxpayers $140,000,000 by the end of 2018. The federal tab for investigating Burge and his confederates and for prosecuting Burge was an additional unknown amount. Burge had collected about $900,000 in pension money, and Chicago police officers implicated in the torture scandal had collected an additional $31 million in pensions, pushing the still mounting total past $170,000,000.

Of this total, Chicago has paid $31.6 million to outside counsel to represent the City, Daley, Burge, and company, the majority of which has gone to line the pockets of the Dykema firm, as well as those of Andrew Hale and Jim Sotos. Hale, who wormed his way back into the city's good graces after being disgraced for tendering prejudicial information to the

Oscar Walden jury, was representing Burge, Byrne, and Dignan in the *Smith* and *Wrice* cases. He has reaped a total of more than $33 million in taxpayer funds defending alleged torturers and other assorted police miscreants, while Terrence Burns and his Dykema buddies have made more than $20 million representing Daley, the City, and its policymakers in these cases.

The County has quietly expended $16.5 million of the total: more than $7,000,000 went to Egan and Boyle for their whitewash investigation and report, and another $6 million has gone to Mike O'Rourke and the next wave of special prosecutors.

On the other side of the ledger, the torture survivors have to date wrested $93,000,000 in verdicts, settlements, and reparations from the City, County, and State. A decade after Steve Whitman made his projections, the high-end $195 million estimate of the potential cost of the torture scandal had appeared on the horizon.

A broken but unrepentant Burge died in September 2018, with his death announced on the front pages of the *Tribune* and *Sun Times*. The *Tribune*'s headline read, "Disgraced ex-Chicago Police Cmdr. Jon Burge, Accused of Presiding over Decades of Brutality and Torture, has Died." The *Sun Times* editorialized, under the title, "Burge's legacy: Torture, deceit and distrust—and the push to stop it all." Darrell, Anthony, and our staff decided to stay silent, but the *Sun Times* published some apt prior quotes of ours, with Darrell saying that Burge headed up a "new wave Klan" that "wore badges, instead of sheets," while my quote condemned their "crimes against humanity."

John Conroy pointed to a lack of supervision. Outside the courtroom where a Cook County jury would later convict officer Jason Van Dyke for the second-degree murder of Laquan McDonald, former FOP president Dean Angelo, loyal to the very end, praised Burge as an "honorable" and "effective" cop who "put a lot of people in prison." Reverend Jesse Jackson spoke as a man of the cloth: "As a person, may his soul rest in peace. As a policeman, he did a lot of harm to a lot of people and left on this city a mark. It stains us for a long time. His legacy, unfortunately, is tied in with forced confessions and wrongful convictions." The *Tribune* concluded:

> Diverging assessments of Burge's legacy have been a lightning rod that further polarized the long-tense relationship between the mostly white Chicago

Police Department and the black and brown communities it patrols. Burge's conduct and the subsequent department cover-ups are a seminal scandal in that history . . . the widespread impact of the allegations against Burge included questions about the conduct of former Mayor Richard M. Daley, who was Cook County state's attorney in the 1980s when much of the alleged torture took place, and former state's attorney Richard Devine, whose office opposed inmates' allegations of torture.

Burge's torture box rests on the bottom of Lake Michigan, and Deep Badge's identity may never be known. But the fight against police torture and violence is far from over. The complete Chicago police torture narrative traces an unbroken line of white supremacist violence from slavery, Black codes, convict leasing, and lynching to Jim Crow laws and police torture in Chicago. Torture is baked in to Chicago's law enforcement agencies and its judiciary, and has been condoned and covered up by politicians at every level, in every party.

Dozens of survivors of Burge's cabal and other victims of police coercion remain in prison on the basis of tortured confessions. Special Prosecutor O'Rourke, still beholden to the Fraternal Order of Police, is pursuing what promises to be a frivolous appeal in Jackie Wilson's case. People of color continue to be brutalized, unjustly imprisoned, shot, and murdered by law enforcement in Chicago and across the country.

Those who continue to fight for the constitutional—and human—right to a fair hearing, free from torture and brutality, encounter added resistance from the public's short attention span and a desire on the part of politicians for "finality," to put the torture scandal "behind us." The truth is that it will never be "behind us," and Chicago's collective conscience will not be cleansed, until and unless the City of Broad Shoulders, and the nation as a whole, reckon fully with the systemic racism of law enforcement, of the criminal courts, of mass incarceration and the death penalty, and of the political power structure.

Until then, *la luta continua*: the struggle must continue.

Acknowledgments

I n some real sense, the hardest part of this three-year odyssey to write *The Torture Machine* has been to compose this acknowledgment. This is so because there are so many wonderful and committed clients, mentors, comrades, activists, and organizations who contributed to the effort to forge the peoples' narrative that I have labored to recount. After much thought, I have decided not to list those whose roles are chronicled in the foregoing pages, but rather to acknowledge the important people who contributed but remained unnamed.

First comes my family. My parents, Elly and Flint Sr., who instilled in their children a strong sense of fairness, justice, and equality and gave us the space and support to pursue the often unpopular causes to which we committed ourselves. My older sister Laurie, a pioneer in writing and teaching women's history, who, through her quiet leadership in opposing the war in Vietnam and supporting the civil rights movement, led me first to question racism and unjust wars. My brother Wally, who has been a lifelong best friend, not only was an unflinching activist in his younger years but also has shown a profound kindness in raising his son and grandchildren, and caring for our parents in their declining years. Likewise their spouses, Clyde and Janice, have also been committed to fighting for human rights, are strong supporters of my work, and are important friends to my family and me.

My wife, Pat, herself a true people's lawyer, has always given me support and constructive criticism while serving over the decades as an intern at the PLO, a Cook County public defender, a human rights administrative law judge, and an elder abuse lawyer. Now, in her "retirement," she, together with Melinda Power and many others, has stepped up to defend the courageous Water Protectors who have fought to stop the DAPL oil pipeline at Standing Rock.

Our daughter, Kate, who as a baby and toddler was present with Pat for the Andrew Wilson closing arguments, the *Wilson* and *Jones* appellate arguments, and the *Buckley* argument before the US Supreme Court, has done us proud ever since. Her heroic basketball exploits in high school, excelling in her pursuit of Africana studies in college, fighting for sentencing reforms for several years, graduating from law school magna cum laude as a public interest scholar, clerking for a federal court of appeals judge, and now serving as a federal public defender are just some of the highlights of her most impressive career to date. She has consistently committed herself to fighting for justice and has become a people's defender in the truest sense of the words.

My late mother-in-law, Jeanne Handlin, a conservative midwestern Republican, without exception always supported my work, as have Pat's aunt Rita, the Wilson family, and my nieces and nephews, Stephen, Flint, Jennifer, Scott, and Michelle.

While I could never in one book, no matter how long, completely describe the collective love, work, commitment, and struggle of all those whom I have named as People's Law Office brothers and sisters in the narrative, I hope that the reader (and those whom I have named) can appreciate their remarkable contributions. Those who escaped mention include many of those folks who were an integral part during the early days of the PLO—Don Stang (a co-founding lawyer), Susan Jordan (our first woman lawyer and a pioneer of the battered-woman defense), Victory Kadish, Nancy Dempsey, Laura Whitehorn, Mona Mellis, Mzizi Woodson, Kalman Resnick, Mary Frank, Mariha Kuechmann, Courtney Esposito, Liza Lawrence, Susie Waysdorf, Eugene Feldman, Lee Tockman, Norrie Davis, Linda Peters, Nancy McCullough, Jim Fennerty, Hank Rose, Marty McDowell, Loren Siegel, Susan Rutberg, Arnie Jochums, Sandy Fogel, Marie Leaner, Steve White, Susan Kaplan, Kathy Swanson, Mimi Harris, and Carrie Shuman come to mind. Later mainstays include Alarie Mack, Ann Campbell Kendrick, Marta Rodriguez, Jill Inglis, Meryl Geffner, Ed Koziboski, Micky Forbes, Brian Glick, Amber Miller, Abby Clough, Rosie Velez, Janet Good, Abiar Poole, Allison Forker, and, most recently, Kristin Maglabe and Jose Gonzalez. Additionally, there are the PLO spouses and significant others—Susan Schrieber, Linda, Pam, Susan Mitchell, Andrea, Bridget, Lilly, Mike, Archer, and Tommy—and the hundreds of law students and interns who have worked with us for a summer, a semester, or longer, many of whom have gone on to be people's lawyers and activists in their own right.

In the same way, I hope that the reader can feel, through their first-person accounts as well as my narration, the strength demonstrated by our clients, from Fred Hampton and the Attica brothers to the Ford Heights Four and the torture survivors. They, and the organizations and movements they led, together with my families both at home and at the PLO, have given me the strength and inspiration to continue fighting when it would have been easier to "just give up." One of the most compelling of those persons who has not appeared in the book is Rafael Cancel Miranda, a revered Puerto Rican independentist freedom fighter, whom Michael and I met in 1970 in Marion Federal Penitentiary, and who inspired us both with his quiet yet powerful leadership during a prisoner work stoppage there. Others include Jose "Cha Cha" Jimenez, the self-made leader of the Young Lords Organization; Michael James, the leader of Rising Up Angry; so many Black Panthers and SDS members; Lolita Lebron; Muhammad Salah; Rasmea Odeh; Oscar Lopez Rivera; Bernardine Dohrn; Bill Ayers; Elizam Escobar; Yaki; and Jose Lopez.

Thanks to all the folks who worked, and continue to work, on torture reparations, including Sarah Ross, Carla Meyer, Mario Venegas, Jasmine Heiss, Ernest Coverson, Kelly Hayes, Amy Partridge, Mary Patten, Sali Vickie Casanova, Debbie Southorn, Lauren Taylor, Laurie Palmer, Christine Haley, Cindy Eigler, Rodney Walker, and Nate Gilham.

Special mention should be given to the women of color who lead the Movement for Black Lives, Black Lives Matter, BYP 100, Assata's Daughters, and Black and Pink, and those who write to spotlight official violence against women of color: Charlene Carruthers, Janae Bonsu, Christian Snow, Mariame Kaba, Page May, Alicia Garza, Aislinn Pulley, Andrea Ritchie, Beth Richie, Barbara Ransby, Kimberlé Williams Crenshaw, and Keeanga-Yamahtta Taylor, to name but a few. Together with those who continue to fight so valiantly at Standing Rock and across the globe for our sacred earth and water, you are an inspiration that parallels that of Dr. King, Malcolm X, SNCC, the Black Panthers, the Young Lords, Angela Davis, and the movement to end the war in Vietnam from decades ago.

Likewise, the National Lawyers Guild has been a bedrock in the legal community for more than eighty years, and its lawyers, law students, and legal workers have fought for human rights in the courts and in the streets over the decades. Many NLG members both worked with us and gave us support and inspiration. Bill Kunstler and Lenny Weinglass showed us how to fight back against unfair judges and opposing counsel in the Conspiracy 8 trial, Marc Kadish revived the NLG in Chicago with the help of Susie Gamm, Lorry Sirkin, Ed Schwartz, and many others, and Ted Stein, Cecile Singer, Mary Rita Luecke, and Cliff Zimmerman started another important Chicago civil rights office. More recently, Bryan Stevenson and the Equal Justice Initiative and Stephen Bright and the Southern Center for Human Rights have given us inspiration by fighting doggedly against racism and the death penalty in the deep South for decades.

The media are also a major part of the story. Changing the narrative in the *Hampton* and torture cases would not have been possible without the courageous and independent writing and reporting that is recounted in the book. Beyond those named, I want to acknowledge other media outlets, editors, and writers who also gave me voice, including WVON, *This Is Hell*, *Live from the Heartland*, *In These Times*, *Truthout*, the *Nation*, the *Big Muddy Gazette*, *Up Against the Bench*, *Law and Disorder*, the *Huffington Post*, Cliff Kelley, Tom Frisbee, Katy Hogan, Joel Bleifuss, Jessica Stites, Maya Schenwar, Micah Uetricht, Alana Price, Michael Smith, Heidi Boghosian, Santita Jackson, Don Terry, Brent Staples, Josh Simon, Ty Wansley, Dave Zirin, Liliana Segura, and Steve Saltzman.

I also want to give a shout-out to my high school history teacher, Charlotte Spinney, who headed me down the path of honest people's history and has supported me ever since, my high school basketball coach, Bob Kirby, and my lifelong high school friends from Westborough, Massachusetts, and Brown University—Bob, Joanne, Chris, Frankie, Steve, Bonnie, Jay, and Rich.

I would also be remiss if I did not acknowledge the inspiration that so many great writers of people's history provided me, first and foremost Howard Zinn and Noam Chomsky, and, more recently, Bryan Stevenson and Ta-Nehisi Coates.

I want to give heartfelt thanks to Haymarket Books, a Chicago monument to people's history in its own right. Their editors believed in me from the beginning, gave me encouragement when the task repeatedly seemed daunting to a first-time author, and supplied me with a magnificent editor, Caroline Luft. Caroline took the manuscript that I wrote, chapter by chapter, and, patiently and skillfully, cut it down to size while zealously protecting its essence. She also fashioned from a manuscript written by a lawyer accustomed to legalese a tract that hopefully can be read and understood by laypeople and lawyers alike. Other important people at Haymarket who contributed mightily to this collective writing effort are Julie Fain, Rory Fanning, and Dana Henricks.

Pat gave me valued insight from beginning to end. Martha, Mary, John Conroy, Jeff, Adam, Rita, Dennis, Mike Smith, Wally, Janice, Heather, Jamie, Bryan, Alison, and Laurie all read some or all of the advance copy and offered constructive input, while Kate's college documentary and her Africana honors thesis also provided me important interviews with torture survivors and historical context for placing police torture in the pantheon of racist official violence from enslavement onward to the present.

Thanks also to those folks who gave the wonderful endorsements that grace the book.

To anyone I have left out, either in the text or here, please accept my sincere apologies and be assured that your effort has been valuable in establishing and writing this people's narrative.

Index

60 Minutes 2, 247, 249, 276, 306
500 Black Men, 150, 170

Aaron Patterson Defense Committee, 289, 291
Abbate, Anthony, 371
Abramsky, Sasha, 270–271
Abu Ghraib, 306, 337, 340, 379, 391, 411, 424
Ackerman, Spencer, 481
ACLU, 376, 490
Acosta, Sergio, 382–83, 394, 395
Adams, Kenneth, 226–27, *260*
Adkins, Phillip, 118–120, 212, 214, 243, 270, 277, 346
Afro American Patrolmen's League, 3, 26, 71, 193, 196, 280, 428, 432
Ainsworth, Russell, 442
Algren, Nelson, 185
Ali, Muhammad, 32
Alinsky, Saul, 185
Allegations of Police Torture in Illinois, 167
Allen, Tom, 380
Alonzo, Jorge, 478
Alvarez, Anita, 393, 407–8, 440, 459, 482, 489
America Never Was America to Me, 235
American Nazi Party, 56–61
Amnesty International, 159, 164, 167–68, 171, 185, 280, 444, 464, 449
    reparations and, 462, 467, 469–70
Analysis of Wilson Case (Sanders), 163
Anderson, Blair, 18–19
Anderson, Monroe, 371
Andrew, Francis "Skip," 4
Angarola, Mike, 37, 46, 48, 51, 53, 72, 506
Angelo, Dean, 509
Anthony, Dwight, 502
Apache Rangers, 204, 228, 330
Arbuckle, Michael, 223
Area 2, 35, 47, 107, 118, 128, 222, 237, 242, 277, 319, 321, 334–35, 393–95, 403, 406, 488, 506. *See also* Chicago Police Department
    Brzeczek and, 46, 91, 346, 348
    Burge and, 67, 203, 283, 306, 334, 346, 347, 459, 478–79, 498
    Burge federal charges and, 431
    Burge federal trial and, 412, 418–19, 421, 423
    Byrd and, 241, 358, 497
    Byrne and, 277, 452
    Cline and, 371, 459
    Deep Badge and, 73–74, 108, 170, 278
    Devine and, 276, 351
    Dignan and, 213–14, 452
    Egan and, 331, 357–59
    facilities of, 304, 488
    files of, 49, 66, 74
    Haas and, 477
    Hoke and, 215
    Hyman on, 140
    Jones and, 64
    Karl and, 360
    Lacey and, 319, 414, 432, 497, 498
    Laverty and, 52, 66, 320, 363
    manhunt in, 35–36, 124, 133
    media on, 221, 271, 275, 302, 337, 348, 381
    Miller at, 38, 49
    OPS and, 113–14, 153, 162, 169, 170, 225, 308
    Orange civil suit and, 308
    Parker on, 177–79, 380
    Ryan on, 293
    Saffold on, 432
    Shaw on, 423
    special prosecutor's report and, 346–49
    Tillman and, 406, 408, 443–44
    torture at, 89–92, 94–98, 107, 114, 122, 124, 159, 164, 222–23, 320, 380, 389, 457
        of Adkins, 119
        of Banks, 331, 358, 414
        of Banks and Bates, 152
        of Benson, 396
        of Brown, 89
        of Caine, 207
        of Cannon, 234, 240
        Daley and, 487
        of Diggins, 206
        of Hammonds, 318
        of Hobley, 221
        of Holmes, 89–90, 90, 313
        of Howard, 150, 228
        Illinois Supreme Court on, 273
        of Jackie Wilson, 422
        of James, 314
        of Jones, 80, 91, 91–92, 101
        of Kidd, 305
        Kirschner on, 243
        Martin and, 174

of Mastin, 317–318
of Michael Johnson, 89–90, 105–7, 129
of Mike, 89
of Mastin, 317
of Mu'min, 160
of Orange, 305
of Patterson, 204–5, 248
of Porch, 94, 111–12
of Poree, 89, 314, 315
of Powell, 89, 316
of Smith, 327, 468, 477
of Thompson, 326
of Tillman, 396–97, 444–45
of Walter Johnson, 111
of Whirl, 478
of White, 117
of White and Williams, 36–37
of Wilson, 38–41, 45, 76, 83, 143, 191–92, 202
of Wrice, 461
plea deals and, 276
police board hearings and, 180
statistics of, 207
Vietnam and, 329
Young on, 319–320
Wilson and, 66, 128, 156, 199, 497
Wilson torture claim and, 497
Young and, 319–320, 329
Area 2 Homicide Division, 315
Area 2 Robbery, 178, 314, 316
Area 2 Violent Crimes Unit, 35, 52, 99, 152, 202, 216, 293, 334, 346, 371, 431, 459
Area 3, 161, 216, 340, 349, 404, 452, 483
Burge and, 172, 188, 283, 306, 319, 346, 404, 428, 479
media on, 188, 190, 271
torture at, 212, 429, 452
Wiggins and, 212, 216, 218
Arias, Lourdes, 452
Arizona Desert Sun, 182
Armstrong, Ken, 227, 273, 278–79
Aspen, Marvin, 361–62, 364–68, 375, 384, 386, 390
Associated Press, 180–81, 332, 341, 357, 386, 471
Attica prison uprising, 5–6, 51, 64, 273–74
Attorney Registration & Disciplinary Commission, 144
Aurora, Illinois, 127
Avila, Frank, Jr., 390–91
Avila, Jim, 190
Axelrod, David, 352

Baden, Michael, 419–20

Bajenski, Leonard, 304, 306
Banks, Gregory, 152–53, 173, 175, 181, 238, 268, 272, 320, 414–15, 418, 494
Burge and, 268, 399, 414–15, 421, 424, 428
Byrne and, 277, 281, 452
Dignan and, 213, 452
Egan and, 331, 357
media on, 172–73, 405
OPS and, 212, 243
Smith and, 478, 480
torture of, 95, 172, 204, 214, 320, 358, 414–15, 452, 480
Bannister, Leonard, 148
Barbosa, Collette, 30
Barker, Sarah, 454, 455
Basile, George, 318
Bates, David, 152, 181, 268, 277, 332, 335, 337–39, 348, 377, 399
Beale, Anthony, 380
Beavers, William, 149
Bedi, Sheila, 489
Bell, Harold, 19
Bell, Louva, 247, 279
Bell, Steven, 397, 406, 447
Bell v. Milwaukee, 453–55, 463–64
Bender, Bill, 4, 8
Benedict, Reverend Don, 166
Benson, Rodney, 396
Berland, Michael, 177, 180, 186
Bermanzohn, Paul, 59–60, 62
Berrios, Jose, 208, 256
Biebel, Paul, 280, 284–86, 289, 298, 335, 340–41, 358, 408, 468, 484–85
Biffl, Betsy, 394, 410, 412, 419
Bilandic, Michael, 24–25
Bill of Rights, 29, 31
Biondi, Martha, 462, 469, 471
Birmingham, Alabama, 476
Birth of a Nation, A, 59
Bishop, Jeanne, 439
Black Bar Association, 36
Black Disciples, 314
Black Gangster Disciples, 106
Blackmun, Harry, 195, 248, 295
Black Officers United for Justice and Equality, 181
Black Panther Party, 1–5, 7–18, 21, 23, 25, 26, 28, 31–34, 80, 96, 150, 253, 285, 356, 413
Black People Against Police Torture, 370–71, 403, 459, 460, 469
Black Power, 370
Blackstone Rangers, 11, 13, 18, 234
Black Youth Project 100, 489
Blagojevich, Rod, 301, 417, 439

Bluhm Legal Clinic, 239, 347, 361, 405
Bohman, Jane, 291
Bonjean, Jennifer, 462
Bonke, Fred, 216
Boss, Richard J. Daley of Chicago (Royko), 185
Boston Globe, 59, 182
Bouza, Tony, 360
Bowman, Locke, *265*, 332, 335, 358, 382, 404,
    407, 408, 450 , 489
    Burge and, 280, 426
    Burge special prosecutor and, 286, 298–299
    Cannon and, 303, 310, 312, 453, 456
    Daley and, 448–49
    Kitchen and, 428, 451, 458
    report on special prosecutors and, 372, 375
    special prosecutor's report and, 340, 347
Boyer, Brian, 3
Boyle, Robert D., 285–86, 297, 334, 345, 352,
    372, 376, 382, 399, 419, 462, 509
    Cook County Board and, 356–57
    county board hearing and, 377–78
    Daley and, 347, 352–54, 356
    Devine and, 352–54, 357
    Kunkle and, 352–54
    media on, 298–99, 331, 347, 350, 351, 400
    special prosecutor's report and, 334–35,
        340–41, 344, 347–48, 350, 353–55, 378
Bradley, Ben, 408
Brennan, Charles, 13
Brennan, William, 63
Brewer, Tommy, 309–310
Brewer, Verlina, 18–20
Brookins, Howard, 351, 355, 378, 384, 391, 393,
    460, 462
Brooks, Marion, 456
Brown, Cortez, 404
Brown, Elaine, 26
Brown, Geraldine Soat, 368
Brown, H. Rap, 9
Brown, Marc, 417
Brown, Roy, 71–74, 76, 83, 89, 110, 127, 133,
    144, 153, 502
Brzeczek, Richard, 36–38, 42, 45, 53–54, 69–71,
    91, 133, 199, 202, 300, 351, 355, 357
    Area 2 and, 46, 91, 346, 348
    Burge and, 46, 70–71, 74, 91, 101, 348, 351,
        360, 420
    Daley and, 69, 70, 73, 300, 324, 341–43,
        348, 351–53, 365, 368, 399, 414
    Devine and, 351–53, 357, 393
    manhunt and, 35–36, 54, 70, 143
    media on, 270–71, 302–03, 341–42, 345,
        347–49, 355, 357

Raba letter and, 45, 71, 118, 341, 347–48, 414
    special prosecutor's report and, 346–47,
        351–55
    Wilson civil retrial and, 96, 109, 127, 129,
        141, 146
    Wilson civil case and, 63, 73–74, 83, 84
Buckley (OPS investigator), 73
Buckley, Steven, 195–96
Bucklo, Elaine, 446
Bueke, Rick, 402, 413, 416, 423–24
Buffalo, New York, 6, 64, 273
Bureau of Alcohol, Tobacco, and Firearms, 56–57,
    62
Burge, Dorothy, 469, 471
Burge, Jeff, 433
Burge, Jon, 67, 95, 131, 154, 194, 196, 231, *265*,
    304–6, 316, 334, 360, 430, 432, 477, 509
    activism against, 118, 148–49, 161–62, 170,
        174, 280, 311, 334–35, 402, 431, 436
    anti-torture legislation and, 430
    appeals and, 189, 197
    Area 3 and, 172, 188, 283, 319, 346, 404,
        428, 479
    Banks and, 172, 268, 421
    Brzeczek and, 46, 70–71, 74, 91, 348, 351,
        360, 420
    Byrd and, 241–42, 318–21, 421, 498
    Byrne and, 119, 150, 152, 172, 249, 276–78,
        323, 404, 414, 419, 428, 452
    Cannon and, 268, 270, 311–12, 402, 456–58
    city coucil and, 161, 166–68, 175, 378–381
    City of Chicago and, 228, 308–9, 311, 349,
        369, 378–79, 383–84, 444–45, 458,
        486, 508
    Cline and, 371, 459
    Conroy and, 154–56, 360
    conspiracy of, 82, 86, 107
    conviction of, 426–27, 508
    Daley and, 108, 187, 192, 287, 351–53, 360,
        362, 365, 392, 418, 444
        Brzeczek letter and, 46, 70–71, 323, 368
        legal fees and, 308, 508
        media on, 372, 399–01, 510
        Wilson and, 466–67
    Deas and, 52, 74
    death row clemencies and, 297
    Deep Badge on, 72, 75, 79, 170, 171
    depositions of, 67–69, 90–91, 116–19, 309,
        311–12, 379, 381, 442, 467–69, 486–88,
        497–98
    Devine and, 232, 246, 280, 284, 287, 357,
        360, 393
    Dignan and, 213–14, 414, 452

Duff and, 122, 124
Egan on, 331, 359
Emanuel and, 445, 446, 466
End of the Nightstick on, 210–11
federal charges against, 151, 242, 347, 380,
    382–85, 387, 389, 394–95, 398, 402, 508
federal trial of, 407, 410–25
Fifth Amendment and, 308, 311, 324, 383,
    431, 442, 468–69, 473–74, 477–78,
    486–87, 492, 498, 503
firing of, 192–94, 208, 211, 215, 225, 231,
    275, 310, 343, 403, 416, 420, 422,
    426–27, 508
Fitzgerald and, 385–86, 398–99, 426
FOP and, 184, 193, 196, 200, 403, 486, 494,
    497, 509
Ford and, 484–85
fraud suit against, 453
going away party of, 203
Hardin and, 506
Hartnett and, 499
Hobley and, 311, 431, 435, 457
Hoke and, 214–15
Hooks on, 504
Hyman and, 139–40
Illinois Supreme Court and, 248, 272–73
incarceration of, 442, 446, 452, 455
in Vietnam, 67, 78, 108, 154, 166, 175, 306,
    327–28, 338, 412, 420, 422, 427
Jackie Wilson and, 469, 486, 496
Jane Byrne and, 357
Johnson and, 106, 122
Jones and, 80–82, 97, 100–2, 106, 122, 420
Kill and, 442–43
Kitchen and, 409, 428–29
Kunkle and, 125, 164, 168, 172, 176, 179,
    191, 193, 216
Lacey and, 319, 432, 498
Laverty and, 53, 320, 421
Logan and, 468
manhunt and, 35–36, 124, 320, 357, 422, 486
Martin and, 172, 183, 319, 321, 360, 444
Maslanka and, 219, 404
McCarthy and, 133
McDermott and, 394, 396, 415–16, 421, 427
McWeeny and, 222
media on, 248–49, 270–71, 299–300, 311–12,
    323, 328, 337–39, 348–49, 426, 432
    Conroy, 221, 283, 302, 306–7, 327–29, 345
    NBC Channel 5, 389, 411, 417
    Southtown Economist, 189, 350–351
    Sun Times, 263, 350, 371, 381, 384, 400,
        407, 410–11, 427, 436, 438–39, 446,
    490, 509
    Tribune, 174–76, 229–31, 282, 285,
        381–82, 438, 509–10
Mogul and, 442
on Holmes, 420
on Mu'min, 421
on Wilson, 420–21
on Wilsons, 395
OPS and, 70, 106, 120, 124, 163, 171, 173, 426
Orange civil suit and, 308
O'Rourke and, 500
Panos and, 395–96, 501
Parker on, 178–79, 380–81
Patterson case and, 209
pension of, 270, 311, 337, 355, 378, 381, 389,
    391–92, 399, 427, 438–39, 445, 465–66,
    486, 508
Pienta and, 204, 478–479
PLO and, 173, 180
police board hearings and, 164, 180, 183–87,
    189–92, 219, 224
polls on, 193
Porch and, 111–12, 114, 122
Powers on, 118
Preib and, 473, 477, 486
Pryweller and, 321
Raoul on, 403
released from prison, 466
Reno and, 242
reparations and, 471, 473, 475, 477
report on special prosecutors and, 372–74
RICO case and, 365
Rodriguez on, 187
Rush on, 297
Ryan on, 293
sentencing of, 430–36, 438–39, 452
Seventh Circuit and, 379, 457–58, 463–64
Shaw on, 423
Shines and, 173
Smith and, 491–92, 500
Sotos and, 195, 509
special prosecutor and, 280–83, 284–86,
    298, 311, 321, 331, 335, 338, 422, 431
special prosecutor's report and, 346–48, 357
suspension of, 174–75
testimony of, 47, 66, 78–79, 122–26, 143,
    185, 328, 402, 420–22
Tillman and, 406–7, 409, 444, 451
TIRC and, 459
torture by, 87–92, 94–98, 120, 124, 206–7,
    224, 240, 316, 318, 379, 414, 439, 457
    of Andrew Wilson, 39–41, 68–69, 78, 96,
        121, 144, 157, 160, 173, 175, 186, 192,

208, 210, 224, 379, 419–20, 422, 502
of Cannon, 379, 474
of Holmes, 88–90, 313–14, 317, 350, 372, 379, 432, 474
of Jackie Wilson, 486, 497, 499, 501, 502
of James, 88–89, 313
of Johnson, 89–91, 95, 106, 116
of Jones, 80–81, 87, 87–88, 90, 96–98, 101–2, 106–7, 183, 201, 233, 249, 413
of Kidd, 304–5
of Kitchen, 229, 405, 429, 442
of Mastin, 317–318
of Mu'min, 160, 176, 183, 211, 243, 394–96, 417–18
of Orange, 207, 304, 304–6, 379
of Porch, 94, 94–95, 111–12
of Poree, 88–89, 91, 313–15
of Powell, 88–89, 91, 316–17
of Safford, 404–5
of Smith, 509
statute of limitations on, 281
of Thompson, 95, 326
of Tillman, 444–45
of White, 117, 126, 131, 486, 496
of Wiggins, 188
of Williams, 37, 496
of Wrice, 509
UNCAT on, 467
Vietnam and, 91
Wiggins and, 191
Williams on, 457
Wilson appeal and, 199, 201, 224
Wilson arrests and, 38
Wilson civil retrial and, 90–91, 94, 99, 111–12, 116–17, 120–26, 129, 136, 141, 143, 146–47, 328, 402
Wilson civil rights case and, 63, 66, 78–79, 85–86, 87–88
Wilson torture claim and, 502
Young and, 319–320
Yucaitis and, 131, 133, 420
Burge/O'Hara/Yucaitis fund, 179–80, 184, 214
Burger, Warren, 63
Burke, Ann, 465
Burke, Ed, 73, 161, 163–66, 187, 193, 197, 207, 378–80, 462, 465, 470
Burns, Terry, 323, 340, 354, 364–65, 367, 446, 449, 457, 491–92, 509
Burroughs, Margaret, 151
Butkovich, Bernard, 57
Butner, North Carolina, 442, 469
Byler, Marjorie, 159
Byrd, Doris, 241–42, 318–21, 334, 358, 414, 421,

497–98
Byrne, Jane, 37–38, 50, 72–73, 108, 184, 233, 357, 365–66
manhunt and, 35, 45, 54, 124, 133, 320, 357, 365
special prosecutor's report and, 352–54, 357, 365
Byrne, John, 95, 119, 150, 216, 222, 304, 308, 335, 365, 373, 383, 428–29, 444, 452–53, 509
Burge and, 172, 249, 276–78, 323, 404, 414, 452
Burge federal trial and, 418, 419, 431
Byrd and, 318–21
Cannon and, 268, 270, 274–75, 310, 453, 456
Deep Badge and, 170, 278
deposition of, 276–78, 383
Dignan and, 276–78
Fifth Amendment and, 308, 311, 324, 383, 405, 452, 462, 478, 492
media on, 249, 274, 276–77, 323, 345, 400, 405, 456
OPS and, 212, 228, 249, 277
Patterson and, 249, 276–77
Smith and, 491, 500
special prosecutor's report and, 347
Tillman-Messenger and, 277
torture by, 221, 237–38, 243, 277, 316, 396
of Banks, 152, 172, 268, 277, 281, 310, 414, 418, 452, 478
of Bates, 152, 181, 268, 277
of Bell, 397, 447
of Cannon, 228, 234–36, 244, 277, 281, 310, 452, 478
of Holmes, 281, 396
of Safford, 404, 405
of Smith, 269, 277, 281, 477, 488, 509
of Tillman, 396–397, 406–7, 447, 452
of Wrice, 396, 461, 478, 509

Caddick, Kenneth, 501
Cain, Albert, 62–63
Caine, Eric, 207, 442, 485
Cambodia, 5, 240
Campaign to End the Death Penalty, 227, 245, 247, 280, 289, 291, 294
Canada, 295
Cannon, Darrell, 237–38, 243, 250–51, 268, 310, 377, 383, 391, 402, 456, 463, 477, 480, 502
appeal of, 237–40, 242–44, 268–70, 272, 274–75, 280
background of, 234
Burge and, 399, 402, 509
Byrne and, 277, 281, 310, 365, 452, 453

City of Chicago and, 453–45
civil suit appeal of, 453, 453–55, 458,
    463–65, 491
civil suit of, 362, 386–87, 395, 396, 443
Daley and, 237, 362, 365, 430, 443
Devine and, 246, 274, 282, 303
Dignan and, 213, 277, 310, 452, 453, 477
media on, 247, 274–75, 310–11, 402, 405,
    471, 474, 476
OPS and, 228–29, 232, 239, 242–43, 270,
    308
parole and, 309–312, 361–63, 375
plea deal of, 274–75, 281, 303
reparations and, 462, 467, 471, 473, 476, 482,
    493–94
at Tamms, 238 39, 312, 362
Tillman-Messenger and, 243–44
torture of, 95, 228, 232, 234–37, 239–40,
    244, 268, 310, 312, 379, 452, 474, 480
Capone, Al, 1, 213, 398, 433
Carbondale, Illinois, 5
Carey, Bernard, 6, 46
Carey, Margaret, 218, 220
Carlos, John, 370
Carmichael, Stokely, 9
Carmody, Edward, 27, 29
Carrothers, Anita, 237
Carrothers, Ike, 376, 380
Carter, Marlene, 161–66, 168
Cassidy, James, 225, 245
Castillo, Ruben, 220, 223–24, 231, 441–42
Cauce, Cesar, 58–59
Cavise, Len, 380, 459
CBS, 168, 190, 247, 306, 323–24, 391, 427
CeaseFire, 456
Center for Constitutional Rights, 333
Center for Justice in Capital Cases, 293
Center for Torture Victims and Families, 460
Center on Wrongful Convictions, 289, 439
Centralia, Illinois, 117, 126
Centralia Prison, 176
Cermak Hospital, 43, 341
Champen, Roger "Champ," 6
Chen, Doris, 488
Cheney, Dick, 382, 411
Chicago, 7, 76, 196, 311, 314, 340, 350, 377, 398,
    401, 432–33, 458. See also City of Chicago
activism in, 247, 338, 462, 467, 469, 482, 489
Altgeld Gardens, 234
Black community of, 7, 30, 54, 301, 355–58,
    411, 446, 474
    Burge and, 170, 197, 199, 351, 510
    Burge special prosecutors and, 286

manhunt and, 35–36, 38, 70, 83–84,
    143–144, 202, 422
    McDonald and, 482–83
Black Panther Party in, 1–3, 10
Bridgeport, 148, 150, 170
Burge federal trial and, 410
Burge in, 311, 402, 404
Burnham Harbor, 203
Canaryville, 148, 150, 169, 186, 196
COINTELPRO papers from, 11–12, 14, 16
Comiskey Park, 148, 150
conscience of, 411, 510
Division Street, 448
Englewood, 225, 493
far southeast side of, 350
far south side of, 320, 416
FBI field office in, 11, 14, 17, 32
Hampton and, 356
Jeffrey Manor, 350
Justice Department and, 242
Loop, 184
Marquette Park, 105
Midway Airport, 488
Mount Greenwood, 196
NATO summit in, 449
north side of, 1, 3, 398
Old Town, 194
Olympics and, 370 371
public opinion in, 197, 221, 344
riot fears about, 187, 193
southeast side of, 95
south side of, 88, 111, 175, 207, 213, 225,
    234, 277, 301, 304, 424, 427, 456, 461
    Burge in, 67, 203, 273
    police murders on, 35, 497
    politicians from, 165, 336, 355
    Wilsons in, 38, 40, 154
southwest side of, 43, 73, 161, 187, 196
"torturable class in," 339
"torture-free zone," 449
UNCAT, 336
war on crime politics in, 67
Washington and, 54
Washington Park, 371
West Englewood, 216, 277, 451
west side of, 2, 38, 148, 165, 226, 377, 408, 481
Wilson civil rights case and, 82
Woodlawn, 213, 234
Chicago City Colleges, 471
Chicago City Council, 355, 375–76, 380, 385, 449
Black Caucus of, 336, 378
county board hearing and, 377–79
Finance Committee of, 378–79, 383–84,

388–89, 451, 462, 466, 470, 471
Fire and Police Committee of, 376, 378–80
media on, 394, 451, 472
reparations and, 375, 460, 469–72, 475, 483
torture settlements and, 384, 386–89
Chicago Committee to Defend the Bill of Rights, 135
Chicago Conference of Black Lawyers, 135, 193
Chicago Council of Lawyers, 280
Chicago Crusader, 349
Chicago Daily Defender, 10, 22, 29, 115, 163, 167, 175
Chicago Daily News, 3, 8, 17, 24
Chicago Defender, 349
Chicago Ethics Board, 166
Chicago Federal District Court, 63
Chicago Fire Department, 39
Chicago Housing Authority, 119
Chicago Innocence Project, 461
Chicago-Kent College of Law, 289, 476
Chicago Law Bulletin, 286–287, 331, 342
Chicago Lawyer, 76–77, *257, 259*
Chicago Police Department, 29, 36, 56, 192, 234, 276–78, 319, 371, 385, 421, 432, 434
activism against, 161, 176, 184, 242, 331, 336–37, 489
Amnesty International and, 171
anonymous tips from, 72–73, 75, 79, 99
assistant state's attorneys and, 288
in Bridgeport, 148–50
brutality by, 54–56, 70–72, 106, 148–50, 371, 393, 467, 473, 482
Burge federal trial and, 412, 418, 421
Burge on, 404, 433
Burge's career in, 67, 433
Burge special prosecutor and, 285–86
city council and, 161–65, 355, 380
county board hearing and, 378
Daley and, 230, 352
Dignan and, 212–13, 478
Duncan and, 315
Egan and, 358
Emanuel and, 451
Fogel on, 150
fraud by, 453
Gang Crimes Unit, 69, 133, 234, 240
Gang Intelligence Unit, 10
Hampton murder and, 1–2, 8, 18–20, 28–29, 32, 34
Hilliard and, 232
Illinois Supreme Court on, 273
independent investigation of, 230, 232
Internal Affairs and, 215

Kunkle on, 47
Laverty and, 52
Lee case and, 63
manhunt by, 44, 66, 74, 85, 126, 502
brutality of, 54, 70–71, 89, 143, 156
Byrne and, 35, 45, 124
Wilson case and, 109–111, 319, 320
Mastin and, 317
McDermott and, 394
McDonald and, 482–83
media on, 223, 323, 328, 337–38, 349, 432
Marin, 445
NBC Channel 5, 176
New York Times, 388, 399
Sun Times, 297, 350, 368–69, 371, 505
Tribune, 192, 229, 230, 350, 408–9, 497, 509–10
murders by, 241, 241–42
murders of, 35, 103, 504
Ninth District, 150, 170
OPS report and, 171
Parker on, 177–78
pattern of abuse by, 65, 69–72, 81, 83–84, 87–88, 92, 96–100, 109–112, 119, 122, 127, 129, 143, 145–47, 199, 225, 443, 482, 508
Amnesty International on, 168
Banks and, 172
city council hearings on, 164
death penalty clemencies and, 303
Fogel on, 151–53
foreman on, 156–57
Goldston report on, 181
Kirschner on, 243
Kitchen and, 229
McClin–Weaver case and, 174
media and, 183
OPS and, 170
police board hearing and, 177
special prosecutor's report and, 346
Wilson appeal and, 202
pensions and, 281, 427, 438, 439, 465
perjury and, 108
PLO and, 404
Preckwinkle on, 389
public opinion on, 197
racial divisions within, 181, 197
Raoul on, 403
reparations and, 472, 473, 490, 494
report on special prosecutors and, 372–73
RICO case and, 366
Seventh Circuit on, 457, 463
Special Operations Section, 386

street files of, 49, 53–54, 63, 66–67, 74, 363
Third District, 213, 304
Tillman civil suit and, 443–44
torture by, 35–41, 64–65, 135, 143, 154, 167,
.   181, 193, 232, 240, 457, 487, 508, 510
    of Brown, 71–72, 83
    city council hearings on, 163–64
    Deep Badge on, 72–73
    Hanhardt and, 179
    Kirchner on, 243
    media on, 169, 176, 181–82, 185, 230–32,
        247, 290, 302
    OPS and, 170, 181
    of Patterson, 203–5, 223, 257, 388
    People's Tribunal and, 151
    reparations for, 161, 370, 375, 460–461
    of Tillman, 409
    Vietnam and, 328
    of Walden, 440–41
    of White, 126–27
    of Wilson, 209, 354, 355
    UNCAT and, 336, 340, 467
    Vanecko and, 448–49
    Washington campaign and, 54
    Wilson civil rights case and, 63, 79
    Wilson torture claim and, 504
Chicago Police Board, 135, 148–49, 283
    Burge decision of, 187–190, 191–92, 198,
        200, 209
    Burge hearings of, 175–77, 180–86, 194, 224
    McClin–Weaver case and, 186
    OPS and, 187, 233
    Tribune on, 186–87
    Wilson and, 201, 413
Chicago Public Schools, 461, 466, 471, 493–94
Chicago *Reader*, 262, 338, 339, 345, 360, 393
    Amnesty International and, 171
    on Burge, 328
    on Byrne, 274
    on Cannon, 275
    on Dignan, 274
    on *Hampton* case, 13, 31
    "House of Screams," 153–59, 165
    on Laverty, 364
    OPS files and, 220
    on Patterson, 282
    "Silent Screams," 159
    "The Police Torture Scandal, a Who's Who,"
        345
    "Town Without Pity," 221
    on Wilson, 387–88
Chicago School of Law and Economics, 198
Chicago Sun Times, 159, 177, 188–89, 232, *259*,

    264–65, *267*, 341, 371, 389, 393–94, 489
    on Burge, 193, 297, 446
    on Burge federal charges, 393, 398, 400, 407
    on *Burge* federal trial, 410–11, 417, 427
    on Burge firing, 192, 211
    on Burge legal costs, 384
    on Burge prosecution, 175
    on Burge sentencing, 436, 438–39
    on Burge suspension, 174
    on CPD, 297, 350, 368–69, 371, 505
    on city council, 166, 381, 394
    on Daley, 162, 352–53, 366–68, 384, 438,
        445, 492
    on Dignan, 275
    on Egan, 357–59
    on Emanuel, 451
    on FOP, 196, 196–97, 403
    on Ford, 484–85
    on Goldston report, 182
    on *Hampton* case, 3, 9, 14
    on Holmes, 350
    on Jackie Wilson, 498–99, 501–5, 507
    on McDonald, 489
    on reparations, 466, 472, 494
    on special prosecutor's report and, 242–43,
        349, 350
    on Taylor, 438
    on Vanecko, 449
    on Whirl, 480
    on Wiggins, 188, 191
    on *Wilson* retrial, 87
Chicago Teachers Union, 466
Chicago Temple, 469, 476
Chicago Tonight, 348
Chicago Torture Justice Center, 493
Chicago Torture Justice Memorials, 460–61,
    466–47, 469–71, 475–76
Chicago Transit Authority, 268
Chicago Tribune, 52, 184, 242, 250, *254*, *261–63*,
    265, 362, 391, 403, 405, 408, 428
    on Andrew Wilson, 92, 125, 175, 388
    on Burge, 231, 282, 285
    on Burge death, 509–510
    on Burge firing, 192
    on Burge pension, 438, 465
    on Burge special prosecutor, 298–99
    on Burge suspension, 174–75
    on Cannon, 247, 274–75, 310
    on Chicago police, 230–32, 247, 408
    on city council hearings, 166, 381–82
    on Cunningham, 278–79
    on Daley, 186, 230–32, 282, 322, 353–55,
        366, 376, 389, 492

on death penalty, 273, 282, 289–90, 293–94
on Devine, 247, 282, 389
on Goldston report, 182–83
on Greensboro Massacre, 59
on Hampton, 3–4, 8, 12–13, 25
on Jackie Wilson, 497, 500, 501, 505, 507
on Obama, 301
on OPS, 181, 187, 229–30, 233
on Patterson, 227, 247, 282, 309, 325
on police board hearing, 176–77, 186–87
on Preckwinkle, 376
"Probing Burge," 230
on reparations, 471–72, 493
Royko and, 185
on special prosecutor's report, 343–44,
    349–51, 354–55, 357
Chile, 246, 332, 461
China, 349
Christenbury, Edward, 15, 17
Christia, Carmen, 244
Church, Frank, 11, 12
CIA, 11, 16, 23
Cieslik, Arthur, 207–8
Citizens Alert, 118, 122, 135, 220, 280, 376
City Colleges of Chicago, 461
City Hall, 162, 175, 183, 336, 352, 367–68, 384,
    463, 467, 469, 471
City of Chicago, 149, 156, 170, 189, 195, 360,
    363, 403, 423, 444, 458, 481, 491, 509
    Amnesty International and, 168, 171
    Burge and, 308–9, 311, 349, 369, 378–80,
        383–84, 444–45, 458, 486, 508
    Burge firing and, 208
    Burge special prosecutor and, 285–86
    Cannon and, 362, 453–56, 463–65
    Citywide Coalition and, 174
    Daley and, 323–24, 348, 354, 361, 364, 375,
        444–46
    depositions and, 229, 232
    Hampton trial and, 21, 27, 34
    Humboldt Park case and, 56
    Kunkle and, 208–9, 224
    McClin–Weaver case and, 174
    McDonald and, 482
    media on, 384, 388, 446
    OPS files and, 71, 113–14, 212, 220, 223–24,
        228–29, 231, 308
    OPS Special Projects reports and, 171, 174,
        179, 181–82
    Orange civil suit and, 308, 310
    Patterson case and, 205, 208, 300
    police board hearings and, 175–76, 180, 183,
        185, 208, 233

reparations and, 469–71, 475–77, 482–83, 509
report on special prosecutors and, 374–77
RICO case and, 366
Seventh Circuit on, 463
sexual and domestic violence policy in, 241
special prosecutor's report and, 340
torture memorials and, 461
torture settlements and, 361–62, 364–67,
    375, 379, 384–90, 430, 450, 458, 509
Walden suit against, 441–42
Wiggins and, 191, 217–18, 220
Wilson appeal and, 199, 202, 209–10, 224
Wilson civil retrial and, 94, 96–100, 103, 105,
    109–11, 120, 123, 126, 129, 133, 136,
    141–43, 145–47, 308, 379, 423
Wilson civil rights case and, 63, 65, 69, 73, 81,
    83, 85–86, 88
Citywide Coalition Against Police Abuse, 135,
    142, 148–49, 151, 161, 174, 188–89
Claps, Joseph, 167
Clark family, 4, 26, 28, 254
Clark, Fannie Mae, 254
Clark, Mark, 1, 12, 17, 19, 27, 30, 89, 94, 433, 490
Clark, Ramsey, 13
Clarkson, Alfred, 136, 141, 156
Claypool, Forrest, 493
Clemency and Pardon Hearings, 260
Clements, Mark, 467
Cline, Phil, 371–72, 376, 448, 459
Clinton administration, 226, 242
Clinton, Bill, 274
CNN, 291, 296, 405
Coalition Against Bashing, 184
Coalition Against the Death Penalty, 280, 289,
    291, 439
Coalition to End Police Brutality and Torture, 124
Coar, David, 228–30, 232–33, 476–77, 482
"Cochise." See Collins
Coffey, Douglas, 87
Coffey, John, 198, 200, 202, 224
Coghlan, John, 7, 21, 23, 27–29, 34
Cohen, Sharon, 438
COINTELPRO, 9, 10–14, 16, 17, 32–33
Coleman, William, 136–42, 145, 156, 189, 198,
    202, 505–6
Collins, Earlean, 377
Collins, Howard, 88, 95
Collins, Roger, 80, 88, 90, 91, 95, 106, 413
Committee against Police Torture, 375
Committee for Civil Rights Under Law, 280
Committee for Justice for Death Row Families of
    Illinois, 289, 291
Committee to End Police Abuse and Torture, 135

Committee to Investigate the Police, 135
Common Ground, 168
Communist Workers Party, 56, 58–59, 62
Community Renewal Society, 334
Compton, James, 196
Congressional Black Caucus, 242
Conlisk, James, 7
Conroy, John, 215, 282–83, 302, 344–45, 387,
    393, 423, 438, 477, 509
    on Abu Ghraib, 306–7
    on Burge, 283, 306, 327–29, 345, 411–12,
        423, 428
    on Cannon, 274–76
    on *Democracy Now!*, 337–39
    "House of Screams," 153–58, 165
    on Laverty, 364
    letter to, 360
    "Town Without Pity," 221–22
Constitution, 29, 49, 53, 60, 76, 82–84, 144–45,
    153, 344
Conyers, John, 225, 375
Cook County, 251, 360, 509
    assistant state's attorney, 284, 412, 418
    bench trials in, 169
    chief judge of, 107, 484
    clerk, 377
    Coghlan, 34
    commissioner, 450
    criminal courts of, 1, 46, 197, 286, 298, 305,
        373, 390, 405, 406, 413, 442, 497
    diversity of, 73
    Felony Review Unit of, 39, 448, 450
    Hanrahan lawyers paid by, 21
    judges of, 71, 112, 167, 207, 480
    media on, 297
    medical examiner, 75
    Orange civil suit and, 308
    PLO research on, 287–88
    prosecutors for, 37, 66, 169, 285
    public defenders in, 136, 280, 284, 478
    reparations and, 509
    sheriff of, 45
    special prosecutors and, 6, 373–74, 377, 431,
        449
    state's attorney, 230, 340, 366, 393, 450, 504
        Alvarez as, 440, 459, 482–83, 489
        Amnesty International and, 167
        Daley as, 69, 175, 322–24, 332, 341, 348,
            353, 361–62, 372–73, 376, 436, 443,
            447, 487, 510
        Davy as, 112
        Devine as, 282, 285–87, 344, 362, 436,
            448, 510

    Hyman as, 418
    Tillman and, 409
    TIRC and, 403
    Van Dyke and, 509
Cook County Bar Association, 109, 280–81,
    286, 442
Cook County Board of Commissioners, 47, 356,
    374–75, 377–79, 414, 450, 458
Cook County Chancery Court, 465
Cook County Department of Corrections, 45
Cook County Hospital, 19, 43, 119
Cook County Jail, 206, 270
    Andrew Wilson in, 43, 82, 97, 137, 342, 354
    Coleman in, 137–38
    George Jones in, 53, 64
    Jackie Wilson in, 43, 136, 507
    Melvin Jones in, 79, 96–97, 100
Cooley, Robert, 207
Cooper, Jerry "Rooster," 59, 61
Corning, New York, 4
Cosey, Robert, 243
Coventry, Dale, 44, 47–50, 71, 90, 207
    Burge federal trial and, 413
    Coleman on, 138, 142
    Jones and, 79, 81
    Wilson and, 63, 65, 66, 69, 83
Coyne, Daniel, 476
Craft, Thomas, 212,, 243
Crane, Clayton, 404–5
Crawford, Cathryn Stewart, 268, 276, 283,
    290–91, 298, 303–4
Crawley, Jerry, 181
Crowe, Brian, 192
Crowe, Michael, 299
Crowley, John J., 47–50
Cruz, Raphael, 55
Cruz, Rolando, 195, 293
Culloton, Dennis, 290
Cunningham, Dennis, 4, 6, 8, 12, 21, 29–31,
    252, 273
Cunningham, Dick, 247–48, 250, 276, 278–79
    Kitchen and, 229, 246–47, 276, 279
    Smith and, 276, 467
Cunningham, Jesse, 278
Cunningham, Maria, 278
Curran, Kevin, 141

Daily Mirror, 139
Daley, Bill, 367
Daley, John, 377
Daley, Maggie, 449
Daley, Richard J., 6, 7, 12, 24, 46, 184–85, 285,
    322, 376, 438, 448

Daley, Richard M., 37, 148–49, 168, 242, *265*, 305, 376, 379, 488, 508–9
  activism against, 161–62, 332, 370
  anonymous police tip about, 72–73
  Boyle and, 347, 356
  Brzeczek and, 69–71, 73, 300, 324, 341–43, 348, 351–53, 365, 368, 399, 414
  Burge and, 55, 70–71, 108, 192, 287, 308, 323, 351–53, 360, 362, 365, 368, 372, 392, 399–401, 444, 466, 508, 510
    Wilson and, 487–88
  Burge conviction and, 428
  Burge federal charges and, 399–401
  Burge federal trial and, 418
  Burge sentencing and, 436
  Burge special prosecutor and, 285
  Byrne and, 50, 444
  Cannon and, 237, 362, 365, 430, 443
  Chicago police and, 230, 352
  City of Chicago and, 324, 354, 361, 364, 375, 444–46
  Davis and, 165, 184
  Death Row Ten and, 249
  deposition of, 322–25, 361, 368, 375, 430, 445–450, 457, 491–93, 495
  Devine and, 97, 245, 282, 311, 357, 361–62, 365, 393
  Dignan and, 233, 444
  End of the Nightstick on, 211
  Fogel and, 152
  FOP and, 169, 187, 197
  Goldston and, 189, 230, 492
  Haas and, 322
  Hyman and, 341, 345
  IPRA and, 376–377
  Kitchen and, 409, 428, 443–44
  Kunkle and, 66
  Lefkow on, 436
  media on, 249, 324–25, 332, 342, 348–53, 443, 445–47, 458
    CBS 2, 323–324
    Conroy, 302, 307, 345
    Democracy Now!, 338
    Spielman, 189, 230–31, 368, 445, 466
    Sun Times, 297, 341, 352–53, 366–67, 368, 371–72, 381, 384, 445, 492
    Tribune, 183, 186, 230, 231–32, 282, 322, 344, 353–35, 357, 366, 376, 389, 492, 510
  Myers on, 170
  Olympics and, 370–71
  OPS reports and, 181–82
  Orange and, 443

  Patterson and, 249, 296, 300, 330, 443
  PLO and, 287, 322
  police board hearing and, 177
  police violence and, 149–50
  Powers on, 118
  Quigley and, 356
  Raba letter and, 45–47, 352–54
  report on special prosecutors and, 361, 373
  retirement of, 443
  RICO case and, 365–66
  Rodriguez and, 186
  Shaw and, 165
  Shines and, 160, 175, 231
  Smith and, 491–92
  special prosecutor's report and, 341, 344–55, 365
  St. Patrick's Day parade and, 196–97
  Task Force and, 210
  Tillman and, 409, 430, 443–45, 447, 451
  torture settlements and, 388, 390–92
  Vanecko and, 448–49, 462
  Washington and, 54, 55
  Wilson and, 125, 341, 347, 352, 354, 438
Danville Penitentiary, 88, 316
Danziger Bridge, 491
Darrow, Clarence, 276
Davis, Andrea, 151–52
Davis, Danny, 165, 166, 184, 242, 332, 380, 429–30
Davis, James "Gloves," 23, 27
Davis, Mrs. (witness), 144, 156
Davy, Thomas, 112–13
Dawson, Eddie, 57, 59–61
Deas, Milton, 37, 52, 74, 128–29, 163, 180, 319
Death Row Ten, 227, 230, 245, 247–49, 275, 281, 286, 290, 297
December 4th Committee, 13, 24
Deep Badge, 119, 160, 168, 170–71, 179, 194, 213–15, *258*, 278, 334, 364, 510
  Area 2 and, 108, 278
  Karl and, 361
  media on, 171, 249, 438
  on Byrd, 241, 320
  on widespread torture, 79–80, 91, 95, 97, 99, 107, 117
  Wilson civil retrial and, 125, 127–28
Del Valle, Vanessa, 489
Democracy Now!, 337–40, 411
Democratic National Convention, 301
Democratic Party, 55, 66, 245,346, 352, 377, 440
  1968 convention of, 371
  Chicago machine of, 6, 46, 47, 54, 108, 149, 164, 271, 285, 331, 351

primaries in, 24, 184, 393, 489
DePaul Law School, 289, 293, 375, 380
Dernbach, Dennis, 305–6
Despres, Leon, 185
Deutsch, Michael, 5–6, *256*, 298, 300, 333, 488
    Attica and, 273
    Burge federal charges and, 410
    Cannon civil suit appeal and, 453
    Cook County courts, 287
    Humboldt Park case and, 55
    on Washington, 149
    Saxner and, 363
    Wilson civil rights case and, 68
Devine, Richard, 37, 46, 164, 250, 281, 286–87,
    325, 345, 357, 436
    Area 2 and, 276, 351
    Biebel and, 298, 408
    Brzeczek and, 351, 357, 393
    Burge and, 232, 246, 280, 284, 287, 357,
        360, 393
    Burge special prosecutor and, 281, 284–85
    Cannon and, 246–47, 274, 275–76, 282, 303
    Daley and, 245, 282, 311, 357, 361–62, 365,
        393
    death row clemencies and, 289, 294
    deposition of, 322, 393
    Illinois Supreme Court and, 248
    Kunkle and, 66, 232, 357, 393
    media on, 349–51
        60 Minutes 2, 249
        Conroy, 302, 307, 345
        Sun Times, 297, 371
        Tribune, 232, 247, 282, 344, 357, 389, 510
        WTTW, 348
    Orange civil suit and, 308
    Patterson and, 245–47, 273, 281, 286, 296,
        300, 330
    Raba letter and, 353–54
    report on special prosecutors and, 373
    RICO case and, 365
    Ryan and, 291, 393
    special prosecutor's report and, 344–48,
        349–55, 357, 365
    Vanecko and, 448
    Wilson and, 97, 357
Diagnostic and Statistical Manual of Mental
    Disorders (DSM-IV), 240
Diggins, Mearon, 206, 479
Dignan, Peter, 95, 213–15, 222, 233, 304, 363
    BOY fund and, 180, 214
    Burge and, 213–14, 414, 452
    Burge federal trial and, 418, 431
    Byrd and, 241, 320–21

Byrne and, 276–278
Cannon and, 213, 268, 274–75, 310, 453,
    456, 477
Chicago of Chicago and, 444
Daley and, 233, 444
Deep Badge and, 170, 213
deposition of, 212–14, 383
Duncan and, 315–16
FBI and, 383, 452
Fifth Amendment and, 311, 383, 452, 462,
    478, 492
fraud suit against, 453
in Vietnam, 306, 478
media on, 274–75, 345, 456
OPS and, 212, 214, 228, 249
Preib and, 477
RICO case and, 365
Shines and, 231
Smith and, 491–93, 500
Sotos and, 509
special prosecutor's report and, 347
Tillman and, 444
torture by, 213–14, 233, 237–38, 396
    Cannon case and, 270
    Duncan on, 316
    Goldston on, 243
    of Adkins, 119, 214
    of Banks, 152, 172, 214, 268, 414, 418,
        452, 478
    of Bates, 152, 268
    of Bell, 397, 406, 447
    of Cannon, 228, 234–36, 244, 277, 452,
        478
    of Smith, 213, 268–69, 327, 477, 488, 509
    of Tillman, 396–97, 406, 447, 452
    of Wrice, 214, 396, 461, 478, 509
    Wiggins and, 310
Dineen, John, 175, 187, 189, 191, 196
Dirksen Building, 11, 13, 25, 103, 197, 402
Dirty Harry, 309, 404
DiStefano, Pam, 58
Dixon, Illinois, 313
Dohrn, Bernardine, 332
Dollinger, Gary, 427
Donahue, Mark, 403
Dong Tam, 327, 328, 329
Dosch, Brian, 206–7, 283–84
Dowell, Pat, 384
Drizin, Steve, 299, 301
Dr. King Movement, 149
Drug Enforcement Agency, 141
Dubuar, Seva, 4
Dudycz, Walter, 188–89

Duff, Brian Barnett, 71, 160, 180, 189, 484, 496
    Burge and, 122, 124, 145
    Burge special prosecutor and, 284
    Chicago Lawyer on, 76–77
    Conroy on, 154–156
    Haas and, 128, 130–31, 136, 138–39,
        140–41, 145
    Kirschner and, 165
    Kunkle and, 68, 92, 115, 118, 121, 124–26,
        129–31, 141, 144–45, 189
    Morrisey and, 242
    police board hearing and, 183
    Stainthorp and, 93, 109, 140, 142
    Wilson and, 120–22, 189
    Wilson appeals and, 198, 201, 209
    Wilson civil retrial and, 87, 91–94, 97–100,
        102–5, 109–111, 115–19, 120–34, 136–47
    Wilson civil rights case and, 63, 65, 73–78,
        81–82, 85–86, 92
Duncan, Melvin, 315–316
Dunne, George, 47, 414
DuPage County, 195
DuSable Museum, 151
Dwight, Illinois, 56, 296

Dwyer, Robert, 181, 221–22, 321
Dykema law firm, 323, 354, 491, 508, 509
"Dynamite Hill," 476
Easterbrook, Frank, 198–99, 202, 224
Edgar, Jim, 188–89
Egan, Edward J., 285–86, 297, 352–54, 357–58,
        376, 382, 399, 462, 509
    Area 2 and, 357–59, 384
    Burge and, 331, 359, 419
    Cook County Board of Commissioners and,
        356–57, 377–78
    Hyman and, 334, 341
    media on, 298–99, 331, 347, 350, 357–59,
        384, 400
    report on special prosecutors and, 372
    special prosecutor's report and, 334–35,
        340–41, 344–45, 347–48, 350–54, 378
Egan, William, 359
Eighth Amendment, 248
Ellison, Eugene, 488
Ellison, Spencer, 488
Ellison, Troy, 488
El Rukn, 234, 276, 463
Elson, Ben, *264*, 333, 396–98, 406–7, 410, 447,
        450, 453, 456, 478, 488
Emanuel, Rahm, 443, 445–47, 450–51, 458, 466,
        470, 472, 475, 466, 482
End of the Nightstick, 210–11

England, 64, 140, 156
Englewood Neighborhood Health Clinic, 493
Epton, Bernie, 55
Erenberg, Debra, 449
Esposito, Stephan, 350
Europe, 295
Evans, Demitrus, 300
Evans, Tim, 149, 485
Evanston, Illinois, 378
Evergreen Park, Illinois, 319
Ewing, Russ, 73
The Exonerated, 291
Exoneration Project, 478

Fagan, Carmella, 313, 318, 329
Fahey family, 193, 459, 497, 502, 503
Fahey, Michael, 433
Fahey, William
    Burge sentencing and, 433
    manhunt and, 35–37, 110, 117, 156, 319, 320
    McCarthy and, 69, 133
    murder of, 35, 131, 176, 354
    Wilson and, 74, 121, 137, 145, 413
FALN, 451
FBI, 21, 31, 104, 141, 151, 310, 395, 407
    BPP files of, 11–12, 14–17, 32–33
    Burge and, 95, 105, 107, 382, 413
    Byrne and, 383, 452
    COINTELPRO and, 9, 11, 14
    conspiracy with Chicago police, 4, 6, 9, 17,
        23, 25, 32, 34
    Dignan and, 383, 452
    Greensboro Massacre and, 56–57, 59, 62
    Hampton murder and, 3, 5, 8–12, 17, 31, 34
    Hobley and, 384–85, 387
    Racial Matters Squad, 10, 14, 16
    Senate and, 11, 16
FBI Domestic Intelligence and Counterintelli-
    gence, 11
Federal Corrections Complex in Butner, 442, 469
Federal Probation Office, 430
Fernwood Boys, 478
Ferro, Mario, 41–43, 145
Ferry, Thomas, 334
Feuer, Kurt, 308, 321, 358, 368, 375, 389
Fifth Amendment, 310–11, 359, 395, 404, 499
    Burge and, 379–81, 383, 418, 431, 442,
        468–69, 473–74, 477–78, 486–87, 492,
        498, 503
    Byrne and, 383, 405, 452, 462, 478, 492
    Conroy on, 345, 364
    Dignan and, 383, 452, 462, 478, 492
    Hyman and, 334, 341, 345, 496, 503

Johnson and, 106
Kill and, 443
McDermott and, 396
McKenna and, 489, 498, 503
Pienta and, 479
Sherer and, 58
Sincox and, 122
Supreme Court and, 308
Wilson and, 48, 74, 83, 413
Zorn on, 400
Final Report With Respect to Intelligence Activities
    (Church Senate Committee), 16
Fink, Liz, 273
Finley, Syd, 175, 196
Fioretti, Bob, 379, 384
First Amendment, 115
Fisher, Maria, 17–18
Fitzgerald, Patrick, 330–31, 339, 375, 387, 415–17
    Area 2 and, 393–94, 452
    Burge and, 385–86, 394, 398–99, 420, 426,
        436
    media on, 345, 350
    on Chicago police, 385–86
    special prosecutor's report and, 347, 383
    Willis and, 382
Fitzgerald, Thomas, 251
Fitzmorris, Charles, 358
Flock, Jeff, 296
Flood, Robert, 96, 101–2, 106, 108, 233, 304
Florida, 219, 278, 297, 327, 337, 381, 470, 488
    Burge in, 270, 271, 309, 398, 404, 427, 488
    city council on, 355, 391
    Vigilante in, 203, 214
Florida State Prison at Starke, 327
Florida Sun Sentinel, 211
Fogel, David, 118, 151, 160, 308, 347
    Chicago police board hearings and, 149–50
    depositions of, 113–14, 151–52
    Wilson civil retrial and, 120, 136, 141
Ford Heights Four, 226–27, 245, *260*, 293, 309
Ford, Nicholas, 483–85
Fort, Jeff, 11, 234
Fourteenth Amendment, 48
Fourth Amendment, 395
Fowler, Jack, 61
Fox, Lawrence, 251, 268, 270, 274–75, 303
Foxx, Kim, 489
Frank, Leo, 83
Fraternal Order of Police, 36, 169, 181, 187, 189,
    196, 210, 310, 377, 386, 484, 498, 503
    Andrew Wilson and, 494, 497–99
    Burge and, 184, 193, 486, 494, 497, 509
    Burge due process case and, 179

Burge federal charges and, 394, 403
Burge prosecution and, 176
float of, 196–97, 200, 339
Hampton and, 355–56
Jackie Wilson and, 504, 510
media on, 403, 501
OPS files and, 220
PLO and, 180, 497
police board hearing and, 175, 177, 184
Preib and, 477, 494, 497
special prosecutor's report and, 340
TIRC and, 459
Van Dyke and, 489
videotaped interrogations bill and, 301
Washington and, 54
Wiggins and, 191
Yucaitis and, 196
Frazier, Carolyn, 405, 429
Freedom of Information Act, 9
Freeman, Edwin, 328
Frenzer, 444–45
Fusco, Chris, 449
Futorian, Aviva, 363
Futterman, Craig, 386, 473, 482

G8, 449
Gacy, John Wayne, 50, 83
Gaines, Carol, 248
Gamboney, William, 412
Gangster Disciples, 71, 106
Garcia, Jesus "Chuy," 469–70
Garippo, Louis, 164
Gaughan, Vincent, 407, 408
Gelsomino, Sarah, *264*, 404, 407, 481
Geneva, Switzerland, 336, 467
Georges, Mara, 308, 354, 379, 392, 450
    city council appearance of, 384–85, 386
    torture settlements and, 361, 365, 367, 390
Geraghty, Tom, 239, 248, 281, 238, 405
    death row clemencies and, 290–91
    Kitchen and, 405, 429
    Orange and, 95, 304
Germany, 83, 156, 164, 188, 355
Gettleman, Robert, 209, 224
Ghezzi, June, 177
Gillis, Kenneth, 406, 447
Gipson, Romarr, 245
Gipson, Shannon, 245
Global Campaign Against Torture, 462, 464
Glover, Danny, 291
Golden, Raymond, 94, 112
Goldston, Michael, 170, 174, 179, 181, 188, 195,
    242, 272, 307, 347,

    Area 2 and, 162, 169, 225
    Daley and, 189, 230, 492
    Police Foundation and, 173, 182
    Wilson and, 152, 159
Gonzalez, Mariano "Dalu," 6
Goodman, Amy, 337–39, 411
Goodman, Bill, 4
Goodman, Dr., 43
Gorman, Joe, 18–19, 27, 89, 94, 111–12, 116,
    123, 326
Gottschall, Judge, 308, 325, 390
Grady, John, 34
Grant, Andre, 226
Green, Adam, 432–33
Greene, Bob, 14
Greensboro Civil Rights Fund, 59, 62
Greensboro Massacre, 56–62
Gregg, Ms., 199
Griffin, Virgil, 57, 59
Griffiths, Keith, 70
Groth, Daniel, 23–24, 33–34, 66
Grunhard, Charles, 95, 170, 268, 431
    torture by, 152, 172, 181, 235–37, 244
Guantánamo, 337, 340, 391, 411, 424
Guardian, 476, 481
Gutierrez, Luis, 353
Gzesch, Susan, 332, 336

Haas, Jeff, 13–14, 25, 27, 88–89 161, 168, 181,
    188, 194, 232, *252–254, 256, 259,* 322
    Burge and, 193, 477
    Chicago Police Board and, 148
    Coleman and, 138–39
    Duff and, 71, 93–94, 128, 130–31, 136, 138,
        140–41, 145
    Hampton case and, 4–5, 29, 29–30
    Hilliard and, 232
    Holmes and, 94
    in contempt, 25–26
    Johnson and, 95, 105
    Jones and, 52–53, 63–64, 102
    Kunkle and, 94, 182
    Mu'min and, 160
    Nanasi and, 124
    O'Neal and, 8–9, 23
    People's Tribunal and, 151
    Perry and, 21, 26
    Piper testimony and, 16
    Porch and, 94–95, 99, 112–15
    Reader on, 31
    Saxner and, 363
    Tribune on, 92
    Watson and, 79, 107

    Wilson civil retrial and, 87, 93–98,
        112–13, 122, 128, 130–31, 136, 138–41,
        145–46, 313
    Wilson civil rights case and, 68, 77–78, 83–85
Haggerty, LaTanya, 242
Hairston, Leslie, 391
Hale, Andrew, 441–42, 459, 500–1, 508
Hall, Marva, 228
Hammonds, Ollie, 318
Hampton, Bill, 34, *254,* 500
Hampton, Dolores, 500
Hampton family, 4, 26, 28, 34
Hampton, Francis, 261
Hampton, Fred, 1–2, 14–15, 19, 26, 30–34, 56,
    184, 282, 294, 298, 322, 430, 489–90
    civil case, 4, 6, 7, 54, 66, 229, 238, 274, 489
    drugging of, 8–9, 17–18, 20, 28
    FOP and, 355–356
    murder of, 1–3, 8–16, 20, 27–31, 54, 69, 238,
        285, 355, 433, 490
    Gorman and, 89, 94, 112, 123, 326
Hampton, Fred, Jr., 28
Hampton, Iberia, 26, 29–30, *261,* 500
Handlin, Patricia, 5, 63, *252,* 278, 447
Hanhardt, William, 36, 179, 319
Hanrahan, Edward, 3–4, 6–10, 17, 21, 23–26,
    33, 184, 322
Hardin, Dewayne, 506
Harold Washington Party, 149
Harris, Brenda, 19, 27
Harris, Ryan, 225, 322
Hartigan, Neil, 159
Hartnett, Michael, 418–19, 499–500
Harvard Law School, 470
Hawkins, Karen, 445
Hawkins, Steve, 471
Heard, Jacquelyn, 311, 384, 401
Henry, James, 363, 375
Herbert, Dan, 489
Hernandez, Alejandro, 195
Hersh, Seymour, 306
Hillard, Terry, 228, 230–31, 307, 345, 360
    deposition of, 232–33, 307, 322
    Tillman civil suit and, 443–45
Hill, Fred, 36–37, 117, 126, 131–33, 502, 506
Hill, Hollis, 13
Hilliard, Terry, 233, 300
Hill, Pat, 196, 370, 403
Hillsborough County Court, 309
Hines, Detective, 397
Hinshaw and Culbertson, 232, 241
HIPAA, 492
History of Allegations of Misconduct by Area 2

Personnel (Goldston), 163
Hobley, Madison, 272, 308, 321, 358, 361, 377
    Burge and, 311, 431, 435, 457
    civil suit of, 304, 311, 333, 361, 365, 367–68,
        383, 386–87, 389, 403, 435
    Conroy and, 221, 223
    death row clemencies and, 291–22
    FBI and, 384–85, 387, 403
    media on, 296, 339
    pardon of, 294, 391
    Ryan and, 293–94
    torture of, 221, 293, 321, 379
Hobley, Robin, 291–93
Hoffman, Charles "Chick," 13, 33, 62–63, 203–4,
    250, *252*, 255, 278, 291, 375, 468
    Cannon and, 303, 310, 453
    death penalty and, 289, 439–40
Hoffman, Hinda, 56
Hoft, Jani, 30, *256*
Hoge, Jim, 3
Hoke, Mike, 88, 95, 108, 212, 214–15, 314
Holderman, James, 208–9, 362, 375, 379
Holland, 156
Holmes, Anthony, 94, 118, 164, 180, 214, 315,
    377, 379, 413, 432, 434, 477, 479
    Burge and, 183, 350
    Burge conviction and, 428
    Burge death and, 509
    Burge federal charges and, 399
    Burge federal trial and, 413, 418, 420, 424
    Burge pension and, 465–66
    Burge sentencing and, 432, 437
    media on, 329, 350, 405, 474
    reparations and, 467, 471, 473, 482, 493–94
    report on special prosecutors and, 372, 374
    torture of, 204, 313–14, 317, 329, 372, 374,
        379, 432, 474
    Wilson case and, 88–89, 129, 136, 141
Holmes, Lee, 95, 152–53, 243, 281, 396
Holocaust, 60, 83, 337
Holt, Lester, 248
Homan Square, 481
Hong Kong, 137, 139, 156
Hooks, William, 286, 442, 485–86, 494–98,
    500–505
Hoover, J. Edgar, 3, 9, 11, 13
Hoover, Larry, 106
Hopkins Symptoms Checklist, 240
Houppert, Justin, 454–56
House Judiciary Committee, 225
Howard, Betty, 396–97, 406, 408
Howard, Connie, 245
Howard Law School, 13

Howard, Stanley, 150–51, 222, 240, 247, 277, 289
    civil suit of, 304, 333, 361, 389, 390
    media on, 302, 339
    OPS and, 153, 228–29, 232, 243
    pardon of, 294, 391
    Ryan and, 293–94
    torture of, 228, 232
Howell, Mary, 490
Hubert, Donald, 286
Huffington Post, 451
Hull, Julie, 188–90, 380
Humboldt Park case, 55–56
Hurricane Katrina, 490
Hurvitz, Ralph, 13
Hussein, Saddam, 168, 306
Hyman, Larry, 53, 418, 499
    Andrew Wilson and, 39–41, 48, 82, 334,
        341–42, 346, 499
    Daley and, 341, 345
    Fifth Amendment and, 496, 503
    Jackie Wilson and, 334, 496, 499
    media on, 302, 342, 344, 345
    special prosecutor's report and, 341–42,
        344–46, 353
    testimony of, 47, 139–40
Hynes, Assistant State's Attorney, 228

Illinois, 53, 117, 301, 441
    attorney general, 159, 167, 230, 374, 375, 439
    death penalty in, 273
        abolition of, 298, 439–40, 508
        activism against, 227–230, 288–89
        Cunningham and, 279
        exonerations from, 245, 250
        Jackie Wilson and, 51
        media on, 249–50, 338–39
        Patterson and, 204, 227–28, 293–97
        popular opinion on, 223
        Ryan and, 288–97
    Dudycz bill in, 188–89
    law of, 209, 224, 274, 276
    Obama and, 301, 367
    prisons in, 2, 84, 95, 316, 396
    Ryan on, 293–94
Illinois Appellate Court, 96, 152–53, 285, 479
Illinois Attorney Registration and Disciplinary
    Commission, 274
Illinois Department of Corrections, 238, 388,
    506–7
Illinois House of Representatives, 71
Illinois Prisoner Review Board, 289–290
Illinois Reparations for Police Torture Victims
    Act, 460–62, 466–67, 471, 473, 475, 493

Illinois Senate, 480
Illinois State Legislature, 7, 17, 245, 377, 439–40
Illinois State Senate, 377
Illinois Supreme Court, 248, 272–73, 456, 462,
    501
    Burge and, 248, 272–73, 465
    Kitchen and, 246–48, 273
    Patterson and, 204, 223, 246–48, 250,
        271–73, 276, 283–84, 390, 449
    special prosecutor's report and, 341, 344–45
    Wilson and, 65, 109, 169, 200–201, 246
        city council hearing and, 166–67
        Coleman and, 138–39, 142
        Fogel and, 114, 120, 151
Independent, 270
Independent Police Review Authority, 376–77,
    490
Indiana, 62–63, 315
Inglis, Jill, *256*
Inter-American Commission for Human Rights,
    332, 375
Internal Affairs, 215
Interstate 55, 206, 247
In These Times, 355
Investigative Reports, 299, 301
Iraq, 306. *See also* Abu Ghraib
Ireland, 139, 156, 502
Irish Republican Army, 137, 154, 307
IRS, 16
Islam, 404
Israel, 154, 243, 307

Jackson, David, 176–77, 183
Jackson, Janice, 494
Jackson, Jesse, 8, 35, 59, 70, 280, 351, 405, 509
Jackson, Jonathan, 405
Jackson Jr., Jesse, 150
Jackson, Michael, 405
Jackson Park Hospital, 397–98
Jackson, Sandi, 379–80
Jalovec, Richard, 4, 6–10, 23, 25
James, Edward, 88–89, 313–14
James, Myron, 218
Japanese American people, 105
Jarrett, Vernon, 197
Jefferson, Arthur, 11–12
Jefferson, Nancy, 148, 190
Jensen, Duane, 74, 82, 260
Jim Crow, 505, 510
Jimerson, Verneal, 227, *260*
Johnson, Carolyn, 190, 217, 380
Johnson, Deborah, 9, 13, 19–20, 27–29
Johnson, Eddie, 490, 493–94

Johnson, Jenette, 247
Johnson, Lyndon B., 57
Johnson, Marlin, 10, 14, 17, 25, 33
Johnson, Mary L., 95, 105–6, 168, 280–81, 348,
    380, 449
Johnson, Michael, 95–96, 129, 380, 449
    Burge and, 68, 81–82, 116, 122
    deposition of, 105–6
    special prosecutor's report and, 346, 348
    Wilson case and, 90–91, 125, 129
Johnson, Nelson, 62
Johnson, Walter, 89–90, 111, 127, 133, 144, 153,
    502
Joliet, Illinois, 88, 310
Jon Burge and His Victims, 379
Jones, Bill, 227
Jones, George, 52–53, 63–64, 74, 215, 320,
    363–64
Jones, Melvin, 95, 118, 156, 172, 179–80, 222,
    270, 423, 432
    AIDS and, 397–400
    Burge conviction and, 428
    Burge federal charges and, 397–400, 410
    Burge federal trial and, 413, 420, 423
    Burge on, 90–91
    deposition of, 96, 100–102
    Duff on, 93–94, 97–100, 103–4, 109, 111,
        130–31, 136, 141, 189
    media on, 249, 250, 400, 427
    OPS and, 135, 229
    police board hearings and, 180, 183, 185,
        191, 233
    special prosecutor's report and, 346
    testimony of, 191, 413
    torture of, 79–82, 233, 249, 413
    Watson on, 106–107
    Wilson case and, 85, 87–88, 122, 125,
        129–30, 199, 201, 208
Jones, Ronald, 276
Jones, Sallie, 14, 30
Jordan, Susan, 95
Justice Coalition for Greater Chicago, 280

Kaba, Mariame, 461
Kadish, Marc, 27
Kalven, Jamie, 386, 473, 482
Kamionski, Avi, 441–42
Kanter, Arnold, 10, 15, 17
Karl, George, 82, 360–31
Kass, John, 351
Katten Muchin, 491
Kay, Dick, 182
Kelly, Cliff, 411

Kelly, Dave, 240
Kendrick Hospital, 398
Kennelly, Matt, 227
Kennon, Larry, 280, 286, 340, 348–49, 358, 370
Kidd, Leonard, 95, 304, 317
Kill, Michael, 429, 442–443, 452
Kim, Alice, 291, 460, 462
King, Derrick, 247–48, 273, 281
King, JX, 11
King, Martin Luther, Jr., 2, 9, 12, 16, 197, 224, 489
King, Peter, 227
King, Rodney, 170, 182, 187, 197, 433
Kinoy, Arthur, 4
Kirkland Ellis, 450
Kirschner, Robert, 75–77, 82, 128, 141, 151, 164, 177, 183, 185, 188–90, 201, 249–50, 290
    Burge federal trial and, 419–20
    Cannon and, 239–41, 243, 270
Kitchen, Ronald, 247, 265, 290, 294, 296, 405, 409, 443
    Bowman and, 451, 458
    civil suit of, 265, 409, 428, 430, 442–43, 446
    Cunningham and, 276, 279
    Illinois Supreme Court and, 246–48, 273
    media on, 438–39, 450
    settlement for, 450–51, 457–58
    torture of, 229, 405, 429, 442
Kling, Richard, 49–51, 499, 501, 502
Klutter, Kris, 468
Korcoras, Charles, 17
Korea, 328
Korecki, Natasha, 398
Korn, Geoffrey, 42–43, 47
Korotkin, Gayle, 58
Kosberg, Rick, 443
Koschman, David, 448, 462
Koschman, Nanci, 448–49
Kowalski, Thaddeus, 43
Kramer, Jeff, 382–83, 395, 398, 407, 452
Ku Klux Klan, 56–62, 227, 476, 509
Kunkle, Bill, 54, 164, 168, 171, 182, 184, 216, 287, 308, 357, 506
    Burge and, 164, 168, 172, 176, 179, 182, 191, 193, 208, 216
    City and, 208–9, 224
    Coleman and, 136–38, 141
    Devine and, 232, 357, 393
    Duff and, 92, 109, 115, 118, 121, 124–26, 129, 141, 144–45, 189
    Haas and, 94, 114–15, 182
    police board hearing and, 175, 177, 179, 183, 186

special prosecutor's report and, 346, 352–54, 365
    Wiggins and, 191, 216
    Wilson appeal and, 200–201, 202
    Wilson civil retrial and, 90–91, 94, 97, 105, 109–110, 112, 114–17, 121–29, 132–33, 138, 141–45
    Wilson civil rights case and, 66–69, 73–74, 77–78, 81–84
    Wilson first criminal trial and, 46–51
    Wilson second criminal trial and, 65–66
Kunz, Jamie, 50
Kurtis, Bill, 190, 299–300, 301
Kuttner, Peter, 176, 210

Lacey, Sammy, 37, 39, 319, 414, 432, 497–98
Lacorte, Lois, 76–77
Lake Michigan, 67, 91, 125, 295, 381, 510
Lambros, Heidi, 462
Landrieu, Mitch, 491
LA Ramparts, 433
LaSalle Street, 31
LA Times, 59, 182
Latin Souls, 451
Laux, Mike, 488
Laverty, Frank, 141, 215, 320, 348, 363, 395
    Burge and, 36, 53, 66, 320, 421, 486
    Deep Badge and, 75, 79, 364
    Dignan and, 213, 363
    Jones case and, 52–53, 63
Lawrence, Leutle, 228–29, 243
Lee, Bill Lan, 242
Lee, Gary, 63
Lefkow, Joan Humphrey, 245, 428, 436
    Burge case and, 402, 407, 410–412, 418, 420, 430–31, 433–36
Leighton, George, 441
Lemon, Don, 324–25, 405
Leonard, Jerris, 5, 13, 25
Leo, Richard, 299
Levi, Edward, 12, 17
Levine, Andrew, 494–95
Lewis, James, 88
Lewis, Karen, 466
Libby, Scooter, 382
Lincoln, Abraham, 247, 294
Litchfield, Lord, 141
Little Rock, Arkansas, 488, 490
"Live from Death Row," 289
Loevy and Loevy, 304, 361, 375, 442, 483
Loevy, Jon, 375, 390
Logan, Alton, 468
Lohraff, Tim, 182, 223, 238, 242, 246, 251, 270,

303
Long Term Prisoner Policy Project, 363
Lopez, Darlene, 414, 421
Los Angeles, 14, 187, 193, 197
Los Angeles Police Department, 170, 197, 433
Lotito, James, 221–22
Louima, Abner, 224–25, 281
Loyola Hospital Burn Center, 82
Loyola Law School, 393
Loyola University, 276
Lyderson, Kari, 470
Lyle, Freddrenna, 336–37
Lyon, Andrea, 293, 304, 321, 375, 477

MacArthur Foundation, 376
MacArthur Justice Center, 280, 289, 448, 489
Madigan, Lisa, 298, 375, 407–8, 439–40, 445, 465
Madoff, Bernie, 442
Magers, Ron, 172
Main, Frank, 393
Malcolm X Grassroots Movement, 184
Maloney, Thomas J., 237
Mandela, Nelson, 295
Mandel Legal Aid Clinic, 280, 386
Mann, Abby, 289, 331, 357, 359
Mann, Myrna, 331
Margolies, Joe, 453
Marin, Carol, 247–50, 297, 368, 372, 393, 400,
    411, 417, 449, 456,
    Byrne and, 276–77
    on Daley, 445–46
    on special prosecutor's report, 348–49
    on Tillman, 446–47
Markham, Illinois, 79
Marshall, Larry, 227, 239, 289–90, 292, 295
Marshall, Prentice, 55–56, 63
Marshall, Thurgood, 63
Martin, Derrick, 502
Martinez, Antonio, 188–190, 216, 218, 223,
    239–40, 270, 290,
Martinez, Iris, 480
Martinez, Oliviero, 299
Martin, Ian, 167
Martin, LeRoy, 66, 163–64, 169–74, 300, 310,
    345–46, 428
    activism against, 149–50, 161
    Burge and, 172, 183, 319, 321, 360, 444
    Burge federal trial and, 418
    Burge suspension and, 175
    media on, 173, 182–83, 345
    OPS and, 163, 171, 181–82
    police board and, 180, 186
    Tillman civil suit and, 443–45

Martin, LeRoy, Jr., 485
Martin, Marc, 420
Maslanka, Anthony, 219–20, 404
Mason, Mary Anne, 479–80
Mason, Michael, 333, 479
Mastin, Barry, 321
Mastin, Rodney, 317–18
Matthews, David Wayne, 59, 61
Maule, Albert, 176–77, 190–94
Maxwell, Andrew, 231, 287
Mayfield, Geoffrey, 96–97, 101, 106
May, Page, 467
Maywood, Illinois, 2, 26
McAllister, Carolyn, 58–59, 61
McCarthy, James, 83, 85, 132, 208
McCarthy, Joseph, 69, 133
McClain, Ray, 4
McClin, Calvin, 148, 150–151, 169, 170, 186
McClory, Robert, 10, 17, 29, 31
McCoun, Thomas B., 398
McDermott, Michael, 394–96, 412, 415–17, 421,
    424–25, 427, 452
McDonald, Laquan, 473, 482–83, 489–90, 509
McDonnell, Herb, 4
McGuire, Detective, 88, 96, 101–2, 304
McKenna, Thomas, 67, 488–89, 497–99, 502–3
McWeeny, Daniel, 101–2, 222, 236, 268, 304,
    310–11, 373, 383
Media, Pennsylvania, 9
Medill Innocence Project, 295
Meisner, Jason, 492–93
Mekong Delta, 67, 328
Mell, Richard, 161–63
Memphis, Tennessee, 89, 314
Menard Correctional Center, 88, 95, 105, 111,
    227, 238, 291, 396, 495
Menendez, Fernando Marino, 340
Mercy Hospital, 42
Merhige, Robert, 57
Metropolitan Correctional Center, 22, 25–26,
    325, 333
Mexico, 246, 295
Meyers, Danny, 273
Midwest Coalition for Human Rights, 335–36,
    467
midwestern United States, 449
Mike, Paul, 89, 110–11, 127, 133, 144
Milan, Bob, 282
Miller, Barry, 382
Miller, Doris, 38–39, 41, 47–49, 141, 496
Mills, Steve, 227–31, 282, 299, 389
    on Cannon, 274, 310–11
    on death row clemencies, 289–90

on Devine, 246, 282
on Morrisey, 250–51
Milwaukee, 453, 473
Milwaukee Journal Sentinel, 182
Miner, Michael, 159
Miskiw, Gregory, 139–42, 189, 198, 202
Mississippi River, 227
Mitchell, John, 13, 25
Mitchell, Roy, 8–11, 14–15, 17, 23, 25, 33
Modell, Jennifer, 168
Mogul, Joey, 218, 238, *262, 264,* 276, 287, 290,
    308, 323, 332, 380, 408, 450
    anti-torture legislation by, 429–40
    Banks and, 415
    Burge and, 280, 442, 467
    Cannon civil suit appeal and, 453, 456
    county board hearing and, 377–78
    Holmes and, 432
    Orange and, 361
    Patterson and, 246, 299–300, 333
    reparations and, 460–63, 466–67, 469–71,
        476, 494
    report on special prosecutors and, 372, 375
    Smith and, 477, 492–93
    Tillman and, 397, 406
    torture settlements and, 384–85, 391
    UNCAT and, 336, 380
Monaco, 156
Monell claims, 70
Montes, Jorge, 310, 312, 375
Montgomery, James, 13, 16, 28–29, 31, 55
Moore, Joe, 380, 384, 449, 462
Moore, Jon, 30, 56
Moore, Phillip, 317
Mora, Antonio, 323
Moran, Cindy, 176, 210
Moreno, "Proco" Joe, 460, 462, 475
Morris, Calvin, 334
Morrissey, John, 206, 223, 237–40, 242–44, 247,
    250–51
Moseley, Don, 446–47
Mother Jones, 270
Mt. Sinai Hospital, 397
Muhammad, Elijah, 9
Mulvaney, John, 41–43, 145, 414
Mu'min, Shadeed, 160, 176, 228, 211
    Burge and, 415–18, 421, 424
    McDermott and, 394–96, 415–17
    police board hearings and, 180, 183, 191, 233
    special prosecutor's report and, 346
    testimony of, 191, 417
    torture of, 243, 394–96, 415, 417
Murder Task Force, 44, 65

Murphy, Clyde, 280
Murphy, Maureen, 113–14, 120, 123, 125–27,
    129–30, 144, 208
Murphy, Morgan, 331
Murphy, Patrick, 183
Murray, Pat, *252*
Muwakkil, Salim, 355–56
Myers, Lew, 150, 170, 226
Myerson, Jimmy, 13

NAACP, 2, 13, 26, 175, 196
NAACP Legal Defense Fund, 280, 476
Nanasi, Mariel, 135, 148, 151, 161, 163, 168, 176,
    241, 477
    Duff and, 76, 92, 124, 125
Natarus, Burt, 66
Narhan, Marty, 58
Nathan, Michael, 61
National Alliance Against Racist and Political
    Repression, 135
National Association of Programming and Televi-
    sion Executives Convention, 270
National Conference of Black Lawyers, 280, 332
National Guard, 6
National Lawyers Guild, 4, 31, 135, 225, 280.
Nation of Islam, 404
NATO, 449
Nazis, 36, 83, 157, 164, 188, 311, 337, 355. *See
    also* American Nazi Party
NBC Channel 5, 9, 171–72, 176, 190, 389, 411,
    417, 456
Needham, Thomas, 228–31, 233, 240, 300,
    443–45
Nelson, Deborah, 188, 191
Nesbitt, Prexy, 13
Newark Police Department, 173
Newhouse, Richard, 17
New Orleans, 225, 490–91
Newsweek, 402
New York, 6, 153, 183, 273, 281
New York City, 224–225
New York Police Department, 210, 224, 363
New York State Police, 6, 273
New York Times, 5, 34, 59, 61–62, 182, 196,
    290–91, 339, 349, 353, 388–89, 399, 426
Nicarico, Jeanine, 195
Nicodemus, Charles, 177, 182, 186, 232
Nixon, Richard, 5, 13
Noland, Dan, 323
Nolan, Nan, 476
Noriega, Manuel, 168
North Carolina, 61, 62
North Carolina A&T, 59

Northcutt, Lance, 501
Northeastern Illinois University in Chicago, 151
Northern District of Illinois, 25, 53, 73, 167, 374
Northern Ireland, 307
Northwestern, 226, 242, 295, 299, 439, 458, 461, 462, 486
Northwestern Hospital, 491
Northwestern Law School, 1, 2, 4, 7, 209, 375, 391. *See also* Bluhm Legal Clinic
    death row clemencies and, 289–90, 294
    Kitchen and, 428, 429
    Marshall and, 227, 239
Northwestern Legal Clinic, 95
Notz, Jenny, 476–77
Novak, Tim, 449
NPR, 336
NSA, 16
Nudelman, Stuart, 408, 442

Oakland Tribune, 180–81
Obama, Barack, 301, 367–68411, 479
    administration of, 489–90
O'Brien family, 459, 497, 502
O'Brien, Richard
    manhunt and, 35–37, 110, 117, 156, 319, 320
    McCarthy and, 69, 133
    murder of, 35, 131, 176, 354
    Wilson and, 74, 121, 137, 145, 413
O'Brien, Thomas J., 208
Obrycka, Karolina, 371
O'Connor, Sandra Day, 195–196
Office of Professional Standards, 109, 118, 146, 149, 153, 165, 167, 169, 171, 180, 187, 347
    activism against, 194–95
    Adkins and, 243
    Area 2 and, 162–63, 169, 212, 308
    Banks and, 153, 212, 243
    Burge and, 124, 135, 173, 426
    Byrne and, 212, 228, 249, 277
    Cannon and, 229, 232, 239, 242–43, 270, 308
    Conroy on, 156, 283
    Craft and, 243
    Dignan and, 212, 214, 228, 249
    files of, 220, 223–24, 228–32, 308
    Fogel and, 113–14, 120, 135, 150, 152–53, 160, 308, 347
    Holmes and, 152–53
    Howard and, 150, 153, 228–29, 232, 243
    Illinois Supreme Court and, 248, 272
    IPRA and, 377–78
    Johnson and, 95, 105–6, 129, 153
    Jones and, 107, 135, 229
    Martin and, 163, 170–71, 173
    Maslanka and, 219
    McDermott and, 395, 416
    media on, 187, 229–30, 438
    Mike and, 89–90, 110
    O'Hara and, 163
    Orange and, 308
    Patterson and, 205, 246
    Porch and, 113
    Powell and, 88
    Richard J. Daley and, 376
    Rodriguez and, 195
    Shines and, 160, 162–63, 169, 195, 212, 228, 232, 443
    Special Projects reports and, 162–63, 169, 174, 179, 181, 198
    Tillman civil suit and, 443
    White and, 126, 135
    Wiggins and, 212
    Wilson and, 70–74, 135, 152–53, 159, 162–64, 308, 438
    Wilson appeal and, 202
    Wilson civil retrial and, 120, 125, 308
    Yucaitis and, 163, 173
Office of the State Appellate Defender, 289
O'Grady, James, 179
O'Hara, Patrick, 67, 117, 126, 128, 131, 176, 187, 196–97, 209, 410
    OPS and, 163, 171
    police board hearings and, 180, 185, 187, 192
    Wilson and, 85–86, 114, 140, 143, 146, 201, 502
O'Hare airport, 52
Ohri, Shubra, 481
Olympic Games, 370–71
O'Malley, Jack, 307
O'Neal, William, 8–11, 14–18, 22–23, 32
Operation PUSH, 150
Oppenheimer, Michael, 226
Orange, Leroy, 95, 180, 260, *262*, 272, 293–94, 308, 317, 391, 443
    civil suit of, 304, 308–9, 333, 361, 389, 391
    death penalty and, 207, 290–91
    media on, 291, 296–97, 339
    torture of, 304–6, 379
Organization of American States, 332
O'Rourke, Mike, 496–500, 504, 509, 510
Orr, David, 377
Osk, Victoria, 58
Osorio, Julio, 55

Page, Clarence, 168
Palestinians, 154, 307

Pallasch, Abdon, 342, 384, 385
Pallmeyer, Judge, 330, 442–45, 447, 449–50, 491
Palmer, Lu, 94, 135
Panos, Diane, 395–96, 414, 421, 501
Paraguay, 332
Paris, Illinois, 440
Parker, Mike, 342, 358
Parker, William A. Sr., 177–79, 380–81
Partee, Cecil, 307
Patterson, Aaron, 204–6, 222–23, 237, 239, 245, 261, 279, 292, 298, 309, 330, 333, 383
    Burge and, 206–7, 300
    Byrne and, 249, 276–77
    Caine and, 442, 485
    civil suit of, 298–300, 308, 325, 386, 389–90
    criminal trial of, 330–31
    Daley and, 249, 296, 300, 330, 443
    death row clemencies and, 290, 291, 293–98
    death sentence of, 203–4, 245, 282
    Devine and, 286, 296, 300, 330
    etching by, 205, 257, 299
    Illinois Supreme Court and, 204, 246–48, 250, 271–73, 276, 390
    "Live from Death Row," 289
    media on, 227–28, 248–49, 282, 296–97, 300–1, 309, 325, 339
    Obama and, 301
    OPS and, 246, 300
    pardon of, 293–94
    plea deal for, 281–82
    PLO and, 291, 310, 333–34
    post-conviction petition of, 283–84, 449
    public defenders and, 205–7
    Ryan and, 291, 293–94
    torture of, 203–5, 245
Patterson, JoAnn, 245, 247, 261, 291, 293–94, 309–10, 388, 391
Patterson, Ray, 248, 277
Patton, Detective, 397
Patton, Steve, 450–51, 456–58, 469–72, 476–77
Pegues, Alexis, 468
Pell, Wilbur, 31
People's Law Office, 1–4, 30, 173, 180, 186, 214, 250, 252, 256, 322, 410, 497, 509
    Attica and, 6, 273
    Bridgeport cases of, 148–49
    Burge and, 173, 180, 280, 423
    Cannon and, 238, 268
    Conroy on, 222, 423
    FOP and, 180, 497
    Hyman and, 341
    Jones case, 52
    Laverty and, 363

Louima and, 225
Martin and, 173
media on, 338, 341, 394, 493
Patterson and, 291, 310, 333–34
report on special prosecutors and, 376
Safforld and, 404
special prosecutor's report and, 344
staff of, 4, 5, 13, 56, 64, 76, 124, 203, 223, 280, 333, 468, 481, 498
    Wilson civil retrial and, 87, 124, 139, 423
    Wilson civil rights case and, 65
People's Tribunal, 150–51
Peoria, Illinois, 1, 19, 56
Percy, Chuck, 71
Perry, April, 410, 415–17, 424–25
Perry, J. Sam, 7–8, 10–15, 21–30, 92, 242, 484
Phelan, Pope and John, 66
Philadelphia, 138
Pienta, James, 204, 206, 478–80
Pierce, Curtis, 58
Pierce, Gorrell, 58
Pincham, Eugene, 96, 226, 242, 280, 286
Pinex, Alfonzo, 336, 346, 394–95, 416
Pinochet, Augusto, 56
Piper, Robert, 10, 16, 33
Pitts, Lewis, 58–60, 62
Plame, Valerie, 339
Police Foundation, 173, 182
Police Memorial Foundation, 459
Police Unbound (Bouza), 360
Ponce, Phil, 168
Pontiac Correctional Center, 65, 68, 88–89, 94, 144, 206, 279, 294
Porch, Willie, 94–95, 111–17, 120, 122–23, 127, 142, 326
Poree, Lawrence, 88–89, 91, 180, 313–15
Porter, Anthony, 230, 245, 293
Posner, Richard, 198–201, 224
Possley, Maurice, 227, 322
Powell, George, 88–89, 91, 180, 316–18
Powers, Mary, 135, 148–49, 188–89, 358, 489
    Burge special prosecutor and, 280–81, 372
    Citywide Coalition press conference and, 174
    Martin and, 171–72
    Wilson civil retrial and, 118, 124
Preckwinkle, Toni, 337, 376, 384, 389, 450, 458
Preib, Martin, 473, 477, 486, 494, 497
Presumed Innocent, 105
Prisoner Review Board, 303, 309–10, 312, 362–63, 375
Project NIA, 467
Protess, David, 226, 295, 317, 461
Pryweller, Eileen, 321

Public Defenders' Office, 376
Puerto Rican Day uprising, 55
Puerto Rico, 451
Purple Steer, 237

Qatar, 349
Queen Elizabeth, 141
Queer Nation, 184
Quigley, Mike, 356
Quinn Chapel AME Church, 242
Quinn, Pat, 403, 440, 459

Raba, Jack, 43–47, 118, 128, 136, 141, 183
    Burge federal trial and, 414, 419
    Daley and, 45–46, 352–53
    letter to Brzeczek, 70–71, 84, 113, 341, 348,
        414
    special prosecutor's report and, 347, 353
Rainbow Coalition, 26
Rainbow/PUSH, 280, 379, 399, 405
Raines, Willie, 227
Ralph, Frank, 237, 280, 283, 294, 303, 310
Ramey, Richard, 207
Raoul, Kwame, 403, 439–40, 480
Rappaport, Diane, 13
Rather, Dan, 249
Reagan, Ronald, 63, 71
Reddick, Erica, 467–68, 477–78, 480
Red Guards, 137
Reeves, Marvin, 405, 429, 458
Rehnquist, William, 195
Reid, Herbert, 13
Reidy, Daniel, 176–77, 179, 183, 185–86
Reno, Janet, 242
Reparations Ordinance. See Illinois Reparations
    for Police Torture Victims Act
"Report on the Failure of Special Prosecutors
    Edward J. Egan and Robert D. Boyle to
    Fairly Investigate Systemic Police Torture in
    Chicago," 372
Republican Party, 6, 34, 54–55, 69, 71, 188, 273,
    291, 346, 406, 440
Reyna, Ralph, 169
Reynolds, Patricia, 42, 47
Rice, Fred, 55, 308, 433
Richardson, Bill, 440
RICO, 93, 340, 345, 361, 365
Ripple, Kenneth, 454
Rising Up Angry, 1
Rivera, Geraldo, 317
Robinson, Michael, 386
Robinson, Renault, 3, 71
Robinson, Stanley, 8, 17

Rockefeller, Nelson, 6
Roddy, Joe, 169, 177, 185, 340, 394
Rodriguez, Alberto, 451
Rodriguez, Matt, 186–87, 195, 219
Romiti, Philip, 6–8, 26
Roosevelt University, 203
Rosenthal, Larry, 210
Rovner, Ilana, 453–57, 463–64
Royko, Mike, 24, 184–85, 351
Rubin, Jeff, 66, 85, 97–98, 100, 106–8, 128, 131
Rugai, Virginia, 187
Rush, Bobby, 2–3, 26, 150, 242, 252, 297–98, 301
Russell, Candice, 211
Russia, 295
Russ, Robert, 242
Ryan, Bill, 291
Ryan, George, 273, 288–91, 294–97, 303, 339,
    346, 391, 393, 404–5, 439

Saffold, Howard, 428, 432
Safforld, Victor, 404–5
Sampson, Dale, 58
Samuels, Ronald, 36, 109, 143, 144
Sanders, Francine, 152, 159–60, 162–63, 169–72,
    179, 270, 272, 426, 438
Sanford, Leroy, 88
Santiago, Marco, 228, 233
"Satan." See Holmes
Satchel, Ronald "Doc," 18–20, 27, 252
Saunders, Warner, 324
Savini, Dave, 323–24
Savory, Johnnie, 405
Sawyer, Eugene, 149, 366
Sawyer, Roderick, 462
Saxner case, 62–63, 253, 255
Saxner, David, 62–63, 363
Scalia, Antonin, 195–96
Schmiedel, Peter, 13, 52–53, 55, 63, 68, 252,
    256, 363
Scholl, Eric, 176, 210
Schroeder, Jeremy, 439
Schwartz, Eddie, 350–51
Scottsboro Boys, 503
Scully, Judith, 193
Search and Destroy, 13
Sears, Barnabas, 6–7
Second Circuit Court of Appeals, 273
Sentencing Reform Act of 1984, 436
Sepulveda, Pedro, 451–52
Serpico, 364
Sessions, Jeff, 490
Seventh Circuit Court of Appeals, 56, 115, 450
    Burge and, 379, 457–58, 463–64

Cannon and, 463–65
   fraud and, 453–56, 463
   Gettleman and, 209
   Perry and, 8, 22, 30–32
   Wilson and, 197, 200, 208–210, 224, 272
Shadur, Milton, 34, 53–54, 174, 179, 181–83, 231
Shapiro, Gary, 384, 452
Shaw, Ricky, 422–23
Shaw, Robert, 165–66, 187, 189–90, 192
Sheehan, Danny, 58
Sherer, Mark, 58, 61
Shines, Gayle, 160, 162–63, 169–71, 174, 181,
      195, 212, 231–32, 300
   Burge and, 173, 175
   Daley and, 175, 231
   deposition of, 229, 231, 232
   Martin and, 170–71, 173–74
   OPS and, 228, 232
   Tillman civil suit and, 443–45
Shine, Shim, 397
Shortstop Inn, 371
Siegel, Mara, 6
Simpson, O. J., 268
Sims, Tyrone, 505
Sincox, Alan, 74, 79, 99, 122
Sixth Amendment, 48, 395
Skinner, Sam, 17
Slosar, Elliot, 267, 483, 495–500, 502, 504,
      506–7
Smith, Alonzo, 276, 305, 500
   Byrne and, 277, 281
   Cannon case and, 268–69
   civil rights case of, 491–93
   exoneration of, 480, 491, 494
   post-conviction petition of, 467–68, 477, 480
   torture of, 213, 268–269, 468, 477, 488
Smith, Ed, 378, 380, 384, 385, 389–91, 394
Smith, Edward, 250
Smith, Eric, 327
Smith, Frank "Big Black," 6, 273
Smith, Jerry Paul, 57–59, 61
Smith, John, 286
Smith, Lindsey, 318
Smith, Maxine, 56, 254
Smith, Mort, 262, 309, 313, 315, 318, 320–21,
      326, 327, 329, 391
Smith, Sage, 262, 391
Smith, Sandy, 62
Smith, Tommie, 370
SNCC, 2
Sneed, Michael, 175
Snow, Christian, 498
Sorrels, James, 488

Sotos, Jim, 195, 456, 508–9
Souter, David, 195
South Africa, 149, 295, 461
South Carolina, 59
southern United States, 61, 356, 505
Southtown Economist, 49, 73, 81, 99, 168, 189,
      197, 350
South Vietnam, 67
Special Grand Jury, 334
Special Prosecutions Unit, 46
Special Prosecutor Committee, 285
Spence, Gerry, 227
Spielman, Fran, 166, 445, 483
   on Burge, 381, 399–401
   on Daley, 189, 230–31, 368, 445–46, 466
   on Emanuel, 458, 466
   on reparations, 473–74
   on torture settlements, 384, 392
   special prosecutor's report and, 352–53
Spitz, Werner, 185
Spoon, Lieutenant, 61
Springfield, Illinois, 247, 367, 403
Stainthorp, John, 64, 95, 151, 160, 168, 178, 182,
      195, 217, 256, 259, 360–61, 370, 441
   Andrew Wilson and, 68–69, 82–84, 183,
      210, 387–88
   Deep Badge and, 73–74
   Duff and, 66, 77, 93, 109, 140, 142
   Jackie Wilson and, 495, 498, 504
   White and, 117, 126
   Wilson appeal and, 197–98, 210, 224
   Wilson civil retrial and, 87, 103–4, 109,
      120–22, 127, 140, 142, 146
Starks, Dana, 378
State of Illinois, 223, 238, 270, 272, 286–87, 305,
      480, 506–7, 509
State of New York, 273
Stateville Penitentiary, 88, 90, 94
Stateville Prison, 310, 375
Steele, John, 167
Stefanich, Brian, 479, 500–501
Steidl, Randy, 439–440
Steinberg, Barbara, 43–44, 138, 145
Stern, Carl, 9
St. Eve, Amy, 443, 453, 491–493, 495
Stevens, John Paul, 195–196
Stewart, Cathryn, *See* Crawford, Cathryn Stewart
St. Louis, 238
Stokes, Dewey, 184
Stone, Randolph, 135, 280, 286, 298–99
Strausberg, Chinta, 167–68
Strayhorn, Earl, 212
Streitor, Reverend, 17

Stroger, John, 378
Stroger, Todd, 378–379
Strong, Johnae, 489
Students for a Democratic Society, 1
Suffredin, Larry, 90, 378–79, 393, 413, 450
Sullivan, William C., 11, 13
Supplemental Summary Report (Sanders), 172
Supreme Court. *See* US Supreme Court; Illinois
    Supreme Court
Susler, Jan, 56, 204–7, 226, 241, *256*, 363, 451
Swygert, Luther, 31–33, 115, 209
Szuc, Jeff, 381

Tamms, Illinois, 238–39
Tamms supermax prison, 238–40, 312, 362, 375
Tampa Tribune, 297
Task Force on Police Accountability, 489
Task Force to Prevent Police Violence, 161, 169,
    176, 182, 184, 194, 210–11, 220, 223
Taylor, James "Bulljive," 108
Taylor, Kate, 235, 429
Tenenbaum, Sam, 361, 375
Terkel, Studs, 185
Ter Molen, Mark, 227
Terre Haute, Indiana, 62, 88
Terry, Paul, 315
Texas, 327
Thielmann, Rachel, 427
Thomas, Charles, 342, 351
Thomas, Clarence, 196
Thomas, David, 459
Thompson, Erica, 181
Thompson, James, 8, 440
Thompson, Tara, 478
Thompson, Timothy, 95, 326
Thompson, Tony, 95, 112, 326, 502
Till, Emmett, 355
Tillis, Darby, 335
Tillman, Dorothy, 151, 355
Tillman, Elizabeth, 408
Tillman-Messenger, Veronica, 228–29, 237, 243,
    277
Tillman, Michael, *264*, 396, 406–9, 444,
    450–52, 491
    civil suit of, 409, 442–45
    Daley and, 430, 443–45, 451
    media on, 408–9, 446–47, 450
    settlement for, 450–51, 457
    torture of, 396–97, 406–7, 447, 452
Tillman, Winter, 408
"Tools of Torture," 328
Toomin, Michael, 276, 283–84, 291, 449, 462
Torture Awareness Month, 451

Torture Inquiry and Relief Commission, 403,
    458–59, 483, 504
Tribune Red Eye, 349
Troutman, Arenda, 355
Truelock, Louis, 19–20
Trump, Donald, 367, 489, 490
Trutenko, Nick, 136, 139
Tucker Telephone, 165
Turkey, 243
Turner, Art, 298
Turner, Bishop, 149
Turner, Linda, 30
Turow, Scott, 105
Tutu, Desmond, 295

UN Committee on the Elimination of Racial
    Discrimination, 460
United Nations, 481
United Nations Committee Against Torture,
    377, 380
United Nations Convention Against Torture, 167,
    335–37, 340, 430, 464, 467, 497
United Nations Manual on the Effective Investiga-
    tion and Documentation of Torture, 243
United Nations Special Rapporteur on Torture,
    246
United States, 3, 21, 51, 154, 156, 225, 295, 306,
    336, 356, 451
    torture and, 329, 337, 340, 464, 467
University of Chicago, 386, 432, 478, 491
University of Illinois, 18, 54
Unspeakable Acts, Ordinary People (Conroy),
    306–7, 338
Urban League, 181, 196
Urso, Joseph, 44
US Army, 67, 88, 328
US Attorney, 15, 340, 426, 436, 452
    Fitzgerald as, 339, 347, 385, 394, 398, 415,
        420, 426, 436
US Congress, 429–30
US Department of Justice, 168, 170, 197, 230,
    374, 382, 394, 426, 482, 489–90. *See*
    also Civil Rights Division
    Civil Rights Division, 5, 25, 242, 489
    Hampton case and, 5, 10, 15, 21
US House of Representatives, 225
US Marine Corps, 213, 276, 286
US Olympic Committee, 370–71
US Senate, 11–12, 13, 16, 209
US Supreme Court, 33, 62–63, 70, 190, 191, 195,
    210, 248, *255*, 308, 456

Vallandingham, Detective, 216

Van Brunt, Alexa, 448–49
Van Dyke, Jason, 483, 489, 509
Vanecko, R. J., 448–49, 462
Velez, Rosie, *256*
Venezuela, 246
Vietnam War, 1
    Burge in, 67, 78, 91, 108, 154, 166, 175, 306,
        327–28, 338, 412, 420, 422, 427
    Dignan in, 213, 306, 478
    torture during, 67, 139, 240, 243, 327–30
    veterans of, 5, 19, 67, 74, 268, 319, 328
Vigilante, 203, 214–215, 263, 278, 311, 422
Village Voice, 153
Volini, Camillo, 21, 24, 27–28
Vrdolyak, Ed, 55

Walden, Oscar, 440–41, 509
Waller, Signe, 58
Walls, William "Doc," 367–68
Walters, Phil, 171–73, 176, 190, 194, 361
Walton, Thomas, 55
Warden, Rob, 17, 289, 372, 413, 439–40, 458–59
Warpeha, Raymond, 82
Warren, Earl, 63
Washington, DC, 11, 32, 62, 141, 332
Washington, Earl, 317
Washington, Harold, 7, 17, 24, 54–55, 64, 69,
        113, 148–49, 233, 366, 433, 485
Washington Post, 59, 196, 293, 461
Watergate, 11, 13, 17, 79
Watson, Cassandra, 79, 101, 106–8, 413
Waxman, Sheldon, 9, 10, 12
WBEZ, 447
Weatherman faction, 1
Weaver, Joseph, 148, 150–51, 169, 170, 186
Webb, Dan, 34, 462
Webber, Linda, 13
We Charge Genocide, 467
Weisman, David, 407, 410, 421–23
Welsh, Jack, 1
Welsh, Kelly, 171
Whirl, Shawn, 478–81, 491, 494.
White, Byron "Whizzer," 195
White, Donald, 72, 117, 126–27, 131–32, 136,
        141, 172, 179–80, 189, 201, 319, 486, 499
    OPS and, 126, 135
    torture of, 36–37, 124, 486, 496, 502
    Wilson torture claim and, 496
White, Lamont, 36, 72, 502
White, Walter, 36–37, 72, 502
Whitman, Steve, 383–384, 397, 509
Wiedrich, Bob, 12–13
Wiggins, Marcus, 190, 219, 239, *259*, 310, 380

at Area 3, 215–16
    confession of, 172, 188–89
    deposition of, 216–18
    Goldston report and, 188
    media and, 190–91
    OPS and, 228, 231
    torture of, 172, 188–91, 212, 216–18, 220,
        404
Williams, Ann, 457
Williams, Anthony, 36, 37, 496, 502
Williams, Anthony "Mertz," 131
Williams, "Clubber," 210
Williams, Dennis, 227, *260*
Williams, Herbert, 173, 182
Williams, Walter, 189
Willis, Stan, 148, *256*, 280, 283, 300, 332, 370,
        382, 403, 460
Wilson, Andrew, 42–44, 63, 65–66, 129, 168,
        193, 241, *255*, *259*, *262*, 284, 357, 395,
        413–14, 433
    appeal of, 175, 189, 197–201, 208
    arrest of, 38, 66, 69, 133, 176, 357
    Brzeczek and, 96, 270, 355
    Burge federal trial and, 413, 418–24, 427
    civil case of, 65–85
    civil retrial of, 103–47, 154, 161, 165, 171,
        177, 229, 238, 302, 328, 379, 402, 487
        Devine and, 246
        media on, 181
        OPS files and, 308
        Shadur on, 179
    Coleman and, 136–39
    confession of, 41, 47–49, 65, 74, 121, 137–39,
        176, 191, 499
    Conroy and, 154–56, 221
    conviction of, 49, 82–83, 109
    Coventry and, 44, 65–66, 69
    criminal trials of, 48–49, 67, 200
    Daley and, 341, 347, 352, 354, 438
    death of, 387–88
    deposition of, 68–69, 500–1
    Duff and, 65–66, 92–93, 120–22, 189
    Egan and, 285, 355
    foreman on, 156–157
    Hardin and, 506
    Hoke and, 215
    Hope and, 131
    Hyman and, 39–41, 334, 341–42, 346, 496
    Illinois Supreme Court and, 109, 114, 120,
        138–39, 142, 151, 166–67, 169, 200,
        201, 246
    Jackie and, 483, 495, 501, 502, 505, 508
    Jones and, 80

Karl and, 360
Kirchner and, 165–66
Martin and, 172
media on, 148, 185, 210, 249, 262, 285
    CBS 2, 323
    Conroy, 307, 345
    Reader, 387
    Tribune, 388
O'Hara and, 131
OPS and, 70–73, 113, 120, 135, 151, 153,
    159, 163, 164, 173, 308, 438
Parker and, 179
Patterson case and, 272
PLO and, 423
police board hearings and, 183–86, 191–92
in Pontiac, 65, 68, 88, 94
Powers on, 118
Raba and, 45–46, 342, 414
Sanders and, 172, 438
sentencing of, 49–51
settlement of, 210, 224
Special Prosecutions Unit and, 46
special prosecutor's report and, 345–47, 355
Stainthorp and, 210, 387–88
testimony of, 74, 76, 120–22, 125, 142, 145,
    183, 210, 387, 410, 413
Tillman and Bell and, 406
torture of, 38–41, 44–45, 97, 102, 125, 143,
    204, 379, 388, 413, 419–20, 422, 488,
    496, 500, 502
    Amnesty International on, 167, 168
    appeal and, 202
    Coleman on, 137–38, 145
    date of, 80, 90, 95
    Hyman and, 139
    investigations of, 140
    jurors on, 87, 147
    Lacey on, 319
    media and, 115, 175
    OPS on, 163
    police board hearing and, 177, 180
    police board on, 191
    police hearings on, 163
    Posner on, 224
    testimony on, 68–70, 73–76, 120–21
    Yucaitis and, 131
Williams, White, and, 37, 117
Yucaitis and, 133, 193
Wilson, Jackie, 37–38, 43–44, 48–51, 67, 131,
    267, 395, 459, 489, 495, 497–9, 501, 505, 508
    arrest of, 40, 66, 357
    Burge and, 486, 496, 501
    Burge depositions and, 469

Burge federal trial and, 419
Coleman and, 136, 139, 505–6
confession of, 41, 47–48, 499, 503, 504
FOP and, 494, 510
Hyman and, 334, 496
media on, 497–99, 503, 507
torture claim of, 483, 485, 494–507
torture of, 40–41, 319, 422, 486, 496, 497,
    499, 500, 502
Wilson, O. W., 490
Winfrey, Oprah, 296
Winnetka, Illinois, 489
Winston-Salem, North Carolina, 57, 61
Winter Soldier investigation, 67
WMAQ, 182
Wolfson, Warren, 238, 239, 270, 275
Wood, Roland Wayne, 60, 61
World War II, 55
Worrill, Conrad, 135
Wrice, Stanley, 214, 396, 461, 461–62, 478, 480
WTTW, 348
WVON, 99

X, Malcolm, 2, 9, 12

Yarborough, Karen, 439–40
Young Lords, 1
Young, Walter, 319–20, 329
Yucaitis, John, 67, 75, 85–86, 170, 176, 187, 193,
    196–97, 201, 209, 314–15
    Burge federal charges and, 410
    Burge federal trial and, 420, 431
    OPS and, 70, 163, 171, 173
    police board hearings and, 180, 187, 192
    torture by, 39, 121, 163, 397
    Wilson civil retrial and, 114, 121, 131, 133, 146

Zimmers, Robert, 21
Zorn, Eric, 275, 344, 351, 400